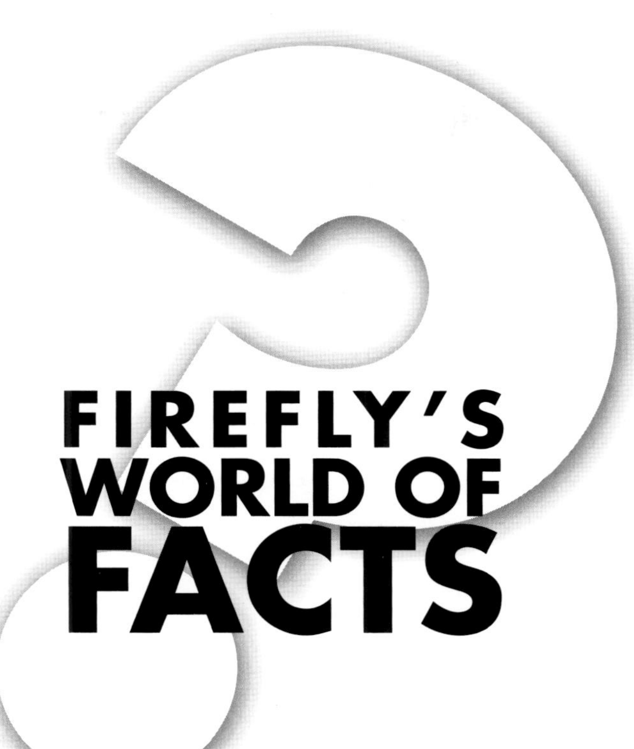

FIREFLY'S WORLD OF FACTS

RUSSELL ASH

FIREFLY'S WORLD OF FACTS

FIREFLY BOOKS

A FIREFLY BOOK

Published by Firefly Books Ltd. 2008

First printing

Publisher Cataloging-in-Publication Data (U.S.)
Ash, Russell.
Firefly's world of facts / Russell Ash.
2nd ed., rev.
[320] p. : col. photos., maps ; cm.
Includes index.
Summary: An illustrated encyclopedia of popular topics, including arts, sciences, health, sports, countries and people.
ISBN-13: 978-1-55407-408-2
ISBN-10: 1-55407-408-8
1. Encyclopedias and dictionaries.
2. Popular culture — Encyclopedias.
I. World of facts. II. Title.
031.02 dc22 AG106.A84 2008

Library and Archives Canada Cataloguing in Publication
Ash, Russell
Firefly's world of facts / Russell Ash. —
2nd ed., rev.
Includes index.
ISBN-13: 978-1-55407-408-2
ISBN-10: 1-55407-408-8
1. Curiosities and wonders.
2. Handbooks, vade-mecums, etc.
I. Title. II. Title: World of facts.
AG106.A76 2008 031.02
C2008-902691-8

Published in the United States by
Firefly Books (U.S.) Inc.
P.O. Box 1338, Ellicott Station
Buffalo, New York 14205

Published in Canada by
Firefly Books Ltd.
66 Leek Crescent
Richmond Hill, Ontario L4B 1H1

Illustrators Alan Baker (Illustration), Julian Baker, KJA-artists
Heraldry consultant
Henry Bedingfeld, College of Arms
Religions consultant
Martin Palmer, ICOREC
Sports consultant Ian Morrison

Printed in China

CONTENTS

Introduction 8

About this Book 9

TIME

The Story of Time 12

Time Periods 14

The Calendar 16

SPACE

The Universe 20

The Solar System 1 22

The Solar System 2 24

Astronomy 26

Space Exploration 28

Astronauts 30

PLANET EARTH

Rocks and Minerals 34

Land Features 36

Rivers and Lakes 38

The World's Oceans 40

Climate 42

Weather 44

Natural Disasters 46

LIFE SCIENCES

Trees and Plants 50

Animal Kingdom 52

Mammals 54

Sea Life 56

Flying Animals 58

Insects and Spiders 60

Reptiles and Amphibians 62

Man and Beast 64

Pet Power 66

Endangered and Extinct 68

Environmental Concerns 70

Garbage and Recycling 72

SCIENCE AND TECHNOLOGY

Science 76

The Elements 78

Inventions 80

Mathematics 82

Weights and Measures 84

Computers and the Internet 86

Telecommunications 88

HUMAN BODY

Human Body 92

Body Facts and Records 94

Health and Medicine 96

Food and Drink 98

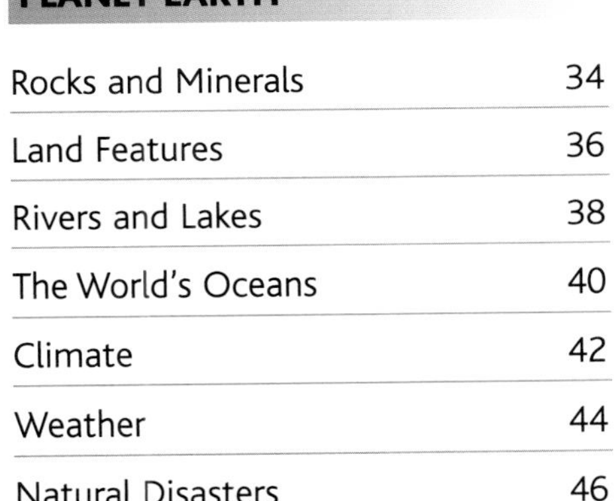

WORLD HISTORY

Historical Ages 102
Historical Events 104
World Civilizations and Empires 106
Rulers and Leaders 108
World Politics 110

COUNTRIES OF THE WORLD

World Map 114
Countries of the World 116
Cities of the World 118
North and Central America 120
Central and South America 122
Europe 124
Africa 130
Asia 136
Australasia 142

PEOPLE

Names 146
Families and Relationships 148
People Who Changed the World 150
Exploration and Endeavor 152
Celebrities 154
Kids' World 156

BELIEFS AND IDEAS

Ancient Religions 160
World Religions 162
Sacred Texts 164
Christianity 166
Festivals 168
Myths and Legends 170
Predictions and Prophecies 172
The Unexplained 174

CONFLICT AND CRIME

Weapons and Forces 178
Wars and Battles 180
The Law 182
Crime 184

WORK AND HOME

Around the House 188
Toys and Games 190
Wealth 192
Energy 194

BUILDINGS AND STRUCTURES

Building Styles 198
Great Buildings 200
Skyscrapers 202
Bridges and Tunnels 204
Wonders of the World 206

TRANSPORTION AND TRAVEL

Water Transportation 210
Land Transportation 212
Rail Transportation 214
Air Transportation 216
Transportation Disasters 218
Tourism 220

LANGUAGE AND LITERATURE

Language 224
Communication 226
Books 228
Authors 230
Children's Books 232
Poets and Poetry 234
Newspapers and Magazines 236

EDUCATION AND THE ARTS

Education 240
Famous Artists 242
Museums and Monuments 244
Collecting 246

MUSIC AND PERFORMANCE

World of Music 250
Classical Music 252
Pop and Rock 254
Theater 256
Dance 258
Ballet 260

FILM, TV AND RADIO

Film Facts 264
Blockbusters 266
Film Winners 268
Animated Films 270
The Stars 272
TV and Radio 274

SPORTS

Sport Facts 278
Sporting Events 280
The Olympics 282
Athletics 284
Ball Games 286
Soccer and Football 288
Racket Sports 290
Combat, Strength and Target Sports 292
Water Sports 294
Wheel Sports 296
Winter Sports 298
Animal Sports 300

LAST LISTS

Dead Ends 304
Last of Everything 306

Index 308
Acknowledgments 318

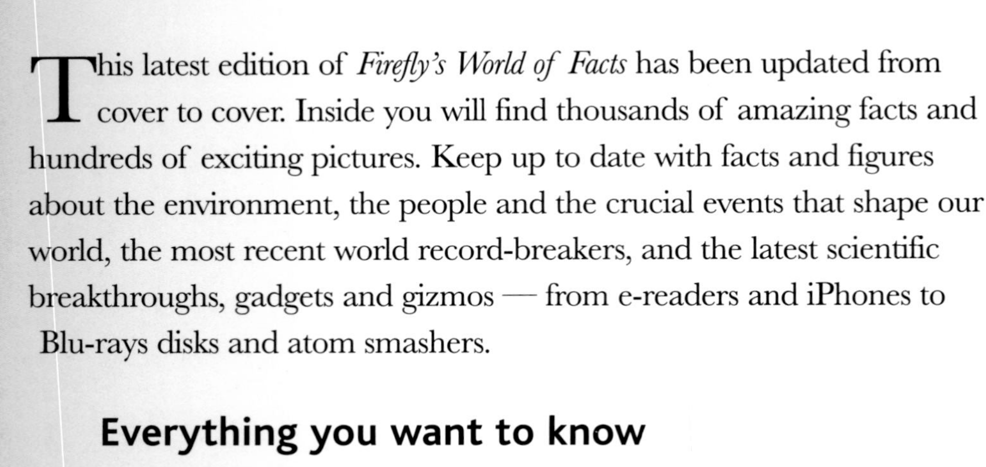

This latest edition of *Firefly's World of Facts* has been updated from cover to cover. Inside you will find thousands of amazing facts and hundreds of exciting pictures. Keep up to date with facts and figures about the environment, the people and the crucial events that shape our world, the most recent world record-breakers, and the latest scientific breakthroughs, gadgets and gizmos — from e-readers and iPhones to Blu-rays disks and atom smashers.

Everything you want to know

Firefly's World of Facts is divided into 20 sections — Space, Planet Earth, World History and Human Body to name but a few. It includes information on a huge range of subjects with data from authoritative sources and specialists on every subject under the Sun, and beyond.

Inside information

Detailed lists and charts show global comparisons, while Special Features and Factdisks provide fast information, revealing everything from how much food you will eat in a lifetime to the highest-earning films and film stars, from the oldest people to the most popular names. An array of oddities are sure to astound you, from the number of ducks in the world, the countries where there are more sheep than people, and the most dangerous things in the home, to the world's tallest garbage dump.

You'll find essential information, including the flags, on every country in the world, detailing population, capital city and currency.

Timelines on subjects such as telecommunications, astronomy, wars and inventions give a see-at-a-glance overview and pinpoint important milestones up to the present day.

Useful maps, tables and formulae include conversions, mathematical symbols and scales, from Beaufort (weather) to Richter (earthquakes).

Other features

Weblink boxes suggest useful websites to explore subjects further. *See also* boxes guide you to information on a particular subject elsewhere in the book. There is an extensive index at the back of the book, as well as a list of sources.

Russell Ash

About this book

216 AIR TRANSPORT

Aviation pioneers

John Alcock (UK, 1892–1919) and **Arthur Whitten Brown** (UK, 1886–1948)
On 14–15 June 1919, they completed the first ever non-stop flight across the Atlantic from Newfoundland to Ireland.

Louis Blériot (France, 1872–1936)
On 25 July 1909 Blériot became the first person to fly across the English Channel.

Samuel F. Cody (USA, c. 1861–1913)
The first person to fly in England, 16 October 1908.

Glenn Curtiss (USA, 1878–1930)
Rival to the Wright Brothers, Curtiss made the first public flight in the USA on 4 July 1908. He set up the first aeroplane manufacturing company in the USA.

Amelia Earhart (USA, 1898–1937)
The first woman to fly the Atlantic. She went on to establish many flying records but disappeared during an attempt to fly round the world.

Amy Johnson (UK, 1903–41)
She made the first solo flight from England to Australia in 1930.

Charles Lindbergh (USA, 1902–74)
The first pilot to fly solo across the Atlantic, from New York to Paris, 20–21 May 1927, in *The Spirit of St Louis*.

Harriet Quimby (USA, 1875–1912)
America's first female pilot. On 16 April 1912 she was the first woman to fly the English Channel – but on the day the sinking of the *Titanic* was reported, so her triumph was barely noticed.

Wilbur Wright (USA, 1867–1912) and **Orville Wright** (USA, 1871–1948)
The Wright brothers, two bicycle mechanics from Dayton, Ohio, made the first ever powered flights on 17 December 1903.

Concorde

Concorde fact file

Concorde, the only passenger aircraft ever to fly faster than the speed of sound, was first named in a speech by General de Gaulle on 13 January 1963. The Anglo-French project began the following year.

- The first prototype Concorde was shown at the Toulouse Air Show on 11 December 1967.
- The first French flight took place on 2 March 1969.
- The first British flight took place on 9 April 1969.
- The first landing at London Heathrow was on 13 September 1970.
- The first Concorde landing in the USA was at Dallas-Fort Worth on 20 September 1973.
- The only Concorde crash was near Paris, 25 July 2000, when 109 passengers and crew and four people on the ground died.
- Concorde's last flight took place on 24 October 2004. All surviving BA and Air France Concordes are on public display in museums and airports in the USA, UK, France, Germany and Barbados.

The Wright brothers demonstrate their Wright Model A plane

The Wright brothers

Orville Wright was the first person to fly a powered aircraft. He also became the first to fly a plane for more than one hour, on 9 September 1908 at Fort Meyer, Virginia, USA. His brother Wilbur became the first to fly for more than two hours, on 31 December 1908 at Auvours, France. On 20 May 1909 French pilot Paul Tissandier became the first person other than the Wrights to fly for more than an hour.

See also
Steve Fossett: page 153
Amelia Earhart: page 153

First manned balloon flights

The first balloons worked on the principle that when air is heated, it rises. They were filled with hot air by burning things under them, such as paper, straw and wool – and even old shoes and rotten meat!

The balloons often caught fire and once the air cooled, they quickly came down. Soon after the first hot-air flights, people realized that the gas hydrogen could be used instead. Hydrogen is the lightest of all elements – almost 15 times lighter than air. Gas balloons can also be filled with helium, which is not as light as hydrogen but does not catch fire so easily. Most balloons today use hot air made by burning propane gas.

The first hot-air balloon flight
The Montgolfier brothers, Joseph and Etienne, tested their first unmanned hot-air balloon on 5 June 1783. On 21 November 1783, François Laurent, Marquis d'Arlandes and Jean-François Pilâtre de Rozier took off from the Bois de Boulogne, Paris, in a Montgolfier hot-air balloon. They travelled about 9 km (5.6 miles) in 23 minutes.

First hydrogen balloon flight
On 1 December 1783, Jacques Alexandre César Charles and Nicholas-Louis Robert made the first flight in a hydrogen balloon. They took off from the Tuileries, Paris, watched by a crowd of 400,000, and travelled 43 km (27 miles) north to Nesle in about two hours. Charles then took off again alone, so was the first ever solo pilot.

First British flight
On 27 August 1784 James Tytler, a doctor and newspaper editor, took off in a home-made balloon from Comely Gardens, Edinburgh. He reached an altitude of 107 m (350 ft) in a 0.8 km (0.5 miles) hop.

First Channel crossing
On 7 January 1785 Jean-Pierre Blanchard made the first Channel crossing in a balloon with Dr John Jeffries (the first American to fly). They also carried the first airmail letter. As they lost height, they had to reduce weight, so they threw almost everything overboard – including their clothes!

First flight in the USA
On 9 January 1793 in Philadelphia, Blanchard made the first balloon flight in America. He took a small black dog with him as a passenger.

Breaking the sound barrier

Charles "Chuck" Yeager became the first person to break the sound barrier on 14 October 1947. His Bell X-1 rocket plane was dropped from a carrier aircraft above Muroc Dry Lake, California. At 12,800 m (42,000 ft) he reached a speed of 1,078 km/h (670 mph). He did not break the air speed record because only aircraft that take off and land under their own power are eligible. The speed of sound is not fixed and varies according to height and air conditions. In dry air at sea level the speed of sound is 1,229 km/h (263.67 mph), but at high altitudes, where air density is less, it is lower.

One and only

The only flight of the Hercules H-4 aircraft, known as the "Spruce Goose", took place on 2 November 1947. It was the largest flying boat ever built. It had the greatest wingspan (97.54 m/320 ft) of any aircraft and eight engines. Millionaire aviator Howard Hughes built and flew it himself, just 20 m (65.6 ft) above the water off Long Beach, California, USA. It travelled only 1.6 km (1 mile). The flight is recreated in the film *The Aviator* (2004).

www.flyingmachines.org search

First hot-air balloon flight

The flight was watched by George Washington, who gave Blanchard a passport permitting his flight, which was the first pilot's licence and America's first airmail document.

First non-stop solo flight
US adventurer Steve Fossett made the first non-stop solo and fastest round-the-world balloon flight, 19 June to 3 July 2002.

217 TRANSPORT AND TRAVEL

190 TOYS AND GAMES

Valuable toys

Some wealthy collectors prize rare toys, especially those that are in good condition – in their original box, and never played with. These are just some of the toys that may have cost very little when they were made, but now sell for high prices.

- GI Joe prototype was sold by Heritage Galleries & Auctioneers of Dallas, Texas for $200,000 (£126,580) in 2003.
- A Kämmer and Reinhardt doll was sold at Sotheby's, London, on 8 February 1994 for £188,500 ($277,981).
- Titania's Palace, a doll's house with 2,000 items of furniture, was sold at Christie's, London, in 1978 for £135,000 ($258,728).
- Dingley Hall, a doll's house dating from 1877, was sold at Christie's, London, in 2003 for £124,750 ($211,938).
- A 1906 train set made by German toymaker Märklin was sold at Christie's, London, in 2001 for £113,750 ($165,290).
- A black mohair Steiff teddy bear, made in about 1912, was sold at Christie's, London, in 2000 for £91,750 ($132,157). It was one of only 494 black Steiff bears made as a mark of respect after the sinking of the *Titanic*. They are known as "mourning teddies".
- A tinplate clockwork motorcycle with Mickey Mouse and Minnie from about 1930 was sold at Christie's, London, in 1997 for £51,000 ($83,650).

Birth of Barbie

The first Barbie doll appeared in February 1959. It was made by Ruth and Elliot Handler, co-founders of American toy manufacturers Mattel, and they named the doll after their daughter Barbara. The doll was dressed in a black and white striped swimsuit, with sunglasses, high heels and gold hoop earrings. In the first year a total of 351,000 Barbies were sold at $3 (£1) each. The doll went on to become one of the bestselling toys of all time.

The first Barbie dolls, in the Barbie Museum, Palo Alto, California

"Teddy Girl" teddy bear made in 1904

Top Teddy

"Teddy Girl" is a teddy bear made by the German manufacturer Steiff in 1904. It was sold at Christie's, London, on 5 December 1994 for a record £110,000 ($171,600). A Japanese collector named Yoshiro Sekiguchi bought the bear for his teddy bear museum near Tokyo.

Toy-buying countries

Forecast sales of traditional toys (eg construction toys, model vehicles, indoor games, dolls and teddy bears) and video games in 2008 are estimated to average £16.9 ($33) for every person on the planet. There are huge differences between countries: North Americans spend the most and people in African countries the least per child.

191 WORK AND HOME

Computer games

The first computer games were played on televisions and appeared in the 1970s. They were basic arcade games like *PONG* (1972), an electronic table-tennis game, and *Pac-Man* (1980), in which a yellow blob is steered round a maze, gobbling up everything in its path.

As computer technology advanced, games and consoles improved, with better graphics, sound and choice of themes. Second generation 8-bit games had removable cartridges, while the fifth 32-bit and 64-bit generation games could be played in 3D. Sixth and seventh generation games are more realistic than ever before and can be played online with anyone around the world. These are popular consoles of different generations.

First generation Atari *PONG* (1975)
Second generation Atari 2600 (1977)
Third generation Nintendo Entertainment System (1983), Nintendo Game Boy (1989)
Fourth generation Sega Mega Drive (1988), Super Nintendo (1990)
Fifth generation Nintendo 64 (1986), Sony PlayStation (1994)
Sixth generation Sega Dreamcast (1998), Sony PlayStation 2 (2000), Microsoft Xbox (2001)
Seventh generation Xbox 360 (2005), PlayStation 3 (2006), Nintendo Wii (2006)

Scrabble

Scrabble was invented in the USA during the 1930s by an architect named Alfred Mosher Butts. First he called it Lexiko, then It and Criss-Cross, before hitting on the name Scrabble. Well over 100 million sets have been sold in more than 130 countries. The numbers of letters included vary according to the language. In Dutch, for example, there are 18 Es, 10 Ns and two Js. The Slovak version has 41 different letters – more than any other version.

Monopoly®

Monopoly was invented in 1934 by an unemployed engineer called Charles Darrow, who lived in Philadelphia, USA. In his first version of the game he used street names from Atlantic City in New Jersey because he dreamed of going there, but could not afford the fare. The game was so successful that Darrow became a millionaire and spent the rest of his life travelling and growing rare orchids.

Monopoly was soon adapted for other countries, using street names from their main cities. The British version uses London place names and Mayfair is the most expensive street. There are also versions of Monopoly based on popular TV series, such as *The Simpsons*. Parkers, the US manufacturers of the game, print more Monopoly money than the US Treasury prints dollars.

Monopoly® around the world

Country	City*	Mayfair becomes
Australia	Canberra + state capitals	Kings Avenue
Canada	Vancouver, etc	Robson Street
China	Hong Kong	Victoria Peak
Egypt	Cairo	Shari Qasr El Nil
France	Paris	Rue de la Paix
Germany	Munich	Schlossallee
Ireland	Dublin	Shrewsbury Road
Netherlands	Amsterdam	Kalverstraat
New Zealand	Auckland	Queen Street
Portugal	Lisbon	Rossio
Russia	Moscow	Arbat
Singapore	Singapore	Queen Astrid Park
South Africa	Johannesburg	Eloff Street/Eloffstraat
Spain	Madrid	Paseo Del Prado
Switzerland	Zurich, etc	Paradeplatz
US	Atlantic City	Boardwalk

* Some feature streets from more than one city

Russian Monopoly board

Coloured bars identify each section of the book

Follow these *web links* for more information

One and Only boxes identify unique facts

Find cross-references throughout the book in these boxes

FactDisks highlight key facts

All new graphics used to illustrate facts and figures

Lists give you the latest facts and figures, dates and top tens for all kinds of subjects

Detailed information and statistics

Time

12 THE STORY OF TIME
14 TIME PERIODS
16 THE CALENDAR

Millenium celebrations — 2, 811 days late

Ethiopians welcomed the year 2000 at midnight on September 12, 2007. The country's Christian Orthodox church uses a calendar that has 13 months and is seven years behind the rest of the world, most of which use the Gregorian calendar.

The Universe in a year!

The American astronomer Carl Sagan (1934–96) first suggested a "cosmic calendar" as a way of helping people understand the history of the Universe. He put everything into the scale of a calendar year: the galaxies are formed over nine months and the Earth appears in September.

Human history is crowded into the last five minutes of the year. Recent time is divided into seconds and fractions of a second. So everything that happened in the last 475 years takes place in less than the last second of the last minute of the year.

Earth's life in a year

Jan 1 (midnight) Big Bang—Universe forms
Mar 15 First stars and galaxies form
May 1 Milky Way galaxy forms
Sep 8 Sun forms
Sep 9 Solar System forms
Sep 12 Earth forms
Sep 13 Moon forms
Sep 20 Earth's atmosphere forms
Oct 1 Earliest known life on Earth
Oct 7 Earliest known fossils
Dec 18 First many-celled life forms
Dec 19 First fish
Dec 21 First land plants; first insects
Dec 23 First reptiles
Dec 24 First dinosaurs
Dec 26 First mammals
Dec 27 First birds
Dec 28 First flowering plants
Dec 28 Dinosaurs extinct
Dec 31 (11:55 p.m.) *Homo sapiens* (modern humans)

The last day

11:59.50.487 p.m. Great Pyramid is built (2520 BC)
11:59.55.333 p.m. Great Wall of China is built (215 BC)
11:59.56.785 p.m. Roman Empire falls (AD 476)
11:59.58.026 p.m. Battle of Hastings (1066)
11:59.58.921 p.m. Columbus lands in America (1492)
11.59.59.128 p.m. Shakespeare writes his first plays (1588–90)
11:59.59.874 p.m. World War II ends (1945)
11:59.59.891 p.m. Mount Everest is climbed (1953)
11:59.59.924 p.m. Man lands on the Moon (1969)
Midnight Today

Royal Observatory, Greenwich; the "time ball" on the roof falls daily at 1:00 p.m.

The world in a single day

In one day (24 hours or 1,440 minutes or 86,400 seconds) the world turns once on its axis. During that time, on average:
364,478 people are born
151,650 people die

Timetellers 1500 BC

The following are some landmarks in the history of telling the time.

1500–1300 BC Sundials are used in Egypt: as the Earth rotates, the gnomon—the upright part of the sundial—casts a shadow that moves to indicate the time.

c. 400 BC Water clocks are used in Greece: as water drains from a container, each level it reaches represents a period of time.

c. AD 890 In England people use candles marked with time intervals.

12th century The hourglass, familiar to us as an eggtimer, is used by monks to show times of prayer.

1325 The first clock with a dial is installed in Norwich Cathedral, England.

1335 The first clock to strike the hours is made in Milan, Italy.

1350 The oldest known surviving alarm clock is made in Würzburg, Germany.

1364 Clocks are first used in people's homes.

1386 The clock is installed in Salisbury Cathedral, England. This is the world's oldest clock in working order.

1462 The earliest description of a watch is written in Italy.

1641 The pendulum clock is proposed by Vincenzio Galilei, son of the astronomer Galileo.

1657 The first pendulum clocks are made in Holland.

Time zones

The Earth is constantly turning on its axis. If people everywhere set their clocks to the same time, midnight would be in the middle of the night on one side of the globe, but the middle of the day on the opposite side. To avoid this problem the Earth is divided into artificial time zones. These generally follow lines of longitude – imaginary lines running from the North to the South Pole. Some large countries, such as the USA, cover several time zones. Mainland USA is divided into Atlantic, Eastern, Central, Mountain, Pacific and Alaska zones, with Hawaii and other islands falling into further zones.

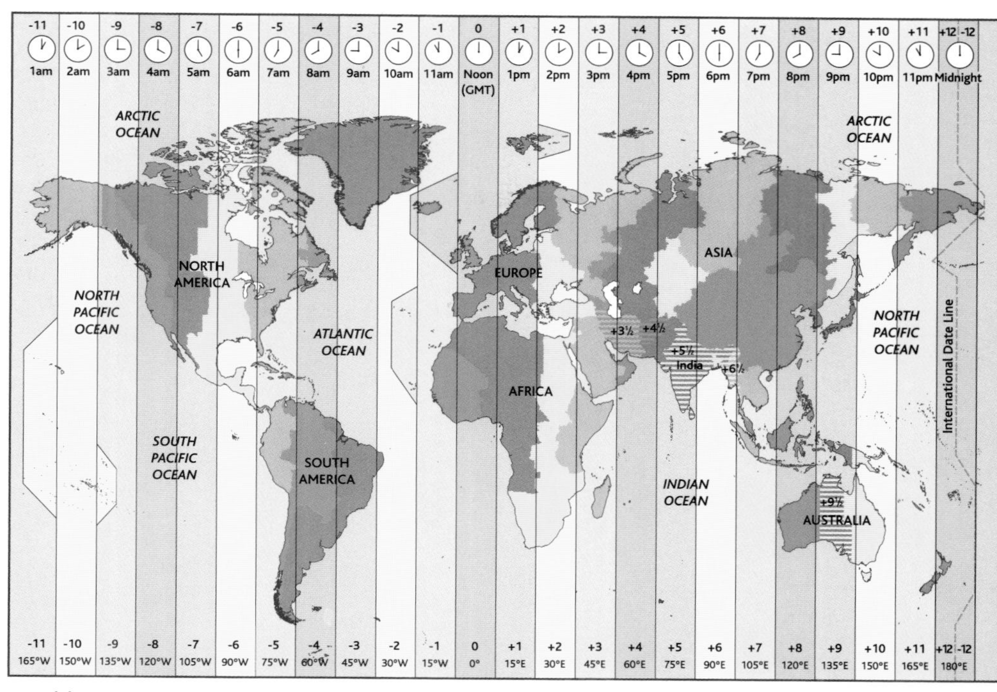

World time zones and the International Date Line

Since the Greenwich Prime Meridian (0°) was established in 1884, there have been 24 time zones, each of 15° longitude and an hour apart. Those to the east are ahead of Greenwich by one hour per zone. Those to the west are behind by one hour each. Some countries, such as India, have chosen zones halfway between those on either side, so that the whole country can use the same time.

Two sides of the Earth

The International Date Line

The Earth makes one complete turn in every 24 hours. In that time, each of the 360 degrees of longitude passes the Sun. This means that time progresses eastwards by four minutes for every degree of longitude.

The International Date Line is an imaginary line between the North and South Poles. It marks the end of one day and the start of another. Countries to the east of the Date Line are always a day ahead of those to the west. Travellers who cross the line gain or lose a day, depending on which direction they are going.

Most of the Date Line follows the 180° Meridian (on the opposite side of the globe from 0°, the Greenwich Meridian). The line generally passes through sea, but where it would pass through or near certain land areas, it is adjusted. It zigzags around islands, putting them either into the west or the east, and avoids dividing Siberia in north-east Asia into two time zones.

See also

Galileo Galilei: page 26

2007

c. 1665 The first watches with minute and second hands are made.

1759 John Harrison's marine chronometer is made. Accurate timekeeping at sea is important for calculating position, but previously the rolling of a ship had made it impossible.

1880 Greenwich Mean Time becomes the standard from which time around the world is set.

1880 The first practical wristwatches are made for the German navy.

1928 The first quartz crystal clock is made in the USA.

1949 The first atomic clock is built in the USA.

1957 The first battery watches are marketed in the USA.

1969 Quartz wristwatches are first sold in Japan.

1970 Digital watches and displays become widely used worldwide and can be made and sold cheaply.

2007 The British national time signal, used by radio clocks, is transmitted from the National Physical Laboratory, Anthorn, Cumbria.

www.rog.nmm.ac.uk search

Thor was the Scandinavian god of thunder and war. He is often shown brandishing a hammer. Thursday, or Thor's day, is named after him.

Names of months

The names of the months in English (as well as in many other languages) come from Latin words.

January
Januarius—this month was dedicated to Janus, the Roman god of doors. Janus had two faces, one looking back at the old year and the other looking forward to the new year.

February
Februarius—Februa was the Roman purification festival, which took place at this time of year.

March
Martius—from Mars, the Roman god of war.

April
Aprilis—from *aperire*, Latin for open, because plants begin to open during this month.

May
Maius—probably comes from Maia, the Roman goddess of growth and increase.

June
Junius—either from a Roman family name, Junius, which means young, or perhaps after the goddess Juno.

July
Julius—after Julius Caesar. This month was named in Caesar's honor by Mark Antony in 44 BC. Previously this month was called Quintilis from the word *quintus*, "five," as it was the fifth month in the Roman calendar.

August
Augustus—named in 8 BC in honor of Emperor Augustus.

September
September—from *septem*, "seven," because it was the seventh month in the Roman calendar.

October
October—from *octo*, "eight" (as in octopus, which has eight legs), the eighth month in the Roman calendar.

November
November—from *novem*, "nine," the ninth month in the Roman calendar.

December
December—from *decem*, "ten," the tenth month in the Roman calendar.

Leap seconds

The rotation of the Earth is slowing down. This means that a solar day (the time it takes Earth to make one complete revolution) and the time shown by atomic clocks would gradually diverge. This problem has been solved by adding "leap seconds." There have been 22 leap seconds since 1972. The last one was added on December 31, 2005, which delayed New Year's Day 2006 by one second!

Naming the days of the week

The ancient Babylonians, then the Romans, named the days of the week after planets and other bodies they saw in the sky. Some names we know today come from the names of Scandinavian gods.

Monday
Moon's day

Tuesday
Tiu's day—Mars, the Roman god of war, was adopted in Scandinavian mythology as the warrior Tiu or Tiw.

Wednesday
Woden's day—the Roman god Mercury became the Scandinavian god Woden.

Thursday
Thor's day—like the Roman god Jupiter, Thor was a thunder god.

Friday
Freyja's day—like Venus, Freyja or Frigg was the goddess of love.

Saturday
Saturn's day

Sunday
Sun's day

How long does it take?

One beat of a fly's wing (1/1,000 second) 0.001 seconds
Flash of lightning (1/1,000 second) 0.001 seconds
One beat of a hummingbird's wing (80 times a second) 0.0125 seconds
Mouse heartbeat (10.8 times a second) 0.09 seconds
Blink of a human eye 0.33 seconds
Human heartbeat 1.0 seconds
Land speed record: car *ThrustSSC* traveling 0.62 mi. (1 km) 2.9 seconds
Record-breaking Jamaican athlete Asafa Powell to run 328 ft. (100 m) 9.77 seconds
Bullet train to travel 0.62 mi. (1 km) 13.75 seconds
Space Shuttle to travel 62 mi. (100 km) 15 seconds
Light reaching Earth from the Sun 497 seconds

Watches at sea

At sea, the 24-hour day is traditionally divided into seven watches, during which some of a ship's crew are on duty.

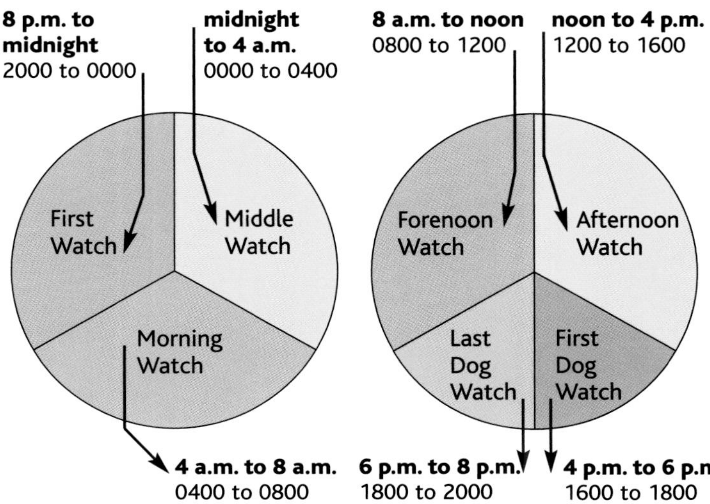

www.physics.nist.gov/Genint search

Just a second

It will take you almost five seconds to read this sentence. During an average-length film more than 5,000 seconds will pass. In a lifetime of 80 years, there are more than 2.5 billion seconds—but you will spend more than 800 million of them asleep!

1 minute 60 seconds
1 hour 3,600 seconds
1 day 86,400 seconds
1 week 604,800 seconds
1 year 31,536,000 seconds

ThrustSCC set the first supersonic land-speed record, at 763,035 mph (1,227,986 km/h).

Time words

Here are some of the words used for units of time.

chronon
One-billionth of a trillionth of a second (the time a photon would take to cross the width of one electron at the speed of light)

femtosecond
0.000000000000001 of a second

picosecond
0.000000000001 (one-trillionth) of a second

nanosecond
0.000000001 (one-billionth) of a second

microsecond
0.000001 (one-millionth) of a second

millisecond
0.001 (one-thousandth) of a second; the blink of an eye takes 50–80 milliseconds

centisecond
0.01 (one-hundredth) of a second

second
1/60 of a minute

minute
60 seconds

hour
60 minutes

day
Sunrise to sunrise, or sunset to sunset, or midnight to midnight; 24 hours

week
Seven days; in Shakespeare's time, it was also called a sennight, or seven nights

fortnight
Two weeks (from the Old English for 14 nights)

month
Full Moon to full Moon; 1/12 of a year; 4 weeks, or 28, 29, 30 or 31 days, depending on month

bimester
Two months

trimester
A period of three months

year
365¼ days, 52 weeks, or 12 months

solar day
The time it takes for a place on the Earth directly facing the Sun to make one revolution and return to the same position (about 23 hours 56 minutes)

solar year
The time it takes for the Earth to make a complete revolution around the Sun, equal to 365.24219 solar days or 365 days, 5 hours 48 minutes, 45.51 seconds; also called a tropical year or astronomical year

leap year
366 days

decade
10 years; also called a decennium

century
100 years

millennium
1,000 years; also called a chiliad

bimillennium
2,000 years

era
A period of time measured from some important event

eon or aeon
A long period of time, usually thousands of years; in geology and astronomy it is one billion years

epoch
A geological era or very long period of time

See also
Geological time chart: page 34

Gregorian calendar

The Gregorian calendar is the one most used nowadays. It is named after Pope Gregory XIII who introduced it in 1582. There is a leap year every four years (or more precisely, 97 leap years every 400 years). This means that the year corresponds closely with the astronomical year (365.24219 days) so that it gets just one day out of sync in every 3,300 years.

Calendar problems

Some non-Catholic countries such as Great Britain refused to adopt the Gregorian calendar at first. The Julian calendar previously used in Great Britain was based on a solar year, the time taken for the Earth to rotate around the Sun. This is 365.25 days, which is fractionally too long (it is actually 365.24219 days), so the calendar steadily fell out of line with the seasons. In 1752 Great Britain decided to correct this by abandoning the Julian calendar in favor of the Gregorian. By doing so, September 3 instantly became September 14—and, as a result, nothing whatsoever happened in British history between September 3 and 13, 1752. Many people believed their lives would be shortened. They protested in the streets, demanding, "Give us back our 11 days!"

1 January 31 days
2 February 28 days*
3 March 31 days
4 April 30 days
5 May 31 days
6 June 30 days
7 July 31 days
8 August 31 days
9 September 30 days
10 October 31 days
11 November 30 days
12 December 31 days

* In a leap year, February has 29 days.

Mayan calendar

The Mayan people lived in the Yucatan area of present-day Mexico and the neighboring region. They built many amazing pyramids and temples, and had an astonishing knowledge of astronomy.

Mayan culture had declined by the time Spanish invaders occupied their territory in the 16th century, but we know something about it from the remains found. The Haab or civil calendar of the Maya had 18 months made up of 20 days each. Five extra days were added at the year's end, known as Uayeb, giving a year of 365 days.

Chichén Itzá, Mexico

Time pyramid

The Mayan pyramid at Chichén Itzá, Mexico, built around 1050, has four stairways, each with 91 steps and one platform. This makes a total of 365, the number of days in a year. The stairways also divide the nine terraces of each side of the pyramid into 18 segments, representing the 18 months of the Mayan calendar.

Calendar timeline

Most of the world's countries and cultures use the Gregorian calendar, but some base their calendars on more ancient systems. Other countries have adopted an alternative calendar at some point in their history.

3761 BC Jewish calendar starts
2637 BC Original Chinese calendar starts
45 BC Julian calendar adopted by Roman Empire
AD 1 Christian calendar starts
AD 79 Hindu calendar starts
597 Julian calendar adopted in Britain
622 Islamic calendar starts
1582 Gregorian calendar introduced in Catholic countries
1752 Julian calendar abandoned, Gregorian calendar adopted in Britain and its colonies, including America
1873 Japan adopts the Gregorian calendar
1949 China adopts the Gregorian calendar

Mayan months

1 Pop
2 Uo
3 Zip
4 Zotz
5 Tzec
6 Xul
7 Yaxkin
8 Mol
9 Chen
10 Yax
11 Zac
12 Ceh
13 Mac
14 Kankin
15 Muan
16 Pax
17 Kayab
18 Cumku

Chinese calendar

Present-day China uses the Gregorian calendar for most purposes, but traditional festivals, such as Chinese New Year, take place according to the ancient Chinese calendar. Legend has it that this was started during the reign of Emperor Huangdi in 2637 BC, and relates to the positions of the Moon and Sun.

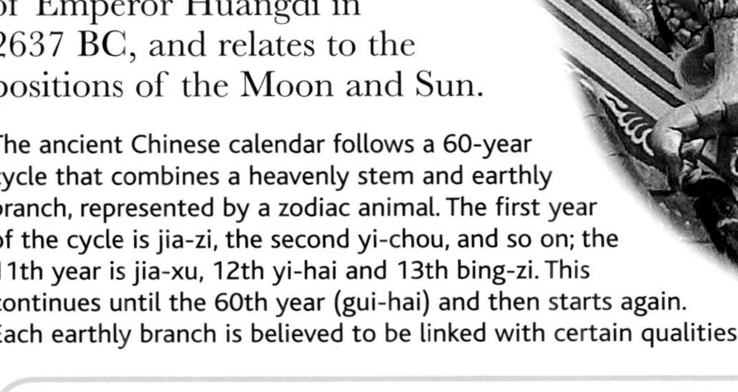

Chinese dragon

The ancient Chinese calendar follows a 60-year cycle that combines a heavenly stem and earthly branch, represented by a zodiac animal. The first year of the cycle is jia-zi, the second yi-chou, and so on; the 11th year is jia-xu, 12th yi-hai and 13th bing-zi. This continues until the 60th year (gui-hai) and then starts again. Each earthly branch is believed to be linked with certain qualities.

Calendars meet

The Islamic year is about 11 days shorter than a year in the Gregorian calendar. The Islamic calendar started 622 years later than the Gregorian so its date is behind. But because the year is shorter, the Islamic calendar is gradually gaining on the Gregorian. The two will eventually coincide—in the year 20874.

webexhibits.org/calendars search

Hebrew and Islamic calendars

The Hebrew (Jewish) and Islamic (Muslim) calendars are based on the lunar (Moon) cycle. Every month starts approximately on the day of a new Moon, or when a crescent moon is first seen.

The visibility of the Moon varies according to the weather so the start date cannot be determined in advance. Printed calendars may vary by a few days. Tishri/Muharram corresponds approximately with September/October in the Gregorian calendar, Heshvan/Safar with October/November, and so on.

Hebrew	Islamic	Hebrew	Islamic
1 Tishri	Muharram* (30 days)	**7 Nisan**	Rajab* (30 days)
2 Heshvan	Safar (29 days)	**8 Iyar**	Sha'ban (29 days)
3 Kislev	Rabi'a I (30 days)	**9 Sivan**	Ramadan † (30 days)
4 Tevet	Rabi'a II (29 days)	**10 Tammuz**	Shawwal (29 days)
5 Shevat	Jumada I (30 days)	**11 Av**	Dhu al-Q'adah* (30 days)
6 Adar	Jumada II (29 days)	**12 Elu**	Dhu al-Hijjah (29 days)

* Holy months † Month of fasting

Indian calendar

The Indian calendar is based on the motions of the Sun and Moon and is dated from the so-called Saka Era, equivalent to AD 79. It is used for dating religious and other festivals, but the Gregorian calendar is used for official dates.

Month	Length	Gregorian calendar
1 Caitra	30 days*	March 22
2 Vaisakha	31 days	April 21
3 Jyaistha	31 days	May 22
4 Asadha	31 days	June 22
5 Sravana	31 days	July 23
6 Bhadra	31 days	August 23
7 Asvina	30 days	September 23
8 Kartika	30 days	October 23
9 Agrahayana	30 days	November 22
10 Pausa	30 days	December 22
11 Magha	30 days	January 21
12 Phalguna	30 days	February 20

* In a leap year, Caitra has 31 days and 1 Caitra = March 21

Chinese calendar and Gregorian equivalents

Heavenly stems	Earthly branches
1 jia	1 zi (rat)
2 yi	2 chou (ox)
3 bing	3 yin (tiger)
4 ding	4 mao (hare or rabbit)
5 wu	5 chen (dragon)
6 ji	6 si (snake)
7 geng	7 wu (horse)
8 zxin	8 wei (sheep or ram)
9 ren	9 shen (monkey)
10 gui	10 you (rooster)
	11 xu (dog)
	12 hai (pig or boar)

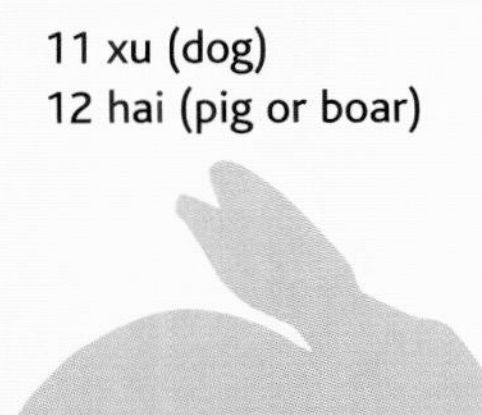

Zodiac animal	Gregorian calendar year beginning	Zodiac animal	Gregorian calendar year beginning
Ox	Feb 7, 1997	Monkey	Jan 22, 2004
Tiger	Jan 28, 1998	Rooster	Feb 9, 2005
Hare	Feb 16, 1999	Dog	Jan 29, 2006
Dragon	Feb 5, 2000	Pig	Feb 18, 2007
Snake	Jan 24, 2001	Rat	Feb 7, 2008
Horse	Feb 12, 2002	Ox	Jan 26, 2009
Sheep	Feb 1, 2003	Tiger	Feb 14, 2010

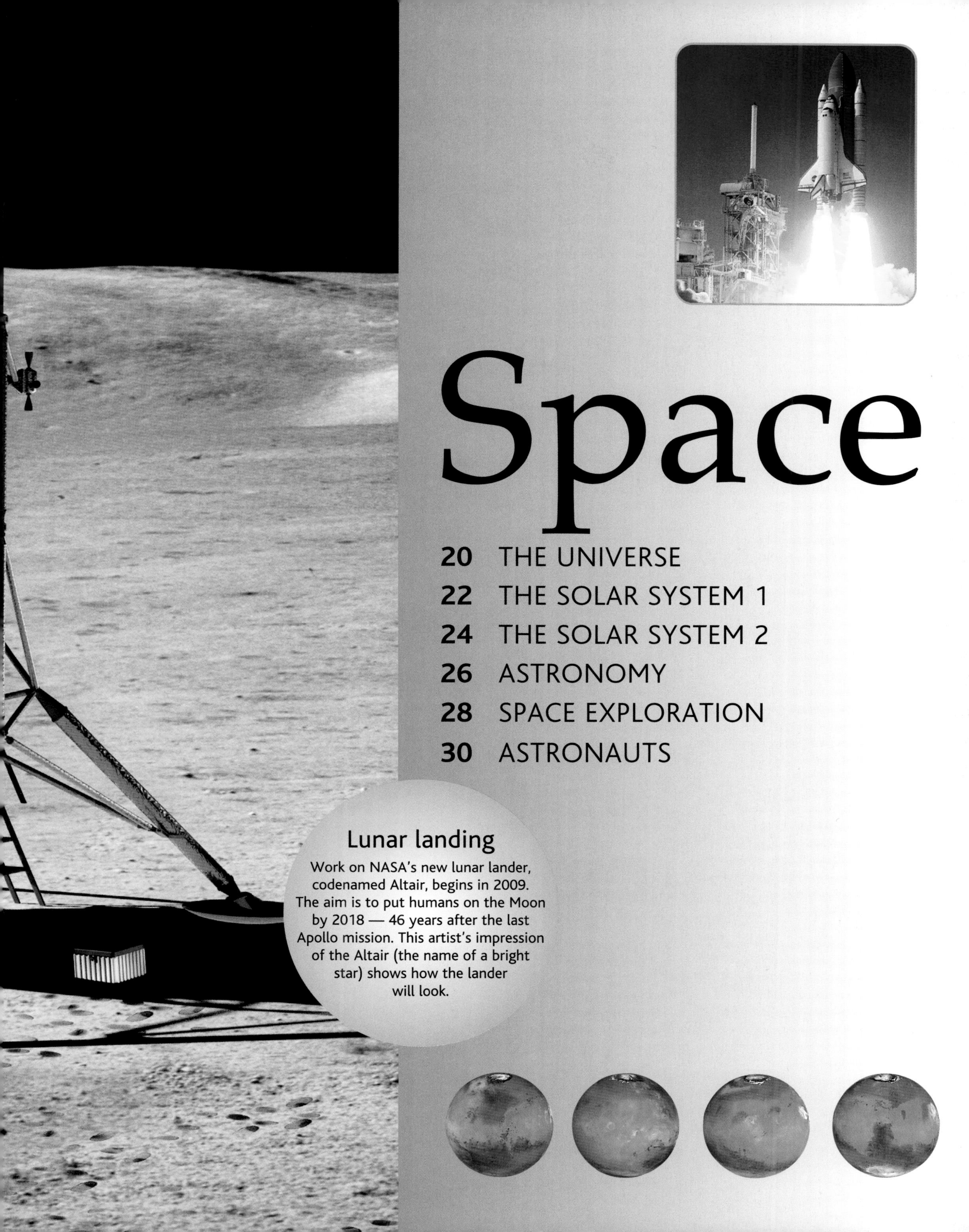

Space

20 THE UNIVERSE
22 THE SOLAR SYSTEM 1
24 THE SOLAR SYSTEM 2
26 ASTRONOMY
28 SPACE EXPLORATION
30 ASTRONAUTS

Lunar landing

Work on NASA's new lunar lander, codenamed Altair, begins in 2009. The aim is to put humans on the Moon by 2018 — 46 years after the last Apollo mission. This artist's impression of the Altair (the name of a bright star) shows how the lander will look.

Twinkle twinkle little star...

Stars appear to twinkle because we see them through the layers of the Earth's atmosphere. Light is distorted as it passes through these layers, so that the amount we see changes constantly. Stars nearest the horizon seem to twinkle the most because the light is passing through a greater depth of atmosphere. Stars do not twinkle when viewed from space, so telescopes in space, such as the Hubble, give the best possible view of distant stars and galaxies.

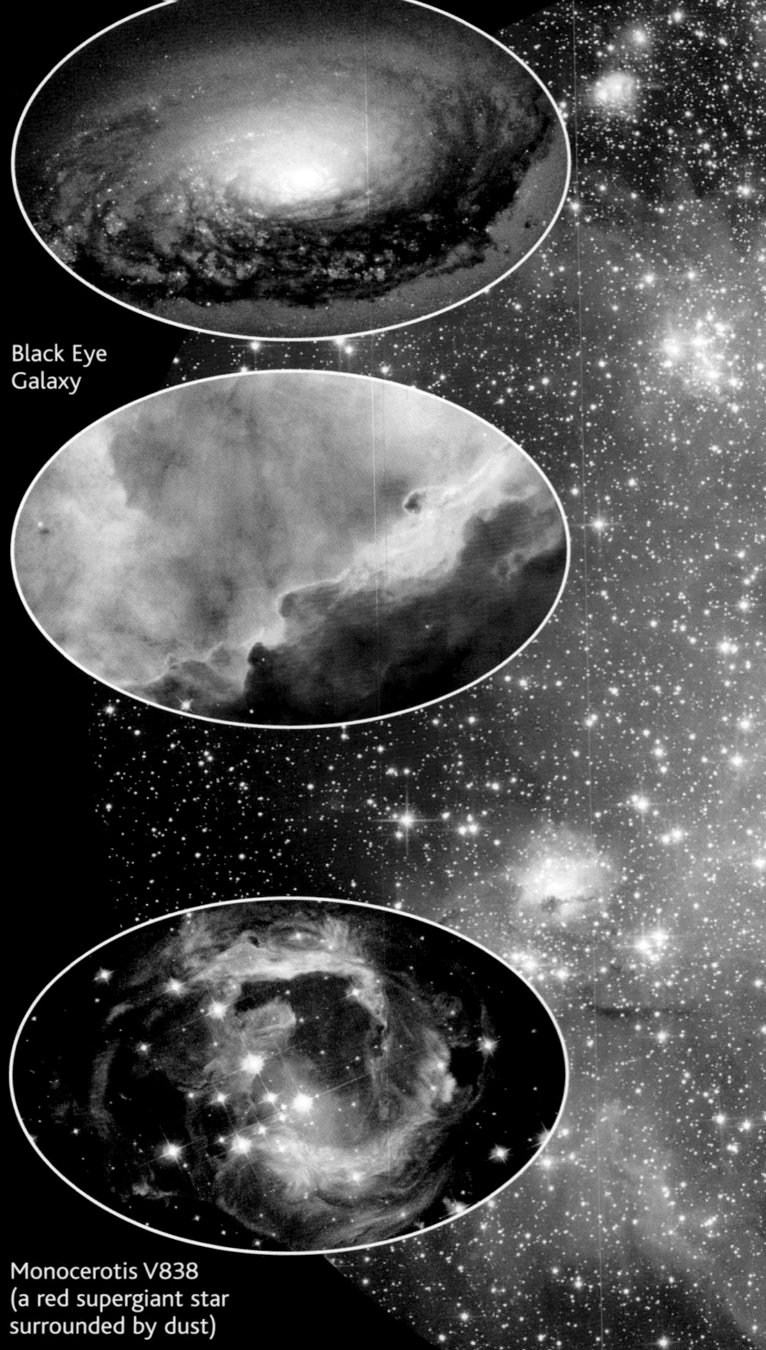

Black Eye Galaxy

Swan Nebula

Monocerotis V838 (a red supergiant star surrounded by dust)

Star facts

A star is a luminous body of gas, mostly hydrogen and helium. Stars generate light, which makes it possible for us to see them with a telescope or the naked eye.

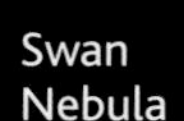

Photographs all taken by the Hubble Space Telescope

Supergiant VY Canis Majoris

The Sun

- **Brightest**
  Not counting the Sun, the brightest star as seen from Earth is Sirius, known as the dog star, in the constellation of Canis Major. It has a diameter of 92,955,900 mi. (149,598,020 km) and is more than 24 times brighter than the Sun. The star LBV 1806–20 in the constellation of Sagittarius may be 40 million times as bright as our Sun, but dust clouds make it almost invisible from Earth.
- **Largest**
  The largest star is VY Canis Majoris, which has an estimated diameter of about 1,950 times greater than the Sun. For comparison, if it were a football, the Sun would be no bigger than a pinhead.
- **Nearest**
  Proxima Centauri, discovered in 1915, is 4.22 light years from Earth. A spaceship moving at 25,000 mph (40,000 km/h)—which is faster than any human has yet traveled in space—would take more than 114,000 years to reach it.
- **Supernovae**
  These are vast explosions in which a whole star blows up. They are extremely bright, rivaling for a few days the combined light output of all the stars in the galaxy. Supernovae are rare—the last one in our galaxy was seen in 1604 by the German astronomer Johannes Kepler.
- **Quasars**
  These are extremely distant radio galaxies—galaxies giving out large amounts of radio energy—and the brightest objects in the Universe. Their radio emission is typically 1,000,000 to 100,000,000 times greater than that of a normal galaxy.
- **Black holes**
  A black hole is a star that has collapsed into itself. It has a surface gravity so powerful that nothing can

Traveling at the speed of light

In space, light travels at a speed of 186,282.4 mi. (299,792.46 km) a second, or 670,616,696 mi. (1,079,252,956 km) an hour. When we look at even the nearest star, we see light that left it more than four years ago. Here are the times it takes light to reach Earth from various bodies in space.

- **Light years**
  A light year measures distance, not time. Distances in space are often described as light years, the distance light travels in a year.

Galaxy facts

Galaxies are groups of billions of stars held together by the force of gravity. Most are either spiral or elliptical, but some are irregular in shape.

- **The Milky Way**

This is the best-known galaxy. The word galaxy comes from the Greek for milk. Before telescopes were powerful enough to prove that they were made up of individual stars, galaxies looked like milky or cloudy areas in the sky. Our Solar System is only one of 100–200 billion stars in the Milky Way, which is 100,000 light years in diameter. The Sun and all the planets take about 200,000,000 years to complete one orbit around its center.

- **Brightest**

The Large Magellanic Cloud, which is visible only in the southern hemisphere, is 170,000 light years from Earth and 39,000 light years in diameter.

- **Largest**

The central galaxy of the Abell 2029 galaxy cluster was discovered in 1990. It is 1.07 billion light years distant and has a diameter of 5.6 million light years, 80 times the diameter of our own galaxy. It has a total light output equivalent to 2 trillion times that of the Sun.

- **Nearest**

Discovered in 1993, the Canis Major Dwarf galaxy is approximately 25,000 light years from the Solar System.

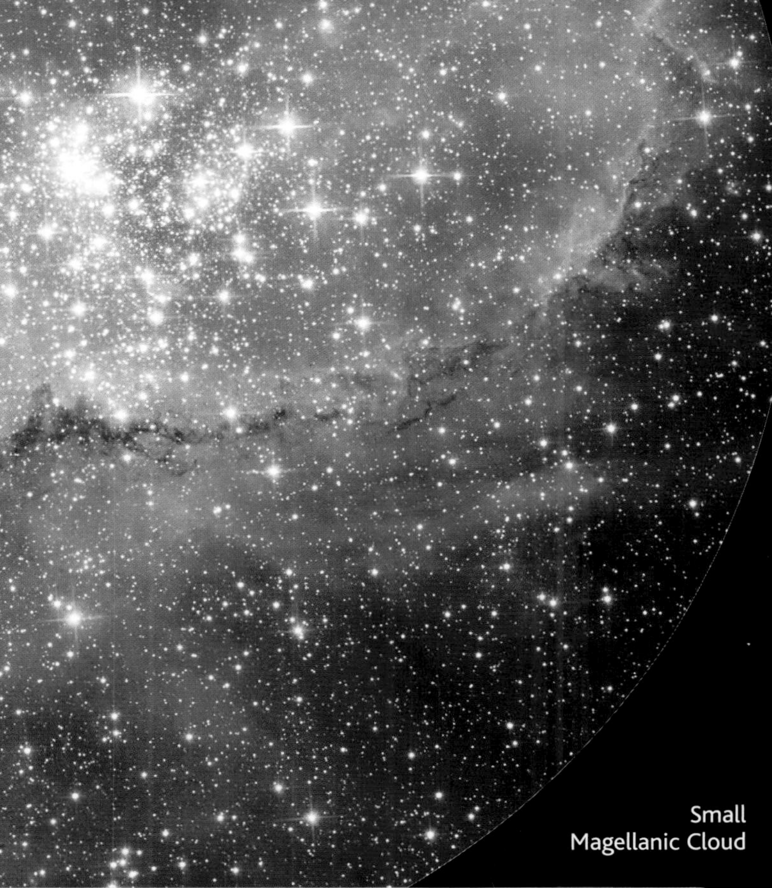

Small Magellanic Cloud

Moon 1.26 seconds
Sun 8 minutes 17 seconds
Furthest planet (Neptune) 4 hrs 21 mins when the planet is at its maximum distance from Earth
Nearest star 4.22 years
Distance at which the Sun would no longer be visible to the naked eye 60 years
Most distant star in our galaxy 62,700 years
From nearest body outside our galaxy 174,000 years
Furthest visible star 2,309,000 years
Most distant known quasar 14,000,000,000 years

Constellations

Groups of stars form patterns in the night sky, which are called constellations. There are 88 known constellations. The Sumerians, a Middle Eastern civilization, probably named them, about 5,000 years ago.

The largest is Hydra, the sea serpent, and the smallest is Crux Australis, the Southern Cross. Centaurus, the Centaur, has the most stars that can be seen with the naked eye (94). Others include Aquila, the Eagle; Canis Major, the Great Dog; and Orion, the Hunter.

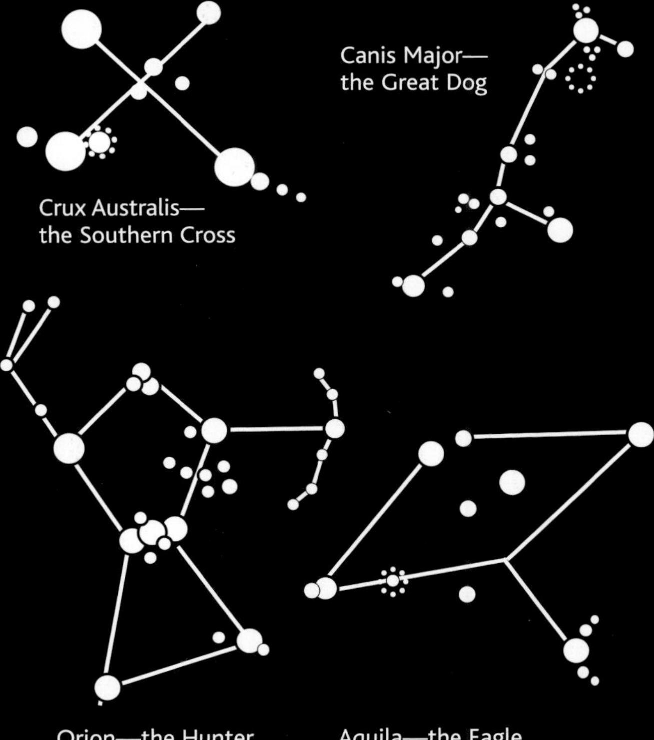

www.astronautix.com search

THE SOLAR SYSTEM 1

The Solar System was formed about 4,560 million years ago. It is made up of the eight planets—Mercury, Venus, Earth, Mars, Jupiter, Saturn, Uranus and Neptune—as well as their moons, comets and other bodies. These all orbit our Sun, which they are attracted to by gravity.

Mercury

Mercury was named after the speedy messenger of the gods because it seemed to move more quickly than the other known planets. In 2004 NASA launched its MESSENGER probe, which is due to reach Mercury in 2011.

Diameter: 3,032 mi. (4,880 km)
Mass: 3.302×10^{23} kg (0.055 Earths)
Average distance from Sun: 35,983,093 mi. (57,909,175 km)
Rotation: 58.6462 days
Orbit: 87.969 days
Average temperature: 332.32°F (166.86°C)
Moons: 0

Venus

In size, mass, density and volume Venus is the planet most similar to Earth. Venus rotates backward, from east to west, so the Sun would appear to rise in the west and set in the east. In April 2006 the European Space Agency's *Venus Express* spacecraft reached Venus. Japan's Venus Climate Orbiter *PLANET-C* will be launched in 2010.

Diameter: 7,521 mi. (12,103.6 km)
Mass: 4.869×10^{24} kg (0.815 Earths)
Average distance from Sun: 67,237,912 mi. (108,208,930 km)
Rotation: 243.0187 days
Orbit: 224.701 days
Average temperature: 854.33°F (456.85°C)
Moons: 0

See also
Planets visited by spacecraft: page 29

Several space probes have flown past or landed on Mars, providing information on its atmosphere and features, such as the volcano Olympus Mons. This stands 17 mi. (27 km) high—more than three times the height of Mount Everest. The latest craft to visit the red planet is *Mars Reconnaissance Orbiter*, which began a four-year orbit in 2006. NASA's *Phoenix* Mars landed in May 2008 (see p. 27).

Diameter: 4,222 mi. (6,794 km)
Mass: 6.4185×10^{23} kg (0.107 Earths)
Average distance from Sun: 141,635,000 mi. (227,940,000 km)
Rotation: 1.025957 days
Orbit: 686.98 days
Average temperature: –81°F(– 63°C)
Moons: 2

Jupiter

Jupiter is the largest planet in the Solar System and is big enough to contain more than a thousand Earths. Four of its many moons were among the first ever astronomical discoveries made with a telescope, by Galileo in 1610. More were identified by later astronomers and in 1979 by the space probe *Voyager 2*. The NASA Juno mission to Jupiter is planned for launch in 2011.

Diameter: 88,846 mi. (142,984 km)
Mass: 1.8986×10^{27} kg (317.8 Earths)
Average distance from Sun: 483,682,799 mi. (778,412,010 km)
Rotation: 9 hours 50 minutes
Orbit: 11 years 314 days
Average temperature: –238°F (–150°C)
Moons: 63

Earth

Earth is a watery planet—70 percent of its surface appears blue—and the only one that can support life. From space, astronauts have observed cities, forest fires, roads, airports, dams and other large structures, such as the Great Pyramid and the Great Wall of China.

Diameter: 7,926 mi. (12,756 km)
Mass: 5.972×10^{24} kg
Average distance from Sun: 92,957,130 mi. (149,600,000 km)
Rotation: 0.99727 days
Orbit: 365.256 days
Average temperature: 59°F (15°C)
Moons: 1

www.nineplanets.org search

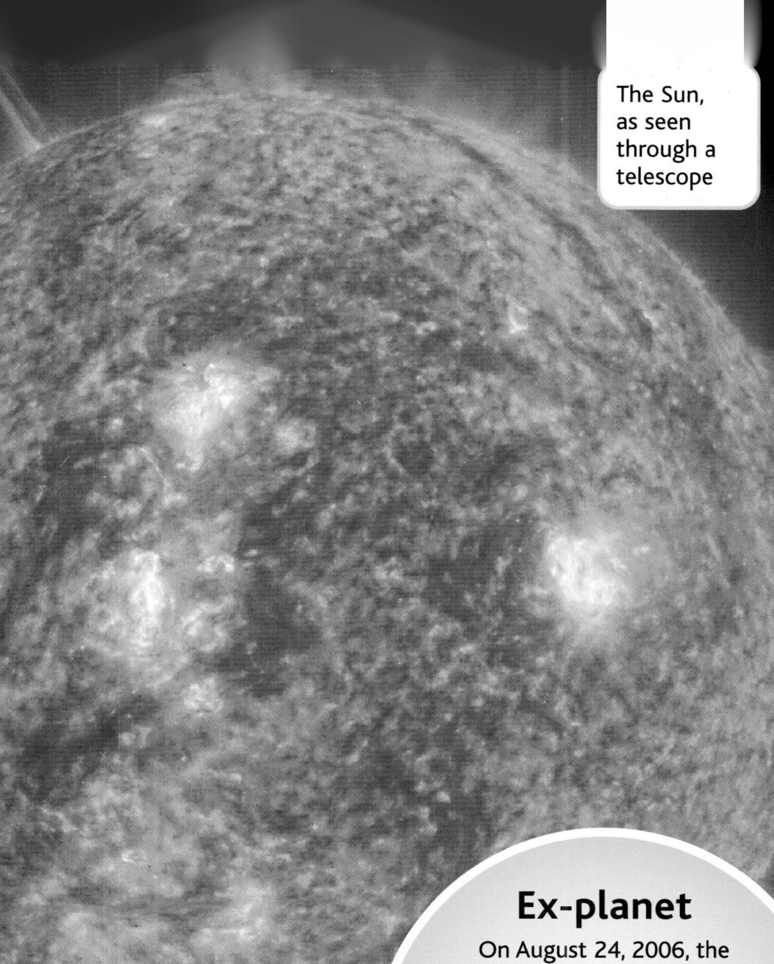

The Sun, as seen through a telescope

Sun facts

The Sun is 92,955,821 mi. (149,597,893 km) from Earth and has a diameter of 864,911 mi. (1,391,940 km). This is more than 100 times larger than Earth. Its mass is equivalent to 99.98 percent of the mass of the entire Solar System.

Elements

The Sun is mostly made up of two light gases, 75 percent hydrogen and 23 percent helium, with relatively small quantities of other elements—including metals such as gold. Helium was discovered in the Sun before it was detected on Earth. Its name comes from *helios*, the Greek word for sun.

Temperature

The Sun has a surface temperature of 5,880 K but it can be 56,000,000 K at its core. (K represents Kelvin, which is an astronomical temperature; it can be converted to Fahrenheit by subtracting 459.67.) At the Sun's center, nuclear fusion constantly changes hydrogen into helium, and the energy and heat released from this process rise to the surface. The yellow surface we see is called the photosphere.

The corona

The outermost layer of the Sun extends millions of miles into space but is visible only during eclipses. At a height of 46,600 mi. (75,000 km) in the corona, the temperature may reach 2,000,000 K.

Rotation

The Sun rotates once every 25.4 days, but because it is not solid, the poles spin at a different rate, taking as much as 36 days to complete a single revolution.

Solar eclipses

When the Moon is between Earth and the Sun, it blocks out the light causing a partial or total eclipse. At this time, astronomers are able to observe the corona in detail.

Ex-planet

On August 24, 2006, the International Astronomical Union downgraded Pluto from planetary status. It is now regarded as belonging to a new "dwarf planet" category, along with Eris, discovered in 2005, and Ceres, which used to be regarded as the largest asteroid. The spacecraft *New Horizons* is scheduled to reach Pluto in 2015.

Saturn

Saturn and its rings are being examined by NASA/European Space Agency's *Cassini* probe, which reached it in 2004. It released the *Huygens* probe to orbit Titan in 2005 and began flybys of Saturn's moons Lapetus in 2007 and Titan in 2008.

Diameter: 74,898 mi.(120,536 km)
Mass: 5.6846 x 10^{26} kg (95.15 Earths)
Average distance from Sun: 886,526,100 mi. (1,426,725,400 km)
Rotation: 10 hours 34 minutes
Orbit: 29 years 168 days
Average temperature: –219.1°F (–139.5°C)

Uranus

All the satellites of Uranus are called after characters from either William Shakespeare's plays or Alexander Pope's poem *The Rape of the Lock*. Uranus has rings like those of Saturn, but they are visible only with a powerful telescope.

Diameter: 31,763 mi. (51,118 km)
Mass: 8.6832 x 10^{25} kg (14.54 Earths)
Average distance from Sun: 1,783,939,400 mi. (2,870,972,200 km)
Rotation: 17 hours 17 minutes
Orbit: 84 years 4 days
Average temperature: -322.87°F (–197.15°C)

Neptune

Neptune is the furthest body from the Sun. Surface winds are the strongest of any planet at up to 2,000 km/h. Neptune's year is so long that it has not completed an orbit round the Sun since its discovery and will not until 2011.

Diameter: 30,772 mi. (49,522 km)
Mass: 10.247 x 10^{25} kg (17.15 Earths)
Average distance from Sun: 2,795,084,800 mi. (4,498,252,900 km)
Rotation: 16 hours 7 minutes
Orbit: 164 years 298 days
Average temperature: –328.27°F (–200.15°C)

Buzz Aldrin, walking on the Moon

The Moon's near side

Our Moon's far side

The far side of our Moon always faces away from Earth, so it was unknown until October 1959, when the Soviet *Luna 3* probe sent pictures of it back to Earth.

Asteroid facts

Asteroids are often called minor planets. They are lumps of rock orbiting the Sun, mostly in the asteroid belt between the orbits of Mars and Jupiter.

- Ceres was once considered the largest asteroid but it has been recently reclassified as a dwarf planet. It is 582 mi. (936 km) in diameter and was found on New Year's Day, 1801. Since then thousands of asteroids have been found. Twelve of them are more than 155 mi. (250 km) wide and 26 are larger than 125 mi. (200 km) in diameter. As telescopes have improved, more and more small asteroids have been detected. There are probably about 100,000 asteroids larger than about a half mile (1 km) in diameter. Some experts think there may be as many as 1.2 million.
- Vesta, the fourth asteroid to be found (in 1807), is the only one bright enough to be seen without a telescope.

Moon facts

Earth's Moon is the most familiar and also the largest satellite in relation to its planet in the Solar System. It is the first body in the Solar System on which vehicles from Earth landed, and the only one to be explored by humans.

Diameter: 2159.6 mi. (3,475.6 km)
Distance from Earth: 252,718 mi. (406,711 km) — furthest 1912; to 221,441 mi. (356,375 km) — closest, 1984; averaging 238,856 mi. (384,403 km)
Mass: 7.3456×10^{23} kg (0.012 Earths) 809,709,000,000 tons; a person weighing 140 lb. (63.5 kg) on Earth would weigh 23.23 lb. (10.5 kg) on the Moon
Rotation: 27 days 7 hours 43 minutes 11.5 seconds
Surface temperature: –261°F to 243°F (–163°C to 117°C)
Largest crater: South Pole Aitken (far side) 1,305 mi. (2,100 km) diameter, 7.5 mi. (12 km) deep (largest in the Solar System)

Part of the Bayeux Tapestry, showing Halley's comet, top left

Halley's comet

British astronomer Edmond Halley (1656–1742) was the first to prove that comets travel in orbits, making it possible to calculate when they will next be seen from Earth. He predicted that the comet he saw in 1682 would return in 1759. It did and was named in his honor. The regular orbit of Halley's comet means that we can find historical accounts of its appearances going back more than 2,000 years. They were often believed to foretell great events.

240 BC

May 25, 240 BC Seen in China
October 10, 12 BC Believed to mark the death of Roman general Agrippa
June 28, AD 451 Believed to mark the defeat of Attila the Hun
March 20, 1066 William (later William the Conqueror) believed the comet foretold victory over King Harold at the Battle of Hastings. The comet and battle are later depicted in the Bayeux Tapestry.

1450s

June 9, 1456 The defeat of the Turkish army by Papal forces was thought to be linked to the comet.

● Astronomers believe that, on average, one asteroid larger than 0.25 mi. (0.4 km) strikes Earth every 50,000 years. Some 65 million years ago a 6 mi. (10 km) diameter asteroid crashing to Earth may have been responsible for wiping out the dinosaurs. It would have caused a catastrophic explosion, affecting the climate and chemical composition of the atmosphere and destroying the plants and animals on which the dinosaurs fed. As recently as 1991 a small asteroid came within 106,000 mi. (170,600 km) of Earth, the closest recorded near miss. On Jan 30, 2052, an asteroid is predicted to pass as close as 74,364 mi. (119,678 km).

● Toutatis (asteroid 4,179) was discovered in 1989. It is named after the Celtic god Toutatis. Toutatis measures 2.9 by 1.5 by 1.2 mi. (4.6 by 2.4 by 1.9 km). It passes Earth every four years and is one of the largest space objects to come so close to us. On September 29, 2004, Toutatis came within 966,740 mi. (1,555,818 km) of Earth. Its next visit will be on November 9, 2008, when it will come within 4,675,677 mi. (7,524,773 km).

Titanic moon

Titan is the largest of Saturn's 34 moons. It is 3,200 mi. (5,150 km) in diameter—larger than the planet Mercury. Dutch astronomer Christiaan Huygens discovered Titan in 1655. We still have no idea what its surface looks like because Titan has a dense atmosphere containing nitrogen, ethane and other gases that shroud its surface—not unlike that of Earth four billion years ago.

Information sent back by the space probe *Voyager 1* during 1980 and recent radio telescope observations suggest that Titan may have ethane "oceans" and "continents" of ice or other solid matter. *Cassini*, a space probe launched by NASA and the European Space Agency, arrived in Saturn's orbit on July 1, 2004. On January 14, 2005, it launched the *Huygens* probe onto the surface of Titan and sent back scientific data.

Neptune's moon

Triton, discovered in 1846, is the only known large moon in the Solar System with a retrograde orbit. It revolves around its planet (Neptune) in the opposite direction to the planet's rotation.

Comet Hale-Bopp as seen from Earth in 1997

Comet Temple 1 as photographed by NASA's *Deep Impact* probe in 2005

Titan, the largest moon of Saturn

Returning comets

More than 20 comets return more often than Halley. The most frequent visitor is Encke's comet, named after the German astronomer Johann Franz Encke (1791–1865). In 1818 he calculated the 3.3-year period of its orbit.

2000s

September 15, 1682 Observed by Edmond Halley, who predicted its return

March 13,1759 The comet's first return, as predicted by Halley, proving his calculations correct

November 16,1835 The American author Mark Twain is born. He always believed that his fate was linked to that of the comet, and soon after it reappeared in 1910, he died.

April 10, 1910 There was panic as many believed the world would come to an end.

February 9,1986 The Japanese *Suisei* probe, Soviet *Vega 1* and *Vega 2* and the European Space Agency's *Giotto* passed close to Halley's comet. Astronomers concluded that the comet is made of dust held together by water and carbon dioxide ice.

July 28, 2061 Next due to appear. The orbit of Halley's comet is not exactly 76 years. Astronomers have to take into account the gravitational pull from planets when calculating its return.

www.spacetoday.org search

Famous astronomers

John Couch Adams (U.K., 1819–92) studied the Leonid meteor shower and predicted the existence of Neptune, which was discovered in 1846.

Edward Emerson Barnard (U.S., 1857–1923) discovered Barnard's Star and Amalthea, a moon of Jupiter.

Nicolaus Copernicus (Poland, 1473–1543) showed that the Sun was at the center of the Solar System.

Galileo Galilei (Italy, 1564–1642) made important discoveries concerning gravity and motion. He built some of the first telescopes used in astronomy and used them to discover many previously unknown space objects.

George Ellery Hale (U.S., 1868–1938) pioneered the astronomical study of the Sun and founded observatories, one with a major telescope named after him.

Edmond Halley (U.K., 1656–1742) predicted the orbits of comets, including the one that bears his name.

William Herschel (Germany/U.K., 1738–1822) built huge telescopes, compiled catalogues of stars and discovered moons of Saturn and Uranus.

Edwin Hubble (U.S., 1889–1953) made important discoveries about galaxies. The Hubble Space Telescope was named in his honor.

Christiaan Huygens (Holland, 1629–95) discovered Saturn's rings and devised the wave theory of light.

Percival Lowell (U.S., 1855–1916) was founder of the Lowell Observatory, Arizona. He predicted that a planet would be found in the region where Pluto was later discovered.

Charles Messier (France, 1730–1817) studied comets and eclipses, but he is best known for his catalogue of stars first published in 1774.

Yerkes Observatory, Wisconsin

Isaac Newton (England, 1643–1727) is considered one of the greatest of all astronomers. His theories of gravity and the motions of planets revolutionized the subject.

Telescopes and observatories

The following are some of the world's most famous telescopes and observatories.

Royal Observatory, Greenwich, London, England

Founded by King Charles II in 1675, but atmospheric and light pollution in London reduced its efficiency. In 1884 the Prime or Greenwich Meridian, 0°, which passes through the Observatory, was adopted as the basis for all mapping and measurements. Longitude measurements refer to west or east of the meridian.

Herschel's "Forty-foot" reflector, Slough, England

A giant telescope built in 1788 with a 48-in. (1.2 m) mirror.

Birr Castle, Co. Offaly, Ireland

The Earl of Rosse's 72-in. (1.8 m) reflecting telescope, built in 1845, was used to discover the spiral form of galaxies. It was the world's largest until the opening of Mount Wilson.

Yerkes Observatory, Williams Bay, Wisconsin

This 40-in. (1 m) telescope is the biggest refracting instrument made up to this time. It was completed in 1897.

Mount Wilson Observatory, California

The telescope was installed in 1917 with a mirror size of 100 in. (2.5 m). It was the world's largest until the Hale.

Hale Telescope, Palomar Observatory, California

The Hale's 200-in. (5 m) telescope was first used in 1949.

Jodrell Bank, Cheshire, England

Great Britain's first, and once the world's largest radio telescope, with a 250-ft. (76 m) dish, began operating in 1957.

Arecibo Observatory, Puerto Rico

Completed in 1963, this is the world's most powerful radio telescope. Its uses include searching for pulsars and quasars and the search for alien life forms under the SETI (Search for Extra-Terrestrial Intelligence) program. Its giant 1,000-ft. (305 m) dish is featured in the final scenes of the James Bond film *Golden Eye* (1995).

Astronomy milestones

Astronomy is the scientific study of the Universe and the bodies it contains (excluding Earth). Astronomers are the scientists who study astronomy.

585 BC First prediction of eclipse of the Sun

130 BC Hipparchus calculates distance and size of Moon

AD 1543 Copernicus shows that the Sun is at the center of the Solar System

1609 Johannes Kepler describes laws of planetary motion

1610 Galileo Galilei discovers moons of Jupiter

1655 Christiaan Huygens discovers Titan, moon of Saturn

1600s

1668 Isaac Newton builds first reflecting telescope

1687 Isaac Newton publishes theories of motions of planets, etc.

1705 Edmond Halley predicts return of comet

1671–84 Giovanni Cassini discovers four moons of Saturn

1774 Charles Messier compiles star catalogue

1781 William Herschel discovers seventh planet, Uranus

1800s

1801 First asteroid, Ceres, discovered by Giuseppe Piazzi

1846 Johann Galle and Urbain Le Verrier discover eight planet, Neptune

1787–89 Herschel finds two moons of Uranus and two of Saturn

1839–40 First photographs of the Moon

1894 Flagstaff Observatory, Arizona, founded

1905 Einstein's Special Theory of Relativity first proposed

Hubble Space Telescope

The HST was launched in 1990 and orbits 366 mi. (589 km) above Earth's atmosphere. It can photograph distant objects with 10 times the detail possible with ground-based telescopes.

Keck I & II Telescopes, Mauna Kea Observatory, Hawaii

The two Keck telescopes were opened in 1992–96. They are situated 13,600 ft. (4,145 m) up a Hawaiian mountain, so above 40 percent of the Earth's atmosphere. They are the world's most powerful ground-based instruments, with a 400-in. (10 m) total aperture made up of 36 hexagonal mirrors.

Hobby-Eberly Telescope, McDonald Observatory, Texas

This telescope is designed to collect light for spectrum analysis rather than for visual exploration. It has been in operation since 1999, and has an overall diameter of 360-in. (9.2 m), making it one of the largest ever optical telescopes.

Large Binocular Telescope, Arizona

The Large Binocular Telescope, completed in 2007, is the largest and most advanced optical telescope ever built. Sited at the Mount Graham International Observatory, it has two 331-in. (8.4 m) mirrors, giving a total area equal to one giant 450-in. (11.4 m) diameter mirror. It is expected to produce images as much as 10 times the resolution of those produced by the much smaller Hubble Space Telescope.

Hubble Space Telescope

First telescopes

The first telescopes were made in 1608 by Dutchman Hans Lippershey. Galileo built his own soon after and used it to discover Jupiter's moons. The earliest type of telescope, known as a refracting telescope, produced a slight distortion of images (called aberration). Since about 1670, astronomers have used reflecting telescopes, which use mirrors that compensate for the distortion.

1900s – 2000s

1908 Giant and dwarf stars described
1923 Galaxies beyond the Milky Way proved
1927 Big Bang theory proposed
1930 Pluto discovered by Clyde Tombaugh
1959 First photographs of the far side of the Moon by Soviet satellite *Luna 3*
1961 First quasars discovered
1967 First pulsars identified
1971 Black hole first detected
1973 *Skylab* space laboratory launched
1976 Rings of Uranus are discovered
1977 *Voyager* deep space probes are launched
1971 *Mariner 9* spacecraft maps Mars
1980 *Voyager 1* explores Saturn
1978 Space probes *Pioneer 1* and *2* reach Venus
1985–89 *Voyager 2* discovers moons of Uranus and Neptune
1994 Comet Shoemaker-Levy observed crashing into Jupiter
1995 *Galileo* probe reaches Jupiter
1997 *Mars Pathfinder* lands
1997 *Cassini* probe launched to Saturn
1998 *International Space Station* construction starts
1999 Chandra X-Ray Observatory launched
2003 *Galileo* probe deliberately crash-landed on Jupiter
2006 *New Horizons* space probe launched to Pluto
2008 *Phoenix* mission to Mars landed on the planet.

www.absoluteastronomy.com search

Animal space pioneers

Before humans went into space animals were used to test equipment. The first animal to be sent up in a rocket – but not into space — was Albert 1, a male rhesus monkey, in 1948. He and his successor, Albert 2, died during the tests.

However, on September 20, 1951, a monkey and 11 mice were recovered after a launch in a U.S. *Aerobee* rocket. Many further animal experiments were carried out before the first manned space flight.

Space dogs, and a cat

Laika, a female Samoyed husky, became the first animal in orbit after being launched by the USSR in *Sputnik 2* in November 1957. There was no way to bring her down and she died after 10 days in space. Two female huskies, Belka and Strelka, orbited successfully in August 1960. Strelka later gave birth to puppies, one of which was given to U.S. President John F. Kennedy. In October 1963, a French *Veronique AGI* rocket put a cat called Félix into space and returned him safely to Earth by parachute.

Monkey business

Able, a female rhesus monkey, and Baker, a female squirrel monkey, were launched by the U.S. in May 1959. They did not orbit and successfully returned to Earth. In November 1961, Enos, a male chimpanzee, completed two orbits and survived. The USSR's first space primates were monkeys Abrek and Bion, who orbited in December 1983 in one of a series of Bion satellite experiments.

Flying frogs

In November 1970, the USA's Orbiting Frog Otolith satellite (OFO-A) launched two bullfrogs into orbit for a week. In December 1990, Toyohiro Akiyama, a Japanese journalist, took six green tree frogs to the Soviet *Mir* space station to conduct weightlessness experiments.

Worldwide web

Arabella, a garden spider, went to the U.S. *Skylab-3* in July 1973. She spent almost 60 days in orbit in an experiment to test the effect of weightlessness on her web-weaving skills.

A space menagerie

The *STS-90* mission of space shuttle *Columbia* (April/May 1998) contained the *Neurolab*—a space menagerie with 170 baby rats, 18 mice, 229 swordtail fish, 135 snails, four oyster toad fish and 1,514 cricket eggs and larvae.

Can of worms

On February 1, 2003, space shuttle *Columbia STS-107* broke up on re-entry and its crew were killed. Onboard animal experiments involving silkworms, spiders, carpenter bees, harvester ants and Japanese killfish were destroyed, but, amazingly, canisters of worms were found alive.

In January 2006, an *Atlas V* rocket launched NASA's *New Horizons* probe on its 9-year journey to Pluto.

kids.msfc.nasa.gov search

Long Duration Exposure Facility satellite (U.S.) orbited the Earth 34,422 times between 1984 – 90. Space Shuttle *Columbia* eventually brought it back to Earth.

Artificial satellites

The USSR's *Sputnik 1* was the first artificial satellite to enter Earth's orbit. This 184 lb. (83.6 kg) metal sphere transmitted signals back to Earth for three weeks before its batteries failed.

In 1958 the U.S. began to launch its own satellites. Five went into orbit. All of the earliest satellites have since crashed back to Earth, except *Vanguard 1* (U.S., 1958) which is still in space—and likely to remain so for another 200 years.

Over the past 50 years, many more artificial satellites have been launched, with a greater range of uses.

Astronomy

The Hubble Space Telescope has been taking photographs of distant galaxies since 1990. In 2008 the Herschel Space Observatory is scheduled for launch. This new telescope will have the biggest mirror ever in space (138 in. [3.5 m] across).

Communications

Over 5,000 satellites have been launched to transmit telephone, radio and television signals around the world. Fewer than half are still orbiting, and many have stopped working.

Earth observation satellites

These transmit images of the weather and the Earth's environment. They helped to show the depletion of the ozone layer.

Military satellites

Governments use these "spies in the sky" for surveillance but their precise functions are secret.

Global Positioning System

This is a system of 24 linked satellites that allows people to pinpoint their exact position anywhere on Earth. The system is operated by the U.S. Department of Defense and is used by aircraft and ships. GPS systems are now common in cars, too.

Space junk

When satellites reach the end of their useful life, they may be deliberately directed back in such a way that they burn up as they re-enter the Earth's atmosphere or come down in the oceans or away from places where they could cause damage. So far, no one has been killed or seriously injured by space debris.

Returned to Earth

The 76-ton (69-tonne) *Skylab* re-entered in 1979, scattering large chunks in the Australian desert, and Russia's *Mir* space station, which weighed 132 tons (120 tonnes), came down in the Pacific.

Orbiting junk

About 100 to 200 objects, each larger than a football, re-enter every year, but there are still many pieces of space junk in orbit. A survey carried out in June 2000 calculated that there are 90 space probes and 2,671 satellites still in space. There are as many as 100,000 objects up to 4 in. (10 cm) in diameter and about 11,000 objects larger than 4 in. (10 cm) including parts of rockets: an *Ariane* rocket booster exploded in 1986, scattering 400 fragments large enough to be tracked. In 1991 space shuttle *Discovery STS-48* narrowly avoided a discarded Soviet rocket.

Space rockets

Thrust is the force required to lift a vehicle such as an aircraft or rocket off the ground. Rockets often have several stages. Each one provides a proportion of the thrust required to carry a satellite, space shuttle or other vehicle into orbit or into space, dropping away as their propellant has been used so that their weight no longer needs to be carried.

Planets visited by spacecraft

No human has yet set foot on any space body other than Earth and the Moon. But unmanned spacecraft have taken photographs, made scientific readings and gathered data from all the planets in the Solar System, either by flying past or landing.

Venus *Mariner 2* (U.S.) flyby 1962; *Venera 4* (USSR) landed 1967; MESSENGER (U.S.) flybys 2006, 2007

Mars *Mariner 4* (U.S.) flyby 1965; *Mars Pathfinder* (U.S.) landed 1997; *Mars Reconnaissance Orbiter* (U.S.) in orbit 2006 – ; *Phoenix Mars* (U.S.) landed in 2008; *Dawn* (U.S.) flyby 2009.

Jupiter *Pioneer 10* (U.S.) flyby 1973; *Galileo* (U.S.) landed* 2003; *New Horizons* (U.S.) flyby 2007

Mercury *Mariner 10* (U.S.) flyby 1974; MESSENGER (U.S.) flybys 2008, 2009 and scheduled to orbit 2011

Saturn *Pioneer 11* (U.S.) flyby 1979; *Cassini/Huygens* (U.S./ESA) orbiter/lander 2004/2005

Uranus *Voyager 2* (U.S.) flyby 1986

Neptune *Voyager 2* (U.S.) flyby 1989

* Deliberately destroyed entering Jupiter's atmosphere, rather than risk contaminating moon Europa with bacteria from Earth.

Manned space missions

During the 1950s, there was a "space race" between the U.S. and USSR to be the first country to send a human into space. NASA's *Mercury* missions were originally unmanned, or carried only animals. The USSR launched the first human into orbit in 1961.

Each country's subsequent space missions had different aims. The U.S. focused on Moon landings with their *Apollo* program and later the reusable space shuttle. The Soviets and later Russia concentrated on long-duration missions, with the *Mir* space station. The latest manned mission is the *International Space Station*, which is four times larger than *Mir*.

Mission	Country	Years
Mercury	U.S.	1959–63
Vostok	USSR	1961–63
Voskhod	USSR	1964–65
Gemini	U.S.	1965–66
Apollo	U.S.	1967–72
Soyuz	USSR	1967–76
Salyut	USSR	1971–82
Skylab	U.S.	1973
Apollo Soyuz	U.S./USSR	1975
Space shuttle	U.S.	1981
Mir space station	USSR/Russia	1986–2001
International Space Station	U.S., Canada, Japan, European Space Agency, Russia, Brazil	1998–
Shenzhou	China	2003–

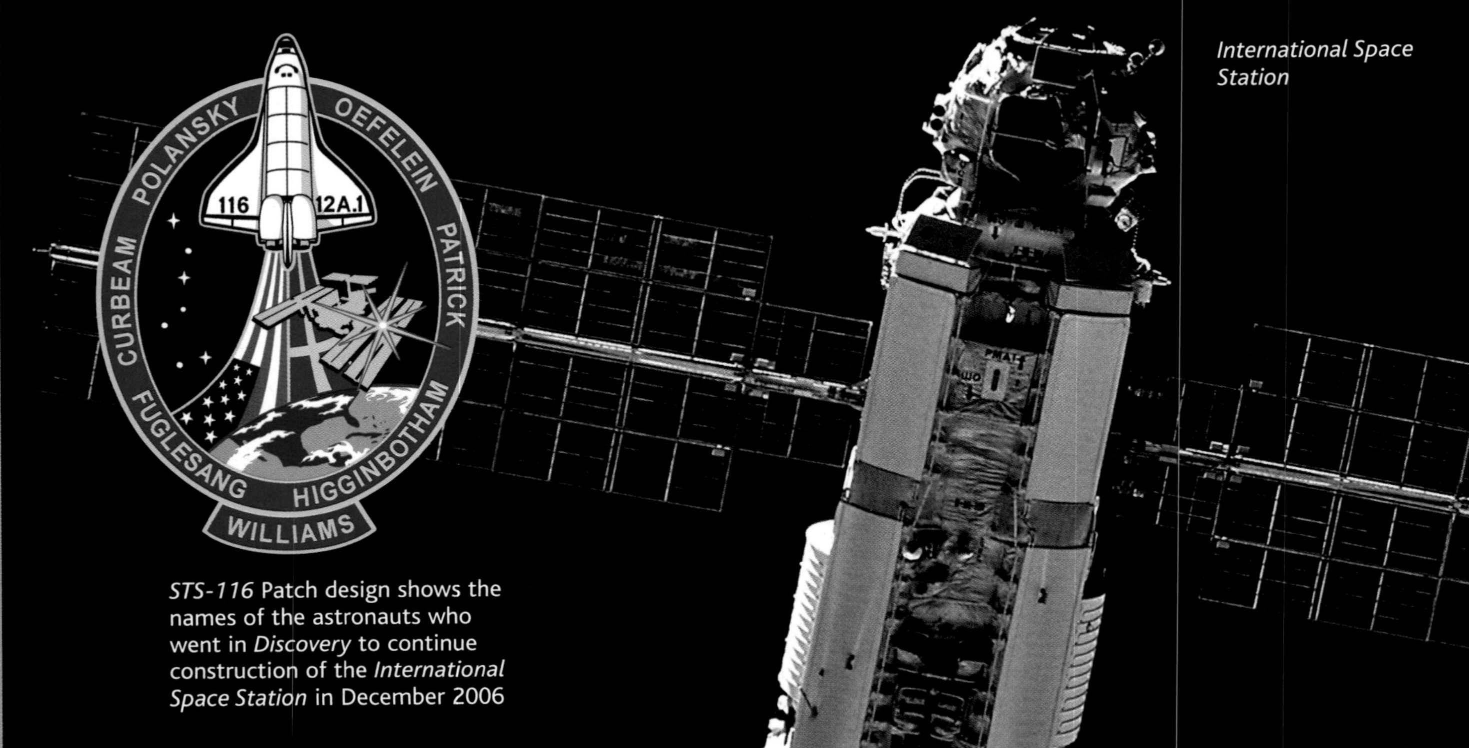

International Space Station

STS-116 Patch design shows the names of the astronauts who went in *Discovery* to continue construction of the *International Space Station* in December 2006

Astronauts and cosmonauts

The word "astronaut" was first used in 1880 by the British writer Percy Greg. It was the name he gave to a spaceship in his novel *Across the Zodiac*. By the 1950s it was the word used for a space voyager. The Russian word is cosmonaut.

April 12, 1961, First person in space Soviet cosmonaut Yuri Gagarin made a single orbit of Earth in *Vostok 1*, a flight that lasted 1 hour 48 minutes.

May 5, 1961, First U.S. astronaut The U.S.'s first astronaut, Alan B. Shepard Jr., entered space aboard *Mercury 3* but did not orbit during his 15-minute 22-second mission.

August 6, 1961, First flight of over 24 hours Gherman S. Titov (USSR) in *Vostok 2* made the first flight of more than 24 hours. He was also the youngest ever astronaut at 25 years, 10 months, 25 days.

February 20, 1962, First U.S. orbit John H. Glenn Jr. in the *Friendship 7* capsule made the first U.S. orbit, completing three orbits in 4 hours, 55 minutes.

June 16, 1963, First woman in space Valentina V. Tereshkova (USSR) in *Vostok 6* was the first woman in space. She spent 2 days, 22 hours, 50 minutes, 8 seconds in space. She remains the youngest (26 years, 3 months, 10 days) woman in space.

March 18, 1965, First space walk Aleskei Leonov (USSR) made the first space walk, from *Voskhod 2*. It took 24 minutes and it almost ended in disaster when his spacesuit ballooned. He was unable to return through the airlock until he reduced the pressure in his suit to a dangerously low level.

March 23, 1965, First two-man U.S. mission John Young and Virgil "Gus" Grissom made the first two-man U.S. mission in *Gemini 3*.

June 3, 1965, First U.S. spacewalk Edward H. White II made a 36-minute spacewalk from *Gemini 4*.

April 24, 1967, First space death After 18 orbits in *Soyuz 1*, Vladimir M. Komarov (USSR) died when his parachute got tangled and his capsule crash-landed.

December 24, 1968, First manned spacecraft to orbit the Moon *Apollo 8* (followed in 1969 by *Apollo* missions 9 and 10) orbited the Moon but did not land.

All the men on the Moon

The human exploration of the Moon lasted just over three years and involved a total of six missions. In each, a pair of U.S. astronauts went down to the surface in a LEM (lunar excursion module) while a third orbited in a CSM (command service module). The missions provided scientists with a huge amount of information about the Moon.

Astronaut	Spacecraft	Total EVA* hr:min	Mission dates
1 Neil A. Armstrong	*Apollo 11*	2:32	Jul 16–24, 1969
2 Edwin E. "Buzz" Aldrin	*Apollo 11*	2:15	Jul 16–24, 1969
3 Charles Conrad Jr	*Apollo 12*	7:45	Nov 14–24, 1969
4 Alan L. Bean	*Apollo 12*	7:45	Nov 14–24, 1969
5 Alan B. Shepard	*Apollo 14*	9:23	Jan 31–Feb 9, 1971
6 Edgar D. Mitchell	*Apollo 14*	9:23	Jan 31–Feb 9, 1971
7 David R. Scott	*Apollo 15*	19:08	Jul 26–Aug 7, 1971
8 James B. Irwin	*Apollo 15*	18:35	Jul 26–Aug 7, 1971
9 John W. Young	*Apollo 16*	20:14	Apr 16–27, 1972
10 Charles M. Duke Jr	*Apollo 16*	20:14	Apr 16–27, 1972
11 Eugene A. Cernan	*Apollo 17*	22:04	Dec 7–19, 1972
12 Harrison H. Schmitt	*Apollo 17*	22:04	Dec 7–19, 1972

* Extra vehicular activity: time spent out of the lunar module on the Moon. The six *Apollo* missions above resulted in successful Moon landings. *Apollo 13*, April 11–17, 1970, was aborted and returned to Earth after an oxygen tank exploded.

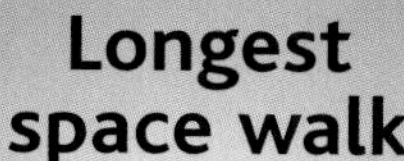

Longest space walk

The record for the longest-ever spacewalk was broken from March 10–11, 2001, when mission specialists James Voss and Susan Helms stepped outside space shuttle *Discovery STS-102* to do construction work on the space station. Their EVA (extra vehicular activity) lasted 8 hours, 56 minutes.

Astronaut Christer Fuglesang resumes construction work on the *International Space Station*, December 2006

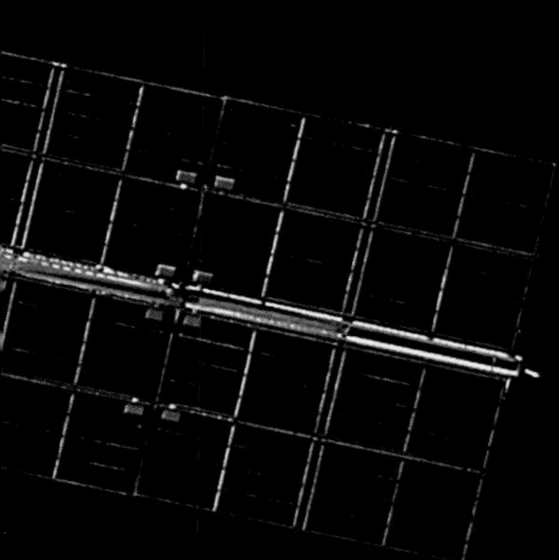

Naming the space shuttles

Unlike space rockets, NASA's space shuttles, or orbiter vehicles, were designed to be re-used. Each has a name, but every mission on which it goes is given a unique number.

The acronym *STS* (Space Transportation System) has been used throughout the shuttle program. The first nine flights were simply numbered *STS-1* to *STS-9*. A more complicated system was then used, but the original system of *STS*+ number has been revived. They do not always follow numerical order, as a mission may be delayed and a later-numbered mission may take its place before it can be rescheduled.

The shuttles

Five space shuttles were built; *Discovery* (first launch 1984), *Atlantis* (1985) and *Endeavour* (1992) remain in service. *Challenger* was destroyed during its 10th mission on January 28, 1986, and *Columbia* was lost on re-entry from its 28th mission on February 1, 2003.

July 20, 1969, First Moon landing Neil Armstrong and Edwin E. "Buzz" Aldrin became the first men on the Moon.

18 June 1983, First U.S. woman in space Sally Ride was launched in the space shuttle *Challenger STS-7*, which was the first reusable space vehicle.

October 5–13, 1984, First Canadian astronaut Quebec-born Marc Garneau traveled on the *STS-41G* space shuttle *Challenger*.

June 29, 1995, First space shuttle/space station docking Space shuttle *Atlantis STS-71* docked with the Soviet space station *Mir*.

September 26, 1996, U.S. endurance record On her 5th mission, U.S. astronaut Shannon Lucid completed 188 days aboard the Russian *Mir* station, setting a world record for women. Lucid was born in China. She flew more missions than any woman and at 53 was the oldest female in space.

December 4, 1998, International Space Station First stage of the *International Space Station* was established.

November 2, 2000, First crew on ISS An American and Russian crew began living aboard the *International Space Station*.

April 28–May 6, 2001 First space tourist U.S. millionaire Dennis Tito became the first space tourist, paying $20 million for his Russian *Soyuz TM-32* flight to the *International Space Station*.

October 15–16, 2003, First astronaut launched by China Chinese astronaut Lang Liwei made eight orbits of Earth in a *Shenzhou 5* spacecraft. China made its second flight, *Shenzhou 6*, with two astronauts on October 12–16, 2005.

2009 Virgin Atlantic plans space tourism flights to greater than 62 miles (100 km) in *SpaceShipOne*, which carries six passengers at a cost of $200,000 per person.

2010 Last space shuttle retires *Atlantis*, *Discovery* and *Endeavour* are to be progressively taken out of service and replaced by NASA's *Orion* spacecraft in a program that will take astronauts back to the Moon and to Mars.

amazing-space.stsci.edu search

Planet Earth

34 ROCKS AND MINERALS
36 LAND FEATURES
38 RIVERS AND LAKES
40 THE WORLD'S OCEANS
42 CLIMATE
44 WEATHER
46 NATURAL DISASTERS

Under the sea

The damage to coral reefs by global warming, pollution and fishing is threatening to destroy Earth's fragile underwater life. Without intervention, 70% of the world's coral reefs will have died within 50 years. 2008 was International Year of the Reef — a worldwide campaign to raise awareness about the value and importance of coral reefs and threats to their sustainability.

Layers of the Earth

The Earth is made up of a number of layers. At the top is the crust—the thinnest layer. Next is the mantle, then the outer and inner cores. The outer core is probably liquid and the inner core solid.

Ocean 2 mi. (3 km)
Crust 13 mi. (21 km)
Mantle 13–1,780 mi. (21–2,865 km)
Outer core 1,780–3,185 mi (2,865–5,125 km)
Inner core 3,185–3,959 mi. (5,125–6,371 km)

Inside the Earth showing the average depth of its layers

The largest meteorite craters

About 500 meteorites reach Earth every year. Many collision sites have been altered by weather over millions of years, and scientists are unsure whether some craters are actually the craters of extinct volcanoes. Those below are all agreed to be meteorite craters.

1 Vredefort, South Africa 185 mi. (300 km) in diameter
2 Sudbury, Ontario, Canada 155 mi. (250 km) in diameter
3 Chicxulub, Yucatan, Mexico 110 mi. (170 km) in diameter
4 Manicougan, Canada 60 mi. (100 km) in diameter
5 Popigai, Russia 60 mi. (100 km) in diameter

Meteor Crater, Arizona

The 10 degrees of hardness

The Mohs scale, named after German mineralogist Friedrich Mohs (1773–1839), is used for comparing the relative hardness of minerals. Each mineral on the scale can be scratched by the harder ones below it.

Mohs scale

No.	Substance	No.	Substance
1	Talc	6	Orthoclase
2	Gypsum	7	Quartz
3	Calcite	8	Topaz
4	Fluorite	9	Corundum
5	Apatite	10	Diamond

Geological time 2007

CENOZOIC ERA
Quaternary period
Recent/Holocene epoch: 11,000 years ago (y.a.) to present day—modern humans
Pleistocene epoch: 1,800,000 to 11,000 y.a. — humans

Tertiary period
Pliocene epoch: 5 to 1.8 m.y.a (million years ago)—apelike human ancestors
Miocene epoch: 23 to 5 m.y.a. —apes and whales
Oligocene epoch: 38 to 23 m.y.a. —cats and dogs
Eocene epoch: 54 to 37 m.y.a.—grasslands
Paleocene epoch: 65 to 54 m.y.a.—large mammals

MESOZOIC ERA
Cretaceous period: 146 to 65 m.y.a.—flowering plants; dinosaurs became extinct
Jurassic period: 208 to 146 m.y.a.—birds and mammals
Triassic period: 245 to 208 m.y.a.—dinosaurs and flying reptiles

Uluru

The rock formerly known as Ayers Rock in Northern Territory, Australia, is believed to be the world's largest free-standing rock. It is made of sandstone and is 1,100 ft. (335 m) high, 2.2 mi. (3.6 km) long and 1.6 mi. (2 km) wide. It was originally named after South Australian premier Sir Henry Ayers, but it is now known by the name given to it by local Aborigines, to whom it is sacred.

Giant meteorites

Many meteorites land in the sea and in unpopulated areas so they are never seen. The Hoba meteorite, the largest in the world, was found in Namibia in 1920.It measures 9 x 8 ft. (2.73 x 2.43 m) and is 82 percent iron and 16 percent nickel. It weighs more than 66 tons (60 tonnes). Second largest is the Tent, found in Greenland in 1894 and now known by its original Eskimo name, Ahnighito. This meteorite weighs about 63.2 tons (57.3 tonnes) and is on display in the New York Museum of Natural History.

Rocks

There are three categories of rocks—igneous, sedimentary and metamorphic.

- Igneous rocks originate deep in the Earth. They erupt from volcanoes as magma and cool or solidify as they rise to the upper layers. Basalt is an igneous rock and so is granite, a very hard rock often used in building. Pumice stone is a soft igneous rock that is ejected from volcanoes. As it cools, it often fills with so many air bubbles that it floats in water.
- Sedimentary rocks can be formed by deposits in water and occasionally by wind. Sandstone is a common example. Organic sedimentary rocks are formed by living plants and animals—coal comes from plant matter and limestone from the calcium from billions of plants and animals. Chemical sedimentary rocks occur when chemical processes take place and minerals are deposited.
- Metamorphic rocks are igneous or sedimentary rocks that have changed as a result of high temperatures or pressures. Slate used on roofs is a familiar example.

www.webmineral.com search

Minerals

Minerals are naturally occurring substances with a definite chemical composition. Most mineral names end in "ite." Many have a practical use or contain a chemical compound or element that can be extracted and used commercially. Bauxite, for instance, is the main source of aluminum. Gems are minerals that are highly prized for their rarity or appearance (e.g., diamonds, sapphires, emeralds and rubies).

4,500,000,000 years ago

PALEOZOIC ERA

Permian period: 286 to 245 m.y.a.—deciduous plants

Carboniferous Pennsylvanian period: 325 to 286 m.y.a.—reptiles

Carboniferous Mississippian period: 360 to 325 m.y.a.—winged insects

Devonian period: 410 to 360 m.y.a.—amphibians

Silurian period: 440 to 410 m.y.a.—land plants and insects

Ordovician period: 500 to 440 m.y.a.—corals and mollusks

Cambrian period: 544 to 500 m.y.a.—fish and shelled creatures

PRECAMBRIAN ERA

Proterozoic period: 2,500 to 544 m.y.a.—earliest fossils; jellyfish

Archaic period: 3,800 to 2,500 m.y.a.—living cells

Hadean period: 4,500 to 3,800 m.y.a.—environment unable to support life; from 4,500 or earlier—the Earth was formed

Largest deserts

Deserts cover about a third of the world's land area. They range from extremely arid and barren sandy deserts (about 4 percent of the total land surface of the globe), through arid (15 percent) to semiarid (just under 15 percent).

Most deserts have features of all these, with one zone merging into the next, so the start and finish of any desert is not exact. Many of the world's largest deserts are broken down by geographers into smaller desert regions—the Australian Desert includes the Gibson, Great Sandy, Great Victoria and Simpson, for example.

1 Sahara, Northern Africa—3,514,000 sq. mi. (9,100,000 sq km)

2 Australian, Australia (Includes Gibson, Great Sandy, Great Victoria and Simpson)—1,313,000 sq. mi. (3,400,000 sq km)

3 Arabian Peninsula, Southwest Asia (Includes an-Nafud and Rub al Khali)—1,004,000 sq. mi. (2,600,000 sq km)

4 Turkestan, Central Asia (Includes Kara-Kum and Kyzylkum)—734,000 sq. mi. (1,900,000 sq km)

5 Gobi, Central Asia—502,000 sq. mi. (1,300,000 sq km)

6 North American Desert, U.S./Mexico (Includes Great Basin, Mojave, Sonorah and Chihuahuan) —502,000 sq. mi. (1,300,000 sq km)

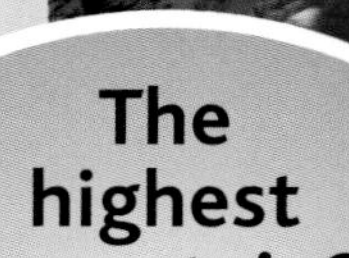

The highest mountain?

The height of mountains is usually measured from sea level. Mauna Kea in Hawaii is only 13,957 ft. (4,245 m) above sea level, but it rises a total of 33,474 ft. (10,203 m) from the floor of the Pacific Ocean, making its real height 4,439 ft. (1,353 m) greater than Mount Everest!

The Devil's Marbles in the Australian desert

Mount Everest, the world's highest mountain

Highest mountains

People used to think that Kangchenjunga in Nepal/India was the highest mountain. Then the Great Trigonometrical Survey of India measured all the country's land features. The survey was completed in 1852 and showed that Everest (then called Peak XV) was the world's highest mountain.

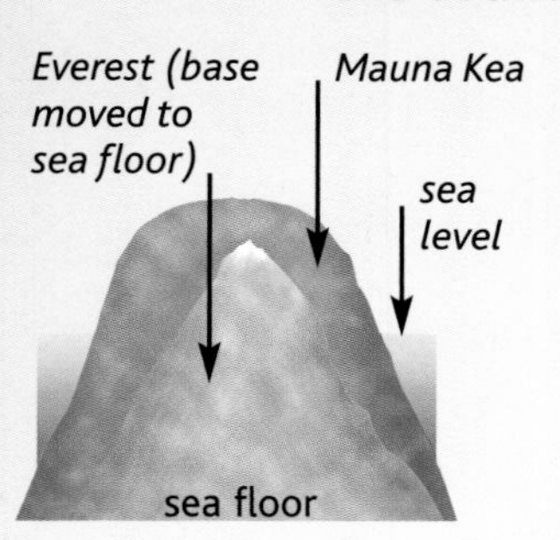

Everest's height was then reckoned to be 29,002 ft. (8,840 m). This has since been adjusted as improved measuring methods have been used. The mountain's name was suggested in 1865 as a tribute to Sir George Everest, the Surveyor General of India, who had led the survey.

Highest mountains

1 Everest, Nepal/China—29,035 ft. (8,850 m)

2 K2 (Chogori), Pakistan/China—28,238 ft. (8,607 m)

3 Kangchenjunga, Nepal/India—28,208 ft. (8,598 m)

4 Lhotse, Nepal/China—27,923 ft. (8,511 m)

5 Makalu I, Nepal/China—27,824 ft. (8,481 m)

Largest island

An island is a piece of land surrounded by water. Australia is so large it is a continent, not an island; otherwise it would rank first. The smallest island with country status is Pitcairn, at 1.75 sq. mi. (4.53 sq km).

1 Greenland (Kalaatdlit Nunaat)—840,070 sq. mi. (2,175,600 sq km)
2 New Guinea—312,190 sq. mi. (789,900 sq km)
3 Borneo—289,961 sq. mi. (751,000 sq km)
4 Madagascar (Malagasy Republic)—226,674 sq. mi. (587,041 sq km)
5 Baffin Island, Canada—195,926 sq. mi. (507,451 sq km)
6 Sumatra, Indonesia—163,011 sq. mi. (422,200 sq km)
7 Honshu, Japan—88,839 sq. mi. (230,092 sq km)
8 Great Britain—84,185 sq. mi. (218,041 sq km)
9 Victoria Island, Canada—83,896 sq. mi. (217,290 sq km)
10 Ellesmere Island, Canada—75,767 sq. mi. (196,236 sq km)
11 Celebes, Indonesia—69,100 sq. mi. (179,000 sq km)
12 South Island, New Zealand—58,676 sq. mi. (151,971 sq km)
13 Java, Indonesia—49,000 sq. mi. (126,900 sq km)
14 North Island, New Zealand—44,204 sq. mi. (114,489 sq km)
15 Newfoundland, Canada—42,031 sq. mi. (108,860 sq km)
16 Cuba—40,519 sq. mi. (104,945 sq km)
17 Luzon, Philippines—40,420 sq. mi. (104,688 sq km)
18 Iceland—39,699 sq. mi. (102,819 sq km)
19 Mindanao, Philippines—36,537 sq. mi. (94,630 sq km)
20 Ireland—32,589 sq. mi. (84,406 sq km)
(Area excludes offshore islands)

Lowest places on land

Sea level is the average height of the sea at a point midway between high and low tides. The shore of the Dead Sea is the lowest exposed ground below sea level. Some land in Antarctica is 8,327 ft. (2,538 m) below sea level, but is covered by a 6,890-ft. (2,100 m) deep ice cap.

1 Dead Sea, Israel/Jordan—1,312 ft. (400 m) below sea level
2 Lake Assa, Djibouti—511 ft. (156 m) below sea level
3 Turfan Depression, China—505 ft. (154 m) below sea level
4 Qattâra Depression, Egypt—436 ft. (133 m) below sea level
5 Mangyshlak Peninsula, Kazakhstan—433 ft. (132 m) below sea level

Geysers

Geysers are jets of boiling water and steam that erupt from beneath the ground where water is heated by volcanic activity. The name geyser comes from a hot spring called Geysir at Haukadalur, Iceland. Yellowstone National Park, Wyoming, has more geysers than anywhere else. There are 500 active ones including Steamboat, which erupts to a height of 375 ft. (120 m), and Old Faithful, which erupts about every 91 minutes.

Geyser erupting in Yellowstone National Park

The seven continents

The Americas are named after the explorer Amerigo Vespucci (1451–1512). Africa was perhaps originally a Berber tribal name. This was adopted by the Romans as the name of their province and later spread to the whole continent.

The name of Europe may simply mean mainland. Asia is probably from the Assyrian, *asu*, meaning sunrise or east. Australis is Latin for southern; Australia, with New Zealand and other islands, is also considered as part of Oceania, a name invented by the geographer Conrad Malte-Brun (1775–1826). Antarctica is Greek for opposite the Arctic. Arctic comes from the Greek for bear, because the region lies under the stars of the Great Bear constellation.

North America
Land area: 9,401,000 sq. mi. (24,349,000 sq km)
% of world total: 16.4

Europe
Land area: 4,053,000 sq. mi. (10,498,000 sq km)
% of world total: 7.1

Asia
Land area: 16,837,000 sq. mi. (43,608,000 sq km)
% of world total: 29.3

Africa
Land area: 11,712,000 sq. mi. (30,335,000 sq km)
% of world total: 20.4

Australasia
Land area: 3,445,000 sq. mi. (8,923,000 sq km)
% of world total: 6.0

South America
Land area: 6,800,000 sq. mi. (17,611,000 sq km)
% of world total: 11.8

Antarctica
Land area: 5,151,000 sq. mi. (13,340,000 sq km)
% of world total: 9.0

Niagara Falls

Longest river

The source of the Nile was discovered by Europeans in 1858 when British explorer John Hanning Speke reached Lake Victoria Nyanza, in what is now Burundi. About a hundred years later, in 1953, the source of the Amazon was identified as a stream called Huarco flowing from the Misuie glacier in the Peruvian Andes mountains.

By following the Amazon from its source and up the Rio Pará, it is possible to sail for 4,195 mi. (6,750 km), which is slightly more than the length of the Nile. But geographers do not consider the entire route to be part of the Amazon basin, so the Nile is considered the world's longest river.

1 Nile* flows through Burundi, Dem. Rep. of Congo, Egypt, Eritrea, Ethiopia, Kenya, Rwanda, Sudan, Tanzania, Uganda—4,158 mi. (6,695 km)
2 Amazon flows through Peru and Brazil—4,007 mi. (6,448 km)
3 Chang Jiang (Yangtze) flows through China—3,964 mi. (6,378 km)
4 Huang He (Yellow) flows through China—3,395 mi. (5,464 km)
5 Amur flows through China and Russia—2,744 mi. (4,415 km)
* In 2006 the British and New Zealand Ascend the Nile team sailed from the mouth to the source of the river. Using Global Positioning, they measured their journey and came up with a total length 66.5 mi. (107 km) longer than the official figure.

Greatest waterfalls

The flow of many waterfalls varies according to the season, and some have been reduced by building dams to harness their power for hydroelectric plants.

The flow of the Boyoma waterfall is equivalent to 36 million gal. (17 million L) a second—enough to fill over 140,000 bathtubs per second, or for every person on Earth to have two baths a day!

1 Boyoma (Stanley), Democratic Republic of Congo—22,235 cu. yd./sec (17,000 cu m/sec)
2 Khône, Laos †—14,819 cu. yd./sec (11,330 cu m/sec)
3 Niagara (Horseshoe), Canada—7,625 cu. yd./sec (5,830 cu m/sec)
4 Grande, Uruguay—5,886 cu. yd./sec (4,500 cu m/sec)
5 Paulo Afonso, Brazil—3,662 cu. yd./sec (2,800 cu m/sec)
(Based on volume of water)
† Also the widest waterfall at 6.7 mi. (10.8 km)

The Nile flowing through Cairo, Egypt

Highest waterfalls

Waterfalls form when a river or stream goes over a drop, often where softer rocks are eroded faster than harder ones. The drop is the distance from top to bottom of the waterfall.

1 Angel Falls, Carrao river, Venezuela —3,212 ft. (979 m)*
2 Tugela Falls, Tugela river, South Africa —3,110 ft. (948 m)
3 Ramnefjellsfossen, Jostedal Glacier, Nesdale, Norway—2,625 ft. (800 m)
4 Mongefossen Falls, Monge river, Mongebekk, Norway—2,540 ft. (774 m)
5 Gocta Cataracta, Cocahuayco river, Peru —2,531 ft. (771 m)
6 Mutarazi Falls, Mutarazi river, Zimbabwe —2,499 ft. (762 m)
7 Yosemite Falls, Yosemite Creek, California—2,425 ft. (739 m)
8 Østre Mardøla Foss, Mardals river, Eikisdal, Norway—2,152 ft. (656 m)
9 Tyssestrengane Falls, Tysso river, Hardanger, Norway—2,120 ft.(646 m)
10 Cuquenán Falls, Arabopo river, Venezuela—2,000 ft. (610 m)
* Longest single drop 2,648 ft. (807 m)

The Great Lakes

The Great Lakes are a group of five freshwater lakes in North America on the border between the U. S. and Canada. Superior is so called because it is higher upstream that the others. Huron takes its name from the name French settlers gave to a local Indian tribe (from *hure*, a boar's head). No one knows where the name Michigan comes from, but Erie and Ontario are both from the Iroquois language. Erie means cat, the animal the tribe used as its symbol. Ontario simply means beautiful lake.

1 Superior, Canada/U.S.—31,820 sq. mi. (82,414 sq km)
2 Huron, Canada/U.S.—23,010 sq. mi. (59,596 sq km)
3 Michigan, U.S.—22,400 sq. mi. (58,016 sq km)
4 Erie, Canada/U.S.—9,930 sq. mi. (25,719 sq km)
5 Ontario, Canada/U.S.—7,520 sq. mi. (19,477 sq km)

Longest glaciers

During the last Ice Age, more than 30 percent of the Earth's surface was covered by glaciers—frozen rivers of ice that move very slowly. Today, as much as 10 percent is covered with glaciers.

The Lambert-Fisher Glacier is the longest in the world and was discovered (from the air) in 1956. The longest glacier in North America is the Hubbard Glacier, Alaska, which measures 91 mi. (146 km). The longest in Europe is the Aletsch Glacier, Switzerland, at 22 mi. (35 km).

1 Lambert-Fisher, Antarctica—320 mi. (515 km)
2 Novaya Zemlya, Russia—260 mi. (418 km)
3 Arctic Institute, Antarctica—225 mi. (362 km)
4 Nimrod-Lennox-King, Antarctica—180 mi. (290 km)
5 Denman, Antarctica—150 mi. (241 km)

Glaciers

Glaciers hold about 75 percent of the world's fresh water. If all the glaciers melted, the world's sea level would rise about 230 ft. (70 m).

Greatest rivers

The volume of water flowing from the mouth of a river varies according to the season. The figures given are highest averages. The outflow of the Amazon would fill almost two million bathtubs every second.

1 Amazon flows into the South Atlantic, Brazil, at 286,441 cu. yd./sec (219,000 cu m/sec)
2 Ganges flows into the Bay of Bengal, Bangladesh, at 57,419 cu. yd./sec (43,900 cu m/sec)
3 Zaïre (Congo) flows into the South Atlantic, Angola/Congo, at 54,672 cu. yd./sec (41,800 cu m/sec)
4 Chang Jiang flows into the Yellow Sea, China, at 41,724 cu. yd./sec (31,900 cu m/sec)
5 Orinoco flows into the South Atlantic, Venezuela, at 41,724 cu. yd./sec (31,900 cu m/sec)
6 Plata-Paraná-Grande flows into the South Atlantic, Uruguay, at 33,614 cu. yd./sec (25,700 cu m/sec)
(Based on rate of discharge at mouth)

Lake fact file

● Largest lake by volume and area

The Caspian Sea (Russia, Kazakhstan, Turkmenistan, Azerbaijan and Iran) has a volume of 18,760 cu. mi. (78,200 cu km) and an area of 144,402 sq. mi. (374,000 sq km), making it the world's largest body of inland water. It would take 400 years for the entire contents of the Caspian to flow over Niagara Falls!

● Largest freshwater lake by area

Some geographers think that Lake Michigan and Lake Huron are one lake. They have a combined area of 45,410 sq. mi. (117,612 sq km) and have a larger area than half the world's countries.

● Largest freshwater lake by volume and deepest lake

Lake Baikal, Russia, contains 5,517 cu. mi. (22,995 cu km) of water. It has an average depth of 2,395 ft. (730 m) and is 5,712 ft. (1,741 m) at its deepest point—deep enough to cover more than four Empire State Buildings piled on top of one another.

● Fastest-shrinking lake

In 1960, The Aral Sea (Kazakhstan and Uzbekistan) was 24,904 sq. mi. (64,501 sq km). Since then, feeder rivers have been diverted for irrigation and the lake has shrunk to about 10,810 sq. mi. (28,000 sq km). It is now in danger of disappearing.

Wave height scale

The wave height scale describes the sort of waves that sailors might meet at sea. Wave height varies according to wind speed. High waves can be very dangerous, especially to small boats which can be turned over and even smashed.

0 Glassy—0 ft. (0 m)
1 Calm—0–1 ft. (0–0.3 m)
2 Rippled—1–2 ft. (0.3–0.6 m)
3 Choppy—2–4 ft. (0.6–1.2 m)
4 Very choppy—4–8 ft. (1.2–2.4 m)
5 Rough—8–13 ft. (2.4–4 m)
6 Very rough—13–20 ft. (4–6 m)
7 High—20–30 ft. (6–9 m)
8 Very high—30–45 ft. (9–4 m)
9 Ultra high—45 + ft (14.0 + m)

Huge waves breaking over a lighthouse in Havana, Cuba, during a hurricane

Tsunami

The word tsunami comes from the Japanese *tsu* (meaning port) and *nami* (meaning wave). A tsunami is not a tidal wave, but a powerful surge of moving water caused by an earthquake or volcanic eruption beneath the sea bed.

There may be advance warning signs, such as bubbling water, a roaring noise and a sudden rise in water temperature. Tsunamis are rarely as high as tidal waves. However, powerful ones can cross huge distances, raising the sea level and destroying entire islands and coastal areas in their path. Lisbon, the capital of Portugal, was almost completely destroyed in 1755 by the combined effects of an earthquake, tsunami and fire. The worst recorded tsunami occurred in 2004 in Southeast Asia.

Animal survivors

Amazingly, few animals died in the tsunami that hit Sri Lanka and other areas in 2004. Elephants, buffalo and tigers, as well as smaller animals, moved to high ground in time. Scientists think that they sensed soundwaves and changes in air pressure in advance of the wave and this gave them time to escape.

Iceberg fact file

An iceberg is a large piece of ice that has broken away from a glacier or ice shelf. Icebergs in the North Atlantic mostly come from glaciers on Greenland, and those in the South Atlantic from the Antarctic.

- The word iceberg probably comes from the Dutch *ijsberg*, or ice hill.
- Icebergs float because they are made of fresh water, which is less dense than sea water.
- Seven-eighths of an iceberg is below the surface of the sea, hence the expression "the tip of the iceberg," which means that more is hidden than can be seen.
- The tallest iceberg measured was 551 ft. (168 m) high. It was seen in 1958 off Greenland and was as tall as a 50-story skyscraper.
- Icebergs less than 3.25 ft. (1 m) high and 16.25 ft. (5 m) wide are known as growlers because of the noise they make.
- Icebergs larger than growlers are called bergy bits; then they are graded small, medium, large or very large. Very large icebergs are those measuring more than 245 ft. (75 m) high and 700 ft. (213 m) wide.
- One of the biggest icebergs of recent times, known as B-15, broke away from the Ross Ice Shelf, Antarctica, in March 2000. It had an average length of 183 mi. (295 km) and width of 23 mi. (37 km), making it about the size of Jamaica!
- About 10,000 to 15,000 new icebergs are formed every year. The process is called "calving."
- The air trapped in icebergs is "harvested" and sold for use in drinks. It may be 3,000 years old.
- At least 500 incidents of ships striking icebergs have been recorded. The worst disaster

Longest coastlines

The coastline of Canada, including all its islands, is more than six times as long as the distance round the Earth at the Equator (24,902 mi. [40,076 km]). Greenland (Kalaalit Nunaat) is not in this list as it is part of Denmark, not a separate country, but its coastline is 27,394 mi. (44,087 km) long.

1 Canada—164,988 mi. (265,523 km)
2 U.S.—82,836 mi. (133,312 km)
3 Russia—68,543 mi. (110,310 km)
4 Indonesia—59,143 mi. (95,181 km)
5 Chile—48,817 mi. (78,563 km)
6 Australia—41,340mi. (66,530 km)
7 Norway—33,056 mi. (53,199 km)
8 Philippines—21,064 mi. (33,900 km)
9 Brazil—20,741 mi. (33,379 km)
10 Finland—19,336 mi. (31,119 km)
11 China—18,652 mi. (30,017 km)
12 Japan—18,032 mi. (29,020 km)

Deepest oceans and seas

The Pacific Ocean is the deepest ocean. Its greatest depth is 35,837 ft. (10,924 m) with an average depth of 13,215 ft. (4,028 m). The Indian Ocean is 24,460 ft. (7,455 m) at its deepest point and has an average depth of 13,002 ft. (3,963 m). The Atlantic Ocean comes next with a greatest depth of 30,246 ft. (9,219 m) and an average depth of 12,880 ft. (3,926 m).

Giant feather stars live 650 ft. (200 m) deep in Cayman Trench, Caribbean.

Deep-sea trenches

There are about 20 deep trenches in the world's oceans. The eight deepest would be deep enough to submerge Mount Everest. The Marianas Trench is the deepest point in the deepest ocean, the Pacific. It was discovered in 1951 and explored in 1960 when Jacques Piccard (Switzerland) and Donald Walsh (U.S.) descended in their bathyscaphe *Trieste 2* to a depth that has since been calculated as 35,813 ft. (10,916 m).

Global warming is melting the world's ice shelves. As ice floes shrink and drift apart, polar bears are forced to swim up to 60 mi. (100 km) between them in search of prey. Some never make it and drown.

Oceans and seas

Ocean is the term used for the world's sea water, except for landlocked seas such as the Caspian.

More than 70 percent of the planet's surface is occupied by oceans—the Pacific Ocean alone is more than 25 percent larger than the planet's entire land area. Smaller divisions of some oceans are separately named as seas.

Pacific Ocean—64,185,629 sq. mi. (166,240,000 sq km)
Atlantic Ocean—33,421,006 sq. mi. (86,560,000 sq km)
Indian Ocean—28,351,484 sq. mi. (73,430,000 sq km)
Arctic Ocean—5,108,132 sq. mi. (13,230,000 sq km)
South China Sea—1,148,499 sq. mi. (2,974,600 sq km)
Caribbean Sea—1,062,939 sq. mi. (2,753,000 sq km)
Mediterranean Sea—969,116 sq. mi. (2,510,000 sq km)
Bering Sea—872,977 sq. mi. (2,261,000 sq km)
Gulf of Mexico—595,749 sq. mi. (1,542,985 sq km)
Sea of Okhotsk—589,798 sq. mi. (1,527,570 sq km)
East China Sea—482,299 sq. mi. (1,249,150 sq km)
Sea of Japan—391,100 sq. mi. (1,012,945 sq km)
Andaman Sea—307,993 sq. mi. (797,700 sq km)
Hudson Bay—282,001 sq. mi. (730,380 sq km)

See also
Worst natural disasters: page 47

involving an iceberg occurred when the *Titanic* struck one on April 14, 1912 and 1,503 people died.

- During WWII, Lord Mountbatten led a program to build artificial icebergs to use as aircraft carriers, but the project, codenamed Habbabuk, was abandoned.
- Cruise ship MS *Explorer* struck an iceberg in the Antarctic and sank on November 23, 2007. All 154 passengers and crew were rescued.

www.oceansatlas.org search

ARCTIC OCEAN
Beaufort Sea
Greenland
Baffin Bay
Bering Sea
Gulf of Alaska
Rocky Mountains
Hudson Bay
Labrador Sea
NORTH AMERICA
Great Basin
Mojave Desert
Sierra Madre
Gulf of Mexico
Caribbean Sea
ATLANTIC OCEAN
PACIFIC OCEAN
SOUTH AMERICA
Andes
Atacama Desert
Patagonian Desert

Climate

Weather and climate are not the same. Weather is how hot, cold or wet a place is at a particular time. Climate is the average weather of an area over time.

Several things decide the climate of an area, including how far it is from the Equator, how far from the sea, its height above sea level and its wind systems. The position of a place on an area of land and the size of that land area also affects the climate. Scientists divide the world into different climate regions: polar and tundra, temperate, tropical, desert and mountain.

Warm temperate

These areas have mild winters and warm to hot summers. There is rain all year round, but there are plenty of sunny days. This is an ideal climate for growing crops such as citrus fruits, grapes and olives.

The sea affects the climate of coastal regions, keeping them warmer than inland areas in winter and cooler in summer.

Climate change

Climates have changed naturally throughout history. But scientists think that human activities, such as burning fossil fuels, are producing greenhouse gases such as carbon dioxide, and these are causing global warming. The effects include ocean currents altering, ice sheets melting, sea levels rising and severe weather, such as cyclones and floods, becoming more common.

Key

- Polar and Tundra
- Cool temperate
- Desert
- Warm temperate
- Tropical
- Mountains

Mountain

The climates of mountain areas vary according to altitude. The higher the mountain, the colder it is. At a certain point, called the tree line, trees can no longer grow. The climate in mountain areas is usually wetter than in the lowlands around them.

Cool temperate

These areas have warm summers and cool winters. In the northern areas the winters can be very cold. Rain falls all year round. Much of this area was once covered with forest.

Polar and tundra

The areas around the North and South Pole are called the Arctic and Antarctic. Both have an average temperature of 0°–10°C (32°–50°F) in summer and as little as -50°C (-58°F) in winter. Few plants can grow. The tundra is land surrounding the Arctic. In summer small plants grow here.

Tropical

These areas are hot all year round. In some parts there is heavy rain all year round, too, and that is where rainforests grow. Rainforest plants fruit and flower all year. In other tropical areas, such as savannas and scrubland, there are dry seasons and rainy seasons, when most of the year's rain falls.

Desert

True deserts are very hot – 40°C (104°F) or more – during the day, but cold at night. They are very dry and what little rain there is falls in short sudden bursts and evaporates quickly. Few plants can grow in deserts but some animals manage to survive.

http://www.wmo.ch search

The Beaufort scale

The Beaufort scale was introduced in 1806 by British Admiral Sir Francis Beaufort (1774–1857) to describe wind effects on a fully rigged man-of-war ship. It was later extended to describe how winds affect land features such as trees.

The Beaufort scale is divided into values from 0 for calm winds to 12 for hurricanes. Forecasters often describe winds by their force number—for example, a force 10 gale. Wind speed can also be measured in knots: 1 knot = 1.15 mph (1.85 km/h).

0 Calm: > 1 mph (0–2 km/h) Smoke rises vertically; the sea is mirror smooth
1 Light air: 1–3 mph (3–6 km/h) Smoke indicates the direction of the wind
2 Slight breeze: 4–7 mph (7–11 km/h) Wind felt on the face and leaves rustle in trees
3 Gentle breeze: 8–12 mph (12–19 km/h) Wind extends a light flag
4 Moderate breeze: 13–18 mph (20–28 km/h) Loose paper blows around; frequent whitecaps at sea
5 Fresh breeze: 19–24 mph (29–38 km/h) Small trees sway
6 Strong breeze: 25–31 mph (39–49 km/h) Wind whistles in telephone wires; some spray on the sea's surface
7 High wind: 32–38 mph (50–61 km/h) Large trees sway
8 Gale: 39–46 mph (62–74 km/h) Twigs break from trees; long streaks of foam on the sea
9 Strong gale: 47–54 mph (75–88 km/h) Branches break from trees
10 Whole gale: 55–63 mph (89–102 km/h) Trees uprooted; sea takes on a white appearance
11 Storm 64–72 mph (103–117 km/h) Widespread damage
12 Hurricane At speeds of more than 73 mph (118 km/h) Structural damage on land; storm waves at sea

A satellite image of Earth shows a hurricane over the Caribbean Sea.

Altocumulus 6,500–23,000 ft. (2,000–7,000 m)
Cirrocumulus 16,500–44,000 ft. (5,000–13,500 m)
Cirrus 16,500–44,000 ft. (5,000–13,500 m)
Cirrostratus 16,500–44,000 ft. (5,000–13,500 m)
Cumulonimbus 1,500–6,500 ft. (450–2,000 m)
Altostratus 6,500–23,00 ft. (2,000–7,000 m)
Stratus below 1,500 ft (450 m)
Stratocumulus 1,500–6,500 ft. (450–2,000 m)
Cumulus 1,500–6,500 ft. (450–2,000 m)
Nimbostratus 3,000–10,000 ft. (900–3,000 m)

Cloud layers

There are 10 types of clouds. Each has a characteristic shape and appears at certain levels in the sky. All types would not appear together as in this diagram.

Hottest and coldest

The hottest place where people live is Djibouti, in the Republic of Djibouti, Africa. The average temperature is 86°F (30°C). Next hottest are Timbuktu in Mali and Tirunelevi in India, both 84.7°F (29.3°C). The coldest place where people live is Norilsk, Russia, with an average temperature of 12.4°F (–10.9°C). Next coldest is Yakutsk in Russia, at 13.8°F (–10.1°C).

World extremes

Windiest place on Earth

Commonwealth Bay, Antarctica, has some consistently high wind speeds, occasionally reaching 200 mph (320 km/h). The highest individual gust of wind measured was 231 mph (371 km/h) at Mt. Washington, U.S., on April 12, 1934.

Tornado wind speed

Fastest: 280 mph (450 km/h) at Wichita Falls, Texas, U.S., on April 2, 1958.

Hurricane wind speed

The fastest sustained winds in a hurricane in the U.S. measured 200 mph (322 km/h), with 210 mph (338 km/h) gusts, on August 17–18, 1969, when Hurricane Camille hit the Mississippi/Alabama coast.

Hottest place on Earth

Dallol in Ethiopia had an average temperature of 94°F (34.4°C) during 1960–66.

Highest shade temperature recorded

Al'Aziziyah, Libyan desert, hit 136°F (57.8°C) on September 13, 1922. A temperature of 134°F (56.6°C) was recorded at Death Valley, California, on July 10, 1913.

Least sunshine

At the South Pole there is no sunshine for 182 days every year, and at the North Pole the same applies for 176 days.

Driest place

Atacama Desert, Chile, where average annual rainfall is officially nil (also longest drought–400 years up to 1971). The average rainfall on the Pacific coast of Chile between Arica and Antofagasta is less than 0.04 in. (1 mm).

Coldest place

Vostok, Antarctica, –129°F (–89.2°C) on July 21, 1983.

Tornados

Tornadoes, or twisters, are columns of air that spin violently, reaching speeds of over 260 mph (420 km/h). They destroy crops and any houses or vehicles in their path. The United State's worst, the Tri-State Tornado of March 18, 1925, struck Missouri, Illinois and Indiana and left almost 700 people dead and over 2,000 injured. In the book and film of *The Wizard of Oz* (1939) Dorothy is carried by a tornado from her Kansas home to the magical land of Oz.

Tools of the trade

Weather forecasters use a range of instruments. Balloons, radar stations and orbiting satellites also provide increasingly accurate weather information, and computer programs are able to make detailed forecasts.

Anemometer

Wind speed is measured by a cup anemometer. This has three or four cups that rotate around a vertical rod. The speed at which the wind spins the cups around is recorded by a counter. A wind vane shows the direction of wind, and an anemograph records the speed on a chart.

Rain gauge

Rain gauges—containers that measure the amount of rain that has fallen—date from ancient China and India. In 1662, British architect Sir Christopher Wren invented a tipping bucket rain gauge, which emptied itself when full.

Thermometer

Galileo invented the thermsocope, a form of thermometer. Later, sealed thermometers using mercury, which expands in a narrow tube as the temperature rises, were developed. Gabriel Fahrenheit's scale dates from 1714, and that of Anders Celsius from 1742. The maximum and minimum thermometer, which records the highest and lowest temperatures reached over a period of time, was invented by James Six at Cambridge in 1780.

A tornado sets down in a field.

www.nws.noaa.gov search

Greatest snowfall in 12 months

At Mt. Rainier, Washington, from February 19, 1971, to February 18, 1972 1,224 in. (3,110.2 cm) fell. This is an incredible 102 ft. (31 m), equivalent to 17 people standing on each other's heads!

Greatest depth of snow

At Tamarac, California, in March 1911: 38 ft. (11.46 m).

Freak snow storm

In the Sahara Desert, Algeria, February 18, 1979.

Heaviest hailstones

Coffeyville, Kansas, 1.65 lb. (0.75 kg), September 3, 1970. The largest hailstone—7 in. (17.8 cm) diameter—fell in Aurora, Nebraska, on June 22, 2003.

Most rainfall in 24 hours

Cilaos, La Réunion, 74 in. (1,870 mm), March 15–16, 1952.

Greatest annual rainfall (extreme example)

Cherrapunji, Assam, India; 1,042 in. (26,461 mm) between August 1, 1860, and July 31, 1861. Also, at the same place, the greatest rainfall in one calendar month—366 in. (9,300 mm)—fell in July 1861.

Greatest annual rainfall (annual average)

Mawsynram, India, with 467 in. (11,870 mm) a year; and Tutunendo, Colombia, 463 in. (11,770 mm).

Most rainy days in a year

Mt. Waialeale, Kauai, Hawaii, can have up to 350 days a year. The total rainfall is about 460 in. (11,684 mm), which approaches the annual record.

Volcanic eruptions

Santorini
The eruption of the Greek island of Santorini in c. 1450 BC is believed to have been one of the most powerful ever.

Vesuvius, Italy
On August 24, AD 79 Vesuvius erupted with little warning, engulfing the Roman city of Herculaneum in a mud flow. Nearby Pompeii was buried under a vast layer of pumice and volcanic ash. This preserved the city, including the bodies of many of its inhabitants, until it was excavated by archaeologists in the 19th and 20th centuries. As many as 20,000 people died. Vesuvius erupted again in 1631, killing up to 18,000 people.

Laki, Iceland
Iceland is one of the most volcanically active places on Earth, but the population is small so eruptions seldom cause many deaths. On June 11, 1783, the largest lava flow ever recorded engulfed many villages in a river of lava up to 50 mi. (80 km) long and 100 ft. (30 m) deep. It released poisonous gases that killed those who managed to escape the lava flow—up to 20,000 people.

Unsen, Japan
On April 1, 1793, the volcanic island of Unsen, or Unzen, completely disappeared, killing all 53,000 inhabitants.

Tambora, Indonesia
On the island of Sumbawa the eruption of Tambora between April 5 and 12, 1815, killed about 10,000 islanders immediately. A further 82,000 died later from disease and famine. This made it the worst-ever eruption for loss of human life.

Krakatoa, Sumatra/Java
The uninhabited island of Krakatoa exploded on August 27, 1883, with what may have been the biggest bang ever heard by humans. People heard it up to 3,000 mi. (4,800 km) away!

Mont Pelée, Martinique
Mont Pelée began to erupt in April 1902, after lying dormant for centuries. The 30,000 residents of the main city, St. Pierre, were told that they were not in danger, so stayed in their homes. They were there on May 8 when the volcano burst apart and showered the port with molten lava, ash and gas, destroying all buildings and killing as many as 40,000 people.

Nevado del Ruiz, Colombia
In 1985 this Andean volcano gave warning signs that it was about to erupt, but the local people were not evacuated soon enough. On November 13, the hot steam, rocks and ash ejected from Nevado del Ruiz melted its icecap, causing a mudslide. This completely engulfed the town of Armero, killing 22,940 people.

Earthquake detector
Chinese astronomer Chan Heng (AD 78–139) invented an earthquake detector made of a vase adorned with dragons' heads and surrounded by metal frogs. In each of the dragons' jaws was a carefully balanced ball. When the first tremors of an earthquake made the device vibrate, the balls fell into the frogs' mouths, making a noise to warn of the coming danger.

Mount St. Helens erupting in 1980

Avalanche!
An avalanche caused by the eruption of the Mount St. Helens volcano, Washington, on May 18, 1980, was believed to have travelled at 250 mph (400 km/h).

A volcano erupts on Réunion Island in the Indian Ocean. (Inset) Lava pouring from an erupting volcano.

The Richter scale

Seismic waves are vibrations from earthquakes that travel through the Earth. Sensitive instruments called seismographs can record the waves, even at great distances, and calculate their strength and location.

The Richter scale indicates the magnitude or strength of an earthquake based on the size of the seismic waves (the distance the ground moves). The biggest earthquake (9 on the Richter scale) is a billion times greater than the smallest.

- **0** Detected by sensitive seismographs (some can detect magnitudes of less than zero!)
- **1** Detected by instruments
- **2** Lowest felt by humans
- **3** Slight vibration; more than 100,000 a year around the world
- **4** Up to 15,000 a year; at 4.5, would be detected by seismographs worldwide, but cause little damage
- **5** About 3,000 a year; the 1960 earthquake in Agadir, Morocco, was 5.6
- **6** About 100 a year worldwide
- **7** About 20 a year; the 1995 earthquake in Kobe, Japan, was 7.2
- **8** Major destructive earthquakes; average two a year; the 1904 San Francisco earthquake was probably 8.25
- **9** No quake higher than 8.9 has been recorded, but 9.0 or even higher is theoretically possible

Earthquake

Earthquakes are movements of the Earth's surface, often as a result of a fault, or fracture, in the crust. They happen more often in some parts of the world than others. In heavily populated areas, they cause great damage to buildings and loss of life.

Worst ever

An earthquake affecting the Middle East and North Africa on May 20, 1202, may have been the worst in human history. Up to 1,000,000 people were killed, 110,000 in Cairo, Egypt, alone.

Most powerful

The worst earthquake affecting an inhabited area was in Assam, India, on June 12, 1897. It is believed to have reached 8.7, killing about 1,500. The Colombia/Ecuador earthquake of January 31, 1906, was 8.9 on the Richter scale. Fortunately, it was 200 mi. (300 km) off the coast, and so resulted in fewer than 1,000 deaths on land.

Worst modern earthquakes

An earthquake in Tang-shan, China, on July 28, 1976, killed 242,419. The Kashmir quake of October 8, 2005, officially killed 87,350 people, but it may have been more than 100,000.

Longest lasting

Most earthquakes last only a minute or two, but the Alaska earthquake of March 27, 1964, continued for at least five minutes and registered 8.6 on the Richter scale. It killed only 131 people but caused more than $450 million worth of damage.

Worst natural disasters

Drought

Serious droughts kill people and livestock and destroy crops. The drought in Australia in 1982 cost $6 billion, and one in Spain in 1995 cost $4.7 billion.

Flood

Floods caused by China's Huang He, or Yellow River, were first recorded in 2297 BC. The river has flooded at least 1,500 times since. In 1887 floods killed between 1.5 million and 7 million people, making it the worst flood ever.

Tsunami

On December 26, 2004, a tsunami created by an undersea earthquake caused catastrophic floods in Indonesia, Sri Lanka, Myanmar (formerly Burma), the Maldives, Malaysia, India and parts of Africa. More than 283,100 people died.

Cyclone

The worst cyclone of the 21st century has been Cyclone Nargis (2008), which killed an estimated 140,000 Katrina (2005), which killed in Myanmar with more than 2.5 million more effected.

On the edge

The rare Malagasy rainbow frog, found off Madagascar, is one of the 100 creatures on the 2008 EDGE (Evolutionary Distinct and Globally Endangered) list. Its striking colors make it popular in the pet trade, which is a significant threat to this critically endangered species.

Life Sciences

50 TREES AND PLANTS

52 ANIMAL KINGDOM

54 MAMMALS

56 SEA LIFE

58 FLYING ANIMALS

60 INSECTS AND SPIDERS

62 REPTILES AND AMPHIBIANS

64 MAN AND BEAST

66 PET POWER

68 ENDANGERED AND EXTINCT

70 ENVIRONMENTAL CONCERNS

72 GARBAGE AND RECYCLING

Top food plants

Every year the people of the world eat more than 2.4 billion tons of cereals, 995 million tons of vegetables and 579 million tons of fruit. These figures (in tons per year) come from the Food and Agriculture Organization of the United Nations, or FAO, which is based in Rome. The aim of the FAO is to help people around the world grow more food and eat a better diet.

Sugar cane	1,534,820,044
Corn/maize	766,357,997
Rice	699,533,077
Wheat	667,940,341
Potatoes	347,338,646
Beets	282,640,255
Cassava	249,494,272
Soybeans	244,162,989
Barley	152,827,262
Tomatoes	138,387,993
Sweet potatoes	136,146,218
Watermelons	110,895,155
Bananas	77,995,522
Cabbages	76,049,979
Grapes	76,007,444
Oranges	71,424,684
Apples	70,332,460
Onions	67,943,069
Sorghum	62,264,363
Coconuts	60,984,627

A woman going to work in rice fields in Vietnam

U.S. plants

Here are some of the plants that originated in the United States—avocado, beans (kidney, French, etc.), cashew nut, cassava, chilli pepper, cocoa, corn, cranberry, loganberry, peanut, pecan, pineapple, potato, pumpkin, quinine, rubber, squash/gourd, sunflower, tobacco, tomato, vanilla

American plants

As many as 30 percent of the world's most useful plants originally came from North, Central and South America. Early European explorers discovered the plants while on their travels and took them back home to grow.

This was not always easy. Pineapples were so difficult and expensive to cultivate in Europe that they became a symbol of wealth—carved stone pineapples are often seen on the gateposts of many grand houses.

avocado

chilli pepper

peanut

tomato

squash

Important crops

These are the most important crops grown for uses other than food.

Cotton (clothing, household items) 79,375,310 tons a year

Rubber (tires, shoes, balls, erasers) 10,933,544 tons a year

Tobacco (cigarettes, cigars) 7,406,775 tons a year

Jute (sacks, rope) 3,429,235 tons a year

World forests

Forests cover 29.6 percent of Earth's land and almost a quarter of these are in Russia. There are three main types of forest, which grow in particular climates in different parts of the world.

- Tropical forests or rainforests grow near the Equator where it is always hot and wet. Here, temperatures are about 68–77°F (20–25°C) and there is more than 80 in. (200 cm) of rain a year.
- Temperate forests grow in places that have hot summers and cold winters. The summers can be as hot as 86°F (30°C) and winters as cold as –22°F (–30°C). Average rainfall is about 30–60 in. (75–150 cm) a year. Many trees are deciduous (drop their leaves in autumn).
- Boreal or taiga forests grow in Russia, Canada and elsewhere in the far north. Winters are long and very cold. There is rainfall of 16–40 in. (40–100 cm) a year, but most falls as snow. Most trees are evergreen conifers (cone-producing trees with needle-like leaves).

Dangerous plants

- Potatoes are safe to eat when cooked, but the stems and leaves of the plants contain a poison called solanine. If potatoes turn green, they may also contain solanine.
- Ricin is extracted from the seeds of the castor oil plant and is more poisonous than cyanide or snake venom. Even minute doses of ricin can be fatal.
- Opium is extracted from the juice of a poppy and contains morphine. Small quantities of both are used legally as painkillers and illegally as drugs. Both can easily cause death.
- The death cap is a highly poisonous mushroom. It is responsible for almost 90 percent of deaths from eating fungi. The poison causes severe diarrhea and vomiting.
- Curare is extracted from the bark of certain trees and is used by South American Native tribes to tip their poison arrows when they go hunting.
- Deadly nightshade is also known as belladonna. It contains a poison called atropine. Less than 0.0004 oz. (10 mg) could kill a child.
- Nicotine is a yellow oily liquid found in tobacco. About 0.002 oz. (50 mg) of nicotine would kill an adult within minutes.
- The leaves of the purple foxglove contain digitalis and eating just a few can be fatal. Digitalis is used in tiny doses to treat people suffering from heart disease.

Purple foxglove

Children investigating a rafflesia flower

Largest and smelliest flower

The flower of the rafflesia, or stinking corpse lily, measures almost 3.3 ft. (1 m) across and weighs 24 lb. (11 kg). It is one of the world's smelliest flowers, with an odor like rotting flesh. The smell attracts flies, which pollinate the plant.

Record-breaking plants

- **Tallest tree**
The world's tallest tree is called the Stratosphere Giant. It grows in the Rockefeller Forest, Humboldt Redwoods State Park, California. At 369 ft. (112.32 m), this redwood is almost three times the height of the Statue of Liberty in New York.

- **Biggest living thing**
The General Sherman giant sequoia in Sequoia National Park, California, is the world's largest living thing. It is 275 ft. (83.8 m) tall and measures 8.3 ft. (2.53 m) around its mighty trunk. Including its huge root system, the tree weighs about 2,200 tons (2,000 tonnes).

- **Oldest trees**
The bristlecone pines in California and Nevada, are almost 5,000 years old and were long believed to be the oldest trees. Latest research suggests that creosote bushes in the U.S.'s Mojave Desert may be even older—some of these plants began life nearly 12,000 years ago.

- **Smallest flowering plant**
Wolffia, a kind of duckweed, is just 0.024 in. (0.6 mm) long and weighs about as much as two grains of salt. Its seeds are also the tiniest known—they weigh only 70 micrograms, as much as a single grain of salt.

www.fao.org search

Grouping living things

Living things are organized by scientists into five groups called kingdoms. These are: animals (Animalia); algae and protozoans (Protista); bacteria (Prokaryotae); mushrooms, molds and lichens (Fungi); plants (Plantae).

The animal kingdom alone has thousands of different species. A species is a type of animal, and animals of the same species can breed successfully with each other. Similar species are grouped in a genus. Genera are grouped into families, families into orders, right up to the level of phylum. The phylum Chordata contains all vertebrate animals—animals with a backbone. Here's how a human and a giant panda are classified.

	Human	**Giant panda**
Phylum	Chordata	Chordata
Class	Mammalia	Mammalia
Order	Primates	Carnivores
Family	Hominidae	Ursidae
Genus	*Homo*	*Ailuropoda*
Species	*sapiens*	*melanoleuca*

Animal species

Below is a list of the animals we know about. No one knows exactly how many species there may be altogether. New species are always being found and there may be tens of millions not yet discovered.

Some experts think there may be millions of species of insects and at least a million species of deep-sea fish that no one has ever seen. About half of all known creatures and plants live in tropical rainforests. In a study of just 19 trees in a tropical rainforest, 1,200 beetle species were found. About 80 percent of these had not been seen before.

- **Arachnids** 75,500 (spiders, scorpions, etc.)
- **Mollusks** 70,000 (snails, clams, etc.)
- **Crustaceans** 40,000 (shrimps, crabs, etc.)
- **Fish** 29,300
- **Nematodes** 20,000 (unsegmented worms)
- **Flatworms** 17,500
- **Segmented worms** 12,000
- **Sponges** 10,000
- **Birds** 9,934
- **Jellyfish, coral, etc.** 9,000
- **Reptiles** 8,240
- **Starfish** 6,000
- **Amphibians** 5,918
- **Mammals** 5,416

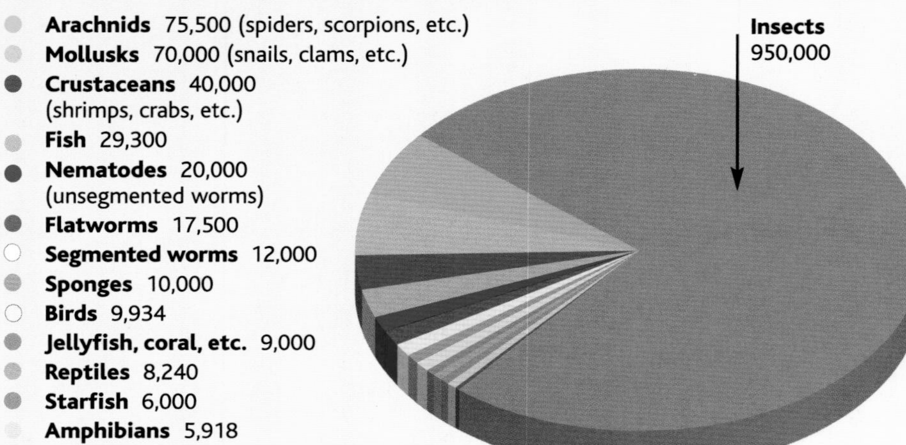

San Diego Zoo

San Diego Zoo in California is one of the largest in the world. Each year, its 4,000 animals in over 800 different species eat:

Apples	3,800 lbs
Bananas	17,600 lbs
Carrots	37,500 lbs
Crickets	9 million
Fish (frozen)	112,000 lbs
Food pellets	241,800 lbs
Hay	4,000 bales
Lettuce	41,448 heads
Mealworms	3,640 lbs
Mice	288,000
Meat	60,000 lbs
Rabbits	2,500
Rats	5,000
Yams	37,000 lbs

Life on Earth

3,900 million years ago (m.y.a)

The first simple life forms began to appear on Earth almost four billion years ago. More familiar animals appeared about 500 million years ago, and humans only within the past two million. We know a little about extinct creatures and early humans from fossil remains found in rocks from each period.

3,900–2,500 m.y.a. Archaean period—the earliest marine life form (blue-green algae)

2,500–540 m.y.a. Proterozoic period—the first many-celled organisms evolve

540–490 m.y.a. Cambrian period—the first fossils of animals with shells and skeletons

490–443 m.y.a. Ordovician period—mollusks, some corals and fishlike vertebrates

443–417 m.y.a. Silurian period—fish develop jaws; first sharks

417–354 m.y.a. Devonian period—fish dominant; amphibians (the first land animals) evolve

354–290 m.y.a. Carboniferous period—insects; first reptiles

290–248 m.y.a. Permian period—insects evolve into modern types; reptiles evolve

248–206 m.y.a. Triassic period—early dinosaurs; marine reptiles

How fast?

Most of the creatures in this list can keep up these speeds for only a short time—less than an hour. The peregrine falcon achieves its speed as it dives through the air to catch prey, not in level flight.

Peregrine falcon (diving speed) 185 mph (298 km/h)
Spine-tailed swift 106 mph (171 km/h)
Eider duck 70 mph (113 km/h)
Sailfish (fastest fish) 68 mph (110 km/h)
Cheetah (fastest on land) 65 mph (105 km/h)
Pronghorn antelope 55 mph (89 km/h)
Racing pigeon 50 mph (80 km/h)
Lion (charging) 50 mph (80 km/h)
Brown hare 45 mph (72 km/h)
Ostrich (fastest flightless bird) 45 mph (72 km/h)
Blue shark 43 mph (69 km/h)
Horse 43 mph (69 km/h)
Greyhound 42 mph (68 km/h)
Killer whale 35 mph (56 km/h)
Death's head hawkmoth (fastest flying insect) 33 mph (53 km/h)
Guano bat (fastest flying mammal) 32 mph (51 km/h)
Skipper butterfly 30 mph (48 km/h)
California sea lion 25 mph (40 km/h)
Dolphin 25 mph (40 km/h)
Fastest human over 328 ft (100 m) 23 mph (37km/h)

Peregrine falcon

Oldest creature?

On March 23, 2006, a giant tortoise called Adwayita died at the Alipore Zoo, Calcutta, India. He was brought to the zoo in the 1860s from the estate of Lord Robert Clive. He may even have been up to 250 years old when he died.

How long do they live?

Who would have thought that a sea anemone could live for 80 years? All these figures are the longest ever recorded. Most of these animals have much shorter lives.

Marine clam 200
Giant tortoise 150
Human 122
Killer whale 90
Sea anemone 80
Asiatic elephant 78
American alligator 66
Blue macaw 64
Horse 62
Chimpanzee 56
Hippopotamus 54
Slow-worm 54
Beaver 50
Bactrian camel 50
Grizzly bear 50
Blue whale 45
Boa constrictor 40
Domestic cat 34
Lion 30
Pig 27
Common rabbit 18
Queen ant 18
Giant centipede 10
Millipede 7
House mouse 6
Bedbug 6 months
Common housefly (male) 2 weeks

A mouse can live for up to six years

206–144 m.y.a. Jurassic period—reptiles dominate land, sea and air; *Archaeopteryx* (first bird) appears; first mammals
144–65 m.y.a. Cretaceous period—dinosaurs become extinct; snakes and lizards appear
65–55 m.y.a. Paleocene period—first large land mammals
55–34 m.y.a. Eocene period—modern land mammals and whales appear
34–24 m.y.a. Oligocene period—modern mammals dominant
24–5 m.y.a. Miocene period—modern mammals, eg., primates; birds
5–1.8 m.y.a. Pliocene period—humanlike apes appear
1.8 m.y.a. to 10,000 years ago Pleistocene period—humans appear
10,000 years ago to present Holocene period—human civilization

animaldiversity.ummz.umich.edu search

Types of mammal

A mammal is a warm-blooded vertebrate (animal with a backbone) with some hair on its body. Female mammals feed their young on milk from their mammary glands. Most mammals give birth to live young which develop inside the mother's body, but echidnas and the platypus lay eggs.

Marsupial mammals such as kangaroos give birth to live young, but they are very small and weak. They finish their development in a pouch on the mother's body. There are 21 main groups, or orders, of mammals. Listed below are the names of the main mammal groups, examples of the animals and the approximate number of known species. Common names are given where possible.

Rodents Beavers, squirrels, mice, rats, porcupines, voles, guinea pigs, chinchillas 2,052
Chiroptera Bats 977
Insectivores Shrews, moles, hedgehogs, tenrecs 440
Marsupials Opossums, koalas, bandicoots, kangaroos, wallabies, numbat 292
Primates Lemurs, lorises, tarsiers, marmosets, monkeys, gibbons, apes, humans 270
Carnivores Dogs, foxes, wolves, cats, bears, hyenas, raccoons, civets, mongooses, weasels, pandas 249
Even-toed ungulates Pigs, peccaries, giraffe, okapi, hippopotamuses, deer, camels, llamas, antelopes, cattle 225
Cetacea Whales, dolphins, porpoises 83
Lagomorphia Rabbits, hares, pikas 80
Pinnipedia Seals, sea-lions, walruses 34
Edentates Anteaters, sloths, armadillos 29
Odd-toed ungulates Horses, asses, zebras, rhinos, tapirs 19
Scandentia Tree shrews 19
Macroscelidea Elephant-shrews 15
Monotremes Duck-billed platypus, echidnas 5
Hyracoidea Hyraxes 8
Pholidota Pangolins 7
Sirenia Manatees, dugong 4
Proboscidea Elephants 3
Dermoptera Flying lemurs 2
Tubulidentata Aardvark 1

African elephant

Big babies

The African elephant has the longest pregnancy of any mammal. She carries her baby for an average of 660 days. When the baby is born it weighs 200–265 lb. (90–120 kg). A baby blue whale is even bigger. It weighs 4,409 lb. (2,000 kg) and is 23 ft. (7 m) long. It puts on weight at the astonishing rate of 200 lb. (90 kg) a day.

Biggest and smallest

The following are the biggest land mammals according to weight:

African elephant 14,400 lb. (7,000 kg)
White rhinoceros 7,900 lb. (3,600 kg)
Hippopotamus 5,500 lb. (2,500 kg)
Giraffe 3,520 lb. (1,600 kg)
American buffalo 2,200 lb. (1,000 kg)
Arabian camel (dromedary) 1,520 lb. (690 kg)
Polar bear 1,320 lb. (600 kg)

The following are the smallest land mammals, according to length:

Kitti's hog-nosed bat 1.1 in. (2.9 cm)
Pygmy shrew 1.4 in. (3.6 cm)
Pipistrelle bat 1.6 in. (4 cm)
Little brown bat 1.6 in. (4 cm)
Masked shrew 1.8 in. (4.5 cm)
Southern blossom bat 2 in. (5 cm)
Harvest mouse 2.3 in. (5.8 cm)

Big cats

Big cats like lions are perhaps the most powerful of all mammal predators. These measurements are from the nose to the tip of the tail. The length of tail varies—a leopard's tail can be as long as 43 in. (110 cm) and a jaguar's tail as short as 18 in. (45 cm).

Tiger (Asia) 130 in. (330 cm)
Leopard (Asia, Africa) 126 in. (320 cm)
Lion (Africa, Asia) 110 in. (280 cm)
Jaguar (North, Central and South America) 107 in. (271 cm)
Cougar (North, Central and South America) 96 in. (245 cm)
Snow leopard (Asia) 94 in. (240 cm)
Cheetah (Africa, Asia) 87 in. (220 cm)
Clouded leopard (Asia) 75 in. (197 cm)

Bears of the world

Scientists have long argued about whether the giant panda should be grouped with the raccoon family or the bears. DNA tests have now proved that it belongs with the bears. The koala, often called koala bear, is actually a marsupial not a bear.

Polar bear (Arctic) Length up to 101 in. (257cm); weight 440–1,760 lb. (200–800 kg)
Brown (grizzly) bear (North America, Europe, Asia) Length up to 114 in. (290 cm); weight 300–860 lb. (136–390 kg)
American black bear (North America) Length 50–75 in. (127–191 cm); weight 130–660 lb. (60–300 kg)
Asiatic black bear (Southern Asia) Length 50–74 in. (127–188 cm); weight 220–440 lb. (100–200 kg)
Sloth bear (Asia) Length 60–75 in. (152–191 cm); weight 175–310 lb. (80–140 kg)
Giant panda (China) Length 48–60 in. (122–152 cm); weight up to 275 lb. (125 kg)
Spectacled bear (South America) Length 60–72 in. (152–183 cm); weight 150–250 lb. (70–113 kg)
Sun bear (Asia) Length 48–60 in. (122–152 cm); weight 60–145 lb. (27–65 kg)

Western lowland gorilla

Champion divers

Lots of mammals can dive underwater, including humans, but whales are the champions. All have to hold their breath. These are average dives.

Northern bottlenose whale 120 min.
Sperm whale 112 min.
Greenland whale 60 min.
Seal 22 min.
Beaver 20 min.
Dugong 16 min.
Hippopotamus 15 min.
Porpoise 15 min.
Muskrat 12 min.
Duck-billed platypus 10 min.
Sea otter 5 min.
Human pearl diver 2.5 min.
Human 1 min

Intelligence

Edward O. Wilson, professor of zoology at Harvard, researched the intelligence of mammals. He defined intelligence on the basis of how fast and how well an animal can learn a wide range of tasks. He also took into account the size of the animal's brain compared with its body. His top 10 most intelligent mammals, in order are: human, chimpanzee, gorilla, orangutan, baboon, gibbon, monkey, small-toothed whale, dolphin and elephant.

Siberian tiger cubs in the snow

Monkeys and apes

Monkeys and apes (and humans) belong to the group of mammals called primates. There are 256 known species of primate. The smallest is the pygmy mouse lemur, which weighs only 1 oz. (30 g). The largest is the gorilla, which weighs 485 lb. (220 kg). Humans comes next at an average 170 lb. (77 kg).

Marine mammals

The biggest creatures in the sea are whales, which are mammals not fish. The blue whale is the largest creature that has ever lived. Whales spend all their lives in the sea, but there are other mammals that spend most of their time in water and some time on land. These include seals, sea lions and otters.

Smallest marine mammals

- The marine otter, which lives off the western coast of South America, is the smallest marine mammal. It weighs up to 10 lb. (4.5 kg) and is about 3.77 ft. (1.15 m) long. The sea otter of North American coasts is slightly larger.
- Small dolphins include Hector's dolphin, which lives off New Zealand. It is rarely more than 3.77 ft. (1.5 m) long and 126 lb. (57.2 kg) in weight.

The most dangerous fish is the great white shark

Biggest marine mammals

- The blue whale is 110 ft. (33.5 m) long and weighs 145 tons (130 tonnes)
- The fin whale is 82 ft. (25 m) long and weighs 50 tons (45 tonnes)
- The right whale is 57.4 ft. (17.5 m) long and weighs 45 tons (40 tonnes)
- The sperm whale is 59 ft. (18 m) long and weighs 40 tons (36 tonnes)

Blue whales can be as long as three buses

Top food fish

Fish and shellfish are popular foods for people. The top catches are:

Type of fish	Total catch in 2006 (tons)
Herring, sardines, anchovies	24,697,030
Carp, barbells, cyprinid	22,255,755
Cod, hake, haddock	9,891,113
Tuna, bonito, billfish	6,907,123
Shrimp, prawns	6,715,136
Clams, cockles, arkshell	5,380,994
Oysters	5,270,751
Squid, cuttlefish, octopus	4,290,373
Salmon, trout, smelts	3,326,063
Tilapia, cichlids	3,063,248
Top 10 total	91,797,586
Aquaculture	155,870,278
Capture	102,794,218
World total caught for food	258,664,496

Danger in the water

Most creatures living in the world's oceans and rivers are harmless to people, but there are a few that can be very dangerous if you encounter or provoke them.

- The tiny candiru fish lives in South American rivers. It can enter your body and kill you unless it is surgically removed.
- Cone-shells, found in the South Pacific and Indian Oceans, have poisonous barbs that cause paralysis and occasionally death if you touch them. The geographer cone is probably the most dangerous of all.
- Freshwater electric eels live in South America and are the most powerful of all the electric eels. They can release up to 650 volts, which is enough to kill a person. Fortunately, this rarely happens.
- Certain parts of the Japanese puffer fish, also known as the maki-maki or deadly death puffer fish, contain a powerful nerve poison that can kill you if you eat it. There is no known antidote. Despite the danger, puffer fish are eaten in Japan, where they are a very expensive delicacy. People are specially trained to prepare them because eating the wrong part causes death in about 60 percent of cases. About 50 people a year in Japan die after eating incorrectly prepared puffers.
- Several species of octopus are dangerous. The sting of the

Big fish

Whale sharks are probably the biggest fish in the world. They are usually up to 39 ft. (12 m) long, though one caught off Thailand in 1919 was believed to be 59 ft. (18 m) long.

Whale sharks eat only plankton—tiny plants and animals that float in water. Basking sharks also eat plankton, but most other big fish hunt.

Whale shark 46,300 lb. (21,000 kg)
Basking shark 32,000 lb. (14,500 kg)
Great white shark 7,300 lb. (3,300 kg)
Giant manta 6,600 lb. (3,000 kg)
Beluga 4,600 lb. (2,100 kg)
Sharptail mola 4,400 lb. (2,000 kg)
Ocean sunfish 4,400 lb. (2,000 kg)

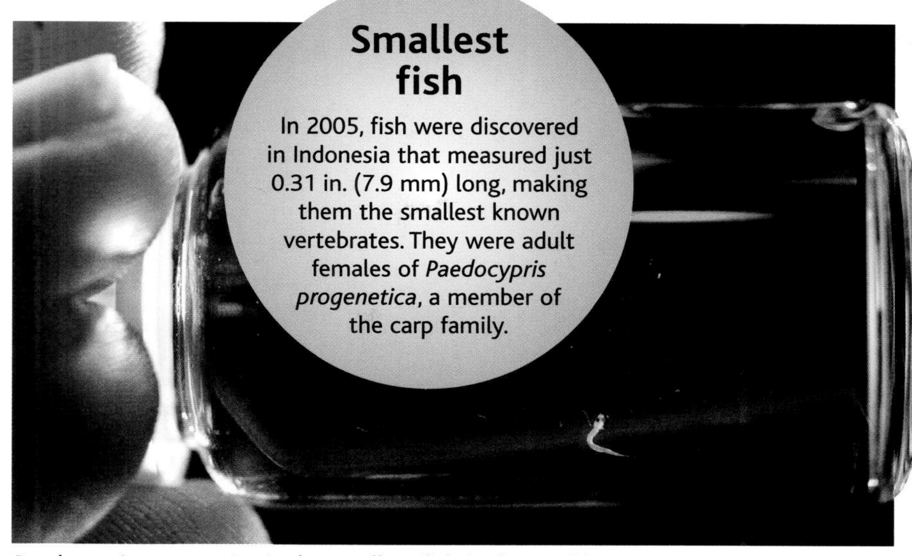

Smallest fish

In 2005, fish were discovered in Indonesia that measured just 0.31 in. (7.9 mm) long, making them the smallest known vertebrates. They were adult females of *Paedocypris progenetica*, a member of the carp family.

Paedocypris progenetica is the smallest fish in the world

Giant Japanese spider crabs

Deep sea divers

Leatherback turtle

- Emperor penguins sometimes dive to depths of 870 ft. (265 m).
- In 1987 a leatherback turtle fitted with a depth-gauge reached a depth of 3,900 ft. (1,200 m).
- Sperm whales regularly dive to 3,900 ft. (1,200 m) and experts think they may sometimes go down to twice this depth.
- Fish called brotulids are the deepest living vertebrate animals. They have been found in deep-sea trenches at 27,230 ft. (8,300 m)—that is almost as deep as Mount Everest is high.

Amazing sea creatures

Most eggs
The black marlin fish lays as many as 226 million eggs.

Largest crustacean
The giant spider crab's body measures up to 12–14 in. (30.5–35.5 cm) across and it has a claw span of 7.8–8.8 ft. (2.4–2.7 m).

Smallest crustacean
Pea crabs measure only about 2.5 in. (6.5 cm) across the shell.

Heaviest crustacean
An Atlantic lobster weighing 42.44 lb. (19.25 kg) was caught off the Virginia State coast in 1934. It was nicknamed Mike.

Heaviest mollusk
A giant squid caught in 1878 had tentacles 35 ft. (10.7 m) long and weighed about 4,000 lb. (1,800 kg).

Largest clam
A clam known as *Tridacna derasa* measures up to 49 in. (124 cm) across and weighs 580 lb. (263 kg).

Largest gastropod
The gastropod group includes snails. The largest gastropod is the trumpet or baler conch. It lives off Australian coasts and weighs up to 40 lb. (18 kg). Its shell measures 30 in. (77 cm) long and 40 in. (101 cm) around.

Largest jellyfish
The lion's mane jellyfish (*Cyanea arctica*) is up to 7.5 ft. (2.3 m) long, with tentacles that add an extra 121 ft. (37 m).

Largest sponge
The barrel sponge of the Caribbean is up to 6–8 ft. (1.8–2.4 m) tall.

blue-ringed octopus, which lives in the Australian seas, can cause paralysis and even death.

- Piranha are small but incredibly ferocious fish that live in rivers in parts of South America. They hunt in groups, attacking any creatures in the water—including humans unlucky enough to encounter them. They strip their prey to the bone in minutes.
- Sea wasps, also known as box jellyfish, live off the coast of Australia. They have tentacles up to 29 ft. (9 m) long and venom as powerful as that of a cobra. Australian lifeguards often wear nylon tights to protect them against stings, which can cause death within three minutes.
- Most sharks are harmless but a few species have been known to attack people. The great white, tiger and bull sharks are the most dangerous. Of the 631 attacks on humans recorded from 1508 to 2007, 135 resulted in death.
- Stonefish lie on the seabed where they resemble rocks encrusted with seaweed. Unsuspecting swimmers who tread on the fish receive a very painful sting from their spines. In severe cases, victims may die.

www.fishbase.org search

Bird fact file

Birds are vertebrate animals with two legs and front limbs that have become adapted to form wings. All birds have feathers and most, but not all, can fly. Birds reproduce by laying eggs from which their young hatch.

Smallest bird

The smallest bird is the bee hummingbird, which is 2.2 in. (5.7 cm) long and weighs 0.056 oz. (1.6 g).

Longest beak

The bird with the longest beak in relation to its body is the sword-billed hummingbird—its beak is 4.1 in. (10.5 cm) long and its body is 5.3 in. (13.5 cm) long. The bird with the longest beak of all is the Australian pelican. Its beak is 18.5 in. (47 cm) long.

Highest flyer

Ruppell's griffon is the highestflying bird. In 1973 one was recorded at 37,000 ft. (11,300 m) above sea level—7,900 ft. (2,400 m) higher than Mt. Everest—after colliding with an airliner.

Longest migration

The Arctic tern migrates farther than any other bird. Every year it flies from the Arctic to Antarctica and back again—a round trip of at least 25,000 mi. (40,000 km).

Largest flying birds

- **Great bustard**: wingspan 9 ft. (2.7 m); weight 46 lb. (20.9 kg)
- **Trumpeter swan**: wingspan 11 ft. (3.4 m); weight 37 lb. (16.8 kg)
- **Mute swan**: wingspan 10 ft. (3.1 m); weight 36 lb. (16.3 kg)
- **Albatross**: wingspan 12 ft. (3.7 m); weight 34.8 lb. (15.8 kg)
- **Whooper swan**: wingspan 10 ft. (3.1 m); weight 34.8 lb. (15.8 kg)

Arctic tern

One and only

The North American whippoorwill is the only bird that hibernates. In autumn the bird dozes off in a rock crevice or an old nest and sleeps through the winter. Its heart rate and breathing slow down and its body temperature drops from its normal 105°F (41°C) down to 55.4°F (13°C) so it uses as little energy as possible.

All about feathers

The body of a feather is called its vane, the shaft is known as the rachis and the individual tufts are known as barbs. The barbs have hooks called barbules that cling to the others like Velcro to make a smooth surface.

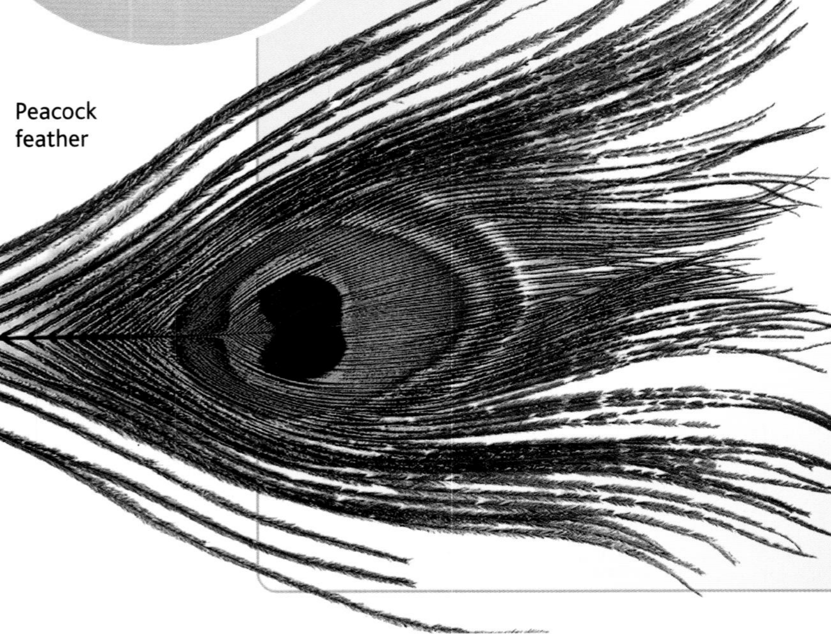

Peacock feather

- Feathers are made of keratin, the same material as our hair and nails.
- Birds shed their feathers at intervals and grow new ones. This process is called molting. Feathers fall in a set pattern and in pairs, one from each side, so that the bird's flight is not unbalanced. Birds that do not fly, such as penguins, molt all over.
- A songbird such as a sparrow has about 3,000 feathers in the summer but as many as 3,500 in the winter to keep it warm. A swan may have 25,200 or more—up to 20,000 of them on its head and neck. The bird with the fewest feathers is the ruby-throated hummingbird with only 940.
- Pens for writing were once made from the quills, or feathers, of geese, turkeys and other birds. The word pen comes from the Latin *penna*, a feather.
- Grebes eat their own feathers. They are thought to form pellets that help the birds regurgitate (bring up) the bones and scales of the fish they eat.
- The Japanese phoenix fowl is a domestic bird. It has tail feathers measuring up to 34.8 ft. (10.6 m), the longest of any bird. Various types of pheasant have tail feathers 6.6 ft. (2 m) long or more and a peacock's tail feathers can be 5 ft. (1.5 m) long.
- Each feather weighs very little, but together they make up a large part of the weight of a bird, especially as flying birds have very light skeletons. The skeleton of the frigate bird, a large bird with a 6.9 ft. (2.1 m) wingspan, weighs just 4 oz. (113 g), less than the weight of all its feathers.

Largest flightless birds

- **Ostrich**: height 9 ft. (2.7 m); weight 345 lb. (156.5 kg)
- **Emu**: height 5 ft. (1.5 m); weight 88 lb. (40 kg)
- **Cassowary**: height 5 ft. (1.5 m); weight 74 lb. (33.5 kg)
- **Rhea**: height 4.5 ft. (1.4 m); weight 55 lb. (25 kg)
- **Emperor penguin**: 4.3 ft. (1.3 m); weight 64.8 lb. (29.4 kg)

Birds' eggs

The biggest ostrich eggs weigh up to 5.2 lb. (2.35 kg), but they are not the largest eggs of all time. The extinct elephant bird (*Aepyornis maximus*) of Madagascar laid eggs that were up to 13 in. (33 cm) long.

This is larger than the eggs of any dinosaur, seven times bigger than an ostrich egg, 180 times bigger than a chicken egg and over 20,000 times the size of a hummingbird's egg!

Ostrich 56.4 oz. (1,600 g)
Albatross 21 oz. (595 g)
Kiwi 15.9 oz. (450 g)
Emperor penguin 15.9 oz. (450 g)
Mute swan 12 oz. (340 g)
Eagle 5.1 oz. (145 g)
Snowy owl 2.9 oz. (83 g)
Domestic hen 2.3 oz. (65 g)
Mallard 1.9 oz. (54 g)
Peregrine falcon 1.8 oz. (52 g)
Sparrow 0.106 oz. (3 g)
Vervain hummingbird 0.013 oz. (0.375 g)

Emperor penguins

The Emperor penguin is the largest penguin. It lives in Antarctica, where there are about 200,000 breeding pairs. The female lays one egg, then goes off to feed for about two months. The male keeps the egg warm on his feet, beneath his body. Chicks stay with their mothers for about seven weeks, then gather together in a group to keep warm.

Flying mammals

Bats are the only mammals capable of true flight. They belong to the order Chiroptera, which means hand-wing. Instead of front legs, bats have wings made of skin that are supported by the bones of the arms and hands.

- There are about 977 species of bats. Flying foxes are among the largest. These bats are 18 in. (45 cm) long, have wings that span 5.6 ft. (1.7 m) and weigh up to 3.5 lb. (1.6 kg). The Kitti's hog-nosed bat, which lives in Thailand, is the smallest. It weighs 0.07 oz. (2 g), which is less than a table tennis ball. It is only 1.1 in. (2.9 cm) long, making it the smallest of all mammals.
- Bats sleep during the day and wake up at night, when they go in search of food. Most bats are insect-eaters—a little brown bat can catch 1,200 insects in an hour—but others eat fruit or nectar from plants. Some larger species catch frogs, birds and fish.
- Many bats live in large groups called colonies. Bracken Cave in Texas, contains the world's largest bat colony, with about 20 million animals. This is one of the densest populations of any mammal and there can be as many as 450 newborn babies per square foot (0.09 sq m). These bats eat 1,102 tons (1,000 tonnes) of insects every night.

Emperor penguins and their young

www.bsc-eoc.org/avibase/avibase.jsp search

Tarantula

Shortest-lived
Male houseflies live for about 17 days and females for about 29 days. Mayflies may live for only a single day as adults, but for two or three years as larvae.

Distance fliers
Butterflies have been tracked flying for 3,000 mi. (4,800 km).

Fastest
Dragonflies can fly at speeds of 18–20 mph (29–32 km/h).

Spiders

Spiders are not insects. They belong to a separate group called arachnids, which also includes scorpions. A spider's body is divided into two parts linked by a narrow waist. It has four pairs of legs tipped with claws, but no wings. All spiders can make silk but not all spin webs.

There are at least 35,000 species of spiders. Most are harmless but a few can be deadly. The banana spider of Central and South America produces enough venom to kill six adult humans. Other deadly spiders are the funnel-web, which lives in Australia, and the wolf spider of Central and South America. The black widow and various tarantulas are also dangerous and can kill.

Biggest spider
The goliath bird-eating spider, which lives in South American rainforests, has legs up to 10 in. (25 cm) long.

Smallest spider
A species called *Patu marplesi* from Western Samoa is the smallest known spider. It is only 0.018 in (0.46 mm) long.

Amazing insects

Most abundant
Insects called springtails live in topsoil all over the world. There are probably as many as 1.5 billion per acre (600 million per hectare) . Together, they weigh more than the entire human race.

Longest
Stick insects have the longest bodies. Some measure up to 20.1 in. (51 cm) long, including their legs.

Heaviest
Goliath beetles can be 4.3 in. (11 cm) long and weigh 3.5 oz. (100 g).

Largest wingspan
The wings of the female Queen Alexandra birdwing butterfly of Papua New Guinea measure 11 in. (128 cm) across.

Smallest
The wings of a battledore wing fairy fly, which is a kind of parasitic wasp, measure only 0.008 in. (0.21 mm).

Longest lived
Jewel beetle larvae, or young, may live inside lumber for up to 30 years or more before emerging and turning into adult insects.

Types of insect

The body of most insects has three parts—head, thorax and abdomen. Insects have three pairs of legs and many have two pairs of wings. Listed here are the main groups, or orders, of insects. Numbers are just the species that we know about and have been named. There may be thousands more still to be discovered. Total numbers are huge. Together, all the insects in the world would weigh at least 12 times as much as all the people in the world.

Coleoptera meaning "hard wings": 370,000 species, e.g., beetles

Hymenoptera "membrane wings": 198,000 species, e.g., ants, bees, wasps

Lepidoptera "scaly wings": 165,000 species, e.g., butterflies and moths

Diptera "two-wings": 122,000 species, e.g., midges, mosquitoes, true flies

Hemiptera "half wings": 82,000 species, e.g., aphids and cicadas

Orthoptera "straight wings": 20,000 species, e.g., crickets and locusts

Trichoptera "hairy wings": 8,000 species, e.g., caddisflies

Collembola "sticky peg": 6,500 species, e.g., springtails

Phthiraptera "louse wings": 6,000 species, e.g., biting and sucking lice

Odonata "toothed flies": 5,500 species, e.g., dragonflies

Bee facts

There are about 20,000 types of bees. The best known is probably the honeybee, but not all bees live in colonies like the honeybee. Many live alone and build their own nests.

- Honeybees are the only insects that make food that humans eat. Bees make honey to feed the inhabitants of their hives during winter. The honey they do not eat is harvested by beekeepers. Bees also make beeswax, which is used for making candles and furniture polish.
- Wallace's giant bees are the world's largest at up to 1.6 in. (4 cm) long. They were first found in Indonesia in 1858 but were then thought to have become extinct. In 1981 the bees were rediscovered.

Honeybee on a flower

Huge colonies of monarch butterflies migrate up to 1,860 mi. (3,000 km) every year.

Eating insects

In many countries insects are a popular food. Insect dishes include omelet made from silkworms and fried honeybees in China, fried locusts in Thailand and red ant chutney in India. Many of us may eat insects without realizing it—the red food coloring cochineal is made from the bodies of a Mexican scale insect.

- Honeybees visit up to five million flowers to make 2.2 lb. (1 kg) of honey. In doing so, they fly a total distance equal to flying four times round the Earth.
- The smallest bee is the Brazilian *Trigona duckei* at 0.08–0.2 in (2–5 mm) long.
- One beehive may contain 50,000 worker bees—these are the bees that collect nectar from flowers to make honey.
- Honeybees' wings beat 11,400 times a minute. These wing movements make the bees' familiar buzz.
- Every year 1.4 million tons (1.3 million tonnes) of honey are produced worldwide. China is the main producer with 304,000 tons (276,000 tonnes), followed by the U.S. with 90,000 tons (82,000 tonnes).
- Some people are allergic to bee stings, which can even be fatal. In 1962 in Rhodesia, Johanne Relleke was stung 2,243 times by wild bees, but survived!
- Queen bees can lay 2,000 to 3,000 eggs a day—as many as 200,000 eggs a year. They may live as long as five years, so can produce a million eggs.

Thysanoptera "fringed wings": 5,000 species, e.g., thrips

Neuroptera "net-veined wings": 4,000 species, e.g., lacewings

Blattodea "insect avoiding light": 4,000 species, e.g., cockroaches

Pscoptera "milled wings": 3,500 species, e.g., hook lice

Isoptera "equal wings": 2,750 species, e.g., termites

Ephemeroptera "living for a day": 2,500 species, e.g., mayflies

Phasmatodea "like a ghost": 2,500 species, e.g., leaf insects

Mantodea "like a prophet": 2,000 species, e.g., mantids

Plecoptera "wickerwork wing": 2,000 species, e.g., stoneflies

Siphonaptera "tube without wings": 2,000 species, e.g., fleas

Dermaptera "leathery wings": 1,900 species, e.g., earwigs

Mecoptera "long wings": 550 species, e.g., hanging flies

Thysanura "fringed tail": 370 species, e.g., silverfish

Archaeognatha "ancient jaw": 350 species, e.g., bristletails

Embioptera "lively wings": 300 species, e.g., web-spinners

Megaloptera "large wings": 250 species, e.g., alderflies

Raphidioptera "embroidered wings": 150 species, e.g., snakeflies

Zoraptera "pure + wingless": 30 species, e.g., angel insects

Grylloblattodea "cricket cockroach": 25 species, e.g., rock crawlers

Reptiles

A reptile is a vertebrate animal with a body covered in tough scales. Most reptiles live on land, but turtles and some kinds of snakes live in water.

Crocodiles and their relatives spend time on land and in water. There are more than 8,000 species of reptiles, which are divided into the following groups.

Lizards 4,765 species
Snakes 2,978 species
Turtles and tortoises 307 species
Amphisbaenians (worm lizards) 165 species
Crocodiles, alligators, caimans 23 species
Tuataras 2 species

Deadly snakes

The coastal taipan of Australia injects the most venom per bite with 0.004 oz. (120 mg). Just 0.00004 oz. (1 mg) would be enough to kill a person. The common krait's venom is even more dangerous—only 0.00002 oz. (0.5 mg) can be fatal.

Alligators and crocodiles

The crocodile family contains 23 species, including alligators, caimans and gavials. All are large reptiles with long bodies and short legs. Most crocodiles have narrow V-shaped snouts, but alligators and caimans have wider, U-shaped snouts. The gavial has long slender jaws—just right for catching fish.

In alligators and caimans the teeth of the lower jaw fit into pits in the upper jaw and cannot be seen when the mouth is closed. In crocodiles the fourth tooth on each side of the lower jaw fits into a notch on the upper jaw, so they are always visible. Crocodiles are generally bigger and more aggressive than alligators.

Alligators

American alligator (southern U.S.) 13.1–14.8 ft. (4–4.5 m)
Chinese alligator (China) 6.6 ft. (2 m)
Spectacled caiman (South America) 6.6–8.2 ft. (2–2.5 m)
Broad-snouted caiman (South America) 6.6 ft. (2 m)
Yacaré caiman (South America) 8.2–9.8 ft. (2.5–3 m)
Black caiman (South America) 13.1–19.7 ft. (4–6 m)
Cuvier's dwarf caiman (South America) 4.9–5.2 ft. (1.5–1.6 m)
Schneider's or Smooth-fronted caiman (South America) 5.6–7.5 ft. (1.7–2.3 m)

Crocodiles

American crocodile (southern U.S., Mexico, Central and South America) 16.4 ft. (5 m)
Slender-snouted crocodile (West Africa) 8.2 ft. (2.5 m)
Orinoco crocodile (northern South America) 19.7 ft. (6 m)
Australian freshwater crocodile (Australia) 8.2–9.8 ft. (2.5–3 m)
Philippine crocodile (Philippines) 9.8 ft. (3 m)
Morelet's crocodile (Central America) 9.8 ft. (3 m)
Nile crocodile (Africa) 16.4 ft. (5 m)
New Guinea crocodile (New Guinea) 11.5 ft. (3.5 m)
Mugger or marsh crocodile (India, Sri Lanka) 13.1–16.4 ft. (4–5 m)
Estuarine or saltwater crocodile (Southeast Asia, Australia) 19.7–23 ft. (6–7 m)
Cuban crocodile (Cuba) 11.5 ft. (3.5 m)
Siamese crocodile (Southeast Asia, very rare) 9.8–13.1 ft. (3–4 m)
African dwarf crocodile (Central and West Africa) 6.2 ft. (1.9 m)
False gharial or gavial (Southeast Asia) 16.4 ft. (5 m)

Gavials

Indian gavial or gharial (India, Pakistan, Bangladesh, Nepal) 16.4–19.7 ft. (5–6 m)

Estuarine or saltwater crocodile

Amphibians

An amphibian is a vertebrate animal that spends at least some of its life in water. Its skin is not scaly. There are about 5,578 species of amphibian, divided into:

Frogs and toads 4,896 species
Newts and salamanders 517 species
Caecilians (legless amphibians) 165 species

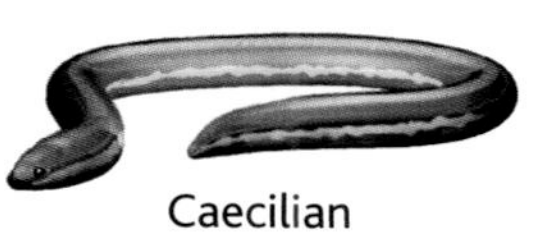
Caecilian

Salamander

Snake facts

Largest snakes

Many people believe that the South American anaconda is the longest snake. There are reports of anacondas up to 120 ft. (36.5 m) long, but this has never been proven. The reticulated or royal python is probably the longest snake at up to 35 ft. (10.7 m), but the anaconda may be the heaviest at up to 500 lb. (230 kg).

Smallest snake

The thread snake is rarely longer than 4.3 in. (10.8 cm). The spotted dwarf adder is the smallest venomous snake at 9 in. (23 cm) long.

Turtles and tortoises

These reptiles all have a hard shell that protects the body. There are about 250 species, some of which live in the sea, others in fresh water and the rest on land.

Biggest

- Fossils of the extinct turtle *Stupendemys geographicus* have been found with shells up to 10 ft. (3 m) long. They would have weighed more than 4,500 lb. (2,040 kg).
- The largest living turtle is the leatherback. A male washed up on the coast of Wales in 1988 holds the record—he was 113.5 in. (291 cm) long and weighed 2,019 lb. (916 kg).
- The Aldabra giant tortoise, which lives on an island in the Seychelles, weighs up to 670 lb. (304 kg) and is the largest land-living tortoise. It is also one of the slowest tortoises. It moves at an average speed of 0.17 mph (0.27 km/h).

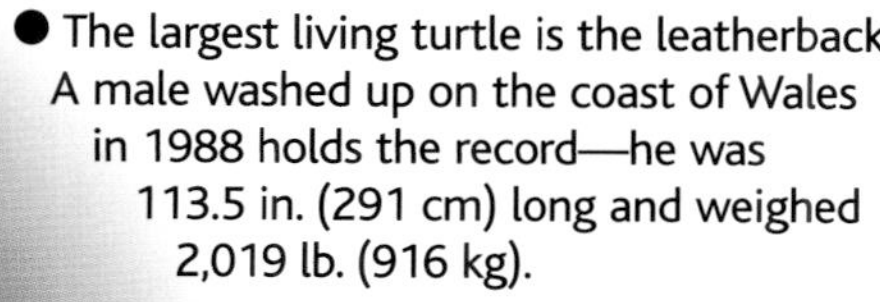

Smallest

The smallest turtle or tortoise is the common musk turtle, which is 3 in. (7.6 cm) long and weighs 8 oz. (230 g).

Blue poison arrow frog

Fantastic frogs and toads

Largest frogs and toads

- The world's largest known frog is the goliath frog, which lives in central Africa. It measures up to 34.5 in. (87.6 cm) long and weighs as much as 8.1 lb. (3.7 kg).
- The largest tree frog is *Hyla vasta*, which lives only on the island of Hispaniola. It is more than 4.7 in. (12 cm) long and has huge round finger and toe disks that grip like superglue.
- The world's largest toad is the South American marine toad. It can have a body length of over 9.1 in. (23 cm) and weigh up to 2.6 lb. (1.2 kg).

Smallest frog

The smallest frog and the world's smallest amphibian is the *Eleutherodactylus limbatus* frog, which measures only 0.3–0.5 in. (8.5–12 mm).

Newest frogs

In 2006, 20 previously unknown frog species were discovered in an expedition to Indonesia (see page 69) including a tiny microhylid frog that measures less than 0.6 in. (14 mm).

Egg laying

The marine toad lays 35,000 eggs a year, but the Cuban arrow-poison frog lays only one egg.

Highest and lowest homes

The green toad has been seen at 26,250 ft. (8,000 m) in the Himalayas and toads have been discovered more than 10,000 ft. (3,050 m) down a coal mine.

Most poisonous

The poison-arrow frogs of Central and South America are the most deadly. The world's most poisonous amphibian is the golden poison-arrow frog of western Colombia. One adult contains enough highly toxic poison in its skin to kill 1,000 people.

Smelliest

The smelliest frog is the Venezuela skunk frog, which was discovered in 1991. It warns off its enemies by releasing a bad-smelling chemical identical to the one produced by skunks.

Longest jumps

- On May 21, 1977, a female sharp-nosed frog leaped 33.5 ft. (10.2 m) in three consecutive jumps at a frog derby at Larula Natal Spa, Paulpietersburg, in South Africa.
- The cricket frog is only 1.4 in. (3.5 cm) and can jump 36 times its own length. If an adult human jumped 36 times his or her own length, the long-jump record could stand at 216 ft. (65.8 m)!

Life on man

As many as 100 trillion viruses and bacteria live on each of us. However much we wash, there are always 10 million or so bacteria on every square centimeter of our skin. There are also many tiny creatures called parasites, which can live inside or on the human body, feeding on our blood.

- Parasites such as roundworms, hookworms, flukes and tapeworms—which can grow as long as 32 ft. (9.8 m)—can live inside our bodies. They may cause such diseases as elephantiasis, in which the patient's limbs swell to gigantic sizes. Head lice live on human heads and feed on blood. The lice lay little white eggs, called nits, which cling to individual hairs.
- Follicle mites are in everyone's hair, even among our eyelashes. They were first described by 19th-century scientist Richard Owen (the man who first named dinosaurs), but are so tiny that few people have ever seen them or are even aware that they are there.
- Some of the tiny creatures that feed on us may also transmit diseases. Tsetse flies carry African sleeping sickness. Mosquitoes can infect humans with diseases such as malaria, dengue fever and yellow fever when they bite. Malaria has killed more people in human history than any other disease.
- Ticks can carry diseases such as encephalitis and Lyme disease. Mites and chiggers (baby mites) cause skin diseases and may transmit typhus.

See also
Black Death: page 104

Head louse with egg

The first teddy bear

Teddy bears are named after U.S. President Theodore (Teddy) Roosevelt. The story began when the president refused to shoot a young bear while on a hunting trip. This incident appeared in a cartoon by Clifford K. Berryman, published in the *Washington Post* on November 16, 1902. Soon after, Morris Michtom, a New York shopkeeper, started making stuffed bears and advertising them as "Teddy's Bears" with Roosevelt's permission.

At about the same time, Margarete Steiff, a German toymaker, started making her first toy bears and exported them to the U.S. to meet the demand created by Teddy's Bears. In 1903 Steiff's factory produced 12,000 bears.

By 1907, the figure had risen to 974,000. Steiff teddy bears, with a distinctive tag on their ear, are still made and are sold internationally. Early examples are prized by collectors.

Counting sheep

There are about 1,084,979,126 sheep in the world—an average of one sheep for every six people. In some countries there are twice as many sheep as humans.

United States 6,230,000 sheep, 298,444,125 people = 48 people for every sheep.

Canada 919,000 sheep and a population of 33,098,932 = 36 people per sheep.

Falkland Islands 690,000 sheep, 2,967 people = 233 sheep per person

New Zealand 39,928,000 sheep, 4,076,140 people = 10 sheep per person

Australia 101,125,000 sheep, 20,264,082 people = 5 sheep per person

Mongolia 11,866,400 sheep, 2,832,224 people = 4 sheep per person

Uruguay 9,712,000 sheep, 3,431,932 people = 3 sheep per person

Mauritania 8,850,000 sheep, 3,177,388 people = 3 sheep per person

Plague carriers

Fleas are perhaps the most dangerous creatures of all—they were the carriers of the deadly bubonic plague that killed millions of people in medieval times.

Humans and animals

Since ancient times humans have used many types of animals for a vast range of different purposes.

Maneater

A tigress known as the Champawat maneater, after the part of India in which she lived, killed a record 436 people over five years. She was shot in 1907 by British big-game hunter Colonel Jim Corbett (1875–1955).

Meat, milk and honey

Humans have always hunted and eaten wild animals. Milk from such animals as cows, goats, sheep, camels, buffalo, reindeer, llamas and yaks is drunk, used in cooking and made into butter and cheese. The eggs from birds such as hens, ducks, geese and quail are another important food. Honey has long been taken from the hives of wild bees, and now from domesticated bees kept in artificial hives.

Wool, fur and skin

Wool is shorn from live sheep, which then regrow their coats. The fur and leather of many other animals can be taken only after the animal has been killed. Cattle, goats, rabbits, mink, seals, wolves, foxes, kangaroos, big cats such as leopards, and alligators and snakes are among the many animals that have been used in this way. There are some very special uses for animal skin: for example, medieval manuscripts were written on vellum, made from calfskin.

Silk

Silk comes from the silkworm, the caterpillar of the silkmoth. Silkworms eat about a ton of mulberry leaves to make 11 lb. (5 kg) of silk.

Beasts of burden and transport

Strong animals such as horses, donkeys, camels, reindeer and buffalo are used to pull agricultural equipment and carts, and to carry people. Elephants drag heavy logs, pit ponies once drew trucks in coal mines, and dogs—usually huskies—pull sleds.

Indian elephant carrying a log at a logging camp

Security

Guard dogs (and even guard geese), police dogs and sniffer dogs (to detect drugs) are widely used.

Helpers

Sheepdogs, hunting hounds, retrievers and guide dogs for the blind are among the best known, but other animals, such as monkeys, can be trained to aid the disabled. Search and rescue dogs help to find missing people, lost walkers and climbers, and earthquake victims. Less well-known human helpers include pigs used to find truffles (edible fungi) and cats kept by the British Post Office to prevent mice from eating the mail! Animals kept as pets also provide millions of people with companionship.

Military

The warhorse is one of the most familiar of all military animals, but elephants have also been successfully used in battles. Many military organizations use dogs, goats and other animals as regimental mascots. Message-carrying dogs and carrier pigeons have been used by armies. During the Iraq war in 2004, dolphins were trained to find mines.

Top farm animals

These are the most popular farm animals worldwide (2005). They are kept for their meat, eggs and milk. The total number of these types of animal alone is three times that of the world's human population.

Bird flu

Avian or bird flu is a disease that affects domesticated and wild birds. In recent years, a type known as H5N1 has killed many birds, as well as a small number of people who have been in contact with them. Experts fear that if the virus mutates it could start to pass from human to human.

Chickens 16,887,556,000
Cattle 1,383,157,265
Sheep 1,101,639,064
Ducks 1,057,677,000
Pigs 989,763,628
Goats 837,235,801
Rabbits and hares 661,821,000

Countries with most pets

These totals include cats, dogs, birds, fish, small mammals (hamsters, guinea pigs, etc.) and reptiles.

U.S. 36,326,869
China 274,103,310
Germany 7,495,000
Brazil 72,062,640
France 67,150,000
Japan 66,451,000
Russia 60,075,000
Italy 59,850,000
U.K. 49,281,000
Turkey 41,001,580
Philippines 31,604,030
Netherlands 29,713,000
Mexico 26,978,440
Canada 25,463,000

Homeward bound

There are amazing stories of cats and dogs that travel great distances home after getting separated from their owners. Bobbie, a collie dog, made one of the longest journeys. He was lost on a family holiday in Indiana, on August 15, 1923. Six months later, he arrived home in Silverton, Oregon, 3,000 miles (4,800 km) away. He became known as Silverton Bobbie, the Wonder Dog of Oregon.

Playful kitten

Top pets

In the United States, 71 million households (63 percent) include a pet, ranging from fish, dogs, and cats to more exotic creatures.

Pet	Number
Freshwater fish	142,000,000
Cat	88,300,000
Dog	74,800,000
Bird	16,000,000
Horse	13,800,000
Saltwater fish	9,600,000
Rabbit	6,171,000
Turtle	1,991,000
Hamster	1,239,000
Lizard	1,078,000
Ferret	1,060,000
Guinea pig	1,004,000
Snake	586,000
Gerbil	431,000

Cat-alogue

Heaviest

Himmy, owned by Thomas Vyse of Queensland, Australia, weighed 47 lb. (21.3 kg). He had a 15 in. (38.1 cm) neck and an 33 in. (84 cm) waist—similar to that of an adult human! He died in 1986 at the age of 10.

Smallest

Tinker Toy, a male Blue Point Himalayan owned by Katrina and Scott Forbes of Illinois, is 2.8 in. (7 cm) tall, 7.5 in. (19 cm) long and weighs 1.4 lb. (625 g).

Biggest breed

Maine Coons are a North American breed of muscular, big-boned cats. Males often reach 13–17.5 lb. (6–8 kg) in weight.

Oldest

There are several contenders for this title. The most reliable record is that of the French-born cat Grandpa Rex's Allen. This was a Sphynx cat owned by Jake Perry of Austin, Texas. The cat died in 1998 at the age of 34.

Largest litter

In 1970 Tarawood Antigone, a female Burmese owned by Valerie Gane of Kingham, Oxfordshire, England, gave birth to 19 kittens. Fifteen of the litter survived.

Racing greyhounds

The fastest dogs

Greyhound 41.72 mph (67.14 km/h)
Saluki 40+ mph (64+ km/h)
Ibizan hound 38–40 mph (60.8–64 km/h)
Whippet 36.52 mph (54.42 km/h)
Sloughi 36 mph (57.6 km/h)

Famous cat lovers

Bill Clinton and Socks

Socks (born c. 1991) moved to the White House with the Clinton family. A cartoon version of Socks appeared on the White House website, in books and as one of the Muppets. Since the Clintons left, Socks has been in the care of Bettie Currie, the President's secretary.

Ernest Hemingway and Crazy Christian

Crazy Christian, Ecstasy and about 40 other cats overran the American writer's Cuban home until a special tower was built for them.

Charles Dickens and Williamina

Williamina was called William until she had a litter of kittens. One of these, known as the Master's Cat, used to put out Dickens' candle with its paw.

Domenico Scarlatti and Pulcinella

The Italian composer's cat used to jump onto his harpsichord keyboard and stroll along the keys. This inspired Scarlatti to compose *The Cat's Fugue*.

Mark Twain and Tammany

Tammany was one of many cats belonging to writer Samuel Clemens, better known as Mark Twain. The others included Apollinaris, Beelzebub, Blatherskite, Buffalo Bill, Sour Mash and Zoroaster. Twain described how one of Tammany's kittens liked to sit in the pocket of his billiard table, watching games in progress.

Dog-alogue

Largest dog

In 1989 Aicama Zorba of La-Susa, an Old English mastiff owned by Chris Eraclides of London, England, weighed 343 lb. (155.58 kg) and measured 8.25 ft. (2.5 m) nose to tail.

Smallest dog

A Yorkshire terrier owned by Arthur Marples of Blackburn, England, in the 1940s was just 2.5 in. (6.3 cm) tall and weighed 4 oz. (113 g).

Oldest dog

Bluey, an Australian cattledog owned by Les Hall of Victoria, Australia, died in 1938 at the age of 29 years, 5 months.

Largest litter

In 1944, Lena, an American foxhound, produced 23 puppies, all of which survived. Other dogs have equaled this record, but not all the pups have survived.

Longest jumper

Bang, a greyhound, jumped 30 ft. (9.2 m) while chasing a hare at Brecon Lodge in Gloucestershire, England.

Greatest climber

Tschingel, a beagle, climbed more than 50 peaks in the Alps, including the 13,664 ft. (4,165 m) Jungfrau and the 13,038 ft. (3,974 m) Eiger.

Famous dog lovers

Lee Duncan and Rin Tin Tin

Rescued as a puppy from a German trench in France at the end of World War I, the German shepherd Rin Tin Tin was taken to the United States where he became famous as an animal movie star.

J.M. Barrie and Luath

Luath, a Newfoundland dog, was the model for Nana in Barrie's book *Peter Pan*.

George Bush and Millie

Millie, the springer spaniel belonging to U.S. President George Bush (Sr.) had a best-selling "autobiography," *Millie's Book*, written by First Lady Barbara Bush.

William Wegman and Man Ray

American photographer Wegman named his Weimaraner after the famous photographer Man Ray, dressing him and other dogs in costumes and posing them in a variety of settings. Wegman's dogs appeared on TV in Sesame Street.

John Gray and Greyfriars Bobby

Bobby was a Skye terrier who faithfully guarded his master's grave at Greyfriars, Edinburgh, Scotland, for 14 years from 1858. The true story of the devoted dog has been the subject of books and films.

Charles Schulz and Spike

American cartoonist Charles Schulz based his comic character Snoopy on his family's basset hound Spike. In later strips a dog called Spike appears as Snoopy's brother.

Intelligent dogs

American psychology professor and pet trainer Stanley Coren ranked 133 breeds of dogs for intelligence. He studied their responses to a range of IQ tests, as well as the opinions of dog obedience judges. The five top breeds were the border collie, poodle, German shepherd, golden retriever and Doberman pinscher.

Tyrannosaurus rex skull and reconstruction (below)

Dinosaurs

Dinosaurs first appeared about 230 million years ago. These amazing reptiles then dominated life on Earth until they became extinct 65 million years ago. The first dinosaurs to be described were *Megalosaurus* (great lizard) by William Buckland in 1824 and *Iguanodon* (iguana tooth) by Gideon Mantell in 1825.

They were named before the word "dinosaur" had been invented. The name *dinosauria* (terrible lizards) was suggested by British scientist Richard Owen in July 1841. Since then 700 species have been identified. Not all dinosaurs were enormous—some measured less than 24 in. (60 cm) long, about the size of a chicken. Sizes of dinosaurs are mostly estimates worked out from the size of bones. The largest known complete skeleton is of a *Brachiosaurus* and is 73.2 ft. (22.3 m) long. The skeleton is in the Humboldt Museum, Berlin, Germany.

Biggest dinosaurs

Seismosaurus weight 220,000 lb. (99,800 kg); length 150 ft. (45.7 m)

Argentinasaurus weight 200,000 lb. (90,700 kg); length 120 ft. (36.6 m)

Supersaurus weight 120,000 lb. (54,400 kg); length 120 ft. (36.6 m)

Ultrasaurus weight 140,000 lb. (63,500 kg); length 100 ft. (30.5 m)

Brachiosaurus weight 120,000 lb. (54,400 kg); length 100 ft. (30.5 m)

Dinosaur facts

- The biggest dinosaurs were all herbivores. *Tyrannosaurus rex*, one of the largest carnivorous dinosaurs, measured up to 49 ft. (15 m) long and weighed 132,000 lb. (60,000 kg) or more. Its huge jaws were packed with 60 teeth, the biggest of which were 9 in. (23 cm) long!
- A new type of tyrannosaur called *Guanlong wucaii* has recently been discovered in China. It lived 160 million years ago, measured about 10 ft. (3 m) long, and looked like a miniature version of *Tyrannosaurus rex*.
- The largest flying prehistoric creatures were pterosaurs. The wings of the biggest pterosaur, *Quetzalcoatlus*, measured 36 ft. (11 m) from tip to tip.
- The largest known dinosaur egg belonged to *Hypselosaurus*. The 100 million-year-old egg measures 10 by 12 in. (25 by 30 cm), about three times the volume of an ostrich egg.
- The fastest dinosaur, *Ornithomimus*, could probably run at a speed of up to 44 mph (70 km/h). The ostrich runs at a similar speed today.
- Dinosaurs have been in space! Fragments of bone and an eggshell of *Maiasaura peeblesorum* were taken into space by astronaut Loren Acton in 1985. A *Coelophysis* skull was taken into space by astronaut Bonnie Dunbar in 1998.

Coelacanth: a living fossil

Paleontologists discovered a large fish known as the coelacanth from fossil remains. They thought it had become extinct about 65 million years ago. But on December 22, 1938, one was caught alive off East London in South Africa. This strange-looking creature, about 5.6 ft. (1.7 m) long, snapped at the hand of Captain Henrik Goosen, but died soon afterward. Captain Goosen realized that he had found something unusual so took the fish to a local museum where scientists identified it as a "living fossil." Since then, more than 200 coelacanths, some measuring up to 6.2 ft. (1.9 m) long, have been caught, mostly off the Comoros islands.

Animals in danger

In the past 500 years, hundreds of species of animals have become extinct—they have disappeared from Earth forever. In many cases this is because of human actions. The animals have been hunted, or the areas where they lived have been destroyed.

Some creatures become extinct in the wild but have survived in artificial settings, such as zoos. If they can be successfully bred, they may be taken back to the wild. Przewalski's horse, for example, became extinct in the wild but has since been bred in captivity. Now there are herds of these wild horses in their old home around the Gobi Desert. Other species are defined as "threatened," or in danger of becoming extinct. According to the degree of threat they may be considered "critically endangered," "endangered" or "vulnerable."

Amphibians 6,199 known species; 1,808 threatened
Birds 9,956 known species; 1,217 threatened
Fish 30,000 known species; 1,201 threatened
Mammals 5,416 known species; 1,094 threatened
Mollusks 81,000 known species; 978 threatened
Insects 950,000 known species; 623 threatened
Crustaceans 40,000 known species; 460 threatened
Reptiles 8,240 known species; 422 threatened
Others 130,200 known species; 42 threatened

Dodo

Last seen alive

Saber-toothed tiger 12,000 years ago
Woolly mammoth 10,000 years ago
Moa 1,000 years ago
Aurochs (giant wild ox) 1627
Aepyornis (elephant bird) 1649
Dodo 1681
Steller's sea cow 1768
Great auk 1844
Tarpan (wild horse) 1851
Labrador duck 1875
Quagga (zebra-like creature) 1883
Pilori muskrat 1902
Badlands bighorn sheep 1905
Japanese gray wolf 1905
Passenger pigeon 1914
Carolina parakeet 1918
California grizzly bear 1922
Schomburgk's deer 1938
Arabian ostrich 1941
Euler's flycatcher 1955
Eskimo curlew 1963
Guam flying fox 1968
Pyrenean ibex 2000
Yangtze River dolphin 2006
Western black rhinoceros 2006
Madeiran large white butterfly 2007

www.dinodata.org search

Lost world

In 2006 a team of 12 scientists returned from an area of rainforest in Indonesia where no humans had ever set foot before. It lies in the Foja Mountains on the island of New Guinea and it is so difficult to reach that the explorers had to be dropped in by helicopter. They discovered dozens of new animals and plants, including an orange-faced honeyeater, a golden-mantled tree kangaroo, 20 new species of frogs, four new species of butterflies, a giant rhododendron flower (about 6 in. [15 cm] across), and a species of bird that had been considered extinct for over 100 years.

The end of the tiger?

Some very familiar animals are under threat of extinction. They include the gorilla, African and Asian elephants, the black rhino, the giant panda and many species of whale, such as the blue, right and fin whales.

Tigers are also in serious danger. A century ago there were more than 100,000 tigers. Of the eight known subspecies of tiger, three—the Bali, Caspian and Javan—became extinct. There are now fewer than 5,000–7,500 tigers left in the wild because their habitats have been destroyed and they have been illegally hunted for their bones and other parts used in traditional Chinese medicines.

Numbers of the Amur or Siberian, the largest tiger, have recovered slightly to 600 in the wild, with fewer than 501 in wildlife parks and zoos. The Sumatran tiger is down to about 400–500, with 232 in captivity. The Bengal, including the rare white tiger, ranges from 3,176–4,556, with about 200 in zoos, and there are only an estimated 1,227–1,785 of the Indochinese, with 60 in zoos.

The rarest tiger of all is the South China tiger. Its population is down to only 20–30 individuals in the wild and 48 in zoos.

Siberian tiger

Pollution fact file

Pollution happens when unwanted gases and other materials escape into the environment. It causes waste, financial losses and damage to human, animal and plant health. Huge growth in industry and in the world's population in the last 100 years have led to more and more industrial processes and pollution. Deliberate dumping and accidents such as oil spills have seriously affected the Earth's air, land and water.

Loggers cutting down rainforest in Borneo

Air pollution

Most air pollution comes from burning fossil fuels (coal, oil and gas) and solid waste, or from gases released into the air. Carbon monoxide from vehicle exhausts is poisonous because it prevents the absorption of oxygen. Nitrogen oxide reacts with sunlight to produce smog (a combination of smoke and fog).

Acid rain

Acid rain is caused when nitrogen oxide, sulfur dioxide and other chemicals from volcanic eruptions and human sources combine with rain and fall as acid. It can damage buildings, kill fish and harm trees and other plants.

Land pollution

Soil can be damaged by the dumping of chemicals, toxic (poisonous), radioactive and other waste as well as the overuse of pesticides and fertilizers. Polluted land is unsafe for anything to live on.

Global warming

Greenhouse gases in Earth's atmosphere, such as carbon dioxide, nitrous oxide, water vapor and methane, help to trap heat and stop too much of it escaping into space. Without these gases, the Earth would not be warm enough for us to live on. But more and more greenhouse gases are being released into the atmosphere from human activities, and too much heat is being trapped. The Earth became 0.5°C (1°F) warmer during the 20th century and a further rise of even a couple of degrees will damage its natural balance.

Reversing pollution

Many countries have become more aware of pollution and the damage it causes and are taking action to reduce it. For example, since the 1990s, laws have been introduced in the United States to ban the use of lead-based paint and leaded gasoline. Clean air laws have reduced pollution in cities, and scientists are making vehicles that do not burn fossil fuels. People and businesses are heavily fined for dumping waste and chemicals. However, pollution is still a huge problem.

Destroying forests

About 35,000 sq. mi. (90,000 sq km) of forest are cut down every year worldwide to obtain lumber or to clear land so it can be used for farming. This is about the same area as the state of Indiana.

Cutting down forests increases the amount of carbon dioxide in the atmosphere, which can affect climate and destroy the homes of many animals and plants.

Country	Average annual forest loss 2000–2005
Brazil	13,382 sq. mi. (34,660 sq km)
Indonesia	5,578 sq. mi. (14,448 sq km)
Sudan	4,548 sq. mi. (11,780 sq km)
Zambia	2,055 sq. mi. (5,322 sq km)
Mexico	1,525 sq. mi. (3,950 sq km)

How much water?

People worldwide use 3,802,300,000,000,000 liters (8,035,600,000,000,000 pt) of water every year. On average everybody in the world uses 633,000 liters (1,337,767 pt) a year, or 1,734 liters (3,665 pt) a day. Of this, 9 percent (156 liters [330 pt]) a day is used in homes, 20 percent (347 liters [733 pt]) by industry and 71 percent (1,231 liters [2,602 pt]) by agriculture.

The United States uses 408 billion gallons of water a day (2000) – 1,450 gallons per person in total. Of this 48% is used in power generation, 34% in irrigation, 11% public supply, 5% industrial and less than 1% each for domestic, livestock and aquaculture

Household water usage

Brushing teeth (tap off) 2.5 liters (5.3 pt)
Brushing teeth (tap on) 5 liters (10.6 pt)
Toilet flush 5–20 liters (10.6–42.3 pt)
Shower (per minute) 22 liters (46.5 pt)
Washing machine 120 liters (253.6 pt)
Bath (full) 170 liters (359.3 pt)
Washing car 200 liters (422.7 pt)
Watering garden (1 hour) 600–1,500 liters (1,268–3,170 pt)

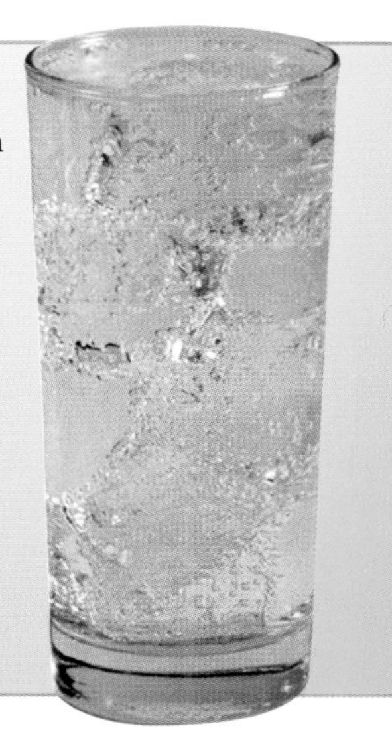

Worst polluters

Carbon dioxide (CO_2) pollution enters the atmosphere from three main sources—burning fossil fuel (coal and oil), cement manufacturing and gas burning.

These figures show the total amounts produced by some of the leading industrial countries in 2004 in tons (tonnes). CO_2 is produced naturally by animals, forest fires and other sources. But natural production has been overtaken by the amount produced by human activities. More carbon dioxide in the atmosphere increases the amount of heat absorbed, and this leads to global warming (see Pollution fact file).

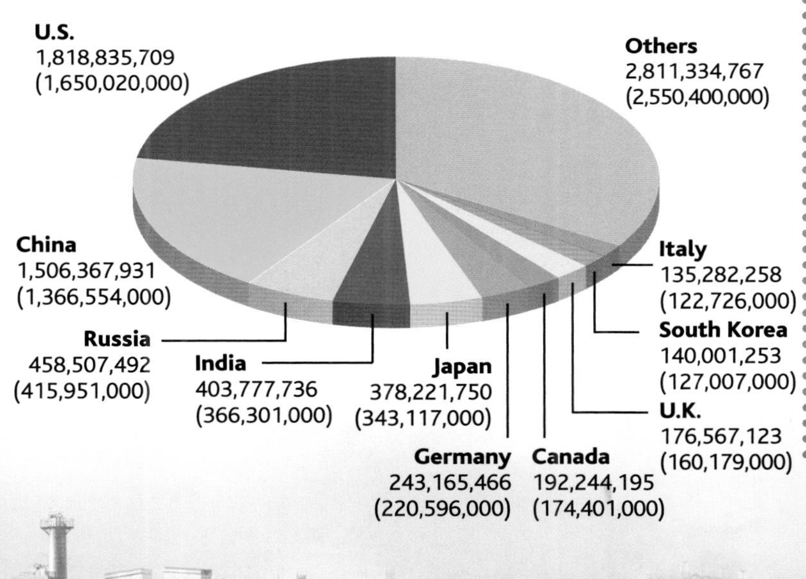

Worst oil tanker spills

About two million tons of oil are spilled into the sea every year from oil tankers, mostly during collisions or other accidents. Most spills are small (tons or less), but some are much more serious. When huge quantities of oil are discharged into the sea and washed up on shorelines they harm many birds and other creatures.

The 1989 grounding of the *Exxon Valdez* in Prince William Sound, Alaska, caused the U.S.'s worst oil spill. The quantity spilled was smaller than the spills listed 38,500 tons (35,000 tonnes), but thousands of birds, fish, otters, seals and whales were killed.

Atlantic Empress and ***Aegean Captain***, off Tobago, 1979, 316,000 tons (287,000 tonnes)

ABT Summer, off Angola, 1991, 286,000 tons (260,000 tonnes)

Castillio de Bellver, off Saldanha Bay, South Africa, 1983, 278,000 tons (252,000 tonnes)

Olympic Bravery, off Ushant, France, 1976, 276,000 tons (250,000 tonnes)

Amoco Cadiz, off Finistère, France, 1978, 246,000 tons (223,000 tonnes)

Water pollution

Increasing quantities of heavy metals such as mercury and lead, chemicals, sewage and oil spills are polluting lakes, rivers and oceans. Water in some places is now unsafe to drink or bathe in and animals are harmed or killed.

www.epa.gov search

A brief history of garbage

The ancient world

In ancient times, nomadic peoples simply left their garbage and moved on. Once people settled in villages, they were faced with the problem of having to dispose of garbage where they lived. Often they just covered it with earth. This caused the ground level in ancient cities, such as Troy, to increase by over 3.3 ft. (1 m) a century. The first anti-dumping law was issued in Athens, Greece in 320 BC, when citizens were compelled to bury their garbage or put it in pits outside the city.

The Middle Ages

In medieval cities, people often threw their garbage into the street, causing the spread of rats, mice—and disease. Free-roaming pigs ate some of it, except in Paris where they were banned after King Louis VI's son was killed when his horse tripped over a pig in 1131. In London, kites and ravens scavenged among the garbage tips. The birds were so important that killing one was punishable by death.

The 19th century

Rag-and-bone men were a common sight in 19th-century streets. They went from house to house with a horse and cart, gathering anything that could be resold. Dustmen collected cinders from home fires to be used in brickmaking; human waste and horse manure were taken to farms for fertilizer; and dog droppings were used in the leather tanning trade. The first garbage-burning incinerator, called The Destructor, was built in Nottingham, England in 1874. The first garbage can appeared in Paris, France, in 1883. It was introduced by Eugène Poubelle, the Prefect of Police. To this day, the French call a garbage can a *poubelle*.

The 20th century

During the 20th century, thousands of new, disposable goods were invented and fewer people had open fires so more garbage was thrown away. Disused electronic equipment including TVs, computers, cell phones and fax machines began to join the growing garbage dumps.

Household waste

per person per year (OECD countries only)

Ireland
1,675 lb. (760 kg)
U.S.
1,630 lb. (740 kg)
Iceland
1,610 lb. (730 kg)
Norway
1,545 lb. (700 kg)
Australia
1,520 lb. (690 kg)
Denmark
1,475 lb. (670 kg)
Switzerland
1,455 lb. (660 kg)
Germany, Luxembourg, Spain
1,435 lb. (650 kg)
U.K.
1,345 lb. (610 kg)
The Netherlands
1,325 lb. (600 kg)

How much garbage is that?

In the contiguous United States (excluding Alaska and Hawaii), there are 1,654 landfill sites. The Fresh Kills Landfill on Staten Island, New York, closed in 2001 after operating for over 50 years.

It was the world's largest garbage dump, covering over 2,000 acres (810 ha) and receiving 29,000 tons (26,300 tonnes) of garbage every day. Following the events of 9/11, 1.8 million tons (1.6 million tonnes) of debris from the World Trade Center site was taken there to be searched for evidence, personal items and human remains. Puente Hills landfill in Whittier, California, is now the United States' largest dump in use.

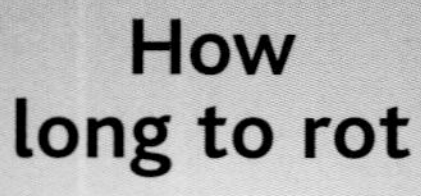

How long to rot

Cotton rags 1–5 months
Paper 2–5 months
Orange peel up to 6 months
Wool socks 1–5 years
Cigarette butts 1–12 years
Plastic-coated drink cartons 5 years
Plastic bags 10–20 years
Photo film 20–30 years
Leather shoes 25–50 years
Artificial fiber clothes (nylon, etc.) 30–40 years
Metal cans 50–100 years

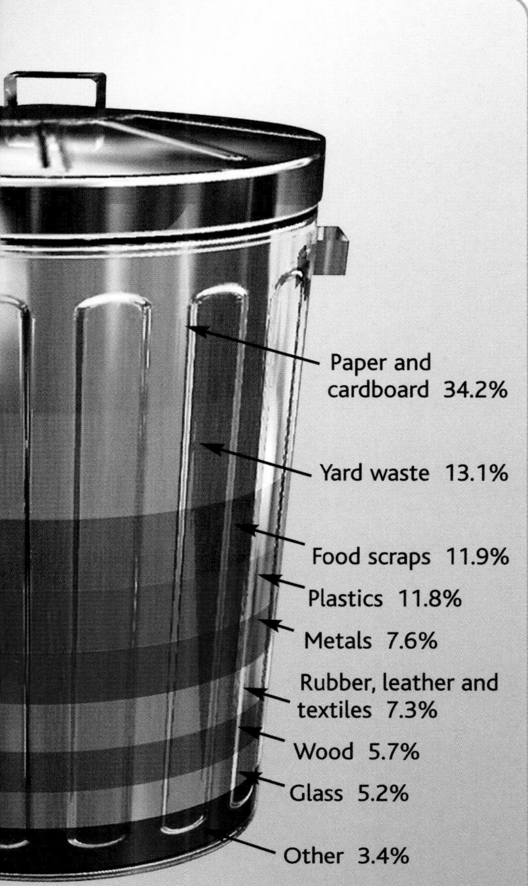

Where does it go?

Landfills

Most waste ends up underground—in giant municipal pits, or landfill sites, where it can rot out of sight. These are usually lined to prevent dangerous chemicals seeping into the ground. However, many discarded objects take decades, even centuries to break down, and we are running out of suitable places to bury waste.

Incineration

Burning garbage is another solution. Burning gets rid of most kinds of waste and the heat can be converted into energy for other uses. The problem is that incineration releases harmful gases, some of which may contribute to global warming.

www.epa.gov/epaoswer/osw/kids search

Compost is recycled organic waste

Recycling

Recycling uses old waste to make new products. It cuts down the amount of garbage and saves natural resources by reducing the need for new raw materials. Items most suitable for recycling are organic matter (plant and animal), which can be composted and used as fertilizer, metals (such as aluminum cans), glass and paper.

Reduce and reuse

The most sustainable solution is to reduce the amount of waste we create. Compared with 50 years ago, food cans are 50 percent lighter, yogurt containers are 60 percent lighter, glass bottles are 50 percent lighter and plastic shopping bags are half as thick. Shoppers can help by choosing not to buy goods with lots of packaging or disposable containers, as these make up 10–20 percent of all domestic garbage.

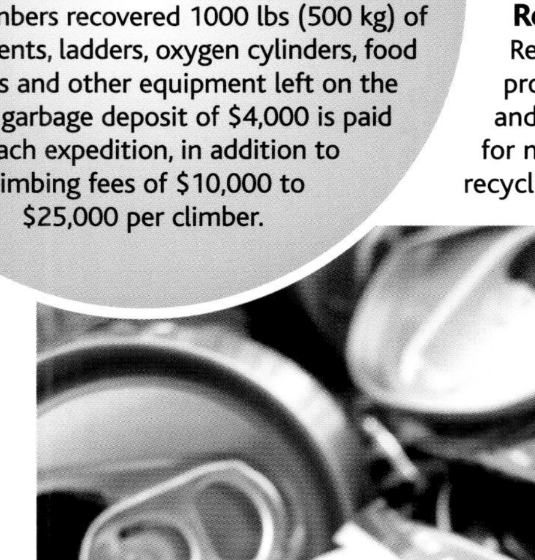

Aluminum cans that could be recycled

A mountain of junk

More than 1,000 people have climbed Mt. Everest since it was conquered in 1953. They, and their support teams, have dropped more than 50 tons (50 tonnes) of garbage, making Everest the world's highest garbage dump. In 2007, climbers recovered 1000 lbs (500 kg) of discarded tents, ladders, oxygen cylinders, food containers and other equipment left on the slopes. A garbage deposit of $4,000 is paid by each expedition, in addition to climbing fees of $10,000 to $25,000 per climber.

Ways to reduce waste

1. Use your own shopping bag and refuse unnecessary plastic bags
2. Buy refills
3. Buy fruits and vegetables loose, not prepacked
4. Buy recycled goods
5. Buy reusable diapers
6. Buy soft drinks in large bottles and pour into smaller bottles for daily use
7. Reuse wrapping paper, packing materials and envelopes
8. Pack your lunch in a reusable box rather than foil or plastic wrap
9. Choose durable products over disposable ones, e.g., rechargeable batteries
10. Donate unwanted clothes to charity or sell at yard sales
11. Donate unwanted furniture to a furniture recycling project
12. Buy drinks in glass bottles—they can be reused 20 times
13. If it's broken, mend it—don't throw it away!
14. Return clothes hangers to dry cleaners
15. Recycle glass, cans, paper and cardboard. If your community doesn't have a recycling program, propose one
16. Compost leftover food, yard waste and vacuum cleaner dust

FIREFLY'S WORLD OF FACTS

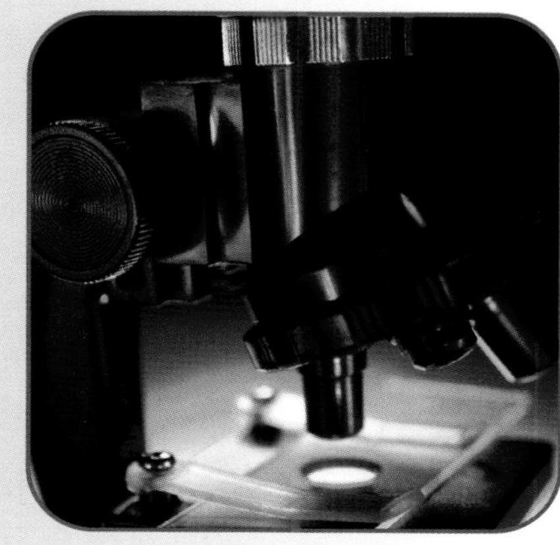

Science & Technology

76 SCIENCE
78 THE ELEMENTS
80 INVENTIONS
82 MATHEMATICS
84 WEIGHTS AND MEASURES
86 COMPUTERS AND THE INTERNET
88 TELECOMMUNICATIONS

Collision course

Completed in 2008, ATLAS, the large particle detector at the CERN laboratory in Switzerland, lies 328 miles (100 meters) underground. It will research the atomic particles created when proton beams collide. Scientists hope this will help them understand the "God particle", one of the remaining mysteries of science.

How dense?

A cubic meter (equal to 35.3 cu. ft.) of pure water weighs 1,000 kg (2,205 lb.) or 1 metric tonne. Materials that have a density greater than water sink, and those that are less dense float.

Lightweight metals such as aluminum and titanium are important to engineers—for example, for building aircraft that need to be strong but light enough to fly. These are the average densities of some of the substances around us.

	kg/cu m	(lb/cu. ft.)
Air at 32°F (0°C)	1.29	(0.08)
Styrofoam	100	(6.24)
Balsa wood	150	(9.36)
Cork	240	(14.98)
Steam	600	(37.46)
Gasoline	730	(45.57)
Oak	750	(46.82)
Butter	900	(56.19)
Paper	900	(56.19)
Ice	920	(57.43)
Olive oil	920	(57.43)
Rubber	940	(58.68)
Wax	950	(59.31)
Pure water at 32°F (0°C)	1,000	(62.43)
Milk	1,030	(64.30)
Sea water	1,030	(64.30)
Ebony	1,200	(74.91)
Spider silk	1,260	(78.66)
Coal	1,400	(87.40)
Bone	1,800	(112.37)
Brick	2,100	(131.10)
Salt	2,165	(135.16)
Carbon	2,267	(141.52)
Chalk	2,300	(143.58)
China	2,300	(143.58)
Concrete	2,300	(143.58)
Sand	2,500	(156.07)
Glass	2,600	(162.31)
Aluminum	2,700	(168.56)
Marble	2,700	(168.56)
Human tooth enamel	2,900	(181.04)
Diamonds	3,500	(218.50)
Titanium	4,507	(281.36)
The Earth (average for whole planet)	5,520	(344.60)
Iron	7,874	(491.56)
Copper	8,920	(556.86)
Silver	10,490	(654.86)
Lead	11,340	(707.93)
Mercury	13,570	(847.15)
Tungsten	19,250	(1,201.74)
Gold	19,300	(1,204.86)
Platinum	21,090	(1,316.61)
Osmium	22,610	(1,411.5)

Strange studies

Angelology Angels
Aphnology Wealth
Biometrology The effect of weather on people
Cereology Crop circles
Cryology Snow, ice and frozen ground
Cryptology Codes and ciphers
Draconology Dragons
Enigmatology Puzzles
Eremology Deserts
Fromology Cheese
Garbology Garbage
Gelotology Laughter
Googlology The Google search engine
Googology Large numbers
Hypnology Sleep
Kalology Beauty
Limacology Slugs
Loimology Plagues
Momilogy Mummies
Nanotechnology Very small objects
Nephology Clouds
Osmology Smells
Pharology Lighthouses
Polemology Wars
Pomology Fruit-growing
Rhinology Noses
Siphonapterology Fleas
Teratology Monsters
Toxicology Poisons
Tsiology Tea
Ufology Unidentified flying objects
Vermeology Worms
Xylology Wood

Cryology is the study of snow, ice and frozen ground

An iceberg is made of almost pure water. This is less dense than sea water, so the iceberg floats.

See also
Conversions: page 84

www.exploratorium.edu search

Acids and alkalis

The pH (potential Hydrogen) system was invented in 1909 by Danish chemist Søren Sørensen (1868–1939). In this, pH is a measure of the concentration of hydrogen ions, which shows whether something is acidic or base (also known as alkali).

Pure water has a pH of 7.0. Substances that have a pH of less are acidic. Substances with a pH of more than 7.0 are base (alkali). Acids make lemon juice and vinegar taste sharp, and acid rain harms trees and other plants. The traditional way of testing pH is by using litmus paper — acidic substances turn blue litmus red, while alkalis turn red litmus blue.

Substance	pH	Substance	pH
Hydrochloric acid	0	Orange juice	3.7
Car battery acid	1.0	Wine/beer	4.0
Gastric (digestive) juices	1–3	Tomato juice	4.3
Lime juice	2.3	Normal rainfall	5.6
Lemon juice	2.4	Saliva	6.4–6.9
Acid rain	2.4–3.6	Milk	6.6
Apple	3.0	Pure water	7.0
Vinegar	3.0	Human blood	7.4
Grapefruit	3.2	Sea water	7.8–8.3

A rainbow is created when sunlight passes through water droplets.

Spectrum colors

The electromagnetic spectrum includes all forms of light, from radio waves and microwaves at one end of the scale to X-rays and gamma rays at the other. In between is visible or white light, which is made up of a range of colors.

We can see the individual colors when they are split up by water droplets and form a rainbow, or by passing white light through a prism. The colors of the spectrum are red, orange, yellow, green, blue, indigo and violet.

Sound levels

The decibel (dB) is a way of measuring sound. Sounds of 80–90 dB or more can damage hearing and it is dangerous for people to work in sound levels of more than 90 dB.

Sounds above 130 dB become painful, and people should wear hearing protectors with sounds of more than 140 dB. A decibel level of more than 150 dB can cause permanent deafness.

Silence	0 dB
Rustle of leaves	10 dB
Quiet whisper at 16 ft. (5 m); library	20–30 dB
Normal conversation; soft music	30 dB
Sailing boat	35 dB
Quiet countryside; ticking watch	40 dB
Inside average home	45–50 dB
Restaurant; office; loud conversation	50–60 dB
Background music; motorboat	60 dB
Hairdryer	60–80 dB
Workshop	65 dB
Radio; telephone ring; busy traffic; orchestra; loud TV	70 dB
Inside car; underground train	80 dB
Pneumatic drill at 50 ft. (15 m); Niagara Falls; top level of comfort	85 dB
Very loud snore	88 dB
Heavy traffic at 50 ft. (15 m); roaring lion	90 dB
Loud shout at 50 ft. (15 m); lawnmower; chainsaw; blender	100 dB
Heavy truck 3 ft. (1 m) away; orchestra playing Beethoven's Ninth Symphony	105 dB
Circular saw at 3 ft. (1 m); car horn at 16 ft. (5 m)	110 dB
Shouting in someone's ear	114 dB
Personal stereo	115 dB
Loud scream; thunder; explosion; submarine engine room	120 dB
Loud rock music	120–130 dB
Racing car	125 dB
Motorbike (without silencer)	130 dB
Jumbo jet takeoff at 100 ft. (30 m)	140 dB
Rock music (peak at 16 ft. [5 m] from speaker)	150 dB
Level at ear of person firing powerful rifle	160 dB
Launch of *Saturn V* space rocket	172 dB
Blue whale call	188 dB
Volcanic eruption	272 dB

Brightness scale

A candela is a unit of light intensity. It was originally equivalent to the amount given out by a candle, but is now more precise.

	Candelas per sq. ft. (sq m)
Overcast sky	185 (2000)
Moon	232 (2,500)
Clear sky (average)	745 (8,000)
Candle (brightest spot)	930 (10,000)
Domestic light bulb	9,300 (100,000)
Sun at Equator	150,000 (1,600,000)
Flash of lightning	7,400,000 (80,000,000)
Atom bomb	185,000,000 (2,000,000,000)

A flash of lightning gives out 80,000,000 candelas

What is an element?

The elements are sometimes called the building blocks of the Universe because everything in the Universe—including ourselves—is made from them. The nucleus of each element consists of atoms with the same number of protons. Each element is unique, although elements can exist in different forms—for example, carbon may be soft graphite or hard diamond. Elements cannot usually be broken down into any other substance.

There are about 118 elements altogether, and 91 occur naturally on Earth. Others can be created in laboratories, but in minute quantities and they have very short lifespans of only thousandths of a second. Each element is also known by a one- or two-letter symbol as well as its name; for example, Fe is iron.

A chemical compound is a combination of two or more elements linked together, which can be broken down again into their constituent parts, but no further. Water, for example, is made up of two hydrogen atoms linked to one oxygen atom. Salt, or sodium chloride, is a compound of sodium and chlorine.

One and only

Element 98 was given the name Californium by the four scientists who discovered it in 1950. They were working at the University of California at Berkeley, and named the element for both the state and their university. One of them, Glen Theodore Seaborg (1912–99), received the Nobel Prize for Chemistry in 1951. The 106th element, Seaborgium, was named after him in 1994. It was the first to be named in honor of a living person.

Highest melting points

1 Carbon 6,381°F (3,527°C)
2 Tungsten 6,192°F (3,422°C)
3 Rhenium 5,767°F (3,186°C)
4 Osmium 5,491°F (3,033°C)
5 Tantalum 5,463°F (3,017°C)

The surface of the Sun reaches 10,121°F (5,605°C), so no element could approach it and remain solid.

See also
Air transportation: pages 216–17

Various weights of gold in a gold refinery

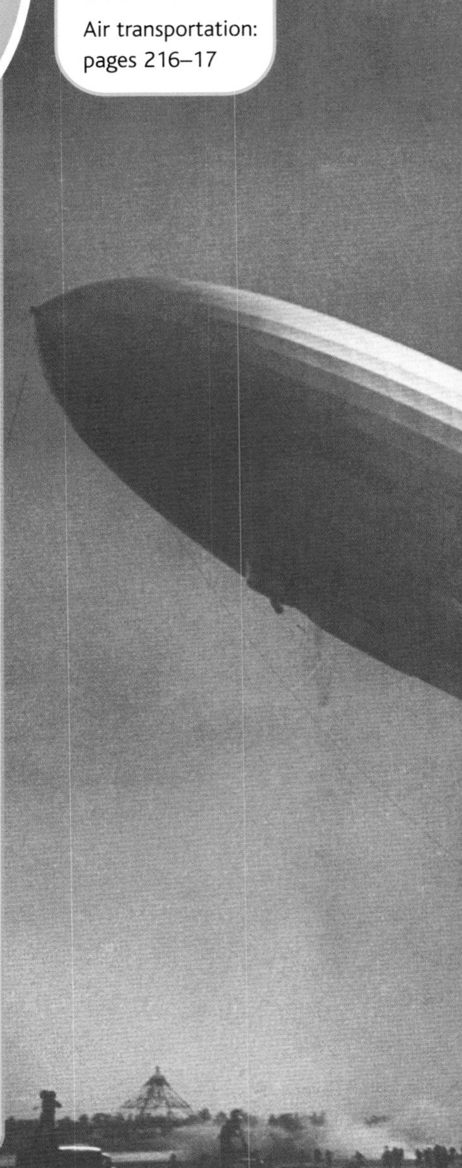

The heaviest elements

● Osmium
Osmium is the heaviest element (13.07 oz./in.^{3} [22.61 g/cm^3]). It was discovered in 1803. It was named after the Greek word for smell because it smelled bad. Osmium is very hard, and is used to make hard-wearing points, such as the nibs of fountain pens.

● Platinum
Platinum was used before anyone realized that it was an element. It weighs almost as much as osmium (12.39 oz./in.^{3} [21.45 g/cm^3]) and is used to make jewelery. It is also used in catalytic converters in cars to reduce the pollution from exhaust gases.

● Plutonium
Plutonium was discovered in 1941 and is a heavy and highly radioactive metal. It is used as a nuclear fuel and in nuclear weapons—1 lb. (0.45 kg) of plutonium produces an explosion equivalent to 10,000 tons (9,070 tonnes) of TNT.

● Gold
Gold is the best-known of all heavy metals—though at 11.15 oz./in.^{3} (19.29 g/cm^3) it is less heavy than the others here. Gold has been prized since ancient times and has many uses beyond coins and jewelery.

The lightest elements

● Hydrogen

Hydrogen is the simplest and lightest element, and the most common — 93 percent of all atoms in the universe are hydrogen atoms. On Earth, it is relatively rare in the atmosphere—only 10.6 of 211 million pints (5 of 100 million L) of air are hydrogen, but hydrogen combined with oxygen forms all the water in the world. Hydrogen is very light. This is why it was used in balloons carrying human passengers: the second-ever flight, in Paris on December 1, 1783, was in a hydrogen balloon. Hydrogen was also used in giant airships until May 6, 1937, when the giant German airship *Hindenburg* exploded, killing 36 people, at Lakehurst, New Jersey. Today, hydrogen fuel cells are used to power clean-energy cars.

● Helium

Helium is twice as heavy as hydrogen, but it is still only one-seventh the weight of air. Unlike hydrogen, helium does not burn, so it is used in modern airships.

● Lithium

Lithium was discovered in 1817 and takes its name from the Latin word for rock, although it is actually a metal. Lithium is so light and so soft that it can be easily cut with a knife. It floats because it is half as heavy as water and lighter than some types of wood. It is used to make lithium batteries.

● Potassium and sodium

Both were discovered in 1807. Both are metals that are lighter than water. In a laboratory, potassium and sodium are usually kept in paraffin wax because if they come into contact with water they will catch fire. Potassium is vital for plant growth and human well-being—our bodies contain about 5 oz. (140 g) of it. Sodium is relatively common as part of a compound: in combination with chlorine it is ordinary table salt.

The *Hindenburg*, a giant airship filled with hydrogen, bursts into flames.

Elements in sea water

Sea water is a treasure chest of elements, but sodium and chlorine, combined as sodium chloride, are the only two that are taken from it in large amounts. Other elements, such as gold, are too expensive to extract, even though there may be as much as 4,595 pounds of gold in a cubic mile of sea water (4,595 lb/ml^3)" with equivalent amount of gold in pounds in 1 cubic mile of sea water (500 kg/km^3).

Elements in the sea

1 Oxygen* 114.43 oz./gal. (857,000 mg/l)
2 Hydrogen* 14.39 oz./gal. (107,800 mg/l)
3 Chlorine 2.65 oz./gal. (19,870 mg/l)
4 Sodium 1.48 oz./gal. (11,050 mg/l)
5 Magnesium 0.18 oz./gal. (1,326 mg/l)
* Combined as water

Elements on Earth

There is calcium in the Earth and ocean in the form of calcium carbonate. Sodium exists in the form of sodium chloride, the salt in the ocean and on our tables.

The quantities of both calcium and sodium are so vast that these elements are considered unlimited.

There are quite small amounts of some precious metals on Earth, which is why they are so valuable. For example, there are about 1.1 million tons (1 million tonnes) of silver and 16,500 tons (15,000 tonnes) of gold. Elements are constantly being taken from Earth, but new discoveries are being made.

www.webelements.com search

Cowboy inventions

All these items, beloved of cowboys, are named after their inventors.

Levi's jeans

Levi Strauss (1829–1902) was a Bavarian immigrant who arrived in San Francisco in 1850 at the height of the California gold rush. Strauss noticed that the gold miners needed strong trousers and began making them, first from tent canvas and later from denim. The company is now one of the world's largest clothing manufacturers.

Bowie knife

The large knife was supposedly invented by James Bowie (1799–1836), a Texan adventurer who died during the siege of the Alamo fortress by Mexican soldiers. In fact, his older brother, Rezin Pleasant Bowie (1793–1841), may have invented the knife. It had a blade 10–15 in. (25–38 cm) long, with a guard between the blade and the handle.

Colt revolver

The Colt was invented by Samuel Colt (1814–62). Colts were used during the American Civil War, and the six-gun, the six-shot, single-action .45-caliber Peacemaker model introduced in 1873, made Samuel Colt a wealthy man.

Stetson hat

John Stetson (1830–1906) was a hat maker from New Jersey. He started the John B. Stetson Manufacturing Company of Philadelphia, which made the famous 10-gallon hat worn by cowboys.

Leonardo da Vinci

Italian Leonardo da Vinci (1452–1519) is best known as a painter, anatomist, sculptor and architect. *The Last Supper* and *Mona Lisa* are among the most famous paintings of all time.

But he is also hailed as one of the greatest inventors. Among his notebooks he left plans for countless advanced machines, often with descriptions written in secret mirror writing. Many of them were never built, but they anticipated modern inventions, often by hundreds of years. They include the following:

- Air conditioner
- Alarm clock
- Crane
- Diving suit and diving bell
- Double-hull ship
- Eyeglasses
- Flying machine
- Gas mask
- Gears
- Giant catapults and crossbows
- Helicopter
- Lifebelt
- Magnetic compass
- Mileometer
- Multi-barreled machine gun
- Parachute
- Revolving stage
- Shrapnel bomb
- Steam engine
- Tanklike armored vehicle
- Telescope
- Water turbine

Crazy inventions

There are many odd items dreamed up by inventors—a self-raising hat (1896) for the polite man with his arms full; spectacles for chickens to protect their eyes from other fowl that might attempt to peck them (1903); a motorized ice cream cone (1998) which rotates against the tongue. Here are some other examples.

Parachute fire escape

This invention was patented in 1879 by Benjamin B. Oppenheimer of Trenton, Tennessee. It was made up of a parachute attached to a helmet and padded shoes that would allow a person to leap out of a blazing building and land safely—if he was lucky enough not to break his neck.

Spider ladder

This invention was perhaps not so crazy for people who are scared of spiders. British inventor Edward Doughney's 1994 patent helps spiders to climb out of a bath.

Over 100 years of everyday inventions 1903

1903 the safety razor was invented by King Camp Gillette

1904 the ice cream cone was invented by Italo Marcioni

1906 the electric washing machine was invented by Alva J. Fisher

1907 vacuum cleaners with bags were invented by J. Murray Spangler

1913 the crossword puzzle was invented by Arthur Wynne

1913 the zipper was invented by Gideon Sundback

1920 the tea bag was invented by Joseph Krieger

1924 frozen food was invented by Clarence Birdseye

1926 the aerosol spray was invented by Erik Rotheim

1927 the pop-up toaster was invented by Charles Strite

1928 elastoplast was invented by Horatio Nelson Smith

1928 sliced bread was invented by Otto Rohwedder

1931 the electric razor was invented by Col. Jacob Schick

1934 the trampoline was invented by George Nissen and Larry Griswold

1938 the ballpoint pen was invented by László Biro

1938 instant coffee was invented by the Nestlé company

1945 the microwave oven was invented by Percy LeBaron Spencer

1945 Tupperware (food containers) was invented by Earl W. Tupper

1947 the long-playing record was invented by Goldmark

1950 the credit card was invented by Frank X. McNamara

Peter Chilvers

Chilvers was 12 when he invented windsurfing (boardsailing) in 1958 off Hayling Island, U.K.

What is a patent?

A patent is granted by a government to an inventor. It gives him or her the right for a limited period — usually 20 years—to stop others from making, using or selling the invention without the inventor's permission. The invention is territorial and protected only in the country in which it is patented. The first patent was granted to Filippo Brunelleschi in Florence in 1421, for a barge crane to transport marble.

Brainchildren: young inventors

Horatio Adams

Adams was only 16 when he assisted his father, Thomas, in his experiments with chicle, the dried sap of a Mexican jungle tree. This led to the invention of chewing gum.

Charles Babbage

Babbage was 19 when he first thought of the idea of the mechanical computer.

Louis Braille

He invented Braille, the raised-dot writing used by blind people, at the age of 15. Louis himself was blind.

Frank Epperson

The Popsicle was invented by 11-year-old Frank Epperson of San Francisco, California, in 1905. He had the idea when he left a fruit drink out during a freezing winter night and originally called it the Epsicle. He did not apply for a patent until 1923, by which time his son had renamed it Popsicle.

Chester Greenwood

Greenwood of Farmington, Maine, was aged 15 in 1873 when he invented earmuffs. He started Greenwood's Ear Protector Factory and made a fortune by supplying his product to U.S. soldiers in World War I.

Jeanie S. Low

At the age of 10 in 1992, Jeanie, of Houston, Texas, was granted a patent for a folding bathroom stool to enable small children to reach the bathroom sink.

John J. Stone-Parker

In 1989, when he was only 4 years old, John and his sister, Elaine W. Stone-Parker, invented a star-shaped gadget to prevent ice from slipping out of a drinking glass. He is the youngest-ever holder of a patent.

Austin Meggitt

U.S. schoolboy Meggitt was 9 when he invented a device for carrying a baseball bat, ball and glove safely on the handlebars of a bicycle. In 2000 he received US Patent No. 6,029,874.

See also

Computer timeline: page 86

2005

1955 Lego was invented by Gotfried Kirk Christiansen

1956 Velcro was invented by Georges de Mestral

1958 videotape was invented by A.M. Poniatoff

1963 the pull-tab can was invented by Alcoa

1971 the digital watch was invented by George Theiss and Willy Crabtree

1971 E-mail was invented by Ray Tomlinson

1971 the pocket calculator was invented by the Sharp company

1974 the personal computer was invented by MITS

1975 the digital camera was invented by Steven Sasson and Kodak

1979 Post-it notes were invented by Spencer Silver and 3M

1979 the mobile phone was invented by NTT

1979 the Walkman was invented by Akio Morita

1981 the compact disc was invented by Philips

1982 the camcorder was invented by Sony

1989 the World Wide Web was invented by Tim Berners-Lee

1994 the GPS (completed) was invented by I. Getting and B. Parkinson

2000 the iPod digital music player was invented by Apple Computer, Inc.

2001 Self-cleaning glass was invented by Kevin Sanderson

2005 YouTube video sharing website launched and becomes a global phenomenon

2008 MyVu launches personal media viewer (video glasses)

Roman numerals

Roman numerals use seven letters (I, V, X, L, C, M and D). A small numeral in front of a larger one is subtracted from it, so 90 is written as X (10) subtracted from C (100)—XC. A small number after a larger one is usually added to it—for example, XI (11).

Roman numerals are still in use today. You can find them in the introduction pages of books (i, ii, iii, iv, etc.), on traditional clock and watch faces, in film and TV credits (2007 will appear as MMVII), in serial film titles (such as *Star Wars: Episode III—Revenge of the Sith*). They are also used in the names of sporting events—the Beijing 2008 Olympics will be the XXIX (29th) Games.

Roman	Arabic	Roman	Arabic	Roman	Arabic
I	1	XX	20	CCC	300
II	2	XXX	30	CD	400
III	3	XL	40	D	500
IV	4	L	50	DC	600
V	5	LX	60	DCC	700
VI	6	LXX	70	DCCC	800
VII	7	LXXX	80	CM	900
VIII	8	XC	90	M	1,000
IX	9	C	100	MM	2,000
X	10	CC	200		

Mega multiples

Certain prefixes are used in the International System of Units (SI). The prefixes are the same whether describing weight, distance, or other measurements.

Prefix	Name	Value
exa-	quintillion	1,000,000,000,000,000,000
peta-	quadrillion	1,000,000,000,000,000
tera-	trillion	1,000,000,000,000
giga-	billion	1,000,000,000
mega-	million	1,000,000
kilo-	thousand	1,000
hecto-	hundred	100
deca-	ten	10
	one	1
deci-	tenth	0.1
centi-	hundredth	0.01
milli-	thousandth	0.001
micro-	millionth	0.000,001
nano-	billionth	0.000,000,001
pico-	trillionth	0.000,000,000,001
femto-	quadrillionth	0.000,000,000,000,001
atto-	quintillionth	0.000,000,000,000,000,001

Useful mathematical formulas

Area of a rectangle	length x height
Area of a triangle	$\frac{1}{2}$ length x height
Area of a circle	π x radius^2
Diameter of a circle	radius x 2
Circumference of a circle	π x diameter
Volume of a sphere	$\frac{4}{3}\pi$ x radius^3
Surface of a sphere	4 x π^2
Volume of a cylinder	π x radius^2 x height
Curved area of cylinder	2 x π x radius x height
Area of a cone	π x radius x length
Volume of a cone	$\frac{1}{3}\pi$ x radius^2 x height

π = pi, pi = 3.14159265

"Big Ben," London, England, uses Roman numerals.

Mathematical symbols

Symbol	Meaning	Symbol	Meaning
+	Plus or positive	%	Percent
–	Minus or negative	>	Greater than
±	Plus or minus, positive or negative	<	Less than
		√	Square root
x	Multiplied by	Σ	Sum of
÷ or /	Divided by	π	Pi
=	Equal to	°	Degree
≠	Not equal to	∞	Infinity
~	Of the order of, similar to		

Big numbers

The bigger the number, the more zeroes, so very large numbers such as a billion, are shown as 10^9, or 1.0×10^9, and so on.

Number	Equivalent to	Zeros	Written as
Thousand	100 hundreds	3	10^{3}
Million	1,000 thousand	6	10^{6}
Billion	1,000 million	9	10^{9}
Trillion	1,000 billion	12	10^{12}
Quadrillion	1,000 trillion	15	10^{15}
Quintillion	1,000 quadrillion	18	10^{18}
Sextillion	1,000 quintillion	21	10^{21}
Septillion	1,000 sextillion	24	10^{24}
Octillion	1,000 septillion	27	10^{27}
Nonillion	1,000 octillion	30	10^{30}
Decillion	1,000 nonillion	33	10^{33}
Undecillion	1,000 decillion	36	10^{36}
Duodecillion	1,000 undecillion	39	10^{39}
Tredecillion	1,000 duodecillion	42	10^{42}
Quattuordecillion	1,000 tredecillion	45	10^{45}
Quindecillion	1,000 quattuordecillion	48	10^{48}
Sexdecillion	1,000 quindecillion	51	10^{51}
Septendecillion	1,000 sexdecillion	54	10^{54}
Octodecillion	1,000 septendecillion	57	10^{57}
Novemdecillion	1,000 octodecillion	60	10^{60}
Vingtillion	1,000 novemdecillion	63	10^{63}

- There are names for even bigger numbers, including a centillion (303 zeros), a trigent-billillion (60,000,003 zeros) and a sextent-billillion (1,800,000,003 zeros).
- In 1938, 9-year-old Milton Sirotta came up with the word googol, which means a 1 followed by 100 zeros. Milton was the nephew of an American mathematician named Edward Kasner (1878–1955).
- A googolplex is an even bigger number — a 1 with a googol of zeros, or 10 to the googol power. This number is so vast that, as Kasner explained, "... there would not be enough room to write it, if one went to the furthest stars, touring all the nebulae in the Universe and putting down zeros every inch of the way."
- There is no such number as a zillion — the word just means a really huge amount.

www.factmonster.com/mathmoney.html search

Prime numbers

A prime number is a whole number that can be divided only by 1 and itself, and not by any other number. Examples include 2, 3, 5, 7, 11 and 13. All prime numbers, except for 2, are also odd numbers. There are 168 prime numbers under 1,000.

Regular polygons

A polygon is a shape enclosed by straight lines. Regular polygons have sides of equal length and the inside angles are all the same. A regular polygon fits inside a circle with all its points touching the circumference. An irregular polygon does not.

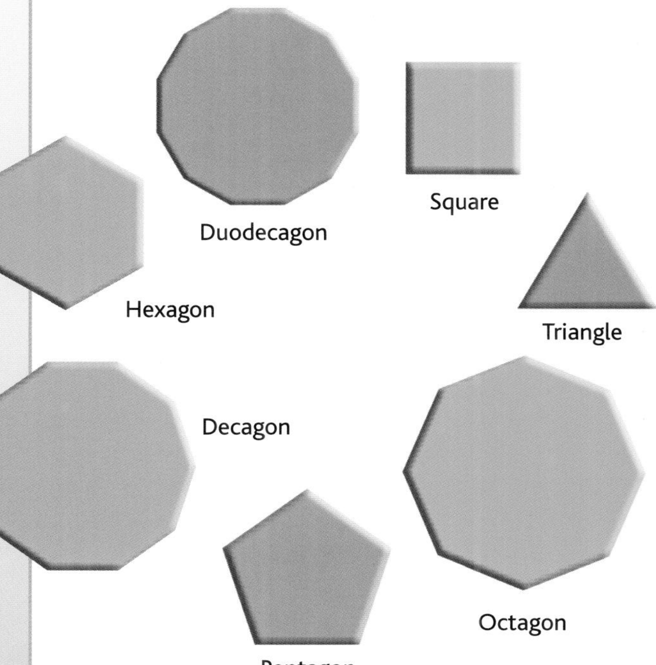

Polygon	Number of sides	Each internal angle	Sum of internal angles
Triangle	3	60°	180°
Square (or quadrilateral)	4	90°	360°
Pentagon	5	108°	540°
Hexagon	6	120°	720°
Heptagon	7	128.57°	900°
Octagon	8	135°	1,080°
Nonagon	9	140°	1,260°
Decagon	10	144°	1,440°
Undecagon	11	147.27°	1,620°
Duodecagon (or dodecagon)	12	150°	1,800°
Quindecagon	15	156°	2,340°
Icosagon	20	162°	3,240°

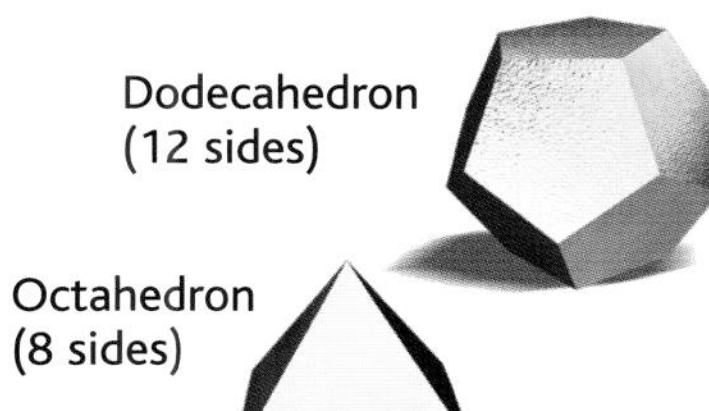
Dodecahedron (12 sides)

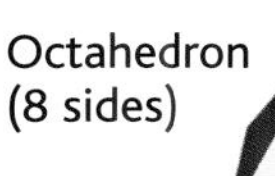
Octahedron (8 sides)

Isosahedron (20 sides)

Cube (6 sides)

Tetrahedron (4 sides)

Regular solids

There are five types of regular solid. All faces on a regular solid are exactly the same shape. If you put a regular solid inside a sphere, all its points will touch the surface of the sphere.

Conversions

There are two systems of measuring length, area, weight, volume and so on—imperial and metric. Here's how to convert between the two different systems.

From	To	Multiply by
Area		
Square centimeters (cm^2)	Square inches (in.^{2})	0.1550
Square inches (in.^{2})	Square centimeters (cm^2)	6.4516
Square meters (m^2)	Square feet (ft.^{2})	10.7639
Square feet (ft.^{2})	Square meters (m^2)	0.0929
Square meters (m^2)	Square yards (yd.^{2})	1.1960
Square yards (yd.^{2})	Square meters (m^2)	0.8361
Square kilometers (km^2)	Square miles (mi.^{2})	0.3861
Square miles (mi.^{2})	Square kilometers (km^2)	2.5900
Hectares (ha)	Acres	2.4711
Acres	Hectares (ha)	0.4047
Speed		
Meters per second (m/s)	Feet per second (ft./s)	3.2808
Feet per second (ft./s)	Meters per second (m/s)	0.3048
Kilometers per hour (km/h)	Miles per hour (mph)	0.6214
Miles per hour (mph)	Kilometers per hour (km/h)	1.6093

From	To	Multiply by
Weight		
Grams (g)	Ounces (oz.)	0.0353
Ounces (oz.)	Grams (g)	28.3495
Kilograms (kg)	Pounds (lb.)	2.2046
Pounds (lb.)	Kilograms (kg)	0.4536
Tonnes (metric)	Tons (long)	0.9842
Tons (long)	Tonnes (metric)	1.0160
Tonnes (metric)	Tons (short)	1.1023
Tons (short)	Tonnes (metric)	0.9072
Length		
Centimeters (cm)	Inches (in.)	0.3937
Inches (in.)	Centimeters (cm)	2.5400
Meters (m)	Feet (ft.)	3.2808
Feet (ft.)	Meters (m)	0.3048
Meters (m)	Yards (yd.)	1.0936
Yards (yd.)	Meters (m)	0.9144
Kilometers (km)	Miles (mi.)	0.6214
Miles (mi.)	Kilometers (km)	1.6093

Namesakes

These measurements were named after the people who discovered them.

Ampere is a measure of electrical current. It was named after André-Marie Ampère (French, 1775–1836).

Beaufort scale measures wind speed and was named after Sir Francis Beaufort (British, 1774–1857).

Marie Curie in her laboratory

Bel/decibel is a measure of sound named after Alexander Graham Bell (Scottish/American, 1847–1922).

Celsius is a temperature measure. It was named for Anders Celsius (Swedish, 1701–44).

Curie is a measure of radiation named after Marie Curie (Polish/French, 1867–1934).

Fahrenheit is a measure of temperature named after Gabriel Fahrenheit (German, 1686–1736).

Joule is a measure of energy named after James Prescott Joule (British, 1818–89).

Kelvin is a temperature measure. It was named after William Thomson, Lord Kelvin (British, 1824–1907).

Mercalli scale measures earthquakes. It was named after Giuseppe Mercalli (Italian, 1850–1914).

Mohs' scale measures hardness and was named after Friedrich Mohs (German, 1773–1839).

Ohm/Mho measures electrical resistance. It was named after Georg Simon Ohm (German, 1787–1854).

Richter scale measures earthquakes and was named after Charles Richter (American, 1900–85).

Volt is a measure of electromagnetic force. It was named after Alessandro Volta (Italian, 1745–1827).

Watt is a measure of power and was named after James Watt (British, 1736–1819).

Volume conversions

From	To	Multiply by
Cubic centimeters (cc)	Cubic inches (in.^{3})	0.0610
Cubic inches (in.^{3})	Cubic centimeters (cc)	16.3871
Cubic feet (ft.^{3})	Cubic meters (m^3)	0.0283
Cubic meters (m^3)	Cubic feet (ft.^{3})	35.3147
Cubic yards (yd.^{3})	Cubic meters (m^3)	1.3080
Cubic meters (m^3)	Cubic yards (yd.^{3})	0.7646
Cubic kilometers (km^3)	Cubic miles (mi.^{3})	0.2399
Cubic miles (mi.^{3})	Cubic kilometers (km^3)	4.1682
Liters (l)	Pints (pt.)	1.7598
Pints (pt.)	Litres (l)	0.5683
Liters (l)	Quarts (qt.)	1.0567
Quarts (qt.)	Liters (l)	0.9464
Litres (l)	U.S. gallons (gal.)	0.2642
U.S. gallons (gal.)	Liters (l)	3.78532

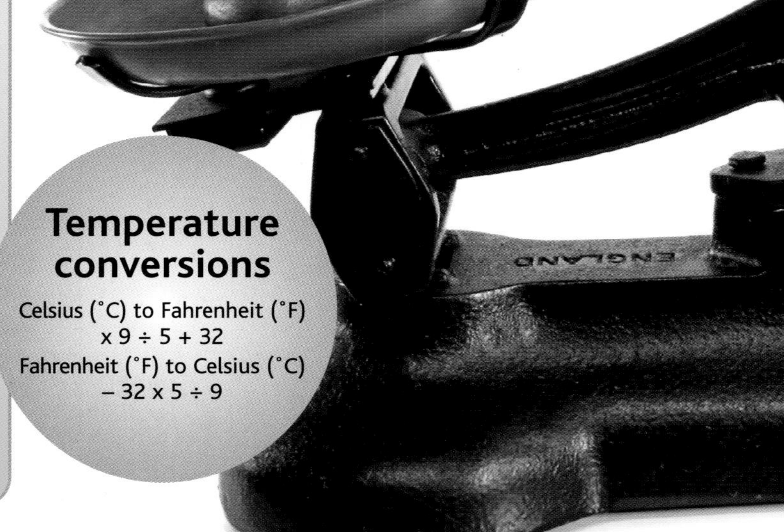

Temperature conversions

Celsius (°C) to Fahrenheit (°F)
x 9 ÷ 5 + 32

Fahrenheit (°F) to Celsius (°C)
− 32 x 5 ÷ 9

The world's smallest

Atomic clock The smallest clock in the world was made in 2004 by the National Institute for Standards in Technology (United States). It measures 0.06 in. (1.5 mm) by 0.16 in. (4 mm) and it is accurate to one second in 300 years.

Robot In 2005 Donald Laboratory (United States) built a micro-robot that measured 250 micrometers by 60 micrometers, which is the thickness of a single hair.

Car The French Ligier Be Up is the smallest car that is still in production and can be driven on public roads. It has two seats and measures 106 in. (268 cm) long, 55.5 in. (141 cm) wide and 61.4 in. (156 cm) high. It weighs 730 lb. (330 kg) and has a top speed of 62 mph (100 km/h).

The Ligier Be Up has a 505 cc engine.

Weighty words

Acre
An acre describes an area of land and comes from the Old English word *aecer*, meaning a plowed field. It was the area a team of oxen could plow in one day. One acre is equivalent to 4,840 sq. yd.

Celsius
A temperature scale invented in 1742 by Swedish astronomer Anders Celsius. A Celsius degree is 1/100th of the difference between the freezing and boiling points of water (0°C and 100°C).

Fahrenheit
This temperature scale was devised by German physicist Gabriel Fahrenheit. On this scale the freezing point of water is 32°.

Foot
Foot originally meant the average length of an adult foot, and has been used since ancient times. Before France invented the metric system, the French foot was based on the length of the Emperor Charlemagne's foot.

Meter
The meter was introduced in France in June 1799. It was first set as one ten-millionth of a quarter of the circumference of the Earth. It was later set as the distance between two lines on a metal bar that was kept in Sèvres, France. The distance is now more precise. It is the distance light travels in a vacuum in 1/299792458th of a second. A centimeter is 1/100th of a meter. A millimeter is 1/1,000th of a meter and a kilometer is 1,000 meters.

Gram/kilogram
Gram comes from the same ancient Greek word that gave us grammar, and means a marked-off division. A kilogram is 1,000 grams. Kilo comes from the Greek *chilioi*, meaning one thousand.

Hectare
This is used for measuring land areas and comes from the ancient Greek *hekaton*, meaning one hundred. One hectare is equivalent to 10,000 square meters or 2.4711 acres.

Tons and tonnes
Tons are imperial weight measurements, whereas tonnes are metric—1 short (U.S.) ton is equal to 2,000 lb. (907 kg), while 1 metric tonne (also simply called a tonne) is 2,204.6 lb. (1,000 kg).

Special measurements

Carat
The weight of diamonds and other valuable gems is measured in carats. The word comes from the carob bean, which has a consistent weight of 0.007 oz. (0.2 gram).

Hand
The height of horses is measured in hands. The measurement is taken from the ground to the highest point on the animal's shoulder. One hand is 4 in. (10.16 cm).

Knot
Speed at sea is measured in knots, which is the time it took a ship to travel the length of a knotted rope. A knot is now the same as a nautical mile, which is 6,076 ft. (1,852 m).

Point
This is used by typographers and printers and refers to the size of a letter such as an x. One point is equal to 0.0139 in. (0.3528 mm), so 6-point type is 0.083 in. (2.116 mm) high.

Troy ounce
This name comes from the city of Troyes, France, where dealers in precious stones and metals gathered in medieval times. Gold and other rare metals are still measured in troy ounces (1.1677 oz./31.1035 g).

Computer use worldwide

In 1943 Thomas Watson, the chairman of IBM, made one of the least accurate predictions ever. He said, "I think there is a world market for maybe five computers."

There are now over one billion personal computers around the world. It is forecast that by 2010 there will be 1.35 billion computers, one for every person on the planet. One in five (290 million) of them will be in the U.S.

Computer speak

Storage

1 bit equals 0.125 (0 or 1/on or off) bytes
1 nibble equals 0.5 bytes
8 bits equals 1 byte
1 kilobyte equals 1,024 bytes
1 megabyte equals 1,018,576 bytes
1 gigabyte equals 1,073,741,824 (over 1 billion) bytes
1 terabyte equals 1,099,511,627,776 (over 1 trillion) bytes
1 petabyte equals 1,125,899,906,842,624 (over 1 quadrillion) bytes
1 exabyte equals 1,152,921,504,606,846,976 bytes
1 zettabyte equals 1,180,591,620,717,411,303,424 bytes
1 yottabyte equals 1,208,925,819,614,629,174,706,176 bytes

What that means in data

Storage

10 bytes equals one word
2 kilobytes equals one page of typewritten text
10 kilobytes equals one page of a reference book
1 megabyte equals a short novel
5 megabytes equals the complete works of Shakespeare
250 megabytes equals the total output of data per year for every person on Earth
500 megabytes equals a CD-ROM
20 gigabytes equals the complete works of Beethoven on CD
10 terabytes equals all the printed works in the U.S. Library of Congress (the world's largest library)
200 petabytes equals everything ever printed
5 exabytes equals every word ever spoken

Computer timeline

1642 Blaise Pascal, France, makes a numerical wheel calculator, an early mechanical adding machine
1694 Gottfried von Leibniz, Germany, makes a machine that can multiply numbers

1800s

1820 Charles Xavier de Colmar, France, makes an "Arithometer" that can add, subtract, multiply and divide
1822 Charles Babbage, England, devises his Difference Engine
1829 Charles Wheatstone uses punched paper tape to store data
1834 Babbage conceives the Analytical Engine
1889 Herman Hollerith's punch card machine used in U.S. Census

1900s

1928 IBM adopts 80-column punched card
1944 Harvard's Mark I, first digital computer
1952 Univac computer accurately predicts the U.S. presidential election winner
1953 First IBM electronic digital computer (IBM 701)
1956 First hard disk drive (IBM). Term "artificial intelligence" devised
1958 First chess game between computer and human
1960 U.S. has 6,000 computers
1963 ASCII (American Standard Code for Information Interchange) introduced
1967 IBM releases floppy disk
1970 Douglas Engelbart patents first computer mouse
1971 Intel builds the micro-processor, "computer on a chip." Wang 1200, first word processor; E-mail invented by Ray Tomlinson.
1972 First electronic video game: *PONG*
1975 Microsoft founded by Bill Gates, later to become the world's richest person
1976 First Apple computer. Cray-1, first supercomputer
1979 Compuserve launches first commercial Bulletin Board (BBN) service
1980 U.S. has more than one

Computers then and now

Computers have come a long way since Charles Babbage (1791–1871) invented his Difference Engine No. 2. His early computer could make complicated calculations and print the results.

However, it had over 4,000 parts, measured 11.2 ft. (3.4 m) wide and 7 ft. (2.1 m) high, weighed 2.9 tons (2.6 tonnes) and was operated by cranking a handle hundreds of times. By comparison, some of the latest personal computers measure less than 1.2 in. (3 cm) thick and weigh as little as 5.6 lb. (2.54 kg), with processing speeds of up to 2.16 GHz.

Babbage's Difference Engine, 1822

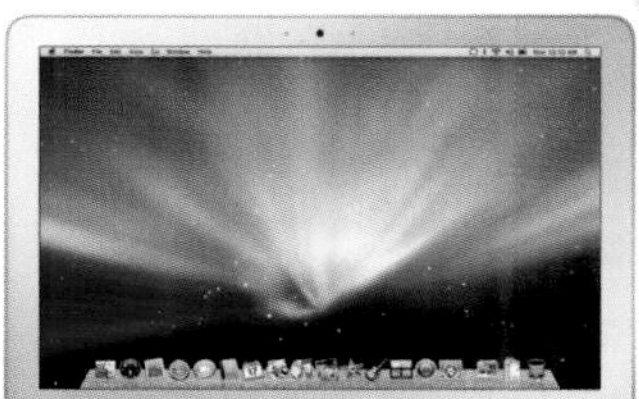

Apple's MacBook Air, 2008

Internet milestones

In a little over 10 years, the Internet has become a global phenomenon. In 1995 it was used by about 45 million people around the world. By 2006 the figure had more than doubled to 1,018,057,389. By the time you read this, the figures will have increased again.

Google

Google is the most-used internet search engine in the world. In 2007, the company employed 16,805 people and had a total revenue of $16.6 billion. In 2008, Microsoft attempted to buy Yahoo to turn it into a rival to Google.

1960s

During the 1960s scientists in the U.S. began trying to work out how organizations could keep in touch with one another after a nuclear attack. In 1965 ARPA (Advanced Research Projects Agency) suggested linking computers. In 1969 computers at four U.S. universities were connected and could "talk" to each other for the first time.

1970s

At the same time, electronic mail (e-mail) was being used more and more to send messages between computers. In 1979 the first Usenet newsgroups (online discussion groups) began.

1980s

By 1981 the ARPA network had 213 hosts (sites to which users could connect). A new host was added approximately every 20 days. In 1982 a language called TCP/IP was invented, which allowed all Internet computers to communicate with each other, and the network was first called an Internet. The Internet began to be used commercially and by governments and universities.

1990s

In 1991 the World Wide Web (www) was created. By 1994 about 40 million people were connected to the Internet. They could exchange information, sell goods and work from any computer with a phone line. Schools started using it as an electronic library. By 1996 users in almost 150 countries around the world were connected to the Internet.

2000s

High-speed broadband and wireless access is now widespread and more and more businesses are using the Internet. The number of people using the Internet more than doubled from 2000 to 2007, with the number in China increasing nearly six times. More than one billion people use the Internet worldwide.

2000s

million computers. First laptop computers
1981 First Nintendo home video game. Commercial introduction of the computer mouse. Microsoft introduces software for IBM personal computers
1982 Worldwide, 200 computers connected to the Internet
1984 Apple Macintosh computers launched
1985 Microsoft ships Windows 1.0
1986 U.S. has more than 30 million computers
1988 4.7 million microcomputers, 120,000 minicomputers and 11,500 mainframe computers sold in U.S.
1989 World Wide Web invented by Tim Berners-Lee. 100,000 hosts on the net
1990 First palmtop computers
1991 First use of the phrase "surfing the net," by Jean Armour Polly
1993 Mosaic, the first graphical Internet browser, launched
1994 135 million PCs worldwide. First ads on the World Wide Web (ad for *Wired* magazine claimed as first)
1995 Amazon.com Internet bookseller founded. Microsoft's Internet Explorer browser launched
1999 150 million people use Internet worldwide (more than half in U.S.)
2000 Dot-com crash
2002 iPod digital music players launched
2005 Nearly 200 million broadband lines worldwide
2007 Sales of iPods top 100 million
2008 More than 330 million broadband lines in use worldwide

computer.howstuffworks.com search

The first telegraph message was sent by Morse code using a hand-operated key.

From fixed cables to satellites

In the early years of telecommunications, the only way of linking one telephone with another was by fixed cables. Links between continents relied on cables under the ocean. The invention of radio brought the first wireless communications, but because the surface of the Earth is curved these signals could not travel far.

Satellites changed everything. They sit at an exact height above the Earth's Equator (usually around 22,000 mi./35,000 km) and they rotate at the same speed as the Earth spins. This means that they stay in a fixed position. Telephone signals can be sent to the satellites and bounced back to Earth. Everywhere on the planet can be covered by only five or six satellites, except for the poles and surrounding areas, which are out of their range.

Cables under the sea

Soon after telegraph cables came into use in the 1840s, attempts were made to lay them across rivers and between islands and mainlands. Most didn't work. In 1850 the first cable was laid across the English Channel. It had to resist attack by salt water, ocean currents and water pressure, so had a thick, water-resistant, steel cover. Inside were copper wires that carried the power and signal.

Technical improvements and the demand for faster communications led to cables being laid over ever greater distances. Several attempts to lay them across the Atlantic failed when the cables snapped, but one was completed in 1858. To mark the occasion, Queen Victoria sent a telegraph message to President Buchanan in the U.S. It took almost 18 hours. Attempts were made to increase the pace by raising the voltage, but this burned out the cable. In 1865 the world's largest ship at the time, the *Great Eastern*, laid the first continuous cable across the Atlantic.

During the 20th century, telegraph cables, which transmitted Morse code, were steadily replaced by telephone cables, which could transmit voices. Hundreds of thousands of miles of underwater cables were laid across the world's oceans and seas. These have been replaced by fiber-optic cables, which offer faster transmission and many more connections.

Telecom timeline

1793 Word "telegraph" first used (in France)

1837 Charles Wheatstone and William Cooke set up first electric telegraph in London

1843 Morse code inventor Samuel Morse (U.S.) sends first telegraph message between Washington and Baltimore

1850s

1850 Telegraph cable laid between England and France across English Channel, but fails; 12,000 mi. (19,300 km) of telegraph line in U.S.

1852 First telegraph line in India; there are now 23,000 mi. (37,015 km) of telegraph line in U.S.

1854 First Australian telegraph line (Melbourne to Williamstown)

1858 First transatlantic telegraph cable laid, but fails

1861 First U.S. transcontinental telegraph

1862 32,000 mi. (51,500 km) of telegraph line and more than five million messages sent in U.S.

1867 First theory suggests using radio waves for telecommunication

1870s

1876 Alexander Graham Bell patents the telephone—beating his rival Elisha Gray by a matter of hours. He makes his historic first call to his assistant, Thomas Watson, who is in the next room: "Mr. Watson, come here, I want to see you." The invention is demonstrated at the Centennial Exposition, Philadelphia, where Emperor Don Pedro of Brazil hears Bell recite the "To be or not to be" speech from *Hamlet* over the phone.

1877 Bell makes the first long-distance call between Boston and Salem, Massachusetts, 14 mi. (22.5 km) away

1878 Bell demonstrates his telephone to Queen Victoria at Osborne House on the Isle of Wight. She becomes the first European monarch to use a phone

1884 First telephone handset is launched

1889 First coin-in-the-slot public phone, U.S.

1894 Guglielmo Marconi invents wireless telegraphy

1897 There are seven phones per 1,000 people in the U.S.

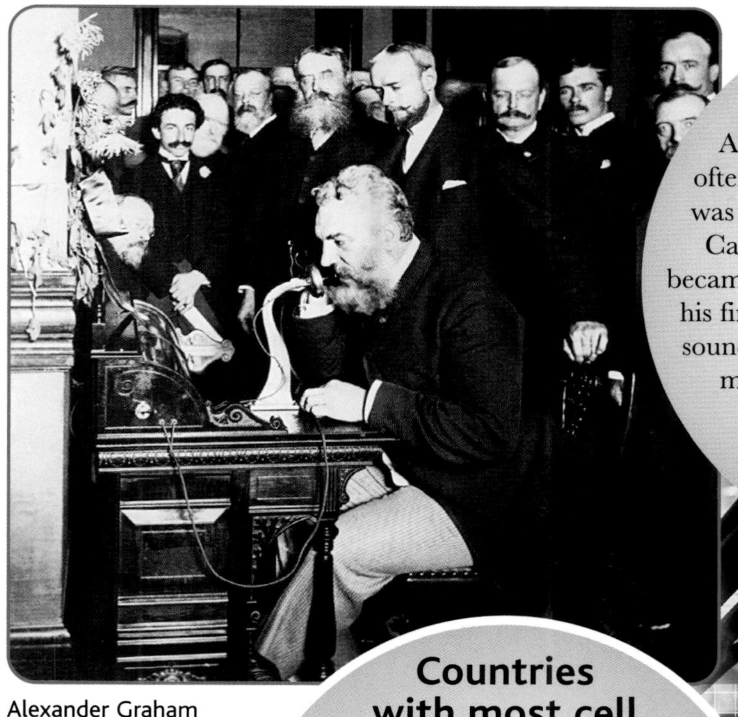

Alexander Graham Bell making the first telephone call between New York and Chicago

Telephone Bell

Alexander Graham Bell (1847–1922) is often called the father of the telephone. He was born in Edinburgh, Scotland, moved to Canada in 1870, and later to the U.S. He became an expert on the science of speech, and his first inventions helped deaf people to hear sounds. During his research, Bell developed a method of transmitting voice messages along a wire. In 1876 he patented the device, which he called the harmonic telegraph. This was the first telephone.

Countries with most cell (mobile) phones

China 534,000,000
India 242,400,000
U.S. 233,000,000
Russia 150,000,000
Japan 100,700,000
U.K. 69,675,000

World total 3,300,000,000

In 2006, India joined the list of countries with more than 100 million cell phones, and has since risen rapidly to take second place on the world list.

2000s

1901 Marconi sends a radio signal across the Atlantic

1902 The trans-Pacific telephone cable connects Canada, New Zealand and Australia

1907 There are an estimated 1,027,348 mi. (1,653,356 km) of land telecommunications lines and 233,823 mi. (376,302 km) of submarine cable worldwide

1914 The first radio message is sent to an aircraft; the first transcontinental telephone call is made in the U.S.

1919 Rotary dial telephones are invented

1945 British writer Arthur C. Clarke proposes putting communications satellites in orbit above the Earth, which move at the same speed as the Earth spins; this means they stay in a fixed position, and communication with the ground is not interrupted

1956 The first transatlantic telephone cable is laid

1965 Intelsat I (*Early Bird*), the first commercial telecommunications satellite, is launched

1967 The first cordless telephones go on sale

1975 The first handheld cell (mobile) phones are sold

1988 The first transatlantic fiber optic cable is laid

2004 There are 1.2 billion telephone lines around the world: 538,981,500 in Asia, 327,657,500 in Europe, 295,292,700 in North and South America, 25,929,800 in Africa and 13,773,000 in Oceania

2005 Cell phone users now number more than two billion worldwide

2006 US company Western Union ends its telegraph service after 150 years, as e-mails replace telegrams

2007 More than three billion worldwide use mobile phones. Apple's iPhone is launched

2008 The iPhone has sold 5 million worldwide and is expected to reach 10 million in 2008.

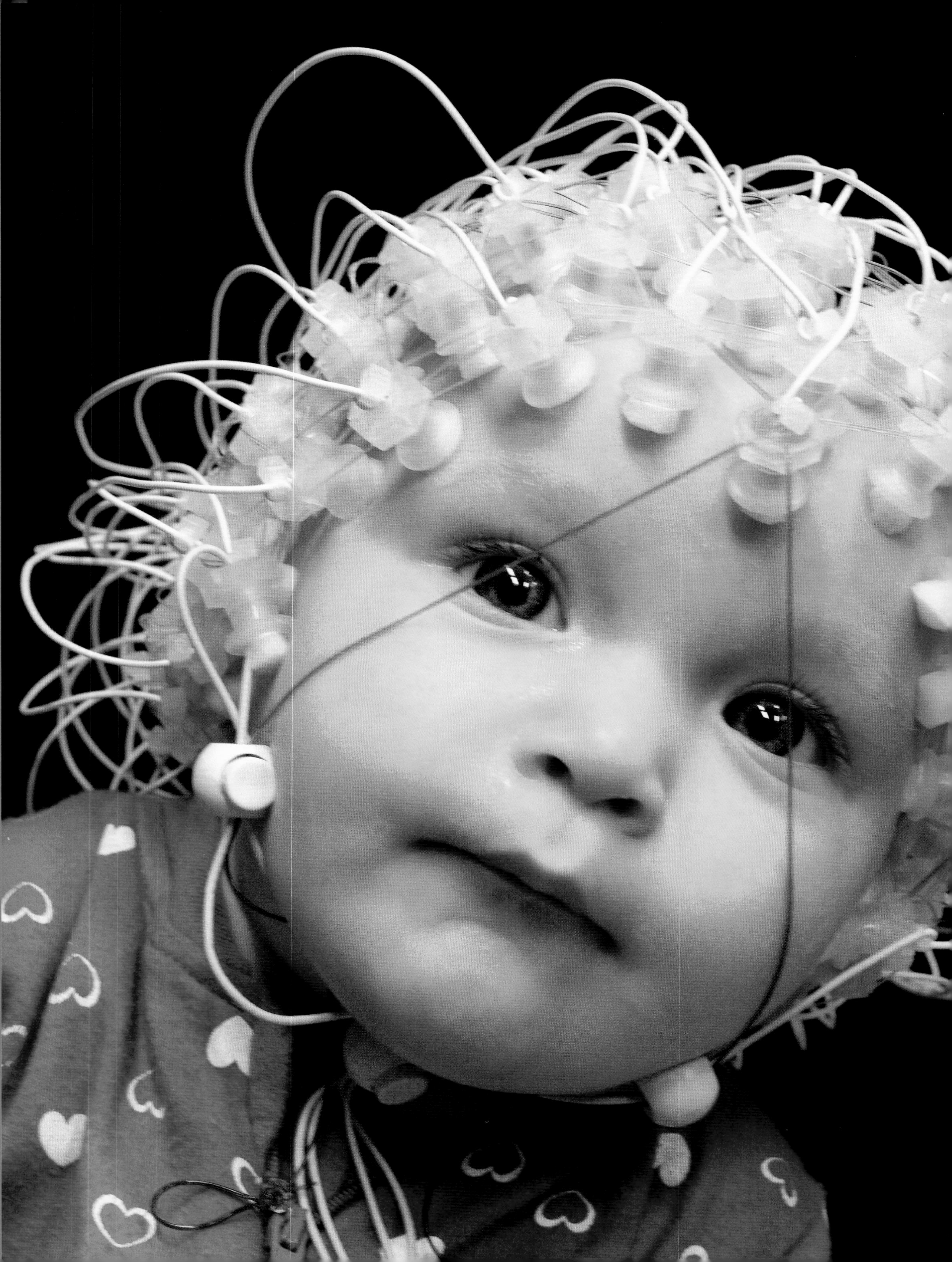

Human Body

92 HUMAN BODY

94 BODY FACTS AND RECORDS

96 HEALTH AND MEDICINE

98 FOOD AND DRINK

Brain waves

In 2008, the "Babylab" research center in Uppsala, Sweden, received widespread media attention for its projects that monitor a baby's brain activity. The study will help scientists understand how the brain develops and to better understand conditions such as autism.

Your amazing body

Blood
An adult man's body contains about 1.3 gal. (5 L) of blood. A woman's contains about 1.1 gal. (4.3 L). The blood travels along 62,000 mi. (100,000 km) of blood vessels. It contains 25 billion to 30 billion red cells. The life span of red cells is only about 120 days, and 1.2 million to 2 million of them are made every second.

Brain power
You lose 100,000 brain cells every day! Luckily you have 100 billion altogether. If the surface area of your brain could be ironed out it would measure 324 sq. in. (2,090 sq cm).

Breathing
The average person inhales 1.6 gal. (6 L) of air per minute, or 2,280 gal. (8,640 L) a day. You take 13 to 17 breaths a minute when sitting still and up to 80 during vigorous exercise.

Cells
There are 50 trillion cells in your body and 3 billion of them die every minute (4,320,000,000,000 a day). Most of these are replaced. You make 10 billion new white blood cells each day. You have a total of 1 trillion white cells, which help fight germs and infections.

Chemicals
There is enough carbon in your body to fill 900 pencils, enough fat to make 75 candles, enough phosphorus to make 220 match heads and enough iron to make a 3 in. (7.5 cm) nail.

Digestive system
Your stomach produces up to 0.5 gal. (2 L) of hydrochloric acid a day. It does not damage the stomach walls because 500,000 cells in your stomach lining are replaced every minute. The small intestine is about 16 ft. (5 m) long. The large intestine is thicker, but only about 5 ft. (1.5 m) long.

Eyes
You blink about 20,000 times a day.

Gas
On average, you release 0.5 gal. (2 L) of gases from your intestines as burps or farts.

Hair
Hair grows about 0.02 in. (0.5 mm) a day.

Heartbeats
Your heart pumps 3,600 gal. (13,640 L) of blood around your body in a day. An average heartbeat rate of 70 beats a minute adds up to more than 100,000 beats a day.

Mouth
You will produce 10,000 gal. (37,800 L) of saliva in your life.

Nerves
Your body has about 13 trillion nerve cells, transmitting messages at speeds of 180 mph (290 km/h).

Sweat
You lose about 0.5 qt. (0.5 L) of water a day through 3 million sweat glands. In hot climates you may lose as much as 3.6 gal. (13.5 L) a day.

Urine
You will pass 0.8 to 4.2 pt. (400 to 2,000 ml) of urine every day, depending on your age, your size and outside conditions, especially temperature.

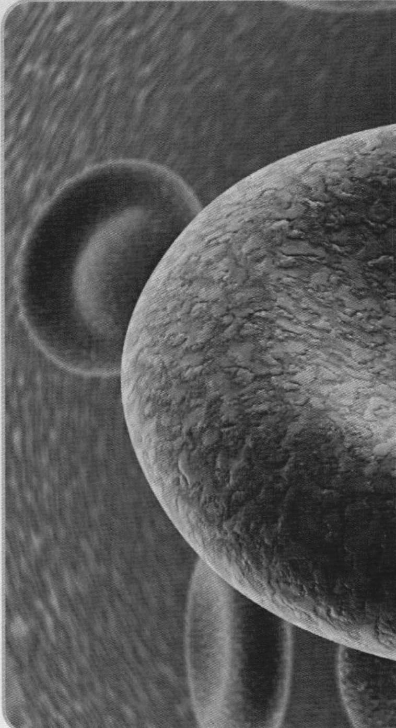

Highly magnified image of red blood cells

Largest human organs

The weights listed below are all averages, but sometimes organs are much larger. Some brains have weighed more than 4.4 lb (2,000 g), but that doesn't mean the owners were super-intelligent!

Skin 384 oz. (10,886 g)
Liver 55 oz. (1,560 g)
Brain male 49.7 oz. (1,408 g)
Brain female 44.6 oz. (1,263 g)
Lungs right 20.5 oz. (580 g)
Lungs left 18 oz. (510 g)
Heart male 11.1 oz. (315 g)
Heart female 9.3 oz. (265 g)
Kidney left 5.3 oz. (150 g)
Kidney right 4.9 oz. (140 g)
Spleen 6 oz. (170 g)
Pancreas 3.5 oz. (98 g)
Thyroid 1.2 oz. (35 g)
Prostate (male only) 0.7 oz. (20 g)
Adrenals left 0.2 oz. (6 g)
Adrenals right 0.2 oz. (6 g)

One and only

The only bone in the human body that is not connected to another bone is the hyoid bone, a U-shaped bone at the base of the tongue. It is supported by the muscles in the neck, but it is not connected to any other bone.

What's your body made of?

Most of the human body is made up of water, or H_2O, which is a combination of hydrogen and oxygen. As much as 99 percent of the body is made up of oxygen, carbon, hydrogen, nitrogen, calcium and phosphorus. There are also small amounts of other elements.

Element	Avg. in 155 lb. (70 kg) person oz. (g)	Element	Avg. in 155 lb. (70 kg) person oz. (g)
Oxygen	1,1517 (43,000)	Potassium	4–5 (110–140)
Carbon	564 (16,000)	Sodium	3.5 (100)
Hydrogen	247 (7,000)	Chlorine	3.35 (95)
Nitrogen	64 (1,800)	Magnesium	0.8 (25)
Calcium	42 (1,200)	Iron	0.1 (4)
Phosphorus	28 (780)	Zinc	0.08 (2.3)
Sulphur	5 (140)	Silicon	0.03 (1)

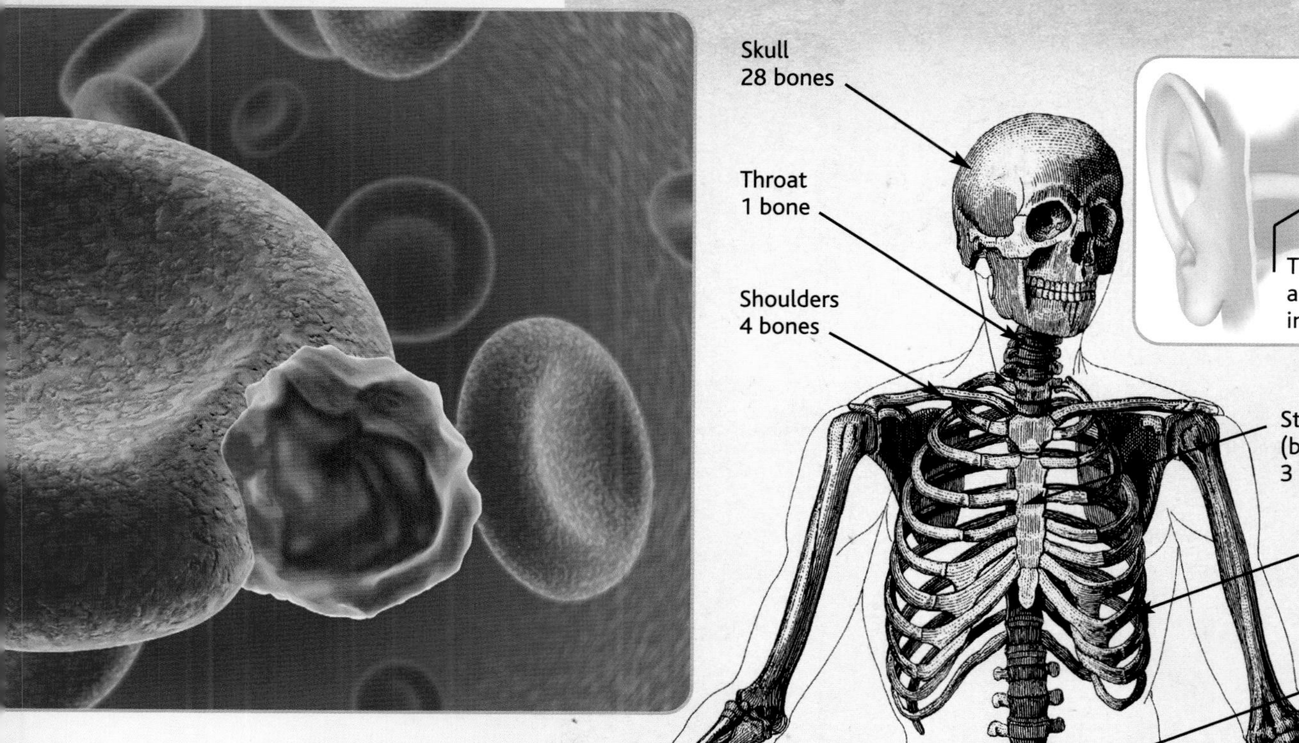

Human skeleton

The skeleton is the body's framework. The bones of the skeleton support the body, protect the internal organs such as the heart and lungs, and allow you to move.

Longest bones in the body

These are the average measurements of the longest bones of an adult male. The same bones in the female skeleton are usually 6 to13 percent smaller, except the breastbone, which is almost the same.

Femur (thighbone, upper leg) 19.88 in. (50.5 cm)
Tibia (shinbone, inner lower leg) 16.94 in. (43.03 cm)
Fibula (outer lower leg) 15.94 in. (40.5 cm)
Humerus (upper arm) 14.35 in. (36.46 cm)
Ulna (inner lower arm) 11.1 in. (28.20 cm)
Radius (outer lower arm) 10.4 in. (26.42 cm)
7th rib 9.45 in. (24 cm)
8th rib 9.06 in. (23 cm)
Hipbone (one half of pelvis) 7.28 in. (18.5 cm)
Sternum (breastbone) 6.69 in. (17 cm)

Nails

Your fingernails grow 0.02 in. (0.05 cm) a week—four times faster than your toenails.

Skin

Your skin weighs up to 8.8 lb. (4 kg) and covers up to 14–18.3 sq. ft. (1.3–1.7 sq m). Getting dressed and undressed, rubbing body parts together and even breathing cause microscopic flakes of skin to fall off at the rate of 50,000 flakes a minute. In a lifetime you will shed 40 lb. (18 kg) of skin.

How heavy?

The human skeleton makes up about one-fifth of a person's entire weight. An average adult weighing 155 lb. (70 kg) will have a skeleton that weighs 31 lb. (14 kg).

www.innerbody.com search

Weighty wonder

Carol Yager (1960–94) of Beecher, Michigan, was claimed to have reached a peak weight of 1,600 lb (727 kg). If true, it would make her the heaviest person of all time. She was unable to stand or walk, and when taken out of her house through specially widened doorways, had to be lifted by a relay team of 20 strong firefighters.

Jon Minnoch (1941–83) of Bainbridge Island, Washington, was reportedly the world's heaviest man at approximately 1,400 lb (635 kg). At one point, he went on a strict diet and shed 952 lb (432 kg), the greatest weight loss ever recorded.

In comparison, the 727.5-lb (330-kg) **Daniel Lambert** (1770–1809) was almost a lightweight.

Daniel Lambert

Body records

Longest beard
Hans Langseth (1846–1927) had a beard that measured 17.5 ft. (5.33 m). It has been in the Smithsonian Institution, Washington DC, since 1967.

Hans Langseth

Longest nails
Shridhar Chillal of Pune, India (1937–) has not cut the nails on his left hand since 1952. By 2000 the total length of his nails on that hand was over 236 in. (600 cm).

Longest mustache
Kalyan Ramji Sain of Sundargath, India, holds the record. His mustache is 11 ft., 11.5 in. (3.29 m) from tip to tip.

Longest hair
Swami Pandarasannadhi was the head of a monastery in Madras, India. When his hair was measured in 1949 it was 26 ft. (7.9 m) long.

Longest sneezing bout
Donna Griffiths of Pershore, England, started sneezing on January 13, 1981, and continued for 978 days.

Math genius
When he was only 8 years old, American Zerah Colburn (1804–40) worked out how many seconds had elapsed since the birth of Christ. He did this in his head within seconds. When Zerah was asked whether 4,294,967,297 was a prime number (one that cannot be divided evenly by another number), he instantly replied that it was not—it is equal to 641 times 6,700,417.

Longest hiccuping
Charles Osborne of Anthon, Iowa, hiccuped from 1922 to 1990.

Infant prodigy
By the age of 4, Kim Ung-Yong of Korea (1963–) could speak fluent Korean, English, Japanese and German, and could solve calculus problems.

Memory
Gon Yang-ling of Harbin, China, has memorized more than 15,000 telephone numbers.

World's oldest people

Below is a list of the world's longest living people, or supercentenarians. It includes only those for whom there are accurate records of their birth and death dates.

Although Christian Mortensen is ninth in the list, he is the world's oldest man. The others in the list are women.

Jeanne Calment (1875–1997), France: 122 years and 164 days
Sarah DeRemer Knauss (1880–1999), U.S.: 119 years and 97 days
Lucy Hannah (1875–1993), U.S.: 117 years and 248 days
Marie-Louise Meilleur (1880–1998), Canada: 117 years and 229 days
Maria Capovilla (1889–2006) Ecuador: 116 years and 347 days
Tane Ikai (1879–1995), Japan: 116 years and 175 days
Elizabeth Bolden (1890–2006) U.S.: 116 years and 118 days
Maggie Barnes (1882–1998), U.S.: 115 years and 319 days
Christian Mortensen (1882–1998), Denmark/U.S.: 115 years and 252 days
Charlotte Hughes (1877–1993), U.K.: 115 years and 228 days

Oldest living person

Edna (Scott) Parker was born in Indiana on April 20, 1893 and celebrated her 115th birthday in 2008, making her the oldest person alive in the world.

Tom Thumb and friends

American showman P.T. Barnum first met Charles Sherwood Stratton (U.S., 1838–83) when he was 4 years old. He was 24 in. (61 cm) tall and weighed 15 lb. (6.8 kg). Barnum persuaded Charles's parents to allow him to exhibit their son for a fee of $3 a week. He was advertised as "General Tom Thumb, a dwarf 11 years of age, just arrived from England." By the time he died, he had grown to 3 ft. 3 in. (1 m) and weighed 70 lb. (32 kg). Lavinia Warren (U.S., 1841–1919) was 31 in. (79 cm) tall. Her first husband was Tom Thumb.

"Commodore" Nutt (U.S., 1844–81) was 29 in. (74 cm) tall. Like Tom Thumb, he was exhibited by P. T. Barnum.

Amazing feats

- In 1997, at Sydney Airport, Australia, David Huxley pulled a 206-ton (187 tonne) Boeing 747-400 a distance of 298.5 ft. (91 m). He had previously hauled a Boeing 737 and a Concorde.
- In 2005, U.S. arm-wrestler Ed Shelton ripped up 55 telephone directories, each 1,044 pages thick. It took him three minutes.
- Sri-Lankan born Arulanantham Suresh Joachim currently holds 30 endurance records, including a drumming marathon (84 hours), the longest time standing still (76 hours, 40 minutes), running 100 mi./160 km on a treadmill (42 minutes, 33 seconds) and crawling 1 mi./1.6 km (37 minutes, 17 seconds). In 2006 he announced his intention to run a mega-marathon through 54 countries in 181 days—over 3,730 mi. (6,000 km).

Run-up records

In the annual Empire State Building Run-Up, runners race up the famous skyscraper's 1,576 steps. In 2006 Andrea Mayr of Austria set a new women's record of 11 minutes, 23 seconds. The overall record-holder is Australian athlete Paul Crake. In 2003, he got to the top in 9 minutes, 33 seconds. In 2008, Thomas Dodd (Germany) won the race for the third consecutive year.

Tallest real giants

These are the most reliable records. All are men, except Trijntje Keever and Jeng Jinlian.

Robert Pershing Wadlow (1918–40), U.S.: 8 ft., 11.1 in. (2.72 m)

John William Rogan (1868–1905), U.S.: 8 ft., 9.8 in. (2.68 m)

John Aasen (1887–1938), U.S.: 8 ft., 9.8 in. (2.67m)

John F. Carroll (1932–69), U.S.: 8 ft., 7.6 in. (2.64 m)

Al Tomaini (1918–62), U.S.: 8 ft., 4.4 in. (2.55 m)

Trijntje Keever (1616–33), Netherlands: 8 ft., 3.3 in. (2.54 m)

Edouard Beaupre (1881–1904), Canada: 8 ft., 2.5 in. (2.50 m)

Bernard Coyne (1897–1921), U.S.: 8 ft., 1.2 in. (2.49 m)

Don Koehler (1925–81), U.S.: 8 ft., 1.2 in. (2.49 m)

Jeng Jinlian (1964–82), China: 8 ft., 1.1 in. (2.48 m)

Väinö Myllyrinne (1909–63), Finland: 8 ft., 1.1 in. (2.48 m)

Louis Moilanen (1885–1913), Finland/U.S.: 8 ft., 1 in. (2.46 m)

Gabriel Estavo Monjane (1944–90), Mozambique: 8 ft., 0.75 in. (2.46 m)

Robert Wadlow

Life expectancy

Life expectancy is the average number of years people in different countries are likely to live. Conditions can improve or sometimes get worse, so life expectancy can get higher or lower.

The country with the highest life expectancy is Andorra at 83.5 years. The country with the lowest life expectancy is Swaziland with 31.8 years. People who live in the United States have an average life expectancy of 75.4 years.

Commodore Nutt, Miss Warren, normal-sized man and Tom Thumb

A fear of snakes is called ophidiophobia.

Common phobias

A phobia is a strong fear of a particular animal, object, situation or activity. The fear is often out of proportion to the reality and may make people vomit, sweat, tremble and even faint. People may go to great lengths to avoid the subjects of their phobias.

Most common phobias

Fear of snakes is called ophidiophobia
Fear of flying is called aerophobia or aviatophobia
Fear of open spaces is called agoraphobia, cenophobia or kenophobia
Fear of confined spaces is called claustrophobia, cleisiophobia, cleithrophobia or clithrophobia
Fear of spiders is called arachnephobia or arachnophobia
Fear of heights is called acrophobia, altophobia, hypsophobia or hypsiphobia

Unusual phobias

Fear of beards is called pogonophobia
Fear of chickens is called alektorophobia
Fear of dancing is called chorophobia
Fear of dolls is called pediophobia
Fear of fish is called ichthyophobia
Fear of frogs is called batrachophobia
Fear of hair is called chaetophobia
Fear of mirrors is called eisoptrophobia
Fear of the number 13 is called triskaidekaphobia
Fear of string is called linonophobia
Fear of teeth is called odontophobia

Calorie counts

A Calorie (with a capital C) is a unit that measures the amount of energy in foods. It is also known as a kilocalorie and is equal to 1,000 calories (with a small c). A calorie is the amount of heat needed to raise the temperature of 1 g (0.035 oz.) of water by 1°C (1.8°F).

An adult might eat up to 3,000 Calories a day. Eating too many Calories that the body does not use for energy may make you fat. The figures below are based on the average number of Calories a 155 lb. (70 kg) adult burns when doing an activity for one hour. A lighter person uses fewer Calories; a heavier person more.

Squash 844 Calories
Skipping, swimming 704 Calories
Basketball, cycling, running, walking upstairs 563 Calories
Canoeing or rowing 493 Calories
Football, ice skating, roller skating, skiing, tennis 493 Calories
Aerobics 422 Calories
Mowing lawn 387 Calories
Gardening, skateboarding 352 Calories
Dancing 317 Calories
Golf, table tennis 281 Calories
Housework, walking dog 246 Calories
Frisbee, surfing 211 Calories
Playing piano 176 calories
Standing 120 calories
Sitting 90 calories
Sleeping 65 calories

Causes of death worldwide

There are big differences between the causes of death in developing countries and in developed countries. In developing countries, many more deaths are caused by infectious diseases and illnesses spread by insects such as malaria.

In developed countries more people become ill from being overweight and eating rich diets. There are about 57,029,000 deaths a year worldwide.

Heart diseases 16,733,000 per year
Cancers 7,121,000 per year
Respiratory infections 3,963,000 per year
Lung diseases 3,702,000 per year
HIV/AIDS 2,777,000 per year
Digestive diseases 1,968,000 per year
Diarrheal diseases 1,798,000 per year
Tuberculosis 1,566,000 per year
Malaria 1,272,000 per year
Road traffic injuries 1,192,000 per year
Neuropsychiatric disorders 1,112,000 per year

Medical milestones 1800s

c. 460 BC The first medical studies were carried out by Hippocrates (Greece)
AD 1543 Accurate anatomical drawings were made by Andreas Vesalius (Belgium)
1628 Blood circulation was discovered by William Harvey (U.K.)
1683 Bacteria were first described by Antonie van Leeuwenhoek (the Netherlands)
1796 The first smallpox vaccination was carried out by Edward Jenner (U.K.)
1805 Morphine was used as a painkiller by Friedrich Sertürner (Germany)
1810 Homeopathy was used by Samuel Hahnemann (Germany)
1816 The stethoscope was invented by René Laënnec (France)
1818 The first blood transfusion was carried out by Thomas Blundell (U.K.)
1842 Ether was administered as an anesthetic by Crawford Long (U.S.)
1844 Nitrous oxide (laughing gas) was used as an anesthetic by Horace Wells (U.S.)
1846 Ether vapor was used as an anesthetic by William Morton (U.S.)
1847 Chloroform was used as an anesthetic by John Bell/James Simpson (U.K.)
1864 The Red Cross was founded by Henri Dunant (Switzerland)
1867 Antiseptic was used before surgery by Joseph Lister (U.K.)
1885 Rabies vaccine was developed by Louis Pasteur (France)
1895 X-rays were discovered by William von Röntgen (Germany)
1895 Psychoanalysis was used by Sigmund Freud (Austria)
1898 Aspirin was made by Felix Hoffman (Germany)
1901 Blood groups were identified by Karl Landsteiner (Austria)

Sleep fact file

- About one-third of our lives are spent sleeping, but very little is really known about it.
- We sleep in different stages. These range from light sleep to deep sleep, with periods of REM (rapid eye movement) in between, during which we dream.
- The connection between REM and dreaming was discovered in 1953. It usually begins about 90 minutes after falling asleep and occurs in bursts, totaling about two hours a night, or 20 percent of total sleep time.
- At least 30 percent of adults snore. Many inventors have come up with anti-snoring gadgets to solve the problem. These include mouth or nose devices that alter breathing by blasting the snorers with sound, giving them electric shocks or shaking their beds.
- Trains have a "dead man's handle," which must be held at all times. If the driver falls asleep and loses his or her grip, the train stops.
- The scientific word for stretching and yawning is pandiculaton.
- Newborn babies can sleep for up to 21 hours out of 24. Children and teenagers need about 10 hours of sleep a night, while most adults need only seven to nine hours. Those over 65 need the least of all—about six hours. Older people also have less deep sleep and less REM sleep than young people.

Sir Winston Churchill

First face transplant

The world's first face transplant was carried out in 2005 on Isabelle Dinoire (born 1967) of Valenciennes, France. Her nose, lips and chin had been seriously injured when she was attacked by her dog. In an operation that lasted 15 hours, she was successfully given the face of a brain-dead donor.

- It is claimed that several famous people have existed on polyphasic sleep—short naps of a few minutes—instead of one long period of sleep. These include Leonardo da Vinci and Winston Churchill.

2000s

1906 Vitamins were discovered by Frederick Hopkins (U.K.)

1922 Insulin was used to treat diabetes by Frederick Banting and John Macleod (Canada) and Charles Best (U.S.)

1927 Iron lung was invented by Philip Drinker (U.S.)

1928 Penicillin was discovered by Alexander Fleming (U.K.)

1940 Penicillin was first used by Howard Florey (Australia) and Ernest Chain (U.K.)

1952 The first artificial heart valve was used by Charles Hufnagel (U.S.)

1953 DNA structure was identified by Francis Crick (U.K.) and James Watson (U.S.)

1955 Kidney dialysis machine was invented by Willem J. Kolff (the Netherlands/U.S.)

1957 First heart pacemaker was used by Clarence Lillehie (U.S.)

1967 The first human heart transplant was performed by Christiaan Barnard (S. Africa)

1970 First artificial heart was used by Robert Jarvik (U.S.)

1971 CAT scanner was first used by Godfrey Hounsfield (U.K.)

1978 First test-tube baby (Louise Brown) was born after procedure perfomed by Patrick Steptoe (U.K.)

1980 Smallpox was eradicated by World Health Organization

1984 Genetic fingerprinting was invented by Alec Jeffreys (U.K.)

1984 AIDS virus was first identified by Centers for Disease Control (U.S.)

1996 First mammal was cloned (Dolly, a sheep) by Ian Wilmut, Roslin Institute (U.K.)

2000 Human DNA genome sequence was completed

2006 Robot heart surgery was performed by Carlo Pappone (Italy)

2008 DNA testing enables people to check for genetic disorders

1928 poster advertising milk chocolate

Roadkill recipes

Eating roadkill (animals that have been killed on the road) has occurred ever since there have been cars. In North America, where deer and other large animals are common victims, a number of recipe books and websites have been devoted to the subject.

Two notable books, both published in 1987, were Buck Peterson's *The Original Road Kill Cookbook* (U.S.), and Richard Marcou's *How to Cook Roadkill: Gourmet Cooking* (Canada). Both are humorous guides, with recipes for "meals from under wheels" including "pavement possum" and "windshield wabbit." However, actually eating an animal scraped off the highway or the fender of a car could make you very sick and is not advisable!

The birth of the burger

The name hamburger is nothing to do with ham, but comes from the German city of Hamburg. A burger was originally called a Hamburg steak. In 1889, the word hamburger first appeared in a restaurant review in the U.S. newspaper *Walla Walla Union*. It was in a phrase that was itself a mouthful: "You are asked if you will have porkchopbeefsteakhamandegg hamburgersteakorliver andbacon."

Burger with all the toppings

What we eat

The U.S. Department of Agriculture compiles annual food consumption statistics. These products are the main food and drink groups, with the total amount an average person would consume on an 80-year lifetime – a total of over 60 tons of food and more than 10,000 gallons of beverages in the major categories alone.

Food	Lifetime consumption (lb)
Fresh vegetables	33,232
Fresh fruit	21,904
Processed vegetables	17,344
Flour and cereal products	15,384
Processed fruit	11,776
Sugar and sweeteners	11,328
Fats and oils	6,840
Beef	4,992
Chicken	4,832
Pork	3,720
Cheese	2,512
Fish	1,280
Ice cream	1,232
Turkey	1,048
Eggs	20,320 eggs

Beverages	(gal)
Carbonated soft drinks	4,120
Bottled water	2,032
Alcoholic beverages	2,000
Coffee	1,936
Milk	1,760
Cream	121

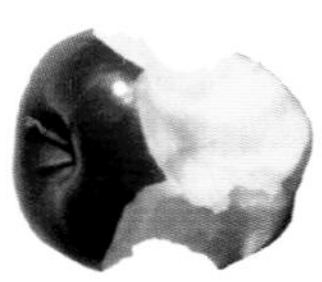
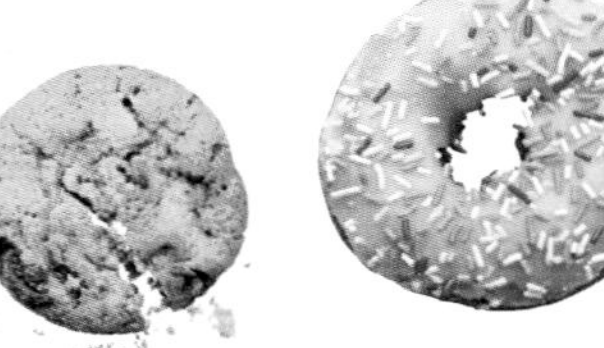

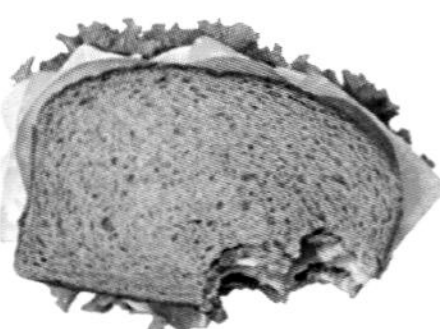

Extraordinary feasts

- Philip, Duke of Burgundy, gave a four-day banquet in 1454. The highlight came when a huge pie was brought into the room. The lid was raised to reveal 28 musicians playing inside the pie.
- On October 23, 1843, the statue of Lord Nelson was due to be hauled to the top of Nelson's Column in Trafalgar Square, London. Before this was done, 14 men sat down to a dinner of rump steak on the plinth on top of the column, 167 ft. (51 m) above the ground.
- Businessman C.K.G. Billings had a dinner at Sherry's restaurant in New York on March 28, 1903, to celebrate the completion of his new stables. All the guests were on horseback. Their horses were brought by elevator and the floor was laid with turf. The main course was served in nosebags, and the champagne in buckets.
- American millionaire George A. Kessler held his birthday party at the Savoy Hotel in London on June 30, 1905. He had the courtyard flooded and decorated Venetian style. His guests sat in a gondola and were served by waiters dressed as gondoliers.

Lunch in a dinosaur

On New Year's Eve 1853, dinosaur expert Professor Richard Owen held a banquet inside the framework of a model of a gigantic iguanodon dinosaur.

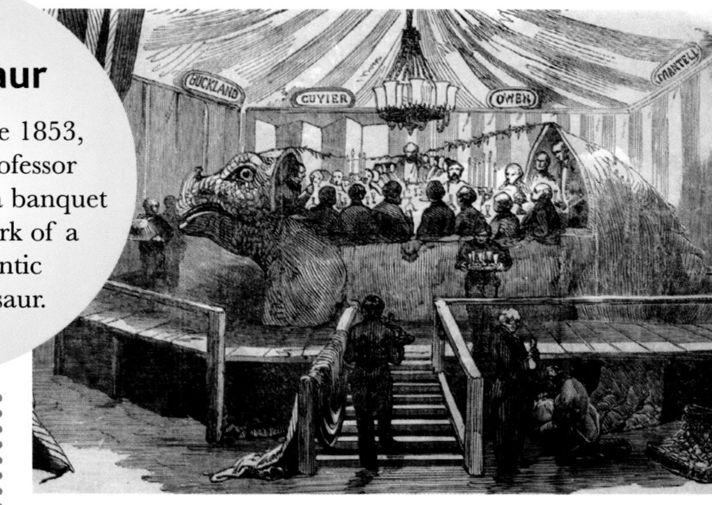

Richard Owen's banquet was held inside a model of a dinosaur

Bottles and barrels

The first bottles were made in sizes that were easy to carry. The 750 ml bottle became the standard size for most types of wine in the 19th century. In the U.S. this has been the legal size since 1979, even though metric measurements are not widely used here.

Some wine and champagne bottle sizes have Biblical names—the name Jeroboam was used for the four-bottle size as early as 1725 in Bordeaux, and others were soon named in the same way.

The origins of the names used for bottles

- Jeroboam (4 bottles), first king of Israel
- Rehoboam (6 bottles), son of Solomon, the first king of Judah
- Methuselah (8 bottles), Biblical leader said to have lived 969 years
- Salmanazar (12 bottles), an Assyrian king
- Balthazar (16 bottles), served wine at a great feast
- Nebuchadnezzar (20 bottles), king of Babylon
- Melchior (24 bottles), one of the Three Wise Men

Barrels were invented during the Iron Age. They gradually replaced the pottery containers or amphorae the ancient Greeks and Romans used for their wine, oil and other liquids. Barrels come in a range of different sizes.

Pin is 4.5 gal. (20.5 L)
Firkin is 9 gal. (40.9 L)
Kilderkin is 18 gal. (81.8 L)
Barrel is 36 gal. (163.7 L)
Hogshead is 54 gal. (245.5 L)
Puncheon is 72 gal. (327.3 L)
Butt is 108 gal. (491.0 L)
Tun is 216 gal. (981.9 L)

Bottled water

Then...

- In the 19th century contaminated water from taps and pumps spread the killer disease cholera. Bottled water became popular as a safe alternative.
- In 1741 the English scientist Dr. William Brownrigg created the first artificial mineral water. He added health-giving minerals and carbon dioxide for fizziness. He was also the first scientist to extract the element platinum.
- In 1792 Joseph Schweppe moved from Vienna to London and began to produce his own brand of artificial mineral water. His company grew to become one of the world's most famous manufacturers of soft drinks.
- French doctor Louis Perrier gave his name to Perrier water, which became the best-known mineral water in the world. In the 1960 James Bond novel *For Your Eyes Only*, Bond insists on drinking only this brand of water.

...and now

- The world drinks over 43 billion gal. (164 billion L) of bottled water every year. That's enough to fill 65,600 Olympic-size swimming pools, In the U.S., the average adult drinks 26.1 gal. (6.9 L) each year, but Italians average the most in the world — 50.5 gal. (191 L) per adult every year.
- Many people choose bottled water over tap water because it lacks substances, such as chlorine, which affect the flavor of tap water and bottles are portable. Bottled water is also produced to strict safety standards, so in some places it may be safer.
- Bottled water removes billions of gallons of underground water, while making and transporting the bottles uses huge amounts of energy. Over 2.75 million tons (2.5 million tonnes) of plastic go into the bottles every year and this has to be disposed of. Bottled water may also lack fluoride and other useful minerals found in tap water so may be less healthy than the water in our homes.

Types of bottled water

The Food and Drug Administration (FDA) sets rules for bottled water in the United States. Mineral water, for example, contains at least 250 parts per million of dissolved solids, with nothing added. Other types are: artesian water, fluoridated water, ground water, purified water, sparkling water, spring water, sterile water and well water.

FIREFLY'S WORLD OF FACTS

World History

102 HISTORICAL AGES

104 HISTORICAL EVENTS

106 WORLD CIVILIZATIONS AND EMPIRES

108 RULERS AND LEADERS

110 WORLD POLITICS

Castro bows out

In 2008, after almost 50 years as President of Cuba, Fidel Castro announced his retirement. His younger brother Raúl has taken power in the country, which remains governed as a communist dictatorship.

Prehistoric ages

Prehistory is the time before events were written down and recorded. Human prehistory is usually divided into three periods.

Stone Age

The period when stone was used for tools. It is divided into two parts: Paleolithic (Old Stone) from about 2 million to 10,000 BC and Neolithic (New Stone) from about 10,000 to 3300 BC.

Bronze Age (c. 3300–c. 2500 BC)

The period when people began to make things with bronze, which was more reliable and hardwearing than stone.

Iron Age (c. 1200 BC–c. AD 50–1000)

The period when iron was used for making tools. Bronze is a better material, but iron was more widely available, so cheaper.

Neolithic burial place, called a dolmen, in Portugal

Historical periods

History is usually divided into different periods to make it easier to study and talk about. The following are the main periods in the history of the Western world since the fall of the Roman empire.

The early Middle Ages (Dark Ages)

This period came after the fall of the Roman empire in AD 476, when so-called barbarians (Germanic tribes) took over areas that had been under Roman control. It became known as the Dark Ages because there was very little writing, science or culture during this time. The lack of writing also means that we do not know much about what happened. The early Middle Ages came to an end after the Norman Conquest when there was a revival in learning.

The Middle (Medieval) Ages

This was a very religious time. Most people believed in an all-powerful God, responsible for bringing order and prosperity. The Church was very influential and wealthy, and many great cathedrals and monasteries were built during this period. It was a great age of learning, and the first universities were founded in Parma and Bologna, then Paris and Oxford. Chartres Cathedral in France was built and the writings of Dante and Chaucer were published.

The Renaissance

The Renaissance began in Italy during the 14th century, and spread to northern Europe in the 16th century. The name Renaissance comes from the French word for rebirth; people looked back to Greek and Roman ideals in arts such as architecture and sculpture at this time. These ideas spread with the help of printing, which was invented by German Johannes Gutenberg in the mid-15th century. The Renaissance was marked by people's belief in progress and personal achievement. The playwright William Shakespeare and the artist Leonardo da Vinci lived and worked during this time.

The Reformation

In 16th-century Europe most people belonged to the Roman Catholic Church, which was headed by the Pope. Some were concerned that the Church was too involved with power and money. Leaders such as Erasmus and Martin Luther wanted people to reject the priests and return to the roots of Christianity and the Bible. This led to the start of Protestantism and its split from the Roman Catholic Church.

The age of colonialism

In 1492 Christopher Columbus discovered the Americas. This encouraged many European countries to invade and conquer other smaller or weaker countries so they could use their resources, trade with them or use them as stopping points for their ships. Portugal gained control of what is now Brazil, and Spain took most of Latin America, as well as large parts of what is now the U.S.. The Dutch gained the Indonesian islands and the French took Canada. Great Britain was the most powerful colonizing power. It gained 13 colonies in North America, plus Australasia, some Caribbean islands and vast tracts of Africa and Asia, including India. European colonization continued throughout the 19th century and up to World War I (1914–18). After the War, the victors divided many of the territories of the losers.

See also
Inventions: pages 80–81

Extent of European colonialism 1815–1914

The Industrial Revolution

The Industrial Revolution began with the invention of steam power and steam-driven machinery (mainly used in the textile industry) in 18th-century Great Britain. During the following century inventions such as steam-powered ships and railways spread throughout the world. This revolution led thousands of people to leave the countryside and move to crowded slum towns where there were large factories employing huge numbers of workers. The new industries needed better transportation to bring supplies and deliver finished goods, so a huge network of roads and canals was built during the 18th century, followed by railways in the 19th. The Industrial Revolution also led to a growth in child labor and a widening divide between rich and poor people.

The modern age

During the 20th century advances in technology led to great changes in society and global politics. New weapons and military techniques changed the way wars were fought. Huge numbers of people died during World Wars I and II. During the Cold War between the U.S. and the USSR there was no fighting, but both sides were afraid of the nuclear weapons they were developing.

Air travel, television and, most recently, the Internet have all enabled more people to experience the world beyond their own country. At the same time, cheap domestic appliances such as washing machines and dishwashers allow people more time to spend on activities such as entertainment and shopping.

Modern living

In the 20th century, factories began to mass-produce cars that ordinary people could afford. This allowed them to live further from their work places and led to the building of suburbs all over the Western world.

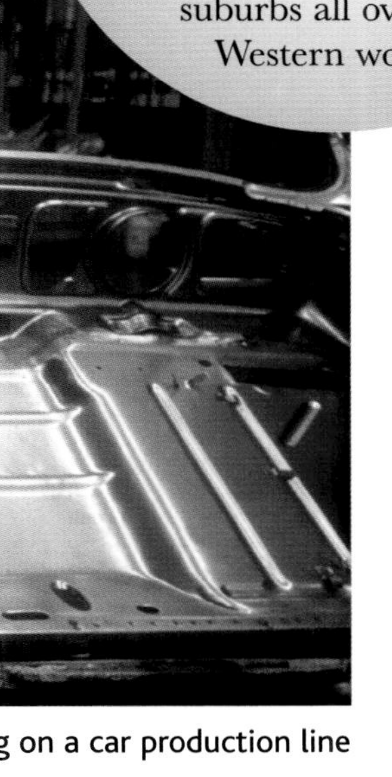

Working on a car production line

View down an elevator inside a shopping center

Romulus and Remus, the founders of Rome, nursed by a she-wolf

753 BC Rome founded

According to legend, Rome was founded by Romulus and Remus, the twin sons of the god Mars and priestess Rhea Silvia. The city is named after Romulus, who killed his brother and ruled as Rome's first king. Rome was the capital of the Roman empire, which controlled the entire Mediterranean region and far beyond by 44 BC.

1789 French Revolution

The French people had many complaints against their system of government, especially the power of the monarchy and the land-owning aristocracy. These erupted in a revolution in which the Bastille prison was seized. The violent period that followed became known as the Reign of Terror, and King Louis XVI and many other members of the ruling class were executed.

Black Death

This epidemic was probably caused by bacteria that were passed on by fleabites and by contact with infected sufferers. It was known as the Black Death because victims suffered from black blotches on their skin before dying. The plague swept across Asia and Europe in the 14th century, killing as many as a third of the people.

The Statue of Liberty in New York has a tablet in her left hand that reads July 4, 1776.

1776 U.S. Independence

The Declaration of Independence was prepared after years of tension between Great Britain and the American colonies over matters such as taxation. It listed the colonies' complaints and expressed the determination of the people of America to separate themselves from their British rulers. The declaration was signed on July 4, 1776. The armed conflict that followed ended with the American victory in 1781. In 1783 the Treaty of Paris recognized the country's independence.

History timeline

1000s **1600s**

753 BC Rome founded

221 BC Qin Shihuangdi becomes first Emperor of China

about AD 33 Jesus crucified

43 Emperor Claudius invades Britain

79 Pompeii, Italy, destroyed by the eruption of Vesuvius volcano

476 Roman empire ends when Goths invade

632 Death of Muhammad, founder of Islam

1066 Battle of Hastings; William the Conqueror becomes king of England

1096–99 First Crusade — European Christians attempt to recover Jerusalem and the Holy Land from Muslim control

1215 King John signs Magna Carta, granting rights to English citizens

1347–80s Black Death kills 75 million in Asia and Europe

1337–1453 Hundred Years' War between England and France; France eventually wins

1415 Henry V of England defeats the French at Agincourt and goes on to conquer Normandy

1431 17-year-old French patriot Joan of Arc leads an army and defeats the English (1429), but is burned at the stake

1455–85 Wars of the Roses (civil war in England)

1476 Caxton begins printing in London

1478 Spanish Inquisition begins the persecution of non-Catholics

1492 Columbus sails from Palos, Spain, to Americas

1517 Reformation starts when Martin Luther publishes protests against Catholic Church

1519-22 Ferdinand Magellan's expedition circumnavigates the globe

1588 Spanish Armada defeated by the English fleet, fireships and storms

1618–48 Thirty Years' War (Catholic v. Protestant) in Europe

1620 The Pilgrim Fathers sail from Plymouth for America and found a new colony

1649 King Charles I executed

1660 Restoration of the monarchy; Charles II becomes king

1664–65 The Great Plague kills 70,000 in London

1666 Great Fire of London

1776 U.S. Declaration of Independence

1776–83 American War of Independence

Lenin addressing a crowd of workers

1917 Russian Revolution

The rule of the Russian royal family led by the tsar ended with the February Revolution in 1917. The revolution was triggered by problems such as food shortages and Russia's involvement in World War I. The October Revolution followed later that year, when Soviet forces seized control. They murdered the tsar and his family and attempted to create a Communist state under the leadership of Lenin. A civil war followed from 1918 to 1922. Soviet rule lasted until 1991.

1989 Fall of Berlin Wall

After World War II, control of the East German city of Berlin was split between West Germany (with U.S., British and French troops) and Soviet East Germany. In 1961 the East Germans built the Berlin Wall to stop its inhabitants fleeing to the West, and 192 people were shot while trying to defect. The wall was a symbol of the divide between the Soviet Union and the West. When the Soviet Union collapsed, the wall was torn down and East and West Germany were reunited, with Berlin as the new capital city.

2008 Centenaries

1509
Henry VIII became king of England. His reign saw the Reformation in England and progress in art, architecture and literature.

1609
The Italian scientist Galileo Galilei demonstrated his first astronomical telescope.

The colony of Virginia was granted a royal charter

1709
Iron smelting using coke in place of charcoal was started in England by Abraham Darby.

Daniel Fahrenheit (Germany) invented the thermometer.

1809
American soldier John Steven's first ocean-going steamship Pheonix sailed from New York to Philadelphia.

1909
Ernest Shackleton (Anglo-Irish) explored Antarctica, discovered the Beardmore glacier and was the first to climb Mt. Eberus

Robert Peary (U.S.) claimed to have reached the North Pole, but his achievement has been disputed.
In his monoplane Blériot XI, Louis Blériot (France) became the first to fly across the English Channel.

See also
First telescopes: page 27
Famous artists: pages 242–43

2000s

1783 First balloon flight (Montgolfier brothers, France)
1788 First European settlers arrive in Australia
1789 French Revolution
1793 Louis XVI of France executed
1815 Battle of Waterloo; Wellington defeats Napoleon
1825 World's first public railway, Stockton to Darlington
1833 Slavery abolished in the British empire
1853–56 Crimean War
1860–65 American Civil War
1869 Suez Canal opens
1869 U.S. transcontinental railway completed
1876 Alexander Graham Bell invents telephone
1901–1910 Peak decade for immigration into U.S. (8.8 million immigrants)
1903 First airplane flights (Wright brothers, U.S.)
1903 Henry Ford begins mass production of cars
1914–18 World War I — 8,545,800 military deaths
1917 Russian Revolution establishes Soviet Union
1929–33 Great Depression (world economic crisis)
1939–45 World War II — 15,843,000 military deaths
1945 Atom bombs dropped on Hiroshima and Nagasaki, Japan
1945–90 Cold War between USSR and the West
1950–53 Korean War
1959–75 Vietnam War (U.S. involved 1961–73)
1961 First man in space (Yuri Gagarin, USSR)
1961 Berlin Wall built, separating East and West Germany
1963 U.S. President John F. Kennedy assassinated
1969 Neil Armstrong becomes first man on the Moon
1989 Fall of the Berlin Wall triggers the end of the Soviet Union
1994 Nelson Mandela becomes president of South Africa
2001 World Trade Center, New York, destroyed by terrorists; U.S. retaliates by invading Afghanistan
2003 Iraq War and Saddam Hussein overthrown; elections later held but violence continues
2006 Saddam Hussein executed
2007 Global warming and environmental issues become increasingly debated

Mesopotamia/Sumeria

Mesopotamia was a region around the Tigris and Euphrates rivers, which is now part of Turkey, Syria and Iraq. The area was controlled by several different peoples, beginning with the Sumerians in around 3500 BC. They set up a number of city-states that constantly battled to control land and trade routes until they were united under one ruler in 2350 BC. The Sumerians are said to have invented the wheel and cuneiform script, which many people claim is the earliest form of writing. They finally became absorbed into other races around 2000 BC.

Ancient Egypt

Egypt is an area in the Nile valley that was ruled as a single state from about 3200 BC. There were 30 dynasties, led by pharaohs who were both kings and gods. The pyramids were built during the fourth dynasty (2575–2467 BC) as tombs for the pharaohs of that time. The Great Pyramid of Giza was the world's tallest building for 4,000 years, and it is the only wonder of the ancient world that still stands. The Egyptians are also famous for their hieroglyphic writing and seagoing ships. Like other powerful empires, ancient Egypt was weakened by invasions, until it was taken over by Alexander the Great in 332 BC.

Ancient Greece

Ancient Greece was called Hellas. The civilization was at its strongest in 500–400 BC, after Greece colonized Cyprus, parts of Italy, Ukraine and the south of France. This era was known as the Golden Age. Some city-states, such as Athens and Sparta, became great centers of art, learning and politics. Many famous thinkers lived in Athens during this period, including Aristotle, Plato, Socrates and Aristophanes. The ancient Greeks also created the idea of democracy: its citizens were encouraged to debate and then vote on issues. The Golden Age ended in wars between the city-states, which paved the way for King Philip of Macedonia to invade Greece, followed later by his son Alexander.

EUROPE
ITALY
GREECE
Black Sea
Caucasus
Caspian Sea
TURKEY
ASIA
Mediterranean Sea
IRAQ
IRAN
AFGHANISTAN
PAKISTAN
EGYPT
Arabian Peninsula
Gulf of Oman

Greek empires
Colonies of the Ancient Greeks
Empire of Alexander the Great

Alexander the Great's empire

Alexander III of Macedonia lived for only 33 years, from 356 to 323 BC. In that short time he built an empire covering Persia (modern Iraq, Iran, Syria and Turkey), Egypt, Greece and Babylon. It was difficult to keep this huge empire together, and it collapsed soon after his death.

Chinese empire

China was one of the first places where people are known to have lived. From 1600 BC it was made up of many small kingdoms, which all united in 221 BC under one leader or emperor. Various dynasties ruled the empire, starting with the Qin dynasty. During this time, the Great Wall of China was built to keep invaders out. China was an extremely learned civilization, ahead of Europe in the arts and sciences by up to 200 years. The empire finally fell apart under the Han dynasty in AD 220 as a result of corruption and poverty.

Roman empire

The Roman empire was formed in 31 BC under the leadership of Caesar Augustus, who ruled over every aspect of Roman life. Caesar Augustus brought peace, prosperity and culture. The empire expanded so much that by the 2nd century AD, Rome had colonies that stretched from the Middle East to Spain, and from Great Britain to North Africa. The sheer size of the empire brought problems. There was not enough money to pay for an army spread across the world, which made the empire vulnerable to enemies. Constant attacks by German barbarians eventually defeated the army, and the empire fell in AD 476. The influence of ancient Rome is staggering: Roman roads still cross Europe, the Roman legal system is still the model for countries in Europe and Latin America, and its language, Latin, is the basis of many languages spoken today.

The Great Pyramid of Giza (seen here in the center), also called the Pyramid of Khufu, stands near the smaller pyramids of Khafre and Menkaure.

Mayan pyramid in Tikal, once the capital of the Mayan empire

Mayan empire

The Mayan empire was made up of city-states that stretched across southern Mexico and northern Central America. There have been Mayan people since 2000 BC but their greatest period was from AD 300 to 900, when architectural wonders such as Palenque and Uxmal were built. These structures and many others show that the Mayans had an advanced knowledge of mathematics. The Mayan empire gradually declined after 900, and the Spanish invaded the area in the 15th century.

Inca empire

The Incas had a great empire that stretched 350,000 sq. mi. (900,000 sq km) across South America, including Colombia, Bolivia and Argentina, with a capital, Cuzco, in Peru. It lasted from around 1200 until 1533. Inca society was very organized: every person was told which job they had to do and where to do it. In return, they were looked after by the state. Like the Aztecs, the Incas were brutally repressed by Spanish conquistadors in the 15th century.

Aztec empire

The Aztecs arrived in Mexico in 1325 and founded the city of Tenochtitlán, home to about 90,000 people. It showed the Aztecs' skill in engineering and included a system of drainage that was far ahead of any in Europe. The Aztecs conquered neighboring city-states and extended their empire until it stretched from the Pacific to the Gulf of Mexico into Guatemala. The empire ended when the Spanish, led by Hernán Cortés, invaded between 1519 and 1522.

Ottoman empire

The Ottoman empire was an Islamic state from the 13th to 20th centuries and the most powerful empire in the world during the 1500s and 1600s. It covered Turkey, parts of southwest Asia, southeast Europe and North Africa. The capital was Constantinople (now Istanbul). The empire began to decline because its rulers refused to modernize and they lost lands in several wars. It allied with Germany in World War I. Defeated, its remaining lands were divided among the victors.

The Taj Mahal in Agra, India

Mogul empire

The Mogul empire was founded in 1526 in northern India by a descendent of Genghis Khan. This was a hugely wealthy civilization and the Moguls greatly valued education, culture and art. The Taj Mahal was built by Moguls from 1632–53. This beautiful mausoleum was made for Emperor Shah Jahan's favorite wife, Mumtaz Mahal, and is built of marble with exquisite inlaid decoration. The empire's Muslim leaders wanted the people to keep Muslim ways, but many of its subjects were Hindu. In 1691 the empire was torn apart by bloody battles between Muslims and Hindus. The Mogul empire was finally overthrown by the British in 1857.

British empire

At the beginning of the 20th century, about a quarter of the world's people lived under British rule. The British had been expanding their empire since the 15th century, and by 1900 its lands included South Africa, Kenya, Egypt, Hong Kong, India, Iraq, Nepal, Singapore, Malta, Australia, New Zealand and Canada. Most of Great Britain's former colonies have now won or been granted independence. Many belong to the Commonwealth, which is a voluntary association of independent states founded in 1931 (see map on pages 102–3).

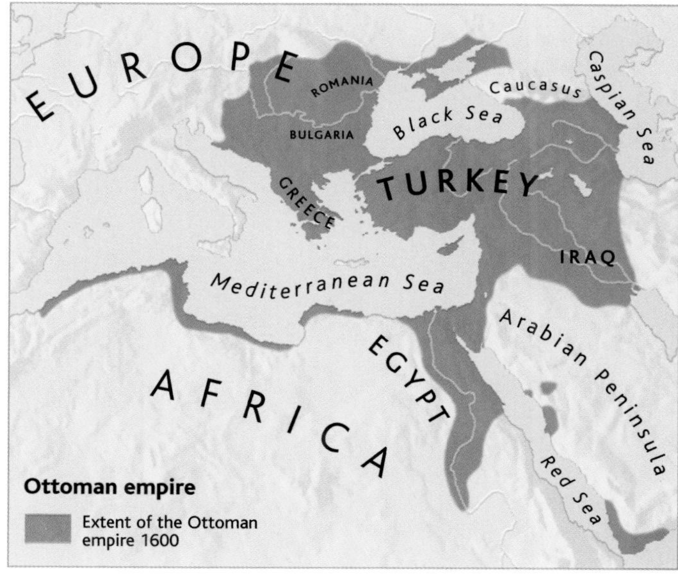

U.S. presidents

United States presidents are elected for a term of four years. George Washington was the first U.S. president and he served two terms. Only Franklin Delano Roosevelt served three terms. He died shortly after he was elected for a fourth term.

In 1951 the 22nd Amendment to the U.S. Constitution ruled that two terms are the most any president may serve. The two main political parties in the U.S. today are the Democratic Party and the Republican Party.

The heads of presidents Washington, Jefferson, Lincoln and Roosevelt are carved into the face of Mt. Rushmore in South Dakota.

Abraham Lincoln on a U.S. 1-cent coin

1 George Washington (Federalist Party) first elected 1789
2 John Adams (Federalist Party) first elected 1797
3 Thomas Jefferson (Dem-Rep Party) first elected 1801
4 James Madison (Dem-Rep Party) first elected 1809
5 James Monroe (Dem-Rep Party) first elected 1817
6 John Quincy Adams (Dem-Rep Party) first elected 1825
7 Andrew Jackson (Democratic Party) first elected 1829
8 Martin Van Buren (Democratic Party) first elected 1837
9 William Henry Harrison (Whig Party) first elected 1841
10 John Tyler (Whig Party) first elected 1841
11 James Knox Polk (Democratic Party) first elected 1845
12 Zachary Taylor (Whig Party) first elected 1849
13 Millard Fillmore (Whig Party) first elected 1850
14 Franklin Pierce (Democratic Party) first elected 1853
15 James Buchanan (Democratic Party) first elected 1857
16 Abraham Lincoln (Republican Party) first elected 1861
17 Andrew Johnson (Democratic Party) first elected 1865
18 Ulysses Simpson Grant (Republican Party) first elected 1869
19 Rutherford Birchard Hayes (Republican Party) first elected 1877
20 James Abram Garfield (Republican Party) first elected 1881
21 Chester Alan Arthur (Republican Party) first elected 1881
22 Grover Cleveland (Democratic Party) first elected 1885
23 Benjamin Harrison (Republican Party) first elected 1889
24 Grover Cleveland (Democratic Party) first elected 1893
25 William McKinley (Republican Party) first elected 1897
26 Theodore Roosevelt (Republican Party) first elected 1901
27 William Howard Taft (Republican Party) first elected 1909
28 Woodrow Wilson (Democratic Party) first elected 1913
29 Warren Gamaliel Harding (Republican Party) first elected 1921
30 Calvin Coolidge (Republican Party) first elected 1923
31 Herbert Clark Hoover (Republican Party) first elected 1929
32 Franklin Delano Roosevelt (Democratic Party) first elected 1933
33 Harry S. Truman (Democratic Party) first elected 1945
34 Dwight David Eisenhower (Republican Party) first elected 1953
35 John Fitzgerald Kennedy (Democratic Party) first elected 1961
36 Lyndon Baines Johnson (Democratic Party) first elected 1963
37 Richard Milhous Nixon (Republican Party) first elected 1969
38 Gerald Rudolph Ford (Republican Party) first elected 1974
39 Jimmy Carter (Democratic Party) first elected 1977
40 Ronald Reagan (Republican Party) first elected 1981
41 George Bush (Republican Party) first elected 1989
42 Bill Clinton (Democratic Party) first elected 1993
43 George W. Bush (Republican Party) first elected 2001

World monarchies

A monarchy is a country where the head of state is a king, queen or other hereditary ruler — someone who inherits the throne from a family member. In some countries, such as Malaysia, the monarch is elected.

Bahrain Shaikh Hamad bin Isa al-Khalifa succeeded to the throne in 1999

Belgium King Albert II succeeded to the throne in 1993

Bhutan King Jigme Singye Wangchuck succeeded to the throne in 1972

Brunei Sultan Haji Hassanal Bolkiah succeeded to the throne in 1967

Cambodia King Norodom Sihamoni succeeded to the throne in 2004

Denmark Queen Margrethe II succeeded to the throne in 1972

Japan Emperor Akihito succeeded to the throne in 1989

Jordan King Abdullah II succeeded to the throne in 1999

Kuwait Shaikh Sabah al-Ahmad al-Sabah succeeded to the throne in 2006

Lesotho King Letsie III succeeded to the throne in 1996

Liechtenstein Prince Hans Adam II succeeded to the throne in 1989

Luxembourg Grand Duke Henri succeeded to the throne in 2000

Amazing monarchs

Oldest monarch to ascend the British throne

William IV (ruled 1830–37) was 64 when he was crowned.

British monarchs with the most children

Edward I had 16 children (6 sons and 10 daughters). Both George III and James II had 15.

Most-married British monarch

Henry VIII had six wives who suffered various fates. They were: Catherine of Aragon (divorced), Anne Boleyn (beheaded), Jane Seymour (died 1537), Anne of Cleves (divorced), Catherine Howard (beheaded) and Catherine Parr, who survived Henry.

Youngest British monarchs

Henry VI was just 8 months old when he became king on September 1, 1422, after the death of his father, Henry V. When his grandfather, Charles VI, died 50 days later on October 21, 1422, Henry also became king of France.

Shortest reigning British monarchs

Queen Jane (Lady Jane Grey), ruled for only nine days in 1553, before being sent to the Tower of London. She was executed the following year. Edward V ruled for 75 days. He was one of the Princes in the Tower, who were allegedly murdered on the orders of their uncle, Richard III. Edward VIII abdicated (gave up the throne) on December 11, 1936, before his coronation. He had ruled for just 325 days.

Longest reigning world monarch

King Louis XIV of France became king at the age of 5. He ruled for 72 years, from 1643–1715.

Longest reigning British monarch

Queen Victoria was 18 years old when she became queen in 1837 and she ruled for 63 years.

Richest world ruler

Although no longer the richest man in the world, the Sultan of Brunei is estimated to have a fortune of $28 million.

Monarchies with the most rulers

Japan's monarchy dates from 40 BC. Since then, it has had 125 rulers.

Henry VIII

Oldest king to be crowned

The British crown usually passes to the next in line when the king or queen dies. Charles, Prince of Wales, is Queen Elizabeth II's oldest son and heir. If he becomes king on or after September 20, 2013, he will have overtaken William IV, who was crowned in 1830 at the age of 64 years, 10 months and 5 days, and currently holds the record as the oldest monarch to ascend the British throne. Queen Elizabeth II celebrated her 82th birthday on April 21, 2008.

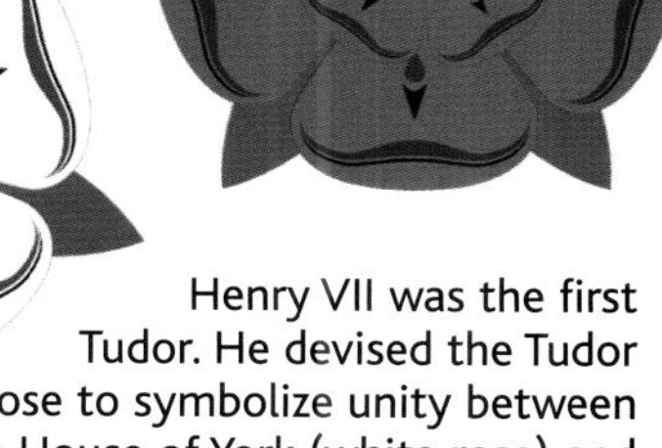

Henry VII was the first Tudor. He devised the Tudor Rose to symbolize unity between the House of York (white rose) and the House of Lancaster (red rose).

See also

Types of government: pages 110–11

Malaysia Sultan Mizan Zainal Abidin succeeded to the throne in 2006

Monaco Prince Albert II succeeded to the throne in 2005

Morocco King Mohammed VI succeeded to the throne in 1999

Nepal King Gyanendra Bir Bikram Shah Dev succeeded to the throne in 2001

Netherlands Queen Beatrix succeeded to the throne in 1980

Norway King Harald V succeeded to the throne in 1991

Oman Sultan Qaboos Bin Said al-Said succeeded to the throne in 1970

Qatar Shaikh Hamad bin Kaalifa al-Thani succeeded to the throne in 1995

Samoa Tuiatua Tupua Tamasese Efi, a member of one of the country's ruling families, was elected head of state in 2007.

Saudi Arabia King Abdullah ibn Abdul Aziz al-Saud succeeded to the throne in 2005

Spain King Juan Carlos I succeeded to the throne in 1975

Swaziland King Mswati III succeeded to the throne in 1986

Sweden King Carl XVI Gustaf succeeded to the throne in 1973

Thailand King Bhumibol Adulyadej succeeded to the throne in 1946

Tonga George Tupou V succeeded to the throne in 2006

United Kingdom Queen Elizabeth II succeeded to the throne in 1952

Votes for women

The Isle of Man was the first place to give women the vote, in 1880, but the island is part of the U.K. and not a separate country. Until 1920 the only European countries that allowed women to vote were Sweden (1919) and Czechoslovakia (1920).

In the United States women were granted the vote in 1920, although some states allowed it earlier. Women could not vote in France or Italy until 1945, in Switzerland until 1971 or in Liechtenstein until 1984. Women were granted the right to vote in Kuwait for the first time in 2005, but they are still not allowed to vote in Brunei, Saudi Arabia and the United Arab Emirates. There are other countries where women have no vote — but neither do men.

1 The first country to give women the vote was New Zealand in 1893.

2 Australia followed suit in 1902 although women had the vote in South Australia in 1894 and in Western Australia in 1898 before the separate states were united in 1901.

3 Finland (then a Grand Duchy under the Russian Crown) granted women the vote in 1906.

4 Norway gave some women the vote in 1907. It was not until 1913 that all women over 25 could vote.

5 Denmark and Iceland (a Danish dependency until 1918) allowed women to vote in 1915.

6 The Netherlands and the USSR both gave women the vote in 1917.

8 Austria, Canada, Germany, Poland, Great Britain and Ireland all gave women the vote in 1918. (In Ireland, part of the U.K. until 1921, only women over 30 got the vote in 1918. This was lowered to 21 in 1928.)

British poster demanding votes for women

Types of government

There have been many different types of government around the world throughout history. Many of the names for them end in the term "-cracy," from a Greek word meaning power.

Aristocracy
Rule by a small group of members of a privileged class.

Autocracy
Government by one person with unrestricted power; also known as despotism and dictatorship.

Fidel Castro was President of Cuba for almost 50 years before handing over power to his brother Raúl.

Communist
Government of a classless state in which private ownership is abolished and the state controls all means of production, as in China and Cuba.

Democracy
Government by the people directly or through elected representatives, as in the U.K. and U.S.

Roosevelt's Four Freedoms

On January 6, 1941, during World War II, U.S. President Roosevelt made a famous speech to Congress. He proclaimed that four freedoms are essential to a democracy: freedom of speech, freedom of worship, freedom from want, and freedom from fear. He looked forward to these freedoms being possible after the defeat of Hitler and the Axis powers. In 1997 a memorial park was opened in Washington DC, honoring Roosevelt. It contains the Four Freedoms fountain as a symbol of his ideas.

Major international organizations

A number of international organizations have been set up to deal with issues that concern the world in general, rather than the interests of individual countries. These organizations are not linked to political parties but often become involved in political matters.

Flags flying outside the United Nations, New York

United Nations

The UN was founded in 1945. Most countries of the world — a total of 192 — are members. The General Assembly of the UN makes decisions about peacekeeping and human rights.

Women in parliament

There are 49 countries with at least 20 percent of their parliament made up of women — but a number of countries still do not have any women representatives at all.

Based on the most recent general election results, these countries have the highest percentages of women in parliament: Rwanda 48.8 percent, Sweden 47 percent, Finland 41.5 percent, Argentina 40 percent, Netherlands 33.3 percent.

Meritocracy
Government by leaders selected according to their ability.

Monarchy
Government in which power is held by a king (or queen, emperor or empress) who can pass power on to their heirs.

Oligarchy
Government by a small group of people.

Plutocracy
A government or state in which wealthy people rule.

Theocracy
Government ruled by or subject to religious authority.

Amnesty International (AI)
Amnesty International is a charitable organization set up in 1961. It campaigns for human rights throughout the world and against the detention of political prisoners.

International Monetary Fund (IMF)
The IMF was established in 1944 and promotes world trade. It has 184 member countries.

International Red Cross and Red Crescent Movement
These organizations help the victims of such events as warfare and natural disasters.

North Atlantic Treaty Organization (NATO)
Nato was founded in 1949. Ten countries signed a defense treaty that committed them to helping each other in the event of attack. There are now 26 country members, and the NATO headquarters are based in Belgium.

Organization for Economic Co-operation and Development (OECD)
The OECD was formed in 1961. It aims to encourage economic and social development in industrialized countries and provide aid to developing countries.

United Nations Children's Fund (UNICEF)
UNICEF was set up in 1947. It works to improve the health and welfare of children and mothers in developing countries.

United Nations Educational, Scientific and Cultural Organization (UNESCO)
UNESCO was set up in 1946. It encourages countries to get together on matters such as education, culture and science.

World Bank
The World Bank was founded in 1944 and has 184 member countries. It helps developing countries by giving loans.

World Health Organization (WHO)
The WHO is part of the UN. It promotes health matters worldwide and aims to raise medical standards and monitor diseases.

World Trade Organization (WTO)
The Swiss-based WTO encourages international trade by establishing trade agreements between countries.

World Wildlife Fund (WWF)
The WWF was set up in 1961 and is the world's largest conservation organization. Its main aims are to protect endangered animals and the places where they live.

G8

The Group of 8 (G8) is made up of the world's leading industrial countries (Canada, France, Germany, Italy, Japan, the U.K., the U.S. and Russian Federation). The heads of the G8 countries meet each year to discuss global issues such as world poverty and security.

Countries of the World

114 WORLD MAP
116 COUNTRIES OF THE WORLD
118 CITIES OF THE WORLD
120 NORTH AND CENTRAL AMERICA
122 CENTRAL AND SOUTH AMERICA
124 EUROPE
130 AFRICA
136 ASIA
142 AUSTRALASIA

A new country is born

The world's newest country, Kosovo, declared its independence from Serbia in 2008. It is the latest development following the years of conflict that led to the break-up of Yugoslavia.

ARCTIC OCEAN
Beaufort Sea
Baffin Bay
Greenland (DENMARK)
Arctic Circle
Alaska (USA)
ICELAND
Hudson Bay
Labrador Sea
Bering Sea
Gulf of Alaska
CANADA
UNITED KINGDOM
IRELAND
PACIFIC OCEAN
UNITED STATES
ATLANTIC OCEAN
SPAIN
PORTUGAL
MOROCCO
MEXICO
Gulf of Mexico
Canary Islands (SPAIN)
Western Sahara (MOROCCO)
Tropic of Cancer
BAHAMAS
Hawaii (USA)
CUBA
DOMINICAN REPUBLIC
JAMAICA
HAITI
Puerto Rico (USA)
ANTIGUA & BARBUDA
ST CHRISTOPHER & NEVIS
DOMINICA
ST VINCENT & THE GRENADINES
ST LUCIA
BARBADOS
GRENADA
TRINIDAD & TOBAGO
BELIZE
HONDURAS
GUATEMALA
EL SALVADOR
NICARAGUA
COSTA RICA
PANAMA
Caribbean Sea
CAPE VERDE
MAURITANIA
MALI
SENEGAL
GAMBIA
GUINEA-BISSAU
GUINEA
BURKINA FASO
SIERRA LEONE
LIBERIA
CÔTE D'IVOIRE
GHANA
VENEZUELA
GUYANA
SURINAME
French Guiana (FRANCE)
COLOMBIA
Equator
Galapagos Islands (ECUADOR)
ECUADOR
PERU
BRAZIL
BOLIVIA
PACIFIC OCEAN
PARAGUAY
Easter Island (CHILE)
CHILE
ARGENTINA
URUGUAY
ATLANTIC OCEAN
Falkland Islands (UNITED KINGDOM)
Antarctica
Key to numbered countries
Europe
1 Netherlands
2 Luxembourg
3 Andorra
4 Monaco
5 Lichtenstein
6 Vatican City State
7 San Marino
8 Slovenia
9 Boznia-Herzegovina
10 Serbia
11 Macedonia
12 Montenegro
Africa
13 Republic of Congo
Asia
14 Singapore

ARCTIC OCEAN
Svalbard (NORWAY)
Barents Sea
Kara Sea
Arctic Circle
RUSSIA
NORWAY
SWEDEN
FINLAND
Baltic Sea
North Sea
DENMARK
ESTONIA
LATVIA
LITHUANIA
Russia
BELARUS
POLAND
GERMANY
BELGIUM
CZECH REP.
UKRAINE
SLOVAKIA
AUSTRIA
SWITZ.
HUNGARY
MOLDOVA
FRANCE
CROATIA
ROMANIA
Black Sea
ITALY
BULGARIA
ALBANIA
GEORGIA
ARMENIA
AZERBAIJAN
Corsica (FRANCE)
Sardinia (ITALY)
Mallorca (SPAIN)
TURKEY
GREECE
MALTA
TUNISIA
CYPRUS
Mediterranean Sea
LEBANON
ISRAEL
SYRIA
JORDAN
IRAQ
KUWAIT
BAHRAIN
QATAR
UNITED ARAB EMIRATES
SAUDI ARABIA
OMAN
YEMEN
ALGERIA
LIBYA
EGYPT
Red Sea
Caspian Sea
Aral Sea
KAZAKHSTAN
UZBEKISTAN
TURKMENISTAN
KYRGYZSTAN
TAJIKISTAN
AFGHANISTAN
IRAN
PAKISTAN
NEPAL
BHUTAN
INDIA
BANGLADESH
MONGOLIA
CHINA
NORTH KOREA
SOUTH KOREA
Sea of Japan
JAPAN
Sea of Okhotsk
PACIFIC OCEAN
Tropic of Cancer
TAIWAN
Philippine Sea
PHILIPPINES
MYANMAR
LAOS
THAILAND
CAMBODIA
VIETNAM
South China Sea
Arabian Sea
Bay of Bengal
SRI LANKA
MALDIVES
NIGER
CHAD
SUDAN
ERITREA
DJIBOUTI
NIGERIA
TOGO
BENIN
CAMEROON
CENTRAL AFRICAN REPUBLIC
ETHIOPIA
SOMALIA
EQUATORIAL GUINEA
GABON
DEMOCRATIC REPUBLIC OF CONGO
UGANDA
KENYA
SÃO TOMÉ & PRÍNCIPE
Angola
RWANDA
BURUNDI
TANZANIA
SEYCHELLES
COMOROS
ANGOLA
ZAMBIA
MALAWI
ZIMBABWE
MOZAMBIQUE
NAMIBIA
BOTSWANA
MADAGASCAR
MAURITIUS
SWAZILAND
LESOTHO
SOUTH AFRICA
INDIAN OCEAN
Tropic of Capricorn
BRUNEI
MALAYSIA
PALAU
MICRONESIA
MARSHALL ISLANDS
Equator
NAURU
KIRIBATI
INDONESIA
PAPUA NEW GUINEA
EAST TIMOR
SOLOMON ISLANDS
TUVALU
Coral Sea
VANUATU
SAMOA
FIJI
New Caledonia (FRANCE)
TONGA
AUSTRALIA
Tasman Sea
NEW ZEALAND
SOUTHERN OCEAN
Antarctic Circle
Antarctica

St Peter's, Vatican City

Largest countries

These figures are based on total land area, including inland water, such as rivers and lakes. If the water area was not taken into account, China would be second largest, at 3,600,947 sq. mi. (9,326,410 sq km), the U.S. third with 3,537,439 sq. mi. (9,161,923 sq km) and Canada fourth at 3,511,023 sq. mi. (9,093,507 sq km).

Largest countries

Country	Area sq. mi.	(sq km)
Russia	6,592,770	(17,075,200)
Canada	3,855,105	(9,984,670)
U.S.	3,794,085	(9,826,630)
China	3,705,405	(9,596,960)
Brazil	3,286,490	(8,511,965)
Australia	2,967,910	(7,686,850)

Smallest countries

Country	Area sq. mi.	(sq km)
Vatican City	0.17	(0.44)
Monaco	0.77	(2)
Nauru	8	(21)
Tuvalu	10	(26)
Bermuda	20	(53)
San Marino	24	(61)
Liechtenstein	62	(160)

Biggest landlocked countries

A landlocked country has no coastline. This means that it has no direct access to the sea and fishing. Also, people and goods traveling to and from the country must go through another country. This may be difficult or expensive.

There are more than 40 landlocked countries in the world. The largest, Kazakhstan, has a coast on the Caspian Sea — which is a landlocked sea. The largest landlocked European country is Hungary (35,637 sq. mi. [92,300 sq km]). Europe also contains the world's smallest landlocked countries — Andorra, Liechtenstein, San Marino and Vatican City. All are less than 200 sq. mi. (518 sq km) in size. Liechtenstein and Uzbekistan are both double-landlocked. This means that they are surrounded by other landlocked countries.

Kazakhstan 1,049,155 sq. mi. (2,717,300 sq km)
Mongolia 603,908 sq. mi. (1,564,116 sq km)
Chad 495,755 sq. mi. (1,284,000 sq km)
Niger 489,190 sq. mi. (1,267,000 sq km)
Mali 478,765 sq. mi. (1,240,000 sq km)
Ethiopia 435,186 sq. mi. (1,127,127 sq km)
Bolivia 424,165 sq. mi. (1,098,580 sq km)

Longest and shortest frontiers

A country's frontier is made up of the combined length of all its land borders.

Longest
China 13,743 mi. (22,117 km)
Russia 12,488 mi. (20,097 km)
Brazil 10,488 mi. (16,885 km)
India 8,763 mi. (14,103 km)
U.S. 7,478 mi. (12,034 km)

Shortest
Vatican City 2.4 mi. (3.2 km)
Monaco 2.7 mi. (4.4 km)
Cuba 18 mi. (29.0 km)
San Marino 24 mi. (39.0 km)
Qatar 37 mi. (60 km)

Biggest and smallest populations

In most countries, more people are born every day than die, so population figures are going up all the time. China has the biggest population, but India is catching up fast.

Biggest population

Country	Population
China	1,313,552,030
India	1,152,342,278
U.S.	305,072,714
Indonesia	227,070,492
Brazil	192,047,523
Pakistan	155,360,000
Nigeria	147,357,690
Bangladesh	143,481,419
Russia	141,833,475
Japan	127,939,307

Smallest population

Country	Population
Vatican City	549
Tuvalu	9,916
Nauru	10,147
Palau	20,548
San Marino	30,684
Monaco	33,639
Liechtenstein	35,406
St. Kitts and Nevis	48,925
Marshall Islands	53,236
Dominica	70,581

Crowded shopping street in Shanghai, China

Country development

These rankings from the United Nations are based on a range of factors, including how long people can expect to live, how much money they earn, education level and quality of life.

Most developed

1 Iceland
2 Norway
3 Australia
4 Canada
5 Ireland
12 U.S.
16 U.K.

Least developed

1 Sierra Leone
2 Burkina Faso
3 Niger
4 Guinea-Bissau
5 Mali
6 Central African Republic

Population density

In densely populated countries, lots of people live on a small amount of land, usually in cities. The least densely populated countries are usually difficult for people to live in. The climate may be very cold or very hot, or there may be large areas of mountain, desert or forest.

Most densely populated countries

Monaco 44,680 people per sq. mi. (17,251 per sq km)
Singapore 18,871 people per sq. mi. (7,280 per sq km)
Malta 3,315 people per sq. mi. (1,280 per sq km)
Vatican City 3,232 people per sq. mi. (1,248 per sq km)

Least densely populated countries

Mongolia 4.37 people per sq. mi. (1.69 per sq km)
Namibia 6.68 people per sq. mi. (2.58 per sq km)
Australia 6.83 people per sq. mi. (2.64 per sq km)
Mauritania 7.56 people per sq. mi. (2.92 per sq km)
Iceland 7.92 people per sq. mi. (3.06 per sq km)

Monaco

www.census.gov/main/www/popclock.html search

Changing names

Many cities change their names after the countries they are in become independent. Others are renamed after political changes, such as those ending the former Soviet Union. Some changes come from variations in the way in which foreign languages are translated from one alphabet to another.

Was called/country	Now called (since)
Batavia, Indonesia	**Jakarta** (1949)
Bombay, India	**Mumbai** (1995)
Christiana, Norway	**Oslo** (1924)
Byzantium/Constantinople, Turkey	**Istanbul** (1930)
Danzig, Poland	**Gdansk** (1945)
Leningrad, USSR	**St. Petersburg**, Russia (1991)
Léopoldville, Belgian Congo	**Kinshasa**, Zaire (1960)
New Amsterdam, America	**New York**, U.S. (1664)
Pretoria, South Africa	**Tshwane** (2005)
Rangoon, Burma	**Yangon**, Myanmar (1989)
Saigon, Vietnam	**Ho Chi Minh City** (1975)
Salisbury, Rhodesia	**Harare**, Zimbabwe (1980)
Santa Isabel, Equatorial Guinea	**Malabo** (1973)
Tsaritsyn/Stalingrad, USSR	**Volgograd**, Russia (1961)

What is a city?

A city is a large town. In some countries, a city has a special status. In the United States it is an urban area with its own government.

A town is a densely populated area with a defined boundary and its own government. A town is smaller than a city and larger than a village.

A village is a small group of houses and other buildings in a country area.

A hamlet is a small village or a cluster of houses in a country area.

A settlement is a small group of inhabited buildings, or a small countryside community, such as a ranch or farm with a few dwellings.

Cities with the most people*

1 Tokyo, Japan	37,203,122
2 New York, U.S.	22,981,510
3 Mexico City, Mexico	22,968,205
4 Seoul, South Korea	22,254,620
5 Mumbai (Bombay), India	20,870,764
6 São Paulo, Brazil	20,218,868
7 Manila, The Philippines	19,195,048
8 Jakarta, Indonesia	18,588,548
9 New Delhi, India	18,362,625
10 Los Angeles, U.S.	18,215,539

*Estimated figures for city and adjoining populated areas 2008. This calculation applies throughout this section.
Source: World Gazetteer

www.citypopulation.de/cities.html search

Highest towns and cities

Some towns and cities are in surprisingly high places. The Chinese city of Wenchuan, founded in 1955, is at more than half the height of Mt. Everest. Even the towns and cities at the bottom of this list are at more than one-third the height of Everest.

1 Wenchuan, China — 16,729 ft. (5,099 m)
2 Potosí, Bolivia — 13,045 ft. (3,976 m)
3 Oruro, Bolivia — 12,146 ft. (3,702 m)
4 Lhasa, China — 12,087 ft. (3,684 m)
5 La Paz, Bolivia — 11,916 ft. (3,632 m)
6 Cuzco, Peru — 11,152 ft. (3,399 m)
7 Huancayo, Peru — 10,659 ft. (3,249 m)
8 Sucre, Bolivia — 9,301 ft. (2,835 m)
9 Tunja, Colombia — 9,252 ft. (2,820 m)
10 Quito, Ecuador — 9,249 ft. (2,819 m)

La Paz, the world's highest capital city

The rediscovered city of Troy

Lost cities

There are some cities that were very famous in the past but have since been destroyed or abandoned.

Angkor, Cambodia

Angkor was once the largest city in the world and more than a million people lived there. The city had an area of more than 30 sq. mi. (78 sq km) and was surrounded by a water-filled moat. It was abandoned in about AD 1100. Frenchman Henri Mouhot was the first westerner to discover the city, in 1861.

One and only

The only city in two continents: Istanbul, Turkey, is partly in Europe and partly in Asia.

The only city center with no cars: Venice. Its only traffic is boats on the canals.

The only non-U.S. capital city named after a U.S. president: Monrovia, the capital of Liberia, in Africa, was named after U.S. president James Monroe.

Grand Canal, Venice

See also

World civilizations and empires: pages 106–107

Atlantis

Some people believe that there was a city and island of Atlantis, perhaps in the Mediterranean Sea, that was destroyed by an earthquake and flooding almost 12,000 years ago. No one knows exactly where it was or even whether it really existed.

Chichén Itzá, Mexico

Chichén Itzá was once the center of the Mayan empire. It was built in about AD 400 and had many buildings used in Mayan rituals. The city was abandoned in AD 1200.

Cliff Palace (Mesa Verde), Colorado, United States

This Native American city was built on a cliffside, but was abandoned during a long drought in the late 13th century. It lay unknown until December 18, 1888, when Richard Wetherill, a local farmer, spotted it while looking for stray cattle.

Machu Picchu, Peru

The fortified Inca city on top of a mountain was stumbled on in 1911 by American explorer Hiram Bingham. He was searching for Vilcabamba, another lost Inca city.

Pompeii, Italy

The entire city was buried by volcanic ash when Mt. Vesuvius erupted in AD 79. Nearby Herculaneum was buried at the same time. Excavations began in 1748, and many treasures have been uncovered, including beautifully preserved murals (wall paintings). Plaster casts have been made of the bodies of inhabitants who were buried beneath the debris.

Troy, Turkey

Troy was once thought to have existed only in legends, but its site was discovered in the 1870s.

Ur, Iraq

Ur was once one of the greatest cities in the world, but was abandoned in the 4th century BC. Its magnificent royal tombs and other sites were excavated by archaeologists in 1922–34 and many treasures were discovered.

Banff National Park, Alberta, Canada

Canada

Canada is the second largest country in the world, after Russia. Almost half of Canada's land area is covered by forest and it exports more lumber, pulp and newsprint than any other country. Canada also has a successful fishing industry and lots of natural resources, such as minerals and metals. Its varied landscape attracts millions of tourists each year. Famous Canadian landmarks include Niagara Falls and the Rocky Mountains.

Area 3,855,105 sq. mi. (9,984,670 sq km)
Country population 32,213,280
Capital city (pop) Ottawa (1,152,721)
Official languages English/French
Currency Canadian dollar

United States

The U.S. is made up of 50 states (including Alaska and Hawaii) and the District of Columbia, which contains the capital city, Washington. It includes a huge variety of landscapes, from hot deserts to snow-covered mountains. The country was once a colony under British rule but has been independent since 1776. It is now the world's wealthiest country and a great economic and military superpower.

Area 3,794,085 sq. mi. (9,826,630 sq km)
Country population 305,072,714
Capital city (pop) Washington, D.C. (8,281,142)
Official language English
Currency U.S. dollar

Mexico

Some of the world's oldest civilizations have lived in Mexico, such as the Aztecs and Mayans. Nowadays, many tourists visit and it has plenty of natural resources. However, almost half the people are very poor and many try to cross the border into the United States every year. Some of them are arrested by border patrols.

Area 761,605 sq. mi. (1,972,550 sq km)
Country population 107,236,677
Capital city (pop) Mexico City (22,968,205)
Official language Spanish
Currency Peso

Guatemala

Guatemala is one of Central America's most beautiful countries, with a dramatic landscape of forests, lakes and volcanoes. It is also one of the poorest and most violent. The country is still suffering from the aftereffects of a long civil war (1960–96). Two-thirds of Guatemalan children live in poverty.

Area 42,045 sq. mi. (108,890 sq km)
Country population 13,994,079
Capital city (pop) Guatemala City (3,293,168)
Official language Spanish
Currency Quetzal

Honduras

Honduras lies in Central America between the Caribbean Sea and the Atlantic Ocean. It is one of the world's poorest countries, although it has valuable stocks of lumber. In 1998 Hurricane Mitch caused $4 billion worth of damages.

Area 43,280 sq. mi. (112,090 sq km)
Country population 7,761,830
Capital city (pop) Tegucigalpa (2,063,368)
Official language Spanish
Currency Lempira

El Salvador

The tiny country of El Salvador is on Central America's Pacific coast. It often suffers hurricanes and earthquakes. Coffee is a major crop, but El Salvador relies heavily on aid money from other countries.

Area 8,125 sq. mi. (21,040 sq km)
Country population 7,218,048
Capital city (pop) San Salvador (1,912,758)
Official language Spanish
Currency U.S. dollar

Nicaragua

Nicaragua is the largest country in Central America. It is one of the poorest countries in the Western world and half its people are very poor indeed. In 1998, Hurricane Mitch caused great damage and left 20 percent of Nicaraguans homeless.

Area 50,000 sq. mi. (129,494 sq km)
Country population 5,353,272
Capital city (pop) Managua (1,752,912)
Official language Spanish
Currency Córdoba

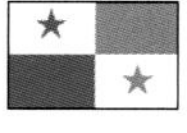

Panama

Panama is a narrow strip of land stretching between North and South America. It has coastlines on the Atlantic Ocean and the Pacific Ocean and has a canal, which connects the two oceans. Panama receives money from the many ships that use the canal each year and has other successful industries, but nearly 40 percent of the people are poor.

Area 30,195 sq. mi. (78,200 sq km)
Country population 3,426,464
Capital city (pop) Panama City (1,242,192)
Official language Spanish
Currency Balboa

Costa Rica

Costa Rica is one of the most successful Central American countries and has a good standard of living. Its landscape is beautiful, with many mountains and tropical forests, and tourism is increasing. However, the country is also becoming more and more involved in the illegal drug trade.

Area 19,730 sq. mi. (51,100 sq km)
Country population 4,572,364
Capital city (pop) San José (1,666,585)
Official language Spanish
Currency Costa Rican colón

St. Kitts and Nevis

The Caribbean islands of St. Kitts (also known as St. Christopher) and Nevis became independent of the U.K. in 1983. Most of the people are descended from slaves brought from West Africa to work on the islands. Sugar has always been the island's main crop, but tourism and financial services are now important industries.

Area 101 sq. mi. (261 sq km)
Country population 48,925
Capital city (pop) Basseterre (13,245)
Official language English
Currency East Caribbean dollar

The Bahamas

The Bahamas is made up of more than 700 islands, which lie southeast of Florida in the Atlantic Ocean. The islands were ruled by the British, but became independent in 1973. Queen Elizabeth II is still the head of state. About 40 percent of people work in tourism, but banking and finance are also important.

Area 5,380 sq. mi. (13,940 sq km)
Country population 335,187
Capital city (pop) Nassau (235,102)
Official language English
Currency Bahamian dollar

Jamaica

The Caribbean island of Jamaica became independent of the U.K. in 1962, but has remained in the Commonwealth. Tourism is its main industry, but many visitors are put off by the island's poverty and violence. Jamaica has one of the world's highest murder rates.

Area 4,244 sq. mi. (10,991 sq km)
Country population 2,687,852
Capital city (pop) Kingston (941,433)
Official language English
Currency Jamaican dollar

Dominican Republic

The Dominican Republic makes up the eastern two-thirds of the island of Hispaniola, sharing it with Haiti. It is the oldest European settlement in America. The Dominican Republic is one of the Caribbean's poorest countries, but it is now very popular with tourists.

Area 18,815 sq. mi. (48,730 sq km)
Country population 9,679,893
Capital city (pop) Santo Domingo (3,338,850)
Official language Spanish
Currency Dominican Republic peso

Belize

Belize was a British colony called British Honduras, but became independent in 1981. Queen Elizabeth II is still the head of state. The coral reef off the coast is the world's second largest after Australia's Great Barrier Reef. Belize is now popular with tourists.

Area 8,865 sq. mi. (22,966 sq km)
Country population 321,243
Capital city (pop) Belmopan (17,570)
Official language English
Currency Belize dollar

Antigua and Barbuda

The Caribbean islands of Antigua and Barbuda were settled by the Spanish, the French and the British before becoming independent in 1981. They are still part of the Commonwealth and Queen Elizabeth II is the head of state. The islands are popular with tourists.

Area 171 sq. mi. (443 sq km)
Country population 85,420
Capital city (pop) St. John's (22,077)
Official language English
Currency East Caribbean dollar

Haiti

Haiti shares the island of Hispaniola with the Dominican Republic. In 1804, Haiti was the first Caribbean state to become independent. Now Haiti is the poorest country in the Americas, after years of dictatorship and violence. Financial help from the EU and U.S. was stopped in 2000 after unfair elections, and drug-trafficking is a big problem.

Area 10,715 sq. mi. (27,750 sq km)
Country population 8,558,135
Capital city (pop) Port-au-Prince (1,720,655)
Official languages Haitian Creole/French
Currency Gourde

Cuba

Cuba is 93 mi. (150 km) south of Florida and is the largest island in the Caribbean. It has a Communist government, which has been led by Fidel Castro since 1959. Cuba attracts more and more tourists, but the collapse of the Soviet Union and trade restrictions put on Cuba by the U.S. have caused financial problems.

Area 42,805 sq. mi. (110,860 sq km)
Country population 11,237,171
Capital city (pop) Havana (2,599,655)
Official language Spanish
Currency Cuban peso

A street in Havana, Cuba

St. Vincent and the Grenadines

This Caribbean nation includes 33 small islands. It became independent from Britain in 1979, but it is still a member of the Commonwealth. Bananas are the main crop. Many tourists visit the islands.

Area 150 sq. mi. (389 sq km)
Country population 102,133
Capital city (pop) Kingstown (16,610)
Official language English
Currency East Caribbean dollar

Boats docked near the island of St. Vincent

Dominica

This tropical, mountainous Caribbean island was once under British rule. It became independent in 1978. Dominica's main exports are bananas and fruit juices, but the crops are often destroyed by hurricanes.

Area 290 sq. mi. (750 sq km)
Country population 70,857
Capital city (pop) Roseau (13,803)
Official language English
Currency East Caribbean dollar

Barbados

This Caribbean island became an independent state in 1966, but it remains part of the Commonwealth. Queen Elizabeth II is the head of state. The main industries are tourism and sugar manufacturing.

Area 166 sq. mi. (431 sq km)
Country population 276,965
Capital city (pop) Bridgetown (92,467)
Official language English
Currency Barbados dollar

Grenada

Grenada lies between the Caribbean Sea and the Atlantic Ocean, north of Trinidad and Tobago. Nearly 400,000 tourists visit Grenada every year. The island exports spices, and about a quarter of the world's nutmeg comes from there.

Area 133 sq. mi. (344 sq km)
Country population 106,478
Capital city (pop) St. George's (5,159)
Official language English
Currency East Caribbean dollar

Trinidad and Tobago

The Caribbean islands of Trinidad and Tobago lie northwest of Venezuela. They have large reserves of oil and natural gas and are among the richest of all Caribbean nations. Tobago is quieter than Trinidad. Both islands are popular with tourists.

Area 1,980 sq. mi. (5,128 sq km)
Country population 1,339,932
Capital city (pop) Port of Spain (49,959)
Official language English
Currency Trinidad and Tobago dollar

St. Lucia

This mountainous island lies between the Atlantic Ocean and the Caribbean Sea. It is famous for its two large, cone-shaped peaks known as the Pitons. Bananas are the island's main crop, but banking and tourism are also important.

Area 238 sq. mi. (616 sq km)
Country population 170,718
Capital city (pop) Castries (9,914)
Official language English
Currency East Caribbean dollar

South America

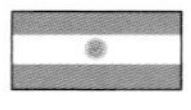

Argentina

Argentina was once ruled by Spain, but it became independent in 1816. This South American country is famous for its beef and has large mineral deposits.

Area 1,068,300 sq. mi. (2,766,890 sq km)
Country population 39,792,277
Capital city (pop) Buenos Aires (14,197,085)
Official language Spanish
Currency Peso

Venezuela

Venezuela is a land of great natural beauty in northern South America. Angel Falls is the world's highest waterfall, and Maracaibo is the largest lake in South America. Venezuela has large reserves of oil, coal and gold, but almost half of Venezuelans live in poverty.

Area 352,145 sq. mi. (912,050 sq km)
Country population 28,522,297
Capital city (pop) Caracas (4,259,737)
Official language Spanish
Currency Bolívar

Suriname

This is the smallest independent nation in South America. It was governed by the Netherlands but became independent in 1975. Suriname has large amounts of lumber as well as bauxite and gold, but 70 percent of the people are still very poor.

Area 63,040 sq. mi. (163,270 sq km)
Country population 439,117
Capital city (pop) Paramaribo (226,124)
Official language Dutch
Currency Suriname dollar

Colombia

Colombia is in the northwest of South America. The main crops are coffee, bananas and sugar, and the country has oil and mineral reserves. Colombia is also the world's leading producer of cocaine.

Area 439,735 sq. mi. (1,138,910 sq km)
Country population 44,459,803
Capital city (pop) Bogotá (8,148,808)
Official language Spanish
Currency Colombian peso

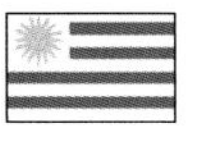

Uruguay

Uruguay is the second-smallest country in South America. It is wealthier than most South American nations because of its livestock, tourism and banking industries. It has a good welfare system and its people are well educated.

Area 68,040 sq. mi. (176,220 sq km)
Country population 3,383,284
Capital city (pop) Montevideo (1,843,196)
Official language Spanish
Currency Uruguayan peso

Ecuador

Ecuador lies on the Equator and stretches across the Andes Mountains. The country's main exports are fish, bananas, cocoa and coffee. Oil was discovered there in 1972.

Area 109,485 sq. mi. (283,560 sq km)
Country population 835,076
Capital city (pop) Quito (1,594,883)
Official language Spanish
Currency U.S. dollar

Bolivia

The Andes mountain range crosses Bolivia. The Bolivian capital La Paz is in the Andes and is the highest capital city in the world. Bolivia is one of only two landlocked countries in South America.

Area 424,165 sq. mi. (1,098,580 sq km)
Country population 10,300,696
Capital city (pop) La Paz (2,175,731)
Official language Spanish
Currency Boliviano

Peru

Peru lies on South America's Pacific coast. It has been home to famous ancient civilizations, including the Inca Empire. Peru has important natural resources, including gold and oil, but they have not yet been developed.

Area 496,225 sq. mi. (1,285,220 sq km)
Country population 26,901,638
Capital city (pop) Lima (8,057,397)
Official languages Spanish/Quechua
Currency New sol

Paraguay

The Republic of Paraguay is landlocked. It has one of the smallest populations in South America. Alfredo Stroessner, the region's longest ruling dictator, was overthrown in 1989, but Paraguay is still struggling with political and financial problems.

Area 157,045 sq. mi. (406,750 sq km)
Country population 6,243,757
Capital city (pop) Asunción (2,014,725)
Official languages Spanish/Guaraní
Currency Guaraní

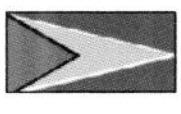

Guyana

Guyana is the only country in South America where English is the official language. Its natural resources include gold and diamonds, but it is very poor and has political problems. The country has many fascinating animals and plants and is popular with tourists interested in nature.

Area 83,000 sq. mi. (214,970 sq km)
Country population 742,165
Capital city (pop) Georgetown (247,588)
Official language English
Currency Guyana dollar

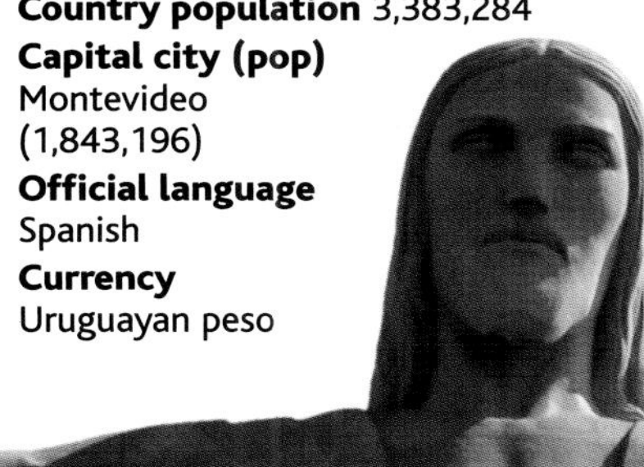

Statue of Christ, Rio de Janeiro, Brazil

Chile

Chile is an extremely long, narrow country, which lies between the Andes Mountains and the Pacific Ocean. It is one of the most successful nations in South America and has many natural resources, including minerals and lumber, as well as thriving agriculture and fishing industries.

Area 292,260 sq. mi. (756,950 sq km)
Country population 16,998,021
Capital city (pop) Santiago (5,099,129)
Official language Spanish
Currency Chilean peso

Brazil

Area 3,286,490 sq. mi. (8,511,965 sq km)
Country population 192,047,523
Capital city (pop) Brasília (2,492,188)
Official language Portuguese
Currency Real

Brazil covers nearly half of South America. It contains the world's second-longest river, the Amazon, and vast tropical rainforests. About 82 percent of Brazil's population lives in cities, which are mostly on the coast in the south and southeast of the country. Brazil is the leading nation in South America but there are wide divisions between rich and poor.

Norway

Norway is famous for its fiords. The population is small and has a very good standard of living, thanks to the country's plentiful natural resources. Only Russia and Saudi Arabia export more oil than Norway, and it is the world's biggest exporter of seafood.

Area 125,021 sq. mi. (323,802 sq km)
Country population 4,714,633
Capital city (pop) Oslo (846,584)
Official language Norwegian
Currency Krone

Oil rig supply boat in Bergen harbor, Norway

Ireland

Ireland was divided in the 1920s, when 26 counties in the south gained independence from the United Kingdom. Since then there has been conflict in Northern Ireland between those who want to remain part of the United Kingdom and those who want a united, independent Ireland. Since Ireland joined the European Community in 1973 it has become a modern, high-tech nation with successful industry. It began using the euro in January 1999, along with 10 other nations.

Area 27,135 sq. mi. (70,200 sq km)
Country population 4,364,523
Capital city (pop) Dublin (1,058,265)
Official languages Irish/English
Currency Euro

Denmark

Denmark shares a border with Germany and is the smallest, most southerly Scandinavian nation. It is a wealthy, high-tech country and has all the oil and natural gas it needs. The standard of living is high. Denmark is a monarchy and the kingdom includes the Faeroe Islands and Greenland.

Area 16,639 sq. mi. (43,094 sq km)
Country population 5,466,444
Capital city (pop) Copenhagen (1,082,884)
Official language Danish
Currency Danish krone

Luxembourg

Luxembourg is landlocked by Belgium, Germany and France. Its inhabitants have an amazingly high standard of living. Steel was once the main industry, but financial services have now become more important.

Area 999 sq. mi. (2,586 sq km)
Country population 463,129
Capital city (pop) Luxembourg (75,552)
Official languages French/German
Currency Euro

Sweden

Sweden is a rich country with a high standard of living. Swedes have one of the world's longest life expectancies. The country has many natural resources including iron ore, lead, granite, zinc and forests. Forests cover about half the land and there are important lumber and paper industries.

Area 173,732 sq. mi. (449,964 sq km)
Country population 9,146,262
Capital city (pop) Stockholm (1,737,995)
Official language Swedish
Currency Swedish krona

Finland

Since the end of World War II, Finland has changed from being a rural country covered with dense forest into a modern nation. It has very successful industries and an excellent welfare system. Finland joined the European Union in 1995 and adopted the euro as its currency in 2002.

Area 130,560 sq. mi. (338,145 sq km)
Country population 5,291,078
Capital city (pop) Helsinki (1,262,805)
Official languages Finnish/Swedish
Currency Euro

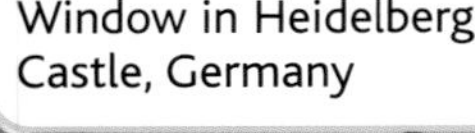

Window in Heidelberg Castle, Germany

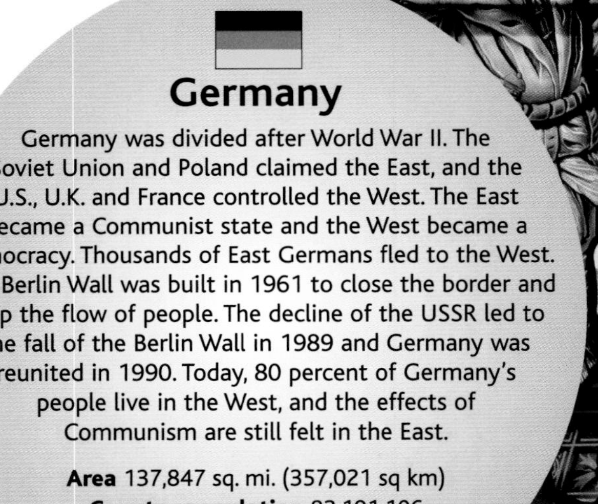

Germany

Germany was divided after World War II. The Soviet Union and Poland claimed the East, and the U.S., U.K. and France controlled the West. The East became a Communist state and the West became a democracy. Thousands of East Germans fled to the West. The Berlin Wall was built in 1961 to close the border and stop the flow of people. The decline of the USSR led to the fall of the Berlin Wall in 1989 and Germany was reunited in 1990. Today, 80 percent of Germany's people live in the West, and the effects of Communism are still felt in the East.

Area 137,847 sq. mi. (357,021 sq km)
Country population 82,191,106
Capital city (pop) Berlin (4,040,690)
Official language German
Currency Euro

People bathing in the Blue Lagoon, Iceland

Iceland

Iceland is a volcanic island and is the most westerly country in Europe. Its capital city is the furthest north in the world. Iceland is a wealthy country with low unemployment and a good welfare system. Fishing provides 70 percent of its exports, which could cause problems as fish stocks decline.

Area 39,769 sq. mi. (103,000 sq km)
Country population 315,450
Capital city (pop) Reykjavíc (201,008)
Official language Icelandic
Currency Icelandic króna

The Netherlands

The Netherlands is a low-lying country and much of it has been reclaimed from the sea. Nearly a quarter of the land lies below sea level, which makes it vulnerable to flooding, despite coastal defences and a network of dikes and canals. Banking, shipping and fishing all are important industries. The Netherlands is the sixth-largest exporter in the world.

Area 16,033 sq. mi. (41,526 sq km)
Country population 16,409,082
Capital city (pop) Amsterdam (749,372)
Official language Dutch
Currency Euro

Belgium

Belgium is divided into Flanders (in the northwest) and Wallonia (in the southeast). Brussels is the headquarters of the European Union. This has brought wealth to the country as multinational companies have settled in the city. Belgium is well known for its fine chocolates and beer.

Area 11,787 sq. mi. (30,528 sq km)
Country population 10,629,889
Capital city (pop) Brussels (2,175,008)
Official languages Flemish/French/German
Currency Euro

France

France is the largest country in Western Europe and a key member of the European Union. It has a varied landscape ranging from coastal plains to the Alps in the southeast. Farms and forests cover a large proportion of the country, and agricultural products — particularly wine and liqueurs — are major exports. France once had one of the world's largest empires. Most of its former colonies are now independent, but French Guiana, Guadeloupe, Martinique, Réunion, Mayotte, St. Pierre and Miquelon, French Polynesia, New Caledonia, Wallis and Futuna and the Southern and Antarctic Territories all still have links with France.

Area 248,428 sq. mi. (643,427 sq km)
Country population 62,015,826
Capital city (pop) Paris (11,818,503)
Official language French
Currency Euro

United Kingdom

The United Kingdom is made up of Great Britain (England, Scotland and Wales) and Northern Ireland. Although it is a small country, the U.K. has had a huge influence on the world because of its cultural, military and industrial strengths. At one time, it controlled a vast empire of lands across the globe and was the world's leading industrial nation. Traditional manufacturing industries are now less important. In the 21st century the U.K.'s main industries are technology, tourism and services such as banking, and it is still an important economic power.

Area 94,525 sq. mi. (244,820 sq km)
Country population 61,264,416
Capital city (pop) London (12,577,225)
Language English
Currency British pound

Monaco

Monaco is a principality — it is ruled by a prince. It is surrounded by France and is the second smallest independent state in the world. It has no income tax and low business taxes so rich people flock there to escape taxes.

Area 0.77 sq. mi. (2 sq km)
Country population 33,639
Capital city (pop) Monaco (955)
Official language French
Currency Euro

Plaza de España in Seville, Spain

Spain

Spain covers most of the Iberian peninsula. The country has many cultures. Basque, Catalan, Galician and Valencian are spoken in different regions, but Castilian Spanish is the official language. There are 19 regions with their own elected authorities. There is a campaign for independence by the Basque country in the north, which has caused ongoing problems for the government. Spain is the world's second most popular tourist destination (after France) and has more than 50 million visitors every year. The fishing industry is one of the biggest in Europe, but unemployment is high.

Area 194,897 sq. mi. (504,782 sq km)
Country population 4,113,018
Capital city (pop) Madrid (6,270,551)
Official language Castilian Spanish
Currency Euro

Portugal

Portugal lies to the west of Spain on the Iberian peninsula. It is one of the European Union's least developed countries and has the highest number of people working on the land. Portugal's economy has grown rapidly since it joined the European Union in 1986. Tourism is one of its fastest growing industries. Portugal once had a vast empire, stretching across the Americas, Africa and Asia. Over 177 million people worldwide speak Portuguese.

Area 35,672 sq. mi. (92,391 sq km)
Country population 10,634,138
Capital city (pop) Lisbon (2,634,878)
Official language Portuguese
Currency Euro

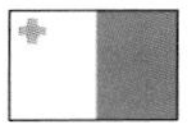

Malta

Malta, which includes the neighboring island of Gozo, used to be under British rule. It became independent in 1964, but remains a part of the Commonwealth. Malta became the European Union's smallest new member in 2004. Tourism is the island's most important industry and Malta has more than a million visitors every year.

Area 122 sq. mi. (316 sq km)
Country population 403,266
Capital city (pop) Valletta (255,377)
Official languages Maltese/English
Currency Maltese lira

Vatican City State

The Vatican City is the smallest country in the world, both in area and population. It is surrounded by the city of Rome. The Vatican is home to the Pope and it is the spiritual center of the Roman Catholic Church. It depends on contributions from Roman Catholics all over the world for its income, and the sale of souvenirs and publications.

Area 0.17 sq. mi. (0.44 sq km)
Country population 549
Capital city (pop) Vatican City (549)
Official languages Latin/Italian
Currency Euro

San Marino

San Marino is entirely surrounded by Italy and it is the third-smallest state in Europe. The tiny republic attracts about three million tourists every year. San Marino's inhabitants (known as Sammarinese) enjoy the world's sixth-highest income per person.

Area 24 sq. mi. (61 sq km)
Country population 30,684
Capital city (pop) San Marino (4,638)
Official language Italian
Currency Euro

Andorra

Andorra is a small principality (a state ruled by a prince), which dates from 1278. It lies in the mountains between France and Spain. Tourism is its main industry, but financial services are also becoming important.

Area 181 sq. mi. (468 sq km)
Country population 86,417
Capital city (pop) Andorra la Vella (25,204)
Official language Catalan
Currency Euro

Estonia

The small Baltic state of Estonia regained its independence in 1991 when the Soviet Union collapsed. It was one of the Eastern European nations that joined the European Union in 2004.

Area 17,462 sq. mi. (45,226 sq km)
Country population 1,339,330
Capital city (pop) Tallinn (394,898)
Official language Estonian
Currency Kroon

Italy

Italy is a long, narrow country reaching into the Mediterranean Sea. It includes the islands of Sicily and Sardinia among others. Italy can be divided into two: the wealthy, industrial north, and the poorer south, where most people work on the land and around 20 percent of the population is unemployed. About 40 million foreign tourists visit Italy every year, many of them to see its beautiful cities, which include Rome, Venice and Florence.

Area 116,305 sq. mi. (301,230 sq km)
Country population 59,279,992
Capital city (pop) Rome (3,858,111)
Official language Italian
Currency Euro

Austria

Austria is a small, mountainous country. It is landlocked by the Czech Republic, Slovakia, Italy, Slovenia, Hungary, Germany, Switzerland and Liechtenstein. It was once the center of the powerful Austro-Hungarian empire, until its defeat in World War I. It was occupied by Nazi Germany and then by the Allies after World War II. Since the war Austria has flourished, and it is now a popular vacation spot.

Area 32,380 sq. mi. (83,870 sq km)
Country population 8,370,759
Capital city (pop) Vienna (2,123,722)
Official language German
Currency Euro

Czech Republic

The Czech Republic was part of Czechoslovakia until it split from Slovakia in 1993. It now attracts investment from other countries and has a thriving tourism industry. The country joined the European Union in 2004.

Area 30,450 sq. mi. (78,866 sq km)
Country population 10,310,957
Capital city (pop) Prague (1,406,142)
Official language Czech
Currency Koruna

Astronomical clock in Prague, Czech Republic

Switzerland

Switzerland is the most mountainous country in Europe. The Alps occupy 60 percent of its land area. It has a very high income per person, low unemployment and its people have a long life expectancy. Switzerland was not involved in either world war and has not joined the European Union.

Area 15,940 sq. mi. (41,290 sq km)
Country population 7,555,082
Capital city (pop) Bern (121,837)
Official languages German/French/Italian/Romansch
Currency Swiss franc

Belarus

Belarus became independent when the Soviet Union collapsed in 1991. It continues to have close ties with Russia. The country still suffers from the effects of nuclear fallout from the 1986 Chernobyl accident, which took place in neighboring Ukraine.

Area 80,155 sq. mi. (207,600 sq km)
Country population 9,615,624
Capital city (pop) Minsk (1,753,547)
Official languages Belarusian/Russian
Currency Belarusian ruble

Poland

Poland is the largest nation in Central Europe and has the highest population. It was devastated by World War II, when more than six million people died — more than in any other country. In 1989 Poland was the first Eastern European nation to topple its Communist leaders. In May 2004 it joined the European Union.

Area 120,730 sq. mi. (312,685 sq km)
Country population 38,077,421
Capital city (pop) Warsaw (2,251,474)
Official language Polish
Currency Zloty

Latvia

Latvia is bounded by the Baltic Sea, Estonia, Lithuania, Belarus and Russia. It became independent of the Soviet Union in 1991 and in 2004 it was accepted into the European Union.

Area 24,938 sq. mi. (64,589 sq km)
Country population 2,268,001
Capital city (pop) Riga (808,248)
Official language Latvian
Currency Lats

Lithuania

Lithuania became independent of the Soviet Union in 1991. It used to depend on Russia, but more recently it has developed trade links with the West. It joined the European Union in 2004.

Area 25,174 sq. mi. (65,200 sq km)
Country population 3,366,913
Capital city (pop) Vilnius (543,642)
Official language Lithuanian
Currency Litas

Liechtenstein

Liechtenstein is the sixth-smallest country in the world. Its low taxes have encouraged extraordinary economic growth, and thousands of foreign companies have bank accounts there.

Area 62 sq. mi. (160 sq km)
Country population 35,406
Capital city (pop) Vaduz (5,088)
Official language German
Currency Swiss franc

Panoramic view of Florence, Italy

View of Rovinj, Croatia

Croatia

Croatia was one of Yugoslavia's most advanced and prosperous areas, and declared its independence in 1991. The country borders the Adriatic Sea and its coast was popular with tourists. The Yugoslavian conflict of 1991–95 threw the country into turmoil, but visitors are now returning.

Area 21,831 sq. mi. (55,542 sq km)
Country population 4,447,495
Capital city (pop) Zagreb (703,185)
Official language Croatian
Currency Kuna

Bulgaria

Bulgaria was Communist until 1990, when it became a democracy. It has now joined the European Union, despite organized crime, corruption, inflation and unemployment. Bulgaria is becoming popular with tourists, especially the historic capital city of Sofia.

Area 42,825 sq. mi. (110,910 sq km)
Country population 7,535,211
Capital city (pop) Sofia (1,205,048)
Official language Bulgarian
Currency Lev

Bosnia and Herzegovina

Bosnia and Herzegovina was recognized as an independent state in 1992 after Yugoslavia collapsed in 1991. Since then clashes between Bosnia's Croats, Serbs and Muslims have caused civil war, which is still not resolved. Despite this, more tourists are beginning to visit the country again.

Area 19,741 sq. mi. (51,129 sq km)
Country population 3,827,694
Capital city (pop) Sarajevo (424,354)
Official languages Bosnian/Croatian/Serbian
Currency Convertible marka

Slovakia

Slovakia is landlocked and mountainous. It became independent in 1993, when Czechoslovakia divided into the Czech Republic and Slovakia. It joined the European Union in 2004.

Area 18,859 sq. mi. (48,845 sq km)
Country population 5,395,346
Capital city (pop) Bratislava (419,211)
Official language Slovak
Currency Koruna

Moldova

Moldova is Europe's poorest country. It has no natural resources and imports all its energy supplies from Russia, from which it became independent in 1991.

Area 13,067 sq. mi. (33,843 sq km)
Country population 3,640,569
Capital city (pop) Chisinau (697,475)
Official language Moldovan
Currency Moldovan leu

Hungary

Hungary became Communist after World War II. In the 1990s, it defied the Soviet Union and began some free trade with the West. This central European country has flourished since the Soviet Union's collapse and it entered the European Union in 2004.

Area 35,919 sq. mi. (93,030 sq km)
Country population 9,981,334
Capital city (pop) Budapest (2,571,504)
Official language Hungarian
Currency Forint

The Millennium Monument in Budapest, Hungary

Ukraine

Ukraine is a vast area between Poland and Russia. It became independent after the collapse of the Soviet Union. In 1986 it was the scene of the world's worst nuclear disaster, when a reactor at the Chernobyl nuclear plant exploded.

Area 233,090 sq. mi. (603,700 sq km)
Country population 46,396,212
Capital city (pop) Kiev (3,000,198)
Official language Ukrainian
Currency Hryvna

Albania

Albania depends mostly on farming, and its main crops are wheat, corn, beets, potatoes and fruit. It has borders with Serbia, Montenegro, Kosovo, Macedonia and Greece.

Area 11,100 sq. mi. (28,748 sq km)
Country population 3,175,119
Capital city (pop) Tirana (399,999)
Official language Albanian
Currency Lek

Georgia

Georgia lies in a key position east of the Black Sea between Russia and Turkey. It has coal deposits, but they have not yet been exploited. The country relies on farming — particularly grapes from which wine is made.

Area 26,910 sq. mi. (69,700 sq km)
Country population 4,658,143
Capital city (pop) Tbilisi (1,310,819)
Official language Georgian
Currency Lari

Slovenia

About half of Slovenia is covered in forest, making it the third most forested country in Europe. Slovenia became independent from Yugoslavia in 1991 and joined the European Union in 2004. Its people now have a reasonably good standard of living.

Area 20,273 sq km (7,827 sq miles)
Country population 2,018,689
Capital city (pop) Ljubljana (258,810)
Official language Slovene
Currency Euro

Azerbaijan

Azerbaijan regained its independence from the Soviet Union in 1991. The country has rich mineral resources as well as oil and natural gas. However, conflict and corruption have kept it from developing a healthy economy.

Area 86,600 sq km (33,436 sq miles)
Country population 8,770,714
Capital city (pop) Baki/Baku (2,176,777)
Official language Azerbaijani
Currency Manat

Greece

The ancient country of Greece lies in an important position between Europe, Asia and Africa. It includes about 2,000 islands as well as the mainland. About 14 million tourists visit Greece every year. However, it has few natural resources and relies on money from the European Union.

Area 131,940 sq km (50,942 sq miles)
Country population 11,205,946
Capital city (pop) Athens (3,829,018)
Official language Greek
Currency Euro

Windmill on the Greek island of Santorini

Macedonia

Macedonia's full name is the Former Yugoslav Republic of Macedonia (FYROM), not to be confused with the Greek region of Macedonia. Macedonia became independent in 1991. Since then there have been clashes between the country's large Albanian minority and its Macedonian majority.

Area 25,333 sq km (9,781 sq miles)
Country population 9,047,846
Capital city (pop) Skopje (589,307)
Official languages Macedonian/Albanian
Currency Denar

Armenia

Armenia was the first country formally to adopt Christianity in AD 301. This mountainous country is bordered by Azerbaijan, Georgia, Iran and Turkey. Its key position between Europe and Asia led to invasions by the Persian, Ottoman, Roman and Byzantine empires, among others.

Area 29,800 sq km (11,506 sq miles)
Country population 3,237,660
Capital city (pop) Yerevan (1,414,740)
Official language Armenian
Currency Dram

Romania

The mountainous Republic of Romania is the largest Balkan nation. The Communist regime was overthrown in 1989 when the dictator Nicolae Ceausescu was executed. The country is still very poor, with almost half of Romanians living in poverty. It is now a member of the European Union.

Area 237,500 sq km (91,699 sq miles)
Country population 21,503,193
Capital city (pop) Bucharest (2,192,372)
Official language Romanian
Currency Leu

Cyprus

The Mediterranean island of Cyprus has been divided since Turkey invaded the north of the island in 1974. The Turkish Republic of Northern Cyprus is recognized only by Turkey. Greek Cyprus attracts many tourists and was accepted into the European Union in 2004. The Turkish part depends heavily on loans from Turkey.

Area 9,250 sq km (3,571 sq miles)
Country population 1,099,421
Capital city (pop) Nicosia (213, 027)
Official languages Greek/Turkish
Currency Cyprus pound

Serbia

This landlocked country was formerly part of Yugoslavia but is now independent.

Area 88,361 sq km (34,116 sq miles)
Country population 9,567,484
Capital city (pop) Belgrade (1,818,237)
Official language Serbian
Currency Serbian dinar

Kosovo

Kosovo declared its independence from Serbia in 2008 and has received partial recognition from United Nations member states.

Montenegro

Montenegro was a former part of Yugoslavia and became independent from Serbia in 2006. It is now a full member of the United Nations and, although not a member of the European Union, it has adopted the Euro as its national currency.

Area 14,026 sq km (5,415 sq miles)
Country population 625,536
Capital city (pop) Podgorica (143,718)
Official language Serbian
Currency Euro

Morocco

Morocco is in northwestern Africa. The country was divided between Spanish and French rule, but gained independence in 1956. It has rich mineral deposits and nearly three-quarters of the world's phosphate. Tourism is becoming increasingly important, but almost half the population work on the land.

Area 172,415 sq. mi. (446,550 sq km)
Country population 30,886,980
Capital city (pop) Rabat (1,754,425)
Official language Arabic
Currency Dirham

Algeria

Algeria became independent from France in 1962. Throughout the 1990s the country was torn apart by civil war, in which 100,000 people are thought to have died. Algeria is still struggling to control its religious militants.

Area 919,595 sq. mi. (2,381,740 sq km)
Country population 34,498,821
Capital city (pop) Algiers (6,253,265)
Official languages Arabic/Berber
Currency Algerian dinar

Tunisia

The North African country of Tunisia shares borders with Algeria and Libya and has a Mediterranean coastline. About one-fifth of the people live by farming and fishing.

Area 63,170 sq. mi. (163,610 sq km)
Country population 10,326,500
Capital city (pop) Tunis (2,050,434)
Official language Arabic
Currency Tunisian dinar

Cape Verde

Cape Verde is made up of the Windward Islands and the Leeward Islands in the Atlantic Ocean off the west coast of Africa. Their main exports are bananas and coffee.

Area 1,557 sq. mi. (4,033 sq km)
Country population 499,362
Capital city (pop) Praia (124,661)
Official language Portuguese
Currency Cape Verdean escudo

Ethiopia

Ethiopia is Africa's oldest independent country. It has suffered many droughts and famines. These, combined with civil war and a border dispute with Eritrea, have made Ethiopia one of Africa's poorest nations. Its natural resources are underdeveloped, and 85 percent of the people still depend upon the land for a living.

Area 435,186 sq. mi. (1,127,127 sq km)
Country population 79,183,659
Capital city (pop) Addis Ababa (3,144,918)
Official language There is no official language, but Amharic is the most widely used of the 70 languages
Currency Ethiopian birr

Eritrea

Eritrea is in eastern Africa and has had violent border disputes with Ethiopia since 1998. The conflict has affected Eritrea's economy, but the government continues to improve the country's roads, schools and transport systems. Its Red Sea ports are an important source of income.

Area 46,840 sq. mi. (121,320 sq km)
Country population 4,936,403
Capital city (pop) Asmara (1,146,822)
Official languages No official language; Arabic, Tigrinya and English are the main working languages; Italian is also spoken.
Currency Nakfa

Libya

Libya has large oil reserves, but its economy has suffered from sanctions imposed by the United Nations. These were in response to the bombing of an airliner over Lockerbie in Scotland in 1988. Sanctions have now been lifted and Libya's leader, Colonel Gaddafi, has promised to bring his country back into the international community.

Area 679,360 sq. mi. (1,759,540 sq km)
Country population 6,455,346
Capital city (pop) Tripoli (1,943,454)
Official language Arabic
Currency Libyan dinar

Camel and rider near the Great Pyramid in Egypt

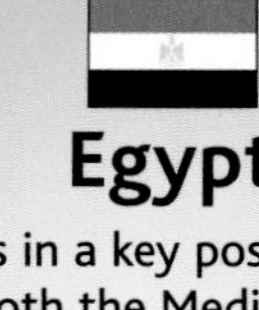

Egypt

Egypt lies in a key position. It has a coastline on both the Mediterranean and Red seas, and borders with the Sudan, Libya, Israel and the Gaza Strip. Egypt also controls the vital Suez Canal. This allows about 15,000 ships each year to travel between the Mediterranean and the Indian Ocean without sailing around Africa. Famous landmarks include the pyramids.

Area 386,662 sq. mi. (1,001,450 sq km)
Country population 75,099,806
Capital city (pop) Cairo (16,078,877)
Official language Arabic
Currency Egyptian pound

Fortified town of Aït Benhaddou in the High Atlas mountains, Morocco

Somalia

Somalia is one of the world's poorest countries and there has been conflict between different groups. The north declared independence under the name Somaliland, but is not recognized by any foreign government.

Area 246,201 sq. mi. (637,657 sq km)
Country population 12,692,376
Capital city (pop) Mogadishu (1,609,050)
Official languages Somali/Arabic
Currency Somali shilling

Mauritania

Mauritania is mainly desert. It became independent from France in 1960. There is conflict between the country's African and Arab peoples. Mauritania has rich mineral deposits, but these have not yet been exploited.

Area 397,955 sq. mi. (1,030,700 sq km)
Country population 3,022,150
Capital city (pop) Nouakchott (775,758)
Official language Arabic
Currency Ouguiya

Sudan

Sudan is the biggest country in Africa. It has large oil reserves, which have been exploited since 1999. However, the country has suffered from civil war since its independence in 1956. This war has been going on longer than any other war in Africa. Since 2003 fighting has been particularly severe in the western region of Darfur, which is one of the poorest parts of the country. The United Nations has described this as the world's worst humanitarian crisis.

Area 967,500 sq. mi. (2,505,810 sq km)
Country population 37,423,543
Capital city (pop) Khartoum (8,873,889)
Official language Arabic
Currency Sudanese dinar

Djibouti

Djibouti lies in a key position between Ethiopia and the Red Sea. The country provides refueling facilities for ships and operates a free port, which bring money into Djibouti.

Area 8,880 sq. mi. (23,000 sq km)
Country population 496,375
Capital city (pop) Djibouti (c. 400,000)
Official languages Arabic/French
Currency Djibouti franc

Senegal

Senegal is almost divided into two by The Gambia. It became independent from France in 1960. It is now popular with tourists, but has few natural resources, high unemployment and more than half its people live in poverty.

Area 75,749 sq. mi. (196,190 sq km)
Country population 11,291,344
Capital city (pop) Dakar (2,485,851)
Official language French
Currency CFA franc

Guinea

Guinea has been placed under great strain by thousands of refugees from its war-torn neighbors, Liberia and Sierra Leone. Guinea has natural resources, including iron ore, gold and diamonds.

Area 94,926 sq. mi. (245,857 sq km)
Country population 10,174,655
Capital city (pop) Conakry (1,857,153)
Official language French
Currency Guinean franc

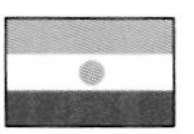
Niger

Niger is the largest nation in West Africa. It is also one of the hottest and poorest countries in the world. Niger borders the Sahara Desert and droughts often kill much of the country's vital livestock. It has one of the world's lowest literacy rates.

Area 489,190 sq. mi. (1,267,000 sq km)
Country population 3,949,837
Capital city (pop) Niamey (931,928)
Official language French
Currency CFA franc

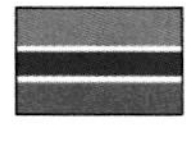
Gambia

The Gambia is a sliver of land and the smallest country in mainland Africa. About 80 percent of Gambians work on the land. It is becoming increasingly popular as a tourist destination.

Area 4,365 sq. mi. (11,300 sq km)
Country population 1,546,400
Capital city (pop) Banjul (33,820)
Official language English
Currency Dalasi

Dogon people from Mali dancing on stilts

Mali

Mali's first democratically elected government came to power in 1992 after more than 20 years of dictatorship. This West African nation is one of the world's poorest countries. About 80 percent of the people depend on farming for a living.

Area 478,765 sq. mi. (1,240,000 sq km)
Country population 12,781,404
Capital city (pop) Bamako (2,111,790)
Official language French
Currency CFA franc

Nigeria

Nigeria has the biggest population of any African country. It is the leading oil producer south of the Sahara. However, about 60 percent of Nigerians live in poverty because of corruption, unequal distribution of money and a rapidly growing population.

Area 356,668 sq. mi. (923,768 sq km)
Country population 147,357,690
Capital city (pop) Abuja (781,199)
Official language English
Currency Naira

Guinea-Bissau

Guinea-Bissau is one of the poorest countries in the world. A civil war in 1998 destroyed many of its roads, schools and hospitals, and ruined its economy. Most people live by fishing and farming. Cashew nuts are the main crop.

Area 13,945 sq. mi. (36,120 sq km)
Country population 1,403,569
Capital city (pop) Bissau (408,627)
Official language Portuguese
Currency CFA franc

Burkina Faso

Burkina Faso is an inland country in West Africa that was called Upper Volta. About 90 percent of people work on the land. It has the lowest literacy rate in the world.

Area 105,870 sq. mi. (274,200 sq km)
Country population 14,337,906
Capital city (pop) Ouagadougou (1,286,529)
Official language French
Currency CFA Franc

Ghana

Ghana was a British colony, but in 1957 it became the first African country to become independent. It contains Lake Volta, the world's largest artificial lake, and it is one of the world's top 10 gold producers.

Area 92,455 sq. mi. (239,460 sq km)
Country population 23,428,820
Capital city (pop) Accra (3,905,009)
Official language English
Currency Cedi

Liberia

The West African country of Liberia was founded by freed U.S. slaves. It has been independent since 1847. Its president is Africa's first elected female head of state.

Area 43,000 sq. mi. (111,370 sq km)
Country population 3,283,000
Capital city (pop) Monrovia (1,690,270)
Official language English
Currency Liberian dollar

Benin

The African country of Benin became fully independent from France in 1960. It now has a thriving tourist industry, which provides much-needed money.

Area 43,485 sq. mi. (112,620 sq km)
Country population 8,052,780
Capital city (pop) Porto Novo (250,262)
Official language French
Currency CFA Franc

Transporting dried grasses by river in Chad

Chad

The Sahara desert covers much of Chad. Since gaining independence from France in 1960, it has suffered conflict with its neighbor Libya. Oil has been found in Chad and is now being exported. Most of its people work on the land.

Area 495,755 sq. mi. (1,284,000 sq km)
Country population 8,988,735
Capital city (pop) N'Djamena (1,518,988)
Official languages Arabic/French
Currency CFA Franc

Republic of Congo

The region of Middle Congo became independent from France in 1960 and was renamed the Republic of Congo. The country has large oil deposits and is one of Africa's largest producers of petroleum. It also produces zinc, lead, gold and diamonds.

Area 132,045 sq. mi. (342,000 sq km)
Country population 3,702,311
Capital city (pop) Brazzaville (1,180,176)
Official language French
Currency CFA franc

Cameroon

Cameroon in West Africa became an independent republic in 1972. It has good natural resources, including bauxite and aluminum, and grows crops such as cocoa, coffee and rubber.

Area 183,570 sq. mi. (475,440 sq km)
Country population 19,018,638
Capital city (pop) Yaoundé (2,075,562)
Official languages French/English
Currency CFA Franc

Côte d'Ivoire

Côte d'Ivoire became independent from France in 1960. It was a peaceful, prosperous African country until its first military coup in 1999. Trouble then began between rebels and the government, which is still going on.

Area 124,500 sq. mi. (322,460 sq km)
Country population 20,794,345
Capital city (pop) Yamoussoukro (226,994)
Official language French
Currency CFA Franc

Sierra Leone

Sierra Leone became independent from Britain in 1971. Between 1991–2002 the country was in a state of civil war. Many thousands of people were killed and thousands more were forced to move from their homes. Sierra Leone has diamond and gold deposits, but its political problems have made it one of the world's poorest countries, along with Somalia and East Timor. Unemployment is high and about three-quarters of its people live on less than U.S. $2 a day.

Area 27,700 sq. mi. (71,740 sq km)
Country population 5,226,221
Capital city (pop) Freetown (819,634)
Official language English
Currency Leone

Traditional woven baskets from the Republic of Congo

São Tomé and Príncipe

The islands of São Tomé and Príncipe lie on the Equator in the Gulf of Guinea and make up Africa's smallest country. Cocoa is the main crop, but São Tomé and Príncipe has other potential sources of income, such as newly discovered oil.

Area 387 sq. mi. (1,001 sq km)
Country population 157,847
Capital city (pop) São Tomé (62,531)
Official language Portuguese
Currency Dobra

Gabon

Gabon has a small population and good oil and mineral reserves. It is one of Africa's richest nations. However, many of its people are very poor because its wealth has been mismanaged and is unequally distributed.

Area 103,346 sq. mi. (267,667 sq km)
Country population 1,725,105
Capital city (pop) Libreville (713,167)
Official language French
Currency CFA franc

Central African Republic

The Central African Republic is a landlocked country in central Africa. It became independent from France in 1960. Since then there have been almost constant political problems and it is now a very poor country. It exports some lumber and diamonds, but most people work on the land.

Area 240,536 sq. mi. (622,984 sq km)
Country population 3,347,188
Capital city (pop) Bangui (752,914)
Official language French
Currency CFA Franc

Togo

Togo was the French territory of Togoland until it became independent in 1960. More than half the people work on the land. Cotton, coffee and cocoa are the main exports. Nearly one third of the people are very poor.

Area 21,924 sq. mi. (56,785 sq km)
Country population 5,582,583
Capital city (pop) Lomé (828,228)
Official language French
Currency CFA franc

Democratic Republic of Congo

The Democratic Republic of Congo, which was called Zaire, is Africa's third-largest country. In 2003 a five-year struggle between government forces and rebels ended, and since then it has been fairly peaceful. The country has good natural resources but has been very poor since the war.

Area 905,565 sq. mi. (2,345,410 sq km)
Country population 64,105,984
Capital city (pop) Kinshasa (9,166,685)
Official language French
Currency Congolese franc

Equatorial Guinea

Equatorial Guinea is made up of five islands and part of the African mainland. It became independent from Spain in 1968 and is one of the smallest countries in Africa. Many people work on the land, but gas and oil have been found and so the country is becoming wealthier.

Area 10,831 sq. mi. (28,051 sq km)
Country population 540,109
Capital city (pop) Malabo (170,964)
Official languages Spanish/French
Currency CFA franc

Rare mountain gorilla in the Democratic Republic of Congo

Namibia

Namibia became independent from South Africa in 1990. The country often suffers from drought so much of its food has to be imported from other countries. Namibia is an important producer of diamonds, but the wealth from this is unevenly distributed. Half of all Namibians are living in poverty.

Area 318,696 sq. mi. (825,418 sq km)
Country population 2,128,560
Capital city (pop) Windhoek (296,366)
Official language English
Currency Namibian dollar

Rwanda

Rwanda is a densely populated country in Central Africa. It is still suffering the effects of a civil war that began in 1990 and lasted for four years. At least 60 percent of the people live in poverty.

Area 10,169 sq. mi. (26,338 sq km)
Country population 8,995,038
Capital city (pop) Kigali (904,779)
Official languages Kinyarwanda/French/English
Currency Rwanda franc

Angola

Angola became independent from Portugal in 1975. Since then, there has been a civil war almost all the time. The country has valuable oil and diamond deposits, but has many financial problems.

Area 481,355 sq. mi. (1,246,700 sq km)
Country population 16,853,679
Capital city (pop) Luanda (2,524,459)
Official language Portuguese
Currency Kwanza

Uganda

Uganda is a landlocked West African nation on the shores of Lake Victoria. It is now a fairly peaceful country, after a devastating civil war and a military dictatorship. The land is fertile and it has natural resources, but Uganda is still being held back by a large international debt.

Area 91,135 sq. mi. (236,040 sq km)
Country population 29,395,836
Capital city (pop) Kampala (1,805,077)
Official language English
Currency Uganda shilling

Burundi

Burundi gained independence in the 1960s. Since then it has been devastated by fighting between the two main tribes, the Hutus and the Tutsis. Burundi lies between the politically troubled countries of Rwanda and the Democratic Republic of Congo, and is being held back by uncertainty over its future.

Area 10,745 sq. mi. (27,830 sq km)
Country population 8,731,814
Capital city (pop) Bujumbura (360,278)
Official languages Kirundi/French
Currency Burundi franc

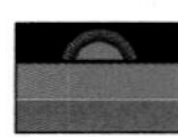

Malawi

In 1964, the British territory of Nyasaland in southeastern Africa became Malawi, which is an independent republic. The country has had many natural disasters and depends on aid from other countries. About 15 percent of the adult population has HIV or AIDS, and Malawi now has one of the world's lowest life expectancies.

Area 45,745 sq. mi. (118,480 sq km)
Country population 13,444,359
Capital city (pop) Lilongwe (866,272)
Official languages Chichewa/English
Currency Kwacha

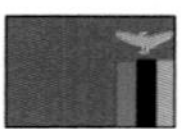

Zambia

The landlocked country of Zambia in Central Africa has a small population. Copper is its chief export, but demand for copper has fallen and Zambia is now one of the world's poorest countries. Almost 90 percent of its people live on less than U.S. $1 a day.

Area 290,586 sq. mi. (752,614 sq km)
Country population 12,450,229
Capital city (pop) Lusaka (2,679,083)
Official language English
Currency Kwacha

Swaziland

Swaziland is one of the world's few absolute monarchies — political parties were banned by the king in 1973. The country relies on South Africa for trade. About 40 percent of the people live on less than U.S. $1 a day. It has one of the highest levels of HIV/AIDS in the world and the world's lowest life expectancy.

Area 6,704 sq. mi. (17,363 sq km)
Country population 1,194,882
Capital city (pop) Mbabane (82,887)
Official languages English/Swazi
Currency Lilangeni

Lesotho

The Kingdom of Lesotho was once called Basutoland and became independent from the U.K. in 1966. It is entirely surrounded by South Africa. Lesotho has diamond mines but few other resources. Most people work on the land or in South African mines.

Area 11,720 sq. mi. (30,355 sq km)
Country population 1,884,897
Capital city (pop) Maseru (240,663)
Official languages Sotho/English
Currency Loti

Tanzania

Tanzania is made up of the country that used to be called Tanganyika on the eastern African mainland, and the island of Zanzibar, which is in the Indian Ocean just off the coast of Tanganyika. The two nations joined in 1964 after becoming independent. The country contains Lake Victoria, Mount Kilimanjaro and Serengeti National Park.

Area 364,900 sq. mi. (945,087 sq km)
Country population 40,120,715
Capital city (pop) Dodoma (203,999)
Official languages Swahili/English
Currency Tanzanian shilling

Botswana

Botswana used to be called the British Protectorate of Bechuanaland, but in 1966 it became an independent Commonwealth republic. It is now one of the wealthiest countries in Africa. Botswana has many natural resources and is one of the world's largest producers of diamonds. However, around one-third of the population has HIV/AIDS.

Area 231,805 sq. mi. (600,370 sq km)
Country population 1,914,815
Capital city (pop) Gaborone (224,990)
Official language English
Currency Pula

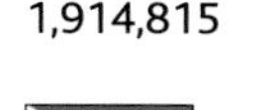

Zimbabwe

Zimbabwe was previously the British colony of Rhodesia. It used to be a fairly well-off country, but since 2000 has suffered a series of political problems and upsets. Zimbabweans now have an extremely low standard of living: one-third have HIV/AIDS and 70 percent live in poverty.

Area 150,805 sq. mi. (390,580 sq km)
Country population 12,352,402
Capital city (pop) Harare (2,999,481)
Official language English
Currency Zimbabwe dollar

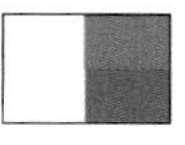

Madagascar

Madagascar is in the Indian Ocean off the coast of Africa. It is the fourth-largest island in the world. More than 80 percent of people work on the land. The country has often suffered natural disasters. In 2000 most of its rice crop was destroyed by cyclones.

Area 226,655 sq. mi. (587,040 sq km)
Country population 18,622,208
Capital city (pop) Antananarivo (1,699,114)
Official languages Malagasy/French
Currency Malagasy franc

Mauritius

Mauritius is a group of islands in the Indian Ocean. It has a stable government, and Mauritians have high incomes. The country exports sugar cane and has a thriving tourist industry. It is home to some of the world's rarest plants and animals.

Area 790 sq. mi. (2,040 sq km)
Country population 1,261,926
Capital city (pop) Port Louis (637,324)
Official languages English/French
Currency Mauritius rupee

Women of the Samburu tribe in Kenya performing a traditional dance

Kenya

Kenya lies on the Equator on the east coast of Africa. It has some of the most fertile land in Africa, and 75 percent of the people work in farming. It is also one of Africa's most popular tourist destinations.

Area 224,962 sq. mi. (582,650 sq km)
Country population 35,527,559
Capital city (pop) Nairobi (3,988,257)
Official languages Swahili/English
Currency Kenya shilling

Mozambique

Mozambique used to be a Portuguese colony. It gained independence in 1975, became a republic in 1990, and held its first free elections in 1994. About 70 percent of its people live in poverty. But since the beginning of the 21st century, things have begun to improve and other countries have started to invest in Mozambique.

Area 309,495 sq. mi. (801,590 sq km)
Country population 21,000,335
Capital city (pop) Maputo (1,994,900)
Official language Portuguese
Currency Metical

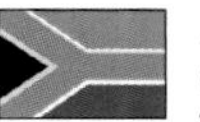

South Africa

South Africa lies on the southern tip of the continent. Until 1994 the country was ruled by its white minority and had an apartheid policy. This segregated the races — kept black and white apart — and denied black citizens the vote. Because of this many other countries refused to trade with South Africa. The African National Congress won South Africa's first inclusive elections in 1994, and it has been in power ever since.

Area 471,011 sq. mi. (1,219,912 sq km)
Country population 48,394,880
Capital city (pop) The seat of government is Tshwane (Pretoria) (2,253,260); the seat of the legislature is Cape Town (4,715,046); the seat of the judiciary is Bloemfontein (495,006)
Official languages There are 11 official languages: Afrikaans, English, Ndebele, Pedi, Sotho, Swazi, Tsonga, Tswana, Venda, Xhosa, Zulu
Currency Rand

Mount Kilimanjaro, Tanzania, is the highest mountain in Africa.

Yemeni women in traditional veils

Israel

After World War II, Israel was created in Palestine as a homeland for Jews. When Great Britain left the area in 1948 the State of Israel was proclaimed, and there was immediate conflict between the Jewish settlers and the Arabs who were living there. The State of Israel gained a great deal of land in the conflict, and many Palestinians were made homeless. There have been many attempts to make peace between the two sides, but the conflict continues.

Area 8,020 sq. mi. (20,770 sq km)
Country population 7,325,999
Capital city (pop) Jerusalem (750,892) Jerusalem is the seat of government but is not recognized as the capital by the UN because East Jerusalem is part of the Occupied Territories captured in 1967. The UN considers Tel Aviv (1,117,842) to be the capital.
Official languages Hebrew/Arabic
Currency Shekel

Yemen

In 1990 North and South Yemen were formally joined as the Republic of Yemen after years of conflict. Yemen is a poor country, affected by drought, political problems and a fast-growing population.

Area 203,850 sq. mi. (527,970 sq km)
Country population 21,175,675
Capital city (pop) Sana'a' (2,304,663)
Official language Arabic
Currency Riyal

Turkey

Turkey is in a key position between Europe and Asia. The territory west of the Bosphorus strait is in Europe, while the much larger area to the east is in Asia. Turkey is popular with tourists, and between seven and ten million people every year visit its coastline and the historic city of Istanbul.

Area 301,385 sq. mi. (780,580 sq km)
Country population 76,375,182
Capital city (pop) Ankara (3,714,056)
Official language Turkish
Currency Turkish lir

Syria

Syria has been home to some of the world's oldest civilizations, and Damascus is probably the oldest city in the world. Syria became independent from France in 1946. Its people come from many different ethnic groups and religions, including Arabs, Kurds, Assyrians and Armenians, and Muslims, Christians and Jews.

Area 71,500 sq. mi. (185,180 sq km)
Country population 19,989,814
Capital city (pop) Damascus (2,688,278)
Official language Arabic
Currency Syrian pound

Kazakhstan

Kazakhstan is an enormous, landlocked nation almost four times the size of Texas. It was part of the former Soviet Union. Kazakhstan is rich in minerals and fossil fuels, including oil, coal, natural gas, gold, silver and lead.

Area 1,049,155 sq. mi. (2,717,300 sq km)
Country population 15,663,189
Capital city (pop) Astana (389,189)
Official language Kazakh
Currency Tenge

United Arab Emirates

The UAE is a group of seven Middle Eastern states and is one of the wealthiest countries in the region. It used to be a very poor country where most people lived by fishing, but is now the Gulf's third-largest oil producer.

Area 32,280 sq. mi. (83,600 sq km)
Country population 5,402,375
Capital city (pop) Abu Dhabi (859,749)
Official language Arabic
Currency UAE dirham

The Burj Al Arab hotel in Dubai, United Arab Emirates

Kuwait

Kuwait has large oil reserves that make up more than 8 percent of the world's total. The country's economy was almost destroyed when Iraqi forces invaded in 1990 and burned oil wells as they retreated. The Kuwaiti government has spent billions of dollars on repairs, and oil production is now higher than it was before the invasion.

Area 6,880 sq. mi. (17,820 sq km)
Country population 2,906,764
Capital city (pop) Kuwait City (2,394,046)
Official language Arabic
Currency Kuwaiti dinar

Jordan

Jordan shares borders with Syria, Israel, the West Bank, Saudi Arabia and Iraq. Despite the problems of its neighbors the country is relatively peaceful. It doesn't have many natural resources, and its vital supplies of Iraqi oil were halted by the Iraq war of 2003.

Area 35,635 sq. mi. (92,300 sq km)
Country population 5,913,809
Capital city (pop) Amman (1,135,733)
Official language Arabic
Currency Jordanian dina

Saudi Arabia

Saudi Arabia is a monarchy. It is ruled by the sons and grandsons of Abdul Aziz ibn Saud, who founded the kingdom. Saudi Arabia is one of the richest countries in the Middle East. It has the largest reserves of petroleum in the world and exports more than any other country. It is about the same size as Western Europe and includes an area called the Empty Quarter, the world's largest sand desert. Saudi Arabia is a Muslim country and includes the city of Mecca (or Makkah). This was the birthplace of the Prophet Muhammad and millions of Muslims make a pilgrimage there every year.

Area 830,000 sq. mi. (2,149,690 sq km)
Country population 24,686,696
Capital city (pop) Riyadh (4,606,888)
Official language Arabic
Currency Saudi riyal

Iran

Iran is a mountainous Middle Eastern country. Until 1935 it was known as Persia. It shares borders with several of the world's most troubled nations, including Iraq, Afghanistan and Pakistan. This discourages investment from other countries and tourism, and Iran's economy depends on oil.

Area 636,295 sq. mi. (1,648,000 sq km)
Country population 71,028,973
Capital city (pop) Tehran (12,664,286)
Official language Farsi
Currency Rial

Iraq

Iraq has had a violent recent history. From 1979 to 2003, Iraq was controlled by the dictator President Saddam Hussein. The U.S., supported by countries including the U.K., Spain, Australia, Poland and Denmark, removed Hussein from power in 2003. Hussein was executed in 2006, but conflict continues in Iraq.

Area 168,754 sq. mi. (437,072 sq km)
Country population 27,141,340
Capital city (pop) Baghdad (10,634,225)
Official language Arabic
Currency New Iraqi dinar

Lebanon

Lebanon is a small country bordering the Mediterranean Sea. It became independent from France in 1943. Since Lebanon's civil war of 1975–91 huge sums have been spent on rebuilding the country and it is heavily in debt.

Area 4,015 sq. mi. (10,400 sq km)
Country population 4,602,431
Capital city (pop) Beirut (1,987,173)
Official language Arabic
Currency Lebanese pound

The GUM department store, Moscow, Russia

Russia

The Russian Federation is the largest country in the world, almost twice the size of the United States. It stretches from Europe to Asia and covers 13 percent of the world's total land area. Russia was the chief republic of the former Soviet Union, which in 1991 was split into 15 separate republics. Oil, natural gas, lumber and metals make up more than 80 percent of its exports. The country is still held back by poor transport and other systems. It also suffers from violent conflict in the Chechnya region.

Area 6,592,772 sq. mi. (17,075,200 sq km)
Country population 141,833,475
Capital city (pop) Moscow (14,744,150)
Official language Russian
Currency Ruble

Bahrain

The island state of Bahrain is 20 mi. (32 km) off the east coast of Saudi Arabia. Oil is its main source of income, but the country is also a center for offshore banking.

Area 257 sq. mi. (665 sq km)
Country population 788,873
Capital city (pop) Manama (668,089)
Official language Arabic
Currency Bahraini dinar

Qatar

Qatar became independent from Britain in 1971 and has changed from being a poor country dependent on pearl fishing to one of the Gulf's richest states. It has large reserves of oil and gas, which have brought great wealth.

Area 4,416 sq. mi. (11,437 sq km)
Country population 928,404
Capital city (pop) Doha (761,019)
Official language Arabic
Currency Qatar riyal

Oman

Oman borders Yemen, Saudi Arabia and the United Arab Emirates so is in a key position for the transportation of oil. Oil makes up more than 80 percent of Oman's exports, but the government wants to encourage tourism and information technology.

Area 82,030 sq. mi. (212,460 sq km)
Country population 2,721,576
Capital city (pop) Muscat (1,090,797)
Official language Arabic
Currency Omani rial

Kyrgyzstan

Kyrgyzstan is a picturesque country of mountains, glaciers and lakes. It became independent from the former Soviet Union in 1991. Since then it has seen many political changes.

Area 76,640 sq. mi. (198,500 sq km)
Country population 5,285,799
Capital city (pop) Bishkek (914,932)
Official languages Kyrgyz/Russian
Currency Som

Tajikistan

Tajikistan lies west of China in Central Asia. It was part of the former Soviet Union. About 50,000 people died in the civil war of 1992–97 and the country is still violent and unsettled.

Area 55,250 sq. mi. (143,100 sq km)
Country population 7,350,401
Capital city (pop) Dushanbe (937,445)
Official language Tajik
Currency Somoni

Bhutan

The mountainous kingdom of Bhutan lies between Tibet (China) and India in the eastern Himalayas. Its main exports are rice, machinery and diesel oil, but tourism is also important.

Area 18,145 sq. mi. (47,000 sq km)
Country population 2,671,887
Capital city (pop) Thimphu (79,185)
Official language Dzongkha
Currency Ngultrum

Afghanistan

Afghanistan is a mountainous country in Central Asia. It has been through more than 20 years of political upheaval. The country was controlled by the Taliban from 1996 until 2001, when the Taliban was overthrown by an alliance led by the U.S. military. At present many people are involved in the drug trade and over one million of the population may be close to starvation.

Area 250,000 sq. mi. (647,500 sq km)
Country population 23,725,835
Capital city (pop) Kabul (2,436,111)
Official languages Dari (Persian)/Pashto
Currency Afghani

Mongolia

Mongolia is a landlocked nation between Russia and China. It is three times the size of France and is a land of deserts, grasslands, forests and mountains. Temperatures range from summer highs of 104°F (40°C) in the Gobi Desert to –40°F (–40°C) during the winter. More than half the population are nomads — they move from place to place with their livestock. Gers (movable tentlike huts) are the most common form of shelter, even in cities.

Area 603,908 sq. mi. (1,564,116 sq km)
Country population 2,644,595
Capital city (pop) Ulaanbaatar (881,218)
Official language Khalkha Mongolian
Currency Tugrik

India

India is the largest democratic country in the world. It became independent from the U.K. in 1947 when it was divided into India and Pakistan. This division has led to three wars. India has the world's largest population, after China. In 1999 its population passed the one billion mark. Most people still live by farming and around 70 percent of the population live in rural areas. India has a booming information technology industry and one of the most successful film industries in the world.

Area 1,269,345 sq. mi. (3,287,590 sq km)
Country population 1,152,342,278
Capital city (pop) New Delhi (18,362,625)
Official languages Hindi/English
Currency Indian rupee

Turkmenistan

Turkmenistan borders the Caspian Sea in Central Asia. About 90 percent of its land is desert. It has the fifth-largest oil and natural gas reserves in the world, but is crippled by debt to other countries.

Area 188,455 sq. mi. (488,100 sq km)
Country population 7,193,046
Capital city (pop) Ashgabat (891,879)
Official languages Turkmen
Currency Manat

Pakistan

Pakistan was created in 1947 as a home for Indian Muslims. It was divided into Pakistan and Bangladesh in 1972. The country is in dispute with India over ownership of the state of Kashmir. This has led to fears of an arms race, as both countries are believed to have nuclear weapons.

Area 310,405 sq. mi. (803,940 sq km)
Country population 155,360,000
Capital city (pop) Islamabad (657,788)
Official language Urdu
(Punjabi is the most commonly used language, and English is used in business, government and higher education)
Currency Pakistan rupee

Sri Lanka

Sri Lanka was called Ceylon until 1948, when it became independent from the UK. It is a tropical island in the Indian Ocean, only 12 mi. (20 km) from the south coast of India. The country has textile, food processing and telecommunications industries. It is held back, however, by nearly 20 years of conflict between some of its people, the Tamils, who want independence, and the government.

Area 25,330 sq. mi. (65,610 sq km)
Country population 20,293,522
Capital city (pop) Colombo (2,588,148)
Official language Sinhala
Currency Sri Lankan rupee

Nepal

Nepal is home to Mt. Everest, the world's highest mountain, and tourism brings vital money into the country. In 2001, Nepal's Crown Prince murdered 10 members of the royal family before taking his own life.

Area 56,827 sq. mi. (147,181 sq km)
Country population 26,942,600
Capital city (pop) Kathmandu (1,611,647)
Official language Nepali
Currency Nepalese rupee

Yak train making its way over the Khumbu glacier, Nepal

China

China is one of the oldest civilizations in the world and has the oldest continuously used language system. It also is home to the world's largest population. The economy of China is growing rapidly and it is now the world's fifth-largest exporter of goods. Tourism has also become a major industry.

Area 3,705,405 sq. mi. (9,596,960 sq km)
Country population 1,313,552,038
Capital city (pop) Beijing (11,941,418)
Official language Mandarin Chinese
Currency Renminbi (also known as the yuan)

Taiwan

The island of Taiwan lies 95 mi. (150 km) from mainland China. Taiwan has a thriving electronics industry. It is one of the world's leading producers of computer technology. Taiwan is home to the world's tallest building, the Taipei 101.

Area 13,890 sq. mi. (35,980 sq km)
Country population 23,195,487
Capital city (pop) Taipei (8,366,945)
Official language Chinese
Currency New Taiwan dollar

Uzbekistan

Uzbekistan has the largest population in Central Asia. It has been independent of the Soviet Union since 1991. It is the second largest exporter of cotton in the world and has mineral deposits. However, its people are poor because the wealth is distributed unequally.

Area 172,740 sq. mi. (447,400 sq km)
Country population 27,363,389
Capital city (pop) Tashkent (3,247,012)
Official language Uzbek
Currency Som

Bangladesh

Bangladesh won independence from Pakistan in 1971. About 70 percent of the people work in farming and the country produces all its own food. The main industries include cotton, tea, leather, sugar and natural gas, and its leading export is clothing.

Area 55,600 sq. mi. (144,000 sq km)
Country population 143,481,419
Capital city (pop) Dhaka (13,240,743)
Official language Bengali
Currency Taka

North Korea

North Korea is one of the world's few remaining Communist states. As many as three million North Koreans have probably died of starvation because of famine and financial mishandling, while the regime spends money on military equipment. North Korea's nuclear program threatens the international food aid that keeps the population going at present.

Area 46,540 sq. mi. (120,540 sq km)
Country population 23,708,186
Capital city (pop) Pyongyang (3,128,617)
Official language Korean
Currency Won

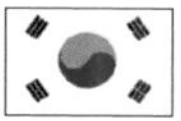

South Korea

During the three-year Korean War in 1953, North Korea attacked the South with Chinese support. The Korean Peninsula was then divided into two. South Korea is a democratic country and has a thriving, high-tech economy and a growing tourism industry.

Area 38,023 sq. mi. (98,480 sq km)
Country population 48,426,195
Capital city (pop) Seoul (22,254,620)
Official language Korean
Currency Won

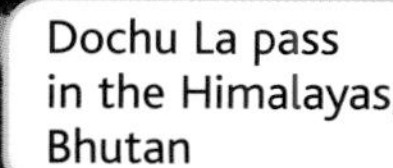

Dochu La pass in the Himalayas, Bhutan

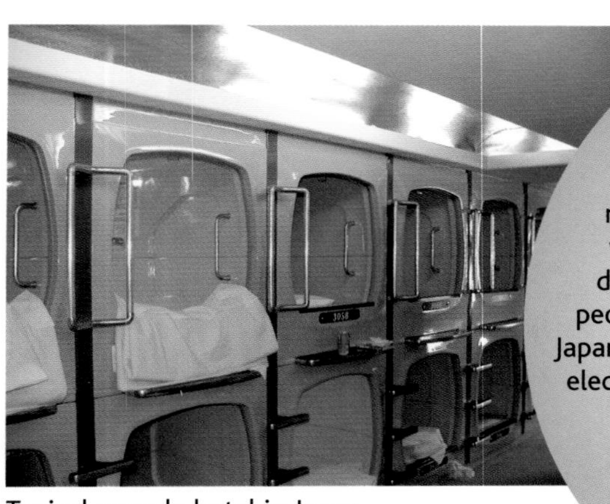
Typical capsule hotel in Japan

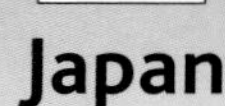

Japan

Japan is made up of four large islands and many smaller islands. This mountainous and volcanic country is one of the world's most densely populated places, and there are more people in Tokyo than any other city in the world. Japan is a wealthy country and a world leader in the electronics, robotics and car production industries.

Area 145,880 sq. mi. (377,835 sq km)
Country population 127,939,307
Capital city (pop) Tokyo (37,203,122)
Official language Japanese
Currency Yen

Myanmar

Myanmar used to be called Burma. The country is ruled by an undemocratic military government and has been accused by foreign governments of severe human rights abuses. It may also be a major producer of heroin. These things have led the U.S. and the European Union to limit trade with the country.

Area 261,970 sq. mi. (678,500 sq km)
Country population 56,950,062
Capital city (pop) Rangoon (4,886,305)
Official language Burmese
Currency Kyat

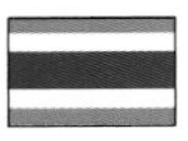

Thailand

Until 1939, Thailand was called Siam. It is the only country in Southeast Asia never to have been under the control of a European power. About 10 million tourists visit Bangkok and the country's beautiful coasts each year. Farming is important and about half the people still work on the land.

Area 198,455 sq. mi. (514,000 sq km)
Country population 63,629,485
Capital city (pop) Bangkok (9,791,333)
Official language Thai
Currency Baht

Laos

Laos is a landlocked, mountainous country bordered by China, Vietnam, Cambodia, Thailand and Myanmar. It is one of the world's last remaining Communist states. Laos is popular with adventurous tourists, but it is extremely primitive. There are few paved roads and no railways.

Area 91,430 sq. mi. (236,800 sq km)
Country population 5,931,809
Capital city (pop) Vientiane (206,211)
Official language Lao
Currency Kip

Malaysia

Malaysia is made up of two regions, separated by about 640 mi. (1,030 km) of the South China Sea. The country used to rely on farming and exports of raw materials, but it is now a leading producer and exporter of high-tech electronic merchandise.

Area 127,315 sq. mi. (329,750 sq km)
Country population 27,737,693
Capital city (pop) Kuala Lumpur (7,239,871)
Official language Bahasa Malaysia (Malay)
Currency Malaysian dollar (Ringgit)

Singapore

The city state of Singapore in Southeast Asia is one of the richest nations in the world. Its people have one of the world's highest standards of living. Singapore's thriving manufacturing industry includes shipbuilding and electronics.

Area 267 sq. mi. (693 sq km)
Country population 4,974,232
Official languages Malay/Mandarin/Tamil/English
Currency Singapore dollar

The Philippines

The Philippines is made up of more than 7,000 islands in Southeast Asia. More than 80 percent of the population is Roman Catholic — the Philippines is the only Asian nation that is mainly Christian. It suffers from natural disasters, such as volcanic eruptions and typhoons, as well as a very high birth rate. Many Filipinos go to work abroad and their country depends on the U.S. $6 billion–7 billion they send home each year.

Area 115,830 sq. mi (.300,000 sq km)
Country population 90,317,981
Capital city (pop) Manila (19,195,048)
Official languages Filipino/English
Currency Philippine peso

Vietnam

North and South Vietnam were rejoined in 1976 after 30 years of war. At first the war was between the Communists and the French colonialists, and later between the Communist North Vietnam and the South, which was supported by the U.S. Nearly four million people died and much of Vietnam's landscape was destroyed. There is now a Communist socialist government. Vietnam is now one of the world's leading rice exporters, and the country's oil production has increased.

Area 127,245 sq. mi. (329,560 sq km)
Country population 86,240,477
Capital city (pop) Hanoi (2,686,290)
Official language Vietnamese
Currency Dong

Villamendhoo Island in the Maldives

East Timor

East Timor became independent from Indonesia in 2002. It is Southeast Asia's youngest nation and the world's newest democracy. East Timor is a very poor country and often suffers floods.

Area 5,794 sq. mi. (15,007 sq km)
Country population 969,816
Capital city (pop) Dili (170,490)
Official languages Portuguese/Tetum
Currency U.S. dollar

Brunei

Brunei gained full independence from Great Britain in 1984. It is ruled by the Sultan, whose family have reigned for six centuries. Brunei is enormously wealthy because of its natural gas and oil fields.

Area 2,230 sq. mi. (5,770 sq km)
Country population 406,849
Capital city (pop) Bandar Seri Begawan (32,331)
Official language Malay
Currency Brunei dollar

The Comoros

The Comoros is a group of volcanic islands between Madagascar and Mozambique. It is one of the world's poorest countries. The Comoros has few natural resources. It exports vanilla, cloves and essential oils, but depends on aid from other countries.

Area 838 sq. mi. (2,170 sq km)
Country population 626,930
Capital city (pop) Moroni (47,040)
Official languages Arabic/French
Currency Comorian franc

Seychelles

The Seychelles is made up of 155 islands in the Indian Ocean, east of mainland Africa. It became independent from Great Britain in 1976. About 90 percent of the islands' people live on the main island of Mahé and are reasonably well off, thanks to successful tourism and tuna fishing industries.

Area 176 sq. mi. (455 sq km)
Country population 86,200
Capital city (pop) Victoria (22,198)
Official languages English/French/Creole
Currency Seychelles rupee

Traditional wayang golek wooden puppets from Indonesia

Indonesia

Indonesia includes more than 17,000 islands. The world's largest Muslim population lives on about 6,000 of these. Indonesia is rich in minerals, and it exports petroleum, textiles, lumber, natural gas and rubber. There are frequent natural disasters.

Area 741,100 sq. mi. (1,919,440 sq km)
Country population 227,070,492
Capital city (pop) Jakarta (18,588,548)
Official languages Indonesian/Bahasa
Currency Rupiah

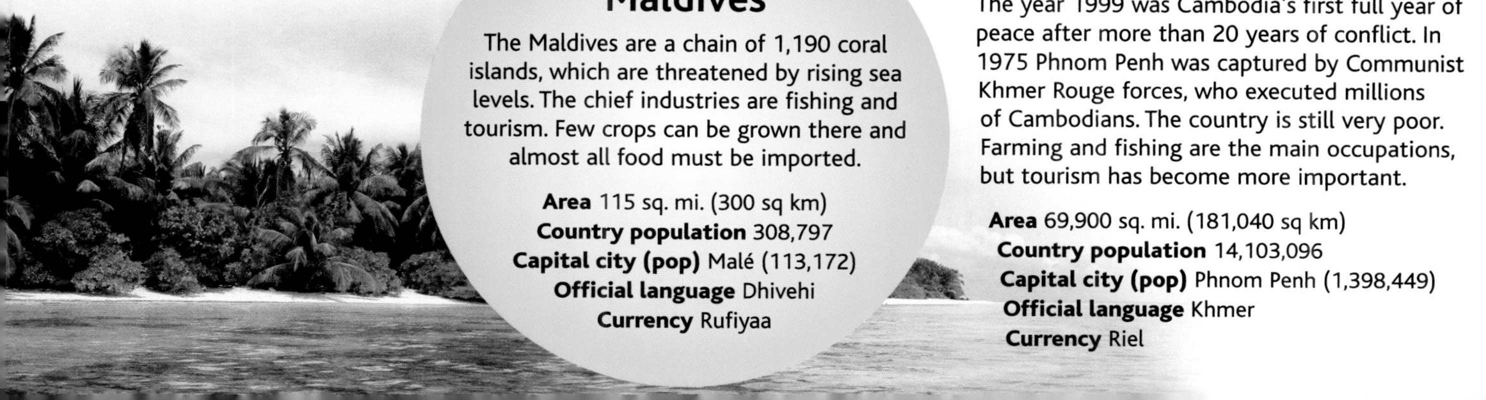

Maldives

The Maldives are a chain of 1,190 coral islands, which are threatened by rising sea levels. The chief industries are fishing and tourism. Few crops can be grown there and almost all food must be imported.

Area 115 sq. mi. (300 sq km)
Country population 308,797
Capital city (pop) Malé (113,172)
Official language Dhivehi
Currency Rufiyaa

Cambodia

The year 1999 was Cambodia's first full year of peace after more than 20 years of conflict. In 1975 Phnom Penh was captured by Communist Khmer Rouge forces, who executed millions of Cambodians. The country is still very poor. Farming and fishing are the main occupations, but tourism has become more important.

Area 69,900 sq. mi. (181,040 sq km)
Country population 14,103,096
Capital city (pop) Phnom Penh (1,398,449)
Official language Khmer
Currency Riel

Papua New Guinea

Papua New Guinea is made up of many small islands and one half of New Guinea, the world's second-largest island. It has mineral deposits such as gold and copper, as well as oil and natural gas. It has been difficult to fully exploit these because the country lacks good roads and transport, and there are large areas of rainforest.

Area 178,705 sq. mi. (462,840 sq km)
Country population 6,315,896
Capital city (pop) Port Moresby (301,817)
Official language English
Currency Kina

Solomon Islands

The Solomon Islands include several densely forested volcanic islands in the South Pacific. People live by farming, forestry and fishing, but since 1998 there has been conflict between different groups in the population. Law and order has broken down, and the islanders' average income has been halved. A peacekeeping force led by Australia arrived in 2003.

Area 10,985 sq. mi. (28,450 sq km)
Country population 506,992
Capital city (pop) Honiara (57,456)
Official language English
Currency Solomon Islands dollar

Kiribati

Kiribati is made up of 33 islands in the Pacific Ocean, halfway between Hawaii and Australia. Kiribati's main exports are coconuts and fish.

Area 313 sq. mi. (811 sq km)
Country population 97,031
Capital city (pop) Tarawa (45,754)
Official language English
Currency Australian dollar

The Olgas, natural rock formations in Australia

Palau

The Republic of Palau is made up of 340 islands in the Pacific Ocean, southeast of the Philippines. It became independent in 1994 and is one of the world's youngest nations. The islands rely mainly on tourism. The waters around Palau are rich in marine life, and visitors come to snorkel and scubadive. The islands also export fish, shellfish and coconuts.

Area 177 sq. mi. (458 sq km)
Country population 20,548
Capital city (pop) Koror (10,650)
Official languages Palauan/English
Currency U.S. dollar

Micronesia

The Federated States of Micronesia is a group of more than 600 islands in the North Pacific Ocean. It gained independence from the U.S. in 1986, but the U.S. has kept the right to have military bases on the islands. This agreement brings Micronesia billions of dollars of financial aid.

Area 271 sq. mi. (702 sq km)
Country population 108,287
Capital city (pop) Palikir (7,321)
Official language English
Currency U.S. dollar

New Zealand

New Zealand lies in the Pacific Ocean, about 1,000 mi. (1,600 km) east of Australia. It is made up of two main islands and several smaller ones. The capital, Wellington, lies further south than any other capital city. New Zealand is mountainous and relatively unspoiled, and is becoming more and more popular with tourists from all over the world.

Area 103,740 sq. mi. (268,680 sq km)
Country population 4,121,662
Capital city (pop) Wellington (364,586)
Official languages English/Maori
Currency New Zealand dollar

A view of the city of Auckland in New Zealand

Australia

Australia was discovered by Captain James Cook in 1770. It became independent in 1931, but it is part of the British Commonwealth and Queen Elizabeth II is the head of state. Australia is the world's sixth-largest country. It has important mineral resources and vast areas are given over to sheep and cattle farming. Some famous landmarks include the Great Barrier Reef and Uluru.

Area 2,967,910 sq. mi. (7,686,850 sq km)
Country population 20,245,629
Capital city (pop) Canberra (329,200)
Official language English
Currency Australian dollar

Tonga

Tonga is a group of 169 islands in the southern Pacific Ocean. It is the only country in the Pacific ruled by a monarchy. The islands have no natural resources and people rely on farming. Tonga exports products such as coconuts, vanilla and yams. Around half of the Tongan people live abroad, particularly in the U.S. and Australasia.

Area 289 sq. mi. (748 sq km)
Country population 101,747
Capital city (pop) Nuku'alofa (23,164)
Official languages Tongan/English
Currency Pa'anga

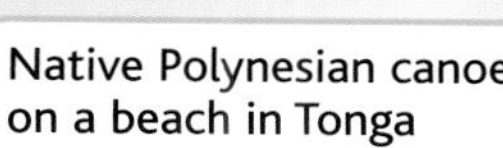

Native Polynesian canoe on a beach in Tonga

Vanuatu

Vanuatu is a chain of 83 volcanic islands in the South Pacific Ocean, between Hawaii and Australia. About 65 percent of the people work on the land, but offshore banking and tourism are growing industries. However, the islands sometimes suffer earthquakes, tsunamis and cyclones, which may limit the growth of tourism.

Area 4,710 sq. mi. (12,200 sq km)
Country population 227,318
Capital city (pop) Port Vila (39,779)
Official languages Bislama/English/French
Currency Vatu

Fiji

Fiji is made up of more than 300 volcanic islands in the South Pacific Ocean, about 1,100 mi. (1,770 km) north of New Zealand. Fiji's main export is sugar cane, and it has a flourishing tourism industry. However, political problems from time to time have discouraged other countries from investing in the islands.

Area 7,055 sq. mi. (18,270 sq km)
Country population 832,390
Capital city (pop) Suva (86,061)
Official languages There is no official language, but the main languages are Fijian and Hindi
Currency Fiji dollar

Nauru

The island of Nauru lies 33 mi. (53 km) south of the Equator in the Pacific Ocean. It is the smallest independent republic in the world. At present, the people have one of the highest incomes per head in the world, thanks to the export of phosphates (fertilizer). However, Nauru's phosphate reserves are running low, and it has few other resources.

Area 8 sq. mi. (21 sq km)
Country population 10,147
Capital city (pop) no official capital
Official languages Nauruan/English
Currency Australian dollar

Samoa

Samoa is a group of islands in the South Pacific Ocean. Samoa's beaches and rainforests have led to a booming tourism industry. This now brings in one-quarter of the islands' income.

Area 1,137 sq. mi. (2,944 sq km)
Country population 188,359
Capital city (pop) Apia (42,141)
Official languages Samoan/English
Currency Tala

Tuvalu

Tuvalu was a British colony until 1975. It is a group of nine coral atolls in the South Pacific Ocean. It is the second-lowest country in the world and is under threat from rising sea levels. Tuvalu has the world's second-smallest population. The country has no known natural resources, and has fewer than 1,000 tourists a year. The islanders rely on exporting fish, stamps and handicrafts, as well as the money sent home from Tuvaluans working abroad.

Area 10 sq. mi. (26 sq km)
Country population 19,916
Capital city (pop) Funafuti (5,008)
Official languages Tuvaluan/English
Currency Australian dollar

Marshall Islands

The Marshall Islands lie in the central Pacific. The islands were occupied by the U.S. after World War II until 1986, and were used for nuclear weapons testing. About half the people work in farming. Coconut oil is the main export.

Area 4,576 sq. mi. (11,854 sq km)
Country population 53,236
Capital city (pop) Dalap-Uliga-Darrit (20,651)
Official languages Marshallese/English
Currency U.S. dollar

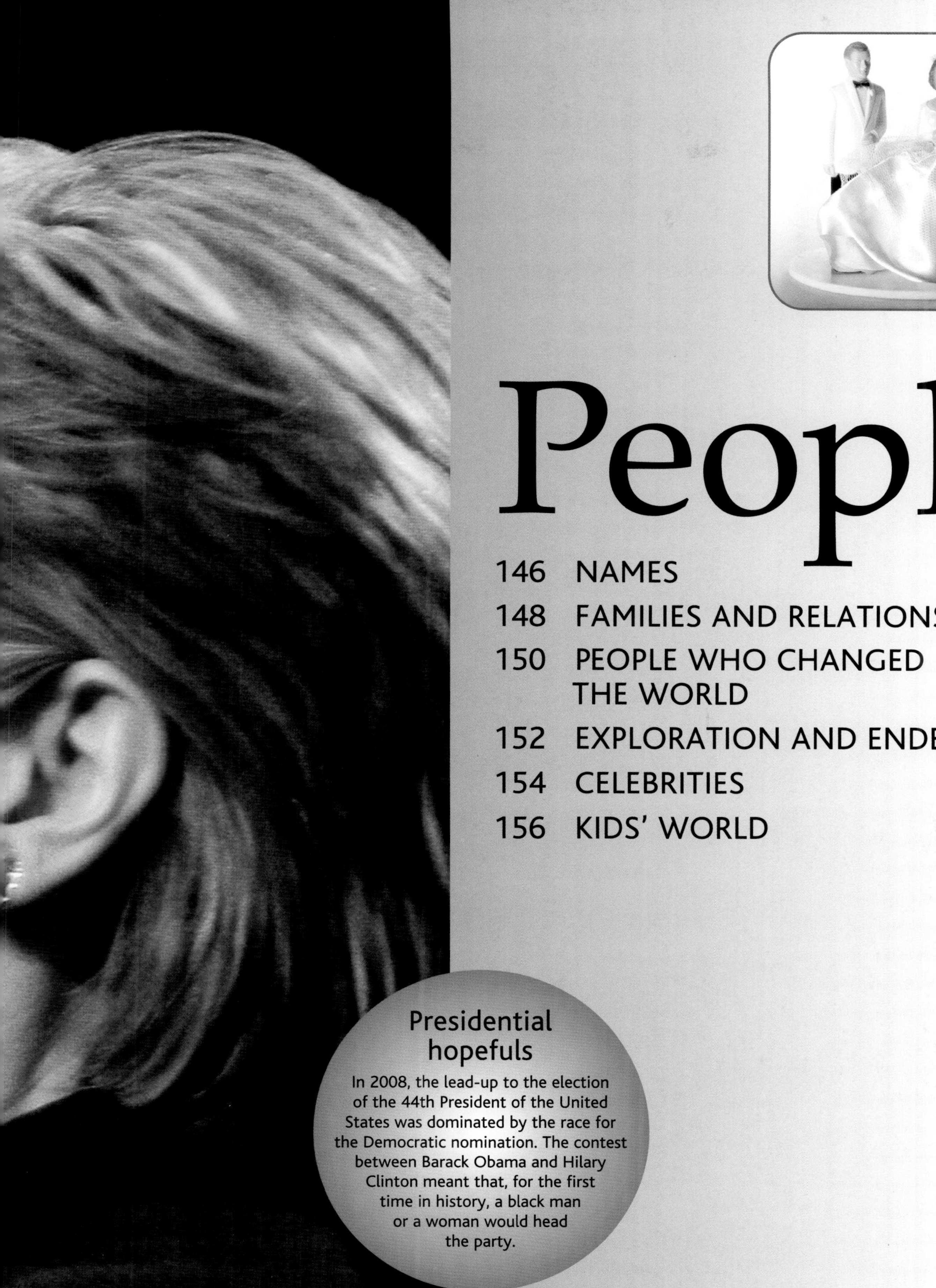

People

146 NAMES

148 FAMILIES AND RELATIONSHIPS

150 PEOPLE WHO CHANGED THE WORLD

152 EXPLORATION AND ENDEAVOR

154 CELEBRITIES

156 KIDS' WORLD

Presidential hopefuls

In 2008, the lead-up to the election of the 44th President of the United States was dominated by the race for the Democratic nomination. The contest between Barack Obama and Hilary Clinton meant that, for the first time in history, a black man or a woman would head the party.

Princes Harry and William: Their names are now two of the favorite boys' names in England and Wales.

Surnames around the world

Surnames were not used in Great Britain until after the Norman Conquest in AD 1066. Until then, most people were known only by their first name. People started to add extra names in order to be able to tell one William from another.

Some surnames came from where a person lived or the person's father's name — so the son of someone called John was known as Johnson. Others were based on a person's occupation (a blacksmith would be called Smith) or their appearance (a brown-haired person might be called Brown). The origins of some surnames have been forgotten.

Popular first names

First name fashions change — especially those for girls. Some traditional names remain popular but new names come into use. Olivia was not in the Top 10 in the United States until 2001, but has kept its popularity. These are the most popular boys and girls names now and 100 years ago in the U.S.

	Girls (current)	Boys (current)	Girls (1908)	Boys (1908)
1	Emily	Jacob	Mary	John
2	Emma	Michael	Helen	William
3	Madison	Joshua	Margaret	James
4	Isabella	Ethan	Ruth	George
5	Ava	Matthew	Anna	Robert
6	Abigail	Daniel	Dorothy	Joseph
7	Olivia	Christopher	Elizabeth	Charles
8	Hannah	Andrew	Mildred	Frank
9	Sophia	Anthony	Alice	Edward
10	Samantha	William	Marie	Thomas

A very long name

Rhoshandiatellyneshiaunneveshenk Koyaanfsquatsiuty Williams, born Beaumont, Texas, September 12, 1984. Soon afterwards, her father James Williams extended her first name to 1,019 letters and the middle name to 36.

Most common surnames

	U.S.	China	Denmark	Eng. & Wales	France	Germany	India	Ireland
1	Smith	Lo	Jensen	Smith	Martin	Müller	Singh	Murphy
2	Johnson	Wáng	Nielsen	Jones	Bernard	Schmidt	Kumar	Kelly
3	Williams	Zhang	Hansen	Williams	Dubois	Schneider	Sharma/Sarma	O'Sullivan
4	Jones	Liú	Pedersen	Taylor	Thomas	Fischer	Patel	Walsh
5	Brown	Chén	Andersen	Brown	Robert	Meyer	Shah	Smith
6	Davis	Yáng	Christensen	Davies	Richard	Weber	Lal	O'Brien
7	Miller	Huáng	Larsen	Evans	Petit	Schulz	Gupta	Byrne
8	Wilson	Zhào	Sørensen	Wilson	Durand	Wagner	Bhat	Ryan
9	Moore	Zou	Rasmussen	Thomas	Leroy	Becker	Rao	O'Connor
10	Taylor	Wú	Jørgensen	Johnson	Moreau	Hoffmann	Reddy	O'Neill

Known by one name

Some people are so famous they are instantly recognizable by just one name.

Aaliyah U.S. singer/actress Aaliyah Haughton, 1979–2001
Barbie U.S. doll Barbara Millicent Roberts, 1959–
Beyoncé U.S. singer Beyoncé Knowles, 1981–
Björk Icelandic singer/actress Björk Gudmundsdóttir, 1965–
Bono Irish rock band U2 singer Paul Hewson, 1960–
Canaletto Italian painter Giovanni Antonio Canale, 1697–1768
Cher U.S. singer Cherilyn Sarkasian, 1946–
Colette French writer Sidonie-Gabrielle Colette, 1873–1954
Dido U.K. singer Dido Armstrong, 1971–
Eminem U.S. rap singer Marshall Mathers, 1972–
Enya Irish singer Eithne ní Bhraonáin, 1961–
Evita Argentinean politician Eva Peron, 1919–52
Flea U.S. Red Hot Chili Peppers bass guitarist Michael Peter Balzary, 1962–
Hergé Belgian Tintin cartoonist Georges Rémi, 1907–83
Houdini U.S. magician Erich Weiss, 1874–1926
Jewel U.S. singer Jewel Kilcher, 1974–
Lulu U.K. singer Marie McDonald McLaughlin, 1948–
Madonna U.S. singer Madonna Louise Ciccone, 1958–
Meatloaf U.S. singer Marvin/Michael Lee Aday, 1947–
Michelangelo Italian painter Michelangelo Buonarroti, 1475–1564
Moby U.S. musician Richard Melville Hall, 1965–
Pelé Brazilian footballer Edson Arantes Nascimento, 1940–
Pink U.S. singer Alecia Moore, 1979–
Ronaldo Brazilian footballer Ronaldo Luiz Nazario de Lima, 1976–
Shaggy Jamaican singer Orville Richard Burrell, 1968–
Sting U.K. singer Gordon Matthew Sumner, 1951–

Another long name!

In the late 19th century, the Reverend Ralph William Lyonel Tollemache of Grantham, Lincolnshire, England, gave his 15 children very long names. These included Lyulph Ydwallo Odin Nestor Egbert Lyonel Toedmag Hugh Erchenwyne Saxon Esa Cromwell Orma Nevill Dysart Plantagenet Tollemache-Tollemache (1876–1961). The initial letters of his first names spell "Lyonel the Second."

Initial impressions

These famous people are known by their initials and surnames, rather than their full first names.

Early Heinz wagon from about 1900

W.H. (Wystan Hugh) Auden was a poet
Rev. W. (Wilbert) Awdry wrote *Thomas the Tank Engine*
P.T. (Phineas Taylor) Barnum was a circus proprietor
J.M. (James Matthew) Barrie was the author of *Peter Pan*
T.S. (Thomas Stearns) Eliot wrote the book on which the musical *Cats* was based
W.C. (William Claude) Fields was a film actor
H.J. (Henry John) Heinz manufactured food
k.d. (Kathryn Dawn) Lang is a singer
D.H. (David Herbert) Lawrence was a writer
T.E. (Thomas Edward) Lawrence was a soldier/writer (Lawrence of Arabia)
C.S. (Clive Staples) Lewis wrote *The Lion, the Witch and the Wardrobe*
A.A. (Alan Alexander) Milne wrote *Winnie the Pooh*
E. (Edith) Nesbit wrote *The Phoenix and the Carpet*
J.K. (Joanne Kathleen) Rowling is the author of *Harry Potter*
O.J. (Orenthal James) Simpson was a football player
R.L. (Robert Lawrence) Stine wrote the *Goosebumps* series
J.R.R. (John Roland Ruel) Tolkien wrote *Lord of the Rings*
J.M.W. (Joseph Mallord William) Turner was a painter
H.G. (Herbert George) Wells was a science-fiction author
E.B. (Elwyn Brooks) White wrote *Charlotte's Web* and *Stuart Little*
F. W. (Frank Winfield) Woolworth was a retailer

Japan	Norway	Russia	Scotland	Spain	Sweden
1 Sato	1 Hansen	1 Ivanov	1 Smith	1 García	1 Johansson
2 Suzuki	2 Olsen	2 Smirnov	2 Brown	2 Fernández	2 Andersson
3 Takahashi	3 Johansen	3 Vasilev	3 Wilson	3 González	3 Karlsson
4 Tanaka	4 Larsen	4 Petrov	4 Campbell	4 Rodríguez	4 Nilsson
5 Watanabe	5 Andersen	5 Kyznetsov	5 Stewart	5 López	5 Eriksson
6 Ito	6 Nilsen	6 Fedorov	6 Thomson	6 Martínez	6 Larsson
7 Yamamoto	7 Pedersen	7 Mikhailov	7 Robertson	7 Sánchez	7 Olsson
8 Nakamura	8 Kristiansen	8 Sokolov	8 Anderson	8 Pérez	8 Persson
9 Kobayashi	9 Jensen	9 Pavlov	9 Macdonald	9 Martín	9 Svensson
10 Saito	10 Karlsen	10 Semenov	10 Scott	10 Gómez	10 Gustafsson

Even longer!

Louis Jullien (1812–60) was a French conductor and composer, born in Sisteron, France. His parents were persuaded by the 36 members of the local Philharmonic Society that they should all be godfathers, and Louis received all their names.

Who's who in the family?

We all know who's who in our immediate family — our mothers, fathers, grandparents, aunts and uncles, sisters and brothers. But who is a second cousin or a cousin once removed?

Nephew
Son of your sister or brother

Niece
Daughter of your sister or brother

Cousin, or first cousin
Child of your aunt and uncle

Second cousin
Child of your first cousin. Second cousins have the same great-grandparents as you, but not the same grandparents. Third cousins have the same great-great-grandparents, and so on.

Removed
A child of your first cousin is called "once removed.'' Removed means a different generation. Once removed is one generation, twice removed is two generations, and so on.

Step
Stepmother, stepfather, stepsister, stepbrother, stepson or stepdaughter is a person who is related to you only by the remarriage of someone in your immediate family after death or divorce. For example, if a woman marries again, her new husband will be her children's stepfather but he has no blood relationship with them.

Half
A half-sister or half-brother has either the same mother or father as you, but not both.

In-law

A relative by marriage — so the wife of your son is your daughter-in-law or the wife of your brother is your sister-in-law. It refers only to immediate members of your family (your own marriage, that of your brothers and sisters, and your children).

Weddings and divorces around the world

The number of people marrying every year varies from country to country. Some are tropical islands and countries that are popular with tourists who travel there for a romantic wedding.

Others have cultures that place a specially high value on marriage. The number of divorces varies greatly from country to country, according to the legal system and religion.

Number of marriages per 1,000 per year*

High rates
China 35.9
Cook Islands 32.8
Barbados 13.1
Cyprus 12.9

Medium rates
U.S. 7.8
Australia 5.4
U.K. 5.1
Canada 4.7

Low rates
Venezuela 3.3
Argentina 3.2
Armenia 3.2
Saudi Arabia 3.2

Number of divorces per 1,000 per year*

High rates
Russia 5.30
Aruba 5.27
U.S. 4.19
Ukraine 3.79

Medium rates
Australia 2.85
U.K. 2.58
Canada 2.24

Low rates
Guatemala 0.12
Belize 0.17
Mongolia 0.28

* In those countries for which data are available

Wedding on a Pacific island beach

www.theheraldrysociety.com search

Till death do us part...

Longest marriages

- Sir Temulji Bhicaji Nariman and Lady Nariman of Mumbai (Bombay), India were married in 1853 at 5 years old. They stayed married for 86 years until Sir Temulji's death in 1940.
- Lazarus Rowe and Molly Weber were allegedly married in Greenland, New Hampshire, in 1743. They remained married for 86 years until 1829 when Lazarus died.

According to the Bible, King Solomon had 700 wives as well as 300 concubines.

Most marriages

- King Mongkut of Siam (1804–68) had 39 wives and 82 children. His life inspired the musical *The King and I* and the film *Anna and the King* (1999).
- American Glynn "Scotty" de Moss Wolfe (1908–97) was married 29 times, which is a U.S. record. His 29th and last wedding was on June 20, 1996, to Linda Essex. It was her 23rd wedding — another U.S. record.

Tommy Manville (1894–1967), a wealthy resident of New York City, the heir to a fortune made from asbestos, married 13 times to 11 different women (he remarried two of them).

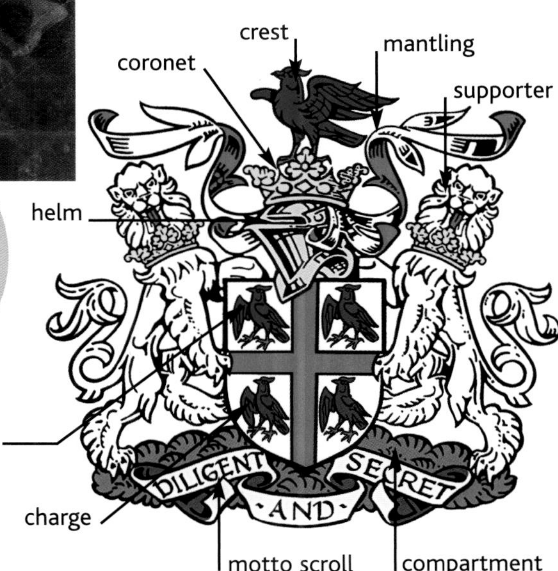

Coat of arms

A coat of arms is the symbol or badge of a family, person or even organization. The idea started in Europe in the Middle Ages, when knights began to add decoration to their armor. This helped soldiers tell the difference between their own army and the enemy on a battlefield. It also helped people to tell knights apart in jousting contests.

The designs on a coat of arms symbolized the achievements of the family, and were passed on from generation to generation. A coat of arms is still put together by people called heralds, and the process is known as heraldry.

Parts of a coat of arms

Each coat of arms has a unique combination of colors and symbols. The positions of the different features are described in special terms, such as sinister (left) and dexter (right).

Ordinaries

The geometric designs in a coat of arms are called ordinaries.

Colors

The background or field uses one of two metals: gold (known as or in the language of heraldry), represented by yellow, and silver (argent), shown as white. There are five basic colors: gules (red), azure (blue), sable (black), vert (green) and purpure (purple). Patterns called furs, such as ermine, are also used. Each color or pattern symbolizes a special feature, such as red for bravery. Special rules dictate how these devices are used: a metal may not be placed on metal, and so on.

Charge, supporters and other features

An object on the body of a shield is called a charge. It may include real and imaginary animals, often lions, eagles or dragons. At each side of the shield are the supporters, which may be animals, birds or people. There may also be other features such as a family motto in a banner above the shield and a crest or helmet, which may feature the same animals used as the charge or supporters.

Anniversary gifts

There is a very old tradition of celebrating wedding anniversaries by presenting special types of gift. For example, for a 25th anniversary people give gifts made of silver. In the U.S. and Canada most people celebrate only the milestone anniversaries: the 25th, 30th, 40th, 50th and 60th.

The 75th anniversary was traditionally the diamond but few married couples live long enough to celebrate it. Since Queen Victoria's Diamond Jubilee was held to mark her 60 years on the throne, the 60th wedding anniversary has become the diamond celebration.

1st paper
2nd Cotton
3rd Leather
4th Linen
5th Wood
6th Iron
7th Wool
8th Bronze
9th Pottery
10th Tin
11th Steel
12th Silk
13th Lace
14th Ivory
15th Crystal
20th China
25th Silver
30th Pearl
35th Coral
40th Ruby
45th Sapphire
50th Gold
55th Emerald
60th Diamond
70th Platinum
75th Diamond (again)

Christopher Columbus landing in the New World

Karl Marx

(1818–83) German

Karl Marx's ideas on economic history and sociology changed the world. Marx was a social philosopher who attacked the state and predicted a future in which everyone was equal. He explained his theories in the *Communist Manifesto* (compiled with Friedrich Engels and published in 1848) and *Das Kapital* (1867–94). His ideas eventually led to the Russian Revolution and communism. By 1950 almost half of the world's people lived under communist regimes.

Christopher Columbus

(1451–1506) Italian

Christopher Columbus is one of the most famous of all explorers. He believed he could reach Asia by sailing west across the Atlantic Ocean and in 1492 he set sail in the *Santa Maria* to prove his theory. Instead, he landed on the islands now known as the West Indies. His discoveries led to the European exploration and settlement of the Americas.

William Shakespeare

(1564–1616) English

William Shakespeare is generally agreed to be the greatest playwright in the English language. He began as an actor and wrote at least 154 love poems and 37 plays, including *King Lear*, *Hamlet*, *Romeo and Juliet* and *Macbeth*. Shakespeare also probably introduced more than 1,700 new words to the English language.

A 1964 U.S. stamp commemorating the 400th anniversary of Shakespeare's birth

Charles Darwin

(1809–82) English

Naturalist Charles Darwin established the theory of evolution. He began forming his ideas when he served as official naturalist on a world voyage on *HMS Beagle* (1831–36) and spent the rest of his life back in England developing them. When his famous book *The Origin of Species by Means of Natural Selection* was published in 1859 there were violent reactions against it. Darwin challenged the Bible's account of creation, and explained that human beings are descended from an apelike ancestor. Another English naturalist, Alfred Russel Wallace, independently developed very similar ideas at the same time as Darwin.

Emmeline Pankhurst

(1858–1928) English

Emmeline Pankhurst was the most famous of the women who campaigned for the right to vote in the U.K. From 1905 she fought for the vote by any means possible and was frequently arrested and imprisoned. She died in 1928 shortly before her aims were realized and every woman over 21 years old was granted the vote.

Emmeline Pankhurst, 1914

Mahatma Gandhi

(1869–1948) Indian

Gandhi began his career as a lawyer but became a great political and spiritual leader. He led the peaceful civil disobedience of Indians against British rule in India and negotiated with the British government until 1947, when India was granted independence. Gandhi became the first icon of a people's struggle against oppression. His simple lifestyle and his belief in religious tolerance have made him a symbol of decency and peace ever since.

Albert Einstein

(1879–1955) German/American

Einstein was one of the greatest of all physicists and his name has become a symbol of genius. When his most famous work, *The General Theory of Relativity*, was proven in 1919, Einstein became the most celebrated scientist in the world, and he won the Nobel Prize for Physics in 1921. Einstein was a firm believer in pacifism, but his scientific theories helped his adopted country, the U.S., to develop the atomic bomb. A week before he died Einstein wrote to Bertrand Russell, a British philosopher and leading anti-nuclear campaigner, asking to put his name to a manifesto urging all countries to give up their nuclear weapons.

Adolf Hitler

(1889–1945) Austrian

Adolf Hitler was Germany's leader from 1933 to 1945, during which time he led the world into the most devastating war in history. Hitler's hatred of Jewish people and his desire for a blue-eyed, blond-haired master race led to the murder of six million people during World War II; most died in concentration camps in Eastern Europe.

Nelson Mandela

(1918–) South African

Nelson Mandela dedicated his life to the fight against apartheid — a policy that kept black and white South Africans apart and denied black citizens the vote. He was imprisoned in 1964 for his aggressive opposition to South Africa's racist government and was held for 26 years. In 1990, after his release, Mandela was elected president of the African National Congress. In 1993 he won the Nobel Peace Prize for his work to end apartheid.

See also
History timeline: page 104

Mao Zedong/ Mao Tse-tung/ Chairman Mao

(1893–1976) Chinese

Mao Zedong was one of the founders of the Chinese Communist Party and the first chairman of the People's Republic of China in 1949. He had an enormous influence on his country and was greatly admired for founding the Chinese republic and for changes in the early years of his rule. During his rule, Mao's image was displayed everywhere— in every school, home, factory and workplace.

James Watson (1928–) American and Francis Crick

(1916–2004) English

American biologist James Watson and English scientist Francis Crick discovered the molecular structure of DNA, using theories already written by Maurice Wilkins. Their theory helps to explain how DNA carries hereditary information and their discoveries have revolutionized our understanding of genetics and the study of disease.

Martin Luther King, Jr.

(1929–68) American

Martin Luther King was a Baptist minister who campaigned against the segregation of blacks in the southern states of the U.S. He was influenced by Gandhi and believed in peaceful protest. He won the Nobel Peace Prize in 1964. King was assassinated in 1968, but will always be remembered for his dignified, passive resistance to an unjust society.

Bill Gates

(1955–) American

Bill Gates created his first computer program while still at high school, co-founded Microsoft in 1977, and by 1993 was the richest man on Earth. In 2000 Gates and his wife formed the Bill & Melinda Gates Foundation, which is the largest charity in the world. One of its aims is to rid the Third World of polio and other deadly diseases.

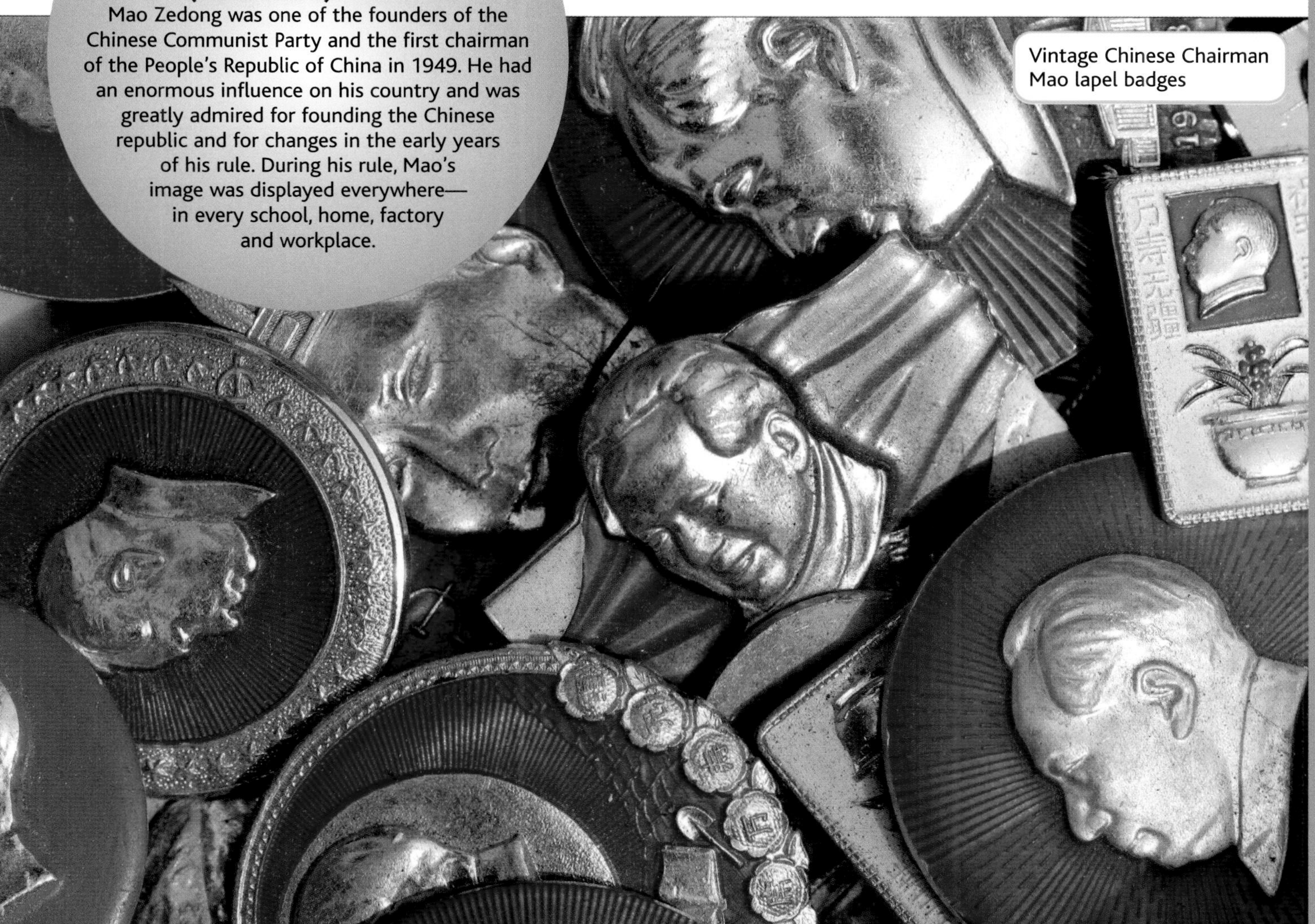

Vintage Chinese Chairman Mao lapel badges

Women adventurers

These are just some of the intrepid women who went where no other woman — in some cases, no man — had gone before.

Amelia Earhart in the cockpit of her plane

- French novelist Jules Verne's novel *Around the World in 80 Days* inspired American journalist Nellie Bly (real name Elizabeth Cochrane, 1864–1922) to beat this time. She set out in 1889, and returned to New York on January 25, 1890 — a record round-the-world trip of 72 days, 6 hours, 11 minutes and 14 seconds.
- Amelia Earhart (U.S. 1898–1937) became the first woman to fly solo across the Atlantic in 1932.
- Cosmonaut Valentina Tereshkova (USSR, 1937–) was the first woman in space. She went into orbit on June 16, 1963.
- Sheila Scott (U.K. 1927–88) was the first woman to fly around the world solo, in 1971. She was also the first woman to pilot a plane over the North Pole.
- Harriet Quimby (U.S. 1875–1912) was the first American woman to gain a pilot's license, and in 1912 became the first woman to fly across the English Channel.
- Jacqueline Cochran (U.S. 1906–80) raced aircraft in the 1930s and set more aviation records than any woman — in 1953 becoming the first to break the sound barrier.

Polar exploration firsts

The North and South Poles are two of the most difficult places on Earth to reach and so have been great challenges for explorers. These are some of the people who reached the poles by one means or another.

First to reach the North Pole

American adventurer Frederick Albert Cook (1865–1940) claimed he and two Inuit companions reached the North Pole on April 21, 1908, but he probably faked his journey. Another American, Robert Edwin Peary (1856–1920), his companion Matthew Alexander Henson (1866–1955) and four Inuit were first at the pole on April 6, 1909.

First to reach the South Pole

Norwegian explorer Roald Amundsen (1872–1928) and four companions reached the South Pole on December 14, 1911. They just beat British explorer Robert Falcon Scott and his team, who got there on January 17, 1912, but died on their return journey.

First swim at the North Pole

British swimmer Lewis Gordon Pugh swam 3,280 feet (1 km) in gaps between ice at the North Pole, July 15, 2007

First manned descent to North Pole seabed

On August 2, 2007, two Russian MIR submarines placed a Russian flag on the seabed beneath the North Pole

First solo overland journey to the North Pole

Japanese explorer Naomi Uemura reached the North Pole on May 1, 1978. He traveled by dog sled, but was then picked up by an aircraft. France's Jean-Louis Etienne made the first solo journey without dogs. He reached the pole on May 11, 1986.

First pole-to-pole journey

British explorer Sir Ranulph Fiennes and his partner Charles Burton were the first people to walk from pole to pole. They crossed the South Pole on December 15, 1980, and reached the North Pole on April 10, 1982.

First woman to reach the South Pole solo

Norwegian Liv Arnesen trekked to the South Pole unaided in 50 days, arriving at the pole on December 25, 1994.

First cat to sail around the world

Trim the cat was born on board *HMS Reliance* in 1799 on the way to Australia. The following year he sailed to England and back to Australia.

First around the world

Since the first voyage around the world, almost 500 years ago, people have been looking for different ways of circumnavigating (traveling right around) the planet by land, sea or air.

First circumnavigation
Juan Sebastian de Elcano and his crew of 17 on *Vittoria* sailed from Spain in 1519 and returned 1,079 days later. The expedition was led by Ferdinand Magellan, but he was murdered in the Philippines on April 27, 1521.

First British circumnavigation
Sir Francis Drake and a crew of 50 left Plymouth, England, in 1577 on the *Golden Hind* and returned on September 26, 1580.

First solo sailing
Canadian-born sailor Captain Joshua Slocum (1844–1910) sailed around the world alone in *Spray*, an oyster boat he built himself. He left the U.S. on April 24, 1895, and returned on June 27, 1898.

First walk
George Matthew Schilling (U.S.) claimed to have walked around the world between 1897 and 1904, but his journey has not been verified. David Kunst (U.S.) made the first confirmed journey from June 20, 1970, to October 5, 1974. He wore out 21 pairs of shoes during his 14,445-mi. (23,250 km) walk.

Explorers and travelers

Today there are few places that have not been explored, but this was not always the case. The Americas were unknown to Europeans until a little over 500 years ago, and Australia was scarcely known by the rest of the world until the late 18th century. These are some of the people who made Europeans aware of the rest of the world.

Marco Polo (c. 1254–1324)
Italian traveler Marco Polo was one of the first Europeans to visit China and other Far Eastern territories. His reports were not believed, but he encouraged the idea of trading with the East.

John Cabot (1450–98)
Italian-born explorer John and his son Sebastian Cabot were employed by British merchants to seek a western route to Asia. During their travels they discovered parts of the northeast coast of North America.

Christopher Columbus (1451–1506)
Italian explorer Christopher Columbus discovered North, Central and South America and the islands of the West Indies.

Vasco da Gama (c. 1460–1524)
Portuguese explorer Vasco da Gama traveled around the Cape of Good Hope and up the East coast of Africa. He discovered a trade route to India.

Ferdinand Magellan (1480–1521)
Magellan was a Portuguese explorer who led the first voyage around the world. He discovered the Strait of Magellan, near the tip of South America.

Abel Tasman (1603–59)
Abel Tasman, a Dutchman, explored Australia. In 1642 he discovered Van Diemans Land (later called Tasmania) and New Zealand.

Henry Hudson (c. 1550–1611)
Henry Hudson was an English navigator who searched for a Northwest Passage (a route to the East by traveling north of North America). He discovered Hudson Bay.

James Cook (1728–79)
British Captain James Cook led several major expeditions. He explored the coasts of Australia, New Zealand and North America.

David Livingstone (1813–73)
Livingstone was a Scottish missionary and explorer of Africa. He discovered and named the Victoria Falls after Queen Victoria.

Sir Richard Burton (1821–90)
Burton was one of the first Europeans to travel to Arabia. With John Hanning Speke he discovered Lake Tanganyika in Africa.

John Hanning Speke (1827–64)
Speke discoverered Lake Tanganyika with Burton. He also discovered Lake Victoria, believed to be the source of the River Nile.

Sir Henry Morton Stanley (1841–1904)
Stanley was a British explorer of Africa and was involved in the search for Livingstone.

Top of the world

The first people to succeed in climbing Everest, the world's highest mountain, were Edmund Hillary from New Zealand and Tenzing Norgay from Nepal. They reached the summit on May 29, 1953.

Steve Fossett in *Virgin Atlantic Global Flyer*

First nonstop flight
USAF B-50A bomber *Lucky Lady II* piloted by Capt. James Gallagher flew from Fort Worth, Texas, on February 26, 1949. The journey took 94 hours, 1 minute, and the plane was refueled four times in mid-air.

First underwater
U.S. Navy nuclear submarine *Triton* traveled around the world underwater between February 16, and April 25, 1960.

First nonstop solo voyage
British yachtsman Robin Knox-Johnston sailed from and returned to Falmouth, U.K., in *Suhali* between June 14, 1968, and April 22, 1969.

First in a wheelchair
Rick Hansen (Canada) went around the world in a wheelchair between March 21, 1985, and May 22, 1987. He traveled through 34 countries.

First balloon flight
Brian Jones (U.K.) and Bertrand Piccard (Switzerland) made a round-the-world voyage in the *Breitling Orbiter 3*. They left on March 1, 1999, and their journey took three weeks.

First solo flight
On March 7, 2005, Steve Fossett (U.S.) achieved the first solo round-the-world flight without refueling in *Virgin Atlantic Global Flyer*. He covered 22,878 mi. (36,818 km) in a flight time of 67 hours, 2 minutes and 38 seconds. On February 1, 2006 he once again took off from the U.S. to fly around the world. This time he carried on to Bournemouth, U.K., making this voyage the longest ever solo, nonstop, round-the-world flight. He traveled a distance of 22,936.5 mi. (36,912.68 km) in 76 hours, 42 minutes, and 55 seconds.

Apollo 8 astronauts James Lovell, William Anders and Frank Borman, 1968 "people of the year"

Late success

As people live longer, many continue to work well into what was once thought of as extreme old age. These are all people who made great achievements in their 80s and beyond.

Alice Porlock, British writer, published her first book at 102 years old.

Ichijirou Araya, Japanese climber, climbed Mount Fuji aged 100 years.

George Burns, U.S. actor, appeared in *Radioland Murders* (1994) at 98.

Dimitrion Yornanidis, Greek athlete, ran a marathon at 98.

Pablo Casals, Spanish musician, conducted the Israel Festival Youth Orchestra when he was 96.

Michelangelo, Italian artist, produced his Rondandini *Pietà* sculpture at the age of 88.

Claude Monet, French painter, completed his waterlily paintings when he was 84 years old.

Against the odds

All these people triumphed over disability or illness to achieve fame.

Lance Armstrong (1971–) U.S. cyclist, contracted cancer that affected his brain and lungs. He recovered and went on to win the gruelling Tour de France cycle race a record seven times in a row, 1999–2005.

Ludwig van Beethoven (1770–1827) was one of the world's greatest composers. He continued to compose music even after he became totally deaf in 1817.

Lord Horatio Nelson

(1758–1805) was a British admiral. He lost an arm and an eye in battle, but won many naval victories, including the Battle of Trafalgar in 1805.

Stephen Hawking

(1942–) a British physicist and celebrated author of *A Brief History of Time*, suffers from motor neuron disease. He is confined to a wheelchair and speaks with the aid of a voice synthesizer.

In the news

Every year the editors of *Time* magazine nominate a person of the year — the individual or group who has most influenced world events during the year. The winner may not always have had a good influence — Adolf Hitler was nominated in 1938.

Nominees may be a man, a couple (Chinese leaders General and Madame Chiang Kai-shek in 1937), a woman (Queen Elizabeth II in 1952), a group of people (three astronauts in 1968), even a machine (a computer in 1982). Here are just some of the winners.

2007 Vladimir Putin (Russian President)
2006 You
2005 Bill and Melinda Gates/Bono
2003 The American Soldier
2000/04 George W. Bush (U.S. president)
1999 Jeff Bezos (founder of Amazon.com)
1994 Pope John Paul II
1992/98 Bill Clinton (U.S. president)
1987/89 Mikhail Gorbachev (Soviet leader)
1966 Young people
1963 Martin Luther King, Jr. (civil rights campaigner)
1961 John F. Kennedy (U.S. president)
1949 Winston Churchill (British prime minister)
1935 Haile Selassie (Ethiopian ruler)
1930 Mohandas Gandhi (Indian leader)

s9.com search

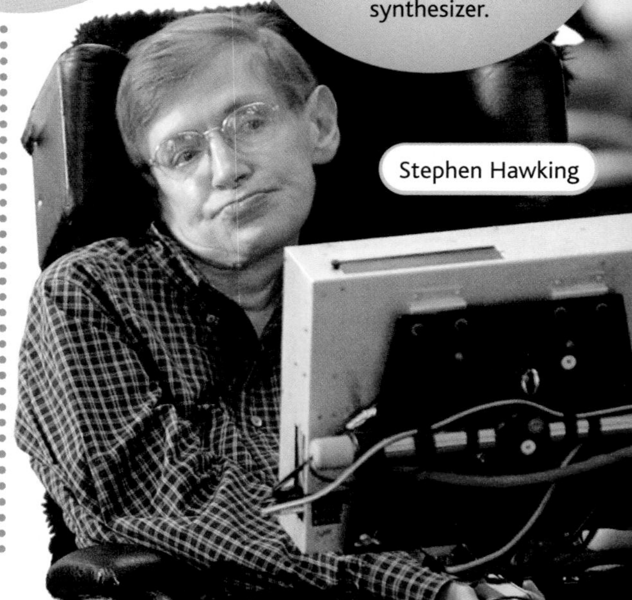
Stephen Hawking

William Gladstone, British politician, became prime minister for the fourth time when he was 82 years old.

Benjamin Franklin, American statesman, helped write the U.S. Constitution when he was 81 years old.

George Cukor, U.S. film director, directed *Rich and Famous* (1981) at 81 years old.

One and only

At the age of 82, Irish playwright George Bernard Shaw won an Oscar for Best Screenplay for *Pygmalion* (1938). He had already won the Nobel Prize for Literature in 1925, so became the only person ever to win both a Nobel and an Oscar.

Sarah Bernhardt
(1844–1923) French actress, lost a leg in 1914 but continued acting.

Andrea Bocelli
(1958–) an Italian opera singer who was blinded at the age of 12. He went on to achieve international singing success.

Louis Braille
(1809–1852) was blind and invented the Braille system of printing with raised dots to enable blind people to read.

Terry Fox
(1958–81) Canadian athlete, lost a leg to cancer. He took up long-distance running, and through this he raised money for a cancer charity.

Mark Inglis
(1959–) In 2006, the New Zealander became the first double amputee to reach the top of Everest.

Helen Keller
(1880–1968) was a famed author and lecturer despite being blind and deaf.

Joseph Pulitzer
(1847–1911) U.S. publisher and founder of the prestigious Pulitzer Prizes, was blind from the age of 40.

Christopher Reeve
(1952–2004) American actor, star of four Superman movies, was paralyzed after a horse riding accident in 1995, but devoted his life to campaigning for disabled people.

Maria Runyan
(1969–) U.S. athlete, who despite being blind competed in the 2000 Olympic Games and in the 2002 New York City Marathon, achieving the second-fastest time by a woman.

Awards

Awards are presented in almost every area of achievement. The ones that receive the most attention in newspapers and on television are those given to famous film stars, writers, artists and singers. Among the best known are the following.

Academy Awards (Oscars)
These are the most famous of all film awards. The Oscar presentations are now watched on television by more than a billion people worldwide. The Academy Awards — also called the Oscars after the statuette that winners receive — were first presented in 1929. Walt Disney has won the most, a total of 20.

Emmy Awards
These are the principal U.S. television awards. First presented in 1949, they are named after the "Immy", the nickname for a type of TV camera. The actual award is a metal statuette of a winged figure holding an atom.

Governor General's Literary Awards
Among Canada's leading literary prizes, they were established in 1937 and are presented in a variety of categories, including children's literature, in both English and French.

Sundance Awards
These awards have been presented at the Sundance Film Festival held in Utah since 1978 and named after the Sundance Kid, a movie character played by the festival's organizer, Robert Redford.

Tony Awards
The Tony Awards were first presented in 1947 to honor outstanding Broadway plays and musicals, actors and actresses, music, costume, and other theatrical contributions. They are named for the actress and director Antoinette Perry (1888–1946).

Golden Globe Awards
These U.S. film awards began in 1943. Julia Roberts has been nominated five times and won three awards, and Tom Hanks has won four of the six awards for which he was nominated.

Grammy Awards
The U.S. music awards have been presented since 1959. The classical awards have been dominated by conductor Sir Georg Solti, who won 38 Grammys. U2 has won more awards than any other band, a total of 22, while Amy Winehouse won in five categories in 2008.

MTV Video Music Awards
The music television channel MTV established its awards in 1984. Madonna is the most successful MTV artist, with 70 nominations and 21 awards.

Nobel Prize
These international awards are named after Alfred Nobel, the inventor of dynamite, and were first presented in 1901. There are now six categories — Physics, Chemistry, Medicine, Literature, Peace and Economics. Famous winners include Winston Churchill (Literature, 1953) and Mother Theresa (Peace, 1979).

Pulitzer Prizes
These U.S. awards are given for achievements in journalism, writing (fiction, non-fiction and poetry) and music. They are named after publisher Joseph Pulitzer and began in 1917.

Turner Prize
This British art prize is named after landscape painter J.M.W. Turner and was established in 1984. The winning works are often controversial, and usually not conventional paintings. Damien Hirst is a notorious winner.

Golden Raspberry awards

The Golden Raspberries, founded in 1980, are joke awards presented to the worst films and actors! Madonna was a notable winner. She also received the Razzies award for worst actress of the 20th century. In 2008, Lindsey Lohan won the worst actress award for both her roles in worst film award-winner *I Know Who Killed Me*.

"Oscar"

Where are the children?

In countries such as India, where people have large families and relatively short lives, there are more children than older people. In North America there are more middle-aged and older people than children. Most people have smaller families so there are fewer young people.

No. of children aged 0–14 yrs

India	362,874,979
China	265,167,835
Indonesia	67,499,548
U.S.	61,482,447
Pakistan	60,993,354
Nigeria	59,666,293
Bangladesh	52,594,517
Brazil	47,463,314
Mexico	32,405,364
Canada	5,388,547

*Estimated for 2009

Schoolchildren in India taking part in a physical education class

Early success

Wolfgang Amadeus Mozart (Austria, 1756–91) began composing music at the age of 5, and a year later began a concert tour across Europe.
William James Sidis (U.S., 1898–1944) went to Harvard University to study mathematics at the age of 11.
Balamurali Ambati (U.S., 1977–) graduated from university at 13 and from medical school at the age of 17, becoming the world's youngest qualified doctor.

Young populations

Countries with a lot of people under 15 usually have high birth rates and high death rates. In countries where families have many children who are too young to work and adults die relatively young, there are not enough people of working age to earn money to feed and take care of the families. As a result, these countries tend to be among the world's poorest.

Population under 15 years old

1 **Uganda** 50 percent
2 **Mali** 48.3 percent
3 **Democratic Republic of Congo** 47.3 percent
4 **Niger** 46.9 percent
5 **São Tomé and Príncipe** 46.8 percent
6 **Chad** 46.7 percent
7 **Republic of Congo** 46 percent
World average 26.9 percent

The U.S. and Canada have a lower than average proportion of children.
U.S. 20.1 percent
Canada 16.9 percent

*Estimated for 2009

Harry Potter fame

Daniel Jacob Radcliffe (born July 23, 1989) was 11 years old when he won the role of Harry Potter in the film *Harry Potter and the Sorcerer's Stone* (2001).

He was reported to have earned $14 million for his appearance in *Harry Potter and the Order of the Phoenix* (2007). With the release of *Harry Potter and the Half-Blood Prince*, he will have earned more than $39 million from the Harry Potter films alone.

Hollywood star Angelina Jolie visiting a refugee camp in her role as Goodwill Ambassador for the United Nations High Commissioner for Refugees

The UN Convention on the Rights of the Child

The United Nations issued its Declaration on the Rights of the Child in 1959 to try to relieve the suffering of children in poor and war-torn countries. It came into force as a convention in 1990. One hundred and ninety three countries are parties to the Convention: Somalia and the United States are not.

All the signatories agree to make sure that children under 18 have certain basic rights, such as housing and medical care. Recent optional additions include one that children will not have to serve in military action.

The Convention on the Rights of the Child states that all children have the right to:

- a name and nationality
- affection, love, understanding and material security
- adequate nutrition, housing and medical services
- special care if disabled — physically, mentally or socially
- be among the first to receive protection and relief in all circumstances
- be protected against all forms of neglect, cruelty and exploitation
- full opportunity for play and recreation and equal opportunity to free and compulsory education, to enable the child to develop his/her individual abilities and to become a useful member of society
- develop his/her full potential in conditions of freedom and dignity
- be brought up in a spirit of understanding, tolerance, friendship among peoples, peace and universal brotherhood
- enjoy these rights regardless of race, color, sex, religion, political or other opinion, national or social origin and property, birth or other status.

International youth organizations

Scouts and Cub Scouts

Sir Robert Baden-Powell (1857–1941), a former general in the British army, launched the scouting movement in 1907. Today there are scouts in almost every country in the world — a total of 28 million. More than six million are in the U.S., but the leading scouting country is Indonesia, with almost nine million members. Scouting is forbidden in some countries, including Cuba and North Korea. The junior division for boys under 11 is called the Cub Scouts and was founded in 1930.

Girl Guides/Girl Scouts and Brownies

The Girl Guide Movement was started in 1910 by Sir Robert Baden-Powell and his sister Agnes (1858–1945). Today the World Association of Girl Guides and Girl Scouts (WAGGGS) has 144 member organizations with a total membership of 10 million. It is the largest international organization for girls and young women. The junior division, for girls under 11, is called the Brownies.

YMCA and YWCA

The YMCA (Young Men's Christian Association) was founded by George Williams in the U.K. in 1844 and in the U.S. in 1851. Its aim was to provide shelter and other support for young men who came into cities to find work. The YMCA now has branches in 122 countries. The YWCA (Young Women's Christian Association), was founded in the U.K. in 1855 and in the U.S. in 1858.

www.unicef.org/crc/crc.htm search

Beliefs & Ideas

160 ANCIENT RELIGIONS
162 WORLD RELIGIONS
164 SACRED TEXTS
166 CHRISTIANITY
168 FESTIVALS
170 MYTHS AND LEGENDS
172 PREDICTIONS AND PROPHECIES
174 THE UNEXPLAINED

Religious movement

The key role played by Buddhist monks in mass protests against the military government of Myanmar (Burma) highlighted the ruling regimes violence to the rest of the world in 2007. The monks are highly revered by the country's predominantly Buddhist population and their involvement drew the attention of the world's press.

Gods and goddesses

In most of the world's major religions today only one god is worshiped. But in many ancient religions, followers worshiped a group of gods. Each god had special characteristics and responsibilities, and some could appear in a variety of forms.

The myths and legends of ancient cultures and the range of gods worshiped often changed over thousands of years as different gods and goddesses rose or fell in importance. Those listed on these pages are a selection of the most revered and long-standing gods of some of the world's ancient cultures.

Chinese gods

The Chinese worshiped a large range of gods for more than 4,000 years, up to the coming of Chinese communism in the 20th century. Some Chinese people continue to worship these gods — often in secret — today.

Dragon Kings Ao-shin (North), Ao-chin (South), Ao-kuang (East) and Ao-jun (West), the gods of rain, rivers and seas
Fu-xi god of arts and creativity
Guan-yin god and goddess of compassion
Guan-yu god of war
Meng-po goddess of the underworld
Nu-guawas serpent goddess of creation
Pan-gu giant creator god
Qi-yu god of the rain (half bull, half giant)
Three Pure Ones supreme trinity of Yuan-shi-tian-zong, Ling-bao-tian-song and Lao-jun
Xi-he goddess of light
Xi-wangmu goddess of immortality
Yi-di god of wine
Zao-jun god of the household

Ancient Egyptian gods

Egyptian religion dates back about 5,000 years and lasted until the coming of Christianity and Islam. Its huge range of gods and goddesses were believed to control almost every aspect of people's lives.

Amun-Ra king of the gods
Anubis jackal god of death and Egyptian mummies
Aten god of the sun-disk
Bast/Bastet cat goddess of fertility
Bes lion-like domestic god
Hathor cow-headed goddess of happiness
Horus falcon-headed sky god
Isis wife of Osiris, mother of Horus, goddess of motherhood and royalty
Month falcon-headed god of war
Nefertum god of the sacred blue lotus and the rising sun
Osiris god of the underworld and agriculture
Ptah creator god and patron of craftsmen
Ra Sun god, ancient Egypt's most important god
Reshef god of war and thunder
Sekhmet/Sakhmet lion-headed goddess of war and destruction
Seth god of storms and violence
Thoth ibis-headed god of the Moon, arts and sciences

Ancient Egyptian falcon-headed god Horus depicted on a mummy mask

See also
World civilizations and empires: pages 106–107
Time: pages 14–16

Greek and Roman gods

The ancient Greeks had 12 major gods and goddesses. They believed the gods all lived on Mount Olympus and influenced the well-being of all humans. As the Greek civilization declined and the Roman empire grew, the Romans renamed the Greek gods and took them as their own.

Greek/Roman
Hera/Juno chief goddess — marriage
Aphrodite/Venus goddess of beauty
Artemis/Diana goddess of hunting
Athena/Minerva goddess of wisdom
Demeter/Ceres goddess of the harvest, nature
Hestia/Vesta goddess of the hearth
Zeus/Jupiter chief god — sky and air
Apollon/Apollo god of poetry, music, Sun
Ares/Mars god of war
Hephaistos/Vulcan god of blacksmiths
Hermes/Mercury messenger of the gods
Poseidon/Neptune god of the sea

The 12 Norse gods

The Norse people lived in ancient and medieval Scandinavia (modern Norway, Sweden, Finland, Iceland and Denmark).

The 12 Norse, or Scandinavian, gods were together called the Aesir, and their homeland was Asgard. There was also a second group of gods called the Vanir, who fought the Aesir. Later some Vanir gods, including Frey and his sister Freya, became Aesir.

- Odin, or Woden, chief god in Norse mythology
- Thor, red-haired and bearded son of Odin and Jord, god of war (his name gave us Thursday — Thor's day)
- Tyr, Tiu or Tiw, another son of Odin, god of warfare and battle (his name is commemorated in Tuesday)
- Balder or Baldur, god of sunlight
- Brag or Bragi, god of poetry
- Vidar, god of silence, stealth and revenge
- Hoder the blind
- Hermód or Hermoder the Brave, Odin's son and his messenger
- Hönir or Hoenir, a minor god
- Odnir, husband of Freya
- Loki, god of strife or mischief, capable of changing shape and performing tricks
- Vali, Odin's youngest son by Rind, a giantess. He slew Hod, who had murdered his brother Balder

Aztec gods

The Aztecs were based in central Mexico. They flourished from the 14th century until their conquest by Spanish invaders in 1522. They sacrificed humans to the gods, who were believed to control daily life and agriculture.

Chalchiuhtlicue goddess of lakes and streams, youth and beauty
Cinteotl god of maize
Coyolxauhqui goddess of the Moon
Ehecatl god of the wind and weather
Huehueteotl god of the hearth, the fire of life
Huitzilopochtli war god
Ilamatecuhtli goddess of the Earth, death and the Milky Way
Itztlacoliuhqui god of stone and the Morning Star
Mayahuel goddess of alcohol and the maguey plant (from which alcoholic drinks were made)
Mictlantecuhtli god of death
Quetzalcoatl creator god — and bringer of chocolate!
Tepeyollotl god of caves and earthquakes
Tezcatlipoca god of night and death
Tlahuizcalpantecuhtli god of dawn
Tonacatecuhtli god of food
Xipe-totec god of spring and agriculture, patron of goldsmiths
Xochipilli god of love, flowers, singing and dancing
Xochiquetzal goddess of love

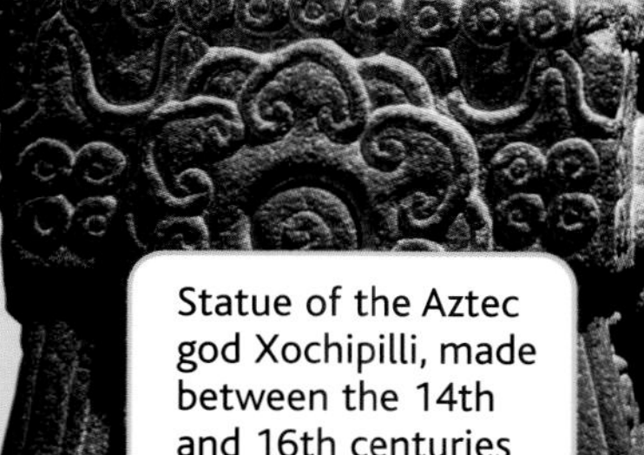
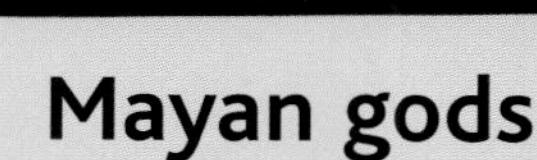

Statue of the Aztec god Xochipilli, made between the 14th and 16th centuries

Inca gods

The Inca people lived in the part of South America that is now Peru from about 1200 to 1533. Inca gods were thought to influence natural events.

Apocatequil god of lightning
Apu Illapu god of thunder
Ilyap'a weather god
Inti Sun god
Kon god of rain and the southern wind
Mama Oello mother goddess, daughter of Inti and Mama Quilla
Mama Quilla Moon goddess, daughter of Viracocha and wife of Inti
Manco Capac creator god, Sun and fire
Pachacamac Earth god
Punchau Sun god
Vichaama god of death
Viracocha god of creation

Mayan gods

The Mayan civilization and neighboring Olmec culture date back 3,000 years. Descendants of the Mayans still live in southern Mexico, Belize and Guatemala.

Bacabs gods of the four directions — Mulac (North), Cauac (South), Kan (East) and Ix (West)
Balu-chabtan god of war and sacrifice
Chak god of rain, fertility and agriculture
Hunahau god of death
Itzamna reptile creator god
Ix-chel Moon goddess
Kinichi-ahau Sun god
Kukulcan feathered serpent god
Xbalanque god of the jaguar
Yum-kaax corn god

The five pillars of Islam

The following are the five most important aspects of the Muslim faith.

1 **ash-Shahada** — profession of faith in Allah and his prophet Muhammad
2 **salat** — prayer five times a day, facing Mecca
3 **zakat** — giving alms to the poor and needy
4 **sawm** — fasting between dawn and dusk during Ramadan
5 **hajj** – pilgrimage to Mecca, at least once in one's lifetime

Jihad, meaning holy war, is sometimes added as an extra pillar.

Religious buildings

- Abbey — a building occupied by monks or nuns and run by an abbot or abbess
- Basilica — a type of early Christian church
- Cathedral — the main church in an area and the seat of the bishop
- Chapel — a place of worship within a larger building, or a nonconformist Christian religious building
- Church — a building used for public worship by Christians
- Convent or nunnery — the home of a community of nuns
- Dagoba — a Buddhist shrine
- Friary — home to friars, members of a religious order
- Meeting house — a place where certain religious groups, such as Quakers, gather
- Monastery — the home to a religious community of monks
- Mosque — a Muslim place of worship
- Pagoda — an Eastern temple
- Priory — a religious house run by a prior; it may be under the control of an abbey

Major religions

Christianity 2,159,141,594*
Islam 1,345,175,832*
Hinduism 859,893,462*
Buddhism 380,567,154*
Chinese folk religions 380,486,297*
Sikhhism 22,199,953*
Judaism 14,678,791*

* followers worldwide

The Golden Temple, Amritsar, India

Holy places

A holy place is somewhere that is especially revered by the followers of a religion. Examples include the birthplace of the founder of a religion, shrines and places of pilgrimage. There has been conflict in some of these holy places when members of other religions have claimed or attacked the sites.

Amritsar, India
This city is the Sikh religion's spiritual center. The Golden Temple is the main shrine.

Athos, Greece
This is a holy mountain for the Greek Orthodox Church where there are many monasteries. Women are forbidden to go on to the mountain.

Benares, India
This Hindu holy city is dedicated to the god Shiva.

Bethlehem, Israel
The birthplace of Jesus

Canterbury, U.K.
The city was once England's most important pilgrimage center.

Ganges, India
The Ganges River is sacred to Hindus, who bathe here and scatter the ashes of their dead in its waters.

Jerusalem, Israel
A holy city for Christians, Muslims and Jews. Sites include the Western Wall, Dome of the Rock and Church of the Holy Sepulchre.

Karbala, Iraq
This city is the center of Shia Islam and contains the shrine of the Prophet Muhammad's grandson al-Husain.

- Shrine — a place of worship connected with a sacred person or saint. It may contain sacred objects or relics
- Synagogue — a building for Jewish religious services
- Tabernacle — a house or tent used for worship, named after the tent used by the Israelites to cover the Ark of the Covenant
- Temple — a place of worship dedicated to a particular god or gods. Also sometimes used instead of synagogue

Gate of a Shinto shrine in Miyajima, Japan

Hindu gods and goddesses

About 80 percent of the people of India are Hindus. Most believe that God takes many different forms, so the Hindu religion has a range of gods and goddesses. Brahma, Vishnu and Shiva are the most important.

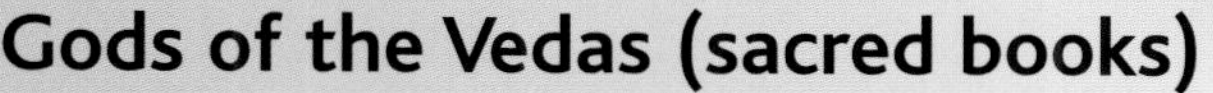

Gods of the Vedas (sacred books)

Indra is the thunder god of battle.
Varuna is the guardian of order.
Agni is the god of fire.
Surya is the sun deity.

Other Hindu gods

Brahma is the creator.
Vishnu is the preserver, who has 10 incarnations:
- Matsya, the fish
- Kurma, the tortoise
- Varah, the boar
- Nrisinha, half-man, half-lion
- Vamana, the dwarf
- Parasurama, Rama with the axe
- Ramachandra, Rama with bow and arrows
- Krishna, god of the Bhagavad-Gita
- Buddha, teacher
- Kalki, "the one to come."

Shiva is the god of destruction.
Ganesh is the elephant-headed god.
Hanuman is the monkey warrior god.

Hindu goddesses

Durga or Amba is the warrior god.
Parvati is the wife of Shiva.
Kali is the goddess of destruction.
Lakshmi is the wife of Vishnu, goddess of beauty, wealth and fortune.
Saraswati is the goddess of learning, arts and music.

Figure of the Hindu god Krishna

Lhasa, Tibet (China)
The center of Tibetan Buddhism. The monastery here was once the home of the Dalai Lama.

Lourdes, France
In 1858 Bernadette Soubirous (later St. Bernadette) saw visions of the Virgin Mary in a grotto at Lourdes. Since then Catholics have made pilgrimages there, seeking cures for their illnesses.

Mecca (Makkah), Saudi Arabia
Every year, millions of Muslims go on pilgrimage to this city. They also turn to face Mecca when they pray.

Medina, Saudi Arabia
This is the site of the tomb of the prophet Muhammad.

Olympus, Greece
The ancient Greeks believed the mountain to be the home of Zeus and other gods.

Salt Lake City, Utah
The headquarters of the Church of Latter-Day Saints (Mormons)

Santiago de Compostela, Spain
In the 9th century a tomb believed to belong to the apostle James the Greater was discovered here. Christians make pilgrimages to a shrine made on the site.

Mount Shasta, California
A dormant volcano and a sacred site for Native Americans

Vatican City
The city-state in Rome, Italy, is the center of the Roman Catholic faith.

www.adherents.com search

The Koran

Allah is the Islamic name for God. Muslims believe that He revealed His wishes for the world to a man called Muhammad. These messages were later collected together as the Koran (also written Qur'an). Muslims believe that the words of the Koran are the exact words of Allah. It is said that it has not been altered since it first appeared in AD 632. The Koran is written in Arabic, the language that Muhammad spoke, and it contains the main teachings of Islam.

The Cairo Koran, made for the Sultan of Morocco in the 18th century

Boy reading from the Torah at a bar mitzvah ceremony

The Torah

The Torah is Judaism's most sacred text. It includes the first five books of the Bible, also known as the Pentateuch. These include the laws that God revealed to Moses on Mount Sinai. The Jewish scriptures also include the books of the prophets, historical writings and the Talmud. The Talmud contains instructions for following a Jewish way of life and understanding Jewish laws.

Sacred books

The Vedas

The four books of the Vedas contain the earliest Hindu beliefs and they have also influenced Buddhism, Sikhism and Jainism. The Rig-Veda is the oldest of the Vedas. It was composed about 1500 BC, although it was not written down until around 300 BC. The Vedas include rituals and hymns that give us a glimpse of life in ancient India. Another important Hindu text is the Bhagavad-Gita, or Song of the Lord. This is one section of a very long epic poem called the Mahabharata. The Bhagavad-Gita is about 700 verses long and sets out Hindu philosophy, explaining the importance of selflessness, duty, devotion and meditation.

The Pali Canon

The Pali Canon is a collection of sacred texts followed by the Theravada school of Buddhism. The teachings of the Buddha were first passed on through the spoken word and were not written down until the 1st century BC. The Pali Canon is written in the Pali language, and is also known as the Tripitaka, meaning three baskets. The texts are divided into three sections that were originally written on palm leaf scrolls and kept in three different baskets. They include rules for Buddhist monks and nuns, tales of the Buddha's life and teachings, stories and philosophical arguments.

Guru Granth Sahib

Sikhs believe that the Guru Granth Sahib is the supreme spiritual authority and head of the Sikh religion, rather than any living person. The original version was compiled by Guru Arjan Dev, the fifth Sikh guru, in 1604. He collected the compositions of previous gurus over a number of years. The text includes almost 6,000 hymns and poems composed at different times and in different languages, which makes it very difficult to translate. It also includes Hindu and Muslim writings, reflecting the religious tolerance of the gurus.

The Bible

The Christian sacred book is called the Bible. It is made up of two parts—the Old Testament and the New Testament. The Old Testament describes the history of the Israelites and contains books of history, law, poetry and wisdom. It was written by different people, probably between 1100 and 200 BC. The New Testament describes the story of Jesus' life and his importance for Christians, and also contains writings by some important early Christians. It was probably written between AD 50 and 150. Passages from the Bible are read at Christian church services, and Christians also see the Bible as containing a code to live by and guidance in following their faith.

The original 12 disciples

1 **Andrew**: a fisherman and brother of Simon Peter; crucifed in Achaia, Greece; the patron saint of Scotland and Russia (November 30)
2 **Bartholomew** (August 24)
3 **James the Great**: son of Zebedee and brother of John; martyred by Herod Agrippa (July 25)
4 **James the Less** (May 3)
5 **John**: son of Zebedee and younger brother of James the Great; also known as John the Evangelist; said to have written the Gospel that bears his name (December 27)
6 **Judas Iscariot**: the disciple who betrayed Jesus in return for 30 pieces of silver; he later hung himself
7 **Jude**: known as Judas, son of James; said to have been martyred in Persia with Simon (October 28)
8 **Matthew**: originally a tax collector before he became a disciple; author of the first Gospel (September 21)
9 **Peter**: a fisherman from Capernaeum; according to tradition he was crucified upside down; usually depicted holding the keys to heaven; considered to have been the first pope (June 29)
10 **Philip** (May 3)
11 **Simon**: also called Peter; a Galilee fisherman (October 28)
12 **Thomas**: known as Didymus, "the twin"; the patron saint of Portugal (December 21)

See also
Bestsellers: page 230

The Last Supper, painted by Pomponio Amalteo in 1574

The Last Supper

The Last Supper is an event described in the New Testament, which took place the day before Jesus was crucified. Jesus' 12 followers, called disciples, were all there. Following his crucifixion, they elected Matthias and Paul of Tarsus to join them, making a total of 14. Together they are known as the apostles and are regarded as the original Christians who acted as missionaries, spreading Jesus' teachings. All except Judas Iscariot later became saints in the Catholic church and have feast days devoted to them, listed above (some dates differ in other church traditions). The historical accounts of their lives contain many conflicting legends and details of their martyrdoms.

The Ten Commandments

The commandments are the divine law handed down to Moses by God on Mount Sinai.

They are key to both Christian and Jewish religions. The commandments appear in the books of Exodus and Deuteronomy in the Old Testament of the Bible, but are also described by Jesus in Matthew's Gospel in the New Testament, where he shortens them to just two — Love God, Love your neighbor.

1 Thou shalt have no other gods before me
2 Thou shalt not make unto thee any graven image
3 Thou shalt not take the name of the Lord thy God in vain
4 Remember the sabbath day, to keep it holy
5 Honor thy father and thy mother
6 Thou shalt not kill
7 Thou shalt not commit adultery
8 Thou shalt not steal
9 Thou shalt not bear false witness against thy neighbor
10 Thou shalt not covet thy neighbor's house, thou shalt not covet thy neighbor's wife, nor his manservant, nor his maidservant, nor his ox, nor his ass, nor any thing that is thy neighbor's

Animals in the Bible

There are many animals mentioned in the Bible. Sheep and lambs are referred to most often, probably because they were important for their meat and wool.

The lion appears because it is a symbol of power, strength and wisdom.

Animal	OT*	NT*	Total
1 Sheep	155	45	200
2 Lamb	153	35	188
3 Lion	167	9	176
4 Ox	156	10	166
5 Ram	165	0	165
6 Horse	137	27	164

* Occurrences in verses in the King James Bible
OT: Old Testament, NT: New Testament

Longest serving popes

Popes are usually chosen from among senior cardinals. They rarely live long enough to serve more than about 20 years. However, Pope Benedict IX is said to have been only 12 years old when he was elected in 1033!

Pius IX was the longest serving pope. He was 85 years old when he died. Leo XIII was even older at 93. The shortest serving pope was Urban VII, who died of malaria 12 days after his election in 1590.

Pius IX was in office for 31 years (June 16, 1846, to February 7, 1878).
John Paul II was in office for 26 years (October 16, 1978, to April 2, 2005).
Leo XIII was in office for 25 years (February 20, 1878, to July 20, 1903).
Pius VI was in office for 24 years (February 15, 1775, to August 29, 1799).
Adrian I was in office for 23 years (February 1, 772, to December 25, 795).
Pius VII was in office for 23 years (March 14, 1800, to August 20, 1823).
Alexander III was in office for 21 years (September 7, 1159, to August 30, 1181).

The Holy Grail

The Holy Grail was the cup that Jesus used at the Last Supper. According to legend, it was taken to England by Joseph of Arimathea but was lost, and King Arthur and his Knights of the Round Table went on a quest to find it. The cup was said to have magical powers — but only for those with a pure heart. The legend featured in many 19th-century paintings, as well as modern films, including *Monty Python and the Holy Grail* (1975), *Indiana Jones and the Last Crusade* (1989) and *The Da Vinci Code* (2006), based on the novel by Dan Brown.

Knights of the Round Table, a painting in the church of Trehorenteuc, France

Largest Christian populations

1 **U.S.** 245,859,613
2 **Brazil** 170,597,790
3 **Russia** 113,863,473
4 **China** 109,576,362
5 **Mexico** 99,945,687
6 **Philippines** 75,520,618
7 **India** 65,962,801

Christianity timeline

300s

1000s

c. 6–4 BC Birth of Jesus Christ, Bethlehem
AD c. 33 Christ crucified
c. 60–100 Gospels written
c. 64 Persecution of Christians by Roman Emperor Nero
312 Emperor Constantine converts to Christianity, leading to it becoming sole religion in the Roman Empire
324 Building of St. Peter's Basilica, Vatican, Rome, begun on site of Circus of Nero
c. 380 Final agreement on which books should be in the Christian Bible
635 Jerusalem and most of Middle East conquered by Muslims
999 Most of Europe converted to Christianity
1054 Christian church splits into Western (Catholic) and Eastern (Orthodox)
1095–1272 Crusades (series of wars by Christians to take holy sites in Middle East away from Muslim control)
1187 Jerusalem captured by Saladin
1209 Franciscan order of monks started
1382 John Wycliffe translates Bible into English
1456 First printed Bible (Johannes Gutenberg, Germany)
1479 Spanish Inquisition begins to persecute heretics
1517 Martin Luther begins Protestant Reformation, Germany

Patron saints

A patron saint is a saint chosen to be the protector of a particular person or group of people, or associated with a particular problem or situation.

Many more saints are called upon for help with problems than are linked with pleasant events. For example, at least 26 saints are connected with difficult marriages, but only one (St. Valentine) with happy marriages.

Patron saints for special problems

Appendicitis Erasmus
Arthritis/rheumatism James the Greater
Broken bones Drogo+
Cold weather Sebaldus
Coughs Blaise+
Dog bites Vitus
Earache Cornelius+
Famine Walburga
Floods Christopher+
Headaches Acacius+
Insect bites Felix+
Knee problems Roch+
Lost articles Anne+
Natural disasters Agatha
Poisoning Benedict+
Shipwreck Anthony of Padua
Snake bites Hilary of Poitiers+
Storms Scholastica+
Toothache Apollonia+
+ More than one saint

Patron saints of professions and groups

Accountants Matthew the Apostle
Actors Genesius of Rome+
Air travelers Joseph of Cupertino
Ambulance drivers Michael the Archangel
Architects Barbara+
Artists Luke the Apostle+
Astronauts Joseph of Cupertino
Athletes Sebastian
Authors Francis de Sales
Bakers Elizabeth of Hungary+
Beekeepers Ambrose of Milan+
Booksellers John of God+
Boys John Bosco+
Bricklayers Stephen of Hungary
Broadcasters Gabriel the Archangel
Cab drivers Christopher+
Carpenters Joseph+
Children Nicholas of Myra+
Comedians Vitus+
Cooks Martha+
Dentists Apollonia
Doctors Cosmas+
Farmers Isidore the Farmer+
Fathers Joseph
Firefighters Florian+
Fishermen Andrew the Apostle+
Gardeners Adelard
Girls Agnes of Rome+
Hairdressers Cosmas+
Librarians Jerome+
Mathematicians Barbara
Mothers Monica+
Motorcyclists Our Lady of Grace
Musicians Cecilia+
Nurses Agatha+
Plumbers Vincent Ferrer
Poets David+
Police officers Michael the Archangel+
Postal workers Gabriel the Archangel
Printers Augustine of Hippo+
Prisoners Dismas
Sailors Francis of Paola+
Scientists Albertus Magnus+
Sculptors Claude de la Columbiere+
Soldiers George+
Teachers Catherine of Alexandria+
+ More than one saint

Stained glass window of Christ with Matthew, Mark, Luke and John

One and only

According to legend, the only female saint to have grown a beard is Wilgefortis. Wilgefortis was the daughter of a king of Spain. She converted to Christianity, vowing to serve God and to remain unmarried. So when her father arranged for her to marry the king of Sicily, she prayed for a way to escape. She promptly grew a huge beard, which made her so unattractive that the wedding was called off. In a rage, her father crucified her. She became a popular saint in the Middle Ages. In Britain, she was known as Uncumber and women with troublesome husbands often prayed to her!

1800s **1900s**

1534 Henry VIII breaks with Rome; leads to the founding of the Church of England
1610–1795 Baptist, Congregationalist, Presbyterian, Quaker (Society of Friends) and Methodist Churches founded
1611 King James Bible published
1800–1900 The Age of the Mission. Western Churches send missionaries to every country in the world. Number of Christians doubles by the end of the century
1830 Church of the Latter-Day Saints (Mormons) founded, Fayette, New York, U.S.
1872 Jehovah's Witnesses founded by Charles Taze Russell, U.S.
1878 Salvation Army founded by William Booth, U.K.
1910 International Missionary Conference marks first attempt in nearly 1,000 years to reunite churches
1948 World Council of Churches founded
1962–65 Second Vatican Council radically reforms the Catholic Church worldwide
2005 Pope John Paul II dies; Pope Benedict XVI elected
2007 Boris Yeltsin's Russian Orthodox funeral is the first of a head of state in Russia since 1894

See also
History timeline: page 104

Buddhist festivals

There are a number of Buddhist traditions, and Buddhists in different countries have their own festivals on different dates. These are the most important Buddhist festivals.

- Wesak, held on the full moon in May, is the most important Buddhist festival and celebrates the birth of Buddha.
- Dharma Day celebrates Buddha's teaching and is held on the full moon of July. On Dharma Day there are readings from Buddhist scriptures, and people spend time reflecting on what they mean.
- Sangha Day is held on the full moon in November and celebrates the spiritual Buddhist community. Buddhists traditionally give presents on this day.
- Parinirvana Day, also known as Nirvana Day, marks the death of Buddha. Celebrations vary from place to place, but generally Buddhists go to temples or monasteries on this day, or meditate.

Losar

Losar is a Tibetan Buddhist festival. It is held in February and marks the New Year. The festival lasts for three days, when people go to monasteries, visit friends and family and exchange gifts.

Tibetan monks blowing horns to celebrate the Buddhist festival of Losar

Christian festivals

Epiphany (also known as Twelfth Night)

January 6 (January 18 in Russia; February 1 in Ethiopia). The Epiphany (*Epiphaneia:* Greek for manifestation) celebrates three events that are all thought to have happened on this day: Jesus' appearance as a newborn to the Magi (three wise men); Jesus' baptism, when God acknowledged his son; Jesus' first public miracle, when he turned water to wine in Galilee.

Ash Wednesday

The first day of Lent (see below). Ash Wednesday is a day of repentance for Christians, when they make amends for the year's sins before the fasting of Lent. Anglican and Roman Catholic churches hold ceremonies at which churchgoers' foreheads are marked with crosses using ash.

Lent

The 44 days before Good Friday (including Sundays). Lent is a period of fasting when Christians identify with Jesus Christ's suffering. The day before the start of Lent is known as Shrove Tuesday or "Fat Tuesday" (Mardi Gras), when Christians traditionally eat up any leftover animal products (often in the form of pancakes), as these cannot be eaten during Lent.

Palm Sunday

The Sunday before Easter Sunday and the first day of Holy Week. Palm Sunday commemorates Jesus' arrival in Jerusalem, when the crowd threw palm leaves in front of his donkey. Later that week, many in the cheering crowd were calling for Christ's execution.

Maundy (or Holy) Thursday

The Thursday before Easter Sunday. Maundy Thursday commemorates the Last Supper, which established the ceremony of Holy Communion, when bread and wine became identified with Jesus' body and blood. It was also the day when Jesus washed the feet of his disciples. At Roman Catholic church services on Maundy Thursday the priest ceremonially washes 12 people's feet.

Good Friday

The Friday before Easter Sunday. Good Friday ("good" meant "holy" in Early Modern English) commemorates the day when Jesus Christ was crucified. The symbol of the cross is an important part of church services on Good Friday, and churchgoers read the psalms and the gospels to remember Christ's experience.

Easter Sunday

The Sunday that follows the first full moon after March 21 (the spring equinox). Easter always falls between March 22 and April 25 in the Western calendar. Easter is up to two weeks later in Orthodox churches. Easter Sunday is the most important day in the Christian calendar, as it celebrates Jesus' resurrection from the dead. Easter Sunday is a day of joy for Christians.

Pentecost/Whitsunday

Fifty days after Easter Sunday. Pentecost celebrates the day the Holy Spirit entered the Apostles, enabling them to speak many new languages and spread the word of God. This event is considered by most Christians to mark the birth of the Church.

Christmas

Christmas is the celebration of the birth of Jesus on December 25 (January 6 in Russia and January 17 in Ethiopia). It comes in midwinter, a time of the year when many faiths hold festivities.

Jewish festivals

The main Jewish festivals celebrate the great events in the history of the people of Israel. The Jewish month in which they fall is given here, with an approximate equivalent in the Gregorian calendar.

Tishri (September/October)
Rosh Hashana: New Year
Yom Kippur: Day of Atonement
Sukkoth: Feast of Tabernacles
Shemini Atzeret: 8th Day of the Solemn Assembly
Simhat Torah: Rejoicing of the Law

Kislev (November/December)
Hanukkah: Feast of Dedication

Adar (February/March)
Tanrit Esther: Fast of Esther
Purim: Feast of Lots

Nisan (March/April)
Pesach (Passover)
Holocaust Remembrance Day

Iyar (April/May)
Lag B'Omer: Counting Day of Barley Sheaves

Sivan (May/June)
Shavuoth: Feast of Weeks

Tammuz (June/July)
Shiva Asar be-Tammuz: Fast of 17th Tammuz

Av (July/August)
Tisha be-Av: Fast of 9th Av

Muslims at the Grand Mosque in Mecca before pilgrimage (Hajj) month

Islamic festivals

Most Islamic festivals (see below) commemorate events in the life of the Prophet Muhammad. New Year's Day, for example, marks the day on which he set out from Mecca to Medina in the year 622. The month of the Islamic calendar in which the festival falls is given.

Every month starts approximately on the day of a new moon, or when a crescent is first seen after a new moon, so the calendar shifts and these festivals fall at different times every year according to the Gregorian calendar.

Sky lanterns lit up in India for the Divali festival

Islamic festival dates

New Year's Day 1 Muharram
Birthday of Muhammad, AD 572 12 Rabi I
Night of Ascent (of Muhammad to Heaven) 27 Rajab
Month of fasting during daylight hours 1 Ramadan
Night of Power (sending down the Koran to Muhammad) 27 Ramadan
Feast of Breaking of the Fast (Eid Ul Fitr) 1 Shawwal (end of Ramadan)
Pilgrimage (Hajj) **month** 8–13 Dhu-al-Hijja ceremonies at Makkah
Feast of the Sacrifice 10 Dhu-al-Hijja

Hindu festivals

These are the main Hindu festivals, held in honor of gods as well as to celebrate important events in mythology and in the heavens. The Hindu month in which they fall is given, with an approximate equivalent in the Gregorian calendar.

Chaitra (March/April)
Ramanavami: Birthday of Lord Rama

Asadha (June/July)
Rathayatra: Pilgrimage of the Chariot at Jaggannath

Sravana (July/August)
Jhulanayatra: Swinging the Lord Krishna
Rakshabandhana: Tying on Lucky Threads

Bhadrapada (August/September)
Janamashtami: Birthday of Lord Krishna

Asvina (September/October)
Durga-puja: Homage to Goddess Durga
Navaratri: Festival of Nine Nights
Lakshmi-puja: Homage to Goddess Lakshmi
Diwali, Dipavali: String of Lights

Magha (January/February)
Sarasvati-puja: Homage to Goddess Sarasvati
Maha-sivaratri: Great Night of Lord Shiva

Phalguna (February/March)
Holi: Festival of Fire
Dolayatra: Swing Festival

www.interfaithcalendar.org search

The Labors of Hercules

The Greek hero Hercules killed his wife Megara and some of their children after being driven mad by his stepmother, the goddess Hera.

As a punishment he had to perform 12 dangerous tasks or labors. When he succeeded in all of them, he was granted immortality.

1 Slay the Nemean lion (its skin resisted weapons, so he strangled it)
2 Kill the Hydra (a many-headed monster) of Lerna
3 Catch the Arcadian stag
4 Destroy the giant Erymanthian boar
5 Clean the Augean stables
6 Destroy the cannibal birds of the Lake Stymphalis
7 Capture the fire-breathing Cretan bull
8 Catch the horses of the Thracian king Diomedes
9 Seize the girdle of Hippolyta, Queen of the Amazons
10 Capture the oxen of the monster Geryon
11 Obtain the golden apples of the Hesperides
12 Bring Cerberus from Hades (hell)

Statue of Hercules fighting with the Cretan bull

Unicorns

A unicorn has the body of a horse, a lion's tail, a goat's beard, an antelope's legs and a single, often twisted, horn growing from its forehead. The unicorn is a popular subject in medieval stories; it is ferocious but good, and can purify water — or neutralize poison — by dipping its horn into it. The way to catch a unicorn is to use a young girl as bait, as a unicorn will lie down peacefully next to a maiden.

Figurehead of *The Unicorn*, a former warship

Mythical creatures

Almost every culture on Earth has legends of imaginary beasts. Some are like humans with supernatural powers; some are part human, part animal; while others are unlike anything we know.

Giants
Giants or ogres are enormous human-shaped creatures. They are usually seen as fearsome but stupid monsters that feed on human flesh. Famous giants include Goliath in the Bible, and Cyclops, Atlas and the Titans in Greek mythology.

Leprechauns
Leprechauns are small Irish fairies who bring good luck. They are helpful creatures, usually shown wearing green clothes, with an apron, buckled shoes and a red cap. Their fun-loving nature means that leprechauns are fond of alcohol, music and sports, but they are also mischievous and love practical jokes. Other "little people," including elves, dwarfs, gnomes and pixies, appear in many European fairy stories.

Centaurs
A centaur is half-horse and half man, with the head and arms o a man and the body of a horse. It is one of the best known of a Greek mythological creatures and is said to have come from Thessaly in northern Greece. The myth may have arisen becau of the skillful horsemanship of the people there.

Fairies
Fairies also feature in many tale They are usually sweet, kindly creatures. In the Middle Ages, however, people believed that fairies stole children and replac them with fairy beings known as changelings.

Heroes of legend

King Arthur
Legend says that Arthur, king of the Britons, won the throne by pulling a sword — the famous Excalibur — from a stone. This was a feat that only the true king was able to achieve. Arthur ruled during a period of peace and prosperity in Great Britain. Some folk tales say that if Great Britain is in danger, Arthur will return with his knights to defend the nation.

Beowulf
Beowulf was a Scandinavian warrior and the hero of *Beowulf*, the oldest poem in the English language. Beowulf was loyal to his king and also extremely brave. He killed Grendel the ogre, Grendel's mother and finally a fearsome dragon, which cost him his own life.

Paul Bunyan
The lumberjack Paul Bunyan is a famous character in American folklore. It is said that he was so enormous, he created the Grand Canyon by dragging his pick behind him, and his giant footsteps formed the lakes of Minnesota. The legend came from stories told by the lumberjacks of the northern United States.

El Cid
El Cid really did exist and many legends have grown up around him. He was also known as El Ci Campeador (meaning my lord, the champion). His real name was Rodrigo Díaz de Vivar and h was a Spanish nobleman who was born in about 1040 and die in 1099. El Cid is a national hero in Spain because he is seen as a brave and accomplished warrior who fought to take control of

Mermaids

Mermaids are beautiful creatures with the head and body of a woman and the tail of a fish. The first mermaid legend is thought to have been the story of Atargatis, a Syrian moon goddess of about 1000 BC. Atargatis had a child with a human. She then killed her lover, abandoned the child and jumped into a lake, where she took the form of a mermaid.

Vampires

Vampires are the "undead" who drink the blood of the living to survive. Ideas about vampires include the belief that plunging a wooden stake through a vampire's heart can destroy it. Some people also think that you can protect yourself against vampires with garlic, holy water, crosses and bibles, and that a vampire cannot enter a home unless invited.

Werewolves

Werewolves, or lycanthropes, are mythical creatures in the folk tales of many cultures. They usually appear as men by day, but may turn into wolves on the night of a full moon. The werewolf is bloodthirsty and ruthless. It devours its prey and shows none of the remorse that it might have felt in human form.

Trolls

Trolls are grotesque, malicious, rather dim-witted creatures in Scandinavian folklore. They are said to steal sleeping children, sometimes replacing them with one of their own. Trolls have poor eyesight, and are active only at night because sunlight turns them to stone.

Dragon at the end of the Dragon Bridge in Ljubljana, Slovenia

See also

Monsters in the movies: page 272

Dragons

Dragons appear in the myths of many cultures, especially China, where the dragon was a symbol of the emperor. A typical dragon has a serpent-like body covered with scales, large wings, and can breathe fire. In legends, dragons often guard a cave of treasure.

Spain from the Muslims. Legend suggests that El Cid fought for both sides at different times.

St. George

St. George was a soldier for the Roman Empire who refused to take part in the Empire's persecution of Christians. He was executed for treachery and became a Christian martyr. Later, King Edward III made him the patron saint of England. St. George is the hero of a legend in which he slays a man-eating dragon that was guarding a city's water supply. The city's inhabitants were so grateful that they converted from paganism to George's Christianity.

Hercules/Heracles

According to Greek and Roman mythology, Hercules was born with superhuman strength. By the time he reached adulthood he had killed a lion. Hercules had a jealous stepmother who drove him to madness. While in this state, Hercules killed his wife and children. In order to regain his honor, Hercules had to perform 12 difficult tasks (see p. 170).

Robin Hood

The Robin Hood of folklore was an English nobleman whose land was seized while King Richard the Lionheart was away fighting in the Crusades (1188–92). He became an outlaw in Sherwood Forest and led a band of Merry Men (and Maid Marian, his true love). They robbed the nobility who traveled through the forest and passed on the valuables they stole to the poor and needy. Robin Hood was a master of disguise and many stories describe how he dressed as somebody else in order to trick his enemies or rescue his friends.

Good and bad luck signs

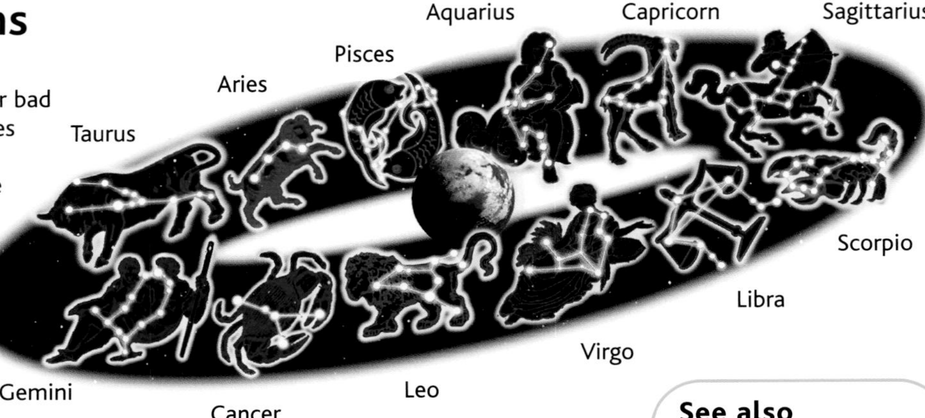

Black cats

Whether you find black cats to be good luck or bad depends on where you live. In the United States and Canada, a black cat is seen as a very bad omen, whereas in the U.K., for instance, people think black cats are lucky, particularly if they cross your path. On the other hand, in the U.S. a white cat is very good luck, while in the U.K., it is a sign of bad luck.

Horseshoes

A horseshoe is a piece of metal fixed to a horse's foot. Some people think that if you find a horseshoe and the open space is facing you it will bring you luck. Traditionally, people also hang horseshoes above the doorway of their home to bring good luck. In some countries, the horseshoe is hung downward — that's believed to let the luck flow out into the house. In others, the shoe must be hung with the opening at the top to keep the good fortune.

Lucky horseshoe

See also
Constellations: page 21

Clovers

Four-leaf clovers are very rare. Anyone who finds one is said to be able to recognize evil influences and avoid them.

Ladders

A ladder leaning against a wall forms a triangle. Some believe it is disrespectful, and unlucky, to walk underneath one because triangles symbolize the Holy Trinity. The bad luck is warded off by crossing the fingers or making a wish while under the ladder.

Magpies

Magpies are generally thought to be unlucky. This belief is said to come from the Bible, as the magpie was the only bird that refused to enter Noah's Ark. In China, however, the magpie is a good omen, and should never be killed.

Mirrors

Breaking a mirror is said to bring seven years' bad luck. This idea may come from the old belief that your reflection is an image of your soul, so anything that changes the reflection may bring evil. The length of the period of bad luck may come from the Roman belief that life renews itself every seven years.

Spilling salt

Salt was once valuable and spilling it was thought to cause bad luck, unless the person who spills it throws a pinch over their left shoulder. In his painting of the Last Supper, Leonardo da Vinci shows Jesus' betrayer Judas knocking over the salt shaker.

The signs of the zodiac

In Western astrology the zodiac has 12 parts. Each is named after a constellation and corresponds to a different time of year. Astrologists believe that the movements of the planets influence what happens on Earth, and that people born under the different signs have certain characteristics.

Aries, the ram
March 21–April 19
Creative, impatient, masculine, competitive, warrior-like, independent, outspoken

Taurus, the bull
April 20–May 20
Determined, resourceful, materialistic, touchy, ruthless, entrepreneurial

Gemini, the twins
May 21–June 21
Intellectual, shallow, inquisitive, selfish, talkative, witty, indecisive, irritable

Cancer, the crab
June 22–July 22
Emotional, sympathetic, moody, sensitive, home-loving, romantic, loyal, tactless

Leo, the lion
July23–August 22
Generous, creative, broad-minded, patronizing, bossy, extroverted, idealistic, arrogant

Virgo, the virgin
August 23–September 23
Diligent, intelligent, modest, conservative, overcritical, pedantic, affectionate, methodical

Libra, the scales
September 24–October 23
Charming, sociable, gullible, flirtatious, attractive, objective, artistic

Scorpio, the scorpion
October 24 –November 22
Forceful, passionate, jealous, obsessive, secretive, intense, outspoken, extreme, rebellious

Sagittarius, the archer
November 23–December 21
Optimistic, honest, philosophical, careless, irresponsible, energetic, adventurous

Capricorn, the goat
December 22–January 20
Disciplined, economical, patient, reserved, pessimistic, serious, organized, rational

Aquarius, the water bearer
January 1–February 19
Inventive, friendly, independent, unpredictable, serious, intelligent, eccentric

Pisces, the fishes
February 20–March 20
Imaginative, compassionate, vague, gentle, sensitive, creative, spiritual, easygoing

Number 13

The belief that the number 13 is unlucky is very ancient. The Romans believed the number 13 was a symbol of death and destruction. Norse legends claimed that the 13th guest at a banquet is the spirit of evil.

The Christian belief that the number brings bad luck is often said to come from the Last Supper, when Christ sat down with his 12 disciples — making 13 people. Some people think that the first person to leave a dinner table at which there are 13 diners will die before the end of the year.

Unlucky for some?

- The 13th *Apollo* space mission was known as *Apollo 13*. On April 13, 1970, there was an explosion on board and the spacecraft began to leak oxygen. This happened two days after it took off at 13:13 (1:13 pm). The spacecraft only just made it back to Earth.
- On Friday, September 13, 1928, a hurricane killed 2,000 people in Puerto Rico, Florida and the Virgin Islands, and caused approximately $25 million in damage.
- In some countries, high-rise buildings do not have a 13th floor. The floor numbering may skip directly from 12 to 14, or what would be the 13th is given another name, for example, "12A," or as in the Radisson Hotel, Winnipeg, Manitoba, where the 13th floor is called the "Pool Floor."
- The 13th of the month costs the U.S. about $1 billion a year through cancellations on trains and planes, absenteeism from work, and reduced business activity.

Lucky for others?

- The number 13 was sacred for the Mayans and Aztecs of Central America, and it is traditionally a lucky number in China.
- Buddhists pay homage to 13 Buddhas, and the orthodox Jewish prayerbook holds 13 principles of faith.

See also
The Last Supper: page 165

Predictions that were wrong

"I give Castro a year."
Former Cuban dictator Fulgencio Batista, 1959. Fidel Castro stayed in power for 49 years.

"It will be years — not in my time — before a woman will become prime minister."
Margaret Thatcher, 1974. She was the British prime minister from 1979 to 1990.

"It is too early for a Polish pope."
Karol Wojitya, 1978, shortly before being elected as Pope John Paul II.

"No, thank you."
Several agents who rejected J.K. Rowling's first Harry Potter book.

Palmistry

Palmistry is the art of telling the future from the lines on the palms of your hands. The lines are unique to each person and are said to show the person's character and what will happen in the future. Palmistry began in India thousands of years ago as a form of counseling.

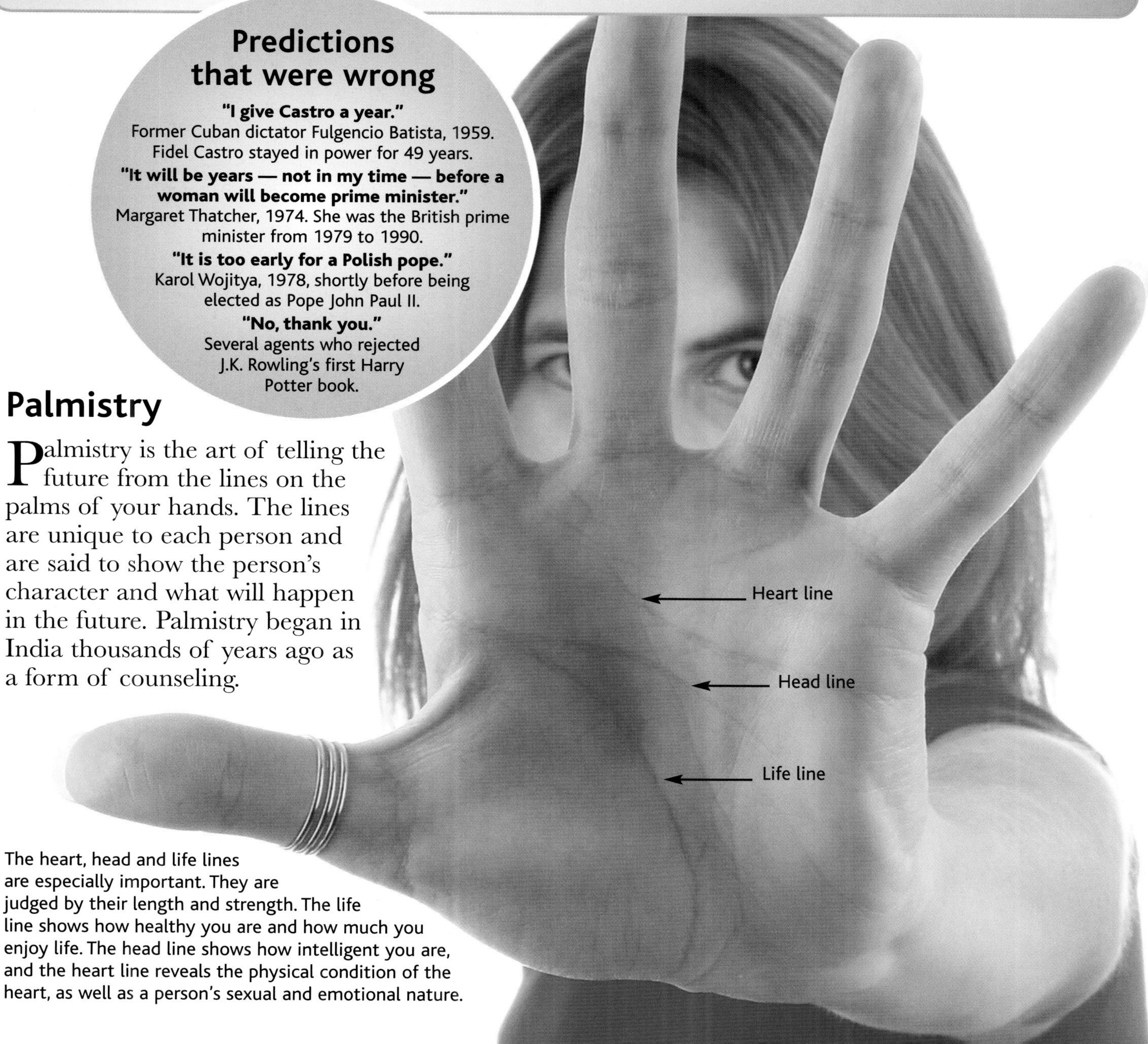

The heart, head and life lines are especially important. They are judged by their length and strength. The life line shows how healthy you are and how much you enjoy life. The head line shows how intelligent you are, and the heart line reveals the physical condition of the heart, as well as a person's sexual and emotional nature.

Mysterious places

The Nazca Lines

The Nazca Lines are enormous drawings on the ground (called geoglyphs) that stretch across the Nazca Desert in southern Peru. They show more than 300 geometric patterns, spirals and animals. The lines are so vast (one extends 40 mi. [65 km]) that they can only be seen properly from a height of about 1,000 ft. (300 m). Most experts agree that they were made by the Nazca Indians who lived in the region between 300 BC and AD 800, but there are many questions yet to be answered about them. For example, why were the pictures made and how are they so precise if their makers had no means to view them from the sky?

Stonehenge

Stonehenge is a circle of 17 upright stones called sarsens that stand on Salisbury Plain in southwest England. The stones weigh up to 55 tons (50 tonnes) and have other stones, called lintels, laid across the top. There is also an inner circle of smaller bluestones weighing up to 4.5 tons (4 tonnes) each. Stonehenge is the only stone circle in the world with lintels across the top of the stones, and experts think it was completed in about 1500 BC. They believe that the sarsen stones were transported from 20 mi. (32 km) away and the bluestones came from an incredible 155 mi. (250 km) away. At least 600 men would have been needed to move each sarsen stone on some of the steepest parts of the journey. Nobody knows exactly why Stonehenge was built, but it may have been a druids' temple or even a kind of astronomical calendar.

Teotihuacán

In AD 600 Teotihuacán in Mexico was the sixth-largest city in the world and about 200,000 people lived there. Just 150 years later, Teotihuacán was almost deserted, and plants had begun to grow over the city's huge pyramids. Nobody knows why Teotihuacán was abandoned, but it may have been devastated by a huge fire in AD 650.

The Bermuda Triangle

The Bermuda Triangle is an area of the Atlantic Ocean off the coast of Florida. It is famous for being the supposed site of many unexplained disappearances. The points of the triangle are Miami, Bermuda and San Juan in Puerto Rico. In the 15th century, Christopher Columbus claimed to have seen a "great flame of fire" falling into the ocean in the area. The Bermuda Triangle first began to attract attention in 1945, when Flight 19, a training mission of five U.S. bombers, vanished off the Florida coast. The plane that was sent to find them also disappeared, and around 100 boats and aircraft have been lost there. Explanations include magnetic fields, sea monsters and abduction by aliens, but most experts agree the disappearances are due to bad navigation and/or extreme weather conditions.

See also
Aztec empire: page 107

Teotihuacán

Easter Island

Easter Island (or Rapa Nui) lies in the South Pacific between Chile and Tahiti, and is one of the most isolated islands in the world. By the 16th century, Easter Island had nearly 10,000 inhabitants, who made huge statues known as *moai*. The 887 *moai* were carved from the island's volcanic rock and have long, angular faces. Some have eyes made from coral. The average *moai* was about 13 ft. (4 m) tall and weighed over 15 tons (14 tonnes), so they would have been extremely difficult for the islanders to transport. Archaeologists believe that the statues symbolize the spirits of Easter Island's most important inhabitants.

Four of the huge *moai* figures on Easter Island

Crop circles

Crop circles are complicated geometric patterns, usually in wheat fields. Some people believe that the patterns are left by the imprint of an extraterrestrial craft, or that they are a message from extraterrestrials themselves.

Another theory is that natural forces such as tornadoes, heat or strong winds create the patterns by flattening the crops, but the regular shapes of most crop circles makes this unlikely. The most likely explanation is that the circles are made by people as a hoax. They gradually build up a design by flattening the wheat, using very basic equipment such as rope and planks of wood.

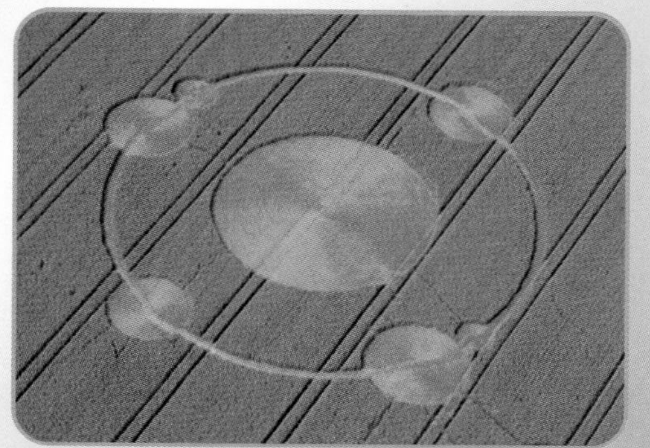

Crop circles in Slovenia

On the Moon, or is this photo a fake?

Conspiracy theories

Many people believe that certain well-known historical events have been manipulated by governments and other secret organizations to conceal the truth. Some of the better-known beliefs are:

- A secret society called the Illuminati controls the world. This shadowy organization features in Dan Brown's novel *Angels and Demons*. Other powerful secret societies, including Opus Dei and the Priory of Sion, feature in his bestselling *The Da Vinci Code*.
- Sinister groups were responsible for plotting the deaths of U.S. President Abraham Lincoln, civil rights leader Martin Luther King Jr., musician John Lennon and Princess Diana. Some people claim that the Mafia were responsible for assassinating U.S. President John F. Kennedy. Others believe it was the work of Russian spies.
- Inventions have been hushed up by big businesses and oil companies who fear loss of income if new technologies become available. These include light bulbs that last for ever and ways of running cars on water.
- Aliens from other planets have crashed on Earth at Roswell, New Mexico. Their bodies and spacecraft have been secretly examined in a place in Nevada, known as Area 51, and the U.S. government has acquired advanced weapon and space travel technology from them.
- Photographs of the *Apollo* Moon landings (July 20, 1969) were faked by NASA in a TV studio. Conspiracy theorists have produced "evidence" such as the wrong sort of shadows and a lack of stars in the photographs, which were supposedly taken on the Moon's surface. They have even suggested that some astronauts were killed as part of the coverup.

Mysterious monsters

The Loch Ness Monster

The Loch Ness Monster, nicknamed Nessie, is said to live in Loch Ness in Scotland. The monster is generally thought to be a long-necked creature with flippers, like a prehistoric reptile. Many people have reported seeing Nessie, and in 2006 it was claimed that it might have been a circus elephant swimming in the Loch! However, there is no real evidence that the creature exists.

Yeti

The Yeti, also called the Abominable Snowman, is believed to live in the Himalayan mountains. People say this legendary creature measures up to 8 ft. (1.4 m), is covered in long brown hair, and walks upright like a human being. Everest mountaineers, including Sir Edmund Hillary and Sherpa Tenzing Norgay, have reported seeing mysterious footprints in the snow.

Bigfoot

Another legendary creature is said to live in the northwest of North America. People who claim to have seen Bigfoot say it is a large, hairy creature that walks upright like the Yeti. There is no firm evidence that Bigfoot exists, but there are some fuzzy photos and videos that are supposed to show this mystery monster.

Elvis sightings

Singing legend Elvis Presley died on August 16, 1977, but many people all over the world have claimed to have seen him since — in supermarkets, at gas stations, even working in burger joints. There is a society devoted to Elvis sightings and an "Elvis is Alive Museum" in Wright City, Missouri. If Elvis were alive today, he would be over 73 years old.

Conflict & Crime

178 WEAPONS AND FORCES
180 WARS AND BATTLES
182 THE LAW
184 CRIME

Genocide in Darfur

The ongoing conflict in Darfur has resulted in the deaths of more than 200,000 people, and has driven at least two million refugees into neighboring countries. Sudan's government has been accused of unleashing Janjaweed militia to commit atrocities against Darfur's ethnic African communities. A plan to install a UN and African Union peacekeeping force of more than 26,000 soldiers by January 2008 failed due to political and logistical problems.

Weapons named after people

● Big Bertha
Big Bertha was a 161 tons (144 tonne) cannon used by the German army to shell Paris from a distance of 76 mi. (122 km) during World War I. The name came from Bertha Krupp von Bohlen und Halbach (1886–1957), who inherited the German Krupp armaments business from her father.

● Browning pistol
Invented in the United States in 1896 by John Moses Browning (1855–1926), the Browning was an automatic pistol used by both civilians and military.

● Gatling gun
In 1862, Dr. Richard Jordan Gatling (1818–1903) patented the hand-cranked machine gun with a fire rate of up to 350 rounds per minute. It appeared too late to be widely used in the U.S. Civil War, and it was soon overtaken by more efficient weapons.
The slang term "gat" for any gun derives from the name.

● Kalashnikov
This machine gun is named after its inventor, Russian Mikhail Kalashnikov (1919–). More than 70 million have been made.

● Lüger
Gunmaker Georg Lüger (1849–1923) pioneered the P-08 pistol that bears his name in 1898. It was adopted by the German army and was widely used during both world wars.

● Mauser
The Mauser bolt-action rifle was developed in 1898 by German brothers Wilhelm (1834–82) and Peter Paul Mauser (1838–1914). They also invented an automatic pistol.

Nuclear explosion

● Maxim gun
U.S. (later British) inventor Sir Hiram Maxim (1840–1916), who was also an aviation pioneer, made this machine gun in 1884.

● Molotov cocktail
This was a crude but effective bomb made with a gasoline-filled bottle and fuse. It was given its name by the Finns in about 1940 who used it during the war against Russia. They called it a cocktail for Molotov. Vyacheslav Mikhailovich Molotov (1890–1986) was the Soviet prime minister at the time.

● Shrapnel
This name was given to exploding shells invented by British officer Henry Shrapnel (1761–1842). Fragments of bombs are now also called shrapnel.

● Tommy gun
The Thompson submachine gun was invented by American army general John Taliaferro Thompson and U.S. Navy commander John N. Blish. It became known as the Tommy gun and was popular with gangsters during the 1920s.

Weird weapons

Combined gun and plow
This was patented by C.M. French and W.H. Fancher of Waterloo, New York, in 1862. It was designed to be used by farmers so they could quickly turn their plows into powerful guns if they were attacked while plowing.

Hard cheese
In 1865 during a war between Uruguay and Brazil, a Uruguayan ship ran out of cannon balls. Instead they fired stale Dutch cheeses, one of which dismasted an enemy vessel and killed two sailors.

Boomerang bullets
These bullets were invented in the United States in 1870, and were designed to fire in a curved line. The danger was that if they traveled in a complete circle, they could kill the person who fired them.

Countries with nuclear weapons

These numbers of nuclear warheads are as estimated by the Carnegie Endowment for International Peace. The total for Israel is not officially acknowledged.

Russia: 7,200–16,000
U.S.: 5,735–9,960
France: 350
U.K.: 200
India: 120–200
Israel: 75–170
China: 130
Pakistan: 30–92
North Korea: 1–10
World total: 27,600

Weapons milestones

1500s

500,000 BC Spears
250,000 BC Stone axes
25,000 BC Boomerang-like weapons (Poland) and knives
15,000 BC Spear-throwers
3000 BC Bows and arrows, shields and war chariots; Galleys (Crete)
2000 BC Armor and swords
865 BC Battering rams and other siege engines (Assyria)
397 BC Catapults propelling darts
332 BC Catapults throwing stones
AD 7th century Gunpowder (China)
8th century Viking longships
11th century Chain mail and crossbows
1150 Longbows
1221 Bombs (China)
1242 English monk Roger Bacon first describes gunpowder
1288 First guns (China)
1324 Cannon used at Battle of Metz
1346 Cannon (siege of Calais)
1370s Arbalests (crossbows)
1492 Leonardo da Vinci invents giant siege crossbows
1514 Man-of-war
1515 Wheel-lock muskets
1590 Bayonets made at Bayonne, France
1776 Submarine torpedoes
1784 Shrapnel shells
1835 Revolvers, Samuel Colt (U.S.)
1838 Breech-loading rifles
1847 Guncotton, invented by Christian Friedrick Schönbein
1847 Nitroglycerin (explosive) invented by Ascanio Solaro
1850 Battleships
1860 Repeating rifle invented by Christopher Spencer (U.S.)
1861 Metal gun cartridges and sea mines
1862 Gatling machine guns and Winchester repeating rifles
1866 Dynamite invented by Alfred Nobel (Sweden)
1872 Automatic pistols
1884 Maxim machine guns
1897 Dum-dum bullets (banned 1908)
1898 Lüger pistols

Largest armed forces

The number of personnel in the armed forces listed below are all active forces, but some countries have many reserves who can be called for service if needed. South Korea may have as many as 4.5 million reserve forces, Vietnam may have 5 million and China 800,000.

1 China 1,600,000 army, 255,000 navy and 400,000 air force personnel. Total: 2,255,000

2 U.S. 593,327 army, 341,588 navy and 336,081 air force personnel. Total: 1,498,157

3 India 1,100,000 army, 55,000 navy and 125,000 air force personnel. Total: 1,288,000

4 North Korea 950,000 army, 46,000 navy and 110,000 air force personnel. Total: 1,106,000

5 Russia 360,000 army, 142,000 navy and 195,000 air force personnel. Total: 1,027,000

Some totals include other forces.

Biological warfare

The aim of biological warfare is to infect enemies with deadly diseases. It is a modern form of warfare. However, in the Middle Ages the rotting carcasses of animals were catapulted into enemy castles to infect the inhabitants. In 1500, Leonardo da Vinci suggested using bombs containing saliva from mad dogs or pigs, or the venom of animals such as toads and spiders.

Gunner on a U.S. army Black Hawk helicopter

2000s

1901 Modern submarines
1902 Armored cars
1911 Aircraft carriers and bombers
1914 Zeppelin airships and large multi-engined aircraft able to carry heavy bombs used in aerial warfare
1914 Flechéttes first used — steel darts, designed to be dropped from aircraft on the enemy beneath
1915 Aircraft machine gun invented by German manufacturer Anthony Fokker
1915 Poisonous gases, such as mustard gas, chlorine and tear gas, first used by German army at Ypres. Gas masks invented to combat them
1915 Rifles with periscopic sights (allowing users to remain hidden) invented by an Australian soldier
1917 Water-cooled Browning machine guns invented by John Browning. Tanks introduced as a way of getting through enemy barbed wire, and increasingly as a battlefield weapon
1936 Nerve gas (Tabun) and Spitfire fighter aircraft
1939 Military helicopters
1940 Bazookas and radar
1942 Napalm and V2 rockets
1942 Dam-buster bombs
1943 Jet bombers and fighters
1945 Atomic bomb
1952 Hydrogen bomb
1955 Nuclear submarines
1960 Harrier jump jets
1970 Exocet missiles
1982 Air-launched cruise missiles
1984 Stun guns
1988 Stealth bombers
1988 IMINT (Imagery Intelligence) satellites
2001 Heckler and Koch MP7 submachine guns
2003 Multiple JDAM (Joint Direct Attack Munition) air-launched smart bombs
2009 (Scheduled launch date) Boeing YAL-1 Airborne Laser (ABL) system capable of shooting down missiles.

Great land battles

●Marathon, Greece, September 490 BC
The Athenians defeated an invading Persian army during the Battle of Marathon.

●Hastings, England, October 14, 1066
In the last successful invasion of England, the Norman and French army under William, Duke of Normandy, defeated the Saxons under King Harold. Harold was killed and William, known as William the Conqueror, was crowned King of England.

●Agincourt, France, October 25, 1415
Despite being heavily outnumbered (5,700 against 25,000), the English army under King Henry V decisively defeated the French. This gained them control of much of France.

●Naseby, England, June 14, 1645
In the English Civil War Oliver Cromwell's New Model Army defeated the Royalist army of King Charles I. The king was later taken prisoner and executed.

●Blenheim, Bavaria, August 13, 1704
This battle took place in the War of the Spanish Succession. English and Dutch troops crossed Germany and defeated the Franco-Bavarian army. The English and Dutch were led by John Churchill, later Duke of Marlborough.

●Yorktown, Virginia, October 6–19, 1781
In the American Revolutionary War, the British were forced to surrender by the U.S army led by General George Washington, later the first president of the United States.

● Waterloo, Belgium, June 18, 1815
During the Napoleonic Wars, the Emperor Napoleon's army was defeated by the British and allies under the Duke of Wellington.

● Gettysburg, Pennsylvania, July 1–3, 1863
During this important American Civil War battle, the Confederate (Southern) army under General Robert E. Lee was defeated by the Union army.

● Somme, France, July 1–November 18, 1916
In World War I, the British army under General Sir Douglas Haig tried to end the stalemate of trench warfare against the Germans. This led to the first of two battles of the Somme River. Neither side gained anything, and both suffered massive casualties.

● El Alamein, Egypt, July 1–27, October 23–November 4, 1942
These two World War II battles were fought in the desert when the British 8th Army under Lieutenant-General Bernard Montgomery eventually crushed the German and Italian armies under Field Marshal Erwin Rommel.

● Desert Shield/Storm/Sabre, Iraq/Kuwait, January 16–February 27, 1991
These Gulf War campaigns were a response to Iraq's invasion of Kuwait. Coalition forces led by the United States drove the Iraqis out through a combination of air and land attack.

Stalingrad

During World War II, the German 6th Army was surrounded by the Soviet army in Stalingrad (now Volgograd), USSR, and suffered huge casualties in an extended siege from August 19, 1942, to February 2, 1943.

Worst battles

The Battle of Stalingrad was one of the longest and bloodiest battles of all time. It was fought between German and Soviet forces and continued from August 19, 1942, to February 2, 1943. The total number of casualties can only be estimated.

1 The Battle of Stalingrad World War II, 1942–43: 2,000,000 casualties
2 The Battle of the Somme River I World War I, 1916: 1,000,000 casualties
3 Po Valley World War II, 1945: 740,000 casualties
4 Moscow World War II, 1941–42: 700,000 casualties
5 Gallipoli World War I, 1915–16: 500,000 casualties
Figures are the estimated total of military and civilian dead, wounded and missing

Soviet troops massing for the Stalingrad Offensive in 1942

Major wars

1600s

431–404 BC Peloponnesian War
Sparta vs Athens

264–146 BC Punic Wars
Rome vs Carthage

1095–1291 Crusades
Christians vs Muslims

1337–1543 Hundred Years' War
England vs France

1455–85 Wars of the Roses
York vs Lancaster

1618–48 Thirty Years' War
Catholic vs Protestant forces in Europe

1642–51 English Civil War
Crown vs Parliament

1701–14 War of the Spanish Succession
France vs Grand Alliance (of other European countries)

1740–48 War of the Austrian Succession
France, Spain, Bavaria, Prussia vs Great Britain, Netherlands, Savoy

1756–63 Seven Years' War
Austria, Russia, France, Sweden, Poland vs Prussia, Great Britain, Portugal

1775–83 American War of Independence
America vs Great Britain

1792–1815 Napoleonic Wars
Great Britain, Austria, Russia, Sweden, Naples vs France

1812–15 War of 1812
U.S. vs Great Britain

1846–48 Mexico-American War
Mexico vs U.S.

1853–56 Crimean War
Russia vs Turkey, Great Britain, France, Sardinia

Trafalgar

On October 21, 1805, during the Napoleonic Wars, the British fleet under Lord Nelson won this sea battle against the French, although Nelson was killed.

The Battle of Trafalgar, painted by John Callow, 1875

Great sea battles

Salamis, October 20, 480 BC (Greco-Persian Wars)
The Greeks overcame a Persian fleet, saving Greece from conquest.

Aegosopotami, 405 BC (Peloponnesian War)
In this battle 180 Athenian triremes were faced with 170 Peloponnesian ships. The Athenians were conquered, and the Peloponnesian War ended.

Actium, September 2, 31 BC (Wars of the Second Triumvirate)
Mark Antony and the Egyptian fleet were defeated by the Romans during this battle.

Lepanto, October 7, 1571 (Cyprus War)
The Spanish force defeated the Turkish fleet, which lost 25,000 sailors in 250 galleys.

Spanish Armada, July 29, 1588 (Anglo-Spanish War)
In July 1588, 130 Spanish ships with 2,500 guns and 30,000 troops set out to attack England. The English fleet badly damaged the Spanish ships with their guns, and the rest of the fleet was destroyed by bad weather.

Jutland, May 31, 1916 (World War I)
During this engagement the Royal Navy took on the German fleet, which withdrew.

Guadalcanal, August 9–November 30, 1942 (World War II)
This series of six naval engagements between the U.S. and Japanese resulted in heavy losses on both sides.

Coral Sea, May 8, 1942 (World War II)
The US.. Navy took on the Japanese in the first major battle fought using aircraft from carriers.

Leyte Gulf, October 22–27, 1944 (World War II)
The U.S. defeated Japan in this battle. The Japanese lost three battleships, four aircraft carriers, 10 cruisers and nine destroyers.

Youngest medal winners

The Victoria Cross is the highest military award in Canada. The youngest winner was Thomas Ricketts (1901–67) of White Bay, Newfoundland, who was 17 when he took part in an action in Belgium for which he received the medal. It was presented to him personally by King George V at Sandringham, U.K. This and his other medals are displayed at the Canadian War Museum, Ottawa.

U.S.: William Johnston was a drummer who won the Congressional Medal of Honor, United States highest military award, when he was 12. The award was for bravery in action during the Seven Day Battle and Peninsular Campaign of 1862.

1900s

1861–65 American Civil War
North vs Confederate (Southern) states

1870–71 Franco-Prussian War
France vs Germany

1894–95 Chinese-Japanese War
China vs Japan

1898 Spanish-American War
Spain vs U.S.

1899–1902 Boer War
Boers (South Africa) vs Great Britain

1904–1905 Russo-Japanese War
Russia vs Japan

1914–18 World War I
Allies vs Germany and others

1931–33 Chinese-Japanese War
China vs Japan

1936–39 Spanish Civil War
Nationalists vs Republicans

1937–45 Chinese-Japanese War
China vs Japan

1939–45 World War II
Allies vs Germany and others (Axis powers)

1950–53 Korean War
North Korea (with Chinese aid) vs South Korea (supported by U.S.)

1957–75 Vietnam War
North Vietnam vs South Vietnam (with U.S. aid)

2000s

1982 Falklands War
Argentina vs Great Britain

1991 Gulf War
Iraq vs Allied forces

2001– "War on Terror"
U.S. and allies vs al-Qaeda, Taliban in Afghanistan

2003 Iraq War
U.S. and allies vs Iraq

Legal language

Accessory — someone who assists a criminal
Accomplice — a criminal's partner in crime
Acquit — to free or release from a charge, find not guilty
Affidavit — a written statement
Arson — deliberately setting a building on fire
Assault — inflicting harm on another person
Bail — a sum of money paid to ensure a person appears in court. The money is forfeited if they fail to appear
Battery — unlawful assault
Blackmail — attempting to obtain money by threats
Burglary — breaking into a building to commit theft
Capital crime — a crime for which the penalty is death
Civil cases — disputes between individuals
Criminal case — deals with acts considered harmful to the community
Damages — money paid as compensation for injury or loss
Defamation — harming a person's reputation by libel or slander
Evidence — information presented to a court to prove or disprove a legal issue, such as a defendant's guilt or innocence
Fraud — deception to gain money, etc.
Homicide — the unlawful killing of another person
Indictment — a written accusation
Kidnap — illegally carrying off a person, for example, to obtain ransom payment
Libel — defamation in writing, such as in a newspaper article
Manslaughter — taking another person's life without deliberate intent
Misdemeanor — United States law distinguishes between serious crimes, or felonies, and less serious, or petty (from the French word for "little") crimes or misdemeanors. The maximum penalty for a person convicted of a misdemeanor is 12 months in prison, but probation or community service are the more usual punishments.
Murder — the deliberate killing of another person
Oath — a promise to tell the truth in court, often sworn on a holy book such as the Bible
Perjury — a false statement made while under oath in a court
Probation — placing an offender under the supervision of a probation officer
Robbery — theft with force or threat of violence
Slander — defamation of a person in spoken language
Sue — to bring legal proceedings against a person, organization, etc.
Summons — an official order to attend court
Trespass — illegal entry of another person's property
Trial — the examination of a case in a court of law
Vandalism — deliberate damage to another's property
Verdict — the outcome of a trial, i.e., whether the accused is guilty or not guilty
Warrant — a legal document allowing for someone's arrest, the search of their property, etc.

Law courts

This is the court system in the United States. In many court rooms there is an image of justice as a woman, which dates from Roman times. It traditionally shows her holding scales in one hand, to show that she is impartial, and a sword to represent the power of the law. Sometimes she is blindfolded to show that justice cannot be influenced.

Juvenile Court

These courts deal with cases involving people under the age of 18, except in New York and North Carolina, where the maximum age is 16.

District Court

These courts deal with civil and criminal cases. There is at least one District Court in each state

Court of Appeals

The United States has thirteen Courts of Appeals that rank between District Courts and the Supreme Court. They try cases where a person who has been convicted can appeal against the lower court's verdict.

Federal Court

This is the name given to all courts acting under the United States Constitution, whether at District or Appeal level.

Supreme Court

The highest court in the United States sits in Washington, DC, and hears cases previously tried in a federal court whose decision is disputed.

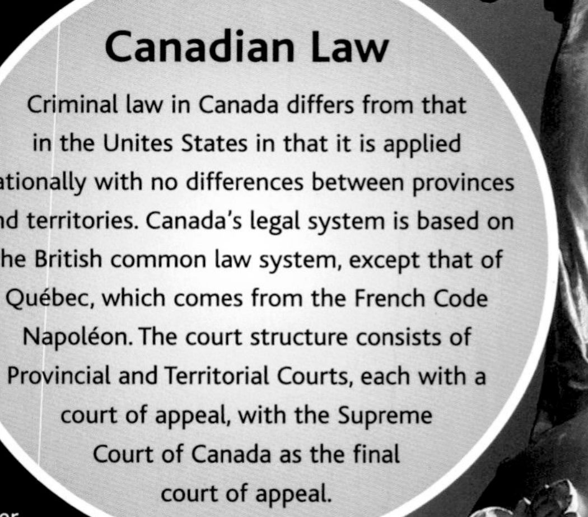

A statue of justice holding scales and sword on the roof of the Old Bailey, the Central Criminal Court in London, U.K.

Canadian Law

Criminal law in Canada differs from that in the Unites States in that it is applied nationally with no differences between provinces and territories. Canada's legal system is based on the British common law system, except that of Québec, which comes from the French Code Napoléon. The court structure consists of Provincial and Territorial Courts, each with a court of appeal, with the Supreme Court of Canada as the final court of appeal.

The death penalty

The death penalty was once the most common punishment for murder and other serious crimes. It has been abolished in more than half the world's countries.

The electric chair at the State Penitentiary in Virginia

- 133 countries have abolished the death penalty. Of these, 91 countries abolished it for all crimes, and 11 abolished it for ordinary crimes, but keep it for exceptional crimes, such as treason and war crimes.
- 62 other countries and territories officially retain the death penalty. Of these, 33 countries keep the death penalty in law, but have not carried out any executions for the past 10 years or more.
- Uzbekistan was one of the most recent countries to abolish capital punishment, on January 1, 2008.
- No executions took place in the United States from 1968 to 1976, when capital punishment was re-introduced. From 1977 to 2007, a total of 1,066 people were executed, including 11 women. Almost one-third of them, a total of 405, were executed in the state of Texas.

Ways of execution

Methods used around the world include shooting (China, Vietnam), hanging (Iran, Singapore), beheading (Saudi Arabia), lethal injection and electric chair (U.S.).

Bear teeth

In the state of Arkansas, it is illegal to extract the teeth of a bear or otherwise surgically alter it.

Strange laws

- Members of parliament are not allowed to wear suits of armor in the British House of Commons.
- It is forbidden to plow fields with elephants in North Carolina.
- Wyoming State Legislature banned the photographing of rabbits during January, February, March and April without an official permit.
- Anyone detonating a nuclear weapon within the city limits of Chico, California, is liable to a $500 fine.
- Owners of monkeys in Indonesia must have an identity card for the animal, complete with a photo of the monkey.
- In France, no pig may be called Napoleon.
- No one may eat a rattlesnake in public on a Sunday in Kansas.
- It is illegal to sell a teddy bear or play with a yo-yo on a Sunday in Memphis, Tennessee.
- A law in Alderson, West Virginia, says that, "No lions shall be allowed to run wild on the streets."
- In Spades, Indiana, you may not open a can with a revolver.
- In the province of Alberta, it is illegal to set fire to a wooden leg.

Who's who in court

Accused – a person charged with an offense.
Attorney/lawyer – a person who is qualified and licensed to act in a court, either for the prosecution or the defense.
Bailiff/marshall – the officer who keeps order and maintains security in the court and issues legal documents. They are often deputy sheriffs.
Defense – a barrister or solicitor who represents the defendant.
Defendant – a person accused of a crime.
Judge – the public official in charge of a trial.
Jury – a group of 12 members of the public (jurors) chosen to hear the evidence and decide whether the defendant is guilty or not guilty.
Court reporter stenographer – a person who records the court proceedings using a stenograph or other equipment.
Magistrate/Justice of the Peace (JP)— a nonprofessional person qualified to try certain cases.
Plaintiff – a person bringing a civil action to court.
Prosecution – a lawyer who presents evidence against the defendant and has to prove his/her guilt beyond reasonable doubt.
Sheriff – the top law enforcement officer for a U.S. county.
Witness – a person who gives evidence in court – someone who saw the offense, a police officer, or a specialist such as a medical expert.

usdoj.gov/usao/eousa/kidspage/index.html search

Punishments

In most countries people who break the law are either fined or imprisoned, but through the ages there have been many other forms of punishment.

Alcatraz, in the Bay of San Francisco, is no longer used as a prison.

Flogging

Whipping or flogging was once common: mutinous sailors were whipped with a cat-o'-nine-tails or keelhauled (dragged beneath a ship on the end of a rope). Flogging was widely used in the U.S. The last state to abolish it was Delaware — but not until 1972!

Stoning

Even today, some countries punish people by pelting them with stones, usually resulting in the victim's death.

Mid-19th-century ball and chain used as restraints when transporting prisoners

Stocks and pillory

Stocks were wooden structures that held the seated victim by the ankles. People threw things at them and ridiculed them—they were literally made a laughing stock. The pillory held victims in place by the neck and wrists. It was worse than the stocks as people could not use their hands to protect their faces from things thrown at them, and could be blinded or even killed.

Ducking stool

This punishment was used in the United States and England. The victims were usually women. They were strapped into a special chair and plunged into a river or pond.

Chain gang

Chain gangs, in which prisoners were chained together as they did heavy labor, such as breaking rocks, were used across the U.S. until 1955. In recent years they have been reintroduced in some prisons.

Branding

In some countries criminals were branded with a hot iron as a combined punishment, a sign that a person was guilty, and to warn other would-be offenders.

Burning at the stake

Many famous people were burned at the stake, including the French patriot Joan of Arc in 1431. In Germany up to 100,000 people accused of witchcraft and other crimes were burned during the 16th, 17th and 18th centuries. In 1589, 133 people were burned in a single day. Contrary to popular belief, witches were never burned in United States, where hanging was the usual punishment.

Great robberies

Mona Lisa
Leonardo da Vinci's famous painting was stolen from the Louvre Museum, Paris, on August 21, 1911, by Vicenzo Peruggia. He kept it for two years, but when he tried to sell it he was caught and jailed.

Art theft
On March 18, 1990, two thieves disguised as policemen stole 12 works of art by Rembrandt, Degas, Vermeer and others from the Isabella Stewart Gardner Museum, Boston. The paintings were valued at $300 million and have never been recovered.

Dunbar Armored robbery
Believed to be the U.S.'s biggest cash robbery, an estimated $8.9 million was stolen in an armed holdup at the Dunbar Armored facility in Los Angeles, California, on the night of September 13, 1997. The gang leader was caught and jailed for 24 years, but most of the money has not been found.

Iraq Central Bank
In March 2003, just before the U.S.-led invasion of Iraq, President Saddam Hussein removed almost $1 billion in cash from the Iraq Central Bank. About $650 million was later discovered in his palace, but the rest has never been located.

Securitas depot robbery
On February 22, 2006, Great Britain's biggest ever robbery took place at the Securitas depot. The gang kidnaped the family of the depot manager and got away with over $105 million in cash. Following a series of police raids, some of the cash was recovered and several people were arrested.

See also
Crime and punishment lasts: page 306

Prison fact file

Longest jail sentence
In Thailand on July 27, 1989, fraudster Chamoy Thipyaso and her seven accomplices were each sentenced to 141,078 years.

Longest in jail
Paul Geidel, a New York State prisoner, was sentenced for murder on September 5, 1911, at the age of 17. He came out on May 7, 1980, at the age of 85, having served 68 years, 245 days.

Famous prisons

Alcatraz
This island in San Francisco Bay, California, is often known as The Rock, but was originally called Isla de los Alcatraces (Isle of the Pelicans). It was first used as a military prison, but then became a prison for the country's most dangerous criminals, among them Al Capone. Robert Stroud, a bird expert who became famous as the Birdman of Alcatraz, spent many years there.

Sing Sing
This New York prison was named after the Sin Sinck Native Americans who originally lived there. It was built from 1825 to 1828, and from 1891 onward many murderers were electrocuted in the electric chair at Sing Sing. In 1969 the prison was renamed Ossining Correctional Facility.

Guantanamo Bay
Since 2002, the detainment camp on the U.S. Navy base at Guantanamo Bay, Cuba, has held hundreds of Al-Qaeda and other prisoners captured in Afghanistan and elsewhere. The camp has been criticized by human rights groups and legal arguments about the status of the prisoners are ongoing.

Newgate
This was once London England's most notorious prison. Public hangings took place outside its gates, and it features in several of Charles Dickens' novels. Newgate was rebuilt several times, and finally demolished in 1902. The Central Criminal Court (Old Bailey) was built on the site of the prison.

Dartmoor
Dartmoor was first used for prisoners of war during the Napoleonic Wars and has served as a high-security, long-term prison ever since. The prison is miles from anywhere on a bleak English moor so if prisoners escape, they are usually recaptured quickly.

Science and crime detection

Modern detectives use a wide range of scientific techniques to help them identify and catch criminals.

Fingerprinting
Fingerprints have been used for more than 100 years to prove whether someone was at a crime scene or held a weapon. Experts dust areas for hidden prints, which can also be revealed under special lights or on contact with certain chemicals. Faint prints can be improved by laser image enhancement.

DNA testing
Now forensic scientists use DNA testing or genetic fingerprinting to prove or disprove a suspect's connection with a crime. Everyone's DNA is unique and even the smallest samples — a single hair or a trace of saliva — can provide evidence.

Psychological profiling
Experts prepare profiles that suggest certain features of the killer, based on the nature of their murders. The profile may give likely age, background and habits. This builds a portrait of the criminal and helps detectives track him or her down.

Ballistics
All guns have a unique "fingerprint" — the marks made on a bullet as it leaves the barrel. Ballistics specialists examine these with microscopes and compare bullets used in crimes with those fired from a suspect's gun to find out whether they are identical.

Identikit
The Identikit system, which was developed in the United States in the 1940s, used transparent layers to build up a picture of a suspect's face. Witnesses' descriptions of eye color, hair styles, etc. were laid over a basic face shape. Modern developments include Photofit and computerized E-fit (Electronic Facial Identification Technique).

Surveillance
Crime fighters increasingly use electronic methods to spy on suspects. They can plant bugs (hidden microphones and video cameras) and intercept telephone calls and computer data.

Most wanted

Since 1950, the FBI (Federal Bureau of Investigation) in the United States has issued a list of its "10 most wanted" criminals. Osama bin Laden, the international terrorist and Al-Qaeda leader, is currently at the top of the list. There is a $25 million reward to anyone who provides information that leads to his capture.

www.bop.gov search

Work & Home

188 AROUND THE HOUSE
190 TOYS AND GAMES
192 WEALTH
194 ENERGY

Playtime

The famous plastic toy Lego (Danish for "play well") turned 50 in 2008. One of the first ever plastic toys to be created, Lego is still popular all over the world. The factory in Denmark makes 2 million pieces every hour.

The first vacuum cleaner

In 1901, Englishman Hubert Cecil Booth invented the first successful vacuum cleaner. The machine worked well and was popular with rich people. It was also used in places such as Westminster Abbey, Buckingham Palace and Windsor Castle. Booth's cleaner was so large that it had to be pulled along by a horse, and six people were needed to operate it. The machines were only rented out, never sold.

The upright vacuum cleaner was invented in the United States by James Murray Spangler in 1907. Spangler realized that his asthma was made worse by dust, and wanted to find a more effective way of sweeping. He made the first upright vacuum cleaner with the help of a pillowcase tied to a broom handle and an electrical pump. Spangler sold the patent to his cousin William H. Hoover, who improved the invention and started a very successful business selling vacuum cleaners.

Fussy sleepers

Benjamin Franklin always slept in rooms with two beds. He liked to move into a fresh bed during the night. Author Charles Dickens always placed his bed north to south and carried a pocket compass so that he could adjust it.

Great Bed of Ware

Amazing beds

One of the largest beds in the world is the Great Bed of Ware. It is 10 ft., 8.5 in. (3.26 m) wide, 11 ft., 1 in. (3.38 m) long and was made in about 1580. The bed is mentioned by Shakespeare in *Twelfth Night*. It is now in the Victoria and Albert Museum in London, England.

In 1882 an Indian maharajah had a bed made of solid silver. At each corner there was a life-sized statue of a naked woman holding a fan. When the maharajah lay on the bed, his weight started a mechanism that made the women wave their fans.

Toilet paper

- Before the invention of toilet paper, people improvized with many different things. The rich used wool or lace, but the poor used anything they could find, including wood shavings, grass, stone, sand, leaves, corn cobs, moss, seashells, water or snow, as well as their hands. Later people began to use newspapers or telephone directories as toilet paper.

In the kitchen

The first washing machine

A washing machine was made in about 1677 by an Englishman named John Hoskin. Fellow English inventor William Bailey made a more efficient version in 1758. The first mass-produced washing machine was invented by American Alva J. Fisher in 1907, and was called the Thor.

The first microwave oven

The Raytheon Company in the United States began using microwave ovens in 1947 to cook food commercially. The idea came from one of their scientists, Percy Spencer. He had been standing near a microwave tube and noticed that a chocolate bar in his pocket had melted, although he had not felt any heat. The first home microwave appeared in 1952 and cost $1,295.

The first refrigerator

People used to pickle, smoke, dry and salt food so they could store it. During the 19th century some households began to use large boxes filled with blocks of ice, and the first electric fridge was made in 1913. It was called the Domelre (Domestic Electric Refrigerator) and was for home use, although it was very bulky. Refrigerators did not really become popular until after World War II, when the design was improved.

The first pop-up toaster

Charles Strite, a U.S. mechanic, invented the pop-up toaster in 1919. There were toasting machines before then, but they had to be watched carefully all the time so the toast didn't burn. Strite worked out a way to put a timer and springs into the design. His first toasters were large machines, used by restaurants, but in 1926 he launched a smaller version called the Toastmaster.

1903 advertisement for refrigerators

● Chinese emperors used toilet paper in the 14th century, but the first commercial toilet paper was produced in 1857 by Joseph Gayetty, a U.S. businessman. Gayetty's paper was sold as individual sheets with his name on them.

● Each person in the United States spends an average of $19.41 on toilet paper every year, while Canadians spend an average of $24.22 each. The world average is $3.36 per person.

Home accidents

We think of our homes and gardens as safe places, but a surprising number of accidents are caused by everyday things. These figures record the number of people in a year who needed hospital treatment after accidents at home.

Estimated injuries
Home and garden (2005)

Stairs, ramps, landings, floors 2,213,829
Beds, mattresses and pillows 531,280
Chairs, sofas, sofa beds 453,424
Non-glass doors and panels 323,477
Tables 298,949
Bathrooms 293,432
Cans and other containers 250,943
Desks, cabinets, shelves, racks 239,850
Ladders and stools 226,709
Clothing 195,781
Glass doors and windows 158,587
Workshop manual tools 121,676
Carpets, rugs 119,572
Miscellaneous furniture 110,460
Fences 109,610
Lawn mowers 84,316
Lawn and garden equipment 73,611
TV sets and stands 58,308

Estimated U.S. injuries in 2005 involving sports and recreation

Basketball 512,213
Bicycle 494,712
Football 418,260
Baseball, softball 262,529
All-terrain vehicles, mopeds, etc. 250,553
Exercise and exercise equipment 243,751
Playground equipment 218,506
Toys 196,052
Soccer 174,686
Swimming 150,553

Toilet fact file

● In medieval Europe people used chamber pots, which they emptied out of the window. In castles there would be a garderobe — a small cupboard with a hole that let waste out into the moat.

● Throwing waste out of the windows into the street, or rivers that provided drinking water, spread disease. The worst epidemic was the Black Death in the 14th century, which killed about one quarter of the people in Europe.

● In London, England a gigantic cesspit was built under 200,000 houses and it often overflowed into them. Cesspits in London were abolished in 1847 and every home had to have a toilet. However, sewage was still diverted into the River Thames, which resulted in the "Great Stink" in the summer of 1858 — the worst smell in the city's history.

● The biggest cities in the U.S. and Europe's major cities started building sewers in the 19th century. Many of these early systems are still in use today. "Sewer tours" are popular in Paris, France, and in Brighton, U.K. The systems are such amazing works of engineering that people travel to these cities just to visit them!

● Today, Japan makes the most advanced toilets. Known as "washlets," they have control panels, water jets, heated seats, dryers and telephones. More improvements are being developed, including voice-activated toilets and some that can do medical tests.

The right path

During the 16th and 17th centuries it was good manners for a gentleman to walk closest to the street when escorting a lady. This meant that he was more likely to be in the path of sewage as it was thrown into the street!

www.historywired.si.edu/index.html search

Valuable toys

Some wealthy collectors prize rare toys, especially those that are in good condition — in their original box, and never played with. These are just some of the toys that may have cost very little when they were made, but now sell for high prices.

- The GI Joe prototype was sold by Heritage Galleries & Auctioneers of Dallas, Texas, for $200,000 in 2003.
- A Kämmer and Reinhardt doll was sold at Sotheby's, in London, U.K. on February 8, 1994, for $277,981.
- Titania's Palace, a doll's house with 2,000 items of furniture, was sold at Christie's, London, in 1978 for $258,728.
- Dingley Hall, a doll's house dating from 1877, was sold at Christie's, London, in 2003 for $211,938.
- A black mohair Steiff teddy bear, made in about 1912, was sold at Christie's, London, in 2000 for $132,157. It was one of only 494 black Steiff bears made as a mark of respect after the sinking of the *Titanic*. They are known as "mourning teddies."
- A tinplate clockwork motorcycle with Mickey Mouse and Minnie from about 1930, was sold at Christie's, London, in 1997 for $83,650.
- In 2006 a rare 1965 Midnight Red Barbie doll was sold for a record $17,000 at an auction at Christie's, London.

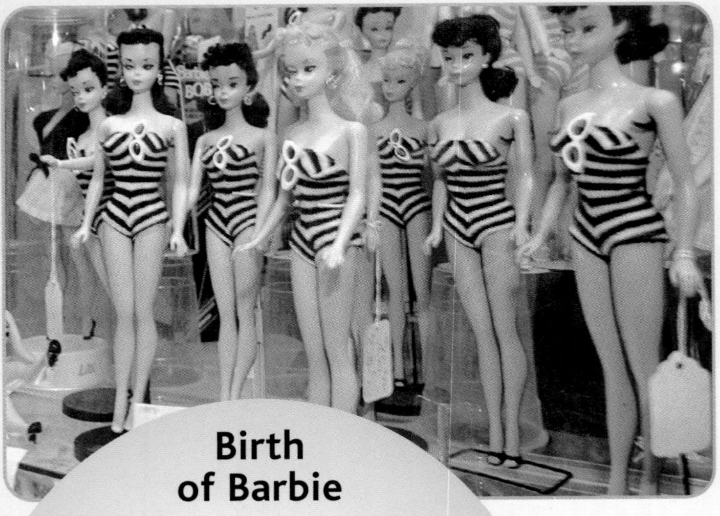

The first Barbie dolls, in the Barbie Museum, Palo Alto, California

Birth of Barbie

The first Barbie doll appeared in February 1959. It was made by Ruth and Elliot Handler, co-founders of U.S. toy manufacturer Mattel, and they named the doll after their daughter Barbara. The doll was dressed in a black and white striped swimsuit, with sunglasses, high heels and gold hoop earrings. In the first year a total of 351,000 Barbies were sold at $3 each. The doll went on to become one of the bestselling toys of all time.

"Teddy Girl" teddy bear made in 1904

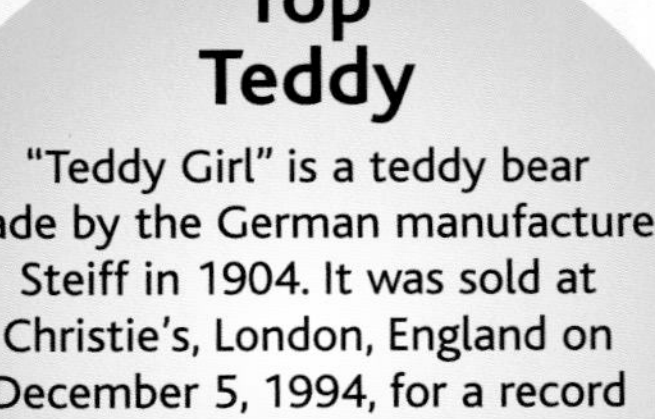

Top Teddy

"Teddy Girl" is a teddy bear made by the German manufacturer Steiff in 1904. It was sold at Christie's, London, England on December 5, 1994, for a record $171,600. A Japanese collector named Yoshiro Sekiguchi bought the bear for his teddy bear museum near Tokyo.

Toy-buying countries

Forecast sales of traditional toys (e.g., construction toys, model vehicles, indoor games, dolls and teddy bears) and video games in 2008 are estimated to average $33 for every person on the planet. There are huge differences between countries: North Americans spend the most and people in African countries the least per child.

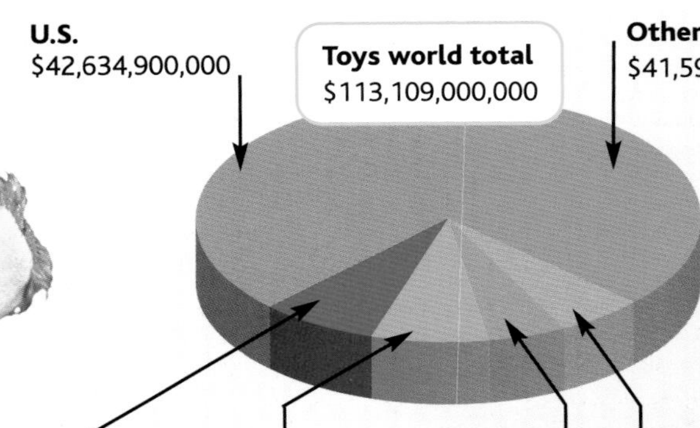

Computer games

The first computer games were played on televisions and appeared in the 1970s. They were basic arcade games like *PONG* (1972), an electronic table tennis game, and *Pac-Man* (1980), in which a yellow blob is steered around a maze, gobbling up everything in its path.

As computer technology advanced, games and consoles improved, with better graphics, sound and choice of themes. Second generation 8-bit games had removable cartridges, while the fifth 32-bit and 64-bit generation games could be played in 3-D. Sixth and seventh generation games are more realistic than ever before and can be played online with anyone around the world. These are popular consoles of different generations.

First generation Atari *PONG* (1975)
Second generation Atari 2600 (1977)
Third generation Nintendo Entertainment System (1983), Nintendo Game Boy (1989)
Fourth generation Sega Mega Drive (1988), Super Nintendo (1990)
Fifth generation Nintendo 64 (1986), Sony PlayStation (1994)
Sixth generation Sega Dreamcast (1998), Sony PlayStation 2 (2000), Microsoft Xbox (2001)
Seventh generation Xbox 360 (2005), PlayStation 3 (2006), Nintendo Wii (2006)

Scrabble

Scrabble was invented in the United States during the 1930s by an architect named Alfred Mosher Butts. First he called it Lexiko, then It and Criss-Cross, before hitting on the name Scrabble. Well over 100 million sets have been sold in more than 130 countries. The numbers of letters included vary according to the language. In Dutch, for example, there are 18 Es, 10 Ns and two Js. The Slovak version has 41 different letters — more than any other version.

Monopoly

Monopoly was invented in 1934 by an unemployed engineer named Charles Darrow, who lived in Philadelphia, Pennsylvania. In his first version of the game he used street names from Atlantic City in New Jersey because he dreamed of going there, but could not afford the fare. The game was so successful that Darrow became a millionaire and spent the rest of his life traveling and growing rare orchids.

There are many national and local versions around the world, as well as specialised versions including those for animal lovers (Birdopoly, Dogopoly and Horse-opoly), those based on films such as James Bond and Shrek, as well as Bible-opoly and Elvis Monopoly. Parker Brothers, the U.S. manufacturer of the game, print more Monopoly money than the U.S. Treasury prints dollars.

Monopoly around the world

Country	City*	Boardwalk becomes
Australia	Canberra + state capitals	Kings Avenue
Canada	Vancouver, etc.	Robson Street
China	Hong Kong	Victoria Peak
Egypt	Cairo	Shari Qasr El Nil
France	Paris	Rue de la Paix
Germany	Munich	Schlossallee
Ireland	Dublin	Shrewsbury Road
Netherlands	Amsterdam	Kalverstraat
New Zealand	Auckland	Queen Street
Portugal	Lisbon	Rossio
Russia	Moscow	Arbat
Singapore	Singapore	Queen Astrid Park
South Africa	Johannesburg	Eloff Street/Eloffstraat
Spain	Madrid	Paseo Del Prado
Switzerland	Zurich, etc.	Paradeplatz
U.K.	London	Mayfair

* Some feature streets from more than one city

Russian Monopoly board

Diamond fact file

- The weight of diamonds is measured in carats. The word comes from the carob which has an amazingly consistent weight of 0.007 oz. (0.2 g). There are about 142 carats to an ounce (5 carats/g).
- Fewer than 1,000 rough diamonds weighing more than 100 carats have ever been found.
- The first ever reference to diamonds is in the Bible in Exodus xxviii.18 and xxxix.11. It mentions a diamond mounted on a priest's breastplate.
- In 1796, Smithson Tennant (1761–1815), a British scientist, was the first person to show that diamonds are made of carbon. The diamond is the only gem in the world made of a single element.
- Diamonds are 180 times harder than emeralds.
- Diamonds melt at 12,450°F (6,900°C), which is two and a half times the temperature needed to melt steel.
- Diamonds come from a rock called kimberlite. About 220 tons (200 tonnes) of kimberlite are mined for every carat of polished diamond.
- The largest diamond ever found is called the Cullinan after Thomas Cullinan, who was president of the diamond company De Beers. The stone weighed 3,106 carats (22 oz. [almost 621 g]) and was found in South Africa in about 1905. It was presented to King Edward VII, who had it cut into 105 separate diamonds. One of the largest of these weighs 317.4 carats and is set in the British Imperial State Crown.

British Imperial State Crown

What's a million?

If you earned $100 a week, it would take you 192 years to earn $1 million. One million dollars in $1 bills would weigh 1.1 tons (1 tonne) and would stand 360 ft. (110 m) high. One million dollars in 1-cent coins would weigh 28 tons (25 tonnes). Placed on top of each other, they would stand 5,085 ft. (1,550 m) high. If they were placed in line edge to edge they would stretch 11.8 mi. (19.05 km).

A 2-euro coin (left) and U.S. $1 coin

Valuable coin

In 1933, 445,500 Double Eagles, gold $20 coins, were minted. They were never officially issued and most were later melted down, but a few found their way into private hands. The only one legally sold fetched $7.59 million in 2002, the highest price ever paid for one coin. In 2005, 10 were returned to the U.S. Mint and are the subject of a legal dispute about their ownership.

Money facts

The first coins Coins made from gold and silver were used in Lydia, an ancient Middle Eastern kingdom, in about 687–652 BC. The coins were known as staters.

Smallest coins The silver quarter-jawa was made in Nepal in about 1740 and weighed only 0.00007 oz. (0.002 g).

Largest coins Swedish 10-daler copper coins (made in 1644) weighed 43.45 lb. (19.71 kg).

Most coins made The U.S. Mint makes up to 20 billion coins every year. In 2007, the U.S. Mint made 7,401,200,000 1 cent coins, worth $74,012,000.

Banknotes Paper money was first made in China in the 13th century. The first European notes were made in Sweden in 1548. Banknotes were issued in 1690 in America and 1695 in England.

Largest banknotes One-guan Chinese notes from the late 14th century measured 9 x 13 in. (22.8 x 33 cm) — bigger than a page of this book.

Smallest banknotes Romanian 10-bani notes of 1917 had a printed area of just 1.08 x 1.5 in. (27.5 x 38 mm) — not much bigger than a postage stamp.

Golden treasures

Gold mask of Tutankhamun

Buddha statue

A 15th-century statue of Buddha is the largest gold object in the world. It is in the Wat Traimit temple, Bangkok, Thailand, stands 10 ft. (3 m) tall and weighs 6 tons (5.5 tonnes).

Gold salt shaker

This was made by Benvenuto Cellini for Francis I of France in about 1540. It is made of solid gold, elaborately decorated, and is one of the greatest works of the goldsmith's art. It is now in the Kunsthistorisches Museum, Vienna, Austria.

Gold stores

The United States Bullion Depository at Fort Knox, Kentucky, contains 5,035 tons (4,570 tonnes) of gold and the Federal Reserve Bank of New York holds about 5,510 tons (5,000 tonnes), the largest amount of gold in one place anywhere in the world.

Tutankhamun's mask

Tutankhamun was king of Egypt in the 14th century BC. In 1922 fabulous treasures were found in his tomb by archaeologist Howard Carter. They are now in the Cairo Museum, Egypt. They include a gold mask, which weighs 22.7 lb. (10.23 kg). It was found inside a solid gold coffin weighing 243 lb. (110.4 kg).

Gold fact file

- People have prized gold since ancient times. It is easy to work with and makes beautiful objects that do not corrode. Even coins and jewelery that have been buried for thousands of years are as bright as the day they were made.
- Gold is rare — it is only the 73rd commonest element in Earth's crust. There are more than 11 million tons (10 million tonnes) of gold in the world's seas, but it would cost too much to get it out.
- Gold is very heavy. A cup of gold would weigh 19.3 times as much as the same cup filled with water.
- Gold can be stretched into very thin wire. Just one gram of gold makes a wire 1.5 mi. (2.4 km) long and 0.0002 in. (5 microns) thick.
- More than 90 percent of all the gold mined in the past 6,000 years has been extracted since 1848.
- Gold is used for making coins and jewelery. It is also used in electronics, dentistry and for making special products such as the coating on astronauts' visors that protects them against harmful radiation.
- Gold bars like those in films about bank robberies are known as "Good Delivery Bars." They measure 7 x 3.6 x 1.75 in. (17.8 x 8.2 x 4.4 cm) and weigh 27 lb. (12.5 kg), about six times as much as a house brick.
- The largest gold nugget ever was found at Moliagul, Australia, in 1869. It is known as Welcome Stranger and weighs 156 lb. (70.92 kg).

Checks The first check was issued in London, England on April 22, 1659. It was for £10 ($20) and made payable to the bearer by Nicholas Vanacker. It was drawn on the bank of Clayton & Morris. The original check was sold for $2,160 at Sotheby's, London, in 1976.

Credit cards The first credit card was invented by Frank X. McNamara in the U.S. and issued in 1950 by Diner's Club. Holograms were first used for security on Visa cards in the U.S. in 1984. Smart cards (cards with built-in microchips) were introduced in France in 1975. There are about 142.8 million credit and debit cards in the U.K. There are more than 1 billion credit cards in use in the U.S.

Travelers' checks The first were issued by American Express in the U.S. in 1891.

ATM The world's first ATM (Automated Teller Machine) began operation on June 27, 1967, at Barclays Bank, Enfield, London, England.

Euro The new European currency was introduced in 1999 and was taken up by most European Union countries on January 1, 2002.

www.gold.org search

Top energy users

These countries guzzle more energy than any others in the world. The figures below show the amount of gas, coal or other power needed to produce the same amount of energy as 1 metric tonne (1.1 tons) of oil. This is the standard way of comparing energy produced and consumed from different sources.

- **Other** Oil 1,601.6, Gas 1,136.4, Coal 636.6, Nuclear 114.7, HEP* 338.8, Total 3,828.1
- **U.S.** Oil 938.8, Gas 566.9, Coal 567.3, Nuclear 187.5, HEP* 65.9, Total 2,326.4
- **China** Oil 363.0, Gas 52.2, Coal 1,198.8, Nuclear 12.3, HEP* 94.3, Total 1,720.6
- **Russia** Oil 128.5, Gas 388.9, Coal 112.5, Nuclear 35.4, HEP* 39.6, Total 704.9
- **Japan** Oil 235.0, Gas 76.1, Coal 119.1, Nuclear 68.6, HEP* 21.5, Total 520.3
- **India** Oil 120.3, Gas 35.8, Coal 237.7, Nuclear 4.0, HEP* 25.4, Total 423.2
- **Germany** Oil 123.5, Gas 78.5, Coal 82.4, Nuclear 37.9, HEP* 6.3, Total 328.6
- **Canada** Oil 98.9, Gas 87.0, Coal 25.0, Nuclear 22.3, HEP* 79.3, Total 312.5
- **France** Oil 92.8, Gas 40.6, Coal 13.1, Nuclear 102.1, HEP* 13.9, Total 262.5
- **U.K.** Oil 82.2, Gas 81.7, Coal 43.8, Nuclear 17.0, HEP* 1.9, Total 226.6

Energy consumption 2006 World total
Oil 3,889.8, Gas 2,574.9, Coal 3,090.1, Nuclear 635.5, HEP* 688.1, Total 10,878.4
* Hydroelectric power

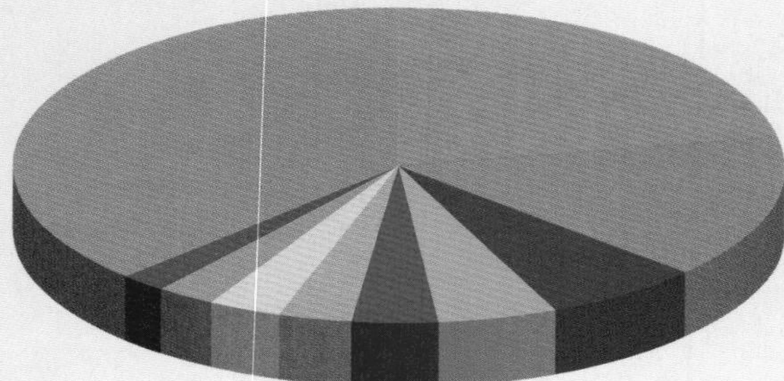

See also
Pollution fact file: page 70

Oil well pump at work

Top coal producers

	Country	2006 production (tonnes oil equivalent)
1	China	1,212,300,000
2	U.S.	595,100,000
4	India	209,700,000
3	Australia	203,100,000
5	South Africa	144,800,000
	World total	3,079,700,000

Top oil producers

	Country	2006 production (tonnes)
1	Saudi Arabia	514,600,000
2	Russia	480,500,000
3	U.S.	311,800,000
4	Iran	209,800,000
5	China	187,700,000
	World total	914,100,000

Top natural gas producers

	Country	2006 production (tonnes oil equivalent)
1	Russia	550,900,000
2	U.S.	479,300,000
3	Canada	168,300,000
4	Iran	94,500,000
5	Norway	78,900,000
	World total	2,586,400,000

Nuclear power

Countries that consume the most energy produced by nuclear power.

	Country	2006 production (tonnes oil equivalent)
1	U.S.	187,500,000
2	France	102,100,000
3	Japan	68,600,000
4	Germany	37,900,000
5	Russia	35,400,000
	World total	635,500,000

Hydroelectricity

Countries that consume the most energy produced by hydroelectric power.

	Country	2006 production (tonnes oil equivalent)
1	China	94,300,000
2	Canada	79,300,000
3	Brazil	79,200,000
4	U.S.	65,900,000
5	Russia	39,600,000
	World total	688,100,000

Wind farm in California

Wind energy

Windmills were used in Persia (now Iran) in the 7th century, and in Europe since the 12th century, but they were first used for making electricity in the late 19th century. Today, the state of California is the world's leading area for wind-generated electricity. Tehachapi Wind Resource, California, produces as much wind energy as the rest of the U.S. combined.

How much power?

All electrical appliances use energy. The amount depends on their size and purpose: an electric heater might use 10 times as much energy as a single light bulb.

The energy an appliance uses is measured in watts. These are named in honor of Scottish engineer James Watt (1736–1819), who first worked out how to measure energy.

Air conditioner 2,500–3,000 watts
Central heating pump 800 watts
Coffee maker 500–750 watts
Computer 400 watts
Deep freezer 1,000–2,000 watts
Dishwasher 2,000–2,500 watts
Electric blanket 50–100 watts
Electric kettle 2,200–3,000 watts
Electric razor 6 watts
Fan 50–100 watts
Fluorescent light 60 watts
Food processor 450 watts
Hair dryer 1,000–1,500 watts
Iron 1,000–1,500 watts
Light bulb 100 watts
Microwave oven 1,500 watts
Photocopier 1,500 watts
Printer 350 watts
Radio, CD player, etc. 40–200 watts
Refrigerator 1,000 watts
Sewing machine 100 watts
Stove 10,000 watts
Toaster 750–1,000 watts
Tumble dryer 2,400 watts
TV (color) 250 watts
Vacuum cleaner 800–1,400 watts
Washing machine 3,000–4,000 watts

The world's energy sources

A century ago, few homes had electricity and cars were a rare sight. Today, much of the world's energy is turned into electricity for homes, to power equipment in factories and to fuel our cars, buses, aircraft and other transportation. These are some of the main sources of this energy.

Oil
The first oil wells were drilled less than 150 years ago but oil, and petroleum that comes from it, has become the most important energy source. Almost 40 percent of the world's energy supply comes from oil. Most oil is found in the Middle East and has to be taken by tankers or pipelines to places where it is used around the world.

Coal
Coal is the world's second most important source of energy. It makes up about 27 percent of the total. Coal is a fossil fuel and is made from plants that lived and died 300 million years ago. The world's coal reserves will last about another 192 years. This is nearly three times as long as gas (67 years) and almost five times as long as oil (41 years).

Natural gas
The third main source of power comes from gas that occurs naturally beneath the Earth's surface. It accounts for 23 percent of the world total. The gas is mainly methane, with some ethane, propane and other gases. It is collected and taken to where it is needed by pipelines.

Grand Coulee Dam, Washington

Nuclear power
The fourth most important power source (7 percent of the world total) is nuclear power. A nuclear reaction releases huge amounts of heat which in turn heats water or other liquid and drives a turbine to produce electricity. The first nuclear power station to produce electricity for public use was Calder Hall, U.K., which opened in 1956.

Hydroelectric power
Flowing water has been used as a power source since the Middle Ages. Modern hydroelectric power uses water flowing through turbines in dams to produce electricity.

Solar energy
The Sun's warmth can be stored to produce energy. Mirrors and glass were used to collect heat in ancient times, but the first houses to use solar heating were not built until 1955. Solar energy is becoming more popular and the technology is getting better all the time. The world's largest solar energy generating plants are in the Mohave Desert, California. They are designed to use the Sun's rays to heat oil, which drives a generator. Each produces enough electricity to power a small town.

Tidal energy
Using waves and marine currents to release energy is expensive and as yet small-scale. The first and largest tidal power station on the Rance River, St. Malo, France, was completed in 1967. It can produce enough energy every year to supply power to 120,000 households.

Buildings & Structures

198 BUILDING STYLES
200 GREAT BUILDINGS
202 SKYSCRAPERS
204 BRIDGES AND TUNNELS
206 WONDERS OF THE WORLD

Rising ambition

The new headquarters of China Central Television in Beijing is scheduled to be completed in time to broadcast the 2008 Olympic Games. It is not a traditional tower, but a continuous loop that required careful planning, as Beijing has strict building regulations due to seismic conditions in the area.

Western architecture

Below are the main styles of Western architecture, from prehistory to the present day and famous examples of each. Styles did not stop and start abruptly; one style blended into another, so all dates are approximate.

Before the Renaissance most buildings had several architects or the architect's name was not recorded. The names of the architects of more recent buildings are given in brackets.

Prehistoric
Wooden post buildings, simple stone buildings, stone circles
Stonehenge, Wiltshire, U.K.

Ancient 3000–337 BC
Ancient Egyptian pyramids, tombs and temples
Great Pyramid, Giza, Egypt

Etruscan 700–200 BC
Alatri Temple, Villa Giulia, Rome, Italy

Greek 600–100 BC
Parthenon, Athens, Greece

Roman 100 BC–AD 370
The Baths of Caracalla, Rome, Italy
The Pantheon, Rome, Italy
The Colosseum, Rome, Italy
Maison Carrée, Nîmes, France

Byzantine 330–1450
Hagia Sophia, Istanbul, Turkey
St. Mark's, Venice, Italy

Pre-Columbian 300–1540
Mayan, Aztec, Inca South and Central American
Mayan temples at Tikal, Guatemala

Carolingian 751–987
Chapel Palatine (now part of cathedral), Aachen, Germany

Romanesque 800–1200
St. James, Santiago de Compostela, Spain
Tournai Cathedral, Belgium

Moorish/Islamic from 8th century
Great Mosque, Cordoba, Spain

Norman 1045–1180
Durham Cathedral, Durham, U.K.
Ely Cathedral, Ely, U.K.

Gothic 1140–1534
Cologne Cathedral, Cologne, Germany
Notre Dame Cathedral, Paris, France
Chartres Cathedral, Chartres, France
Salisbury Cathedral, Salisbury, U.K.

Renaissance 1400–1600
Hampton Court Palace, London, U.K.
Little Moreton Hall, Cheshire, U.K.
Florence Cathedral, Florence, Italy (Filippo Brunelleschi)
Ducal Palace, Urbino, Italy (Luciano Laurana)
Château de Chambord, France (Domenico da Cortona)

Baroque 1585–1750
St Paul's Cathedral, London, U.K. (Sir Christopher Wren)
Versailles Palace, France (Louis Le Vau and Jules Hardouin Mansart)
Greenwich Hospital (Royal Naval College), London, U.K. (Inigo Jones and Sir Christopher Wren)
Blenheim Palace, Oxfordshire, U.K. (Sir John Vanbrugh)

American Colonial 1600–1780
Governor's Palace, Williamsburg, Virginia, (rebuilt 1930)

Jacobean 1618–25
Ham House, Twickenham, Middlesex, U.K.
Blickling Hall, Norfolk, U.K.

Rococo 1650–1790
Vierzehnheiligen Church, Banz, Germany (Johann Balthasar Neumann)

Georgian 1714–1837
The Circus, Bath, U.K. (John Wood, Sr. and Jr.)
Charlotte Square, Edinburgh, U.K. (Robert Adam)

Neoclassical/Federalist U.S. 1750–1880
Panthéon, Paris, France (Germain Soufflot)
Brighton Pavilion, Brighton, U.K. (John Nash)
University of Virginia, Charlottesville, Virginia (Thomas Jefferson)

Greek
The Parthenon, Athens, Greece, 447–438 BC. Doric is the first and simplest classical Greek building style and this is the finest Doric building still standing. When it was first built, the Parthenon was decorated with marble sculptures painted in bright colors. Some of these, known as the Elgin Marbles, were removed and are now in the British Museum, London.

See also
Mysterious places: page 174

The Parthenon

Skyline of Chicago, Illinois, with skyscrapers and other modern buildings

Victorian 1837–1901
Houses of Parliament, London, U.K. (Sir Charles Barry and A.W.N. Pugin)
Crystal Palace, London, U.K. (Joseph Paxton)
American Surety Building, New York, N.Y. (Bruce Price)

Arts and crafts 1860–1900
The Red House, Kent, U.K. (Philip Webb)

Art Nouveau 1890–1905
Glasgow Art School, Glasgow, U.K. (Charles Rennie Macintosh)
Paris Metro stations, Paris, France (Hector Guimard)
La Sagrada Familia, Barcelona, Spain (Antonio Gaudí)
Secession Building, Vienna, Austria (Joseph Maria Olbrich)

Art Deco 1925–35
Chrysler Building, New York, N.Y. (William Van Alen)

Bauhaus 1919–37
Bauhaus, Dessau, Germany (Walter Gropius)

International modernism 1920–50
Fallingwater, Pennsylvania (Frank Lloyd Wright)

Brutalism 1950s
Unité d'Habitation, Marseilles, France (Le Corbusier)
Seagram Building, New York, N.Y. (Mies van der Rohe)

High-tech 1970s–
Centre Georges Pompidou, Paris, France (Richard Rogers and Renzo Piano)
Swiss Re Building (The Gherkin), London, U.K. (Norman Foster)

Post-modern 1970s
Staatsgalerie, Stuttgart, Germany (James Stirling)

Deconstruction 1990s–
Guggenheim Museum, Bilbao, Spain (Frank Gehry)

Art Deco

Chrysler Building, New York, N.Y., 1930.
The Chrysler is one of the best-known Art Deco buildings. The gleaming metal spire was based on the Chrysler cars of the time and skyscrapers are still a key feature of the New York skyline.

High-tech

Swiss Re Building (The Gherkin), London, U.K., 2004.
This building is London's first eco-friendly skyscraper. Its shape allows maximum natural light and ventilation inside so it uses only half the amount of energy consumed by a normal building block.

Japanese architecture

Eastern countries, such as Japan, had their own strong traditions of architecture. The Katsura Palace in Kyoto was built in the early 17th century, at the time of Baroque and Jacobean architecture in Europe. It is a simple, elegant building and one of the most perfect examples of traditional Japanese architecture.

American Colonial

Governor's Palace, Williamsburg, Virginia, 1722
European settlers in the New World used architectural ideas from their home countries. The historic district of Williamsburg in Virginia has some of the most famous colonial buildings, dating from before the American Revolution. The Governor's Palace is one of the finest.

Great religious buildings

The world's major religions, including Christianity, Islam, Judaism, Buddhism, Hinduism and Sikhism, have inspired many of the world's greatest buildings. Some are shrines to the religion's founders. Others are places of pilgrimage. Several are among the world's largest structures. These are the tallest churches.

1 The Chicago Methodist Temple* Chicago, Illinois, built 1924, 568 ft. (173 m)
2 Ulm Cathedral Ulm, Germany, built 1890, 528 ft. (161 m)
3 Notre Dame de la Paix Yamoussoukro, Côte d'Ivoire, built 1989, 519 ft. (158 m)
4 Cologne Cathedral Cologne, Germany, built 1880, 513 ft. (156 m)
5 Rouen Cathedral Rouen, France, built 1876, 485 ft. (148 m)
* Built on top of a 25-story, 330 ft. (100 m) building

Sagrada Familia

Spanish architect Antonio Gaudí's Sagrada Familia Cathedral in Barcelona, Spain, was begun in 1883, but it is still not finished. Its tallest spires are planned to be 558 ft. (170 m).

Sagrada Familia Cathedral, Barcelona, Spain

Largest churches

Salt Lake Temple, Utah, (1893) has a floor area of 253,015 sq. ft. (23,506 sq m). St Peter's in the Vatican (1612), the center of the Roman Catholic Church, is 717.5 ft. (218.7 m) long and covers an area of 247,570 sq. ft. (23,000 sq m). It was the largest Christian cathedral in the world until 1989, when it was overtaken by the 322,920 sq. ft. (30,000 sq m) basilica in Yamoussoukro, Côte d'Ivoire.

Tallest mosques

The Great Hassan II Mosque, Casablanca, Morocco (1993) is the tallest mosque at 689 ft. (210 m). The Saddam Mosque, Baghdad, Iraq was designed to be the largest in the Middle East, with a record-breaking 919 ft. (280 m) minaret, but it has not been completed.

Largest mosque

The Masjid al Haram is the holy mosque of Mecca (Makkah), the birthplace of the Prophet Muhammad. Millions of Muslim pilgrims visit the mosque every year. The mosque covers 882,640 sq. ft. (82,000 sq m) and the surrounding yards cover another 10,602,440 sq. ft. (985,000 sq m). Together they can accommodate up to 1.2 million worshipers.

Largest Buddhist temple

The largest Buddhist temple in the world is Borobudur (Many Buddhas), near Yogyakarta, Java, Indonesia. It was built between AD 750 and 842. The temple covers 645,835 sq. ft. (60,000 sq m) and contains 2 million cu. ft. (56,634 cu m) of stone.

Largest Hindu temple

Angkor Wat, Cambodia, built between AD 879 and 1191, is the largest religious structure in the world. The complex of buildings inside its walls and moat covers 894,590 sq. ft. (83,110 sq m).

Largest synagogue

The world's largest synagogue is Temple Emanu-El, New York City. It opened in 1929 and occupies an area of 37,921 sq. ft. (3,523 sq m).

Lighthouses

Tallest in the world

The biggest lighthouse ever built was the Pharos of Alexandria, which stood 407 ft. (124 m) tall. It was one of the Seven Wonders of the World. The world's tallest lighthouse today is in Yamashita Park, Yokohama, Japan, and is 348 ft. (106 m) tall.

Tallest in Canada

Built in 1858, the Cap des Rosiers Lighthouse, Northeast Gaspé Peninsula, Quebec, is situated near the mouth of the St. Lawrence River and stands 112 ft. (34 m) high. Its light can be seen from a distance of 24 nautical miles. It is open to the public from June to September.

Tallest in the U.S.

The Cape Hatteras lighthouse in North Carolina was built in 1870. It is the tallest in the U.S. at 196 ft (59.7 m). The lighthouse was being eroded by the sea so between 1999 and 2000 the entire 2,800-ton (2,540-tonne) building was moved 2,900 ft. (884 m) inland, very slowly, on tracks.

See also
Holy places: page 162

Millennium Dome, London, U.K.

Biggest domes and roofs

In 1434, the Duomo Cathedral in Florence, Italy, had the largest dome in the world. It was 149.3 ft. (45.5 m) across and was still the world's largest dome 400 years later.

The diameter of the Millennium Dome is almost eight times greater, thanks to modern building techniques and materials. Some of the domes in the list below are supported by struts and cables, others are free-standing. Some can even be opened.

The Millennium Dome, London, U.K., was completed in 1999. It measures 1,175 ft. (358 m) in diameter. The span is supported by steel masts that project through the dome.

Wembley Stadium, London, U.K., was completed in 2007. It has the largest single-span roof in the world (supported only at the sides). It measures 1,033 ft. (315 m) in diameter.

The Georgia Superdome, Atlanta, Georgia, was completed in 1992 with a diameter of 840 ft. (256 m). It has the world's largest cable-supported fabric roof.

The Fantasy Entertainment Complex, Kyosho, Japan, was completed in 2002. It has a diameter of 710 ft. (216 m).

The Houston Astrodome, Houston, Texas, was completed in 1966. It measures 710 ft. (216 m) in diameter.

The Louisiana Superdome, New Orleans, Louisiana, was completed in 1975. It measures 680 ft. (207 m) in diameter.

SkyDome, Toronto, Ontario, Canada, was completed in 1989 with a diameter of 674 ft. (205 m). It has the world's largest retractable roof.

The Multi-Purpose Arena, Nagoya, Japan, was completed in 1997. It measures 614 ft. (187 m) in diameter.

Tacoma Dome, Tacoma, Washington, was completed in 1983 with a diameter of 532 ft. (162 m).

The Superior Dome, Marquette, Michigan, was completed in 1991 and has a diameter of 523 ft. (160 m).

Obelisks and columns

Obelisks are stone columns made in ancient Egypt almost 4,000 years ago. Some were taken as trophies by invading armies and are now in cities such as Istanbul, Rome, London, Paris and New York. More recently, people have built memorials based on the design of obelisks.

- A column commemorating the battle of San Jacinto (1836) near Houston, Texas, USA, is the world's tallest monument at 570 ft. (174 m). It was completed in 1939.
- The Washington Monument, Washington DC, was completed in 1884. It is 555 ft. (169 m) tall, made of 36,491 stone blocks on an iron frame and weighs 90,854 tons (82,421 tonnes). It was the world's tallest structure for five years until it was overtaken by the Eiffel Tower in 1889.
- The Wellington Monument in Dublin, Ireland, is a stone obelisk made to celebrate the victories of the Duke of Wellington. It was completed in 1861 and is Europe's tallest obelisk at 206 ft. (63 m).
- The Monument in London commemorates the Great Fire of London in 1666. It was built in 1667 and is 202 ft. (62 m) tall.
- Nelson's Column in Trafalgar Square, London, U.K., was completed in 1842 to celebrate Great Britain's naval commander. The column is 145 ft. (44m) high and has a 17 ft. (5 m) statue of Nelson on top.
- The tallest Egyptian obelisk is in the Piazza San Giovanni in Laterano, Rome, Italy. It measures 106 ft. (32 m). The tallest still in Egypt is in Karnak and is 97 ft. (30 m) tall. The ancient Egyptian obelisk in New York is 73 ft. (22 m) and the London obelisk, Cleopatra's Needle, is 69 ft. (21 m).

Modern pyramids

The ancient Egyptian pyramids are the best known, but this style of building has also been used in modern times.

Luxor Hotel and Casino, Las Vegas, Nevada
This was opened in 1993. It is 350 ft. (107 m) tall, and at its peak is a fixed spotlight that shines straight upward — its light is said to be visible from space.

Louvre Museum Pyramid, Paris, France
The architect I.M. Pei designed the 71 ft. (22 m) glass pyramid that was built in 1989 as the main entrance to the Louvre Museum, Paris, France.

Christa McAuliffe Planetarium, Concord, New Hampshire
Christa McAuliffe was killed in the *Challenger* Space Shuttle disaster. The pyramid-shaped planetarium named after her opened in 1990.

"Mad Jack" Fuller's tomb, Brightling, England
Jack Fuller, an eccentric landowner and Member of Parliament, had his own 25 ft. (8 m) pyramid tomb built in 1811. It is said that his body is inside, wearing a top hat!

Rainforest Pyramid, Galveston, Texas
This 125-ft. (38 m) tall pyramid, finished in 1993, houses one of the world's largest indoor rainforests.

Tallest skyscrapers over the last 100 years

New York's 391 ft. (119.2 m) Park Row Building was the tallest office or apartment building in the world when it was completed in 1899. Since then it has been overtaken many times by the progressively taller skyscrapers on this list. The latest world record holder, the Burj Dubai, is more than 5 times the size of Park Row.

	Building	Year completed	Floors	Height ft*	m
1	Metropolitan Life, New York, N.Y.	1909	50	700.1	213.4
2	Woolworth Building, New York, N.Y.	1913	57	792.0	241.4
3	The Trump Building, New York, N.Y.	1930	70	926.8	282.5
4	Chrysler Building, New York, N.Y.	1930	77	1,045.9	318.8
5	Empire State Building, New York, N.Y.	1931	102	1,250.0	381.0
6	One World Trade Center, New York, N.Y. †	1972	110	1,368.1	417.0
7	Sears Tower, Chicago, Illinois	1974	108	1,450.1	442.0
8	Petronas Towers, Kuala Lumpur, Malaysia	1998	88	1,482.6	451.9
9	Taipei 101, Taipei, Taiwan	2004	101	1,669.9	509.0
10	Burj Dubai, Dubai, U.A.E.	2008	164	2,034.0	620.0

* Excluding masts, etc.

† Destroyed in terrorist attack of September 11, 2001

See also
Cities of the World: pages 118–19

Until 1930 the Eiffel Tower, Paris, was the world's tallest building.

Tallest structure

The world's tallest free-standing structure is the CN Tower in Toronto, Ontario, Canada. It measures a mighty 1,815 ft. (553.33 m) to the tip of its antenna. There are taller masts, but they are supported with guy wires. The CN Tower also has the world's highest graffiti. It was painted — with permission — in 1976 by 20,000 children before the antenna was lifted into position by helicopter.

The Eiffel Tower

The Eiffel Tower in Paris, France, was built as a temporary structure for the Universal Exhibition held in Paris in 1889. The tower was so popular that it has been there ever since.

- Engineer Gustave Eiffel (1832–1923) also built the framework of the Statue of Liberty. A workforce of 300 steelworkers completed the tower in two years, two months and five days.
- The Eiffel Tower contains 18,038 pieces of steel, weighing a total of 7,910 tons (7,175 tonnes). They are connected by 2.5 million rivets.
- The tower's 2,368,060 sq. ft. (220,000 sq m) of surfaces are hand-painted every 10 years (last in 2003) with 66 tons (60 tonnes) of paint.
- The tower is 986 ft. (300.5 m) tall — 1,052 ft. (320.8 m) with its antenna — but it can expand or shrink by up to 6 in. (15 cm) depending on how hot or cold it is. It was the world's tallest structure until the Chrysler Building in New York overtook it in 1930.
- The tower is lit by 352 1,000-watt projectors and 20,000 lights (installed in 2003). These are switched on after dusk for the first 10 minutes of every hour.
- More than 200 million people have visited the tower. Most take the elevators, although there are 1,665 steps for the very energetic. It also attracts publicity-seeking climbers. "Birdmen," parachutists and even cyclists have made descents — some of them fatal.
- The Eiffel Tower features in many films, including the James Bond film *A View to a Kill* (1985).

Cities with most skyscrapers*

1 Hong Kong, China, has 199
2 New York City, N.Y., has 190
3 Chicago, Illinois, has 90
4 Shanghai, China, has 71
5 Tokyo, Japan, has 69

* Habitable buildings of more than 500 ft. (125 m)

A view of the skyscrapers of Hong Kong from Victoria's Peak

Taller and taller

Scheduled for completion in 2009, the Burj Dubai, Dubai, United Arab Emirates, is planned to be more than 2, 034 ft. (620 m) tall, with a spire reaching 2, 684 ft. (818 m), making it the highest structure in the world. It will have cost more than $4 billion to build.

Currently, the world's tallest building is the Taipei 101 in Taipei, Taiwan. It is so called because it has 101 stories above ground level. Some experts consider that its spire should not be included in its total height, but international rules count all parts of a skyscraper except masts, antennae and flagpoles. So this building qualifies as the tallest. It also has the highest occupied floor of any building.

The Empire State Building

New York's tallest building is the Empire State Building, which stands on Fifth Avenue, New York, between 33rd Street and 34th Street. It was built on the site of the Waldorf-Astoria Hotel and took 410 days at a rate of 4½ floors a week to complete. The building was opened on May 1, 1931, by remote control, when President Herbert Hoover pressed a button in Washington DC.

The Empire State Building towers 1,250 ft. (381 m) above ground, and measures 1,454.1 ft. (443.2 m) to the top of the TV tower. A further 54.8 ft. (16.7 m) is below ground. The spire on top was designed as an airship mooring mast, but after a German airship, the *Hindenburg*, burned at its mooring mast in New Jersey in 1937, the mast was never used. For more than 40 years, the Empire State held the record as the world's tallest office or apartment building, until the twin towers of the World Trade Center were completed. Since their destruction in 2001, it is once again New York's tallest. More than 2.5 million tourists a year go up to the observatories on the 86th and 102nd floors.

- The workforce — 3,400 at its peak — took seven million man-hours to complete the building.
- The cost was $40,948,900 including the land (the building cost only $24,718,000).
- It weighs 365,000 tons (331,120 tonnes), including a 60,000-ton (54,430 tonne) steel frame, 10 million bricks and 730 tons (662 tonnes) of aluminum and stainless steel.
- The Empire State is served by 73 elevators and contains 3,194,547 light bulbs, 50 mi. (80 km) of radiator pipes and 70 mi. (113 km) of water pipes.
- The lightning conductor was struck 68 times in the building's first 10 years.
- In 2003 Australian runner Paul Crake broke his own record for racing up the 1,575 steps to the 86th floor in 9 min., 33 sec.
- On July 28, 1945, a B-25 bomber crashed in fog between the building's 78th and 79th floors, killing the pilot and 13 other people. It happened on a Saturday so most offices were empty, or the casualties would have been higher.
- On St. Valentine's Day, couples can marry on the 80th floor.
- The building's colored lights are changed for seasonal celebrations. They are red, white and blue on Independence Day and green on St. Patrick's Day. The lights are turned off when birds are migrating to avoid confusing them.

Bridge types

Arch An arch bridge is a very strong curved structure made of stone, concrete or steel. It is firmly supported on both sides.

Bascule A bascule bridge has a central section that opens to allow tall ships to pass. The Tower Bridge in London, England, is one of the most famous bascule bridges.

Beam A beam bridge is supported by the shore at both ends. This is the simplest and oldest type of bridge — a log across a stream is a very simple beam bridge. It is not very strong and may need to be strengthened by supports underneath.

Cantilever This type of bridge has two long arms held in place at the ends by anchors. Some can swing to let large ships through. Cantilever bridges are closest in length to suspension bridges.

Suspension This bridge is supported by steel cables fixed to high towers on the banks. All the world's longest bridges are suspension bridges because they are very strong.

Swing A swing bridge can be swung to one side to allow ships through. The Gateshead Millennium Bridge across the Tyne in England is a unique swing bridge, which rotates upward to allow boats to pass beneath.

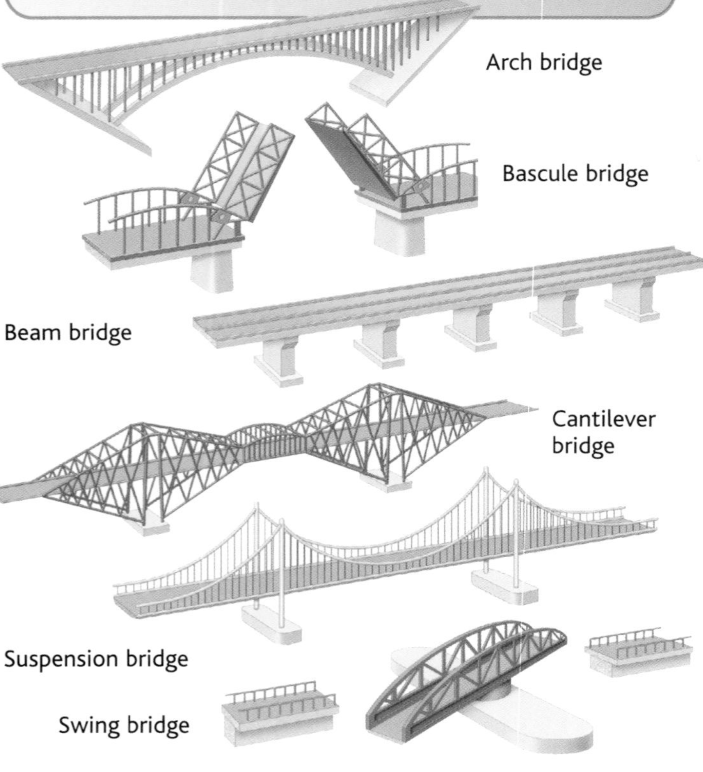

Famous bridges

Pont d'Avignon, France
This bridge was built in the 12th century. It was made famous by the song "Sur le Pont d'Avignon" (On Avignon Bridge).

Bridge of Sighs, Venice, Italy
The Bridge of Sighs was designed in 1560. It connects the Doge's Palace with the city jail, and prisoners who had been sentenced to death had to cross the bridge to reach the jail. Its name is said to come from their sighs of despair.

Pont Neuf, Paris, France
Pont Neuf was completed in 1604. The bridge is in two halves and links the Right and Left Banks of the River Seine to Ile de la Cité, the island on which Notre Dame Cathedral stands.

Kintai-Kyo Bridge, Iwakuni, Japan
This wooden arch bridge was built across the Nishiki River in 1673. It has been damaged and rebuilt many times.

Hartland Bridge, New Brunswick, Canada
Opened in 1901, the bridge across the St. John River is the world's

Longest bridges

1800s

All these bridges were the world's longest when they were built. Today's longest, the Akashi Kaikyo in Japan, is nearly 54 times longer than the Martorell bridge in Spain.

† No longer standing

217 BC Martorell, Spain
A stone arch bridge with a span of 121 ft. (37 m)

27 BC Augustus, Narni, Italy
A stone arch bridge with a span of 142 ft. (43 m)

AD 104 Trajan, Danube, Romania
A timber arch bridge with stone piers and a span of 170 ft. (52 m)

1371 Trezzo, Adda, Italy †
A stone arch bridge with a span of 236 ft. (72 m)

1757 Schaffhausen, Switzerland †
A timber bridge with a span of 390 ft. (119 m)

1816 Schuylkill Falls, Philadelphia, Pennsylvania †
A suspension bridge with a span of 407 ft. (124 m)

1820 Union/Tweed, Berwick, U.K.
An iron chain suspension bridge with a span of 449 ft. (137 m)

1826 Menai Strait, Anglesey, U.K.
A chain suspension bridge with a span of 580 ft. (177 m)

1834 Fribourg, Switzerland †
Wire-cable suspension bridge with a span of 896 ft. (273 m)

1849 Wheeling, West Virginia,
A suspension bridge with a span of 1,010 ft. (308 m)

1851 Lewiston-Queenston, Niagara, U.S./Canada
A suspension bridge with a span of 1,043 ft. (318 m)

The Golden Gate Bridge, San Francisco, California, was completed in 1937. It was the world's longest bridge for many years.

Road and rail tunnels

The first tunnel built especially for passenger trains was the 2,513 ft. (766 m) Tyler Hill Tunnel in Kent, United Kingdom. It opened on May 4, 1830. The first underwater rail tunnel was the Thames Tunnel, London, U.K., which opened in 1869.

Some of the most amazing tunnels are made under the sea. The Seikan tunnel was built to link the Japanese islands of Honshu and Hokkaido. 14.5 mi. (23.3 km) is below the sea bed. The Channel Tunnel has 23.6 mi. (38 km) under the sea. The tunnels listed are all for railways, except the Laerdal in Norway, which is a road tunnel.

Longest tunnels

1 **Gotthard Base Tunnel** (Alp Transit Link) Switzerland, 2018*, will be 35.46 mi. (57.07 km)
2 **Seikan** Japan, 1988 is 33.46 mi. (53.85 km)
3 **Channel Tunnel** France/England, 1994 is 31.35 mi. (50.45 km)
4 **Moscow Metro** (Serpukhovsko-Timiryazevskaya line) Russia, 1983, is 24.17 mi. (38.9 km)
5 **Lötschberg Base Tunnel** Switzerland, 2007, will be 21.49 mi. (34.58 km)
6 **Guadarrama** Spain, 2007, will be 17.63 mi. (28.38 km)
7 **London Underground** (East Finchley/Mordern, Northern Line) U.K., 1939, is 17.29mi. (27.84 km)
8 **Hakkoda** Japan, 2010*, will be 16.44 mi. (26.46 km)
9 **Iwate** Japan, 2002, is 16.04 mi. (25.81 km)
10 **Pajares** Spain, 2011*, is 15.33 mi. (24.67 km)

* Still being built

One and only

London Bridge was taken from the U.K. to the U.S. The five-arched stone bridge was made between 1823 and 1831. In the 20th century, London Bridge needed to be replaced by one better suited to modern traffic. U.S. businessman Robert P. McCulloch bought it for $2,460,000. The bridge was shipped out stone by stone. It was rebuilt in Lake Havasu City in Arizona and completed in 1971. It is the largest structure ever moved and the largest antique ever sold!

longest covered bridge at 1,282 ft. (390.8 m).

Tower Bridge, London
Tower Bridge was completed in 1894. It opens and lifts in the middle to allow tall ships to pass underneath.

Brooklyn Bridge, New York
After many setbacks, Brooklyn Bridge was finally opened in 1883. For a short time it was the world's longest bridge.

Sydney Harbour Bridge, Sydney, Australia
Sydney Harbour Bridge was built in 1932 to carry road and rail traffic across the harbor. It is a famous feature of the Sydney harbor skyline.

Tower Bridge, London, U.K.

1990s

1867 The Cincinnati-Ohio River, Covington
A suspension bridge with a span of 1,057 ft. (322 m)

1869 Niagara-Clifton, Niagara, U.S./Canada †
A suspension bridge with a span of 1,268 ft. (387 m)

1883 Brooklyn, New York
A suspension bridge with a span of 1,596 ft. (486 m)

1890 Firth of Forth Rail, Scotland
A cantilever bridge with a span of 1,710 ft. (521 m)

1917 Quebec Rail, Canada
A cantilever bridge with a span of 1,800 ft. (549 m)

1929 Ambassador, Detroit, U.S./ Windsor, Canada
A suspension bridge with a span of 1,850 ft. (564 m)

1931 George Washington, New York
A suspension bridge with a span of 3,500 ft. (1,067 m)

1937 Golden Gate, San Francisco, California
A suspension bridge with a span of 4,200 ft. (1,280 m)

1964 Verazzano Narrows, New York, N.Y.
A suspension bridge with a span of 4,260 ft. (1,298 m)

1980 Humber Estuary, Hull, U.K.
A suspension bridge with a span of 4,626 ft. (1,410 m)

1997 East Bridge, Denmark
A suspension bridge with a span of 5,328 ft. (1,624 m)

1998 Akashi Kaikyo, Japan
A suspension bridge with a span of 6,529 ft. (1,990 m)

See also
Rail Transport: pages 214–15

The Seven Wonders of the Ancient World

Early Greek writers drew up lists of the most important buildings in the world they knew. Of these only the Great Pyramid survives, but we know about the others from writers' accounts and archaeologists.

The Great Pyramid of Giza
The Great Pyramid of Giza, Egypt, is the oldest, and the only one of the Seven Wonders to survive. It was made as a tomb for King Khufu, who ruled Egypt from about 2551–2528 BC, and it is the largest stone structure ever built. Its sides are 754 ft. (230 m) long and it covers an area the size of 200 tennis courts.

The Hanging Gardens of Babylon
The legendary gardens of King Nebuchadnezzar II may not have existed. Some people believe they were created in about 600 BC in Babylon, 55 mi. (88 km) south of present-day Baghdad, the capital of Iraq. "Hanging" suggests that they were a series of terraces made of bricks, some glazed and brightly colored.

The Statue of Zeus at Olympia
This was an enormous statue of the Greek god, carved by the sculptor Phidias. It was inside the Temple of Zeus, built about 466–456 BC. The statue was 43 ft. (13 m) high and one of the largest indoor sculptures ever made. Today little remains of the temple and nothing of the statue.

The Temple of Artemis
The Temple of Artemis at Ephesus, Turkey, was built to honor the Greek goddess of hunting and nature. The temple was completed in 550 BC. It was the largest of all ancient Greek buildings and measured 180 x 375 ft. (55 x 114 m). Archaeologists have found the foundations and some columns of this ancient wonder.

The Mausoleum at Halicarnassus
This was the tomb of Persian ruler Mausolus, who ruled part of the Persian empire in 377–353 BC. Halicarnassus (modern-day Bodrum) in Turkey was his capital. After his death his widow built this magnificent tomb, which measured 344 x 794 ft. (105 x 242 m) and was 140 ft. (43 m) high. It was damaged by an earthquake and demolished in 1522. The word mausoleum has come to mean any great tomb.

The Colossus of Rhodes
The huge statue of Sun god Helios stood in Rhodes harbor, Greece. In 305–304 BC warrior king Demetrius Poliorcetes attacked the city of Rhodes. When he abandoned his siege, the people built the giant statue as an offering to the god Helios. It took 12 years to build and stood 110 ft. (33 m) high, but in 226 BC it was destroyed by an earthquake.

See also
Holy places: page 162

The belief that the Great Wall can be seen from space is a myth. Apparently, it can be seen from low orbit, but this is not a unique trait, as many other humanmade objects can also be seen from low orbit.

The Great Pyramid of Giza and the Sphinx

The Pharos of Alexandria

This was a lighthouse off the coast of the city of Alexandria. Work started on it in about 299 BC and it took about 20 years to build. It was 407 ft. (124 m) tall—the tallest lighthouse ever made. It was damaged by earthquakes and toppled into the sea in 1375. A few remains have been found.

Seven modern wonders

There are many candidates for this list and here is a selection.

Hoover Dam, U.S.
When it was built in 1936, the 725 ft. (221 m) high Hoover Dam was the largest in the world. A record 128.19 million ft.^{3} (3.63 million m^3) of concrete were used to make the structure, which controls the flooding of the Colorado River.

Deltawerken flood barrier, Netherlands
After a disastrous flood in 1953, engineer Johan van Veen designed the Delta Project, or Deltawerken. This is a series of interconnected dams that forms a movable sea barrier while preserving the habitat and sea life within it.

Kansai International Airport, Japan
This airport was opened in 1994. It stands on a 0.75 x 2.5 mi. (1.2 x 4 km) island which is entirely humanmade. It was built with 48,000 huge blocks, made from earth excavated by flattening three mountains, and designed to withstand typhoons and earthquakes. Its terminal building was designed by Italian architect Renzo Piano.

Channel Tunnel, England/France
Work on the second longest underwater rail tunnel in the world began in 1987. It took seven years and 15,000 workers to create the 31.35 mi. (50.45 km) tunnel (23.6 mi. [38 km] under sea), which opened in 1994. The tunnel links Folkestone in England to Sangatte, France.

Guggenheim Museum, Bilbao, Spain
The Guggenheim was built in 1997 to the design of Canadian-born architect Frank Gehry. It houses a collection of modern art in a striking, ultramodern setting. The structure combines limestone blocks of varied shapes, curved sections covered in panels of titanium (a light, strong metal) and large areas of glass.

The Eden Project, Cornwall, U.K.
About 2 million tons (1.8 million tonnes) of earth were moved to make the foundations for the world's largest greenhouses. These are a series of domes, each devoted to a particular type of climate, and housing 100,000 plants. The Eden Project was designed by Nicholas Grimshaw and opened in 2001. It is one of the U.K.'s most popular tourist attractions.

Panama Canal, Panama
It took 34 years, from 1880 to 1914, to build the ship canal that connects the Atlantic and Pacific Oceans. The 48-mi. (77 km) canal was a remarkable feat of engineering, but cost the lives of up to 27,500 workers.

Leaning Tower of Pisa

The Seven Wonders of the medieval world

People have never been able to agree on the Seven Wonders of the medieval world, and this is just one of several lists that have been made. It includes the Leaning Tower of Pisa (pictured right). In 2007, an organisation compiled a new list of Seven Wonders according to a voting system that included the Colossuem, Italy, and the Great Wall of China, along with the Taj Mahal, India, Chichén Itzà, Mexico, Macchu Picchu, Peru, Jordan and the statue of Christ the Redeemer, Rio do Janiero, which was completed as recently as 1931.

Stonehenge
The circle of huge stones was built in stages from about 3000 BC. The origin of the stones, how they were transported and the purpose of the site remain a mystery. It was possibly some sort of ancient observatory.

The Great Wall of China
This was a defensive wall designed to protect China from its warlike neighbors to the north. It was built in stages after 220 BC, using a huge labor force of as many as 300,000 workers. The main part is 2,150 mi. (3,460 km) long and wide enough for an army to march along it ten abreast.

The Colosseum, Rome, Italy
This amphitheater was opened in AD 80 with a huge spectacle lasting 100 days. It is oval and measures 157 ft. (48 m) high, 617 ft. (188 m) long and 512 ft. (156 m) wide. It could hold up to 50,000 spectators and could be flooded for re-enactments of sea battles.

The Catacombs of Alexandria (Kom El Shoqafa), Egypt
These Roman tombs beneath the city of Alexandria, Egypt, were discovered in 1900 when a donkey fell into them. The beautifully preserved, carved catacombs had been made in solid rock during the 2nd century AD.

Hagia Sophia, Istanbul, Turkey
Hagia Sophia (Holy Wisdom), Istanbul, Turkey, was originally built in AD 360 by the Emperor Constantius. It was later rebuilt as one of the world's finest churches, with many mosaics and ornate details. In 1453 the church was converted into an Islamic mosque.

The Porcelain Pagoda of Nanking, China
The Porcelain Pagoda was built in about 1412 by Emperor Yung-lo. It was an eight-sided structure covered in glazed tiles, and soared to 260 ft. (79 m). It was destroyed during a rebellion in 1853.

Leaning Tower of Pisa

Building began on the bell tower of Pisa Cathedral, Italy, in 1173. Soon the foundations began to sink on one side. The design was adjusted, but by the time the tower had reached its full height of 179 ft. (55 m) it was leaning sharply. The tilt increased over the centuries and it is amazing that the 15,400-ton (14,000-tonne) structure is still standing.

FIREFLY'S WORLD OF FACTS

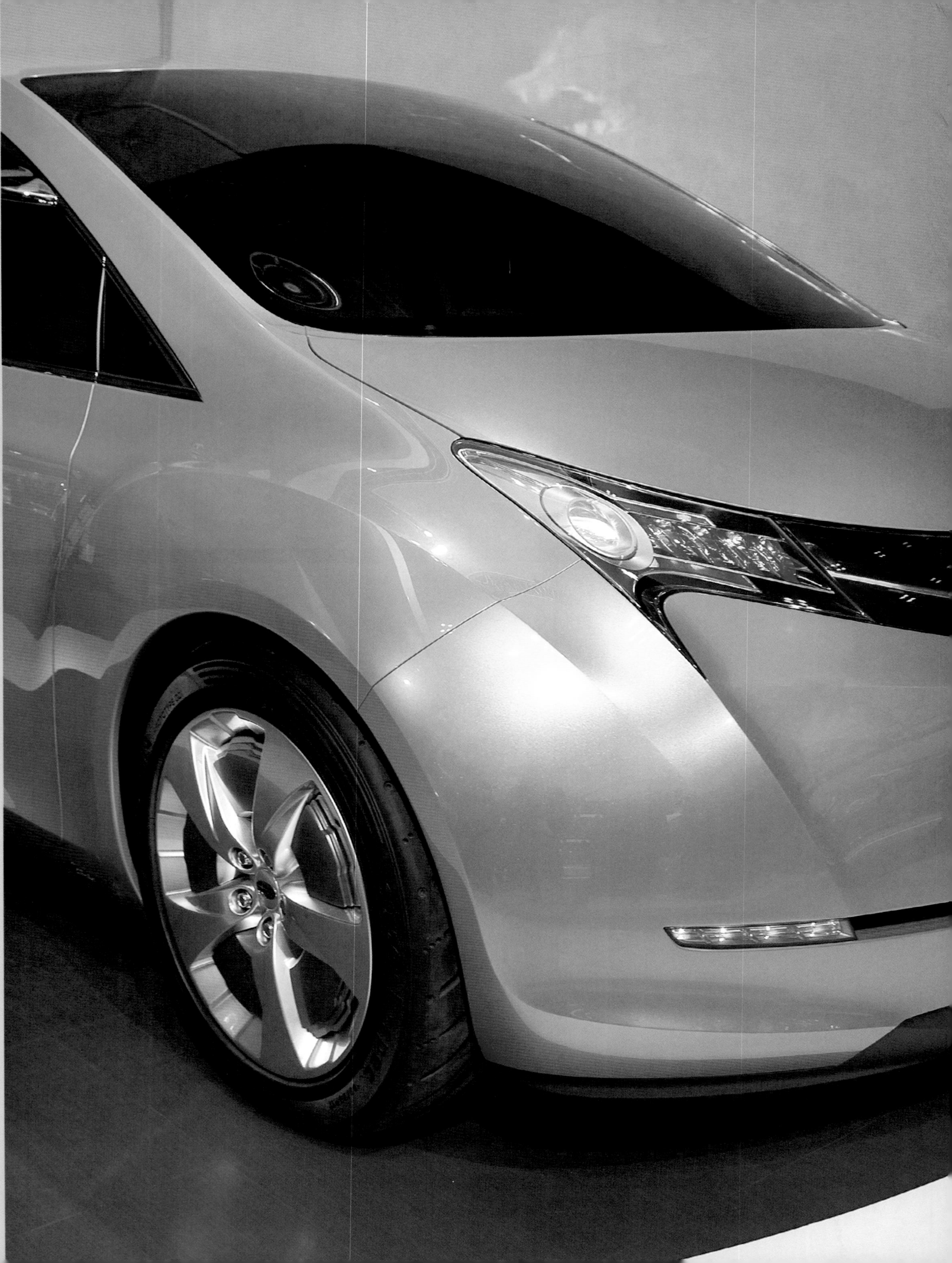

Transportion & Travel

210 WATER TRANSPORTION

212 LAND TRANSPORTION

214 RAIL TRANSPORTION

216 AIR TRANSPORTION

218 TRANSPORT DISASTERS

220 TOURISM

Green car

This battery-powered Subaru is one of the new generation of environmentally friendly cars, invented in response to the rapidly changing natural world. Attempts to make functional and popular alternatives to the internal combustion engine have been going on for many years. At least 11 companies are planning to release electric cars between 2008 and 2011.

Types of ships

Passenger and commercial ships

Barge
This name is used for various types of ships, ranging from a slow canal boat to a small sailing cargo boat or a decorated rowing boat used by royalty.

Catamaran
A boat with two hulls side by side. There are different types of catamarans, including ferries and yachts.

Container ship
A cargo ship designed to carry standard-sized containers, making it easy to load and unload.

Ferry
A ship that takes passengers and vehicles from one port to another.

Galleon
A medieval sailing ship. The word was first used in 1529.

Galley
An ancient warship driven by oars. Biremes have oars on two levels, and triremes on three.

Hydrofoil
A boat with a special device to lift its hull out of the water, thus increasing speed.

Junk
A high-sterned (the stern is the aft, or back end), flat-bottomed, Chinese or Japanese sailing ship with two or three masts.

Liner or cruise ship
An ocean-going ship once used to take passengers on long journeys, such as across the Atlantic. Cruise ships are luxury liners designed to take people on pleasure cruises.

Oil tanker
A large vessel that carries oil from oil fields to refineries in other countries.

Yacht
A sailing or engine-powered ship used for pleasure cruises or racing.

Skyscraper?

During the 18th century, a skyscraper was a small, triangular flag flown from the tip of a sailing ship's main mast. In the 19th century, the word began to be used to describe a tall horse or even an exceptionally tall person. And when the first very tall buildings were constructed in the 1890s people called them skyscrapers.

Sailors racing a catamaran at top speed

Top speeds

Go-fast boat
These high-speed boats are used by the United States Coast Guard to intercept smugglers, who also use them. They have powerful engines and can travel at up to 80 knots (95 mph [150 km/h]).

Aircraft carrier
The U.S. Navy's Nimitz class nuclear-powered aircraft carriers can travel at more than 35 mph (56 km/h).

Submarine (submerged)
Russian Alfa class nuclear submarines could probably travel at 52 mph (83 km/h), but these are no longer in use. U.S. Navy Los Angeles class subs are said to achieve 46 mph (74 km/h), but the precise figures are military secrets.

Sailing vessel
During the 19th century, clippers could average 23 mph (37 km/h). The modern sailing yacht record is held by Simon McKeon and Tim Daddo of Australia. On October 26, 1993, they sailed their yacht *Yellow Pages Endeavour* at 53.57 mph (86.21 km/h).

Car ferry
The Spanish-built Australian catamaran *Luciano Federico L* can carry 52 cars and 450 passengers at a top speed of 67 mph (107 km/h).

Hovercraft
On January 25, 1980, a U.S. Navy Bell SES-1008 experimental vehicle achieved a speed of 106 mph (170 km/h).

Hydroplane
These super-fast racing motor boats are capable of great speeds: Dave Villwock set a record average speed of 213.4 mph (343.5 km/h) in *Miss Budweiser* at Oroville, California, on March 13, 2004.

Ocean liners
Steam ships began carrying passengers across the Atlantic between Europe and the U.S. in 1838. In the early years, the journey (about 3,000 miles/4,800 km) could take 18 days or longer. Shipping companies competed with each other and the fastest ship carried a blue flag, or Blue Riband. There were separate Blue Ribands for westbound and eastbound crossings, and after 1934 an award, the Hales Trophy, was presented to the ship with the fastest average speed. In 1952 the newly launched liner SS *United States* won both the westbound and eastbound Blue Riband with a time of 3 days, 10 hours, 40 minutes, and the Hales Trophy with an average speed of 40.95 mph (65.9 km/h). *Cat-Link V*, a Danish catamaran ferry, is the current Blue Riband and Hales Trophy holder. In 1998, it set a new transatlantic record of just 2 days, 20 hours and 9 minutes, and an average speed of 47.5 mph (76.5 km/h).

Warships

Aircraft carrier A warship from which aircraft can take off and land.

Cruiser A medium-sized, fast, long-range warship.

Battleship A large armored warship.

Destroyer A small, fast warship.

Frigate A warship that escorted cargo convoys to protect them from attack by submarines, introduced during World War II.

Minesweeper A naval ship designed to find and destroy mines.

Submarine Military submarines can travel long distances under water to avoid detection, and can fire torpedoes and missiles. Special civilian submarines are used for undersea research.

See also
The World's Oceans: pages 40–41

Biggest ships

All the ships listed here held the record as the biggest ship in the world when they were launched. The first, the *Great Western*, was a giant in its time but was less than 1/100 the size of the current record holder *Queen Mary 2*, which is 1,132 ft. (345 m) long. The *Great Eastern* measured 692 ft. (211 m) and the *Titanic* was 882 ft. (269 m) long.

Some of these ships are still sailing, but many have been scrapped. The *Titanic* and *Lusitania* sank with the loss of many lives.

Great Western (launched in1838) gross tonnage*: 1,340
President (1840) gross tonnage: 2,360
Great Britain (1845) gross tonnage: 3,448
Great Eastern (1858) gross tonnage: 18,914
Oceanic (1899) gross tonnage: 17,274
Baltic (1904) gross tonnage: 23,884
Lusitania (1907) gross tonnage: 31,550
Mauretania (1907) gross tonnage: 31,938
Titanic (1912) gross tonnage: 46,232
Bismarck/Majestic/Caledonia†, (1922) gross tonnage: 56,621
Normandie/Lafayette† (1935) gross tonnage: 79,301
Queen Elizabeth (1938) gross tonnage: 83,673
Voyager of the Seas (1999) gross tonnage: 137,276
Explorer of the Seas (2000) gross tonnage: 137,308
Navigator of the Seas (2002) gross tonnage: 138,279
Queen Mary 2 (2003) gross tonnage: 142,200
Liberty of the Seas (2007) gross tonnage: 160,000
Genesis class (2009) gross tonnage: 220,000

* Weights given are the weight of the ship when empty, without cargo, crew, supplies or passengers.
† Renamed

Liberty of the Seas, launched in 2007

World's biggest ship

Built in Finland, *Liberty of the Seas* is 1,212 ft. (339 m) long and carries 4,370 passengers and a crew of 1,360. Among its luxurious facilities are an ice-skating rink and a water park with a wave-generator that allows swimmers to surf.

Famous ships

Some ships, such as the *Titanic*, are famous because they sank, but here are some famous ships that are celebrated for a variety of other reasons.

Niña, Pinta **and** ***Santa Maria***
The three ships on Christopher Columbus' voyage to America in 1492.

Mayflower
The ship that took the settlers known as the Pilgrim Fathers from Plymouth to America in 1620.

Endeavour
Captain James Cook's ship on his exploration of Australia and New Zealand in 1768–71.

Bounty
The crew of this British ship mutinied against Captain William Bligh in 1789.

Victory
Captain Horatio Nelson's flagship at the Battle of Trafalgar, 1805. It is now on display in Portsmouth, England.

Beagle
The research ship on which British scientist Charles Darwin visited the Galápagos Islands in 1835.

Cutty Sark
A tea clipper (a sailing ship designed to bring tea from China as fast as possible) launched in 1869. The ship is preserved in dry dock at Greenwich, London.

Replica of the *Mayflower*, moored in Plymouth, Massachusetts

Great Eastern
This ship was designed by Isambard Kingdom Brunel and launched in 1858. It laid the first transatlantic cable in 1866, but was scrapped in 1888.

Marie Celeste
A U.S. ship found abandoned in the Atlantic in 1872. The fate of its crew remains a mystery.

Kon-Tiki
A balsawood raft on which Norwegian anthropologist Thor Heyerdahl sailed from South America across the Pacific to Polynesia in 1947. He made the voyage to prove his theory that Polynesian people came from South America.

Famous cars

● Mercedes

The German luxury car, which has been made since 1901, took its name from Mercédès, the daughter of Daimler car company director Emil Jellinek.

● Rolls-Royce

British car enthusiasts Henry Royce and Charles Rolls joined forces to form Rolls-Royce in 1906 and set new standards for a luxury vehicle. The company's engines are also used in many of the world's aircraft.

● Model T Ford

The first Model T Ford, nicknamed the Tin Lizzie, was made in the U.S. in 1908 by the Ford Motor Company, which was founded in 1903 by Henry Ford. By 1927, when production finished, a total of 16,536,075 had been built. At one point, more than half the new cars in the world were Model Ts.

● Aston Martin

This luxury sports car has been made in the U.K. since the 1920s. It became one of the most featured and gadget-laden cars in the James Bond films.

● Bugatti Royale

Only six Bugatti Royales (1926) were ever made. The Royale was designed by Italian Ettore Bugatti and was one of the largest vehicles of all time. It was 22 ft. (6.7 m) long with a 12.7 L engine originally designed for aircraft. In 1980 one of these rare vehicles set a new world record price when it was sold for $15 million.

● Volkswagen Beetle

The Volkswagen Beetle was designed by Ferdinand Porsche and first manufactured in Germany in 1937. When production

James Bond's Aston Martin

Top vehicle-owning countries

There are so many cars today that there is one car for every 10.2 people in the world. In the United States there are 2.2 people per car, but in some countries the ratio is amazingly high. In Myanmar (formerly Burma, for example, there are 6,203 people for every car!

Germany
Cars 46,090,303
Commercial vehicles 3,133,197

Italy
Cars 34,667,485
Commercial vehicles 4,422,269

France
Cars 29,990,000
Commercial vehicles 6,139,000

U.K.
Cars 30,651,700
Commercial vehicles 3,942,700

Japan
Cars 57,090,789
Commercial vehicles 16,733,871

U.S.
Cars 132,908,828
Commercial vehicles 104,788,269

Rest of the world
Cars 285,621,064
Commercial vehicles 105,949,439

World total
Cars 617,020,169
Commercial vehicles 245,108,745

Car timeline

1800s

1883 First experimental gas car (France)
1886 Karl Benz and Gottlieb Daimler (Germany) build first cars
1892 First U.S. car built by Charles and Frank Duryea
1893 Rudolf Diesel patents engine
1893 First electric car in Canada made for F.B. Featherstonhaugh of Toronto, Ontario
1895 First car race, Paris-Bordeaux-Paris, France, 732 mi. (1,178 km)
1895 Michelin (France) makes first pneumatic car tires
1896 First car theft (France)
1896 First motoring death (U.K.)
1897 First gas-driven car in Canada built by George Foote Foss of Sherbrooke, Quebec
1898 First woman driver in U.S. Genevra Mudge
1899 Jacob German arrested for speeding in New York (12 mph/ 19 km/h)

1900s

1900 There are 8,000 vehicles on the road in U.S.
1902 First Canadian production car, the LeRoy, was built in Berlin (now Kitchener), Ontario
1903 A total of 11,235 cars made in the U.S.
1903 First driving licences issued, Paris, France
1904 There are 535 vehicles in Canada
1907 First Rolls-Royce made, the Silver Ghost (U.K.)
1908 First Model T Ford made (U.S.)
1910 There are 468,500 vehicles in U.S.
1912 First gas station built (U.S.)
1912 Thomas Wilby and F.V. "Jack" Haney are the first to drive across Canada, coast to coast; it took them 51 days, from August 27 to October 17 to travel from Halifax to Victoria
1915 Headlight dipping and stoplights introduced (U.S.)
1919 Mechanical windshield wipers developed (U.S.)
1919 There are 9,158 vehicles in Canada
1921 First autobahn (high-speed road or motorway) built in Germany

ended in 2003 a total of 21,529,464 Beetles had been made, the last of them in Brazil and Mexico. A new version of the Beetle was introduced in 1998.

● MINI
The MINI was launched in the U.K. in August 1959, when it cost just under $1,400. It was designed by Alec Issigonis (1906–88). More than 5.3 million MINIs had been made by 2000. The new MINI was launched in 2001. By 2007 more than one million had been sold.

Fastest car

ThrustSSC is the most powerful car ever built. It uses two Rolls-Royce engines from Phantom fighter aircraft. In 1997, driven by Royal Air Force fighter pilot Andy Green, *Thrust* set a new land speed record of 763.035 mph (1,227.986 km/h). It was also the first road vehicle to break the sound barrier.

See also
ThrustSSC: page 15

Driving on the left

People in most countries drive on the right. But in more than 70 countries and territories they drive on the left. These include the U.K., Japan, Australia, South Africa, Thailand, Ireland, Malaysia, Indonesia, India, New Zealand and Pakistan. The tradition of keeping to the left dates back to the time when most road users were on horseback. One explanation is that as most people are right-handed, riding on the left allowed them to use a sword to defend themselves against approaching riders.

Amazing vehicles

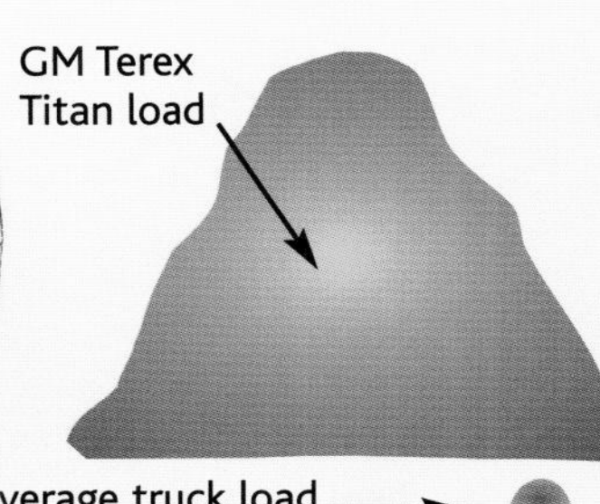

● Biggest dumper trucks
The General Motors Terex Titan 33-19 mine truck, first made in 1974, can carry 350 tons (317.5 tonnes). An average truck carries about 5.5 tons (5 tonnes).

● Biggest fire engines
Fire trucks made by the Oshkosh Truck Corporation of Wisconsin for airports have eight wheels, 860-hp engines and weigh 66 tons (60 tonnes).

● Longest limos
The current record-holder, built by Jay Ohrberg of California, measures 100 ft. (30.5 m) and has 26 wheels. It is so long that it has to be hinged in the middle to enable it to turn corners.

● Biggest bus
The articulated Super City Train Buses used in the Democratic Republic of Congo are 105.7 ft. (32.2 m) long. They can carry 110 seated passengers and 140 standing in the first part, and 60 seated and 40 standing in the second—a total of 350 people.

● Fastest electric car
The *White Lightning Electric Streamliner* holds the official record for the fastest electric vehicle. In 1999, driven by Patrick Rummerfield (U.S.), it went at a speed of 245.952 mph (395.821 km/h). It is powered by two 200-hp motors and a 420-volt battery pack.

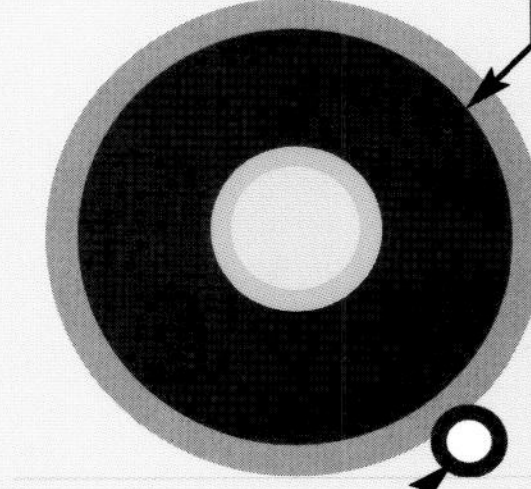

● Biggest tires
The largest road vehicle tires are 12.5 ft. (3.82 m) in diameter. They are made by the Bridgestone Corporation, Tokyo, Japan, for giant dumper trucks. Normal car tires are about 24 in. (60 cm) in diameter.

2000s

1930 First traffic light installed in New York
1933 First drive-in theater built (U.S.)
1935 First parking meters installed in Oklahoma City
1940 There are 1,500,829 vehicles in Canada
1940 There are 32,453,200 vehicles in U.S.
1960 There are 5,256,341 vehicles in Canada
1960 There are 73,868,600 vehicles in U.S.
1962 The 200 millionth car produced in U.S.
1969 Czechoslovakia becomes first country to make seat belts compulsory
1970 Unleaded fuel introduced in U.S.
1978 Bosch (Germany) patents first satellite navigation
1980 There are 155,796,000 vehicles in the U.S.
1985 Seat belts made compulsory in New York
1999 Peak year for U.S. vehicle manufacture (13,024,978 made)
2005 The Bugatti Veyron 16.4 is the fastest, most powerful and most expensive car ever built
2007 Tesla Roadster electric cars capable of 210 km/h (130 mph) and 400 km (250 miles) on a single charge
2008 The Tata Nano, the world's cheapest car ($2,500) is launched in India.

www.lemaymuseum.org search

Types of trains

Not all trains are the same. These are just some of the variations around the world.

Rubber-tired metro
These electric trains run along a tracked roadway. They are quiet, can accelerate quickly and tackle slopes. They first ran in Paris, France, in the 1950s, and are now used in other urban centers, including Montreal, Quebec, and Mexico City.

Funicular
Funiculars (from the Latin *funiculus*, a thin rope) are designed to go up and down steep hills or mountains. Cars are drawn up by cables and descend by gravity. Funiculars are used in mountain and other resorts, and in hilly parts of cities, such as Montmartre in Paris, France. The steepest passenger funicular is the Katoomba Scenic Railway in New South Wales, Australia.

Cog railway
Cog or rack-and-pinion railways are used in mountains. The train has a rotating cog wheel that meshes with a rack rail, so the train can climb steep slopes. The highest one in the U.S. is Manitou and Pike's Peak Railway, Colorado, operating since 1891. The peak is 14,110 ft. (4,300 m) high.

Maglev

The name Maglev comes from the words magnetic and levitation. These trains do not run on a track, but float above it by means of magnetic repulsion. They can travel very smoothly at high speeds (up to 400 mph [650 km/h]) — and use little energy. A new 100-mi. (160 km) Maglev line is being built between Shanghai and Hangzhou, China — the first inter-city Maglev service.

A Maglev train in Germany

Monorail
A monorail train runs on a single rail, instead of on a track or two rails. It is either suspended from the rail or straddles it. The Tokyo Monorail in Japan carries 100 million passengers a year. There are also monorails in the U.S., Malaysia, Australia.

The Ghan on its first journey across Australia

One and only

The only time a train has been powered by fish was during a coal shortage in Turkestan in 1919. Dried fish, caught in the Aral Sea, were used as fuel. Almost 9,900 tons (9,000 tonnes) were used to stoke the train's boilers.

Famous trains

Orient Express
The Orient Express began trips from Paris, France, to Bulgaria on October 5, 1883, and from 1889 went as far as Constantinople (now Istanbul), Turkey. It was the first trans-European train and traveled a total of 1,700 mi. (2,735 km) across six countries. It stopped running in 1977, but was relaunched five years later.

20th Century Limited
The luxurious 20th Century Limited ran between New York and Chicago from 1902 to 1967.

Trans-Siberian Express
The Trans-Siberian Express travels 5,777 mi. (9,297 km) between Moscow and Vladivostok. The line opened in 1914 and is the world's longest continuous rail line.

The Canadian
The streamlined stainless steel transcontinental train originally operated by Canadian Pacific (now VIA Rail Canada) has run between Toronto, Ontario, and Vancouver, B.C., since 1955.

Golden Arrow
From 1929 to 1971, the Golden Arrow ran from Victoria, London, to Dover on the south coast of England. From there passengers could sail across the Channel and then take the French Flèche d'Or to Paris.

Blue Train
This is one of the world's most luxurious trains and it has operated between Cape Town and Tshwane (Pretoria), South Africa, since 1939. The train, carriages and decor are mainly blue — hence the name.

Subways

A subway, or underground railway, is an urban train line that runs mostly, or completely, underground. The world's first subway system was the London Metropolitan Line in London, England.

Although New York had a short pneumatic (air-powered) system running down part of Broadway as early as 1868, the main New York City Subway opened to the public on October 27, 1904. On its first day, 111,881 people paid 5 cents each for a ticket to ride. It was the Unites State's second (after Boston) and the world's seventh underground railway to be opened.

First subways

London, England opened January 10, 1863
Budapest, Hungary opened May 2, 1896
Glasgow, Scotland opened December 14, 1896
Boston, Massachusetts opened September 1, 1897
Paris, France opened July 19, 1900

Longest subway lines

City (stations)	Total track length mi. (km)
London, U.K. (275)	253.5 (408)
New York, N.Y. (468)	228.7 (368)
Tokyo, Japan (274)	181.6 (292.3)
Seoul, South Korea (264)	178.6 (287.4)
Moscow, Russia (172)	172.9 (278.3)
Paris, France (369)	132 (212.5)

Busiest subway systems

Annual passengers

Tokyo 2,819,000,000
Moscow 2,603,000,000
Seoul 1,465,000,000
New York 1,449,000,000
Mexico City 1,442,000,000
Paris 1,336,000,000
London 976,000,000

Longest rail networks

These countries have more than 7,000 mi. (11,265 km) of railways. At the other end of the scale, Djibouti, Puerto Rico, St. Kitts, and Nevis, Nepal and Nicaragua have less than 60 mi. (100 km). Some countries have none at all.

U.S.: 140,810 mi. (226,612 km)
Russia: 54,157 mi. (87,157 km)
China: 46,875 mi. (75,438 km)
India: 39,284 mi. (63,221 km)
Germany: 29,959 mi. (48,215 km)
Canada: 29,868 mi. (48,068 km)
Australia: 23,945 mi. (38,550 km)
Argentina: 19,823 mi. (31,902 km)
France: 18,250 mi. (29,370 km)
Brazil: 18,203 mi. (29,295 km)
Japan: 14,586 mi. (23,474 km)
Poland: 14,336 mi. (23,072 km)
Ukraine: 13,964 mi. (22,473 km)
South Africa: 12,969 mi. (20,872 km)
Italy: 12,092 mi. (19,460 km)
Mexico: 10,997 mi. (17,665 km)
U.K.: 10,294 mi. (16,567 km)
Spain: 9,304 mi. (14,974 km)
Kazakhstan: 8,513 mi. (13,700 km)
Sweden: 7,163 mi. (11,528 km)
Romania: 7,074 mi. (11,385 km)
World total: 851,764 mi. (1,370,782 km)

Bullet Train
Japanese bullet trains (shinkansen) are the world's fastest scheduled rail services. They were introduced in 1964 to coincide with the Tokyo Olympic Games.

TGV
The French TGV (Train à Grande Vitesse, or high speed train) was launched in 1981 and is an electric train service between Paris and Lyon. A specially modified TGV, the Atlantique, set a world speed record of 320.2 mph (515.3 km/h) on May 18, 1990.

Eurostar
The Eurostar service was launched on November 14, 1994 to carry passengers between London, Paris and Brussels through the Channel Tunnel. It can reach speeds of 186 mph (300 km/h). In its first 10 years it carried a total of 59 million passengers.

Ghan
The Ghan is the first rail service from Adelaide to Darwin on the north–south route across Australia. It was named after the camel trains that were once the only way to cross the desert. The first train ran in 2004. It had 43 carriages, measured more than 0.6 mi. (1 km) in length, and carried 330 passengers.

www.nationalrrmuseum.org search

Aviation pioneers

John Alcock (U.K., 1892–1919) and **Arthur Whitten Brown** (U.K., 1886–1948)
On June 14–15, 1919, they completed the first ever nonstop flight across the Atlantic from Newfoundland to Ireland.

Louis Blériot (France, 1872–1936)
On July 25, 1909 Blériot became the first person to fly across the English Channel.

Samuel F. Cody (U.S., c. 1861–1913)
The first person to fly in England, October 16, 1908.

Glenn Curtiss (U.S., 1878–1930)
Rival to the Wright Brothers, Curtiss made the first public flight in the U.S. on July 4, 1908. He set up the first airplane manufacturing company in the USA.

Amelia Earhart (U.S., 1898–1937)
The first woman to fly the Atlantic. She went on to establish many flying records but disappeared during an attempt to fly around the world.

Amy Johnson (U.K., 1903–41)
She made the first solo flight from England to Australia in 1930.

Charles Lindbergh (U.S., 1902–74)
The first pilot to fly solo across the Atlantic, from New York to Paris, May 20–21, 1927, in *The Spirit of St Louis*.

Harriet Quimby (U.S., 1875–1912)
The U.S.'s first female pilot. On April 16, 1912 she was the first woman to fly the English Channel — but on the day the sinking of the *Titanic* was reported, so her triumph was barely noticed.

Wilbur Wright (U.S., 1867–1912) and **Orville Wright** (U.S., 1871–1948)
The Wright brothers, two bicycle mechanics from Dayton, Ohio, made the first ever powered flights on December 17, 1903.

Concorde

Concorde fact file

Concorde, the only passenger aircraft ever to fly faster than the speed of sound, was first named in a speech by General de Gaulle on January 13, 1963. The England-France project began the following year.

- The first prototype Concorde was shown at the Toulouse Air Show on December 11, 1967.
- The first French flight took place on March 2, 1969.
- The first British flight took place on April 9, 1969.
- The first landing at London Heathrow was on September 13, 1970.
- The first Concorde landing in the U.S. was at Dallas-Fort Worth on September 20, 1973.
- The only Concorde crash was near Paris, on July 25, 2000, when 109 passengers and crew and four people on the ground died.
- Concorde's last flight took place on October 24, 2004. All surviving British Airways and Air France Concordes are on public display in museums and airports in the U.S., U.K., France, Germany and Barbados.

The Wright brothers demonstrate their Wright Model A plane

See also

Steve Fossett: page 153
Amelia Earhart: page 153

The Wright brothers

Orville Wright was the first person to fly a powered aircraft. He also became the first to fly a plane for more than one hour, on September 9, 1908, at Fort Meyer, Virginia. His brother Wilbur became the first to fly for more than two hours, on December 31, 1908, at Auvours, France. On May 20, 1909, French pilot Paul Tissandier became the first person other than the Wrights to fly for more than an hour.

Breaking the sound barrier

Charles "Chuck" Yeager became the first person to break the sound barrier on October 14, 1947. His Bell X-1 rocket plane was dropped from a carrier aircraft above Muroc Dry Lake, California. At 42,000 ft. (12,800 m) he reached a speed of 670 mph (1,078 km/h). He did not break the air-speed record because only aircraft that take off and land under their own power are eligible. The speed of sound is not fixed and varies according to height and air conditions. In dry air at sea level the speed of sound is 763 mph (1,227 km/h), but at high altitudes, where air density is less, it is lower.

One and only

The only flight of the Hercules H-4 aircraft, known as the "Spruce Goose," took place on November 2, 1947. It was the largest flying boat ever built. It had the greatest wingspan (320 ft./97.54 m) of any aircraft and eight engines. Millionaire aviator Howard Hughes built and flew it himself, just 65.6 ft. (20 m) above the water off Long Beach, California, USA. It traveled only 1 mi. (1.6 km). The flight is recreated in the film *The Aviator* (2004).

www.flyingmachines.org search

First manned balloon flights

The first balloons worked on the principle that when air is heated, it rises. They were filled with hot air by burning things under them, such as paper, straw and wool — and even old shoes and rotten meat!

The balloons often caught fire, and once the air cooled they quickly came down. Soon after the first hot-air flights, people realized that the gas hydrogen could be used instead. Hydrogen is the lightest of all elements — almost 15 times lighter than air. Gas balloons can also be filled with helium, which is not as light as hydrogen but does not catch fire so easily. Most balloons today use hot air made by burning propane gas.

The first hot-air balloon flight

The Montgolfier brothers, Joseph and Etienne, tested their first unmanned hot-air balloon on June 5, 1783. On November 21, 1783, François Laurent, Marquis d'Arlandes and Jean-François Pilâtre de Rozier took off from the Bois de Boulogne, Paris, in a Montgolfier hot-air balloon. They traveled about 5.5 mi. (9 km) in 23 minutes.

First hydrogen balloon flight

On December 1, 1783, Jacques Alexandre César Charles and Nicholas-Louis Robert made the first flight in a hydrogen balloon. They took off from the Tuileries, Paris, watched by a crowd of 400,000, and traveled 43 km (27 miles) north to Nesle in about two hours. Charles then took off again alone, so was the first ever solo pilot.

First Channel crossing

On January 7, 1785 Jean-Pierre Blanchard made the first Channel crossing in a balloon with Dr. John Jeffries (the first American to fly). They also carried the first airmail letter. As they lost height, they had to reduce weight, so they threw almost everything overboard — including their clothes!

First flight in the U.S.

On January 9, 1793, in Philadelphia, Pennsylvania, Blanchard made the first balloon flight in the United States. He took a small black dog with him as a passenger. The flight was watched by President George Washington, who gave Blanchard a passport permitting his flight, which was the first pilot's license and the United States first airmail document in the United States.

First hot-air balloon flight

First nonstop solo flight

U.S. adventurer Steve Fossett made the first nonstop solo and fastest around-the-world balloon flight, June 19 to July 3, 2002.

Shipwrecks

Shipping disasters as a result of collisions, storms, fires, explosions or military action are among the most famous of human tragedies. Some wrecks were carrying treasure that has since been recovered.

The *Mary Rose*, which sank in 1545

Mary Rose
This Tudor galleon sank in 1545 as Henry VIII watched from the shore. It was found in 1968, raised in 1982, and is exhibited in Portsmouth, UK.

Spanish Armada
Between August and October 1588, military action and storms combined to destroy the Spanish fleet off the British coast. About half the 130 ships that set out were wrecked, killing about 4,000 men.

Empress of Ireland
In the St. Lawrence River, Canada, on the night of May 29, 1914, the liner was struck by the Norwegian coal ship Storstad and quickly sank. Of 1,477 passengers and crew on board, 1,012 were killed; out of 318 children, only four were saved. The wreck is still at the bottom of the river.

Tek Sing
This Chinese junk carrying 2,000 passengers and 350,000 pieces of porcelain sank in 1822. It was found in 1999 and its treasures sold for high prices.

Sultana
On April 27, 1865, the *Sultana*, a steamboat on the Mississippi River near Memphis, Tennessee, was destroyed by a boiler explosion. This was the worst ever marine accident in the U.S. and a total of 1,547 people died.

Princess Alice
On September 3, 1878 the pleasure steamer *Princess Alice* was taking people down the Thames in London. It collided with the *Bywell Castle* and 786 people died.

Titanic
On the night of April 14, 1912, the "unsinkable" *Titanic* struck an iceberg on its maiden voyage and sank the next day, killing 1,517. The wreck was discovered and explored by Robert Ballard in 1986.

Lusitania
The British liner was torpedoed off the Irish coast by a German U-boat on May 7, 1915, with the loss of 1,198 lives.

Wilhelm Gustloff
The German liner, laden with refugees, was torpedoed off Gdansk, Poland, on January 30, 1945, by a Soviet submarine, S-13. Between 5,348 and 7,800 people died, making this the worst ever marine disaster.

Dona Paz
The *Donna Paz* sank off the Philippines on December 20, 1987, killing up to 3,000 people. This was the world's worst passenger ferry disaster.

Kursk
This Russian nuclear submarine sank in the Barents Sea on August 12, 2000, with the loss of all 118 crew.

Rail disasters

Rail travel is one of the safest ways of journeying from place to place, taking into account the large numbers of passengers carried and distances traveled. But there have been accidents.

World's worst
At Telwatta, Sri Lanka, on December 26, 2004, the *Queen of the Sea* train was struck by the Indian Ocean tsunami. The exact number killed is unknown, but is estimated to be between 1,700 and 2,000.

North America
On April 3, 1955, an express train was derailed and fell into a canyon near Guadalajara, Mexico, leaving about 300 people dead.

U.S.
Two U.S. accidents resulted in 101 deaths. On August 10, 1887, a bridge at Chatsworth, Illinois caught fire and collapsed as a train was passing over. As many as 372 people were injured and 101 died. The second accident happened on July 9, 1918, at Nashville, Tennessee, when two trains collided head-on.

Canada
At St. Hilaire, Quebec, on June 29, 1864, a train filled with German and Norwegian immigrants failed to stop at a swing bridge and plunged into the Richelieu River. About 99 people were killed and many seriously injured in Canada's worst rail disaster.

Subway
On October 28, 1995, at Baku, Azerbaijan, an underground train caught fire one evening, killing more than 300 people.

U.S. subway
America's worst subway accident was on November 1, 1918, in Brooklyn, New York. A train was derailed in the Malbone Street tunnel, leaving 97 dead.

Road disasters

Many people are killed and injured on the roads — more than 40,000 a year in the U.S. — but accidents involving more than a few drivers or pedestrians are rare.

Worst road disaster On November 3, 1982 an oil tanker collided with a Soviet army truck and exploded in the 1.7 mi. (2.7 km) Salang Tunnel in Afghanistan. At least 2,000, and perhaps as many as 3,000, people died as a result of the explosion, fire and fumes.

U.S. road disaster The worst U.S. road disaster took place on December 15, 1967. The Silver Bridge across the Ohio River from Kanauga, Ohio, to Point Pleasant, West Virginia, collapsed during heavy pre-Christmas rush-hour traffic. About 60 vehicles plunged into the river and 46 people died.

Canadian road accident On September 3, 1999, dense fog caused pileups near Windsor, Ontario, the worst of which killed eight people and left 33 injured.

The Ashtabula Bridge disaster

On December 29, 1876, a train traveling from New York to Chicago, and pulled by two locomotives, crossed the Ashtabula Bridge, Ohio, in a snowstorm. At 7:28 p.m., after the first locomotive, Socrates, had crossed, the bridge collapsed behind it.

The second engine, Columbia, broke away, and it and all 11 carriages plunged 75 ft. (23 m) into the ravine. About 92 people were killed and many injured in what at that time was the worst rail disaster in the U.S.

Two hijacked planes crash into the World Trade Center, New York

Air disasters

Worst ever

Two terrorist attacks on the twin towers of the World Trade Center, New York, on September 11, 2001, killed everybody on both hijacked planes (92 on one and 65 on the other). More than 2,000 people also died in the buildings.

On the ground

On March 27, 1977, two Boeing 747s collided on the runway of Los Rodeos airport in Tenerife in the Canary Islands. The aircraft were carrying 614 passengers and 30 crew between them. A total of 61 people managed to escape.

Single-aircraft disaster

On August 12, 1985 a JAL Boeing 747 on a domestic flight from Tokyo to Osaka crashed, killing 520.

Midair collision

At Charkhi Dadri, India, on November 12, 1996, a Saudi Airways Boeing 747 collided with a Kazakh Airlines Ilyushin IL-76 cargo aircraft. A total of 349 people died.

The Hindenburg disaster

The *Hindenburg* was the world's biggest airship at 804 ft. (245 m) long. The airship made several successful transatlantic crossings, then flew from Frankfurt, Germany, to Lakehurst, New Jersey. It arrived on May 6, 1937, after a three-day trip. As the airship was moored, it caught fire and turned into an inferno.

See also
Hydrogen: page 79

History of tourism

People have been traveling from place to place since ancient times. Nomadic people moved around to graze their livestock. Later people traveled to trade, or to seek their fortunes in gold rushes, and millions emigrated to other countries to escape persecution or to seek better lives.

Apart from a few historical examples, tourism — traveling for pleasure — is a relatively modern idea. Today, people spend nearly $500 billion a year on tourism.

Space tourism

The first fare-paying space tourist was American millionaire Denis Tito. In 2001 he paid $20 million to spend a week on the *International Space Station*. Anglo–South African Mark Shuttleworth paid a similar amount for a trip in 2002. Several companies, such as Virgin Galactic, are planning to take passengers to a height of about 60 mi. (100 km) in 2009.

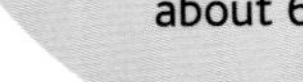

Taking the waters
The Romans placed great value on bathing. They settled in many places with natural springs and developed cities as spas (the name comes from Spa in Belgium). In the 18th century, it became fashionable to visit these spas to "take the waters" — drinking and bathing as cures for various illnesses. Bath, in England, is a well-known Roman spa.

Package tours
On July 5, 1841, British travel pioneer Thomas Cook took 570 members of the Temperance Society (an organization opposed to drinking alcohol) on the newly opened railway from Leicester to Loughborough. This was the first package tour, and the beginning of what was to become the world's best-known travel company. When the Paris Exhibition opened in 1851, Cook took "excursionists" abroad for the first time. By the time Thomas Cook died in 1892, he had made travel possible for the masses.

The Roman baths in Bath, England

Exhibitions
During the 19th and 20th centuries, major exhibitions in the U.S. and Europe brought millions of people to the big cities of the world. Many had never traveled before. The Great Exhibition in London, England in 1851 had more than six million visitors. The Paris Exposition of 1889, for which the Eiffel Tower was built, had 28 million visitors, and more than 51 million visited the New York World's Fair of 1964–65.

Sleeping Beauty's Castle, Disneyland, Paris

Festivals
The world's major arts and music festivals receive millions of visitors. The annual Texas State Fair in the U.S. attracts as many as three million, and many other North American fairs receive one million or more. Festivals such as the carnival held in Rio de Janeiro, Brazil, and Mardi Gras in New Orleans, Louisiana, are attended by large crowds.

Sport tourism
Winter sports such as skiing, water sports and adventure sports such as white-water rafting have become very popular. When the Olympic Games are held, the host country can expect a huge boost to its tourist industry.

Amusement parks
The world's most-visited amusement park is Disney World, Florida, which attracts 16.64 million visitors a year. The total number of visitors at all Disney attractions around the world is 112.5 million a year.

See also
Countries of the World: pages 116-117

Serengeti National Park, Tanzania

Serengeti National Park

This vast park in Tanzania was founded in 1951 and covers 5,700 sq. mi. (14,760 sq km) Wildebeest, gazelles and zebras graze here, along with lions, elephants, giraffes and other animals. It is one of Africa's most popular tourist attractions.

National parks

National parks are established by governments to preserve areas of land and the plants and animals they contain. Yellowstone National Park, set up in 1872, was the first. There are now more than 1,200 national parks in 100 or more countries. These are a few examples of the different types.

Banff National Park (founded 1885; 2,564 sq. mi./6,641 sq km)
Canada's oldest national park, in the Canadian Rockies in Alberta. Its forests and glaciers attract about four million visitors a year.

Everglades (founded 1934; 2,289 sq. mi./ 5,929 sq km)
The Everglades, Florida is the only subtropical park in North America. Many different types of creatures live in its swamps, including alligators.

Great Barrier Reef (founded 1979; 132,742 sq. mi./ 343,800 sq km)
Australia's Great Barrier Reef, off the coast of Queensland, is the world's largest coral reef system, supporting many rare marine animals and plants.

Galápagos Islands (founded 1986; 2,678 sq. mi./6,937 sq km)
These volcanic islands off the coast of Ecuador are home to birds, seals and unique creatures including giant turtles and marine iguanas.

Lake District (founded 1951; 885 sq. mi./ 2,292 sq km)
The largest and most visited of Great Britain's national parks. The parks receive a total of 100 million visitors a year.

Wrangell-St. Elias (founded 1980; 13,057 sq. mi./ 33,820 sq km)
This national park in Alaska is the largest in the U.S.. It contains the most glaciers and peaks higher than 16,010 ft. (4,880 m) in North America, as well as many wild animals, including bears, wolves and moose.

Xingu (founded 1961; 8,500 sq. mi./22,000 sq km)
This large area of Brazilian rainforest is teeming with tropical wildlife. It is also inhabited by tribes of indigenous peoples who have little contact with outsiders.

Yellowstone (founded 1872; 3,471 sq. mi./ 8,991 sq km)
This area of the Rocky Mountains in the U.S. is famed for its hot springs and geysers. Most famous is the Old Faithful geyser which sprays steam and water up to 184 ft. (56 m) high.

Top tourist countries

In 2006, one in every eight people in the world traveled as tourists to another country — a total of 846 million. Of these, almost half visited the top 10 destinations below. By the year 2020 the number of international tourists is likely to more than double to 1.5 billion.

Country	Visitors	% of world total
1 France	79,100,000	9.3
2 Spain	58,500,000	6.9
3 U.S.	51,100,000	6.0
4 China	49,600,000	5.9
5 Italy	41,100,000	4.9
6 U.K.	30,700,000	3.6
7 Germany	23,600,000	2.8
8 Mexico	21,400,000	2.5
9 Austria	20,300,000	2.4
10 Russia	20,200,000	2.4
Top 10 total	395,600,000	46.7

Language & Literature

224 LANGUAGE
226 COMMUNICATION
228 BOOKS
230 AUTHORS
232 CHILDREN'S BOOKS
234 POETS AND POETRY
236 NEWSPAPERS AND MAGAZINES

Shaken not stirred

2008 was the centenary of the birth of Ian Fleming, creator of James Bond. Fleming's bestselling novels are still in print and James Bond is still the most famous fictional spy in the world. The latest film, Quantum of Solace, starred Daniel Craig in his second appearance as Bond.

Most spoken languages

Chinese (Mandarin)
Approximately 885,000,000 speakers. Chinese has many dialects, but about two-thirds of the people speak Mandarin. Wu is the next most common dialect, with approximately 77 million speakers. At least 30 million people around the world are learning Mandarin Chinese because China is becoming an important economic power.

Spanish
Approximately 332,000,000 speakers. Spanish is one of the most widely used of all languages. It is spoken not only in Spain but also in the U.S., South America, and the west coast of Africa.

English
Approximately 322,000,000 speakers. Far fewer people have English as their main language than Chinese, but millions more know at least some English and it is spoken in every corner of the globe. The United States dominates film, television, pop music, technology (Internet) and business, and this has increased the importance of the English language. At least 800 million people use the Internet and about 35 percent of them communicate in English. There are probably more than one billion people worldwide learning English.

Arabic
Approximately 246,000,000 speakers. Arabic is the official language of 17 countries and it is also the language of the Muslim religion. As a result, many millions of Muslims in other countries have some knowledge of the language.

Hindustani
Approximately 182,000,000 speakers. Hindustani includes Hindi and Urdu, which are almost the same language. Hindustani is the official language of Pakistan, where it is written in modified Arabic script and called Urdu. It is also the official language of India, but there it is written in the Devanagari script and called Hindi.

Portuguese
Approximately 177,500,000 speakers. Portuguese is spoken as a first language by the people of Portugal and also by many of the inhabitants of Brazil, Angola and other former colonies in Africa and elsewhere. These stretch from the Caribbean to Macau, China.

Languages spoken in most countries

English: 57 countries
French: 33 countries
Arabic: 23 countries
Spanish: 21 countries
Portuguese: 7 countries

Other major languages

Bengali
Approximate number of speakers: 189,000,000

Russian
Approximate number of speakers: 170,000,000

Japanese
Approximate number of speakers: 125,000,000

German (standard)
Approximate number of speakers: 95,450,000

Chinese (Wu)
Approximate number of speakers: 77,200,000

French
Approximate number of speakers: 77,000,000

A stop sign in English and Inuktituk (the language of the Inuit people)

Disappearing languages

There are about 6,912 living languages but 516 of these are considered almost extinct as they are spoken only by a few elderly people.

Alphabets

An alphabet is the basis of a system of writing, using letters or characters to represent sounds or words. These are some of the oldest and most important alphabets.

Greek
The Greek alphabet is the oldest surviving European alphabet. The early Greek alphabet was written from right to left, but by about 500 BC it was written from left to right. The Greeks introduced an uppercase (capital letters) and a lowercase (small letters).

Cyrillic
The Cyrillic alphabet was invented in the 9th century by two Greek missionaries, St. Cyril and his brother St. Methodius. It is used for Slavonic languages such as Russian, Bulgarian and Ukrainian. The Russian Cyrillic alphabet originally had 43 letters, but the number was reduced to 33 after the Russian Revolution of 1917. Like the Greek alphabet, Cyrillic also has uppercase and lowercase versions of the alphabet.

Hebrew
Hebrew is written horizontally from right to left. Also, sometimes the letters are used as numerals.

Arabic
Arabic evolved from Aramaic in the 4th century, and is written from left to right. It consists of 28 consonants. Vowels are shown by marks placed above or below the consonants but are not always used. Arabic letters are

Writing in Braille

Braille cell

The basic unit of Braille is called a cell. It is made up of six dots, which allows for 63 possible combinations to represent letters, numbers and punctuation marks.

Braille

Braille is a system of raised dots that allows blind people to read by touch. It was invented in the 19th century by a blind French man named Louis Braille. The dots are embossed on to paper, either by hand or using a machine. They are read by moving the fingers across the top of the dots.

The reader uses both hands — the right works out the message while the left feels ahead for the beginning of the next line. A skilled Braille reader can understand up to 150 words a minute, which is about half the speed of a sighted person reading ordinary text.

written differently depending upon where they appear in a word. The positions of characters are known as final (end), medial (middle), initial (beginning) and isolated (on its own).

Chinese and Japanese

These are logographic writing systems. This means that each symbol represents a word, or part of a word, instead of a sound. The Chinese system has 40,000–50,000 characters and the Japanese system has 18,000, but you need to know only about 2,000 and 1,850, respectively, to get by in these languages. In 1966 the Chinese language changed quite dramatically, when books and newspapers were printed with the characters running horizontally from left to right rather than vertically from right to left. There is now a phonetic alphabet known as pin-yin, made up of 25 letters taken from the Roman alphabet.

Most Chinese characters are made up of eight basic strokes. These are all in the character for eternity. Words in a Chinese dictionary are in order of the number of strokes they contain. Chinese verbs and adjectives usually contain only one character or syllable, but nouns often consist of two characters or more. The examples below show how some compound words are made up.

tree woodland (2 trees) forest (3 trees)

Chinese symbol in the background means eternity

Phonetic alphabet

You may have heard pilots and soldiers on television and in films using the phonetic alphabet in radio messages. The alphabet is used to spell out parts of a message that might be difficult to recognize in unclear radio transmissions. The version generally used was developed in the 1950s.

It is known as the NATO (North Atlantic Treaty Organization) Phonetic Alphabet and was designed to be understood and easily pronounced by all NATO members. They chose words that were used in lots of different languages and could not be confused with other common words or those used for another letter. Aircraft and ship crews also use the phonetic alphabet. For example, in the phonetic alphabet "over and out" becomes Oscar Victor Echo Romeo Alpha November Delta Oscar Uniform Tango.

A Alpha
B Bravo
C Charlie
D Delta
E Echo
F Foxtrot
G Golf
H Hotel
I India
J Juliet
K Kilo
L Lima
M Mike
N November
O Oscar
P Papa
Q Quebec
R Romeo
S Sierra
T Tango
U Uniform
V Victor
W Whiskey
X X-ray
Y Yankee
Z Zulu

See also
Brainchildren: young inventors: page 81

Hieroglyphics on the pillars of Habu Temple in Luxor, Egypt

Keeping in touch

From cave paintings onward, there have always been ways of conveying information and ideas to other people. Pictographs are pictures or symbols that represent words. Egyptian hieroglyphics are pictographs. They eventually developed into alphabets so that languages could be written down.

People have also used signs and flags to communicate with each other and found ways of turning language into codes to send messages quickly. Until inventions such as Morse code, the fastest anyone could send information from place to place was at the speed of a horse. Now electronic messages can be sent around the world instantaneously via e-mail.

Hieroglyphics

The simplest of all writing systems use pictures. These are called pictograms and look like the things they describe — just like many road signs and computer icons today.

Writing or carving pictograms is very slow and a lot of work, so people began to use simpler versions of images, such as hieroglyphics. Ancient Egyptian hieroglyphics were used on obelisks, wall paintings, tombs and papyrus (documents on a type of paper made from reeds). They are symbols that represent an object, a sound or an idea. They are not a code: you cannot simply convert an Egyptian hieroglyph into a letter and read it as we read words in a book. People stopped using hieroglyphics in the 1st century AD. From then on, no one could understand them until 1822 when French scholar Jean François Champollion worked out how to translate the text of the Rosetta Stone in the British Museum.

Morse code

By using Morse code you can send a signal in a series of dots and dashes. The signal can be sent by sound or by flashing lights. There are five parts to the code: a dot, a dash, a short gap or pause (between letters), a medium gap (between words) and a long gap (between sentences).

Morse was created by and named after the U.S. artist and inventor Samuel Finley Breese Morse (1791–1872). He sent the first Morse code message from Washington D.C., to Baltimore, Maryland, on May 24, 1844. It read, "What hath God wrought!" An international version of Morse code became widely used to send telegrams by wire. Once people could send messages by radio transmissions they still used Morse code in situations such as warfare, when clear voice signals were not always possible.

A ·-	**N** -·	**0** -----
B -···	**O** ---	**1** ·----
C -·-·	**P** ·--·	**2** ··---
D -··	**Q** --·-	**3** ···--
E ·	**R** ·-·	**4** ····-
F ··-·	**S** ···	**5** ·····
G --·	**T** -	**6** -····
H ····	**U** ··-	**7** --···
I ··	**V** ···-	**8** ---··
J ·---	**W** ·--	**9** ----·
K -·-	**X** -··-	
L ·-··	**Y** -·--	
M --	**Z** --··	

Semaphore

In 1791 French inventor Claude Chappe (1763–1805) and his brothers developed a way of signaling called semaphore. They used two wooden arms which could both be set to seven positions. This made a total of 196 combinations, each representing a letter or other symbol. The signaling device was mounted on a high building. It could be seen from a distance by an operator viewing it through a telescope from the next semaphore station. From this, a system of signaling using human arms and flags was developed and used at sea to send information from ship to ship. This system was kept up to the 1960s, even after radio was commonly used to send messages at sea.

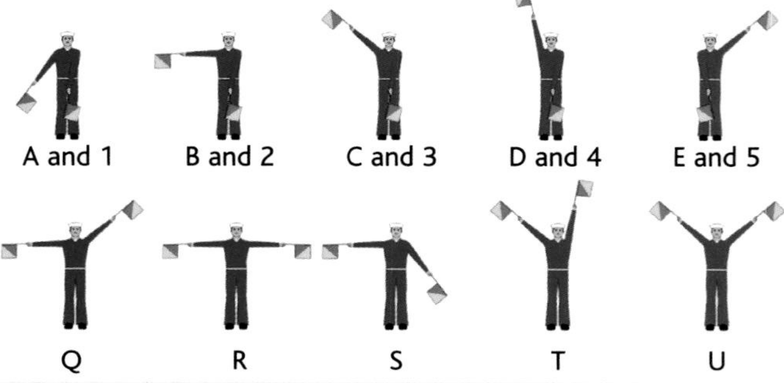

Deaf children learning sign language with their teacher

Sign language

Everyone makes hand gestures to show certain feelings: you might rub your stomach to show you are hungry, raise your fist as a threat or hold your thumb up to show approval.

Sign languages for the deaf were first used in 17th-century Europe. In the 18th century, schools were set up where national systems of sign language developed. Signers use the different finger positions, a variety of hand movements — upward, downward and so on — and make the signs against certain parts of the body such as the neck, arm and wrist. Sign languages differ around the world — some spell words using one hand, while others use both.

Postal firsts

First air letter England to France, by balloon, 1785
First mail carried by rail U.K., 1830
First transatlantic mail, Quebec, Canada, to London, U.K., 1833
First postage stamps in regular use Penny Blacks, U.K., 1840
First Christmas cards invented by Henry Cole, U.K., 1843
First U.S. stamps 1847
First perforated stamps Penny Reds, U.K., 1847
First letter boxes in U.K. (St Helier, Jersey), 1852
London postal districts first used 1858
First postcard sent U.S., 1861
First picture postcard Switzerland, 1872
First commemorative stamps Germany, 1887
First Christmas stamp Canada, 1898
First airmail service India, 1911
First transatlantic airmail service 1939
First postcodes Germany, 1942
First zip (Zone Improvement Plan) codes, U.S., 1963
First self-adhesive stamps Sierra Leone, 1964

Swedish Treskilling Yellow stamp

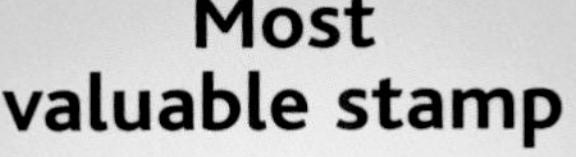

A Morse key for sending messages

Most valuable stamp

The world's most valuable single stamp is a Swedish Treskilling Yellow. It was issued in 1855 and used in 1857 to mail a letter. The stamp was printed with the wrong color ink (yellow instead of green), so it is unique. It was sold for $2.3 million at an auction in Switzerland in 1996, making it the world's most valuable object by weight. The stamp is now part of a private stamp collection in Denmark.

The semaphore alphabet

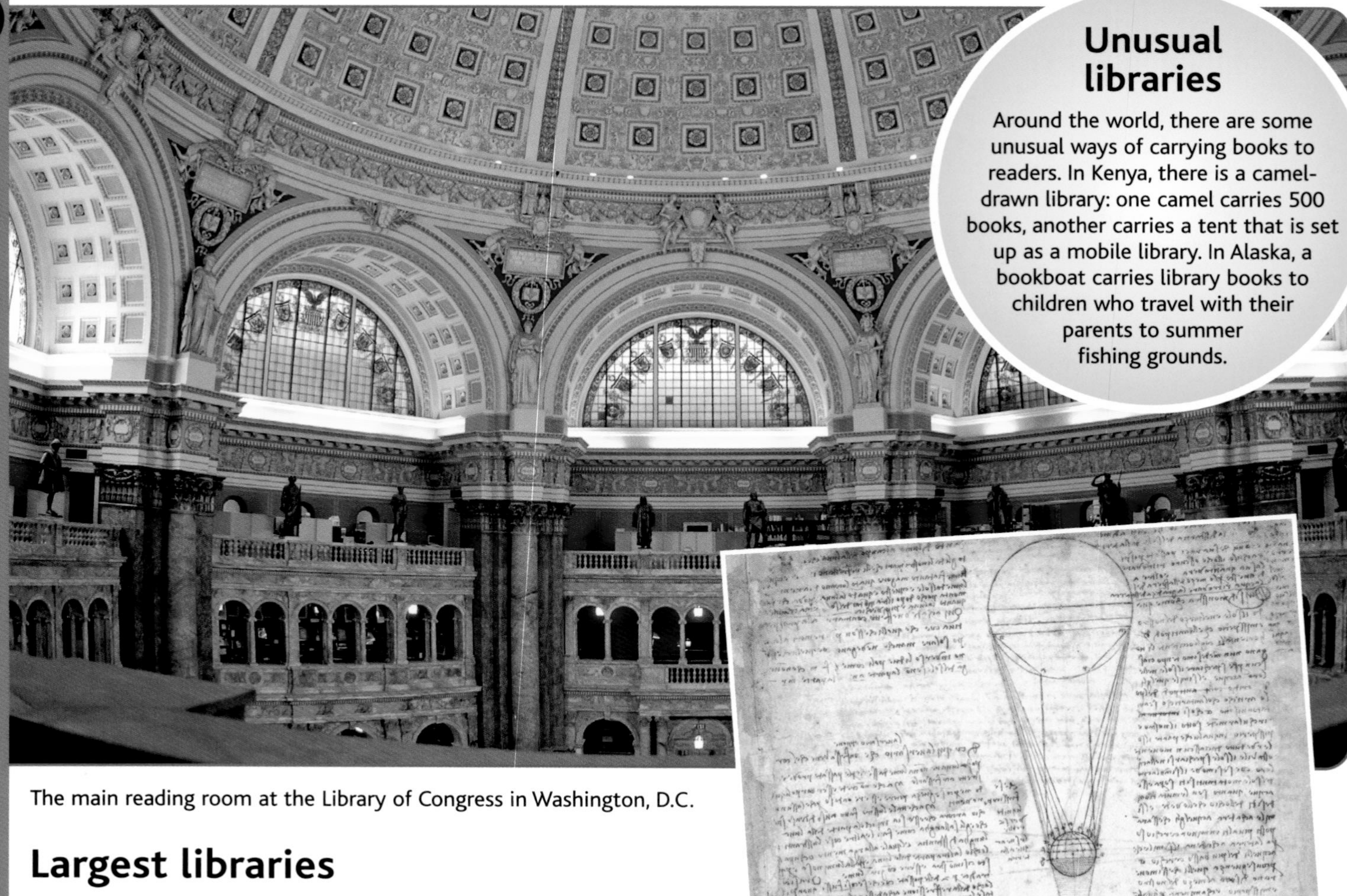

Unusual libraries

Around the world, there are some unusual ways of carrying books to readers. In Kenya, there is a camel-drawn library: one camel carries 500 books, another carries a tent that is set up as a mobile library. In Alaska, a bookboat carries library books to children who travel with their parents to summer fishing grounds.

The main reading room at the Library of Congress in Washington, D.C.

Page from the Codex Hammer

Largest libraries

A library is a collection of books and other printed material. The word library can also be used to describe the building where a collection of books is kept, as well as manuscripts, maps, periodicals and photographs. Below are the world's largest libraries, each containing over 15 million books.

The Library of Congress, Washington, D.C., was founded in 1800 and holds 32,124,001 books.

The British Library*, London, England, was founded in 1753 and holds 29,000,000 books.

Library of the Russian Academy of Sciences, St. Petersburg, Russia was founded in 1714 and holds 22,500,000 books.

Deustche Bibliotek, Frankfurt, Germany was founded in 1990 and holds 22,200, 000 books.

National Library of Canada, Ottawa, Canada, was founded in 1953 and holds 19,500,000 books.

The Russian State Library, Moscow, Russia, was founded in 1862 and holds 17,000,000 books.

Harvard University Library, Cambridge, Massachusetts, was founded in 1636 and holds 15,826,570 books.

* Founded as part of the British Museum, 1753; became independent in 1973

Valuable books and manuscripts

- The Codex Hammer (previously called the Codex Leicester) was sold in New York, N.Y., in 1994 for $28,800,000. It was bought by Bill Gates, the billionaire founder of Microsoft. The Codex is one of Leonardo da Vinci's notebooks and includes many of his scientific drawings and diagrams.
- John James Audubon's *The Birds of America* (1827–38) was sold in New York, N.Y., in 2000 for $8,000,000, making it the most expensive printed book. Its giant pages feature more than 400 hand-colored engravings of birds.
- One of the first-ever printed books was Geoffrey Chaucer's *The Canterbury Tales* (c. 1477). A copy was sold in London, England, in 1998 for $7,570,941.
- A "first folio" (early edition) of the works of William Shakespeare dating from 1623 was sold in London, England, in 2001 for $6,166,000.
- A rare copy of the Gutenberg Bible, one of the first books ever printed, was sold in New York, N.Y., in 1987 for $5,390,000.

Types of book

Almanac
This is an annual calendar of dates and events. It originally contained astronomical facts and figures, but now includes useful statistics and other information. Almanac is sometimes spelled almanack.

Anthology
A collection of writings by one author or on a theme, such as an anthology of animal poems.

Atlas
A book of maps.

Autobiography
An account of a person's life written by himself or herself. Sometimes a "ghost" writer may help someone write an autobiography.

Bibliography
A list of books or sources on a particular subject.

Biography
A book about someone's life written by another person.

Chronology
A dictionary of dated events.

Dictionary
An alphabetical list of words and their meanings. There are also dictionaries on a single subject, for example *Dictionary of Art*.

Dictionary of quotations
A listing of interesting remarks or extracts from the writings of famous people.

Directory
An alphabetical list of names and addresses of people or organizations.

Encyclopedia
A book of articles on many subjects, arranged alphabetically. Encyclopedias are often published in many volumes or, today, on CD-ROM or on the Internet.

Gazetteer
A book that lists and describes places (countries, cities, etc).

Glossary
A list of words and phrases used in a particular subject area, for instance *A Glossary of Computer Terms*.

Language dictionary
A dictionary that gives translations of words and phrases to and from other languages, for example a *French-English/English-French Dictionary*.

Monograph
A book on a specialized subject, such as the work of a particular artist.

Novel
A work of fiction, usually involving imaginary people. A historical novel may be about real historical characters.

Novella
A short work of fiction.

Phrasebook
A book for travellers, with translations of words and phrases into and from a foreign language.

Pop-up book
A book, usually for children, made so that pictures stand up or move when the pages are opened.

Thesaurus
A book organized to show words with similar meanings.

Travel guide
A book of information about a particular country or area.

Who's who or biographical dictionary
Alphabetical summaries of the lives of famous people, living or dead, sometimes by their subjects (such as a *Dictionary of Scientists*).

Yearbook
An annual reference book with information about the events of the previous year. Yearbooks containing statistical information about a country are often called *Abstracts*.

Book firsts and records

First printed books
Books were printed in China in the 8th century using woodblocks, and in 14th-century China and Korea using movable type.

First books printed in English
In 1474 William Caxton printed the first book in English, *Recuyell of the Historyes of Troye*. It was printed in Bruges, Flanders. Chaucer's *Canterbury Tales* was probably the first book in English to be printed in England, in about 1477.

First books printed in America
Massachusetts Bay Colony: The Oath of a Free-Man (1638) and *An Almanack for the Year of Our Lord* (1639) are the first two books known to have been printed in the new American colonies.

Longest novel
A science-fiction novel by French writer Georges-Jean Arnaud, *La Compagne des Glaces* (1980–92), runs to 62 volumes and has about 11,000 pages.

First sequel
Daniel Defoe wrote *The Farther Adventures of Robinson Crusoe* in 1719, after the success of *Robinson Crusoe* earlier that year.

First American novel
The Power of Sympathy (1789) was the first novel published in America. It was published anonymously, but is believed to have been written by William Hill Brown.

First detective story
Murders in the Rue Morgue, by American author Edgar Allan Poe, was first published in *Grahame's Magazine* in 1841.

Smallest book
This was produced by a German typographer Josua Reichertand called *The World's Smallest Book*. It measures 2.4 x 2.9 mm (0.09 x 0.1 in) – the size of a match head.

Largest book
The largest book was published in 2003. It is a collection of photos called *Bhutan: A Visual Odyssey Across the Last Himalayan Kingdom*. When opened out it measures 2.1 x 1.5 m (7 x 5 ft) – almost the size of a table-tennis table! It costs $15,000 (£30,000) a copy.

Electronic books
Electronic books, or eBooks, have been around for over 20 years. The earliest ones could not store much information and had tiny screens that were difficult to read, such as an electronic Bible (1991) that could display four lines at a time. The latest electronic books are small, light, and hold huge volumes of data that can be downloaded from the Internet.

The Amazon Kindle, launched in 2007, can hold the complete text of up to 200 novels.

www.fireflybooks.com search

Famous diaries

People have kept personal diaries for more than 500 years. Most were written as personal records about the times the writers lived through or events that happened to them, and they are often fascinating to read.

Samuel Pepys (1633–1703)

Pepys kept a diary for nearly 10 years from 1660. He lived in London and wrote about events such as the Great Plague and Great Fire of London. He wrote in a special code, which was not translated until the 19th century. Pepys' original diaries are kept in the library of Magdalene College, Cambridge.

Anne Frank (1929–1945)

Anne Frank was forced to hide with her family in Amsterdam, Netherlands, during World War II, when Jewish people were being persecuted by the Nazis. Anne kept her diary while she was in hiding, but left it behind when she and her family were found. She was deported and died in a German concentration camp. Her father survived and edited her diary, which was published after the war. *The Diary of Anne Frank* became a bestseller and was translated into more than 55 languages. It has also been made into an award-winning play and a film. The house in which the Frank family hid is now a museum.

Adolf Hitler (1889–1945)

In 1993, the German magazine *Stern* paid 10 million marks ($8 million) to journalist Gerd Heidemann to publish extracts from what were claimed to be the diaries of the German dictator Adolf Hitler. The diaries were soon discovered to have been forgeries written by Konrad Kujau. He and Heidemann were imprisoned for their deception.

Bestsellers

These are some of the bestselling books ever. But the Bible has outsold them all. It is believed to have sold more than six billion copies in hundreds of versions and translations.

- One of the bestselling books of all time is a collection of quotations by Chinese leader Mao Zedong, known as his *Little Red Book*. Between 1966 to 1971 every Chinese adult had to own a copy and 900 million were printed.
- J.R.R. Tolkien's *The Lord of the Rings* trilogy was first published in 1954–55. It has sold well over 100 million and its sales received a further boost when the films based on the books were released between 2001 and 2003.
- *The American Spelling Book* by Noah Webster (1783) was used in American schools for generations. It has sold nearly 100 million copies.
- *The Common Sense Book of Baby and Child Care* by American doctor Benjamin Spock came out in 1946. Since then more than 50 million copies have been sold.
- British crime writer Agatha Christie has sold at least one billion copies of her novels in English and another billion in 45 foreign languages. In 1935 her novel *The Mysterious Affair at Styles* was one of the first Penguin paperbacks ever published.
- American author Margaret Mitchell's only book, *Gone With the Wind* (1936), has sold around 30 million copies. It is one of the bestselling novels ever.

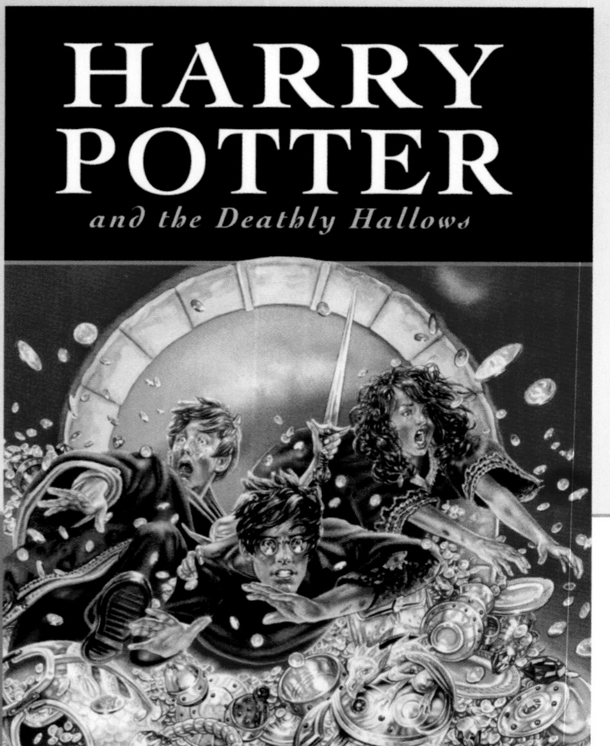

Covers for two *Harry Potter* books

J.K. Rowling

J.K. Rowling was born on July 31, 1965, as Joanne Rowling (she later borrowed the name Kathleen from her grandmother to create a middle initial). Her first Harry Potter book, *Harry Potter and the Philosopher's Stone*, was published in 1997. It has been followed by six more books with sales now over 375 million copies in 64 languages. If all Harry Potter books ever sold were placed end to end, they would stretch 47,734 mi. (76,819 km) — more than one and a half times round the Equator! Earnings from the book sales and films have made J.K. Rowling the richest author ever, and the first to make more than $1 billion from writing. She has given large amounts to charities. The final book, *Harry Potter and the Deathly Hallows*, was published on July 21, 2007.

Translations

These are the 10 most translated authors in the world, according to UNESCO's *Index Translationum* (1979–2005).

Author	Translations
Walt Disney Productions	8,677
Agatha Christie	6,632
Jules Verne	4,021
V.I. Lenin	3,497
William Shakespeare	3,435
Enid Blyton	3,433
Barbara Cartland	3,315
Danielle Steel	2,767
Hans Christian Andersen	2,624
Stephen King	2,591

Imaginary lands

Writers usually invent the characters in their books, but some have also created imaginary lands in which the action of the book takes place. These are some of the best known fictional worlds, and the books in which they first appeared. Some featured again in later books by their authors.

Thomas Moore — **Utopia** in *Utopia* (1516)
Jonathan Swift — **Lilliput** in *Gulliver's Travels* (1726)
Voltaire — **Eldorado** in *Candide* (1759)
Lewis Carroll — **Wonderland** in *Alice's Adventures in Wonderland* (1865)
Samuel Butler — **Erewhon*** in *Erewhon* (1872)
Anthony Hope — **Ruritania** in *The Prisoner of Zenda* (1894)
L. Frank Baum — **Oz** in *The Wonderful Wizard of Oz* (1900)
J.M. Barrie — **Neverland** in *Peter and Wendy* (1911)
James Hilton — **Shangri-La** in *Lost Horizon* (1933)
J.R.R. Tolkien — **Middle Earth** in *The Hobbit* (1937)
C.S. Lewis — **Narnia** in *The Lion, The Witch and The Wardrobe* (1950)
Terry Pratchett — **Discworld** in *The Colour of Magic* (1983)

* An anagram for nowhere

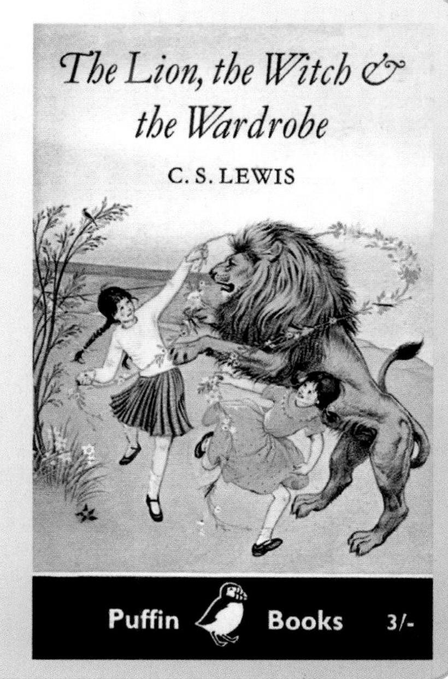

Early cover for *The Lion, the Witch and the Wardrobe*

J.K. Rowling

Nobel Prize for Literature

Nobel prizes have been given every year since 1901 for achievements in different fields, including literature. Nobel Prize winners for literature include poets, playwrights and authors from all over the world. Below are some of the best-known winners.

2007 Doris Lessing (U.K., 1919–)
2006 Orhan Pamuk (Turkey, 1952–)
2005 Harold Pinter (U.K., 1930–)
2004 Elfriede Jelinek (Austria, 1946–)
2003 J.M. Coetzee (South Africa, 1940–)
2001 V.S. Naipaul (U.K., 1932–)
2000 Gao Xingjian (China, 1940–) first win by a Chinese writer
1999 Günter Grass (Germany, 1927–)
1993 Toni Morrison (U.S., 1931–)
1991 Nadine Gordimer (South Africa, 1923–)
1983 William Golding (U.K., 1911–93) author of *The Lord of the Flies*
1976 Saul Bellow (Canada/U.S., 1915–2005)
1971 Pablo Neruda (Chile, 1904–73)
1969 Samuel Beckett (Ireland, 1906–89)
1962 John Steinbeck (U.S., 1902–68) author of *The Grapes of Wrath*
1958 Boris Pasternak (Russia, 1890–1960) author of *Doctor Zhivago*
1954 Ernest Hemingway (U.S., 1899–1961)
1953 Winston Churchill (U.K., 1874–1965) British prime minister and writer
1948 T.S. Eliot (U.S.-born, U.K., 1888–1965) author of the book that inspired the musical *Cats*
1938 Pearl Buck (U.S., 1892–1973)
1936 Eugene O'Neill (U.S., 1888–1953)
1925 George Bernard Shaw (U.K., 1856–1950)
1923 William Butler Yeats (Ireland, 1865–1939)
1907 Rudyard Kipling (U.K., 1865–1936) author of *The Jungle Book*
1901 Sully Prudhomme (France, 1839–1907) the first winner

www.jkrowling.com search

Children's firsts

First children's book
The first English children's book for entertainment (not a school book) was a collection of rhymes called *A Booke in Englyssh Metre, of the Great Merchante Man called Dives Pragmaticus, very preaty for Children to reade*. It was printed in London, England, in 1563.

First children's book printed in the U.S.
John Cotton's *Milk for Babies* was printed in Cambridge, Massachusetts, in 1641–45.

First children's encyclopedia
Pera Librorum Juvenilium (Collection of Juvenile Books) was compiled in Germany by Johann Christoph Wagenseil in 1695.

First story for children
The History of Little Goody Two-Shoes was published by John Newbery in London, England, in 1765. Some experts believe it was written by the famous British poet and playwright Oliver Goldsmith.

First nursery rhyme book
Tommy Thumb's Pretty Song Book was published in London, England, in 1744. It contained well-known rhymes such as "London Bridge is falling down," "Hickory, dickory dock" and "Sing a song of sixpence."

First children's library
The Bingham Library for Youth was set up in Salisbury, Connecticut, in January 1803 when Caleb Bingham, who came from the town, donated 150 books.

First winner of the Newbery Medal
The Newbery Medal is awarded by the American Library Association to the author of the outstanding American book for children. The first writer to receive it, in 1922, was Hendrik Willem van Loon for *The Story of Mankind*. In 2007 it was won by Susan Patron for *The Higher Power of Lucky*.

Fairy tale authors

Fairy tales are fantastic stories for children that do not always involve fairies. They are traditional tales that were retold from generation to generation. The writers below collected the stories and wrote or rewrote them in books that became hugely popular all over the world. Many fairy tales have been made into films—especially animated films by Disney.

Charles Perrault
French writer Charles Perrault (1628–1703) put together a collection of stories with the help of his son Pierre (1678–1700). Their collection contained *Cinderella*, *Little Red Riding-Hood*, *Sleeping Beauty* and *Puss in Boots*. The stories were translated into English in 1729. Later editions had the French title, *Contes de ma mère l'Oye*, or *Mother Goose's Tales*.

Brothers Grimm
German brothers Jacob Ludwig Carl Grimm (1785–1863) and Wilhelm Carl Grimm (1786–1859) were the authors of *Grimm's Fairy Tales*, which were first published for Christmas 1812. This was a collection of traditional stories, rewritten for a young audience. It included many famous fairy tales, such as *Hansel and Gretel*, *Rumpelstiltskin* and *Snow White and the Seven Dwarfs*. They were translated into English in 1823 and became a worldwide bestseller.

Hans Christian Andersen
Danish author Andersen (1805–75) wrote 156 fairy tales, including *The Little Mermaid*, *The Emperor's New Clothes* and *The Ugly Duckling*. His stories first appeared in English in 1846.

Glass slippers

In Perrault's retelling of the story of Cinderella, he used the French phrase *pantoufle de verre*, which means glass slipper. However, it may be that he mistook *verre*, glass, for *vair*, an old French word for fur, and what Cinderella was actually wearing were furry slippers!

Illustration for *The Ugly Duckling,* a fairy tale by Hans Christian Andersen

Lucy Maud Montgomery

Lucy Maud Montgomery (1874–1942) is the Canadian author best known for Anne of Green Gables. The first book she wrote, it was published in 1908 and became a worldwide bestseller, along with Anne of Avonlea (1909) and other sequels. The original book has been made into a film, a television drama series and a stage musical.

Multi-million sellers

J.K. Rowling (U.K., 1965–)
At the end of 2007, the seven Harry Potter books had sold more than 375 million copies worldwide. In 2007, *Harry Potter and the Deathly Hallows* sold 2,652,656 copies in the U.K. on its first day of release — the biggest one-day sale ever recorded.

Enid Blyton (U.K., 1897–1968)
Enid Blyton wrote more than 700 children's books. Total sales of her works are more than 400 million. She was the bestselling English-language author until the arrival of J.K. Rowling.

René Goscinny (France, 1926–77) and Albert Uderzo (France, 1927–)
René Goscinny and Albert Uderzo created the comic-strip character Astérix the Gaul in 1959. They jointly produced 24 books, and Underzo went on to create nine more after Goscinny's death. Their total worldwide sales are more than 330 million copies.

R.L. Stine (U.S., 1943–)
The 138 books in R.L. Stine's *Goosebumps* series and its sequels have sold over 330 million copies worldwide. *Goosebumps HorrorLand* (2008–09) is Stine's latest series.

Beatrix Potter (U.K., 1866–1943)
The Tale of Peter Rabbit (1901) and her other books have sold more than 150 million copies in 30 languages.

Lewis Carroll (U.K., 1832–98)
There are no world figures for sales of Lewis Carroll's books, *Alice in Wonderland* and *Alice*

The Cat in the Hat, a character from one of Dr. Seuss' most popular books

Famous illustrators

Below are some of the artists who have produced the best-loved illustrations for children's books. Some, such as Beatrix Potter, also wrote the books they illustrated.

Honor C. Appleton (American, 1879–1951) *Josephine and Her Dolls*

Quentin Blake (British, 1932–) Illustrated Roald Dahl's books and others

Raymond Briggs (British, 1934–) *The Snowman* and *Father Christmas*

Jean de Brunhoff (French, 1899–1937) *Babar the Elephant* series

Hergé (Belgian, 1907–83) the *Tintin* books

Tove Jansson (Finnish, 1914–2001) the *Moomin* series

Arnold Lobel (American, 1933–87) the *Frog and Toad* books

Henriette Willebeek Le Mair (Dutch, 1889–1966) *Our Old Nursery Rhymes*

Tintin by Hergé

Beatrix Potter (British, 1866–1943) the *Peter Rabbit* books and others

Arthur Rackham (British, 1867–1939) illustrated classics

William Heath Robinson (British, 1872–1944) illustrated classics

Maurice Sendak (American, 1928–) *Where the Wild Things Are* and others

Ernest Shepard (British, 1879–1976) *The Wind in the Willows*, *Winnie the Pooh*

Dr. Seuss (Theodor Seuss Geissel; American, 1904–91) *The Cat in the Hat* and many others

Jessie Willcox Smith (American, 1863–1935) *The Water Babies*

Albert Uderzo (French, 1927–) the *Astérix* books

Chris Van Allsburg (American, 1949–) *Jumanji*, *The Polar Express*

Young authors

At the age of 6, Dennis Vollmer (U.S.) wrote and illustrated his book *Joshua Disobeys*, published in 1988.

British author Libby Rees (born 1995) was only 9 when she wrote *Help Hope & Happiness*, which was published in 2005.

Through the Looking Glass, but these two books have never been out of print. They have appeared in hundreds of editions and in many languages.

Dr. Seuss (U.S., 1904–91)
Green Eggs and Ham, one of Dr. Seuss' most popular books, has sold more than 8 million in the U.S. alone. Worldwide, he has sold more than 100 million copies of his books.

Rev. W. Awdry (U.K., 1911–97)
Rev. Awdry began writing his *Thomas the Tank Engine* books in 1946. The books have sold more than 950 million copies.

E.B. White (U.S., 1899–1985)
E.B. (Elwyn Brooks) White's first children's book, *Stuart Little* (1945), was a bestseller and in 1999 was made into a movie that has earned more than $300 million worldwide. His story *Charlotte's Web* (1952) was even more successful. It has sold more than 45 million copies in 23 languages and was made into a film twice, in 1973 and 2006.

Mark Twain (U.S., 1835–1910)
Book sales in the U.S. were not accurately recorded before 1895. *The Adventures of Tom Sawyer* (1876) and *The Adventures of Huckleberry Finn* (1884) have probably each sold more than 20 million copies worldwide.

www.nea.org/readacross/resources/catalist.html search

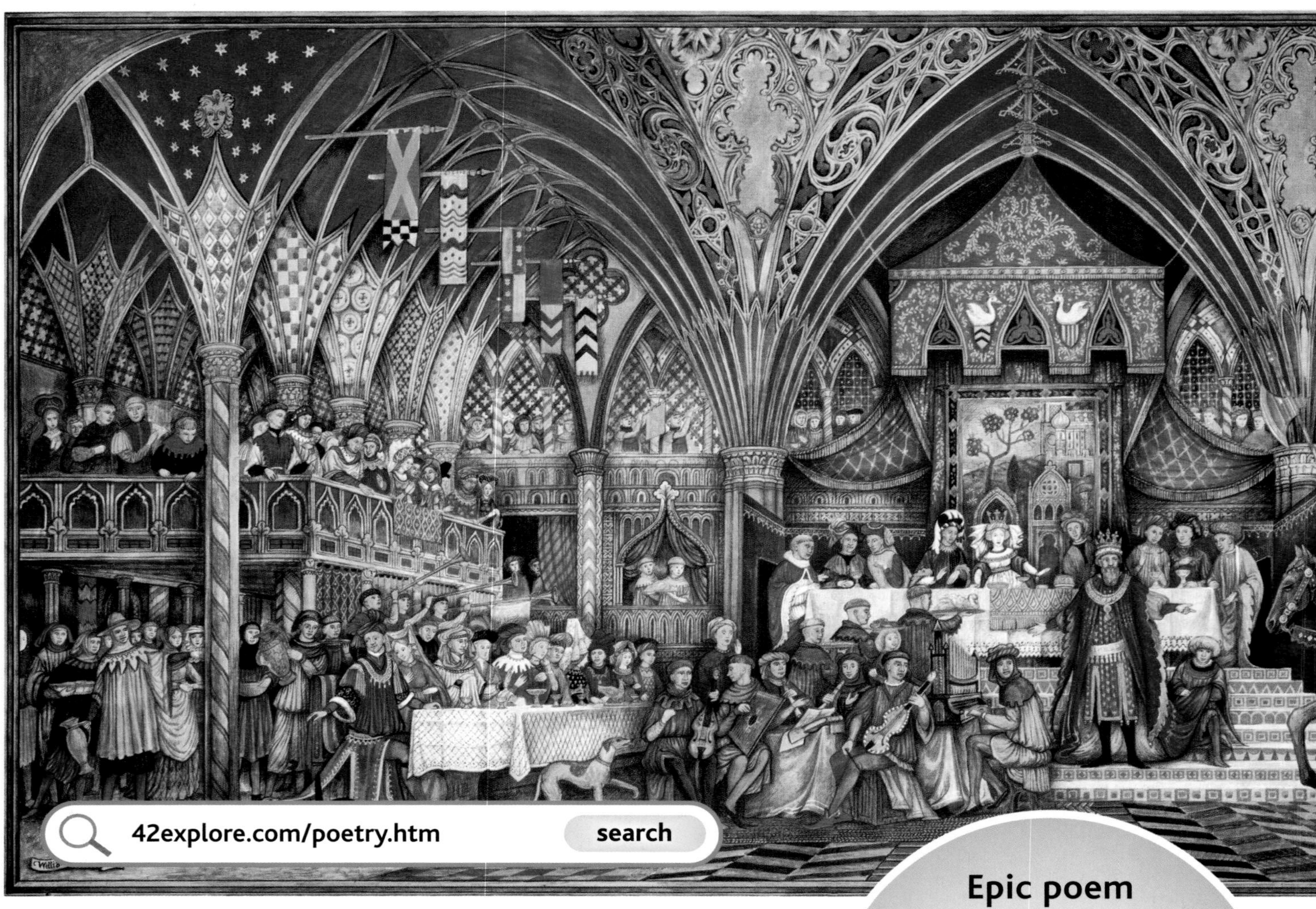

Ancient poems

Before stories and poems were written down they were passed on orally. Some of the most famous long narrative, or story, poems were passed on this way for hundreds of years before being written down by the poet who is now known as the author.

***The Iliad* — Homer**
This Greek poem dates from 850 BC and tells the story of the final year of the war between the Greeks and the Trojans. It describes the great battle and the story of how beautiful Helen left her husband Menelaus for the Trojan prince Paris. It also tells us about the interference of the gods and their quarrels about the action on the battlefield below them.

***The Odyssey* — Homer**
This describes Odysseus' journey home from the Trojan war. Odysseus features briefly in *The Iliad*. Again, human characters work side by side with the gods, who are given human characteristics. Although they are so powerful, the gods bear grudges, seek revenge and are very proud. The word odyssey has now come to mean any long, hard journey. The poem has strongly influenced other works of literature — most famously the novel *Ulysses* by the Irish writer James Joyce.

Rubáiyat
Omar Khayyám was a Persian writer, mathematician and astronomer who lived in the 11th and early 12th centuries. His *Rubáiyat* was introduced to the rest of the world in 1859, when it was translated by Edward Fitzgerald. Each verse contains a complete thought.

Beowulf
An epic poem of almost 3,200 lines written in Old English (or Anglo-Saxon). This is an early form of the English language that modern readers find hard to understand. The main theme is the struggle of the hero Beowulf with the water monster Grendel. Details of the poem's exact date and author are not known, but it may have been written in the 8th century by more than one person.

Epic poem

An epic is an extended narrative poem, written in a grand style about the life of a heroic or mythological person. *The Mahabharata*, a famous Indian epic, is about four times longer than the Bible and seven times longer than Homer's great epics, the *Odyssey* and the *Iliad*.

Sir Gawain and the Green Knight
This poem was written by a monk from the northwest of England during the second half of the 14th century. Its 2,530 lines describe events in King Arthur's court and the testing of Sir Gawain, a model knight. There are many opportunities for the character to fail, but he does not.

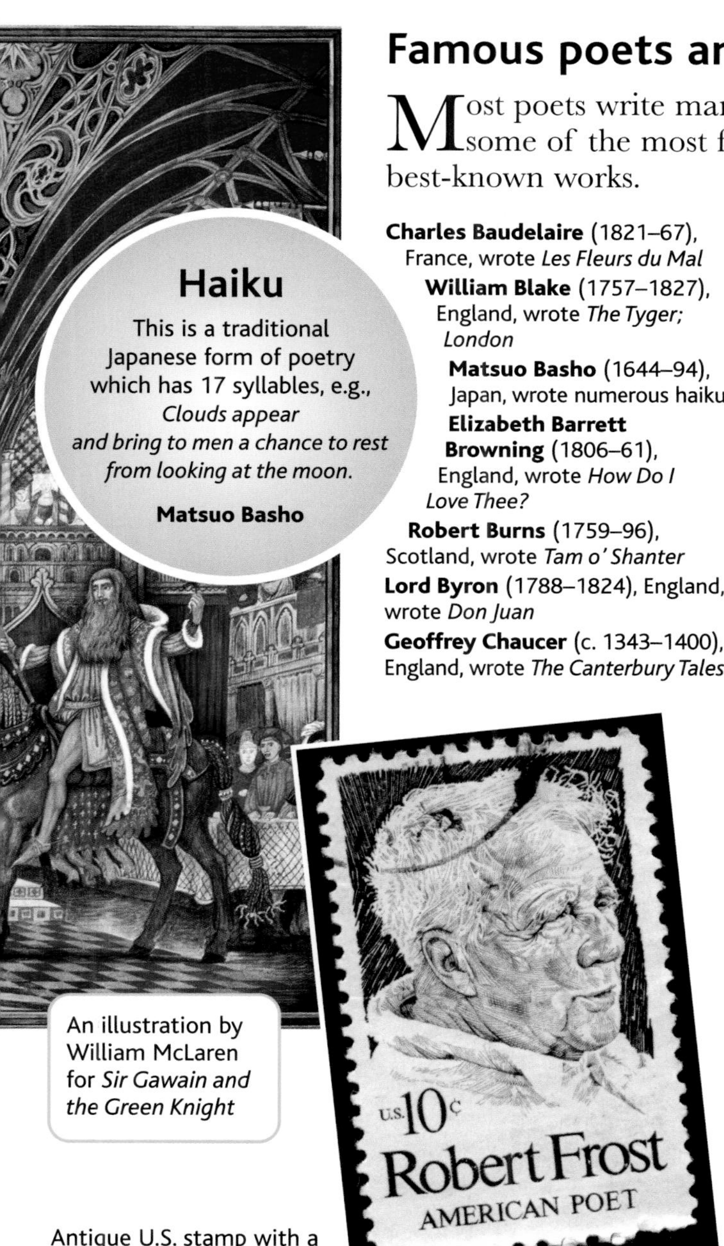

Haiku

This is a traditional Japanese form of poetry which has 17 syllables, e.g.,
Clouds appear
and bring to men a chance to rest
from looking at the moon.

Matsuo Basho

An illustration by William McLaren for *Sir Gawain and the Green Knight*

Famous poets and poems

Most poets write many poems. Below are some of the most famous poets and their best-known works.

Charles Baudelaire (1821–67), France, wrote *Les Fleurs du Mal*
William Blake (1757–1827), England, wrote *The Tyger; London*
Matsuo Basho (1644–94), Japan, wrote numerous haiku
Elizabeth Barrett Browning (1806–61), England, wrote *How Do I Love Thee?*
Robert Burns (1759–96), Scotland, wrote *Tam o' Shanter*
Lord Byron (1788–1824), England, wrote *Don Juan*
Geoffrey Chaucer (c. 1343–1400), England, wrote *The Canterbury Tales*
Samuel Taylor Coleridge (1772–1834), England, wrote *Kubla Khan; The Rime of the Ancient Mariner*
Dante Alighieri (1265–1321), Italy, wrote *The Divine Comedy*
Emily Dickinson (1830–86), U.S., wrote *Because I Could Not Stop for Death*
T.S. Eliot (1888–1965), U.S./England, wrote *The Waste Land*
Robert Frost (1874–1963), U.S., wrote *Stopping by Woods on a Snowy Evening; The Road Not Taken*
Allen Ginsberg (1926–97), U.S., wrote Howl
Homer (c. 8th century BC), Greece, wrote *The Iliad*; *The Odyssey*
John Keats (1795–1821), England, wrote *Ode to a Nightingale*; *La Belle Dame Sans Merci; To Autumn*
Rudyard Kipling (1865–1936), England, wrote *If*
Mikhail Lermontov (1814–41), Russia, wrote *The Novice*
Li Po (701–762), China, wrote *Drinking Alone Under the Moon*
John Milton (1608–74), England, wrote *Paradise Lost*; *Paradise Regained*
Pablo Neruda (1904–71), Chile, wrote *Canto General*
Nezami (1140–c. 1217), Iran, wrote *Khamseh* (or *The Quinary*)
Ovid (43 BC–AD 17), ancient Rome, wrote *Metamorphoses*
Sylvia Plath (1932–63), U.S., wrote *Ariel*
Edgar Allan Poe (1809–49), U.S., wrote *The Raven*
Arthur Rimbaud (1854–91), France, wrote *Une Saison en Enfer* (or *A Season in Hell*)
William Shakespeare (1564–1616), England, wrote *Sonnet 18* (or *Shall I Compare Thee to a Summer's Day*)
Percy Bysshe Shelley (1792–1822), England, wrote *Ozymandias*
Edmund Spenser (1552–99), England, wrote *The Faerie Queene*
Alfred Tennyson (1809–92), England, wrote *In Memoriam* and *The Lady of Shalott*
Dylan Thomas (1914–53), Wales, wrote *Fern Hill*
Virgil (70–19 BC), ancient Rome, wrote *The Aeneid*
Walt Whitman (1819–92), U.S., wrote *Song of Myself*
William Wordsworth (1770–1850), England, wrote *The Prelude* and *Daffodils*
William Butler Yeats (1865–1939), Ireland, wrote *Sailing to Byzantium*; *The Lake Isle of Innisfree*

Antique U.S. stamp with a portrait of Robert Frost

Poets laureate

The word laureate means crowned with laurel. The expression dates back to ancient Rome, where a successful person was traditionally crowned with a wreath of laurel leaves.

In Great Britain, the position of poet laureate was created as a royal office in 1668 with the appointment of John Dryden by King Charles II. The position was traditionally held for life, but is now restricted to 10 years. When it becomes vacant the prime minister has a list of names drawn up and the monarch chooses a new laureate. The poet laureate's main task is to write odes to celebrate royal birthdays, marriages and important state occasions. Poets laureate receive a salary of $140 (£70) per year — the same as in the 17th century! Some famous poets laureate in the U.K. include William Wordsworth, Alfred Tennyson, Sir John Betjeman and Ted Hughes. The present laureate is Andrew Motion.

In the United States the first poet laureate (Joseph Auslander) was appointed in 1937. A new laureate is appointed every year. He or she serves from October to May and is paid $35,000.

Statue of Dante Alighieri in Florence, Italy

Most valuable comics

Copies of American comic books with the first appearances of superheroes Superman and Batman are the most valued by collectors. In perfect condition, an *Action Comics* No. 1, with the first Superman story, could be worth up to $5,800,000. *Detective Comics* No. 27, the first to feature Batman, is valued at up to $4,000,000.

Captain America

All about comics

Comic strips

A comic strip is a story told in a series of pictures published in a newspaper. The New York *Daily Graphic* was the first newspaper to feature a comic strip. It started on September 11, 1875, with *Professor Tigwissel's Burglar Alarm*. The first regular strip was The Yellow Kid, which began in a supplement of the *New York World* on May 5, 1895. A syndicated comic strip is one that appears in more than one newspaper. Some appear in hundreds of papers all over the world.

Comics

In the United States, series of cartoon strips began to appear in newspapers from the 1890s, and were syndicated nationwide. The *Katzenjammer Kids*, which was first published in *The American Humorist*, a Sunday supplement of the *New York Journal* on December 12, 1897, still appears in many newspapers and magazines.

Comic books

The first U.S. comic book was called *Funnies on Parade* and came out in 1933. The first to be published regularly was *Famous Funnies* in 1934. Many comic books were about the adventures of a single superhero, such as Batman or Superman, who used special powers to fight crime and defeat evil villains.

Top newspaper-reading countries

1 Norway 626*
2 Japan 634*
3 Finland 518*
4 Sweden 481*

*daily copies per 1,000 people

See also
Book firsts and records: page 229

Newspaper fact file

First newspapers

From 59 BC onward Roman emperor Julius Caesar had handwritten reports on news posted in public places in Rome. China had newspapers from about AD 713. The first European printed newspapers appeared in Germany in 1609. The first daily newspaper, *Einkommende Zeitungen*, also started in Germany, in 1650. Great Britain's first daily paper was the *Perfect Diurnall*, published in London in 1660. America's first successful newspaper was the *Boston News-Letter*, which appeared in 1704.

Smallest

Newspaper publishers sometimes produce miniature editions for publicity purposes. The smallest regular publication was the *Daily Banner*, published in 1876 in Oregon. It measured just 3 x 3.75 in. (7.6 x 9.5 cm).

Largest

The edition of the Belgian newspaper *Het Volk* published on June 14, 1993, had pages measuring 39.2 x 55.9 in. (99.5 x 142 cm), which is more than six times the area of an ordinary broadsheet (large page size) newspaper.

First appearances

Some comic strip and comic book characters are older than you might think. Below is a list of some famous comic characters' first appearances.

Rupert Bear appeared as a strip in the *Daily Express* (U.K.) on November 8, 1920
Tintin *Le Vingtième Siècle* (Belgium) on January 10, 1929
Popeye appeared as a strip in *Thimble Theatre* (U.S.) on January 17, 1929
Dick Tracy appeared as a strip in the *Chicago Tribune* (U.S.) on October 4, 1931
Flash Gordon appeared as a syndicated strip (U.S.) on January 7, 1934
Desperate Dan *Dandy* (U.K.) on December 4, 1937
Superman *Action Comics* No. 1 (U.S.) in June 1938
Batman *Detective Comics* No. 27 (U.S.) in May 1939
Captain Marvel *Whiz Comics* No. 1 (U.S.) in February 1940
The Green Lantern *All American Comics* No. 16 (U.S.) in July 1940
The Flash *Flash Comics* No. 1 (U.S.) in January 1940
Robin (Batman's assistant) *Detective Comics* No. 38 (U.S.) in April 1940
Wonder Woman *All-Star Comics* No. 8 (U.S.) in December 1941
Captain America *Captain America Comics* No. 1 (U.S.) in March 1941
Dan Dare *Eagle* (U.K.) on April 14, 1950
Peanuts appeared as a syndicated strip (U.S.) on October 2, 1950
Dennis the Menace (U.S.) appeared as a syndicated strip (U.S.) on March 12, 1951
Dennis the Menace (U.K.) *Beano* (U.K.) on March 17, 1951
Astérix the Gaul *Pilote* (France) on October 29, 1959
Supergirl *Action Comics* No. 252 (U.S.) in May 1959
Spiderman *Amazing Fantasy* No. 15 (U.S.) in August 1962
The Incredible Hulk* *Hulk* (U.S.) in March 1962
X-Men *The X-Men* (U.S.) in September 1963
Daredevil *Daredevil* (U.S.) in June 1964

* The Hulk had gray skin in March 1962, but became The Incredible Hulk, with green skin, in the May issue two months later.

Magazine fact file

First-ever popular magazine
Mercure Galant, a gossip magazine, was first published in Paris, France, in March 1672.

First women's magazine
The Ladies' Mercury was first published in London, England, on June 27, 1693.

First American magazine
The American Magazine, published in Philadelphia, probably began on February 13, 1741.

First children's magazine
The *Lilliputian Magazine* appeared in the U.K. in June 1751 and ran for just over a year. The first in the U.S. was the *Children's Magazine*, published in January 1789.

First fashion magazine
The Paris magazine *Le Cabinet des Modes* was first published in 1785.

Longest-running U.S. magazine
Scientific American was launched on August 28, 1845, and is the longest continuously published magazine in the U.S. At first, it was a four-page newspaper and included features on science and technology as well as topics such as religion and poetry. Later it began to focus on science and is now the world's most popular scientific journal.

First photograph in a magazine
Each copy of the June 1846 issue of the *Art Union* (U.K.) contained a photograph by Henry Fox Talbot, one of the inventors of photography.

Heaviest

The Sunday edition of the *New York Times* for September 14, 1987, contained 1,612 pages and weighed 12 lb. (5.4 kg). At one time 314 acres (127 hectares) of forest containing almost 63,000 trees had to be chopped down to make one edition of the paper. Nowadays, much of the paper used for newspapers is recycled.

Top selling

The *Yomiuri Shimbun* (Japan) sells more than 14.2 million copies a day. *Bild-Zeitung* (Germany) is the highest circulation newspaper outside Japan, selling more than 4.2 million copies a day. *The Sun* (U.K.) sells 3.4 million copies, more than any other English-language newspaper in the world. The U.S.'s biggest-selling newspaper is *USA Today*, which sells 2.6 million a day.

Most mistakes

The Times (U.K.) of August 22, 1978, contained 97 misprints in one story about the Pope. He was called "the Pop" throughout the article.

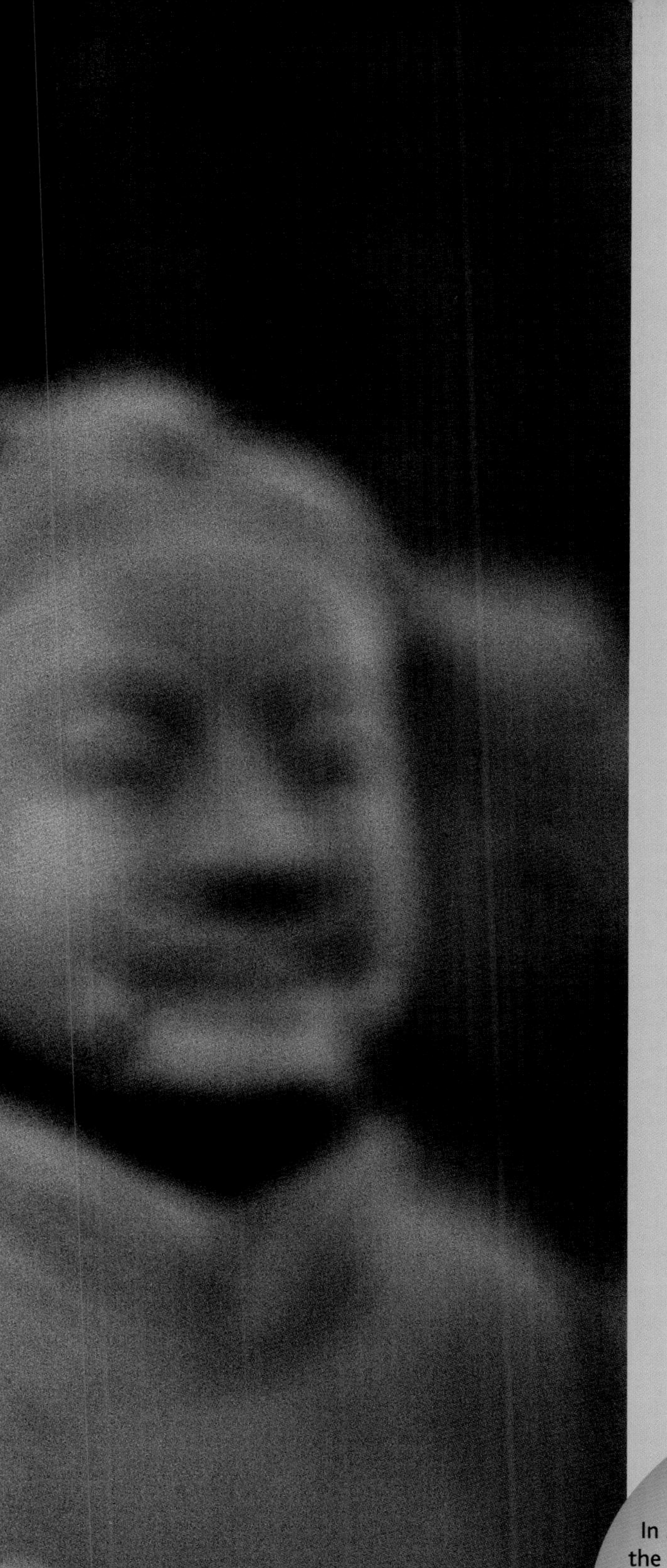

Education & the Arts

240 EDUCATION

242 FAMOUS ARTISTS

244 MUSEUMS AND MONUMENTS

246 COLLECTING

On the march

In 2007, the Terracotta Army was the focus of an exhibition in London that boasted the biggest loan of these magnificent, life-sized and individual figures ever to leave China. The exhibition at the British Museum received over one million visitors, and sparked a new interest in Chinese culture.

Students in higher education

The figures give the percentage of students enrolled in higher education. These countries have the highest number of students, but information is not available for all countries.

Country	%	Country	%	Country	%	Country	%
Finland	92	Latvia	74	Argentina	65	U.K.	60
South Korea	91	Lithuania	73	Hungary	65	Ireland	59
Greece	89	Australia	72	Belgium	63	Israel	58
U.S.	83	Russia	71	Poland	63	France	56
Sweden	82	Iceland	71	Canada	62	Libya	56
New Zealand	82	Ukraine	69	Bermuda	62	Portugal	56
Slovenia	81	Spain	67	Belarus	62	Japan	55
Norway	80	Italy	66	Netherlands	61	World average	24
Denmark	80	Estonia	66	Cuba	61		

U.S. grade system

American children have 12 years of schooling. They start at age 5 and the first year at school is called kindergarten. The grade system begins in the second year with 1st grade (6-year-olds) and continues to 12th grade (18-year-olds). In high schools, years have names instead of numbers: 9th grade is known as the freshman year, 10th as the sophomore year, 11th as the junior year and 12th as the senior year.

Harvard University, Cambridge

Education timeline

1100s

3000 BC The Sumerians pioneer the idea of teaching. Education available only to those who could afford to pay a teacher for each lesson

590 BC The city of Athens becomes the first to offer public education to all men for a small fee. Free education available to the sons of war veterans

597 King's School in Canterbury opens — the first school in the U.K.

859 The world's first university still in existence is founded in Fez, Morocco

1064 The first European university is founded in Parma, Italy

1160 Oxford University becomes the first university in England

1538 The first university of the New World opens in Santo Domingo (now the Dominican Republic)

1635 The first publicly funded high school in the U.S. opens in Boston

1636 Harvard University becomes the first university in the U.S.

1760 The first school for deaf children opens in Paris, France. Pupils are taught an early version of sign language

1781 The first nursery school is opened in Scotland for parents who have to go to work

1783 Poland becomes the first country to ban corporal punishment in schools

Countries with the most...

Primary school pupils

The country with the most primary school pupils is India, where there are 140,012,901 children in primary school. In China there are 112,739,964 primary school children.

Secondary school pupils

China has the most secondary pupils — 100,631,925 — although not all children go on from primary to secondary school. In India there are 89,461,794 secondary school children.

University students

China recently overtook the U.S. for the number of students at university, 21,335,646 compared with the U.S.'s 17,272,044. There are 11,777,296 at university in India and 9,019,556 in Russia.

Pupils per teacher at primary school

Primary school children in some African nations are taught in classes of more than 50: there are 72 pupils per teacher in Ethiopia and up to 83 in Congo. At the other end of the scale, there are only 10 per class in Italy, Norway and Sweden.

Pupils per teacher at secondary school

In secondary schools in Eritrea there are as many as 55 pupils for each teacher. The average class size in Malawi is 51. Schools in Azerbaijan, Belarus, Georgia, Greece, Montserrat, Norway and Portugal have only nine pupils, Lebanon eight and Andorra and Bermuda only seven.

See also
Largest countries: page 116

Children at a Chinese boarding school doing their morning exercises

Schooling around the world

Time spent at school

- School children in China spend more time at school than children in any other country. They have 251 schooldays a year — 71 days more than American children.
- In the United States, Canada , the United Kingdom, France, Germany, Belgium, the Netherlands, Australia and New Zealand children have 10, 11 or 12 years of education. In most African countries and parts of South America children spend just five or six years at school. Only two African countries, Gabon and Tunisia, have 10 years of compulsory schooling.
- In Italy and China, children can legally finish school at the age of 14. In Myanmar (formerly Burma), Angola and Pakistan, children are allowed to finish at the age of 9, after only four or five years at school. In several European countries, including Croatia, Denmark, Sweden and Switzerland, parents don't have to send their children to school until they are 7 years old—two years later than in many other countries.

Largest school

The largest school in the world is the City Montessori school in Lucknow, northern India; it has more than 31,000 pupils.

1900s

1784 The first school for blind children is started in Paris
1785 The University of New Brunswick, Canada's first English-language university, founded
1841 Oberlin College becomes the first university in the U.S. to award degrees to women
1871 A school in New York introduces the first distance-learning courses for young people who live too far away from schools to travel to them
2001 No Child Left Behind Act passed in U.S. extends federal control over state schools and increases parental choice
2004 India launches EDUSAT, the first satellite dedicated to transmitting educational materials to remote places
2007 The National Education Budget in the United States is $1.14 trillion

Most remote school

The world's most remote school is Kiwirrkurra Remote Community School in Australia. It is a 25-hour road journey from the nearest major town. The 100 pupils and seven teachers at another school in the region, Oombulgurri Remote Community School, can only get to school by light aircraft or by boat. The aircraft takes just 35 minutes, but the boat can take up to 12 hours.

Art Deco interior of Helsinki railway station, Finland

Stolen Screams

The Norwegian artist Edvard Munch painted several versions of *The Scream* (1893). One hung in the National Gallery in Oslo, Norway. In 1994 it was stolen and held for ransom for $1 million, but was recovered a few months later. Another version was stolen from the Munch Museum, Oslo, in 2004. The thieves were caught and jailed and the painting, which had been damaged, was recovered.

Western art styles

Medieval
Paintings, mosaics and miniatures in manuscripts, mostly of religious subjects.

Renaissance
The word means rebirth — the Renaissance art of the 15th and 16th centuries replaced medieval styles and revived the art of the Greek and Roman period.

Mannerism
A style of 16th-century Italian art, which uses bright colors and distorts scale and perspective.

Baroque/rococo
An ornate style that was popular in Italy during the 17th and 18th centuries.

Neoclassicism
A style of the 18th century modeled on classical (Greek and Roman) art.

Romanticism
This late 18th/early 19th-century style explores emotion and shows nature in its untamed state.

Realism/naturalism
A 19th-century style that showed real life, including its unpleasant side such as poverty.

Pre-Raphaelitism
This short-lived style, inspired by medieval history and myths, was invented in 1848. The aim was to go back to the simplicity of painting before Raphael.

Impressionism
This style of painting developed in France and was named in 1874. The aim was to convey an impression of what the eye sees rather than what the mind knows is there.

Symbolism
An attempt by late 19th-century artists to link the real and the spiritual worlds in their work.

Post-Impressionism
A development from Impressionism, which includes the Pointillism (dot painting) of Seurat and others. In Pointillism, small dots of color are applied to the canvas. These appear to fuse when seen from a distance.

Art Nouveau
A flowing ornamental style of the late 19th/early 20th centuries that influenced architects, furniture makers and painters.

Expressionism/abstract expressionism
Early 20th-century styles in which the emotions of the painter are powerfully expressed.

Cubism
An abstract style which is mostly about shape and color.

Art Deco
An angular, decorative style popular in the 1920s and 1930s.

Surrealism
A style that emerged between the World Wars, in which artists explore dreams and fantasy.

Abstract art
Non-naturalistic art in which shapes, lines and color are more important than the objects they represent.

Action painting
Popular from the 1940s to 1960s, a style in which paint is splashed and smeared onto canvases.

Pop art
Style conceived in the 1950s, using images from popular culture such as comics and advertising.

Environmental art
Art in which the landscape is decorated or altered. The artists use natural objects such as stones to create their work.

Giant eggs decorate the Dali museum in Rosas, Spain.

Famous artists

Artist	Famous work
Fra Angelico (c. 1400–55) Italian	*Deposition of Christ*
Sandro Botticelli (1445–1510) Italian	*Birth of Venus*
Hieronymus Bosch (c. 1450–1516) Flemish	*Garden of Earthly Delights*
Leonardo da Vinci (1452–1519) Italian	*Mona Lisa*
Albrecht Dürer (1471–1528) German	*Four Apostles*
Michelangelo (1475–1564) Italian	Sistine Chapel ceiling
Raphael (1483–1520) Italian	*Madonna*
Hans Holbein (1497–1543) German	*Sir Thomas More*
El Greco (1541–1614) Greek	*Burial of Count Orgaz*
Sir Peter Paul Rubens (1577–1640) Flemish	*Descent from the Cross*
Rembrandt Van Rijn (1606–69) Dutch	*The Night Watch*
Jan Vermeer (1632–75) Dutch	*Girl with a Pearl Earring*
Antonio Canaletto (1697–1768) Italian	*The Grand Canal and the Church of the Salute, Venice*
Thomas Gainsborough (1727–88) British	*Blue Boy*
Francisco Goya (1746–1828) Spanish	*Maja Nude/Clothed*
J.M.W. Turner (1775–1851) British	*Rain, Steam, and Speed*
Dante Gabriel Rossetti (1828–82) British	*Proserpine*
Sir John Everett Millais (1829–96) British	*Ophelia*
Sir Edward Burne-Jones (1833–98) British	*The Golden Stairs*
Edgar Degas (1834–1917) French	*The Rehearsal*
James McNeill Whistler (1834–1903) American	*Symphony in White*
Paul Cézanne (1839–1906) French	*Large Bathers*
Claude Monet (1840–1926) French	*Waterlilies*
Berthe Morisot (1841–95) French	*The Cradle*
Pierre Renoir (1841–1919) French	*Luncheon of the Boating Party*

Art terms

acrylic
Quick-drying plastic-based paint

cartoon
A preliminary sketch for a painting

chiaroscuro
Light and shade in painting

collage
A work made from pieces of paper and other materials stuck on to a background

composition
The arrangement of the elements and color within a work

fresco
A painting on a freshly plastered wall

gouache
Water-based paint

icon
A portrait of a religious subject, such as a saint

impasto
Thickly applied paint

landscape
A painting of the natural world

medium
The material used to create a work of art

montage
Cut-out objects mounted on a surface

palette
The surface used by an artist for mixing paints, but also used to refer to the selection of colors

pastel
Colored pigments in stick form used for drawing

still life
A painting of an object or a group of objects

tempera
Pigments mixed with egg yolk and oil or water

trompe l'oeil
A painting that plays tricks on the eye to look as if it is three-dimensional

watercolor
Colored pigments mixed with water

Portrait of Dr. Gachet (1890), by Vincent van Gogh

Most expensive paintings

Jackson Pollock's *No. 5, 1948*, was sold privately in New York in 2006 for a price believed to have been about $140 million, making it the most expensive painting not sold at an auction. Among the highest prices paid at auctions are:

- Pablo Picasso, *Boy with a pipe*, $104.2 million, May 2004
- Pablo Picasso, *Dora Maar with Cat*, $95.2 million, May 2006
- Gustav Klimt, *Portrait of Adele Bloch-Bauer II*, $87.9 million, November 2006
- Vincent van Gogh, *Portrait du Dr Gachet*, $82.5 million, May 1990
- Pierre-Auguste Renoir, *Ball at the Moulin de la Galette, Montmartre*, $78.1 million, May 1990
- Sir Peter Paul Rubens, *Massacre of the Innocents*, $75.9 million, July 2002

Record price for a photograph

German photographer Andreas Gurskey (1955–) broke the world record for a photograph at auction in London on February 7, 2007. His large double print *99 Cent*, which shows the interior of a supermarket, was sold for $3.3 million. The previous record holder was *The Pond – Moonlight* by Edward Steichen (U.S.), which was sold in 2006 for $2.9 million.

www.artcyclopedia.com search

Artist	Famous work
Mary Cassatt (1844–1926) American	*The Bath*
Paul Gauguin (1848–1903) French	*Nevermore*
Vincent van Gogh (1853–90) Dutch	*Sunflowers*
Georges Seurat (1859–91) French	*Sunday Afternoon on the Island of La Grand Jatte*
Henri de Toulouse-Lautrec (1864–1901) French	*Aristide Bruant* (poster)
Henri Matisse (1869–1954) French	*The Dance*
Piet Mondrian (1872–1944) Dutch	*Broadway Boogie Woogie*
Pablo Picasso (1881–1973) Spanish	*Guernica*
Edward Hopper (1882–1967) American	*Nighthawks*
Georgia O'Keeffe (1887–1986) American	*Light Iris*
Tom Thomson (1887–1917) Canadian	*The Jack Pine*
Grant Wood (1891–1942) American	*American Gothic*
Norman Rockwell (1894–1978) American	*Dr. and Doll*
Salvador Dali (1904–89) Spanish	*The Persistence of Memory*
Francis Bacon (1909–92) British	*Study after Velazquez's Portrait of Pope Innocent X*
Jackson Pollock (1912–56) American	*No. 5, 1948*
Lucien Freud (1922–) British	*Girl with Roses*
Roy Lichtenstein (1923–97) American	*Whaam!*
Jasper Johns (1930–) American	*Flag*
Andy Warhol (1930–89) American	*Marilyn Monroe*
David Hockney (1937–) British	*A Bigger Splash*
Damien Hirst (1965–) British	*The Physical Impossibility of Death in the Mind of Someone Living* (shark)

Art exhibitions and world fairs

Major art exhibitions and world fairs have been held for more than 200 years. Art exhibitions focus on a particular artist or style. World fairs promote the trade or image of a country and display new inventions.

Great Exhibition, London, U.K.,1851
This was a showpiece of the arts and industries of the world and the first exhibition of its kind in the U.K. It was seen by 6,039,195 visitors.

First Impressionist Exhibition, Paris, France, 1874
Many Impressionist painters, including Claude Monet, first showed their work at this exhibition, which was shocking to many people.

Philadelphia Centennial Exposition, Philadelphia, Pennsylvania, 1876
This first major show in the U.S. was held to celebrate the 100th anniversary of the Declaration of Independence. It was seen by 9,910,966 people. Inventor Alexander Graham Bell first demonstrated the telephone at the Exposition.

Exposition Universelle, Paris, France, 1889
The Eiffel Tower was built as a temporary exhibit for this show, which commemorated 100 years since the French Revolution. It attracted 28,121,975 visitors.

World's Columbian Exposition, Chicago, Illinois, 1893
This show celebrated the 400th anniversary of Columbus' discovery of America and had more than 27.3 million visitors. Many Americans experienced electricity and handheld cameras for the first time.

Armory Show, New York, 1913
This was the first exhibition of modern art in the United States and included the work of Picasso. It influenced American artists, collectors and museums.

Exposition Internationale des Arts Décoratifs et Industriels Modernes, Paris, 1925
This exhibition of art marked the beginning of Art Deco style and attracted 5,852,783 visitors.

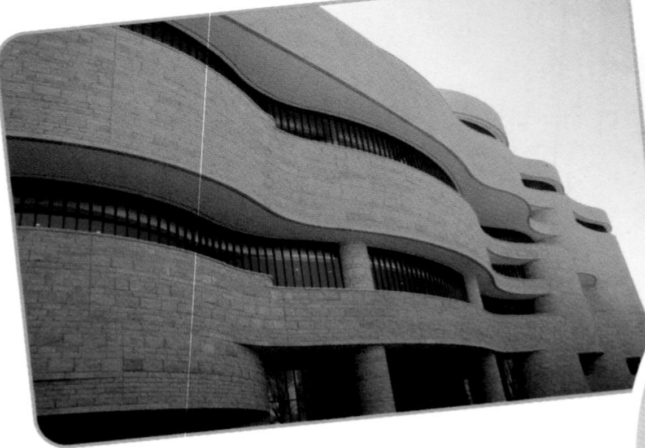

National Museum of the American Indian, in the Smithsonian Institution, Washington, D.C.

World's Fair, Flushing Meadow Park, Queens, New York, 1939–40
The fair had 44,932,978 visitors and first introduced television to the public.

Festival of Britain, London, U.K. 1951
This was a celebration of post-war life, held 100 years after the Great Exhibition. It attracted 8.5 million visitors.

Treasures of Tutankhamun, Metropolitan Museum, New York, 1978–79
This was one of the most popular exhibitions to travel the world, including the United States, Canada, England and Japan. It is still the Metropolitan Museum's most-visited show to date, with 1,226,467 admissions.

Expo 2005, Japan
Over 22 million people visited the show, themed "Nature's Wisdom." All the exhibition pavilions were built from recycled materials.

Museum fact file

First museum open to the public
Uffizi Gallery, Florence, Italy, 1591.

First public museum in the U.S.
Charleston Museum, Charleston, South Carolina, opened 1773.

Oldest museum in Canada
The Niagara Falls Museum was opened by Thomas Barnett in 1827. It once displayed the mummy of Egyptian pharaoh Ramses I, but this was returned to Egypt on October 24, 2003.

Canada's oldest art museum
The Montreal Museum of Fine Arts (Musée des Beaux-Arts de Montreal) was founded as the Art Association of Montreal in 1860. The museum itself opened in 1912.

First open-air museum
Skansen, Stockholm, Sweden, opened in 1891.

First children's museum
The Brooklyn Children's Museum in New York City, opened in 1899 and was the first of more than 300 children's museums worldwide.

First interactive museum
The Exploratorium, San Francisco, California, U.S., opened in 1969 and has hundreds of hands-on exhibits.

Largest museum complex
The Smithsonian Institution in Washington, D.C., consists of 16 museums with a total of more than 140 million items in their collections.

The Buddhas of Bamian (Bamiyan)

Two giant buddhas 180 ft. (55 m) and 121 ft. (37 m) were carved into the side of a cliff in Afghanistan between the 5th and 9th centuries. They were listed as a UNESCO World Heritage site, but were blown up in 2001 by the Islamic fundamentalist Taliban who then ruled the country. A plan has been proposed to project laser images of the statues on the rock face where they once stood.

Giant statues

There are many larger than life statues and monuments around the world. Here are some of the largest and most famous.

Chief Crazy Horse, South Dakota
This is the world's biggest monument. It is carved into Thunderhead Mountain and is 563 ft. (172 m) high and 641 ft. (195 m) long. Work on the carving started in 1948 and continues to this day.

Ushiku Daibutsu (Buddha), Tokyo, Japan
This was unveiled in 1993. It weighs 1,100 tons (1,000 tonnes) and is 394 ft. (120 m) tall.

Leshan Giant Buddha, China
Work on this huge statue began in AD 713 and was completed 90 years later. It is 234 ft. (71 m) high, with shoulders 92 ft. (28 m) across. Its feet measure 28 ft. (8.5 m) and the head is 48 ft. (15 m) high, with ears 23 ft. (7 m) long.

Statue of Liberty, New York
This statue was presented to the U.S. by the people of France. It was shipped in sections and unveiled in 1886. The statue is made of sheets of copper on an iron frame, and weighs 252 tons (229 tonnes). The height of the statue is 151 ft. (46 m) from the base to the top of the torch. It stands on a massive pedestal which more than doubles the overall height to 305 ft. (93 m). The hands are 16 ft., 5 in. (5 m) long, the eyes are 2 ft., 6 in. (0.76 m) across and the nose measures 4 ft., 6 in. (1.48 m). The statue was originally called Liberty Enlightening the World.

Abu Simbel, Egypt
The four huge statues, each standing 66 ft. (20 m) high, used to guard a temple. They were moved in 1966 when the Aswan High Dam was built and the area flooded.

Angel of the North, Gateshead, U.K.
The Angel stands 65 ft. (19.8 m) high, has a wingspan of 175 ft. (53.3 m) and weighs 220 tons (200 tonnes). It was designed by Antony Gormley and erected in 1998.

Antony Gormley's *Angel of the North* sculpture

Christ the Redeemer, Rio de Janeiro, Brazil
This statue stands high above the city. The figure of Christ is 125 ft. (38 m) tall and weighs 1,282 tons (1,163 tonnes). It was unveiled in 1931 by Guglielmo Marconi, who had designed its lighting. He unveiled it by sending a radio signal from his yacht in Genoa, Italy.

Sphinx, Giza, Egypt
This statue was carved in about 2500 BC. It is about 66 ft. (20 m) high and 240 ft. (73 m) long, and has the huge body of a lion, with the head of a pharaoh.

Mount Rushmore, South Dakota
This is a massive sculpture of the heads of U.S. presidents George Washington, Thomas Jefferson, Theodore Roosevelt and Abraham Lincoln. Each one is about 60 ft. (18.3 m) high. It was carved out of a cliff face between 1927 and 1939.

Statues of Abu Simbel

Unusual museums

Cockroach Hall of Fame, Plano, Texas
Record-breaking cockroaches, and insects dressed as famous people

Colman's Mustard Museum, Norwich, Norfolk.
Tells the fascinating history of mustard

The Prince Edward Island Potato Museum, O'Leary, PEI, Canada
Tells the story of potato cultivation and contains a large exhibit of potato artifacts

Gallery of Also-Rans, Norton, Kansas
A collection celebrating people who came second or lost political campaigns and other contests

The Lunch Box Museum, Columbus, Georgia
Over 2,500 lunch boxes from the 1950s to the present

The Medieval Crime Museum, Rothenburg, Germany
Medieval crime, punishment and torture implements

National Wool Museum, Geelong, Australia
The only museum devoted to wool, opened in 1988

Nut Museum, Old Lyme, Connecticut
Nut carvings, 7.9 ft (2.4 m) long nutcrackers and other nut-related exhibits

Philips Mushroom Museum, Kennett Square, Pennsylvania
A museum focusing on all types of mushrooms and other fungi

The Piggy Bank Museum, Amsterdam, Netherlands
Displays 12,000 piggy banks from all periods

Porter Thermometer Museum, Onset, Massachusetts
More than 3,000 devices for taking temperatures

Amazing collectors

Louis XIV

The French king owned a collection of 413 ornate beds. He kept them in different places all over France, so wherever he traveled, he could sleep in his own bed.

The Schlumpf brothers

French factory owners Hans and Fritz Schlumpf built up one of the world's largest car collections. They had 427 vehicles, including 120 rare Bugattis. These are now on public display at the National Auto Museum of France in Mulhouse.

Sir Thomas Phillips

Eccentric English book collector Sir Thomas Phillips (1792–1872) wanted to own a copy of every book ever printed — and he almost succeeded. He acquired more than 50,000 books and 100,000 manuscripts. His collection plunged his family into debt, but he rescued many priceless treasures from destruction. Sales from his collection have continued almost every year since his death.

George Gustav Heye

Heye (1874–1957) of New York built up the world's largest collection of Native American artifacts, which became the basis of the Smithsonian Institution's National Museum of the American Indian, Washington, D.C.

Harold LeMay

Millionaire LeMay (1919–2001) of Tacoma, Washington, collected more than 3,000 vehicles, which will become the core of the world's largest automobile display in America's Car Museum, opening in 2009.

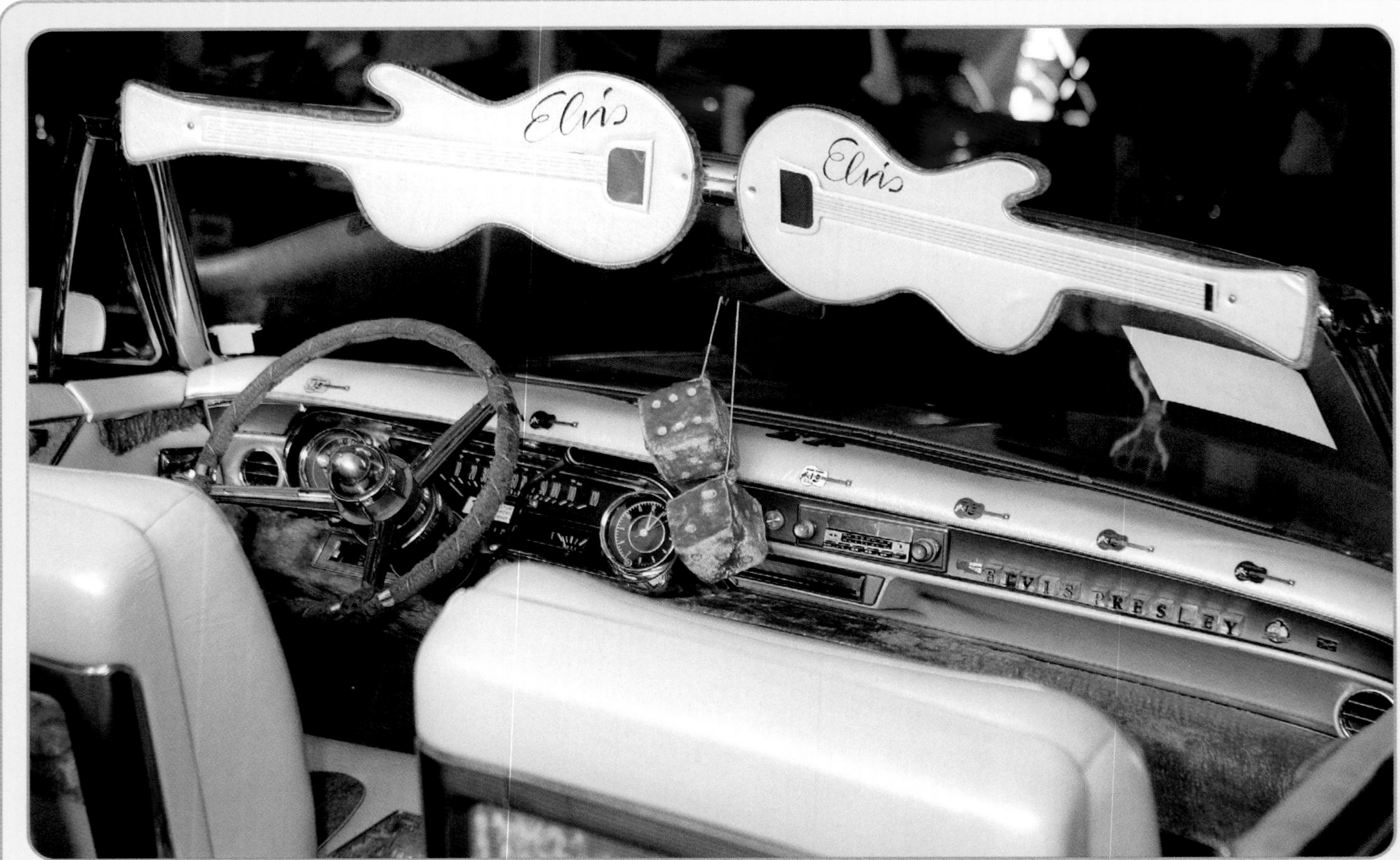

In 2005, George Barris, the "King of Customizers," auctioned his film and television cars, including this one he made for Elvis Presley.

Unusual auction items

- The skull of the Swedish philosopher Emanuel Swedenborg was sold at Sotheby's, London, U.K. in 1978 for $2,900. Stockholm Royal Academy of Science bought the skull and reunited it with the rest of his body, which was buried in Uppsala Cathedral.
- A pair of Napoleon's socks was sold at Sotheby's, London, in 1996 for $4,660.
- A pair of Queen Victoria's underpants were sold at Sotheby's, London, in 1996 for $395. A pair of Victorian rollerblades dating from c. 1860 was sold at the same sale for $900.
- Several pairs of glasses belonging to John Lennon of the Beatles have sold for up to $1.5 million.
- A dish containing a sample of penicillum mold prepared by penicillin inventor Alexander Fleming in 1935 was sold by Christie's, London, in 1997 for $23,770. At the same sale a box of 300 glass eyes was sold for $4,390.
- More than 2,000 items that had belonged to the singer Elvis Presley were sold at an auction in Las Vegas in 1999. These included clothing as well as letters, one of Elvis's school report cards and 29 dry-cleaning bills made out to Elvis.
- In 2007, Christie's auction house in Paris, France, sold a Siberian mammoth skeleton for 312,000 euros ($422,242) and a dinosaur egg for 1,800 euros ($2,436).
- The Texas Schoolbook Depository window from which President Kennedy was shot was sold on eBay in 2007 for $3,001,501.

Young enthusiasts sorting a collection of baseball cards

Who collects what?

As soon as someone starts to collect something a word is invented to describe the collector. Most end in -ist, which means a person who does something (as a motorist is someone who drives a car or a violinist someone who plays a violin). Another ending is -phile or -philist, which means a lover of something.

Collectable	Collector
airmail	**aerophilatelist**
autographs	**philographist**
badges and patches	**scutelliphilist**
banknotes	**notaphilist**
beer bottle labels	**labeorphilist**
beer coasters	**tegestologist** or **tegetologist**
books	**bibliophile** or **bibliophilist**
butterflies and moths	**lepidopterist**
cameos	**cameist**
cheese labels	**laclabphilist**
cigar bands	**brandophilist** or **cigrinophilist**
coins, money, medals	**numismatist**
corkscrews	**helixophile**
dolls	**plangonologist**
eggs	**oologist** (illegal in many countries)
egg cups	**pocillovist**
flags and banners	**vexillologist**
gramophone records	**discophilist**
keyrings	**copoclephilist**
keys	**cagophilist**
match books	**phillumenist**
matchboxes	**cumyxaphilist**
money boxes	**argyrothecologist**
postcards	**deltiologist**
prints and book illustrations	**iconophilist**
shells	**conchologist**
stamps	**philatelist**
sugar packets	**sucrologist**
teddy bears	**arctophilists**
telephone cards	**fusilatelist**

Stamp collection themes

Many philatelists (stamp collectors) follow topical philately, which means they collect stamps by theme.

They may acquire stamps from many different countries and periods. Here are some of the hundreds of popular themes.

aircraft
animals
art and artists
authors
bicycles
birds
butterflies
cars
castles
cats
chess
children
Christmas
cinema
costumes
dance
dinosaurs
dogs
dolls
exploration
famous people
fish
flags
flowers
food
heraldry
horses
insects
lighthouses
literature
maps
medicine
mountains
mushrooms
music
Nobel Prize
Olympic Games
police
railways
religion
scouting
seashells
ships
space
sports
stamps
theater
uniforms

Postage stamps from around the world

www.smithsonianeducation.org.idealabs/collecting/index.html search

A collection of shells

Music & Performance

250 WORLD OF MUSIC

252 CLASSICAL MUSIC

254 POP AND ROCK

256 THEATRE

258 DANCE

260 BALLET

Motown half-century

The Tanla-Motown record label was founded in 1959 with Diana Ross and the Supremes as one of its first and most successful acts. It launched the careers of artists such as the Temptations and Four Tops in its early years, and more recently, Boyz II Men.

Musical instrument records

Double bass

A double bass 14 ft. (4.3 m) long and weighing 1,300 lb. (590 kg) was built by Arthur K. Ferris of Ironia, New Jersey, USA, in 1924.

Drum

The University of Texas Longhorn Band has a drum nicknamed Big Bertha which is 24.9 ft. (7.6 m) in circumference.

Guitar

A giant version of a Gibson guitar 38.2 ft. (11.63 m) long was made in 1991 by students at Shakamak High School, Jasonville, Indiana. Large stringed instruments that are bigger than the span of human hands are difficult or even impossible to play.

Pianos

In 1935 in London, England, Charles H. Challen built a piano which is probably the largest in the world. It weighs 1.4 tons (1.25 tonnes) and is 11.6 ft. (3.6 m) long. One of the lightest pianos ever made was a baby grand weighing just 397 lb. (180 kg). It was made mostly of aluminium covered in yellow pigskin. It was made by the Blüthner company of Germany for the airship *Hindenburg*, and was destroyed when the airship exploded in 1937.

Tuba

In 1896 John Philip Sousa, who is the American inventor of the sousaphone, played a 7.48 ft. (2.28 m) tuba on a world tour. This is the largest brass instrument ever made and had 38.7 ft. (11.8 m) of tubing.

Organs

The world's loudest instrument is the Auditorium Organ in Atlantic City, N.J. It was built in 1930 at a cost of $500,000, has more than 32,000 pipes and is powered by a 365 horsepower blower.

The world's largest cathedral organ was built in St. Stephen's Cathedral, Passau, Germany, in 1928. It has 17,774 pipes.

The world's largest church organ is in St. Stephen's Cathedral, Passau, Germany.

See also
Inventions: pages 80–81

Large orchestras

- In 1958, the Norwegian National Meeting of School Bands assembled 12,600 players at Trondheim, Norway.
- A total of 6,452 musicians from the Vancouver Symphony Orchestra and Canadian music students played together in Vancouver, Canada, on May 15, 2000.
- An ensemble of 1,013 cellists played on November 29, 1998, in Kobe, Japan.
- On July 14, 1999, Piers Adams conducted 710 recorder players performing "Roaring Rag" by Beverley Wragg at Cressing Temple Barn, Essex, U.K.

Large choir

In 1872 Austrian composer Johann Strauss conducted an orchestra of 987 (including 400 first violinists) and a choir of 20,000. The performance was in Boston, Massachusets.

Recording timeline

1800s

1877 Thomas Alva Edison first recorded a human voice (singing "Mary Had a Little Lamb") on a tinfoil cylinder phonograph

1878 Edison is granted phonograph patent

1885 "Graphophone" with wax cylinders is invented by Alexander Graham Bell and Charles Tainter

1888 "Gramophone," with 7-inch (17.8 cm) flat disk, is patented by Emile Berliner

1895 First spring-driven phonograph is sold by Edison

1896 Improved gramophone produced by Eldridge Johnson

1897 Shellac disks introduced

1898 First magnetic recorder, with steel wire, patented by Valdemar Poulsen

1900s

1904 First mass-produced, double-sided disks are sold in Germany

1925 First electrically recorded disks make it possible to record entire orchestral works. Sound recordings for films are introduced

1927 First coin-operated juke box is produced

1931 Stereo recording introduced

1934 First hi-fi (high-fidelity sound) records are made

1935 "Magnetophone" (tape recorder) is demonstrated in Berlin, Germany

Musical terms

Many musical terms are derived from Italian words. Here are the meanings of some common ones.

Musical tempos

Tempo	Meaning
Larghissimo	As slow as possible
Largo	Very slow and solemn
Largementa	Slow, broad
Larghetto	Slightly less slow
Lento	Slow
Adagissimo	Very slow
Adagio	Slow (from the Italian for at ease)
Adagietto	Slightly faster
Andante	Moderately slow (from the Italian for walk)
Andantino	Slightly slower than andante
Moderato	At a brisk walking pace
Allegretto	Fairly lively
Allegramente	Lightly
Allegro	Lively, fast (from the Italian for cheerful)
Vivace	Fast
Vivacissimo	Very quick
Presto	Very fast
Prestissimo	Extremely fast

Other musical terms

Term	Meaning
Agitato	Agitated or excited
Brillante	Sparkling, brilliant
Brio	Spirit or vigor
Crescendo	Gradual increase in volume
Dolce	Sweet, soft and gentle
Dolente	Sad
Forte	Loud or strong
Fortissimo	Very loud
Grave	Slow and serious
Legato	Smoothly and evenly
Molto	Much or very
Pianissimo	Very soft
Piano	Soft
Ritenuto	Slowing in tempo
Scherzo	Lively
Sotto voce	Quiet and subdued
Tutti	All the players

Famous songs

Yankee Doodle

"Yankee Doodle" dates from the period of the French and Indian War of 1754–63. It was originally sung by British troops as a criticism of North American soldiers, but they turned the tables by adopting it as a patriotic song – it even became the state anthem of Connecticut.

Auld Lang Syne

The words of this song come from verses written by Scottish poet Robert Burns in 1788. The music is based on an old ballad. "Auld Lang Syne" (meaning old long since) is traditionally sung at midnight on New Year's Eve, except in Taiwan where it is a graduation song.

Happy Birthday to You

In 1893 two American sisters, who were teachers, wrote this song to sing in school assemblies. Mildred J. and Patty Smith Hill originally called the song "Good Morning to You." After the words were changed in 1924, it became known the world over. The song will be in copyright until 2030, but only for commercial purposes. Singing it at a birthday party does not infringe copyright!

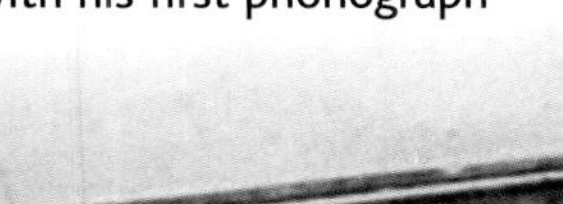

Thomas Edison (1847–1931) with his first phonograph

2000s

1948 First 12-in. (30.5 cm) 33-1/3 rpm, microgroove LP vinylite record is produced, with 23-minute capacity per side
1949 First 7-in. (17.8 cm), 45 rpm, microgroove EP (Extended Play) vinylite record and player are introduced
1958 First stereo LPs are sold
1963 First compact audio cassette is produced
1969 Dolby Noise Reduction is introduced
1979 First Sony Walkman portable audio cassette players are sold
1980 First camcorders are sold
1982 First CDs are sold
1987 DAT (Digital Audio Tape) players are launched
1992 Mini-disks are introduced
1997 MP3 format is launched
1999 DVD-Audio format is introduced
2001 Apple Computer's iPod is launched
2005 Total U.S. recorded music sales (albums, singles, video and downloads) top one billion for the first time.
2006 MSI launches the solar-powered MP3 player
2007 It is estimated that 200 billion CDs have been sold since the launch of the format 25 years ago.

www.recording-history.org search

Strings

The viola is larger and deeper-voiced than the violin, and is played in the same way.

The violin has a hollow wooden body that resonates when the violinist pulls a bow over the four strings. There may be 30 or more violins in a modern orchestra.

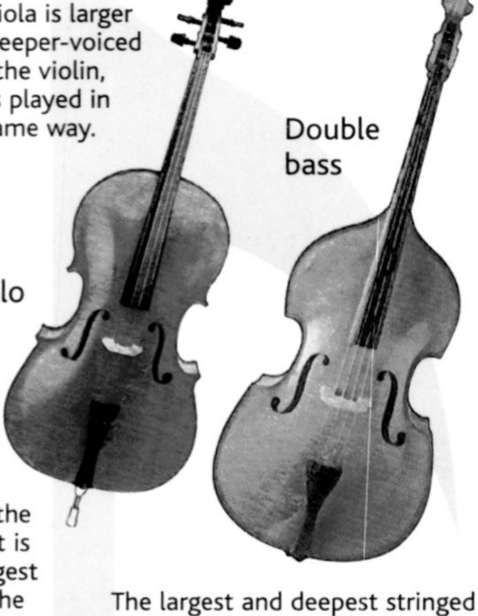

The cello's full name is the violoncello. It is the third-largest member of the violin family and is played sitting down.

The largest and deepest stringed instrument in an orchestra is the double bass. Double bass players usually stand to play, pulling a bow across the strings, or plucking them.

The orchestral harp has 48 strings of different lengths, attached to the top and side, and seven pedals at the base.

Opera terms

aria
A song for a single voice

comic opera
Opera with a comic plot

finale
The ending, when the whole cast often sing together

libretto
The text of an opera, from the Italian for little book

operetta
A light (rather than serious) opera, usually with an amusing story

prima donna
First lady (from the Italian) — the main female singer, or diva

recitative
A part in an opera that is spoken rather than sung

Instruments of the orchestra

The range and number of instruments in a modern orchestra varies enormously. There may be as many as 100 or more, and less familiar instruments are brought in for special performances. The ones illustrated here are the most common instruments.

Brass

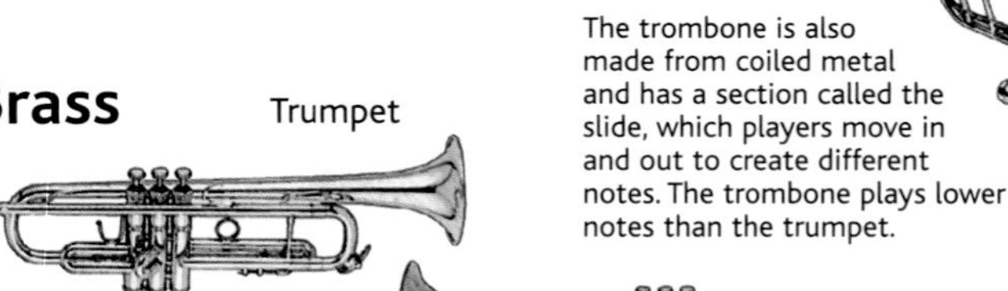

A trumpet is a tightly coiled metal tube with a cone called the bell at one end. Trumpets have three small buttons called valves that make different notes when pressed.

The trombone is also made from coiled metal and has a section called the slide, which players move in and out to create different notes. The trombone plays lower notes than the trumpet.

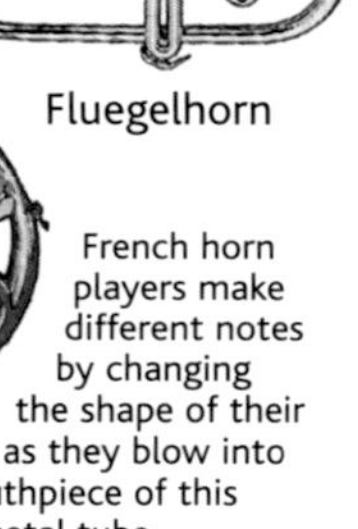

French horn players make different notes by changing the shape of their lips as they blow into the mouthpiece of this coiled metal tube.

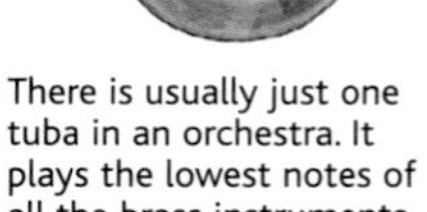

There is usually just one tuba in an orchestra. It plays the lowest notes of all the brass instruments.

Singing parts

Name	Female voices
Soprano	The highest female voice
Mezzo soprano	Between a soprano and a contralto
Contralto	The lowest female voice
	Male voices
Alto	The highest male voice, traditionally sung by choirboys
Tenor	A high male voice. A countertenor voice is very high
Baritone	A voice higher than a bass, but lower than a tenor
Bass	The lowest male voice. Basso profundo is the lowest possible voice
Falsetto	An unnaturally high voice sung by tenors and basses

Woodwind

The concert flute is played through a blow hole at one end. Alto and bass flutes are larger versions which play lower notes. The piccolo is half the size of the concert flute and plays the highest notes in the orchestra.

Oboe players blow through a double reed made from two small slices of cane tied together and inserted into the mouthpiece of the instrument.

The clarinet is also played through a reed. There are several different types of clarinet. B flat and A are played most often.

The bassoon plays the lowest notes of the woodwind instruments. It is a doubled-up wooden tube with a curved metal crook at one end, which holds the reed.

Opera facts

Most-performed operas

Puccini's *La Bohème* is the most-performed opera in New York. It has been staged 1,140 times at the Metropolitan Opera House in New York City. *Aïda* and *Carmen* are the closest runners-up.

Longest operas

Richard Wagner's *Gotterdämmerung* is the longest regularly performed opera. The opera can last up to six hours, including intermissions.

Largest opera venues

The two largest opera houses where operas are regularly performed are in Italy and the United States. They are the Arena di Verona in Verona, which holds 16,663 people, and the Municipal Opera Theater in St. Louis, Missouri, which holds 11,745. The Teatro alla Scala, Milan, Italy, which has 3,600 seats, is one of the world's largest indoor opera theaters, although several U.S. opera houses come close in size.

Poster advertising *Madama Butterfly* by Puccini

Nellie Melba

Grandest grand opera

The opera *Aïda* has often been performed on a grand scale, with a huge cast including elephants and other animals. It has been staged at the pyramids, Egypt, and in the year 2000 was performed in a football stadium in Shanghai, China, with a cast of 3,000 and an audience of 45,000.

Dame Nellie Melba

The real name of Australian opera singer Dame Nellie Melba (1881–1931) was Helen Mitchell. She was a great food lover and inspired the famous chef Escoffier to create several new dishes for her at the Savoy Hotel, London, U.K. These included Peach Melba (a raspberry and redcurrant sauce poured over peaches and ice cream), Melba Toast (crisp dried bread) and Melba Garniture (chicken, truffles and mushrooms stuffed into tomatoes).

Percussion

Timpani/Kettledrums

Orchestras usually have three or four timpani or kettledrums. They are made of copper with a plastic skin stretched over the top.

Triangle

Cymbals

Side drum

Bass drum

Various other instruments are sometimes played in orchestras, including keyboards (piano, organ, celesta, etc.), bells, castanets, glockenspiels, gongs, marimbas, rattles, tambourines, wind machines, wood blocks, xylophones, guitars, mandolins and saxophones.

Top singles of all time*

The numbers of singles sold outside the U.S. and some other countries have only been recorded fairly recently, so world sales here are estimates.

"White Christmas" was the world's bestselling single for more than 50 years until it was overtaken by Elton John's tribute to Princess Diana in 1997.

*These figures are for singles sung in the English language.

Artist/single/year	Estimated sales (millions) U.S.	World total
Elton John, "Candle in the Wind" (1997)/ "Something about the Way You Look Tonight" (1997)	11	37
Bing Crosby, "White Christmas" (1945)	n/a	30
Bill Haley and His Comets, "Rock Around the Clock" (1954)	n/a	17
Elvis Presley, "It's Now or Never" (1960)	1	12
The Beatles, "I Want to Hold Your Hand" (1963)	0.5	12
The Beatles, "Hey Jude" (1968)	4	10
Whitney Houston, "I Will Always Love You" (1992)	4	10

Downloads fact file

- Digital downloads have been included in the Billboard Hot 100 since 2005.
- In 2005 Gwen Stefani's "Hollaback Girl" became the first single to be downloaded more than one million times in the U.S.
- In January 2007, Fergie's single "Fergalicious" became the fastest-selling downloaded track when 295,000 digital downloads were sold in a single week in the U.S.
- In 2006, over 525 million individual tracks and 32.6 million full albums were downloaded in the U.S.
- In 2006, a total of 22 digital tracks were downloaded more than one million times in the U.S.; Canadian Daniel Powter's "Bad Day" was the first with over two million downloads.
- From 2003 to January 2008, iTunes had sold 4 billion downloads, over 70% of all online music sales.

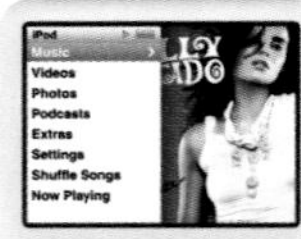

Apple's iPod

The Beatles, 1963

See also
Entertainment lasts: page 306

One and only

The Beatles had all top five positions in the U.S. singles chart on April 4, 1964, with:

1 "Can't Buy Me Love"
2 "Twist and Shout"
3 "She Loves You"
4 "I Want to Hold Your Hand"
5 "Please Please Me"

Rock and pop facts

First CD single by a band
Dire Straits, "Brothers in Arms," 1985

Loudest rock band
During the 1960s and 70s, British group The Who played at 140 decibels — as loud as a jet at takeoff. Members of the band suffered hearing loss.

Biggest-selling group in the world ever
The Beatles' total sales of singles and albums on vinyl, tape and CD are well over one billion.

Bestselling album in the U.S.
The Eagles' *Their Greatest Hits, 1971–1975* (1976) has sold over 29 million copies in the U.S. It was the first album ever to be certified platinum (for sales of over one million copies). It is closely followed by Michael Jackson's *Thriller* (1982), with sales of more than 27 million in the U.S. Only six other albums have ever sold more than 20 million copies in the U.S.

Biggest-selling album by a teenage solo singer
Britney Spears holds the record for her album *Baby One More Time* (1999). She is also the biggest-selling teenage artist—she'd sold more than 37 million records worldwide before her 20th birthday on December 2, 2001.

Group with most No. 1 singles in the U.S.
The Beatles, with 20 No. 1 singles. They also hold the record of bestselling single by a group, with over five million copies of "Hey Jude" (1968) sold in the U.S.

Bestselling album by a female singer in the U.S.
Canadian singer Shania Twain's *Come On Over* (1997) has sold over 20 million copies in the U.S. and twice that number worldwide.

Major rock events

The following are among the best-attended rock events ever. The Live Aid concerts (July 13, 1985) and Live 8 concerts (July 2, 2005) had smaller audiences split over several venues but were believed to have had the greatest TV audiences of all time.

About 1.5 billion people, or one quarter of the world's population, watched Live Aid on television. The figure for Live 8 was over 2 billion.

Event/date	Est. audience
Rod Stewart, Copacabana Beach, Rio de Janeiro, Brazil, December 31, 1994	3,500,000
Golden Jubilee Concert, Buckingham Palace, London, U.K., June 3, 2002	over 1,000,000
Live 8: 10 free concerts in nine countries, July 2, 2005 (The largest single audience was 200,000 in Hyde Park, London, U.K.)	over 1,000,000
Garth Brooks in Central Park, New York, N.Y., August 7 1997	750,000
US Festival, San Bernardino, California, May 28–30, 1982	725,000
Summer Jam, Watkins Glen, New York, July 28, 1973	600,132
Third Isle of Wight Festival, U.K., August 30, 1970	up to 600,000
Simon and Garfunkel in Central Park, New York, N.Y., September 19, 1981	500,000
Rolling Stones Free Concert, Hyde Park, London, U.K., July 5, 1969	up to 500,000
Molson Canadian Rocks for Toronto, Toronto, Ontario, July 30, 2003	489,176
Woodstock Festival, Bethel, New York, August 15–17, 1969	over 400,000

Jimi Hendrix playing at Woodstock Festival, Bethel, New York, 1969

Top albums of all time worldwide

The U.S. has always led the world in album sales. Total worldwide sales are less easy to find, but using the best estimates available these albums can claim to be world-beaters.

Michael Jackson, *Thriller* (1982) 104 million copies (27 million U.S.)
Eagles, *Their Greatest Hits 1971–1975* (1976) 42 million copies (29 million U.S.)
AC/DC, *Back in Black* (1980) 42 million copies (21 million U.S.)
Backstreet Boys, Millenium (1999) 40 million copies (13 million U.S.)
The Bodyguard (soundtrack) (1992) 42 million copies (17 million U.S.)
Saturday Night Fever (soundtrack) (1977) 40 million copies (15 million U.S.)
Pink Floyd, *The Dark Side of The Moon* (1973) 40 million copies (15 million U.S.)
Shania Twain, *Come On Over* (1997) 39 million copies (20 million U.S.)
Meatloaf, *Bat out of Hell* (1978) 37 million copies (14 million U.S.)
Led Zeppelin, *Led Zeppelin IV* (1971) 32 million copies (23 million U.S.)
The Beatles, *Sgt Pepper's Lonely Hearts Club Band* (1967) 32 million copies (11 million U.S.)

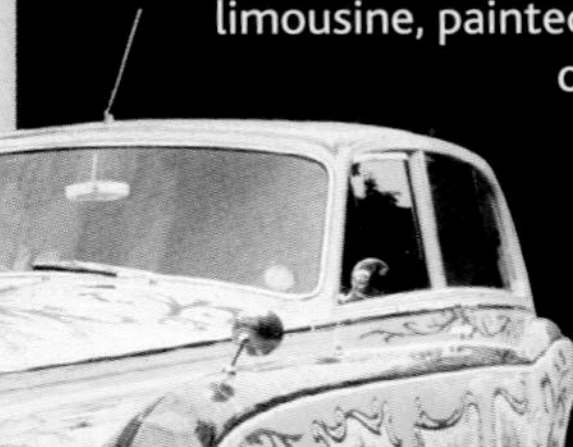

John Lennon's Rolls-Royce

Youngest male artist with a No. 1 single in the U.S.

Jimmy Boyd was just 12 years, 11 months old when his single "I Saw Mommy Kissing Santa Claus" reached No.1 in the U.S. charts in 1952

Bestselling singles by a female band in the U.S.

Rose Royce's "Car Wash" (1976), the Spice Girls' "Wannabe" (1997) and Destiny's Child's "No, No, No" (1998) have each been certified platinum, with sales of more than one million copies.

www.billboard.com search

Treasures of rock

Fans of rock music often like to buy items that belonged to their favorite singers and bands. The more successful the artist, the higher the price.

- The 1965 Rolls-Royce Phantom V touring limousine, painted in psychedelic colors, owned by John Lennon of The Beatles. Sold at auction in New York, on June 29, 1985 for $2,299,000.
- Steinway Model Z upright piano owned by John Lennon. Sold in an online auction on October 17, 2000 for $2,098,860.
- "Tiger" guitar owned by Jerry Garcia of Grateful Dead. Sold in New York, U.S., on May 9, 2002 for $957,500.
- "Blackie" Fender Stratocaster guitar owned by Eric Clapton. Sold in New York, U.S., on June 25, 2004 for $959,500.
- Bernie Taupin's handwritten lyrics for the re-written "Candle in the Wind", sung by Sir Elton John in Westminster Abbey at the funeral of Diana, Princess of Wales. Sold in Los Angeles, U.S., on February 11, 1998 for $400,000.

Canadian circus troupe Cirque du Soleil (French for "Circus of the Sun")

See also
Tom Thumb: page 95

A quick history of circus

Open air-circuses with acrobats, chariot races, bareback riders and comedy acts were popular in ancient Rome. In the 18th century fixed buildings were used, and in the early 19th century traveling circuses appeared in Europe and the U.S. Troupes moved from place to place, setting up a large tent, or "big top." The most famous U.S. circus proprietor was Phineas T. Barnum (1810–91).

His shows were spectacular, with trick riding, juggling, trapeze acts, tightrope walking, strong men and wild-cat tamers. They also featured "human oddities," or freak shows, in which Siamese twins, giants or bearded ladies were often paraded before the curious crowd. Since the 20th century, all-human Chinese and Russian circus companies have toured the world, as well as alternative circus troupes such as Circus Oz, Ra Ra Zoo and Archaos, whose acts have included juggling with chainsaws and jumping over blazing motorbikes.

Famous playwrights and their famous plays

Aeschylus (Greek, c. 525–546 BC) — *The Oresteia*
Edward Albee (American, 1928–) — *Who's Afraid of Virginia Woolf?*
J.M. Barrie (Scottish, 1860–1937) — *Peter Pan*
Samuel Beckett (Irish, 1906–89) — *Waiting for Godot*
Anton Chekhov (Russian, 1860–1904) — *The Cherry Orchard*
Noël Coward (English, 1899–1973) — *Private Lives*
Euripides (Greek, c. 484–406 BC) — *The Trojan Women*
Federico García Lorca (Spanish, 1898–1936)— *Blood Wedding*
Henrik Ibsen (Norwegian, 1828–1906) — *Hedda Gabler*
Ben Jonson (English, 1572–1637) — *The Alchemist*
David Mamet (American, 1947–) — *Glengarry Glen Ross*
Christopher Marlowe (English, 1564–93) — *Doctor Faustus*
Arthur Miller (American, 1915–2005) — *The Crucible*
Molière (French, 1622–73) — *Tartuffe*
Eugene O'Neill (American, 1888–1953) — *Long Day's Journey into Night*
Harold Pinter (English, 1930–) — *The Birthday Party*
Peter Shaffer (English, 1926–) — *Amadeus*
William Shakespeare (English, 1564–1616) — *Hamlet*
George Bernard Shaw (Irish, 1856–1950)— *Pygmalion*
Neil Simon (American, 1927–)— *Plaza Suite*
Sophocles (Greek, c. 496–405 BC)— *Antigone*
August Strindberg (Swedish, 1849–1912) — *Miss Julie*
Tom Stoppard (Czech, 1937–)— *Rosencrantz and Guildenstern are Dead*
J.M. Synge (Irish, 1871–1909)— *The Playboy of the Western World*
John Webster (English, 1580–1625)— *The Duchess of Malfi*
Oscar Wilde (Irish, 1854–1900)— *The Importance of Being Earnest*
Tennessee Williams (American, 1911–83)—*A Streetcar Named Desire*

Theater records

First actor
Thespis was the first performer ever recorded. He was an actor in Greece in 534 BC. At this time, Greek actors used masks, and Thespis was the first to use stage makeup.

World's oldest theaters
The oldest indoor theater in the world is the Teatro Olimpico, Vicenza, Italy, which opened on March 3, 1585. London's oldest theater, and one of the world's oldest still operating, is the Theatre Royal, Drury Lane, which opened on May 7, 1663. It burned down in 1672 and was rebuilt by Sir Christopher Wren. The oldest surviving theater in the U.S. is the Walnut Street Theater in Philadelphia, Pennsylvania, which opened in 1809.

World's biggest theaters
The National People's Congress Building Theatre, Beijing, China was built in 1959 and can hold audiences of 10,000. The Perth Entertainment Centre, Australia (1976) has up to 8,500 seats, the Chaplin (originally Blanquetta), Havana, Cuba (1949) has 6,500 and Radio City Music Hall, New York, U.S., has 6,200. The 3,483-seater Hammersmith Odeon is the largest theatre in Britain, but the Royal Albert Hall in London can hold up to 7,000, depending on the event and how the seating is organized.

The Teatro Olimpico in Vicenza, Italy

Worst disasters at a theater

Fires, in which people were burned or trampled to death, have caused the worst disasters at theaters. The worst ever was at Canton (now Guangzhou), China, in 1845 when 1,670 died. The worst in the U.S. was at the Iroquois Theater, Chicago, in 1903, which left 602 dead. Europe's worst was at the Ring Theatre, Vienna, Austria, in 1881, which killed at least 620 people. These are the worst single-building (rather than city or forest) fires in history.

Longest-running shows

The Golden Horseshoe Revue (Disneyland, California, 1955–86) 47,250 performances
The Mousetrap (London, 1952–) *23,026 performances
The Fantasticks (New York, 1960–2002) 17,162 performances
La Cantatrice Chauve (*The Bald Soprano*) (Paris, 1957–) *16,743 performances
Shear Madness (Boston, 1980–) *11,783 performances
Les Misérables (London, 1985–) *9,934 performances
The Mousetrap (Toronto, 1977–2004) over 9,600 performances
The Drunkard (Los Angeles, 1933–59) 9,477 performances
Shear Madness (Washington, 1987–) *8,930 performances
Cats (London, 1981–2002) 8,949 performances
The Phantom of the Opera (London, 1986–) *8,900 performances
Perfect Crime (New York, 1987–) 8,506 performances
The Phantom of the Opera (New York, 1988–) *8,355 performances
Tubes (New York, 1991–2005) 8,006 performances
Cats (New York, 1982–2000) 7,485 performances
Shear Madness (Chicago, 1982–2007) 7,697 performances

* Still running, total as of March 1, 2008

Longest play

Neil Oram's *The Warp* was first performed at the ICA (Institute of Contemporary Art) in London, U.K. from January 18–20, 1979. It lasted 18 hours and 5 minutes.

Short runs

A play is expensive to stage, so everyone involved hopes that it will run for long enough to earn back the money spent on it. Shows that run for years earn back their initial investment many times over, but some fail on their first night—or even earlier!

- On December 18, 1816, the one and only performance of J.R. Ronden's *The Play Without an A* took place at the Paris Théâtre des Variétés. It was written with words without the letter "a," which made it very hard to perform and understand. The audience rioted and did not allow the play to finish.
- In 1888, at London, England's Shaftesbury Theatre, *The Lady of Lyons* failed to make its first night when the safety curtain jammed.
- The *Intimate Revue* opened and closed at the Duchess Theatre, London, on March 11, 1930. It was a disaster from start to finish. The scenery changes took so long that seven scenes were abandoned to allow the long-suffering audience to go home before midnight.
- *Little Johnny Jones*, a musical starring Donny Osmond, opened and closed at the Alvin Theater, New York, on March 21, 1982.
- *Carrie* closed in New York on May 17, 1988, after struggling through five performances. It is said to have cost the Royal Shakespeare Company, who performed it, $7 million.

Oberammergau

Oberammergau is a town in Bavaria, Germany, where a Passion play (a play dealing with the crucifixion of Christ) is performed. The first play was put on in 1634 after an outbreak of plague in the town. The people vowed to repeat the play every 10 years from then on. More than 2,000 people take part in the play, nearly all of them from Oberammergau, and the performance lasts six hours.

Scene from the Singapore production of *Les Misérables*

library.thinkquest.org/5291/ search

John Travolta in *Saturday Night Fever*, 1977

Highest-earning dance films

The most successful dance film of all time is *Saturday Night Fever*. It starred John Travolta as a talented disco dancer and has earned nearly $300 million around the world. Below are some of the other highest-earning dance films in the world.

1 *Saturday Night Fever* (1977)	$285.4 million
2 *The Full Monty* (1997)	$257.9 m.
3 *Dirty Dancing* (1987)	$214.0 m.
4 *Shall We Dance* (2004)	$170.1 m.
5 *Save the Last Dance* (2001)	$131.7 m.
6 *Staying Alive* (1983)	$127.6 m.
7 *Step Up* (2006)	$114.2 m.
8 *Coyote Ugly* (2000)	$113.9 m.
9 *Billy Elliot* (2000)	$109.3 m.
10 *Flashdance* (1983)	$94.9 m.

Girl breakdancing

Dance spectaculars

American choreographer Busby Berkeley (1895–1976) staged the most spectacular dance films ever made. He used his knowledge of organizing military parades during World War I to create dance numbers with casts of hundreds.

They were often photographed from cranes high above them, on huge sets and sometimes with giant mirrors so that they formed geometrical patterns apparently vanishing into infinity. His films included *42nd Street* (1933) and *Gold Diggers of 1933* (1933), which was hit by an earthquake during filming in Los Angeles. The quake cut all power and nearly collapsed the set.

Breakdancing

Breakdancing began in New York in the late 1970s and early 1980s. Some of its movements came from martial arts such as kung fu and from gymnastics. It became a feature of hip-hop culture.

Popular dances

Barn dances
These developed from traditional Scottish dancing. They were popular in the U.S. in the 1890s when they were held to celebrate the building of a barn on a farm. Barn dances are still held today in country areas.

Belly dance
The popular name of a style of dance that originated in the Middle East, especially Egypt. It was originally danced only by women, and men were not permitted to watch. A British woman named Eileen Foucher set a belly dance record. She danced for 106 hours, from July 30, to August 3, 1984.

The Charleston
The Charleston was named after the city in South Carolina, and was one of the most popular dances of the 1920s.

The conga
People dance the conga in a line, each dancer holding on to the person in front. The conga began in Latin American carnivals and spread to the U.S. in the 1930s. The Miami Super Conga was held on March 13, 1988. The conga line was made up of 119,986 people—only 14 short of 120,000.

The hula
The hip-swaying hula is danced by Polynesian islanders who settled in Hawaii. It was banned by Christian missionaries for a while, but became popular again in the late 19th century.

The limbo
This competitive dance comes from Trinidad. Dancers lean back to pass under a bar, which is placed lower and lower. The winner is the dancer who passes under the lowest bar. On March 2, 1991, American Dennis Walston, known as King Limbo, limboed under a bar 6 in. (15 cm) high.

Lindy Hop
The Lindy Hop was a version of the Charleston and another dance called the Breakaway. It was named after U.S. aviator Charles Lindbergh (nicknamed Lindy). In 1927 he became the first person to fly solo across the Atlantic.

Line dancing
Line dancing grew in popularity in the 1990s. Although often associated with Western or cowboy dances, it developed from various traditional dances in which people dance in lines.

The polka
The polka was originally a Czech peasant dance that developed in Bohemia in the 1830s. It became

Dance marathons

Dance marathons began in New York in 1923, when Alma Cummings won a contest by dancing for 27 hours with six different partners. Marathons were popular during the Depression years of the 1930s, when unemployed people danced nonstop for many days to win money.

See also
Film Winners: pages 268–69

The last couple standing won. Dancers were allowed only very short breaks and partners pinched and kicked each other to stay awake or tied themselves together to prevent one from falling down. Dance marathons were banned in many places because they were so dangerous for people's health.

Mike Ritof and Edith Boudreaux danced from August 29, 1930, to April 1, 1931, at the Merry Garden Ballroom, Chicago, Illinois, to win a prize of $2,000. They danced for a total of 5,154 hours, 28 minutes, 30 seconds (215 days) with only short rest breaks.

Dance dummy

In 1921 Sidney E. Feist of Brooklyn, New York, patented a female dummy to help men practice their ballroom dancing steps. The dummy partner had a telescopic leg with a rotating wooden ball at the end so that she could be wheeled around the floor.

popular in Paris in the 1840s and eventually spread worldwide.

The twist
The twist started when Hank Ballard recorded the song of this name in 1959. It became popular when Chubby Checker performed his cover version on U.S. television on October 22, 1961. A woman called Ra Denny holds the twist record. She twisted for 100 hours at Christchurch, New Zealand, in March 1962.

The waltz
The waltz began in Austria in the late 18th century. Its name comes from a German word meaning to revolve. Many people were shocked by the dance when it first came to England in 1812 because it involved men and women dancing close to each other.

Flamenco dancing

Flamenco is popular in Andalusia, Spain, and comes from Moorish and gypsy dancing. It is lively and exciting; the dancers usually play castanets and are accompanied by guitars, clapping and drumming.

www.streetswing.com/histmain.htm search

Best-known ballets

Ballet	Composer	Choreographer	First performed
La Bayadère	Minkus	Petipa	1877
Cinderella	Prokofiev	Ashton	1948
Coppélia	Delibes	Saint-Léon	1870
The Firebird	Stravinsky	Fokine	1910
Giselle	Adam	Perrot/Coralli	1841
The Nutcracker	Tchaikovsky	Ivanov	1892
Romeo and Juliet	Prokofiev	Lavrovsky	1940
The Sleeping Beauty	Tchaikovsky	Petipa	1890
Swan Lake	Tchaikovsky	Petipa	1895
La Sylphide	Schneitzhoeffer	F. Taglioni	1832
Les Sylphides	Chopin	Fokine	1909

Best-known ballet companies

Alvin Ailey American Dance Theater (New York), founded 1958
American Ballet Theater (New York), founded 1940
Australian Ballet (Melbourne, Australia), founded 1962
Ballet Rambert (London, U.K.), founded 1926
Ballets Russes* (Moscow, Russia), founded 1909
Bolshoi Ballet (Moscow, Russia), founded 1776
Dance Theater of Harlem (New York), founded 1961
English National Ballet (London, U.K.), founded 1950
Kirov/Marlinsky Ballet (St. Petersburg, Russia), founded 1935
Martha Graham Dance Company (New York), founded 1927
Merce Cunningham Dance Company (New York), founded 1953
National Ballet of Canada (Toronto, Canada), founded 1951
New York City Ballet (New York), founded 1948
Paris Opéra Company (Paris, France), founded 1669
Royal Ballet (London, U.K.), founded 1936
Royal Danish Ballet (Copenhagen, Denmark), founded 1748

* not in existence today

Ballet terms

arabesque
Position in which the dancer stands on one leg, with arms extended, the body bent forward and the other leg stretched back

ballerina
A female ballet dancer

barre
The bar dancers hold on to while they practice, to help them balance

choreographer
The person who works out the steps and movements in a ballet

corps de ballet
Chorus of dancers (not those dancing solo)

entrechat
Rapid crossing and uncrossing of the feet during a jump

fouetté
A turn in which one leg is whipped round

glissade
A gliding movement

jeté
A jump from one foot to the other

pas
A dance step

pas de deux
A dance for two (usually the principal male and female dancers in the company)

pas seule
A solo dance

pirouette
A complete turn on one leg

plié
A knee-bending movement

pointes
On the tips of the toes. Dancers wear special point shoes with blocks in the toes to help them stand on their toes

positions
A range of five positions that are the basis of ballet dancing

prima ballerina
The leading ballerina in a company

tutu
The stiff skirt worn by ballerinas performing classical ballet

Sleeping Beauty by the Royal Ballet

See also
Famous last words: page 304

Darcey Bussell dancing with Igor Zelensky

Ballet firsts and records

First ballet
In the late 16th century, performances that included dancing, music and acting were given at the French court of Henri II and Catherine de Médici. The ballet *Comique de La Reine* (1581) was the first recorded.

First professional ballerina
On January 21, 1681, Mademoiselle de La Fontaine appeared in Jean Baptiste Lully's *The Triumph of Love* at the Paris Opéra.

First ballet in the U.S.
On February 7, 1827, Francisquy Hutin performed a ballet in the play *The Deserter* at the Bowery Theatre, New York. The women in the audience were so shocked by it that they fled from the theater.

Most curtain calls for a ballet performance
In October 1964 Margot Fonteyn and Rudolf Nureyev received 89 curtain calls after their performance in *Swan Lake* at the Staatsoper, in Vienna, Austria.

Most pirouettes
Delia Gray (15) performed 166 consecutive turns at The Playhouse, Harlow, Essex, U.K., on June 2, 1991.

First tutu and first on points

Ballerina Maria Taglioni (1804–84) wore a muslin dress known as a tutu when she danced in *La Sylphide* at the Paris Opéra on March 12, 1832. The dress allowed more freedom of movement so became popular in classical ballet. In the same ballet she danced on points without support — the first time any dancer had done so.

Famous ballet dancers

Carlos Acosta (Cuban, 1973–) Trained in Cuba and became a principal dancer with the Royal Ballet in London, U.K.. He has also staged his own show.

George Balanchine (Georgian-American, 1904–83) Dancer and choreographer with the New York City Ballet and other major companies.

Mikhail Baryshnikov (Russian, 1948–) One of the greatest male dancers. He began with the Kirov in Russia but later joined the American Ballet Theater.

Darcey Bussell (British, 1969–) Became a principal dancer with the Royal Ballet at the age of 20. She is one of their most popular soloists, and in 1995 she was awarded an OBE for her work in dance. She retired in 2006.

Sir Anton Dolin (British, 1904–83) Originally danced with Diaghilev's Ballets Russes. He founded the London Festival Ballet (now English National Ballet).

Sir Anthony Dowell (British, 1943–) He was principal dancer with the Royal Ballet for many years and was Director of the Royal Ballet for 15 years from 1986.

Dame Margot Fonteyn (British, 1919–91) Royal Ballet prima ballerina, she is most famous for her long-term partnership with Rudolf Nureyev.

Dame Beryl Grey (British, 1927–) Prima ballerina at the Sadler's Wells Ballet, London, U.K. and the first English ballerina to perform with the Bolshoi.

Sylvie Guillem (French, 1965–) Principal guest artist with the Royal Ballet, she is a versatile and athletic dancer, famous for her extraordinarily high leg extensions.

Karen Kain (Canadian, 1951–) Principal dancer with the National Ballet of Canada and later its artistic director.

Dame Alicia Markova (British, 1910–2004) She danced with Anton Dolin and they are most famous for their *Giselle*. Dolin and Markova formed a ballet company.

Rudolf Nureyev (Russian, 1938–93) Former Kirov star who defected to the West and became the most popular male dancer of his generation.

Anna Pavlova (Russian, 1881–1931) Became the most famous ballerina of her generation through her world tours.

Dame Marie Rambert (Polish/British, 1888–1982) Dancer and teacher whose dance company promoted many new works.

Maria Taglioni (Swedish/Italian, 1804–84) One of the first ballet stars, famous for her role in *La Sylphide*.

Vaslav Nijinsky

(Russian, 1890–1950) One of most famous of all male dancers. He was a leading dancer with the Ballets Russes and best known for his performance in Stravinsky's *Rite of Spring*.

www.national.ballet.ca search

Mutt

Film, TV & Radio

264 FILM FACTS
266 BLOCKBUSTERS
268 FILM WINNERS
270 ANIMATED FILMS
272 THE STARS
274 TV AND RADIO

Indiana's back!

Eighteen years after the "Last Crusade" came the realease of a fourth film in the Indiana Jones series. Harrison Ford was 65 years old when *Indiana Jones and the Kingdom of the Crystal Skull* was released. He first played the part in 1981. The first three films have earned more than $1.2 billion worldwide.

Poster advertising the Indian film *Ek Kali Muskai* (1968)

Top cinema-goers

1 India 3,997,000,000
2 U.S. 1,448,500,000
3 France 188,700,000
4 China 176,200,000
5 Mexico 165,500,000
6 Japan 164,300,000
7 S. Korea 163,900,000
8 U.K. 156,600,000
9 Germany 136,700,000
10 Spain 121,700,000

Top feature film producing countries

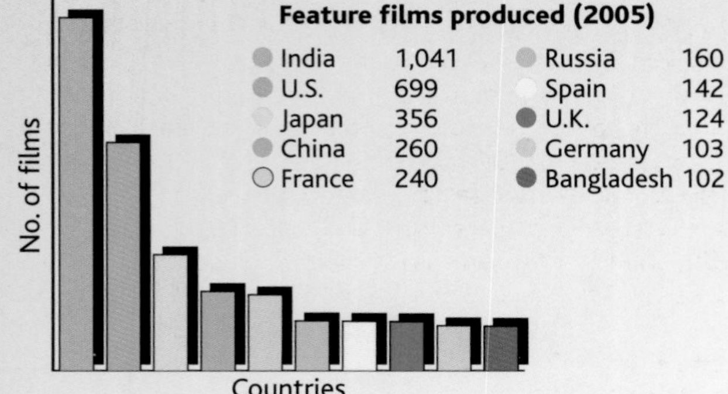

Casts of thousands

About 200,000 of the extras in *Gandhi* were volunteers, but another 94,560 were paid a small fee. They appeared in the scene showing Gandhi's funeral, which lasted just 2 minutes and 5 seconds after editing.

In *Around the World in 80 Days* (1956), there were animal extras too — 3,800 sheep, 2,448 buffalos, 950 donkeys, 800 horses, 512 monkeys, 17 bulls, 15 elephants, 6 skunks and 4 ostriches. In recent films, such as the *Lord of the Rings* trilogy, scenes with thousands of people were computer-generated, so huge numbers of extras were not needed.

Film	Extras
Gandhi (U.K., 1982)	294,560
Kolberg (Germany, 1945)	187,000
Monster Wangmagwi (South Korea, 1967)	157,000
War and Peace (USSR, 1968)	120,000
Ilya Muromets (*The Sword and the Dragon*) (USSR, 1956)	106,000
Dun-Huang (Ton ko) (Japan, 1988)	100,000
Razboiul Independentei (*The War of Independence*) (Romania, 1912)	80,000
Around the World in 80 Days (U.S., 1956)	68,894
Intolerance (U.S., 1916)	60,000
Dny Zrady (*Days of Betrayal*) (Czechoslovakia, 1973)	60,000

Who does what in a film?

Director The director controls everything, gives orders to the cast and crew and makes sure that the script is followed.

Producer(s) There can be more than one producer, who is responsible for raising the money to make the film and for other important activities, such as casting and controlling the costs.

Cast The actors and actresses who appear in the film.

Screenplay writer The person who writes the script. This gives the actors and actresses their lines and explains how the action takes place.

Extras The people who appear in crowd scenes but do not have speaking parts.

Animatronic engineer The person who makes the robotic creatures used in science-fiction and fantasy films.

Art director The art director coordinates the costumes, sets and makeup to set the overall style of the film.

Best boy The deputy electrician, assistant to the gaffer.

Casting director The person who chooses the actors for each role in the film.

Caterer The caterer supplies meals so that the cast and crew can work all day.

Cinematographer The person who directs the lighting and films the action, originally called the cameraman.

Clapper loader Details of each scene are written on a special board called a clapper board. The clapper loader snaps it shut in front of the camera as filming begins to record what is being filmed.

Film budgets

The production budgets of a film include the salaries paid to the director, writer(s), stars and crew, the designing and building of sets, costumes, the transport and location costs (filming away from the studio) and the cost of making and editing the film. Other costs include P & A (Prints and Advertising) — making thousands of copies of the film, distributing them to theaters, and advertising the film in the press, on television and on the Internet.

An average Hollywood feature film takes eight weeks to film. It may cost $5 million or more a week, depending on how lavish the production is and how expensive the stars are. *Titanic* (1997) held the record for largest production budget ($200 million) until it was equaled by *Spider-Man 2* (2004), then broken by *King Kong* (2005) at $207 million. It has since been overtaken by *Superman Returns* (2006) at $270 million and *Spider-Man 3* (2007) at $258 million.

Most movie screens

Country	Estimated number of screens (2006)
1 U.S.	38,415
2 China	37,753
3 India	11,183
4 France	5,632
5 Germany	4,848
6 Spain	4,299
7 Italy	3,987
8 Mexico	3,762
9 U.K.	3,569
10 Canada	2,986

Costs and income of a typical big-budget Hollywood film, *Spider-Man 2* (2004)

COSTS

Estimated cost ($U.S. million)	
Actors	
Toby Maguire	17
Kirsten Dunst	7
Alfred Molina	3
Rest of cast	3
Director (Sam Raimi)	10
Story rights	20
Screenplay	10
Producers	15
Production costs	45
Special effects	65
Music	5
Total production budget	**200**
Prints and advertising	75
Income	
U.S. box office	374
Rest of world	410
Home video/DVD sales and rentals	58.5
TV broadcast rights	15.0
Total	**784**
Profit	**509**

Video and DVD sales and rentals and TV broadcast rights would also add to the total income

La Géode cinema stands in the Parc de la Villette, Paris, France. Inside the enormous dome is a giant screen measuring 10,765 sq. ft. (1,000 sq m).

Composer The composer writes the music or adapts an existing score as a backing track for the film.

Costume designer The costume designer is responsible for designing and supplying the clothing worn by the cast.

Editor The editor cuts and connects the best versions of each section of film to create the final version.

Gaffer The chief electrician, who is responsible for lighting the set. The word may come from slang for grandfather — a senior person respected by everyone. Gaffer tape is the heavy-duty tape used on sets to secure cables and almost anything else.

Key grip A grip is responsible for moving the sets and for laying the tracks on which the camera runs. The key grip is in charge of all the other grips.

Makeup artist He or she applies the cosmetics that alter or improve an actor's looks under the studio lights.

Sound engineer This engineer makes sure that the dialogue and other sounds heard on the film are properly recorded and synchronized with the action.

Special-effects coordinator This person is responsible for creating spectacular scenes with photographic, mechanical and computer methods.

Stunt man/woman A specialist who performs the actions that are too difficult or dangerous for an actor. Stunt doubles are stunt men or women made up to look like the actors so it looks as though the actors have performed a feat themselves.

Wardrobe The wardrobe mistress or master is in charge of the costumes, making sure they fit, are in good condition and available when they are needed for a scene.

R2D2 and C3PO, robots from the *Star Wars* films

Top documentary films

Documentary films present true factual situations and real people, instead of stories acted out by film stars.

These include the exploration of the world and space, and actual events filmed as they happen. Some of the most successful documentaries are IMAX (large format) films that have earned steadily over several years, unlike feature films, which have more limited runs.

Film	Subject	World total ($U.S. million)
*Grand Canyon: The Hidden Secrets** (1984)	Exploration	239.0
Fahrenheit 9/11 (2004)	War on terrorism	222.4
*The Dream is Alive** (1985)	Space Shuttle	200.0
*Everest** (1998)	Exploration	134.0
March of the Penguins (2005)	Nature	128.0
*To Fly** (1976)	History of flying	120.7
Mysteries of Egypt (1998)	Historical	102.6
T-Rex: Back to the Cretaceous (1998)	Dinosaurs	97.0
*Space Station 3D** (2002)	International Space Station	96.3
Jackass: Number Two (2006)	Comedy stunts	84.6
Jackass: The Movie (2002)	Comedy stunts	79.5
*Blue Planet** (1990)	Earth from Space	71.9

*IMAX film

Highest earning films

These films have made the most money at the box office.

Film	World total ($U.S. million)
Titanic (1997)	1,845.0
The Lord of the Rings: The Return of the King (2003)	1,129.2
Pirates of the Caribbean: Dead Man's Chest (2006)	1,065.7
Harry Potter and the Sorcerer's Stone (2001)	985.8
Pirates of the Caribbean: At World's End (2007)	961.0
Harry Potter and the Order of the Phoenix (2007)	938.5
Lord of the Rings: The Two Towers (2002)	926.3
Star Wars: Episode I — The Phantom Menace (1999)	924.3
Shrek 2 (2004)*	920.7
Jurassic Park (1993)	914.7
Harry Potter and the Goblet of Fire (2005)	896.0
Spider-Man 3 (2007)	890.9
Harry Potter and the Chamber of Secrets (2002)	879.0
The Lord of the Rings: The Fellowship of the Ring (2001)	871.4
*Finding Nemo** (2003)	864.6
Star Wars: Episode III — Revenge of the Sith (2005)	850.0
Spider-Man (2002)	821.7
Independence Day (1996)	817.0
Star Wars: Episode IV — A New Hope (1977)	797.9
Shrek the Third (2007)	797.8
Harry Potter and the Prisoner of Azkaban (2004)	795.5
E.T. the Extra-Terrestrial (1982)	792.9
Harry Potter and the Prisoner of Azkaban (2004)	789.8
Spider-Man 2 (2004)	784.0
*The Lion King** (1994)	783.8
Star Wars: Episode IV — A New Hope (1977)	775.4
The Da Vinci Code (2006)	758.2
Spider-Man 3 (2007)	751.2
The Chronicles of Narnia: The Lion, The Witch and The Wardrobe (2005)	744.8
The Matrix Reloaded (2003)	738.6
Transformers (2007)	706.5
Forrest Gump (1994)	677.4
The Sixth Sense (1999)	672.8
Pirates of the Caribbean: The Curse of the Black Pearl (2003)	654.3
*Ice Age: The Meltdown** (2006)	651.6
Star Wars: Episode II – Attack of the Clones (2002)	649.4
*The Incredibles** (2004)	631.4
Ratatouille (2007)	620.6

* animated film

Computer games and films

Computer games are big business and a number of recent blockbuster films have been based on some of the most popular games.

These include *Lara Croft: Tomb Raider* (game 1996, film 2001), *Mortal Kombat* (game 1992, film 1995) and *Super Mario Bros* (game 1985, film 1993).

The link between films and games also works the other way, with games based on live-action and animated films — for example, *The Incredibles* (film and game 2004) and *The Lord of the Rings: Battle for Middle Earth* (2004) — a game based on *The Lord of the Rings* trilogy (2001–2003).

James Bond films

Including the latest, *Quantum of Solace*, Ian Fleming's 12 James Bond books have been made into 22 official and two unofficial films. The unofficial ones were the original *Casino Royale* (1967), a comedy featuring David Niven as the retired spy Sir James Bond, and *Never Say Never Again* (1983), which was a remake of *Thunderball* (1965).

Film	Bond actor	World total ($U.S. million)
Quantum of Solace (not yet released)	Daniel Craig	
Casino Royale (2006)	Daniel Craig	594.2
Die Another Day (2002)	Pierce Brosnan	456.0
The World is Not Enough (1999)	Pierce Brosnan	390.0
GoldenEye (1995)	Pierce Brosnan	350.7
Tomorrow Never Dies (1997)	Pierce Brosnan	339.3
Moonraker (1979)	Roger Moore	202.7
For Your Eyes Only (1981)	Roger Moore	195.3
The Living Daylights (1987)	Timothy Dalton	191.2
The Spy Who Loved Me (1977)	Roger Moore	185.4
Octopussy (1983)	Roger Moore	183.7
Licence to Kill (1989)	Timothy Dalton	156.2
A View to a Kill (1985)	Roger Moore	152.4
Thunderball (1965)	Sean Connery	141.2
Live and Let Die (1973)	Roger Moore	126.4
Goldfinger (1964)	Sean Connery	124.9
Diamonds Are Forever (1971)	Sean Connery	116.0
You Only Live Twice (1967)	Sean Connery	111.6
The Man with the Golden Gun (1974)	Roger Moore	97.6
From Russia with Love (1963)	Sean Connery	78.9
On Her Majesty's Secret Service (1969)	George Lazenby	64.6
Dr. No (1963)	Sean Connery	59.7

Daniel Craig as James Bond in the remake of *Casino Royale*

Unofficial Bond films

Released in 2008, the 22nd official James Bond film takes its title from a short story in a collection by Bond creator, Ian Fleming, *For Your Eyes Only* (1960). The film's events follow on from *Casino Royale* (2006) in which David Craig first starred as Bond.

George Clooney as Batman

See also
All about comics: page 236

Top films based on comic books

Comic book characters have been popular subjects for filmmakers ever since the 1930s. The characters are already familiar, so are immediately appealing to audiences. The exploits of superheroes such as Superman and Batman are perfect for exciting action films, many of which have been hugely successful.

Film	Film released	Comic first published	World total ($U.S. million)
Spider-Man 3	(2007)	1962	890.9
Spider-Man	(2002)	1962	821.7
Spider-Man 2	(2004)	1962	784.0
Men in Black	(1997)	1990	589.4
X-Men: The Last Stand	(2006)	1963	459.3
300	(2007)	1998	456.1
Men in Black II	(2002)	1990	441.8
Batman	(1989)	1939	413.4
X2: X-Men United	(2003)	1963	407.6
Superman Returns	(2006)	1938	391.1
Batman Begins	(2005)	1939	371.9
The Mask	(1994)	1991	351.6

The American Film Institute's top films

The American Film Institute has listed greatest films in a number of categories, based on the views of a panel of 1,500 film experts.

Funniest films

1 *Some Like It Hot* (1959)
2 *Tootsie* (1982)
3 *Dr. Strangelove, or: How I Learned to Stop Worrying and Love the Bomb* (1964)
4 *Annie Hall* (1977)
5 *Duck Soup* (1933)
6 *Blazing Saddles* (1974)
7 *M*A*S*H* (1970)
8 *It Happened One Night* (1934)
9 *The Graduate* (1967)
10 *Airplane!* (1980)

Love stories

1 *Casablanca* (1942)
2 *Gone With the Wind* (1939)
3 *West Side Story* (1961)
4 *Roman Holiday* (1953)
5 *An Affair to Remember* (1957)
6 *The Way We Were* (1973)
7 *Doctor Zhivago* (1965)
8 *It's a Wonderful Life* (1946)
9 *Love Story* (1970)
10 *City Lights* (1931)

Thrillers

1 *Psycho* (1960)
2 *Jaws* (1975)
3 *The Exorcist* (1973)
4 *North by Northwest* (1959)
5 *The Silence of the Lambs* (1991)
6 *Alien* (1979)
7 *The Birds* (1963)
8 *The French Connection* (1971)
9 *Rosemary's Baby* (1968)
10 *Raiders of the Lost Ark* (1981)

Greatest American movies of all time

1 *Citizen Kane* (1941)
2 *Casablanca* (1942)
3 *The Godfather* (1972)
4 *Gone with the Wind* (1939)
5 *Lawrence of Arabia* (1962)
6 *The Wizard of Oz* (1939)
7 *The Graduate* (1967)
8 *On the Waterfront* (1954)
9 *Schindler's List* (1993)
10 *Singin' in the Rain* (1952)

Orson Welles in *Citizen Kane*

The Oscars

What is an Oscar?

The Academy Awards or "Oscars" have been presented since 1929. The award is a gold-plated statuette made of tin, copper and antimony. It is 13.5 in. (343 cm) high and weighs 8.4 lb. (3.8 kg). Winning an Oscar is important because it encourages more people to see the film and helps the individual winners' careers.

Why is it called an Oscar?

According to legend, Academy librarian Margaret Herrick named it when she declared that the statuette looked like her Uncle Oscar!

Who decides who wins?

Members of the U.S. Academy of Motion Picture Arts & Science members, including previous nominees and winners, vote to create a shortlist of five nominees in each of 24 categories, other than special, honorary and technical awards.

Who can win an Oscar?

The main categories are Best Picture, Best Director, Best Actor, Best Actress, Best Supporting Actor and Best Supporting Actress. There are other awards, e.g., screenplay, cinematography, soundtrack, documentary, animated feature, foreign film.

Oscar winners

These are the Best Picture, Best Actor and Best Actress winners for the last 25 years. The date given is the date of release. Oscars are awarded the following year.

Year	Best Picture	Best Actor	Best Actress
2007	*No Country For Old Men*	Daniel Day-Lewis	Marion Cotillard
2006	*The Departed*	Forest Whitaker	Helen Mirren
2005	*Crash*	Philip Seymour Hoffman	Reese Witherspoon
2004	*Million Dollar Baby*	Jamie Foxx	Hilary Swank
2003	*The Lord of the Rings: The Return of the King*	Sean Penn	Charlize Theron
2002	*Chicago*	Adrien Brody	Nicole Kidman
2001	*A Beautiful Mind*	Denzel Washington	Halle Berry
2000	*Gladiator*	Russell Crowe	Julia Roberts
1999	*American Beauty*	Kevin Spacey	Hilary Swank
1998	*Shakespeare in Love*	Roberto Benigni	Gwyneth Paltrow
1997	*Titanic*	Jack Nicholson	Helen Hunt
1996	*The English Patient*	Geoffrey Rush	Frances McDormand
1995	*Braveheart*	Nicholas Cage	Susan Sarandon
1994	*Forrest Gump*	Tom Hanks	Jessica Lange
1993	*Schindler's List*	Tom Hanks	Holly Hunter
1992	*Unforgiven*	Al Pacino	Emma Thompson
1991	*The Silence of the Lambs*	Anthony Hopkins	Jodie Foster
1990	*Dances With Wolves*	Jeremy Irons	Kathy Bates
1989	*Driving Miss Daisy*	Daniel Day-Lewis	Jessica Tandy
1988	*Rain Man*	Dustin Hoffman	Jodie Foster
1987	*The Last Emperor*	Michael Douglas	Cher
1986	*Platoon*	Paul Newman	Marlee Martin
1985	*Out of Africa*	William Hurt	Geraldine Page
1984	*Amadeus*	F. Murray Abraham	Sally Field
1983	*Terms of Endearment*	Robert Duvall	Shirley MacLaine
1982	*Gandhi*	Ben Kingsley	Meryl Streep

AFI's top 10 film songs

Song	Film
1 "Over the Rainbow"	*The Wizard of Oz* (1939)
2 "As Time Goes By"	*Casablanca* (1942)
3 "Singin' in the Rain"	*Singin' in the Rain* (1952)
4 "Moon River"	*Breakfast at Tiffany's* (1961)
5 "White Christmas"	*Holiday Inn* (1942)
6 "Mrs. Robinson"	*The Graduate* (1967)
7 "When You Wish Upon a Star"	*Pinocchio* (1940)
8 "The Way We Were"	*The Way We Were* (1973)
9 "Stayin' Alive"	*Saturday Night Fever* (1977)
10 "The Sound of Music"	*The Sound Of Music* (1965)

See also

Awards: page 155

Highest paid actress

Julia Roberts earned a record $25 million for *Mona Lisa Smile* (2003). These are the highest paid actresses per film in 2007.

	Pay per film $U.S. million
Reese Witherspoon	15–20
Angelina Jolie	15–20
Cameron Diaz	15+
Sandra Bullock	10–15
Nicole Kidman	10–15
Julia Roberts	10–15
Renee Zellweger	10–15
Drew Barrymore	10–12
Jodie Foster	10–12
Halle Berry	10

Reese Witherspoon, Best Actress in 2005

Most wins

These three films have each won 11 Oscars, including Best Picture: *Ben-Hur* (1959), *Titanic* (1997) and *The Lord of the Rings: The Return of the King* (2003).

A no-win situation

The Turning Point (1977) and *The Color Purple* (1985) had 11 nominations each but neither of them won a single Oscar. *Gangs of New York* (2002) received 10 nominations, also without winning anything.

Long and short

Gone with the Wind (1939) was the longest film (238 minutes) and the first color film to win Best Picture. *Marty* (1955) was the shortest Best Picture winner at 91 minutes.

Black and white

Marty was also one of the last black and white films to win Best Picture. *The Apartment* (1960) and *Schindler's List* (1993) are the only black and white films to have won since.

First appearances

These are the films in which some of the most famous animated characters made their first appearances.

Mickey Mouse *Plane Crazy* (1928)

Plane Crazy was Walt Disney's first Mickey Mouse cartoon and was silent. Two months later Mickey appeared in Disney's *Steamboat Willie*, the first Mickey Mouse cartoon with sound. Mickey starred in *Fantasia* (1940), and his *Lend a Paw* won an Oscar in 1941.

Popeye *Popeye the Sailor with Betty Boop* (1933)

Popeye was born in 1929 as a newspaper comic strip by Elzie Crisler Segar. Animator Max Fleischer adapted it for the screen. Popeye cartoons were made for movies and TV until the 1980s, and the live-action *Popeye* film was released in 1980.

Donald Duck *The Wise Little Hen* (1934)

Clarence Nash was the voice of Donald Duck for 50 years. The Donald Duck anti-Hitler film *Der Fuehrer's Face* (1942) won an Oscar.

Bugs Bunny *Porky's Hare Hunt* (1938)

A Wild Hare (1940) was the first cartoon in which Bugs Bunny said "Eh, what's up, Doc?" but he was not named until *Elmer's Pet Rabbit* (1941). *Knighty-Knight Bugs* (1958) won an Oscar.

Tom and Jerry *Puss Gets the Boot* (1940)

The very first Tom and Jerry cartoon was nominated for an Oscar. The characters also appeared in the 1992 film *Tom and Jerry: The Movie*. This full-length film is the only one in which they speak.

Casper the Ghost *The Friendly Ghost* (1945)

Casper starred in more than 50 cartoons and in a part live action/part computer animated feature film in 1995, which earned nearly $300 million around the world.

The Flintstones *The Flintstone Flyer* (1960)

This was the first episode of *The Flintstones* to be broadcast on TV. It went on to become the longest running cartoon series until it was overtaken by *The Simpsons*. The live-action film *The Flintstones* (1994) was one of the top-earning films of the year.

Simpsons *Simpsons Roasting on an Open Fire* (1989)

Matt Groening's hugely successful animated series began in 1987 as short episodes screened on *The Tracey Ullman Show*. It was developed into longer weekly episodes and has become the longest running and most successful cartoon series ever.

Walt Disney's first animated features

Walt Disney (1901–66) produced short animated films, including Mickey Mouse cartoons, before making main features. *Snow White* was Hollywood's first full-length animated feature film and earned Disney an honorary Oscar. The film made $188 million in the U.S. alone.

Film	First released in cinemas
1 *Snow White and the Seven Dwarfs*	December 21, 1937
2 *Pinocchio*	February 7, 1940
3 *Fantasia*	November 12, 1940
4 *Dumbo*	October 23, 1941
5 *Bambi*	August 9, 1942

Walt Disney in his studio

A zoetrope — when the viewer spins the zoetrope and looks through a slit, the pictures inside appear to be moving.

Types of animation

The word animation comes from the Latin *animatus*, meaning filled with life. Even before the invention of cinema, people realized that if the human eye sees a series of images that change at a rate of at least 24 frames a second, the brain can be tricked into thinking it is seeing a live moving image. Nineteenth-century optical toys such as zoetropes worked on this principle.

Traditional animation
Individual frames of a story are hand drawn on cels — transparent sheets of plastic. They are then photographed as a sequence against painted backgrounds.

Cutout
In this type of animation, two-dimensional drawings are placed on a fixed background. These are moved and photographed to create the impression of movement.

CGI
CGI (Computer Generated Imagery) has been used since the 1970s, originally for short films. The 1989 film *The Abyss* used some CGI visual effects, but the hugely successful

A scene from *Ratatouille* (2007)

That's all folks

Mel Blanc was the voice of many famous cartoon characters, from Bugs Bunny to the *Flintstones'* Barney Rubble. The headstone on his grave in the Hollywood Forever Cemetery has the sign-off line used at the end of Looney Tunes cartoons: "That's All Folks."

Most expensive animated films

Making animated films has become more and more expensive. In 1937 *Snow White and the Seven Dwarfs* cost $1.49 million — a record-breaking sum at the time. *Tarzan* (1999) and *The Polar Express* (2004) are the costliest films ever made and were more than 100 times as expensive as *Snow White*.

Film	Year	Budget ($U.S. million)
The Polar Express	2004	170
Shrek the Third	2007	170
Shrek 2	2004	150
Bee Movie	2007	150
Ratatouille	2007	150
Tarzan	1999	145
Flushed Away	2006	143
Treasure Planet	2002	140

Toy Story (1995), from the Disney and Pixar Animation Studio, was the first CGI feature film. Another development known as 3D motion capture has been used in films such as *Beowulf* (2007), a $150 million budget film with Ray Winstone in the title role, in which the motions of live actors are converted into computer images.

Stop motion

This type of animation is created by moving three-dimensional figures and other objects a tiny amount between shots. This method has been used since 1925, but the best-known modern examples of this technique are the *Wallace & Gromit* films by Aardman Animation.

Scene from Wallace & Gromit: *The Curse of the Were-Rabbit* (2005)

Highest earning animated films

Shrek 2 (2004) – $U.S. 920.7 million
Finding Nemo (2003) – $U.S. 864.6 m.
Shrek the Third (2007) – $U.S. 797.8 m.
The Lion King (1994) – $U.S. 783.8 m.
Ice Age: The Meltdown (2006) – $U.S. 651.6 m.
The Incredibles (2004) – $U.S. 631.4 m.
Ratatouille (2007) – $U.S. 620.6 m.
Madagascar (2005) – $U.S. 532.7 m.
Monsters, Inc. (2001) – $U.S. 529.1 m.
The Simpsons Movie – $U.S. 526.5 m.
Aladdin (1992) – $U.S. 504.0 m.
Toy Story 2 (1999) – $U.S. 485.0 m.
Shrek (2001) – $U.S. 484.4 m.
Cars (2006) – $U.S. 462.0 m.
Tarzan (1999) – $U.S. 449.4 m.
Happy Feet (2006) – $U.S. 375.3 m.

Marlene Dietrich

Top 10 screen legends

This is the top 10 of the American Film Institute's list of the greatest American screen legends.

	Actor	Actress
1	Humphrey Bogart	Katharine Hepburn
2	Cary Grant	Bette Davis
3	James Stewart	Audrey Hepburn
4	Marlon Brando	Ingrid Bergman
5	Fred Astaire	Greta Garbo
6	Henry Fonda	Marilyn Monroe
7	Clark Gable	Elizabeth Taylor
8	James Cagney	Judy Garland
9	Spencer Tracy	Marlene Dietrich
10	Charlie Chaplin	Joan Crawford

Actors who have played Superman

Kirk Alyn (1910–99)
The Adventures of Superman (1948) and *Atom Man vs. Superman* (1950), both made as cinema serials

George Reeves (1914–59)
Superman and the Mole Men (1951) and the *Superman* TV series (1953–57)

Christopher Reeve (1952–2004)
Superman (1978), *Superman II* (1980), *Superman III* (1983) and *Superman IV: The Quest for Peace* (1987)

Brandon Routh (1979–)
Superman Returns (2006)

Dean Cain (1966–)
Lois & Clark: The New Adventures of Superman (TV series, 1993–97)

Tom Welling (1977–)
Smallville: Superman the Early Years TV series (2001–) about Superman as a teenager

...and Supergirl

Helen Slater (1963–)
Supergirl (1984)

Stars of the most $100 million-plus films

These are the stars who have appeared in the most films that have made more than $100 million at the US box office. A number of less well-known actors who have supplied their voices to animated films have made as many or even more high-earning films.

Johnny Depp

Star	$100 m. + films
Tom Hanks	17
Tom Cruise	15
Eddie Murphy	13
Jack Angel	12
Will Smith	11
Harrison Ford	11
Mel Gibson	11
Morgan Freeman	11
Robin Williams	11
Samuel L. Jackson	11

Top stars

Since the 1920s, theaters across the U.S. have nominated the top stars of the year according to the number of people who pay to watch their films. These are the top stars of 2006.

1 Johnny Depp
2 Will Smith
2 George Clooney
4 Matt Damon
5 Denzel Washington
6 Russell Crowe
7 Tom Cruise
8 Nicholas Cage
9 Will Ferrell
10 Tom Hanks

Movie monsters

Ever since movies began, filmmakers have played on everyone's fear of monsters. These are some of the most popular monster films.

Aliens
Hundreds of films have been made about alien monsters attacking Earth. The most successful of these was *Independence Day* (1996).

Dinosaurs
One of the first cartoons was *Gertie* (1914). It featured a drawing of a brontosaurus that comes to life. Dinosaur films *Jurassic Park* (1993) and its two sequels, *The Lost World: Jurassic Park* (1997) and *Jurassic Park III* (2001), are among the biggest blockbusters of all time.

Egyptian mummies
The Mummy (1932) featured an Egyptian mummy that comes to life and attacks people. *The Mummy* was remade in 1999 and its sequel, the comedy-adventure *The Mummy Returns* (2001), has made more than $433 million.

Frankenstein's monster
Frankenstein is the name of the creator of the monster, not the monster itself. The original story was written in 1816 by English writer Mary Shelley. It was first made into a silent film in 1910 by the inventor Thomas Edison and has been remade many times since. *Mary Shelley's Frankenstein* (1994) is the highest earning of all the versions.

Stage names

Actors and actresses choose stage names for a variety of reasons. Their real names may be the same as or similar to those of other people, or they may be difficult to spell or pronounce.

Here are some famous performers who decided to change their names.

Film name	Real name
Woody Allen	Allan Stewart Konigsberg
Jennifer Aniston	Jennifer Linn Anastassakis
Mel Brooks	Melvin Kaminsky
Nicolas Cage	Nicholas Kim Coppola
Michael Caine	Maurice Joseph Micklewhite
Jackie Chan	Chan Kong-sang
Tom Cruise	Thomas Cruise Mapother IV
Kirk Douglas	Issur Danielovitch Demsky
Whoopi Goldberg	Caryn Elaine Johnson
Cary Grant	Archibald Alexander Leach
Richard E. Grant	Richard Grant Esterhuysen
Goldie Hawn	Goldie Jean Studlendegehawn
Hulk Hogan	Terry Gene Bollea
Angelina Jolie	Angelina Jolie Voight
Ben Kingsley	Krishna Bhanji
Queen Latifah	Dana Elaine Owens
Jet Li	Li Lian Jie
Marilyn Monroe	Norma Jean Baker
Demi Moore	Demetria Gene Guynes
Natalie Portman	Natalie Hershlag
Winona Ryder	Winona Horowitz
Susan Sarandon	Susan Abigail Tomalin
Christian Slater	Christian Michael Leonard Hawkins
Sigourney Weaver	Susan Weaver

Poster for the original horror-adventure film *King Kong* (1933); the film has been remade twice, most recently in 2005

Funny monsters
Some of the most successful cartoon monsters are those in *Monsters, Inc.* (2001). The monsters are led by Sulley, whose secret is that the monsters are scared of children!

Killer creatures
Giant ape King Kong is one of the most famous animal monsters and the star of the film *King Kong* (1933, 1976 and 2005). Giant spiders have featured in films such as *Arachnophobia* (1990) and *Eight Legged Freaks* (2002). Harry Potter also meets an army of huge spiders in *Harry Potter and the Chamber of Secrets* (2002). Other famous killer creatures include sharks (*Jaws*, 1977), alligators (*Lake Placid*, 1999) and snakes (*Anaconda*, 1997 and *Snakes on a Plane*, 2006).

Vampires
Irish writer Bram Stoker's vampire novel *Dracula* was first published in 1897. Since then it has been made into countless films. The version starring Bela Lugosi (1931) is one of the most famous. *Bram Stoker's Dracula* (1992) and *Van Helsing* (2004) have been the most successful at the box office.

Zombies
Zombies are the "undead"—bodies that come out of their graves and terrorize the living. They have been the subject of many films, including *Night of the Living Dead* (1968) and the comedy *Shaun of the Dead* (2004). This was billed as the first "Rom-Com-Zom" (Romantic Comedy Zombie film).

See also
Mythical creatures: pages 170–71

www.afi.com search

Video and DVD fact file

- The terms video recording and videotape were first used in the early 1950s, but only among TV professionals.
- The abbreviation VCR (video cassette recorder) was first used in the U.S. in 1971.
- The first domestic video cassette recorders were sold in 1974, but were very expensive and few people bought them.
- The VHS (video home system) was launched in 1976 in the U.S.
- By 1980 about 7,687,000 homes had VCRs; by 1996 the global figure was put at 400,976,000.
- DVD (digital video disk or digital versatile disk) players and disks were launched in Japan and the U.S. in 1997.
- Worldwide, sales of DVDs overtook video sales in 2002.
- By 2006, 81.2 percent of U.S. households had DVD players compared with 79.2 percent with VCRs. On average, Americans rent DVDs twice a month. In 2006 High Definition DVD players and disks went on sale. These next-generation formats are able to store much more high-quality data.
- In 2007, most major film studios stopped releasing films on video. DVD became the most popular format and the first High Definition (HD) DVD and Blu-ray high-density optical discs go on sale.

TV-owning countries

Country	TVs per 1,000 people in 2006	Country	TVs per 1,000 people in 2006
Norway	1,552	Latvia	859
Bermuda	1,070	Japan	843
U.K.	1,101	Netherlands	761
Denmark	975	Australia	724
Romania	893	Canada	706
U.S.	882	Ireland	694

TV viewing

- In the average U.S. home, the TV is switched on for 7 hours, 40 minutes a day.
- U.S. children aged 2 to 17 watch an average of 19 hours, 40 minutes' TV every week. That is 1,023 hours a year compared with 900 hours a year in school.
- There are 2.55 people and 2.73 TVs in the average American home.
- The average American watches TV for 4 hours, 35 minutes a day.

A 1950s U.S. magazine advertisement for TVs

First countries to have television*

The British Broadcsting System's first broadcasts used Baird's mechanical television system. In this, spinning disks were used to scan images.

This was later dropped in favor of U.S. inventor Philo Taylor Farnsworth's electronic system. Electronic television did not rely on moving parts, was more reliable and gave a better picture.

Country	Year
U.K.	1936
U.S.	1939
USSR	1939
France	1948
Brazil	1950

* High-definition regular public broadcasting service

TV milestones 1930s 1940s

1922
October 18, BBC (British Broadcasting Company) founded

1929
First transmissions of Philo T. Farnsworth's electronic television system in the U.S. and Scottish inventor John Logie Baird's experimental mechanical TV system.

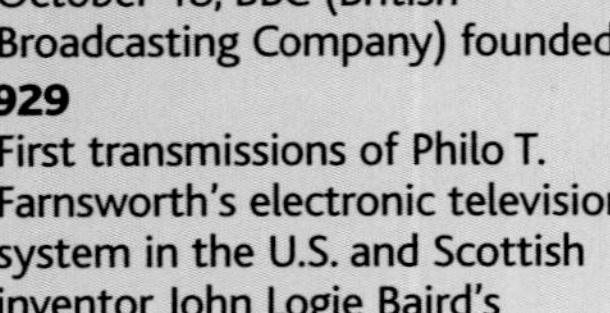

1938
May 31, first movie broadcast on U.S. TV, *The Return of the Scarlet Pimpernel*

1939
April 30, Franklin D. Roosevelt is the first president to appear on TV, opening the World's Fair in New York

May 17, first live sports event: Columbia vs. Princeton baseball game

June 10, the first king and queen on TV in the U.S. are King George VI and Queen Elizabeth, seen visiting the World's Fair

October 25, first live NFL game: Brooklyn Dodgers vs. Philadelphia Eagles

1940
February 25, first live hockey game broadcast: New York Rangers vs. Montreal Canadiens, from Madison Square Garden, New York

February 26, first TV quiz show, *Spelling Bee*

1941
July 1, the first ever TV commercial, for a Bulova clock, is broadcast by WNBT New York, during a game between the Brooklyn Dodgers and the Philadelphia Phillies

1947
February 21, the first American regular daytime serial, or soap opera, *A Woman to Remember*, begins its run

1948
July 29, Olympic Games in London England, are televised

One million U.S. homes have televisions

1949
January 17, first TV sitcom: *The Goldbergs*

1951
September 4, first coast-to-coast TV broadcast, from San Francisco to stations across the U.S., featuring an address by President Harry S. Truman

December 24, in the U.S. *Amahl and The Night Visitors* becomes

Radio milestones

1896
June 2, Italian inventor Guglielmo Marconi applies for first British "wireless" patent

1901
December 12, in St. John's, Newfoundland, Marconi receives the first transatlantic radio signal, broadcast from Cornwall, U.K.

1906
December 24, first radio program (music and speech) broadcast by Professor Reginald Fessenden from the U.S. coast and received by ships. The first radios were crystal sets, operated by adjusting metal wires known as cat's whiskers

1919
Canada's first broadcasting license issued to XWA (later CFCF), Montreal, Quebec

1920
Detroit, Michigan, station 8MK (now WWJ) makes the first regular radio broadcasts in the U.S.
June 15, Marconi broadcasts a concert by opera singer Dame Nellie Melba

1933
U.S. inventor Edwin H. Armstrong patents FM radio

1941
CBC (Canadian Broadcasting Company) News Service launched
U.S. Peabody Awards for radio broadcasting first presented

1945
Radio Canada International (CBC) begins regular international radio broadcasts

1970
February 24, National Public Radio launched in the U.S.

1971
May 3, *All Things Considered*, the longest-running program on National Public Radio (NPR), first broadcast

1977
National Association of Broadcasters establishes its Hall of Fame

1993
First Internet radio broadcasts

2005
December 1, Sirius satellite radio station launched in Canada

2007
U.S. has 4,789 AM and 8,961 FM stations; Canada has 245 AM and 582 FM stations; Internet radio becomes available to cell phones

Why soap opera?

Radio (and later TV) serials about everyday life in the U.S. have been sponsored by soap manufacturers since the 1930s. They advertised their products during the shows. The name of these serials has been shortened to soaps since 1943.

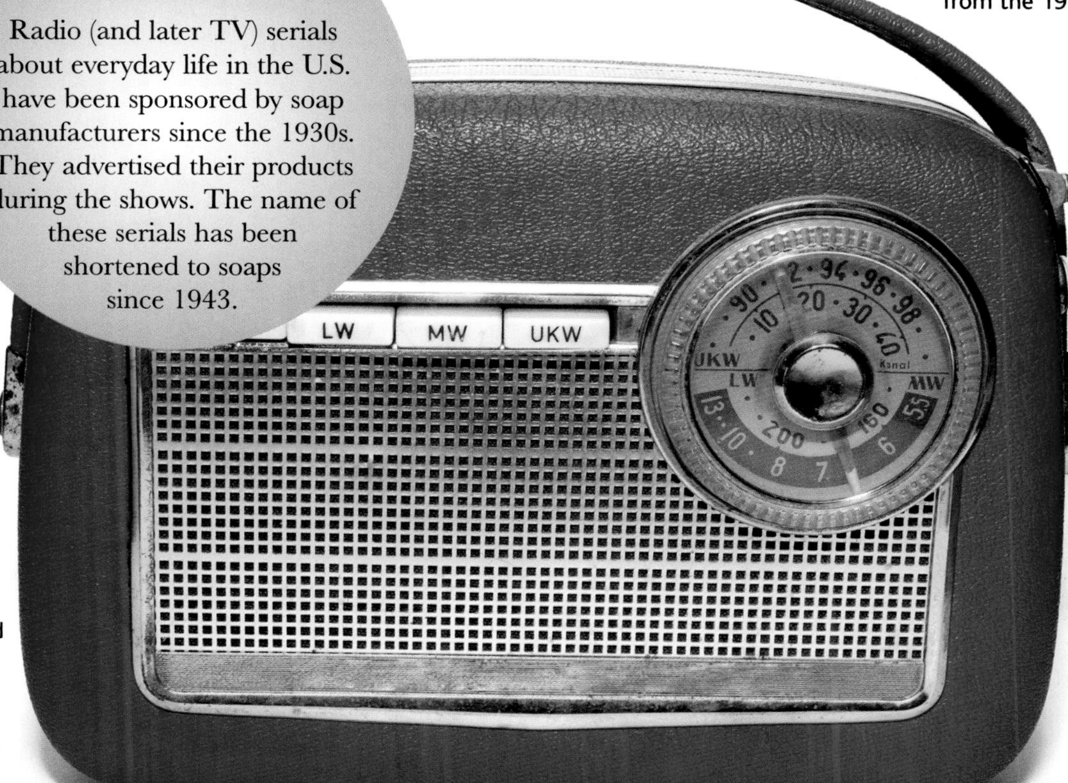

Portable radio from the 1950s

2000s

the world's first commercial color broadcast

1952
September 6, TV starts in Canada with opening of CBS, Montreal
October 11, Hockey Night in Canada first broadcast — the world's longest-running TV sports program

1953
June 2, the coronation of Queen Elizabeth II is watched live by about 200 million people worldwide

1954
January 1, the *Tournament of Roses* parade at Pasadena, California, becomes the first program ever broadcast coast-to-coast

1956
American inventor Robert Adler's Zenith Space Commander is the first TV remote control

1968
October 14, first live broadcast from an orbiting spacecraft: *Apollo 7*
First year in which color TV sets (5.8 million) outsell black and white (5.5 million) in the U.S.

1969
July 21, first live broadcasts from the Moon (*Apollo XI*) November 10, *Sesame Street* first broadcast

1979
Over 300 million TV sets in use worldwide

1981
August 1, MTV launched; The Buggles' *Video Killed the Radio Star* the first music video to be broadcast

1983
February 28, 105.9 million Americans watch the last episode of M*A*S*H

1996
More than 1 billion TV sets in use worldwide

2000
July 18, U.K. launch of *Big Brother* starts a fashion for reality TV that soon spreads to North America

2006
High Definition television (HDTV) becomes available

2007
The U.S. announces that all TV broadcasts will be digital only from 2009

2008
The 108-inch (274-cm) flat-screen liquid crystal display (LCD) TV, the world's largest, is launched by Sharp.

FIREFLY'S WORLD OF FACTS

Sports

278 SPORT FACTS

280 SPORTING EVENTS

282 THE OLYMPICS

284 ATHLETICS

286 BALL GAMES

288 FOOTBALL

290 RACQUET SPORTS

292 COMBAT, STRENGTH AND TARGET SPORTS

294 WATER SPORTS

296 WHEEL SPORTS

298 WINTER SPORTS

300 ANIMAL SPORTS

Track record

2008 was the year of the 50th Daytona 500, regarded by many as the most important race on the NASCAR calendar. Lee Petty won the golden anniversary of the race and the trophy was plated in gold instead of the usual silver.

Teams and competitors

Team sizes

These are the number of players allowed on a field at any one time. The full team can also include some substitutes. In football, for example, there are 45 full-time team members. Different players come on the field for defensive and offensive moves.

Sport	Team on pitch
Australian Rules football	18
Rugby Union	15
Rugby League	13
Canadian football, women's lacrosse	12
Football (American), cricket, field hockey, soccer, speedball (paint ball)	11
Men's lacrosse, slow-pitch softball	10
Baseball, fast-pitch softball	9
Tug-of-war	8
Team handball, netball, water polo	7
Ice hockey, volleyball	6
Basketball, roller hockey	5
Polo	4

Most competitors

- The Boston Marathon centenary race in 1996 attracted a record 38,706 competitors, the most ever for a marathon.
- The Athens Olympic Games (2004) had 11,099 competitors, the most of any Olympics.
- The world's biggest road race is the 7.5 mi. (12 km) Bay to Breakers race in San Francisco, California. It has been held every year since 1912. The 1988 race had a record 78,769 official entries, but the total number of people taking part was probably about 110,000, many of them in fancy dress.
- In 1929 the Grand National horse race had a record 66 runners, but only nine reached the finish line.

Most-watched sporting event

The 2000 Olympic Games in Sydney was the most-watched sporting event ever on television, with 3.7 billion viewers worldwide. A total of 1,159,249 tickets for watching the events live were sold.

Sporting sizes

	Dimensions and distances
Blade of an ice skate (width)	1.3 in. (3.3 cm)
Tenpin height	15 in. (38 cm)
Parallel bars in gymnastics (distance between)	16.5 in. (42 cm)
Dartboard diameter	17.7 in. (45 cm)
Basketball (diameter)	29.5–30.25 in. (34.9–76.8 cm)
Tennis net height (at center)	35.8 in. (91 cm)
Hurdles height (men's 400 m)	3 ft. (91.4 cm)
Water polo pool depth (minimum)	3.3 ft. (1 m)
Women's javelin length (minimum)	7.2 ft. (2.2 m)
Soccer goal height	8 ft. (2.44 m)
Men's javelin length (minimum)	8.5 ft. (2.6 m)
Basketball net rim (above floor)	10 ft. (3.05 m)
Table tennis table	5 x 9 ft. (1.5 x 2.7 m)
Snooker table (full size)	6.1 x 12 ft. (1.9 x 3.7 m)
Boxing ring	20 x 20 ft. (6.1 x 6.1 m)
Soccer goal width	24 ft. (7.32 m)
Basketball court (NBA)	50 x 94 ft. (15 x 29 m)
Hockey rink	85 x 200 ft. (26 x 61 m)
Football field (U.S.)	160 x 360 ft. (49 x 110 m)
Indianapolis Motor Speedway (oval track length)	2.5 mi. (4.023 km)
Marathon distance	26 mi., 385 yd. (42.2 km)
Longest hole in open golf (14th at St. Andrews)	1,853 ft. (565 m)
Iditarod dog sled race, Alaska	
north route (even-numbered years)	1,112 mi. (1,790 km)
south route (odd-numbered years)	1,131 mi. (1,820 km)
Le Mans 24 hour race (greatest distance covered in the time, 1971)	3,314.2 mi. (5,333.7 km)
Tour de France cycle race (record longest, 1926)	3,470 mi. (5,745 km)
Around alone (solo around-the-world yacht race)	28,754.6 mi. (46,276.7 km)

Marathon sprint!

If athletes could run a marathon at the same rate as a 100 m sprint, they would finish in 43 minutes. In reality, no one has run a marathon in under two hours.

Sport origins

Who invented baseball?

Baseball is a much older game than you might think. Medieval manuscripts show ball games with bats, while a game called "base-ball" appears in a picture published in London, England, in 1744. Baseball is also mentioned in Jane Austen's novel *Northanger Abbey*, which she began writing in 1798. The game of "rounders" was first described 30 years later, and this or a similar game was known among British settlers in the U.S. Abner Doubleday is sometimes said to have invented baseball in 1839, but Alexander Joy Cartwright Jr. wrote the game's rules in 1845. He founded the first team, the Knickerbocker Base Ball Club of New York.

When did basketball start?

The inspiration for basketball may have been the Aztec game *ollamalitzli* and other ball and hoop games played by South American peoples. The modern game was invented in 1891 by Canadian physical education teacher Dr. James A. Naismith at the International YMCA College at Springfield, Massachusetts. He wanted to find a game that could be played indoors during the winter. Peach baskets were originally used as goals — players had to climb a ladder to fetch the ball after scoring. Then someone hit on the idea of removing the bottom! The baskets were soon replaced by metal rings with netting.

Sport top speeds

Sport	mph	km/h
Competition rifle bullet	2,353	3,787
Longbow arrow	340	547
Drag racer (0.25 mi./0.4 km from standing start)	332	535
Freefall skydiver	330	531
Pelota (jai-alai) ball	188	302
Indy 500 racing car (record, 1990)	186	299
Golf ball (leaving tee)	170	273
Downhill skier (record)	154	248
Squash ball (record, 1988)	151	243
Tennis serve (record, 2004)	150	241
Racing car (Formula One)	148	238
Water skiing (record, 1983)	143	230
Snowboarding (record)	126	202
Ice hockey puck	118	190
Ski-bike (record, 1999)	115	185
Table tennis ball	106	170
Baseball (pitched)	101	162
Badminton shuttlecock	162	261
Luge	85	137
Frisbee	74	119
Cyclist (record)	65	105
Skateboard (record, 1998)	63	101
4-man bobsled	56	90
Racehorse	45	72
Greyhound	42	67
100-m sprinter	37	59
Boxing punch	35	56
Speed skating	34	50
Karate chop	32	51

Famous U.S. basketball player Michael Jordan about to score

Longest events

- In Formula One motor racing the 18-race (2008) season is spread over seven-and-a-half months.
- The Tour d'Afrique cycle race includes 100 days of cycling and 20 days of rest.
- The Tour de France lasts 22 days (with rest days).
- The Iditarod dog sled race, held in Alaska, lasts nine days.
- The Global Challenge around-the-world yacht race covers some 29,000 nautical mi. (54,000 km). The 72-ft. (22 m) yachts are at sea for six months. The race has been held every four years since 1992, with the next in 2008–2009.
- The longest boxing match with gloves was a 100-round bout between Andy Bowen and Jack Burke (both U.S.). It started at 9:15 p.m. on Thursday, April 6, 1893, and finished at 4:34 a.m. on Friday, April 7, — a total of 7 hours, 19 minutes.

Oldest sporting events

Doggett's Coat and Badge Race is the world's oldest continuous sporting event. It is a rowing contest held on the River Thames in England and has been held every year since 1715. The Newmarket Town Plate horse race is even older, but the race was discontinued for a while.

Event	First held
Newmarket Town Plate horse race	1665
Doggett's Coat and Badge Race (rowing)	1715
Real Tennis Championship	1740
St. Leger horse race	1776
Epsom Derby horse race	1780
County Cricket Championship	1827
Oxford and Cambridge Boat Race	1829
Grand National steeplechase	1836
Henley Regatta	1839
British Open golf championship	1860
Melbourne Cup horse race	1861
America's Cup yachting series	1870
Football Association Challenge Cup	1872
Kentucky Derby horse race	1875
Wimbledon Lawn Tennis Championships	1877
Stanley Cup ice hockey competition	1893
U.S. Open golf championship	1895
Davis Cup tennis tournament	1900
Baseball World Series	1903
Tour de France cycle race	1903
Ryder Cup golf tournament	1927
Commonwealth Games	1930
FIFA Soccer World Cup	1930
NASCAR racing	1949
Formula One World Championship	1950
Canadian Grand Prix (Formula One)	1967
Super Bowl football championship	1967
Athletics World Cup	1977
World Athletics Championships	1983
Breeders' Cup horse race series	1984

Grand National steeplechase (19th century)

Top sporting events

These are the leading events in the world's most popular sports, in addition to the Olympic Games.

Athletics IAAF (International Association of Athletic Federations)

Auto racing NASCAR Nextel Cup, Indianapolis 500, World Formula One Championship

Baseball World Series

Basketball NBA (National Basketball Association) Final

Cycling Tour de France

Football Super Bowl

Golf U.S. Open, U.S. Masters, U.S. PGA, British Open

Hockey Stanley Cup

Horse racing Kentucky Derby, Breeders' Cup, Epsom Derby, Grand National

Marathons New York City Marathon

Rallying (off-road race) Dakar Rally

Soccer FIFA World Cup (every four years)

Tennis U.S. Open, Wimbledon Championships

See also

Major rock events: page 255

Sports timeline

Experts argue about the exact origins of many sports. The dates here are generally agreed to be when these sports were first played or contested on an organized basis.

Athletics	3800 BC
Horse racing	AD 1540
Boxing	1681
Rowing	1715
Ice skating	1742
Cricket	1744
Golf	1744
Swimming	1791
Baseball	1839
Soccer	1848
Tenpin bowling	1850
Show jumping	1864
Cycling	1867
Badminton	1873
Lawn tennis	1873
Football	1874
Hockey (field)	1875
Hockey (ice)	1887
Motor racing	1887
Basketball	1891
Darts	1896
Motorcycling	1896
Speedway	1902

Bare-knuckle boxing match (1820)

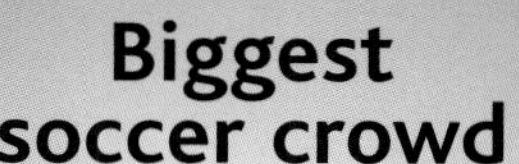

Biggest soccer crowd

The biggest-ever crowd for a soccer match was at the 1950 World Cup Final. The match between Brazil and Uruguay at the Maracanã Stadium (now called the Journalista Mário Filho Stadium) in Brazil was watched by 199,854 people.

The Journalista Mário Filho Stadium in Rio de Janeiro, Brazil, was built for the 1950 World Cup and held almost 200,000 people.

Biggest crowds

In the past, more than 100,000 people at a time crammed into the Rose Bowl Stadium in Pasadena, California, and other venues to watch their favorite sports. Today, there are laws that limit the number of people allowed in a sports stadium. Outdoor events such as the New York City Marathon and the Tour de France now draw the biggest crowds. They are held over open roads and people don't have to pay to watch them.

- About 2.5 million people watch the New York Marathon — the biggest crowd for a single day at a sporting event.
- As many as 15 million people turn out to see the Tour de France during its three weeks.
- The record crowd for a golf tournament was set at the U.S. Open, Flushing Meadows, 2005, which was attended by 659,538 people.
- Some of the biggest crowds at U.S. and Canadian sporting events are for Indy car races. About 270,000 fans attend the Indianapolis 500 every year and as many as 332,000 attended the 2006 Canadian Grand Prix in Montreal.
- In horse racing, a record 163,628 saw Cannonade win the 100th Kentucky Derby in 1974. A total of 156,635 attended the Kentucky Derby in 2007.

Strange sport

A world championship in cell phone throwing has been held in Finland every year since 2000. Competitors take part in individual or team events. There is also an under-12 category. The current world record stands at 314 ft., 4 in. (95.83 m) for men and 175 ft., 7 in. (53.52 m) for women.

Most-watched sporting events

Event	Percentage of U.S. households watching
Super Bowl XVI (49ers vs. Bengals), January 24, 1982	49.1
Super Bowl XVII (Redskins vs. Dolphins), January 30, 1983	48.6
XVII Winter Olympics: Women's figure skating, February 23, 1994	48.5
Super Bowl XX (Bears vs. Patriots), January 26, 1986	48.3
Super Bowl XII (Cowboys vs. Broncos), January 15, 1978	47.2
Super Bowl XIII (Steelers vs. Cowboys), January 21, 1979	47.1
Super Bowl XVIII (Raiders vs. Redskins), January 22, 1984	46.4
Super Bowl XIX (49ers vs. Dolphins), January 20, 1985	46.4
Super Bowl XIV (Steelers vs. Rams), January 20, 1980	46.3
Super Bowl XXX (Cowboys vs. Steelers), January 28, 1996	46.0
Super Bowl XXI (Giants vs. Broncos), January 25, 1987	45.8
Super Bowl XXVIII (Cowboys vs. Bills), January 30, 1994	45.5
Super Bowl XXVII (Cowboys vs. Bills), January 31, 1993	45.1
Super Bowl XXXII (Broncos vs. Packers), January 25, 1998	44.5
Super Bowl XI (Raiders vs. Vikings), January 9, 1977	44.4
Super Bowl XV (Raiders vs. Eagles), January 25, 1981	44.4
Super Bowl VI (Cowboys vs. Dolphins), January 16, 1972	44.2
XVII Winter Olympics: Women's figure skating, February 25, 1994	44.1
Super Bowl XXIII (49ers vs. Bengals), January 22, 1989	43.5
Super Bowl XXXI (Packers vs. Patriots), January 26, 1997	43.3
Super Bowl XXXIV (St. Louis Rams vs. Titans), January 30, 2000	43.3
NFL Championship Game (49ers vs. Cowboys), January 10, 1982	42.9
Super Bowl VII (Dolphins vs. Redskins), January 14, 1973	42.7
Super Bowl XLI (Colts vs. Bears), February 4, 2007	42.6
Super Bowl IX (Steelers vs. Vikings), January 12, 1975	42.4
Super Bowl X (Steelers vs. Cowboys), January 18, 1976	42.3
Super Bowl XL (Steelers vs. Seahawks, February 5, 2006	41.6
Super Bowl VIII (Dolphins vs. Vikings), January 13, 1974	41.6
Super Bowl XXXVIII (Patriots vs. Panthers), February 1, 2004	41.4
Super Bowl XXIX (49ers vs. Chargers), January 29, 1995	41.3
Super Bowl XXXIX (Patriots vs. Eagles), February 6, 2005	41.1
Super Bowl XXXVII (Buccaneers vs. Raiders), January 26, 2003	40.7
Super Bowl XXXVI (Patriots vs. Rams), February 3, 2002	40.4
Super Bowl XXXV (Ravens vs. Giants), January 28, 2001	40.4
Super Bowl XXXIII (Broncos vs. Falcons), January 31, 1999	40.2

Summer Olympics

The modern Olympic Games have been held every four years since 1896, except during World Wars I and II. Over this time the numbers of competitors, events and nations taking part have all increased dramatically.

Winter Paralympic events for athletes with disabilities have been held since 1976. The Summer Paralympics began in 1960 and were first held in conjunction with the regular Summer Olympics in 1988.

Year/City/Country	Competitors	No. of nations	Events	Most golds	Most medals
1896 Athens, Greece	245	14	43	U.S. 11	Greece 47
1900 Paris, France	1,225	26	95	France 26	France 95
1904 St Louis, U.S.	687	13	91	U.S. 79	U.S. 245
1906 Athens, Greece	884	20	76	France 15	France 40
1908 London, U.K.	2,035	22	110	U.K. 54	U.K. 138
1912 Stockholm, Sweden	2,547	28	102	U.S. 25	Sweden 64
1920 Antwerp, Belgium	2,669	29	154	U.S. 41	U.S. 95
1924 Paris, France	3,092	44	126	U.S. 45	U.S. 99
1928 Amsterdam, Netherlands	3,014	46	109	U.S. 22	U.S. 56
1932 Los Angeles, U.S.	1,408	37	117	U.S. 41	U.S. 103
1936 Berlin, Germany	4,066	49	129	Germany 33	Germany 89
1948 London, U.K.	4,099	59	136	U.S. 38	U.S. 84
1952 Helsinki, Finland	4,925	69	149	U.S. 40	U.S. 76
1956* Melbourne, Australia	3,342	72	145	USSR 37	USSR 98
1960 Rome, Italy	5,348	83	150	USSR 43	USSR 103
1964 Tokyo, Japan	5,140	93	163	U.S. 36	U.S. 90
1968 Mexico City, Mexico	5,531	112	172	U.S. 45	U.S. 107
1972 Munich, West Germany	7,123	121	195	USSR 50	USSR 99
1976 Montreal, Canada	6,028	92	198	USSR 49	USSR 125
1980 Moscow, USSR	5,217	80	203	USSR 80	USSR 195
1984 Los Angeles, U.S.	6,797	140	221	U.S. 83	U.S. 174
1988 Seoul, South Korea	8,465	159	237	USSR 55	USSR 132
1992 Barcelona, Spain	9,367	169	257	EUN† 45	EUN 112
1996 Atlanta, U.S.	10,744	197	271	U.S. 44	U.S. 101
2000 Sydney, Australia	10,651	199	300	U.S. 39	U.S. 97
2004 Athens, Greece	11,099	202	301	U.S. 35	U.S. 103

* The equestrian events in 1956 were held in Stockholm, Sweden, from June 10–17, because of quarantine restrictions in Australia at the time.

† The Unified Team (EUN) was made up of the former Soviet republics of Russia, Ukraine, Kazakhstan and Uzbekistan.

The big five

Only five sports have been contested at every Summer Olympics since the first Modern Olympics in 1896. These are cycling, fencing, gymnastics, swimming and track and field. Rowing would have been on this list, but the events in 1896 were canceled due to bad weather.

One and only

Softball is the only sport that women contest at the Olympics but men do not. The sport has been played at three Olympics (1996, 2000, 2004) and the U.S. has won gold each time.

Out of the Olympics

Various sports have been dropped from the Olympic Games over the years. These include croquet, underwater swimming, dueling pistol shooting, stone-throwing, lacrosse, archery with live birds, tug-of-war, club-swinging and rope climbing.

The Olympic flag

The five-ring Olympic flag was first raised at the 1920 Antwerp Olympics. The rings on the flag represent the five major regions of the world: the Americas, Europe, Asia, Africa and Australasia. At least one of the colors on the flag (blue, yellow, black, green and red) can be found on the flags of every nation in the world.

Olympic firsts

1800s

1896 First modern Olympics. Doves released to symbolize peace

1896 First American gold medal winner, James Connolly (triple jump)

1900s

1900 First women competitors. First woman to win a gold medal, Charlotte Cooper from Great Britain for tennis

1908 First parade of athletes with national flags

1908 First athlete to win 10 gold medals (in four Olympics, 1900, 1904, 1906 and 1908), Ray Ewry (U.S.)

1912 Electronic timing and photo-finish equipment first used

1920 Olympic oath, "We swear that we will take part in the Olympic Games in a spirit of chivalry, for the honor of our country and for the glory of sport," first taken, by Belgian fencer Victor Boin

1920 Olympic flag first raised

1924 First Olympics with more than 100 women competitors (there were 136 women and 2,956 men)

1924 First live radio transmissions of events

1928 First Olympic flame, large results display board first used

Olympic history

The ancient Olympic Games were dedicated to the Olympian gods and held at Olympia, on the border between Greece and Macedonia. They began in 776 BC and were held every four years. There were fewer events than now, and only Greeks could take part. The 293rd and last Olympiad was held in AD 392. After this, they were banned by the Emperor Theodosius. The games were revived in 1896 when the first modern Olympic Games were held in Athens.

Top medal winners

These athletes have won the most medals in the history of the Summer Olympics from 1896–2004.

Athlete	Sport	Years	Gold	Silver	Bronze	Total
Larissa Latynina (USSR)	Gymnastics	1956–64	9	5	4	18
Nikolai Andrianov (USSR)	Gymnastics	1972–80	7	5	3	15
Boris Shakhlin (USSR)	Gymnastics	1956–64	7	4	2	13
Edoardo Mangiarotti (Italy)	Fencing	1936–60	6	5	2	13
Takashi Ono (Japan)	Gymnastics	1952–64	5	4	4	13
Paavo Nurmi (Finland)	Athletics	1920–28	9	3	0	12
Sawao Kato (Japan)	Gymnastics	1968–76	8	3	1	12
Alexei Nemov (Russia)	Gymnastics	1996–2000	4	2	6	12

Athlete Ray Ewry (U.S.) won only 10 medals but they were all gold! He still holds the record for the most individual gold medals. Ewry won his medals between 1900 and 1908 in the standing jump events: high jump, long jump and triple jump. Amazingly, Ewry had suffered polio as a child, but overcame his illness to become one of the greatest athletes ever.

The opening ceremony of the 2004 Olympics was watched by 72,000 spectators in the Olympic Stadium in Athens, Greece.

2000s

1928 First women competitors in track and field events

1932 First Olympic logo, three-tier victory stand, national anthem played and flag raised for winner

1936 Introduction of Olympic torch relay (from Olympia, Greece, to Berlin, Germany)

1936 Games televised for the first time

1956 Athletes enter closing ceremony together to symbolize unity

1956 First games in the southern hemisphere (Melbourne, Australia)

1960 First Summer Paralympics, held in Rome, Italy

1960 Worldwide TV coverage for the first time

1984 Professionals allowed to compete for the first time

2004 Women competed in freestyle wrestling for the first time. Ukraine, Japan and China all won gold medals

2004 First Olympics broadcast over the Internet

2008 BMX cycling events introduced

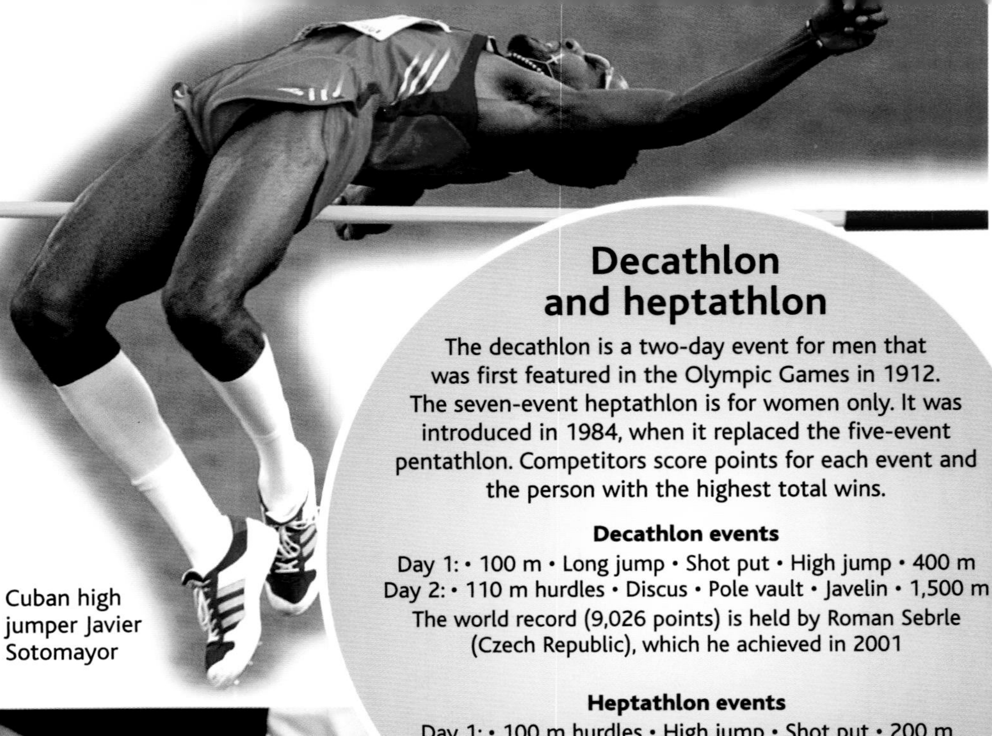

Cuban high jumper Javier Sotomayor

Decathlon and heptathlon

The decathlon is a two-day event for men that was first featured in the Olympic Games in 1912. The seven-event heptathlon is for women only. It was introduced in 1984, when it replaced the five-event pentathlon. Competitors score points for each event and the person with the highest total wins.

Decathlon events

Day 1: • 100 m • Long jump • Shot put • High jump • 400 m
Day 2: • 110 m hurdles • Discus • Pole vault • Javelin • 1,500 m
The world record (9,026 points) is held by Roman Sebrle (Czech Republic), which he achieved in 2001

Heptathlon events

Day 1: • 100 m hurdles • High jump • Shot put • 200 m
Day 2: • Long jump • Javelin • 800 m
The world record (7,291 points) is held by Jackie Joyner-Kersee (U.S.), which she achieved in 1988

Running a mile

For decades, athletes struggled to run a mile in less than four minutes. At 6:07 p.m. on May 6, 1954, British runner Roger Bannister eventually broke the record. He ran a mile in 3 minutes, 59.4 seconds at the Iffley Road track in Oxford.

Since that historic day, Bannister's record has been beaten many times. The current record speed for running a mile is 3 minutes, 43.13 seconds.

Marathon

The race takes its name from a place called Marathon in Greece, which was the scene of a battle between Athenian and Persian troops in 490 BC.

The Athenians won and supposedly sent a messenger named Pheidippides from Marathon to Athens to spread the news — a distance of about 25 mi. (40.2 km). It is said that Pheidippides dropped dead after delivering his message! The current marathon distance of 26 mi., 385 yd. (42.2 km) was first used at the 1908 Olympics in London, England. It was worked out so that the race from Windsor would finish in front of the Royal Box at the White City Stadium. This distance has been the standard for all marathons since 1924.

Marathon fact file

Hundreds of marathon races are held all over the world every year. There is an Antarctica Marathon, a Sahara Marathon and even a nighttime marathon, run in Marburg, Germany. The following are some of the biggest and most popular events.

Boston Marathon
This race has been held since 1897 and is run on Patriots' Day every April. It is the oldest marathon in the United States and one of the world's most important road races. Clarence DeMar won it a record seven times between 1911 and 1930.

New York City Marathon
First held in 1970, the race goes through all five boroughs of New York and finishes in Central Park. It is usually held on the first Sunday in November. Norway's Greta Waitz won the women's race an amazing nine times between 1978 and 1988.

Chicago Marathon
The Chicago Marathon began in 1977. It was originally called the Mayor Daley Marathon after Chicago mayor Richard J. Daley, who died in office in 1976. Khalid Khannouchi of Morocco won the men's race a record four times between 1997 and 2002.

Track and field records

These are the current world records for major track and field events as of January 1, 2008. Most events have both male and female record holders. A few events are contested by only men or women. (Country abbreviations are found on page 318.)

Event		Time (hr:min:sec)	Record holder	Date
100 m	(m)	9.74	Asafa Powell (Jamaica)	2007
	(w)	10.49	Florence Griffith-Joyner (U.S.)	1988
200 m	(m)	19.32	Michael Johnson (U.S.)	1996
	(w)	21.34	Florence Griffith-Joyner (U.S.)	1988
400 m	(m)	43.18	Michael Johnson (U.S.)	1999
	(w)	47.60	Marita Koch (GDR)	1985
800 m	(m)	1:41.11	Wilson Kipketer (Den)	1997
	(w)	1:53.28	Jarmila Kratochvílová (Cze)	1983
1,500 m	(m)	3:26.00	Hicham El Guerrouj (Mar)	1998
	(w)	3:50.46	Qu Yunxia (Chn)	1993
1 mile	(m)	3:43.13	Hicham El Guerrouj (Mar)	1999
	(w)	4:12.56	Svetlana Masterkova (Rus)	1996
5,000 m	(m)	12:37.35	Kenenisa Bekele (Eth)	2004
	(w)	14:16.63	Meseret Defar (Eth)	2007
10,000 m	(m)	26:17.53	Kenenisa Bekele (Eth)	2005
	(w)	29:31.78	Wang Junxia (Chn)	1993
3,000 m steeplechase	(m)	7:53.63	Saaeed Shaheen (Qat)	2004
	(w)	9:01.59	Gulnara Samitiva (Rus)	2004
110 m hurdles	(m)	12.88	Liu Xiang (Chn)	2006
100 m hurdles	(w)	12.21	Yordanka Donkova (Bul)	1988
400 m hurdles	(m)	46.78	Kevin Young (U.S.)	1992
	(w)	52.34	Yuliya Pechonkina (Rus)	2003
4 x 100 m relay	(m)	37.40	U.S.	1992/1993
	(w)	41.37	GDR	1985
4 x 400 m relay	(m)	2:54.20	U.S.	1998
	(w)	3:15.17	USSR	1988
		Ht/lgth (m)		
High jump	(m)	2.45	Javier Sotomayor (Cub)	1993
	(w)	2.09	Stefka Kostadinova (Bul)	1987
Pole vault	(m)	6.14	Sergey Bubka (Ukr)	1994
	(w)	5.01	Yelena Isinbayeva (Rus)	2005
Long jump	(m)	8.95	Mike Powell (U.S.)	1991
	(w)	7.52	Galina Chistyakova (USSR)	1988
Triple jump	(m)	18.29	Jonathan Edwards (GBR)	1995
	(w)	15.50	Inessa Kravets (Ukr)	1995
Shot put	(m)	23.12	Randy Barnes (U.S.)	1990
	(w)	22.63	Natalya Lisovskaya (USSR)	1987
Discus	(m)	74.08	Jürgen Schult (GDR)	1986
	(w)	76.80	Gabriele Reinsch (GDR)	1988
Hammer	(m)	86.74	Yuriy Sedykh (USSR)	1986
	(w)	77.80	Tatyana Lysenko (Rus)	2006
Javelin	(m)	98.48	Jan Zelezny (Cze)	1996
	(w)	71.70	Osleidys Menéndez (Cub)	2005

Florence Griffith-Joyner

World's fastest

The world's fastest man is Asafa Powell (Jamaica) who ran the 100 m in 9.74 seconds at Rieti, Italy, on September 9, 2007

The world's fastest woman was Florence Griffith-Joyner (U.S.), who died in 1998. She ran the 100 m in 10.49 seconds in Indianapolis in 1988. The fastest living woman is Marion Jones (U.S.). She ran the 100 m in 10.65 seconds in Johannesburg in 1998.

London Marathon
Dionicio Ceron (Mexico) and António Pinto (Portugal) have each won the men's race a record three times. Ingrid Kristiansen (Norway) won the women's race four times between 1984 and 1988.

Marathon record holders
The current male record holder is Haile Gebreselassie (Ethiopia) ran the Berlin Marathon in 2 hours, 4 minutes, 26 seconds on September 30, 2007. The female record is held by Paula Radcliffe (U.K.), who ran the London Marathon on April 13, 2003, in 2 hours, 15 minutes, 25 seconds.

See also
Ancient Greece: page 106

www.ingnycmarathon.org search

Yankees All-Star Alex Rodriguez

Baseball World Series

Major League baseball started in the U.S. when the National League was formed in 1876. The rival American League was started in 1901, and in 1903 the World Series, a best-of-nine game event, was held between the winners of each league's championship. In the first series the Boston Red Sox beat the Pittsburgh Pirates 5–3. The World Series has been a best-of-seven games series since 1905, except in 1919–21 when it went back to a nine-game series.

Most wins American League: New York Yankees — 26 between 1923 and 2000; National League: St Louis Cardinals — 10 between 1926 and 2006

Most consecutive wins New York Yankees — 5 (1949–53)

Baseball

Baseball is one of the most popular sports in Canada and the U.S. and is also played in Japan, Mexico and a number of South American countries. It is played by two teams of nine players each.

Games that resemble baseball are shown in medieval manuscripts and are referred to in 18th-century books in England. Such games were taken to the United States where Alexander Joy Cartwright Jr. drew up baseball's first rules on September 23, 1845. He also founded the first organized team, the Knickerbocker Base Ball Club of New York. The first game of baseball played according to the Cartwright Rules took place at the Elysian Fields, Hoboken, New Jersey, on June 19, 1846 between the New York Nine and the Knickerbocker Club.

Golf majors

The four big competitions in golf are known as the majors. They are the U.S. Masters, British Open, U.S. Open and U.S. PGA Championship, and are played in that order every year.

The Masters, founded in 1934, is the only one of the four played on the same course each year, at Augusta National in Georgia. The oldest of the majors is the British Open, which was first held in 1860. It is also the only one played outside the U.S. The U.S. Open was first played in 1895 and the U.S. PGA in 1916.

Players with most professional major wins

Jack Nicklaus (U.S.) 18: 3 British Open; 4 U.S. Open; 5 U.S. PGA; 6 Masters

Tiger Woods (U.S.) 13: 3 British Open; 2 U.S. Open; 4 U.S. PGA; 4 Masters

Walter Hagen (U.S.) 11: 4 British Open; 2 U.S. Open; 5 U.S. PGA

Ben Hogan (U.S.) 9: 1 British Open; 4 U.S. Open; 2 U.S. PGA; 2 Masters

Gary Player (S. Africa) 9: 3 British Open; 1 U.S. Open; 2 U.S. PGA; 3 Masters

Tom Watson (U.S.) 8: 5 British Open; 1 U.S. Open; 2 U.S. Masters

Tiger Woods

Tiger Woods

At just 21 years, 3 months and 14 days old, Tiger Woods was the youngest ever Masters champion. In 2001 Tiger won his second U.S. Masters and became the first player to hold all four professional major championships at the same time.

Basketball

Basketball is hugely popular in the U.S. and is now played in other parts of the world, as well as at the Olympics. The game is played by two teams of five players each, usually on an indoor court.

Players score points by shooting the ball through the basket. The National Basketball Association (NBA) in the U.S. was formed in 1949. It contains 30 teams divided into two conferences, Eastern and Western. At the end of the season the two conference winners meet in a best-of-seven series for the NBA Championship.

Record breakers

Outstanding player Kareem Abdul-Jabbar (Milwaukee Bucks and Los Angeles Lakers) scored a record 38,387 points during his career.

Teams with most wins

Boston Celtics: 16
Minneapolis/Los Angeles Lakers: 14
Chicago Bulls: 6

Corliss Williamson (Sacramento Kings) drives for the basket

Rugby

The game of rugby probably started in 1823 at Rugby School in England, when William Webb Ellis picked up a football and ran with it. The first rules were drawn up in 1848 and the Rugby Football Union (RFU) was formed by Edwin Ash in 1871.

Today's game of Rugby Union is played between two teams of 15 players. The two biggest events are the International Championship and the World Cup. The International Championship began in 1884 and was originally played by four teams: England, Ireland, Scotland and Wales. France joined in 1910 and Italy in 2000, making it a six-nation tournament. The Rugby World Cup was launched in 1987 and has been held every four years since then. In 2003, 20 teams took part and more than 2.25 million people watched the 48 live matches at an average of 47,150 per game.

Rugby League

Rugby League dates from August 29, 1895, when 21 major clubs in the north of England formed a league outside the RFU. They were protesting against the RFU's refusal to pay players who had to take time off work. To make Rugby League less like Rugby Union they changed various rules, including reducing the team size from 15 to 13. Rugby League is now played in Australia, New Zealand, France, Russia and some Pacific nations, as well as in Britain. One of the major events in Rugby League is the Challenge Cup, open to British, French and Russian teams. There is also a Rugby League World Cup; the last was in 2000 and the next will be in Australia in 2008.

Softball

Softball (fastpitch and slowpitch) is a form of baseball invented in 1887 as a form of "indoor baseball", although these days it is generally played outdoors.

Some major differences between baseball and softball include: the bat is smaller, and the ball in softball, which is pitched underhand, is bigger than a baseball ball, but not as dense. On the pitch, the base lines are only 60 ft. (18 m) apart in softball (90 ft. [27.4 m] in baseball), the outfield fence is a constant distance from the home plate, and there is no pitcher's mound. There are normally seven innings in softball as opposed to baseball's nine. Both games are played with nine players (slowpitch softball has ten players).

Little league baseball

Little League baseball was inaugurated in 1938 by Carl Stotz, a clerk from Williamsport, Pennsylvania, when, with the help of his nephews and their friends, they started playing their own form of baseball. He felt it would have an appeal to local children and, the following year he and two friends each managed a team in what became the first Little League. The three teams obtained local sponsorship, and the first Little League game was played on June 6, 1939.

From its humble beginnings, Little League baseball has now spread and is played in every state of the U.S. and in more than 100 countries worldwide. There are believed to be more than three million boys and girls between the ages of five and 18 playing either Little League baseball or softball.

www.nba.com search

Little League World Series

The first Little League World Series was held in Williamsport, Pennsylvania in 1947 when the home team beat Lock Haven, 16–7 in the final. Originally for teams from the United States only, teams from all over the world now take part and in 1960 Berlin (then in West Germany) became the first European team to participate. In that same year, the World Series was broadcast on National Television for the first time.

Children aged 11 to 13 can take part in the Little League World Series, and 16 teams take part each year in two brackets, or 'pools'. Each bracket is sub-divided into two brackets of four teams who play each other once. At the completion of the round robin matches, the top two in each bracket take part in semi-finals, with the eventual winners of the U.S. bracket meeting the International winners in the Little League World Series.

The World Cup

The first soccer World Cup was played in 1930 in Uruguay. Thirteen teams took part and the hosts beat Argentina 4–2 in the final in Montevideo.

They won the Jules Rimet trophy, named after the president of FIFA (Fédération Internationale de Football Association) when the competition began. Brazil were allowed to keep the trophy after winning it for the third time in 1970 and it was replaced by the FIFA World Cup trophy. The World Cup final takes place every four years.

Winning country	Year	Winning country	Year
Uruguay	1930	Brazil	1970
Italy	1934	West Germany	1974
Italy	1938	Argentina	1978
Not held	1942	Italy	1982
Not held	1946	Argentina	1986
Uruguay	1950	West Germany	1990
West Germany	1954	Brazil	1994
Brazil	1958	France	1998
Brazil	1962	Brazil	2002
England	1966	Italy	2006

The Italian team that won the 2006 World Cup

World Cup facts

- The first World Cup goal was scored by Lucien Laurent of France. The goal came 19 minutes into the first World Cup game on July 13, 1930.
- The first player to score four goals in a World Cup game was Ireland's Paddy Moore in a qualifying game against Belgium in 1934. It was Ireland's first ever World Cup game.

Most World Cup wins

Brazil	5
Italy	4
West Germany	3
Uruguay	2
Argentina	2

U.S. soccer

Organized soccer was first seen in the United States in 1862. It became a prominent collegiate sport in the 1870s, and on November 28, 1885, the U.S. played Canada in the first soccer international outside Britain.

The United States entered the first World Cup in 1930, losing 6–1 to Argentina in the semi-final, and 20 years later enjoyed their greatest World Cup moment when they beat a star-studded England team 1–0 in one of the biggest World Cup shocks.

The United States won its first major soccer tournament in 1991 beating Norway to win the FIFA Women's World Championship in China

Most goals (as of January 1, 2008)

Player	Years	Goals
Landon Donovan	2000–2007	34
Eric Wynalda	1990–2000	34
Brian McBride	1993–2006	30
Joe–Max Moore	1992–2002	24
Bruce Murray	1985–1993	21
Earnie Stewart	1990–2004	17
DaMarcus Beasley	2001–2007	15
Cobi Jones	1992–2004	15
Marcelo Balboa	1988–2000	13
Hugo Perez	1984–1994	13
Clint Mathis	1998–2005	12
Frank Klopas	1987–1996	12
Peter Vermes	1988–1998	11
Eddie Johnson	2004–2007	10
William Roy	1965–1973	10

Soccer timeline 1800s

500 BC Football (*tsu chu*, meaning to kick a ball) played in China

1314 First reference to "football" in England when Edward II prohibited the game because "too many people were bustling over footballs on London streets"

1848 The first rules of soccer drawn up at Cambridge University, England

1852 First interschool scoccer game, Westminster vs. Harrow

1855 Sheffield football soccer club, the oldest still in existence, formed in England

1862 Notts County, the oldest current League club, formed

1863 Football Association (FA) formed in England

1870 First international game, England vs. Scotland, played at Kennington Oval

1871 FA Cup launched

1872 Corner kick introduced

1873 Scottish FA formed; Scottish Cup started

1874 Shin pads first worn

1875 The crossbar replaced a tape across the top of the goals

1876 Welsh FA formed

1878 Irish (now Northern Ireland) FA formed

1878 Referee's whistle first used

1885 Professional soccer legalized

1888 Football League of professional soccer clubs from England and Wales formed

1889 The term "soccer" first used in the world; may be an abbreviation of association football — the FA was formed to standardize the rules of the game

1890 Scottish League formed

1891 Goal nets first used

1891 Linesmen (now assistant referees) replace umpires

1891 Penalty kick adopted by the FA

Football records

The first international American football game took place at Cambridge, Massachusetts, on May 14, 1874, between Harvard University and McGill University of Montreal, Canada.

The first Rose Bowl college football game was at Pasadena, California, on January 1, 1902 between the Universities of Michigan and Stanford. It has been held annually since 1916.

The New England Patriots (wearing blue and white) have won three Super Bowls this century.

Football

Football, know as American football in other parts of the world, is the number one sport in the United States. The National Football League (NFL) is split into two conferences, the American Football Conference (AFC) and National Football Conference (NFC). Each conference is split into four divisions — North, South, East and West — and each division has four teams.

Each team plays 16 games and the six teams with the best records in both the AFC and NFC take part in the playoffs with the winner of each conference then meeting for the Super Bowl early in February. The winning team receives the Vince Lombardi Trophy.

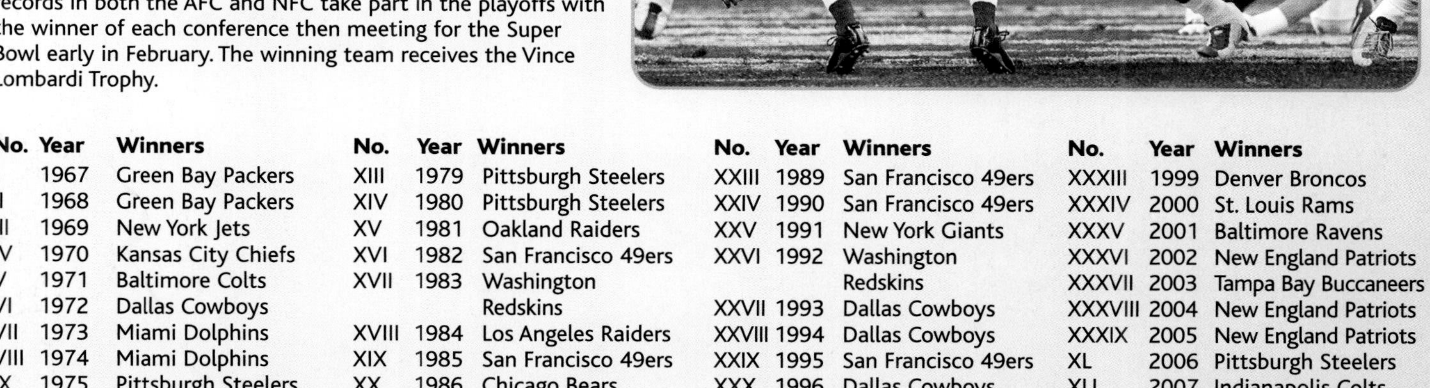

No.	Year	Winners
I	1967	Green Bay Packers
II	1968	Green Bay Packers
III	1969	New York Jets
IV	1970	Kansas City Chiefs
V	1971	Baltimore Colts
VI	1972	Dallas Cowboys
VII	1973	Miami Dolphins
VIII	1974	Miami Dolphins
IX	1975	Pittsburgh Steelers
X	1976	Pittsburgh Steelers
XI	1977	Oakland Raiders
XII	1978	Dallas Cowboys
XIII	1979	Pittsburgh Steelers
XIV	1980	Pittsburgh Steelers
XV	1981	Oakland Raiders
XVI	1982	San Francisco 49ers
XVII	1983	Washington Redskins
XVIII	1984	Los Angeles Raiders
XIX	1985	San Francisco 49ers
XX	1986	Chicago Bears
XXI	1987	New York Giants
XXII	1988	Washington Redskins
XXIII	1989	San Francisco 49ers
XXIV	1990	San Francisco 49ers
XXV	1991	New York Giants
XXVI	1992	Washington Redskins
XXVII	1993	Dallas Cowboys
XXVIII	1994	Dallas Cowboys
XXIX	1995	San Francisco 49ers
XXX	1996	Dallas Cowboys
XXXI	1997	Green Bay Packers
XXXII	1998	Denver Broncos
XXXIII	1999	Denver Broncos
XXXIV	2000	St. Louis Rams
XXXV	2001	Baltimore Ravens
XXXVI	2002	New England Patriots
XXXVII	2003	Tampa Bay Buccaneers
XXXVIII	2004	New England Patriots
XXXIX	2005	New England Patriots
XL	2006	Pittsburgh Steelers
XLI	2007	Indianapolis Colts
XLII	2008	New York Giants

1900s — **2000s**

1904 FIFA formed in Paris; first international game outside Great Britain — Belgium vs. France played near Brussels

1907 Professional Footballers' Association (PFA) formed in the U.K. (as the Football Players and Trainers Union)

1921 FA of Ireland (Republic of Ireland) formed

1923 First Wembley Cup Final (Bolton vs. West Ham)

1928 Players' numbers introduced

1930 First World Cup in Uruguay

1932 Substitutes formally agreed by FIFA

1954 Union of European Football Associations (UEFA) formed

1955 European Cup started

1960 Football League Cup started

1965 Football League agrees on use of substitutes

1968 Red cards introduced (at the Mexico Olympic Games)

1975 Scottish Premier Division (now Premier League) formed

1981 Football League changed the number of points for a win from two to three

1982 Professional foul rule introduced

1992 FA Premier League formed

1993 Ch League replaces the European Cup

2004 Greece are surprise winners of the European Championship

2007 David Beckham moves to Los Angeles Galaxy for $150 million over five years

2008 Fabio Capello (Italy) becomes England Manager

www.fifa.com search

Badminton

Badminton probably came from an old children's game called "battledore and shuttlecock." The battledore is a small wooden bat that the player uses to hit the shuttlecock. The game was popular in India and other Asian countries, and the aim was to keep the shuttlecock in the air as long as possible. British army officers played the game in India in the 1860s and they added a net to hit the shuttlecock over. They called the game "poona."

When the officers returned to England they continued enjoying poona. The game was renamed badminton at a garden party at the home of the Duke of Beaufort in 1873. His home was called Badminton House. By 1877 the first official rules of the game were drawn up and in 1893 the first governing body, The Badminton Association of England, was set up. The Badminton Club of New York began in 1878, although the game did not become popular until the 1930s.

Badminton's greatest player

Rudy Hartono from Indonesia won the world's oldest badminton tournament, the All-England Championships, a record eight times between 1968 and 1976. He was also the 1980 world champion at the age of 32, and unbeaten in six Thomas Cup ties.

New rules for table tennis

Traditionally, the winner of a table tennis game was the first player to score 21 points, but in 2001 the International Table Tennis Federation (ITTF) announced changes in the rules. These included a new scoring system in which the first player to score 11 points wins the game. In national and international tournaments all matches are played to either the best-of-five games or the best-of-seven.

Pelota

Pelota is the name given to a variety of sports that are played by hitting a ball with the hand, a racquet, or a basket attached to the hand. Pelota and its variations were first played during the 13th century in the Basque region of Spain. There are variations of the game depending upon the equipment used.

- Played with the hand it is called *pelota mano*, or just pelota.
- Played with a racquet, it is called *frontenis*.
- Played with a hand basket, it is called *jai-alai*.

The game is similar to squash — players hit the ball against the end wall of a three-sided court, if possible, out of reach of their opponent. Pelota is popular in Spain, Mexico, South America, Cuba, Italy and many U.S. states, including Florida.

Pelota player in action

Lawn tennis timeline 1800s 2000s

1877 First Wimbledon Championship
1881 First U.S. Championship
1891 First French Championship—until 1925 for French nationals
1896 Tennis played at the first Modern Olympics in Athens
1900 Davis Cup began after Dwight F. Davis donated a trophy
1905 First Australian Open
1913 International Lawn Tennis Federation founded in Paris with 12 member countries
1922 Seeding (method of ranking players) first used, at the U.S. National Championships
1923 Women's tennis became international with the launch of the Wightman Cup (named after U.S. team captain Hazel Wightman)
1938 Donald Budge (U.S.) became the first player to complete the Grand Slam
1950 Louise Brough (U.S.) became the first woman to complete the Grand Slam
1963 The Federation Cup, the women's equivalent of the Davis Cup, began
1968 Tennis tournaments were opened to professional players, effectively ending the amateur game
1971 The tie-break was introduced by the British LTA as an experiment
1972 Davis Cup changed from being run on a challenge basis to a knockout tournament involving all competing nations
1973 Introduction of official world rankings by the ATP and LTA
1988 Tennis revived as an Olympic sport after 64 years
2004 World ranking points first allocated to competitors in the Olympic Games
2008 On January 1, 2008, Roger Federer achieved a record 205th consecutive week at No.1 in the ATP rankings.

Tennis scoring

No one knows exactly how the tennis scoring system came about, but it may have started in France in medieval times. People think the system may be based on the movement of the hand of a clock at one end of the court: on winning a point, the hand would be moved 15 minutes, or a quarterway around the clock. Next comes 30, half the clock, and so on. As a player had to win four points to win the game, the first around the clockface won. The score 40 may be used instead of 45 because in French *quarante* (40) is easier to say than *quarante-cinq* (45). When both sides reach 40 the score is deuce. This comes from the French *quarante à deux*, or 40 to both, or simply from *deux*, two, as players must gain two points to win. "Love," the zero score, may come from the French word *l'oeuf*, meaning egg, as the symbol for zero is egg-shaped.

Serena and Venus Williams

Serena Williams (born 1981) has won eight Grand Slam singles titles, which is two more than her older sister Venus (born 1980). Both players have been ranked World No. 1 and have each earned more than $18 million in prize money.

Serena Williams

Lawn tennis Grand Slam events

The Grand Slam consists of the Australian, French, Wimbledon and U.S. Championships. A player is said to have completed the Grand Slam if he or she holds all four titles simultaneously, although not necessarily in the same year. These events were originally for amateur players but are now open to all, including professionals.

Wimbledon Championships

First held in 1877, Wimbledon is the world's most famous tennis championship. From 1877 to 1921 it was a challenge event with the defending champion qualifying for the next year's final. Women first took part in 1884. Since 1968 Wimbledon has been an open event. This means it is open to all players, including professionals.

U.S. Open

This was first held in 1881. Until 1911, the U.S. tournament operated as a challenge system, with the defending champion automatically going through to the following year's final. Women first competed in 1887. Two championships were held in 1968 and 1969, one for amateurs and an open championship. It became completely open in 1970.

French Open

The French Open was first held in 1891 and until 1925 it was only for French nationals. It became the French Open in 1968 and has been played at the Stade Roland Garros (named after a famous French aviator) since 1928. Women have competed since 1897.

Australian Open

This competition was first held in 1905 as the Australasian Tennis Championship. Women first competed in 1922. The competition became the Australian Championship in 1927, and since 1969 has been the Australian Open. It is played at Melbourne every January.

Most titles in Grand Slams

Australian Roy Emerson won 28 Grand Slam titles between 1961 and 1967. He is the only male player to win singles and doubles titles at all four Grand Slam events. Margaret Court (née Smith), also from Australia, won a record 62 Grand Slam titles, between 1960 and 1973.

Squash champions

Jahangir Khan

Jahangir Khan is the greatest male squash player of all time. He has won six World Open titles, three World Amateur titles, four World Masters and 10 consecutive British Open titles. Khan was born in Karachi in 1963. His father, Roshan, was a British champion, as were Roshan's cousins Hashan and Azam. At one point in his career, Jahangir competed for an amazing five years and eight months without defeat, playing more than 800 games. He was voted Pakistan's Sportsman of the Millennium and elected President of the World Squash Federation in 2002.

Heather McKay

Heather McKay (née Blundell) dominated ladies' squash during the 1960s and 1970s. She was born in New South Wales, Australia, in 1942, the eighth of 11 children. Between 1962 and 1977 she won 16 consecutive British Open titles and remained undefeated for 17 years before her retirement. She lost just two games in her career. In 1999 Heather McKay became a founder member of the WISPA Hall of Fame, and was awarded the Australian Sports Medal in 2000.

Boxing weights

Boxing matches are held between two contestants of similar weight. The weight classes were first used in the 19th century and more were added during the 20th century.

Weight class	Max lb.	(kg)
Strawweight/Mini flyweight	106	(48)
Junior flyweight/ Light flyweight	108	(49)
Flyweight	112	(51)
Junior bantam/ Super flyweight	115	(52)
Bantamweight	119	(54)
Junior featherweight/ Super bantamweight	121	(55)
Featherweight	126	(57)
Junior lightweight/ Super featherweight	130	(59)
Lightweight	134	(61)
Junior welterweight/ Super lightweight	143	(65)
Welterweight	148	(67)
Junior middleweight/ Super welterweight	154	(70)
Middleweight	161	(73)
Super middleweight	168	(76)
Light heavyweight	174	(79)
Cruiserweight	201	(91)
Heavyweight	201	(>91)

Muhammad Ali defeating Sonny Liston in 1965 to retain his world title.

Boxing's greatest champions

- "Sugar" Ray Robinson was one of the best boxers in any weight division. His first world title was at welterweight in 1946. Moving up a division, he beat Jake La Motta in 1951 to capture the middleweight title. He even had a crack at the light heavyweight title, but failed after a 14th-round knockout. Robinson was born in Detroit in 1920 and turned professional in 1940. He went on to have 201 fights and won 174 of them, 109 with knockouts.

- "Sugar" Ray Leonard was born in Wilmington, North Carolina, in 1956. He began boxing at 14 and in 1976 won the Olympic light welterweight title. He turned professional in 1977. Two years later he won the first of many world titles when he beat Wilfred Benitez to become welterweight champion. Leonard went on to become the first man to win world titles at five different weights, all within 10 years. He held welterweight, light middleweight, middleweight, light heavyweight and super middleweight titles.

- Oscar de la Hoya from Los Angeles, California, first became famous at the 1992 Barcelona Olympics — he won the U.S.'s only boxing gold that year. La Hoya turned professional after the Olympics. He went on to become only the third man to capture world titles at five different weights, from junior lightweight to junior middleweight. His greatest win was beating his idol Julio Cesar Chavez in four rounds at Caesar's Palace, Las Vegas, in 1996.

Muhammad Ali

Muhammad Ali was born Cassius Clay in Louisville, Kentucky, in 1942. He burst on to the boxing scene at the 1960 Rome Olympics where he took the light heavyweight gold medal. In 1964, aged 22, he won his first world heavyweight title by beating Sonny Liston. He beat George Foreman 10 years later to become only the second man to regain his title. In 1978, at the age of 36, he beat Leon Spinks to become the first man to win the title a third time. He lost his last world title fight to Larry Holmes in 1980.

www.wwe.com search

Snooker and pool

Snooker was first played by British army officers in India and later became popular in Great Britain, while pool began in the U.S. One of pool's top events is the Mosconi Cup, named after the great American pool player and 14 times world champion Willie Mosconi. It is now an annual contest in the U.K. and pits the best pool players from the U.S. against those from Europe.

Pool champion

Earl Strickland from Greensboro, North Carolina, has won three world Nine-ball titles (1990, 1991, 2002). He has also been the U.S. Open Nine-ball champion five times. Nicknamed "The Pearl," he has appeared in 11 Mosconi Cups, winning 37 games out of 56.

Snooker champions

The greatest players of the modern game still playing are Steve Davis and Stephen Hendry. Between them they have won the Embassy World Professional Snooker title 13 times, and both have won all the other major trophies in the game. Davis won six world titles between 1981 and 1989. Scottish-born Hendry has won a record seven, including five consecutive titles between 1992 and 1996.

Wrestling

The World Wrestling Federation was started in the 1960s as the WorldWide Wrestling Federation (WWWF) by Vince McMahon. In the early 1980s Vince's son, Vince McMahon Jr., renamed it WWF.

The sport changed and became widely popular. Characters such as Hulk Hogan became household names, attracting huge crowds to live matches and millions of followers via TV. The WWF is now known as WWE, World Wrestling Entertainment, Inc. The two biggest events in the WWE calendar are Wrestle Mania, which decides the world champions, and the Royal Rumble. The first WWF Wrestle Mania was at Madison Square Garden on March 31, 1985.

Top wrestlers

- Texan Shawn Michaels is one of the most popular of all wrestlers. He weighs in at about 256 lb. (116 kg). Michaels has won the WWE title, WWE World Heavyweight title, the WWE World Tag Team title and twice won the Royal Rumble, among many other top honors and titles.
- The Rock (real name Dwayne Johnson) is 6.36 ft. (1.94 m) tall and weighs 260 lb. (118 kg). He has been the WWE Champion, the WWE World Tag Team Champion and was the winner of Royal Rumble 2000. He took to the sport after a brief professional football career, and has also appeared in several films, including *The Mummy Returns* (2001), *The Scorpion King* (2002), *The Game Plan* (2007), *Be Cool* (2005), and *Get Smart* (2008).
- Triple H, or "The Game," made his WWE debut in 1995 as Hunter Hearst Helmsley. He weighs about 260 lb. (118 kg). He has been WWE Champion, WWE World Heavyweight Champion, WWE World Tag Team Champion, King of the Ring and Royal Rumble. He is the only man to win the Grand Slam, King of the Ring and Royal Rumble.

Hulk Hogan

Hulk Hogan's real name is Terry Bollea. He is 6.66 ft. (2.03 m) tall and weighs a massive 269 lb. (122 kg). His first ring name was Sterling Golden and then he became Terry Boulder before settling with Hulk Hogan. He played the wrestling villain Thunderlips in *Rocky III* in 1982. Hogan's latest appearance is as Zeus in *Little Hercules in 3-D*, which is scheduled to release in 2008.

Hossein Rezazadeh

Hossein Rezazadeh (Iran) holds the men's weightlifting record. He lifted 1,041.7 lb. (472.5 kg) at the Sydney Olympics in September 2000. This is heavier than a cow!

Iranian weightlifter Hossein Rezazadeh

Weightlifting records

In an Olympic weightlifting competition, contestants perform two types of lifts, the snatch, and the clean and jerk. They have three attempts at each. The score is the total of the best of each type of lift.

In the snatch the contestant lifts the bar from the floor directly above the head and holds it for two seconds. In the clean and jerk the contestant first takes the bar from the floor to the shoulders and then above the head.

The women's world record stands at 703.4 lbs (319 kg) set by Mu Shuangshuang of China on September 26, 2007.

Olympic water sports

Sailing

The first Modern Olympics in 1896 should have included sailing, but the races could not be held because of bad weather. Sailing was included for the first time four years later in Paris and has been a full Olympic sport since 1908. Boardsailing made its debut in 1988. Men and women have competed together in sailing events over the years, but in 1988 women had events of their own. Until the 2000 Olympics, sailing was known as yachting.

Top gold-medal winning nations (1900–2004)

Great Britain 24
Norway 17
U.S. 17

Rowing

Rowing was to have been part of the 1896 Olympics, but the events were canceled. It was first included in Paris four years later, and has appeared at every Olympics since. Women first competed in 1976.

The top gold-medal winning nations (1900–2004)

East Germany 33
U.S. 30
Germany/West Germany 27
Great Britain 22

Canoeing

Canoeing was first included as a demonstration sport in 1924, and did not become a full Olympic sport until 1936. Women took part for the first time in 1948.

Top gold-medal winning nations (1936–2004)

USSR/Unified Team 30
Germany/West Germany 28
East Germany 14
Hungary 17
Sweden 15

Michael Phelps swimming in the 2004 Olympic Games

Mark Spitz

When swimmer Mark Spitz took part in the 1968 Mexico Olympics he was already a record holder—he set a total of 26 world records during his career. He predicted he would win six gold medals at the Olympics, but he won just two, both in relay events.

But in 1972, in Munich, Spitz became the first and only person to win seven gold medals at one Summer Olympics. He also set new world records with all his medals.

Mark Spitz's gold medals at the 1972 Olympics

Event	Time (min:sec)
200 m butterfly	2:00.70
4 x 100 m freestyle	3:26.42
200 m freestyle	1:52.78
100 m butterfly	0:54.27
4 x 200 m freestyle	7:35.78
100 m freestyle	0:51.22
4 x 100 m medley	3:48.16

Start of the men's coxless fours rowing final at the 2004 Olympic Games.

Rowing knights

British rower Steve Redgrave won gold medals at five consecutive Olympic Games (1984–2000), while Matthew Pinsent won gold medals at four consecutive Games — in coxless pairs (with Steve Redgrave) in 1992 and 1996 and coxless fours in 2000 and 2004. Pinsent and Redgrave were knighted for their rowing achievements.

Olympic swimming

These are the top medal-winning Olympic swimmers. Totals include medals won in relays.

Swimmer	Gold	Silver	Bronze	Total
Men				
Mark Spitz (U.S.)	9	1	1	11
Matt Biondi (U.S.)	7	2	1	10
Aleksandr Popov (Russia)	4	5	0	9
Zoltán Halmay (Hungary)	3	5	1	9
Women				
Jenny Thompson (U.S.)	8	1	1	10
Dara Torres (U.S.)	4	1	4	9
Dawn Fraser (Australia)	4	4	0	8
Kornelia Ender (GDR)	4	4	0	8
Shirley Babashoff (U.S.)	2	6	0	8

www.fina.org search

Olympic Tarzans

Johnny Weissmuller won the 100 m freestyle at the 1924 Paris Olympics. He went on to win a total of five golds and one bronze medal during his Olympic career. While training for the 1932 Olympics, he was offered a $500-a-week contract to advertise swimwear. A Hollywood executive saw the adverts and offered Weissmuller the role of Tarzan. In 1932 he made his debut in the film *Tarzan the Ape Man*. He played the character in 11 more films over the next 16 years. He was the first of four Olympic medalists to play the film role. The others were Buster Crabbe (freestyle swimmer), Herman Brix (shot put) and Glenn Morris (decathlon).

The America's Cup

The America's Cup is the top sailing trophy and one of the best known trophies in the sporting world. It began in 1851 when the English Royal Yacht Squadron organized a 6-mi. (10 km) regatta of 17 boats around the Isle of Wight. The 102-ft. (31 m) American schooner *America* entered and won the trophy, then called the One Hundred Guinea Cup.

Competitors in the America's Cup, 2003

After *America*'s win, the trophy was renamed the America's Cup and given to the New York Yacht Club. There it remained unless won by a challenger. Over the next 132 years the New York Yacht Club successfully defended the trophy against 25 challengers, until in 1983 it was won by Australia. In 2003 the trophy returned to Europe when Russell Coutts in *Alinghi* won for Switzerland — a landlocked country! The latest Cup was held at Valencia, Spain, in 2007, and was once again won by *Alinghi* for Switzerland.

Swimming strokes

Breaststroke
The breaststroke was the first stroke used in competitive and recreational swimming. It is also the stroke that many people learn when they first take up swimming. The first reference to the breaststroke was in a French book in 1696. The sidestroke, with a scissor leg action, developed from breaststroke. Top swimmers can swim the breaststroke at 4.5 ft. (1.37 m) a second.

Backstroke
The backstroke is the only stroke in which the swimmers start in the water, rather than diving in. The stroke, in which swimmers lie on their backs and use their arms in a windmill motion, was first made popular in the U.S. by Harry Hebner in 1912. An earlier form of the backstroke was first seen at the 1900 Olympics. For this fast stroke, top speed is about 5 ft. (1.52 m) a second.

Butterfly
In this stroke, both arms enter and leave the water at the same time, while the legs perform a dolphin kick. It was developed in the 1930s and evolved from the breaststroke. Swimming coach David Armbruster developed the arm movement of the stroke at the University of Iowa in 1934 and the following year one of his swimmers, Jack Sieg, developed the foot and leg movements. The two combined produced the butterfly. The stroke was not officially approved until 1953 and became an Olympic event in 1956. Maximum speed is 5.5 ft. (1.67 m) a second.

Front crawl/freestyle
In 1844 two Native Americans competing in a swimming regatta in London, England, introduced their new revolutionary overarm stroke. Flying Gull beat Tobacco to take the winner's medal. The stroke was later developed by Englishman John Trudgen, and then by Australian Richard Cavill, who realized the importance of kicking the feet at the same time as moving the arms. Front crawl is the fastest swimming stroke and has a maximum speed of 5.6 ft. (1.71 m) a second.

Tour de France

The oldest and best-known of the world's great cycling tours is the Tour de France. The others are the Vuelta (Tour of Spain) and Giro (Tour of Italy).

- The Tour de France was first staged in 1903 when the course was made up of six stages over 1,509 mi. (2,428 km). Now the race is 3,000 mi. (4,830 km) or more and the course takes in more than 20 stages, often going into neighboring countries.
- The famous yellow jersey (*maillot jaune*) is worn by the current overall time leader in a race. It was first worn in 1919.
- The longest race was in 1926 when Lucien Buysse of Belgium won after 3,570 mi. (5,745 km).
- Around 15 million people every year line the streets to watch the Tour de France over its three weeks.
- The first U.S. winner of the Tour de France was Greg LeMond who won it in 1986, and again in 1989 and 1990. He was also the first English-speaking winner of the race.
- Eddie Merckx has won more of the big three tours than any other man. He has won the Tour de France five times, the Giro five times and the Vuelta once.

Lance Armstrong

Lance Armstrong (U.S.) has won the Tour de France a record seven times, two more than Jacques Anquetil (France), Eddie Merckx (Belgium), Bernard Hinault (France) and Miguel Indurain (Spain).

Olympic cycling

Cycling was included in the first Modern Olympics in 1896. Léon Flameng (France) won the first cycling gold in the 100 km race. Only two men competed — Flameng and Georgios Kolettis of Greece — and they had to race around a 1,093.5 ft. (333.3 m) track 300 times! During the race, Kolettis's bicycle needed repairing, so Flameng waited for him while the repairs were carried out. Cycling has been included in every Olympics since then. Below are the current Olympic events (BMX racing will be introduced in 2008).

Men

Track
Sprint (1,000 m)
Time trial (1,000 m)
Individual pursuit (4,000 m)
Team pursuit (4,000 m)
Points race (40 km)
Madison (60 km)
Keirin (2,000 m)

Road
Road race (individual)
Time trial (individual)
BMX (individual)

Mountain bike
Cross-country

Women

Track
Sprint (1,000 m)
Time trial (500 m)
Individual pursuit (3,000 m)
Points race (25 km)

Road
Road race (individual)
Time trial (individual)
BMX (individual)

Mountain bike
Cross-country

Lance Armstrong

Mountain biking

Mountain biking, or off-road biking, was started in 1974 by a group of Californian enthusiasts, who modified their bikes. By 1977, there was so much interest in the sport that manufacturers started to produce mountain bikes, and in 1983 the National Off-Road Bicycle Association (NORBA) was formed.

There are two principle types of mountain bike competitions — downhill riding and cross-country — and the first world championships were held in 1990. Cross-country mountain biking was first held at the Olympics in 1996. Competitors ride over a hilly, sometimes mountainous, natural course. Men race 25 to 30 mi. (40 to 50 km), and women 19 to 25 mi. (30 to 40 km).

The top male and female riders are both French. Nicolas Vouilloz won seven men's downhill world titles between 1995 and 2002. Anne-Caroline Chausson (France) has won 16 World Championship titles. She won the downhill event every year from 1996 to 2003 and again in 2005.

Olympic women's mountain bike race

Formula One

The Formula One World Championship normally lasts from March until October. In 2008 the schedule consisted of 18 races. Since 2003 the points system has been:

winner – 10 points
2nd – 8 points
3rd – 6 points
4th – 5 points
5th – 4 points
6th – 3 points
7th – 2 points
8th – 1 point.

The driver with the most points at the end of the season is the champion. There is also a manufacturers' championship.

In 2007, in his first season in Formula One racing, British racing driver Lewis Hamilton (born 1985) won four Grand Prix races (Canada, U.S., Hungary and Japan) and became the youngest ever to lead the Formula One World Championship.

World champion

German Michael Schumacher is the world's most successful Formula One driver. He has won a record seven world titles (1994, 1995, 2000, 2001, 2002, 2003, 2004) and also has the most race wins in a season — 13 in 2004.

Motor cycle racing

Grand Prix bikes come in engine sizes 125 cc, 250 cc and Moto GP (which replaced the old 500 cc event). Grand Prix bikes are made in small numbers just for racing. Superbikes are made in larger quantities and can be used on the road.

Top manufacturers

- An Aprilia machine first won at 250 cc in 1987, and the make is now dominant in both the 125 and 250 cc classes. They enjoyed their first Superbike success in 2000.
- Honda are the most successful manufacturer in motor cycle racing. They have won 48 Grand Prix world titles and have had 607 race wins. They are now also making a name for themselves in Superbike racing.
- Kawasaki bikes won their first world title (125 cc) in 1969. They have now won nine world titles in three classes as well as producing the 1993 Superbike world champion.
- The Yamaha company started in 1887 as musical instrument manufacturers and made their first motor cycle in 1955. They entered a bike in the 1961 French Grand Prix, but did not compete regularly until 1964, when they won the world 250 cc title.
- Suzuki began life as clothing makers before starting to make motor cycles. They won their first Grand Prix in 1962 and in the same year won the first ever 50 cc title.
- Ducati have been in Grand Prix racing since the 1950s. They are now by far the most successful manufacturer in Superbike history.

One and only

One of the great Indy 500 drivers was A.J. Foyt, the first of only three men to win the race four times. He won in 1961, 1964, 1967 and 1977. He drove a record 11,785 mi. (18,966 km) in 34 Indy 500 races. Foyt started racing in 1953. He is the only man to win the Indy 500, the Daytona 500 and the Le Mans 24 Hour races.

Young winners

- In 2005 Fernando Alonso (Spain) became the youngest ever winner of the Formula One World Driver's Championship aged 24 years, 2 months.
- In 1952 Troy Ruttman (U.S.) won the Indianapolis 500 (at that time part of the Formula One World Championship) aged 22 years, 3 months. Bruce McLaren (New Zealand) was the same age when he won the U.S. Grand Prix in 1959.
- Other young Formula One World Champions are Emerson Fittipaldi (Brazil), aged 25 years, 9 months, in 1972; Michael Schumacher (Germany), who won in 1994 at the age of 25 years, 10 months.

Indianapolis 500

The biggest single auto racing event in the United States is the Indianapolis 500, which is not just a race but a day-long festival. The race is part of the Memorial Day celebrations at the end of May, and crowds of 250,0000 flock to Indianapolis Motor Speedway from all over the U.S.

The course, which opened in 1909, is known as the Brickyard because the original circuit was made out of thousands of bricks. The first Indy 500 was held in 1911 and was won by Ray Harroun in his Marmon Wasp. Contestants race over 200 laps of the 2.5-mi. (4 km) oval track.

www.formula1.com search

Winter Olympics

The Winter Games (officially the International Winter Sports Week, but later recognized as the first Winter Olympics) was first held in 1924. It included five events: Nordic skiing, figure skating, speed skating, bobsledding and ice hockey.

Winter Olympics were held in the same years as the Summer Olympics until 1992, but since 1994 they have taken place every four years between the Summer Games. The sports being contested at the 2010 Vancouver Games are:

- Alpine skiing
- Biathlon
- Bobsled
- Cross-country skiing
- Curling
- Figure skating
- Freestyle skiing
- Ice hockey
- Ice sledge hockey
- Luge
- Nordic combined
- Short-track speed skating
- Skeleton
- Ski-jumping
- Snowboarding
- Speed skating
- Wheelchair curling

Snowboarding

Snowboards were invented in the 1970s, and the sport started to become popular in the 1980s. In 1998 snowboarding was included in the Winter Olympics for the first time, with Halfpipe and Parallel giant slalom events. Snowboard cross was added in 2006.

Top medal winners at the Winter Olympics (1924–2006)

Athlete — Men	Sport	Gold	Silver	Bronze	Total
Bjorn Dählie (Norway)	Cross-country	8	4	0	12
Sixten Jernberg (Sweden)	Cross-country	4	3	2	9
Ole Einar Bjoerndalen (Norway)	Biathlon	5	3	1	9
Ricco Gross (Germany)	Biathlon	4	3	1	8
Kjetil André Aamodt (Norway)	Alpine skiing	4	2	2	8
Sven Fischer (Germany)	Biathlon	4	2	2	8

Athlete — Women	Sport	Gold	Silver	Bronze	Total
Raisa Smetanina (USSR/Unified Team)	Cross-country	4	5	1	10
Stefania Belmondo (Italy)	Cross-country	2	3	5	10
Lyubov Egorova (Unified Team/Russia)	Cross-country	6	3	0	9
Uschi Disl (Germany)	Biathlon	2	4	3	9
Claudia Pechstein (Germany)	Speed skating	5	2	2	9

www.vancouver2010.org search

Top medal-winning nations at the Winter Olympics (1924–2006)

Country	Gold	Silver	Bronze	Total
USSR/Unified Team/ Russia	122	89	86	297
Norway	96	102	84	282
U.S.	78	81	59	218
Germany/ West Germany	76	78	57	211
Austria	50	64	71	185

Winter Olympics facts and figures 1900s

1924 Chamonix, France
There were 294 competitors from 16 nations. Norway won the most medals (17) and tied with Finland for gold medals (4).

1928 St. Moritz, Switzerland
Twenty-five nations and 495 competitors took part. Norway won the most medals (15) and the most golds (6).

1932 Lake Placid, U.S.
A total of 306 competitors from 17 nations competed. The U.S. won the most medals (12) and the most golds (6).

1936 Garmisch-Partenkirchen, Germany
There were 755 competitors from 28 nations. Norway won the most medals (15) and most gold medals (7).

1948 St. Moritz, Switzerland
A total of 28 nations and 713 competitors took part. Norway, Sweden and Switzerland tied for top medal position (10). Norway and Sweden tied for most golds (4).

1952 Oslo, Norway
A total of 732 competitors from 30 nations took part. Norway held both top medal (16) and top gold (7) position.

1956 Cortina D'Ampezzo, Italy
Thirty-two nations and 818 competitors took part. USSR were top medal winners (16) with the most gold wins (7).

1960 Squaw Valley, U.S.
Thirty nations took part with 665 athletes. USSR again won the most medals (21) and most golds (7).

1964 Innsbruck, Austria
Thirty-six nations and 1,186 athletes took part. The USSR won the most medals (25) and most golds (11) for the third time.

1968 Grenoble, France
A total of 1,293 athletes competed from 37 nations. Norway won the most medals (14) and most gold medals (6).

Competitors in the Men's Snowboard Cross final at the Turin 2006 Winter Olympics

The Stanley Cup

Every player on the winning team takes the Stanley Cup home for 24 hours to show off to family and friends. New York Islander Clark Gillies used it in 1980 to feed his dog, and in 1996 Colorado Avalanche defenceman Sylvain Lefebvre baptized his daughter in it.

Ice hockey

Ice hockey probably developed from a game called bandy that was played on ice-covered fields. The modern game is played over three 20-minute periods between two teams. Each team has six players on the ice at any one time. The object is to move the puck (a hard rubber disk) across the ice with a stick (maximum length 63 in. [160 cm]) and put it into the opponent's goal.

The National Hockey League (NHL) was formed in 1917. Today the NHL is made up of 30 teams split into two conferences. The Eastern Conference has 15 teams divided into three divisions: Atlantic, North-East and South-East. The Western Conference is also divided into three divisions: Central, North-West and Pacific. At the end of season the leading teams in each conference play each other. The winner of each plays for the Stanley Cup.

NHL's top goal scorers

Player	Goals
Wayne Gretzky	894
Gordie Howe	801
Brett Hull	741
Marcel Dionne	731
Phil Esposito	717
Mike Gartner	708

Top Stanley Cup winning teams

Montreal Canadiens	24
Toronto Maple Leafs	13
Detroit Red Wings	10
Boston Bruins	5
Edmonton Oilers	5

Ice skating

Famous skaters

- Ulrich Salchow, born in Sweden in 1877, was the greatest men's figure skater of all time. He won the first Olympic skating title at the 1908 London Olympics and between 1901 and 1911 he was the world champion on 10 occasions.
- Norway's Sonja Henie won Olympic golds in 1928, 1932 and 1936. She also won 10 world titles. She won nearly 1,500 cups and medals during her career. After leaving the sport in 1936 she became a film star and appeared in 11 films.

Fastest speed skaters

- Finland's Pekka Koskela set a new men's world record at Salt Lake City, Utah, on November 10, 2007 when he covered 1000m in 1 minute 7 seconds, knocking 3/100ths of a second off the old record.
- Cindy Klassen of Canada set a women's world record of 1 minute, 13.46 seconds for the 1,000 m at Calgary on March 24, 2006. The next day, she lowered the record further to 1 minute, 13.11 seconds.

Young star

The first athlete aged under 14 to win a Winter Olympic gold was Kim Yoon-mi of South Korea. She was in the winning 3,000 m speed-skating relay team at Lillehammer, Norway, in 1994.

Ski-jumping

In 2005 the world ski-jumping record was broken three times within 75 minutes! At the final meeting of the 2004–2005 Ski Jumping World Cup Bjørn Einar Romøren (Norway) set a new mark at 769.3 ft. (234.5 m). Then Matti Hautamaeki (Finland) put the record up to 772.6 ft. (235.5 m) before Romøren retook the record with a leap of 784.1 ft. (239 m).

2000s

1972 Sapporo, Japan
There were 1,232 competitors from 35 nations. USSR were top of the overall medal table (16) and won most gold medals (8).

1976 Innsbruck, Austria
Thirty-seven nations and 1,128 athletes took part. USSR won the most medals (27) and most gold medals (13).

1980 Lake Placid, U.S.
There were 1,067 competitors from 37 nations. USSR won the most medals overall (22) and most golds (10).

1984 Sarajevo, Yugoslavia
A total of 1,278 competitors from 49 nations took part. USSR won the most medals (25) but East Germany topped the gold medal table (9).

1988 Calgary, Canada
Fifty-seven nations fielded 1,423 athletes. USSR won the most medals (29) and most golds (11).

1992 Albertville, France
Sixty-three nations with 1,801 competitors took part. Germany won the most medals (26) and most gold medals (10).

1994 Lillehammer, Norway
A total of 1,739 athletes from 67 nations took part. Norway won the most medals (26) but Russia won most golds (11).

1998 Nagano, Japan
There were 72 nations taking part and 2,302 athletes. Germany won the most medals (29) and most gold medals (12).

2002 Salt Lake City, U.S.
Seventy-eight nations fielded 2,399 athletes. Germany again won the most medals (35) and most golds (12).

2006 Turin, Italy
A record 2,663 athletes from 82 nations took part. Germany was the top medal winner for the third time in a row (29) and also won the most gold medals (11).

See also
The Olympics: pages 282–83

Greyhound racing

Dog racing has been popular since ancient times, when dogs were used for hunting. Modern greyhound racing takes place on an oval-shaped track over distances from 690 ft. (210 m) to 3,600 ft. (1,100 m). An electric "rabbit" goes around the track, and the dogs are released from traps to chase it.

In the United States, greyhound races are run with eight dogs. There is a draw before the race to decide which trap each dog starts from. Each dog wears a colored jacket that matches its starting trap.

Hambletonian harness race

Harness racing

In harness racing the horses pull the drivers who sit in a two-wheeled cart called a sulky. There are two forms of harness racing — pacing and trotting.

The difference between pacing and trotting is in the way the horse moves. A pacing horse moves its right front and back legs together, then its left front and back legs. A trotter moves its left front leg and right back leg at the same time, followed by its right front leg and left back leg.

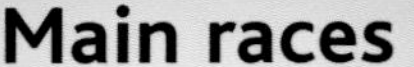

Main races

The leading race for trotters is the Hambletonian. This race was first held at Syracuse, New York, in 1926 and is now run every year at The Meadowlands, East Rutherford, New Jersey. It is named after a trotter called Hambletonian. The leading race for pacers is The Little Brown Jug, named after a 19th-century horse. It has been held at Delaware, Ohio, every year since 1946.

Top drivers

Herve Filion, born in Quebec, Canada, is the most famous driver in harness-racing history and set many records in his 35-year career. In 1968 he became the first driver to win 400 races in a season. He went on to achieve 400 or more wins per season in 14 other years. He was forced to retire in 1995 but made a comeback in 2002. He achieved his goal of reaching 15,000 wins before finally retiring the following year with a total of 15,086 wins.

John Campbell, from Ontario, Canada, is the top money-winning jockey in the sport. He started driving in 1972 at the age of 17 and was the first man to pass the $100 million and $200 million milestones in career earnings. He won the Hambletonian six times.

Top horse

Moni Maker was the first horse to pass the $5 million mark. Remarkably, she achieved this during a four-year career between 1997–2000. She won 60 of her 91 trotting races and won the Horse of the Year Award in 1998 and 1999. In 2003, the Italian-bred horse Varenne surpassed Moni Maker's career winning record.

Rodeo

Professional rodeo developed from the early days of ranching, when bull riding and calf roping were common activities. The first known rodeo with prize money was held at Deer Trail, Colorado, in 1869. The All-Round Cowboy World Champion is decided each year — the champion is the cowboy who wins the most money over a series of events. Top cowboys win more than $250,000 a year.

Record horse jumps

- The highest officially recognized horse jump is 8.1 ft. (2.47 m). The jump was made by Captain Alberto Larraguibel Morales (Chile) on Huasó on February 5, 1949, at Santiago, Chile. Richard "Dick" Donnelly (U.S.) claimed to have cleared 8.3 ft. (2.51 m) on a horse named Heatherbloom in Richmond, Virginia, in 1902, but this is an unofficial record.
- The world record height jumped by a horse in a puissance competition (in which horses jump a limited number of obstacles) was set on June 9, 1991. German rider Franke Sloothaak on Obtibeurs Leonardo cleared 7.9 ft. (2.4 m) in Chaudfontaine, Switzerland.
- The longest horse jump over water is 27.5 ft. (8.4 m). The jump was made by André Ferreira (South Africa) on April 25, 1975, in Johannesburg, South Africa, on a horse named Something.

The Breeders' Cup

The Breeders' Cup Limited was started in 1982 to encourage thoroughbred racing throughout the U.S. The first Breeders' Cup day was held on November 10, 1984, at Hollywood Park, Inglewood, California. Between 1984 and 2006 the championship was a single day event, but since 2007 has been spread over two days. It is held at a different course each year.

There are eight races on Breeders' Cup Day, which is held at a different course each year in October or November. The total prize money for the 2008 Breeders' Cup is $25.5 million. The top race is the Breeders' Cup Classic which runs over 1 mile, two furlongs. The prize money for this race in 2008 is $5 million with the winner receiving more than $2.7 million.

Winner of the Breeders' Cup Classic 2002

Most successful jockey

Laffit Pincay Jr. was the first man to win more than 9,500 races. He won the Breeders' Cup seven times, and the Kentucky Derby once. He retired in 2003 having won more than $225 million In December 2006, Russell Baze (Canada) passed Pincay's world record of 9,530 wins.

Top horse races

England

- The Epsom Derby was first held in 1780 and is now run over 1.5 mi. (2.4 km) at Epsom Downs each June. The first winner was a horse named Diomed. Jockey Lester Piggott won the Derby a record nine times.

- The Grand National is the world's best-known steeplechase, a horse race over a course with obstacles to be jumped. It was first run as the Grand Liverpool Steeplechase in 1839. The race now takes place every spring over 4.5 mi. (7.2 km) at Aintree in England and the winning horse has to clear 30 challenging fences. The famous horse Red Rum won the race a record three times between 1972–76.

France

- The Prix de L'Arc de Triomphe was first run in 1920. It takes place on the first Sunday in October every year and covers 1.5 mi. (2,400 m) over the Longchamps race course, Paris. Alleged, ridden by Lester Piggott, won the race in 1977 and 1978 and was the last horse to win two years in a row.

Australia

- The most important horse race in Australia is the Melbourne Cup, which dates from 1861. It is run on the first Tuesday in November at the Flemington Park race track in Victoria. Trainer Bart Cummings won the race a record 11 times between 1965 and 1999.

United States

- The Kentucky Derby was first held in 1875. It is run over 1 mile, 2 furlongs at Churchill Downs, Kentucky, on the first Saturday in May and is the most famous of all U.S. horse races. Eddie Arcaro and Bill Hartack have been the most successful jockeys with five wins each.

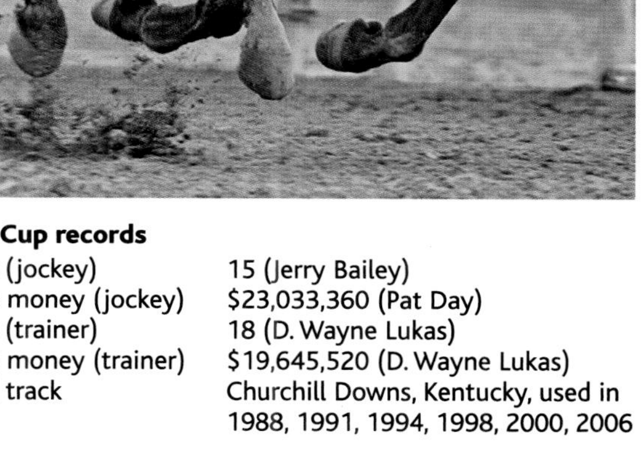

Breeders' Cup records

Most wins (jockey)	15 (Jerry Bailey)
Most prize money (jockey)	$23,033,360 (Pat Day)
Most wins (trainer)	18 (D. Wayne Lukas)
Most prize money (trainer)	$19,645,520 (D. Wayne Lukas)
Most used track	Churchill Downs, Kentucky, used in 1988, 1991, 1994, 1998, 2000, 2006

Breeders' Cup firsts

The 2003 Breeders' Cup produced two firsts. Julie Krone, who rode Halfbridled to victory in the Juvenile Fillies race, was the first woman to ride a winner at the event. One race ended in a dead heat — the first in Breeders' Cup history.

www.usef.org search

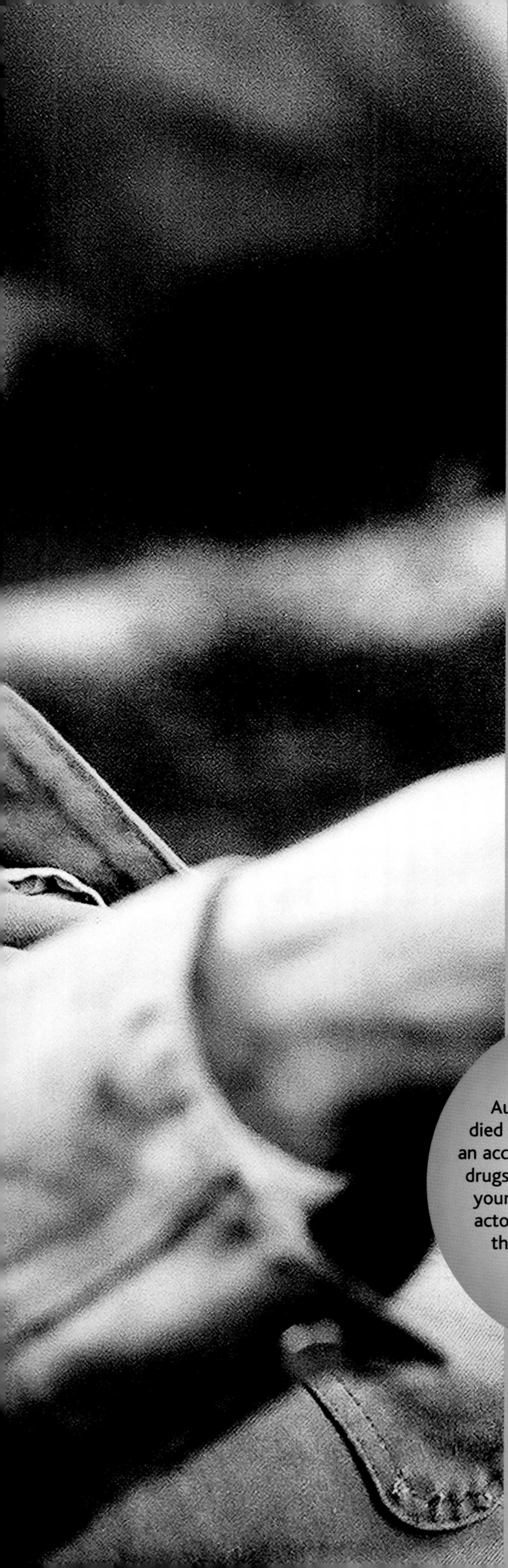

Last Lists

304 DEAD ENDS
306 LAST OF EVERYTHING

Young loss

Australian actor Heath Ledger died in 2008 at the age of 28, from an accidental overdose of prescription drugs. One of Hollywood's brightest young stars, the Oscar-nominated actor's death was a huge shock to the world and highlighted the dangers of combining prescription medication.

Unusual deaths

Aeschylus
Aeschylus was a famous Greek dramatist who died in 456 BC. A prediction that he would be killed by a blow from heaven came true when an eagle carrying a tortoise dropped it on his head.

King Alexander of Greece
He died after being bitten by his pet monkey in 1920.

Francis Bacon
This Elizabethan philosopher caught a chill while trying to deep-freeze a chicken by stuffing it with snow. He died in 1626.

Hilaire Belloc
Although born in France, Hilaire Belloc was an English writer and member of parliament. He died in 1953 after a burning coal fell out of his fire and set him ablaze.

Madéleine-Sophie Blanchard
Madame Blanchard was the widow of pioneer balloonist Jean-Pierre Blanchard. She was killed in Paris, France, in 1819, when fireworks set fire to her balloon.

Jerome Cardan
Cardan was an Italian physician, mathematician and astrologer. He starved himself to death in 1576 to make sure that his own prediction of his death would come true.

Lord Carnarvon
Carnarvon was an amateur Egyptologist who financed the excavation of Tutankhamun's tomb in 1922. Several months after opening the tomb, Carnarvon died suddenly from a mosquito bite. This began the legend of the curse of Tutankhamun.

Isadora Duncan
This American dancer was strangled in 1927 by her scarf. It became caught in the wheel of a Bugatti sports car in which she was a passenger.

Anton Dvorák
The Czech composer died in 1904 of a chill which he caught while trainspotting.

Frederick, Prince of Wales
Frederick was the son of George II and heir to the British throne. He died in 1751 after being hit by a cricket ball.

Harry Houdini (Erich Weiss)
Houdini was a famous escapologist who claimed he could withstand being punched in the stomach. He died in 1926 — after being punched in the stomach.

William Huskisson
Huskisson was a British member of parliament. He was run down by a train during the opening of the first railway in 1830.

Jean-Baptiste Lully
This Italian-French composer died in 1687 after accidentally stabbing his foot with a stick while beating time. The short conductor's baton came into use soon afterward.

Thomas Midgley
Midgley was an American inventor who was strangled in 1944 by a machine he had invented to help him move after contracting polio. He invented three products that have since been found to be environmentally harmful: lead in gasoline, CFCs in fridges and aerosols, and the insecticide DDT.

Forever young

The following are some of the most famous people who died early and so remain forever young in our minds.

Name/cause/year	Age at death
King Edward V of England, murdered, 1483	12
Saint Agnes martyred, c. AD 304	13
King Edward VI of England, natural causes, 1553	15
Anne Frank German diarist, in concentration camp, 1945	15
Lady Jane Grey Queen of England, executed, 1554	16
Thomas Chatterton English poet, took poison, 1770	17
Anastasia Grand Duchess of Russia, assassinated, 1918	17
Ritchie Valens American rock singer, plane crash, 1959	17
King Tutankhamun Egyptian pharaoh, c. 1340 BC	18
Heliogabalus Roman Emperor, assassinated, AD 222	18
Joan of Arc French heroine, burned at the stake, 1431	19
Catherine Howard Queen of Henry VIII, beheaded, 1542	20
Billy the Kid (William H. Bonney) American outlaw, shot, 1881	21

Name/cause/year	Age at death
Eddie Cochran American rock singer, car accident, 1960	21
Pocahontas Native American Indian princess, smallpox, 1617	22
Buddy Holly American rock singer, plane crash, 1959	22
Aaliyah (Aaliyah Haughton) singer, plane crash, 2001	22
River Phoenix actor, drug overdose, 1993	23
Clyde Barrow U.S. outlaw, shot by Texas Rangers, 1934	24
James Dean American film actor, car crash, 1955	24
Lee Harvey Oswald assassin of John F. Kennedy, murdered, 1963	24
John Keats English poet, tuberculosis, 1821	25
"Red Baron" Manfred von Richthofen German flying ace, shot down, 1918	25
Jean Harlow film actress, illness, 1937	26
Brian Jones Rolling Stones guitarist, drowned, 1969	26
Jimi Hendrix rock guitarist, drugs, 1970	27
Kurt Cobain Nirvana lead singer, shooting suicide, 1994	27
Anne Brontë British writer, tuberculosis, 1849	29

Famous last words

Julius Caesar, 44 BC
Roman emperor, who was assassinated by conspirators, including Brutus, a man he thought was his friend. According to legend and Shakespeare, Caesar said: "Et tu Brute?" (You as well, Brutus?)

Caligula, AD 41
Roman emperor who was assassinated: "I am still alive!"

Catherine de Medici, 1589
Queen of France: "Ah, my God, I am dead!"

Joseph Henry Green, 1863
British doctor, after checking his own pulse: "Stopped."

General John Sedgwick, 1864
In the American Civil War, Sedgwick was shot by a sniper as he remarked: "They couldn't hit an elephant at this distance."

Viscount Palmerston, 1865
British Prime Minister: "Die, my dear doctor? That's the last thing I shall do."

Billy the Kid (aka William Bonney, Henry McCarty), 1881
American outlaw, before being shot by Sheriff Pat Garrett: "Who is it?"

Marie Antoinette, 1893
French queen, who accidentally trod on her executioner's foot as she went to the guillotine: "Pardonnez-moi, monsieur." (Pardon me, sir.)

Oscar Wilde, 1900
Opinions differ about the Irish writer's last words. Some people claim he said: "Either these curtains go/that wallpaper goes, or I do."

Prince Philippe
Prince Philippe, heir to the French throne, was killed when his horse tripped over a pig in the streets of Paris in 1131.

Pliny the Elder
Roman writer Pliny was choked by the fumes of the erupting volcano Vesuvius in AD 79.

Sir Thomas Urquhart
Urquhart was the Scottish author of books with extraordinary titles such as *Logopandecteision*. He died laughing when told of the Restoration of Charles II in 1660.

William III
This British king died in 1701, after a fall from his horse when it stumbled over a molehill. His opponents drank a toast to the mole, calling it "The little gentleman in black velvet."

See also
Volcanic eruptions: page 46

Poster for Houdini show

Joan of Arc, 15th-century French heroine who was burned at the stake aged 19

Queen Victoria, 1901
British queen: "Oh, that peace may come" (a reference to the war at the time in South Africa). "Bertie!" (her husband, Prince Albert).

Captain Lawrence Oates, 1912
Oates was a member of Scott's expedition to the South Pole. He was terribly injured from frostbite and went to his death rather than hold up his companions. When he left the tent he said, "I am going outside and may be some time."

Anna Pavlova, 1931
Ballerina: "Get my swan costume ready!"

Lytton Strachey, 1932
English writer: "If this is dying, then I don't think much of it."

Douglas Fairbanks Sr., 1939
American film actor: "I've never felt better."

Heinrich Himmler, 1945
Nazi leader, as he committed suicide by taking poison: "I am Heinrich Himmler!"

H.G. Wells, 1946
English novelist, author of *The Time Machine*: "I'm all right."

John F. Kennedy, 1963
Moments before he was shot, Kennedy replied to "You certainly can't say that the people of Dallas haven't given you a nice welcome, Mr. President" with his final words, "No, you certainly can't."

www.findagrave.com search

Entertainment lasts

Shakespeare's last play
Most people agree that *The Tempest* (1611), is the last play Shakespeare wrote, although some think he may have written a later play that has been lost. Shakespeare died in 1616, and *The Tempest* was first published in 1623.

Charles Dickens' last story
The Mystery of Edwin Drood was Charles Dickens' last novel. It was published in monthly episodes, but ended, unfinished, when Dickens died in 1870.

Beethoven's last symphony
Ludwig van Beethoven's *Ninth Symphony* was the last he composed before his death in 1827. He promised the London Philharmonic Society that he would write his *Tenth Symphony* for them, but died before he could begin work on it.

The last Beatles concert
The Beatles last played together in public at Candlestick Park, San Francisco, on August 29, 1966. Their last publicly performed song was "Long Tall Sally."

The last silent film
The Four Feathers (1929) was the last silent film released by a major studio. The 1976 film *Silent Movie* does contain one word, "Non!" (French for no), which is spoken by Marcel Marceau, a mime artist.

The sixth and last Star Wars film
Star Wars: Episode III — Revenge of the Sith was released in 2005. It made almost $850 million worldwide, bringing the total for the series, which started in 1977, to $4.3 billion.

Crime and punishment lasts

Last executions for witchcraft in the U.S.
On September 22, 1692, seven women and one man were hanged for witchcraft at Salem and other places in New England.

Last beheading in the U.K.
On April 9, 1747, 80-year-old Simon Fraser, Lord Lovat, was beheaded for treason at Tower Hill, London.

Last stagecoach robbery in the U.S.
Surprisingly, this was committed by a woman, Canadian-born Pearl Hart, with her partner Joe Boot. On May 29, 1899, they held up a stagecoach near Globe, Arizona, robbing the passengers of $421. They were caught and Hart was sentenced to five and Boot to 30 years in Yuma Prison.

Last public hanging in the U.S.
On August 14, 1936, in Owensboro, Kentucky, Rainey Bethea was hanged for murder in front of a crowd of 20,000 people. Public hanging was banned in the U.S. soon afterward.

Last executions in Canada
Murderers Ronald Turpin (Canada) and Arthur Lucas (U.S.) were hanged at Toronto's Don Jail on December 11, 1962. Capital punishment was officially abolished in Canada on July 14, 1976.

Last witness to the assassination of Abraham Lincoln
Samuel James Seymour, who died on April 13, 1956, was the last surviving witness to the assassination of the American president. Seymour was only 5 years old when he saw John Wilkes Booth shoot Abraham Lincoln at Ford's Theatre, Washington D.C., on April 14, 1865.

Last person executed by guillotine
The last person to be executed in public was the murderer Eugene Weidmann who had his head cut off at Versailles, France, on June 17 ,1939. The last official use of the guillotine in France was on September 10, 1977, when Hamida Djandoubi was executed for murder at Baumetes Prison, Marseilles.

Last Prisoner of Alcatraz

Alcatraz Island in the Bay of San Francisco, California was a prison for over 100 years. Surrounded by freezing water, it was considered impossible to escape. Armed robber Frank Clay Weatherman was its last prisoner. He left the island on March 21, 1963, after which Alcatraz closed.

Last Aztec emperor

Montezuma II was removed from power by Spanish invaders and killed in June 1520.

Montezuma II, the last Aztec emperor

Royal lasts

The last Egyptian pharaoh
Cleopatra VII ruled from 69 BC, when she was 17 years old, until 30 BC, when Egypt became a province of the Roman empire.

The last Roman emperor
Romulus Augustus was about 14 when he was removed from power in AD 476. The Roman empire split into western and eastern divisions.

The last British king killed in battle
Richard III was killed at the battle of Bosworth on August 22, 1485.

The last British king born abroad
George II was born in Hanover, Germany, on November 10, 1683.

The last king of France
Louis-Philippe (1773–1850) reigned from 1830 until February 24, 1848, when he gave up his throne. Disguised as "Mr. Smith," he traveled to England where he lived until his death.

The last emperor of China
Hsüan T'ung gave up his throne on February 12, 1912, and later took the name Henry Pu-yi. The film *The Last Emperor* (1987) is about his life.

The last tsar of Russia
Nicholas II was removed from power by the Russian Revolution of 1917, and murdered with his family at Ekaterinburg in July 1918. Their remains were reburied in St. Petersburg in July 1998.

Pharos of Alexandria

Last of the Seven Wonders

The last of the Seven Wonders of the world to be built was the 406.9 ft. (124 m) Pharos (lighthouse) of Alexandria, Egypt, which was completed in 279 BC. It was partly knocked down by invaders and later destroyed by an earthquake. The only one of the Seven Wonders that survives today is the Great Pyramid at Giza in Egypt.

Transportation lasts

Last Pony Express

The Pony Express service carried urgent mail by horse in the United States, but died out when coast-to-coast telegraph lines were connected near Salt Lake City, Utah, on October 26, 1861.

Last horse car in New York

The last horse car — a horse-drawn bus — operated on the Bleecker Street Line, New York City, on July 26, 1917.

The last Model T Ford

The Model T, first produced in 1908, was one of the most popular cars of all time. The last U.S.-made Model T (number 15,007,033) rolled off the production line on Thursday May 26, 1927.

Last transatlantic airships

The giant German airship Hindenburg exploded in Lakehurst, New Jersey, on May 6, 1937. At the same time, the Graf Zeppelin flew from Brazil to Germany — it was the last to cross the Atlantic and made its final flight on June 19, 1937.

Last flight of Concorde

Concorde was the world's only supersonic airliner. It was in service for 34 years until it made its last commercial flight, from New York to London, on October 24, 2003.

Last voyage of the Titanic

The last voyage of the *Titanic* was also its first. It sank on April 15, 1912, after striking an iceberg, killing 1,517 people.

Prow of the wreck of the *Titanic*

See also
The Seven Wonders of the ancient world: pages 206–207

See also
Shipwrecks: page 218

Bold type indicates entries with two or more pages of information about them.

A

abbey, 162
Abominable Snowman, 175
abstract art, 242
Abu Simbel, 245
Academy Awards, 155, 268–69
acid rain, 70
acids, 77
Acosta, Carlos, 261
acre, 85
action painting, 242
Actium, 181
actresses, 269
Adams, John, 26
Adar, 169
adventurers, **152–53**
Aegosopotami, 181
Afghanistan, 138
Africa, 130–35
Agincourt, 180
Aida, 253
aircraft carriers, 210
air disasters, 219
air pollution, 70
air transportation, 216–17
Albania, 128
albums, 255
Alcatraz, 184, 185
Alcock, John, 216
Algeria, 130
aliens, 175
alkalis, 77
alligators, 62
almanacs, 229
alphabets, 224
aluminum, 76
amazing feats, 95
Ambati, Balamurali, 156
American colonial architecture, 199
American Film Institute, 268
American plants, 50
America's Cup, 295
Amnesty International, 111
ampere, 84
amphibians, 62–63
Amun-Ra, 160
amusement parks, 220
ancient architecture, 198
Ancient Egypt, 106
Ancient Egyptian gods, 160
Ancient Greece, 106
ancient poems, 234
ancient religions, 160
Anderson, Hans Christian, 232
Andorra, 126
Andrew, 165
anemometer, 45
Angel of the North, 245
Angkor, Cambodia, 119
Angola, 134
animals, 52–54, 69
  kingdom, 52–53
  life expectancy, 53
  sizes, 54
  space pioneers, 28–29
  sports, 300–301
animated films, 270–71
anniversary gifts, 149
anthologies, 229
Antigua, 121
Anubis, 160
apes, 55
Aphrodite, 161
Apollo, 161
  Moon landings, 175
Apollo 8, 154
Apollo 13, 173
Apollon, 161
Aquarius (water bearer), 172
Aquila, 21
Arabic alphabets, 224–25
Arabic language, 224
arch bridges, 204
Ares, 161
Argentina, 122
Aries (ram), 172
armed forces, 179
Armenia, 129
Armory Show, 244
Armstrong, Lance, 154, 296
art, 243
  theft, 184
Art Deco, 199, 242
Artemis, 161
art exhibitions, 244
artists, 242, 242–43
Art Nouveau, 242
Ashes, 287
Ashtabula Bridge disasters, 218
Ash Wednesday, 168
Asia, 136–41
asteroids, 24
Aston Martin, 212
astronauts, 30–31, 154
astronomy, 26–27
Atacama Desert, Chile, 45
Aten, 160
Athena, 161
athletics, 284–85
Atlantis, 119
atlases, 229
auctions, 246
Audubon, John James, 228
Auld Lang Syne, 251
Australia, 142–43
Australian Desert, 36
Australian Open, 291
Australian Rules football, 287
Austria, 127
authors, 230–31
automated teller machine (ATM), 193
Av, 169
avalanches, 46
aviation pioneers, 216
awards, 155
Awdry, W., 233
Azerbaijan, 129
Aztec empire, 107
Aztec gods, 161

B

Babbage, Charles, 87
backstroke, 295
Baden-Powell, Robert, 157
badminton, 290
Bahamas, 121
Bahrain, 137
Balanchine, George, 261
ballet, 260–61
  companies, 260
  dancers, 261
  terms, 260
ball games, 286–87
ballistics, 185
Baltic, 211
Banff National Park, 221
Bangladesh, 139
banknotes, 192
Bannister, Roger, 284
Barbados, 122
Barbie doll, 190
Barbuda, 121
barges, 210
Barnard, Edward, 26
barn dances, 258
Barnum, Phineas T., 256
baroque, 242
  architecture, 198
Barris, George, 246
Bartholomew, 165
Baryshnikov, Mikhail, 261
bascule bridges, 204
baseball, 279, 286
basketball, 279, 287
baslica, 162
bassoon, 252
Bast/Bastet, 160
Batman, 267
battery-operated cars, 208–9
battledore and shuttlecock, 290
Battle of Stalingrad, 180
Battle of the Somme River, 180
Beagle, 211
beam bridges, 204
bears, 55
Beatles, 254
Beaufort, Francis, 44
Beaufort scale, 44, 84
beds, 188
bees, 61
Beijing, 276–77
Belarus, 127
Belgium, 125
beliefs and ideas, 165–76
Belize, 121
Bell, Alexander G., 88
belly dance, 258
Bengali language, 224
Benin, 132
Beowulf, 170
Beowulf, 234
Berkeley, Busby, 258
Berlin wall, 105
Bernhardt, Sarah, 155
Bes, 160
bestsellers, 230, 232
Bhutan, 138
Bible, 165, 230
Bible animals, 165

bibliographies, 229
Bibliothèque Nationale, 228
Big Ben, 82
Big Bertha, 178
Bigfoot, 175
biggest ships, 211
big numbers, 83
bin Laden, Osama, 185
biographical dictionaries, 229
biographies, 229
biological warfare, 179
bird flu, 65
bird migration, 58
birds, 58–59
eggs, 59
sizes, 58
Birds of America, 228
Bismark, 211
black cats, 172
black death, 64, 104
Black Hawk helicopter, 179
black holes, 20
Blanchard, Jean-Pierre, 217
Blenheim, 180
Blériot, Louis, 216
blockbuster films, 266–67
blue poison arrow frog, 63
blue train, 214
Bly, Nellie, 152
Blyton, Enid, 232
board games, 191
body records, 94
Bolivia, 123
Bollea, Terry, 293
Bond, James, 223–3, 267
books, 228–33
books firsts and records, 229
boomerang bullets, 178
Booth, Hubert Cecil, 188
Borman, Frank, 154
Bosnia and Herzegovina, 128
Boston Marathon, 278
Boston Public Library, 228
Botswana, 135
bottled water
types, 99
Bounty, 211
Bowie, James, 80
Bowie knife, 80
boxing, 292
Brachiosaurus, 68
Braille, 225
Braille, Louis, 225
Braille cell, 225
brain power, 92
branding, 184
brass instruments, 252
Brazil, 123
break dancing, 258
breastroke, 295
Breeders' Cup Limited, 301
Bridge of Sighs, 204
bridges and tunnels, 204–5
brightness scale, 77
British empire, 107
British Imperial State Crown, 192
British Library, 228
Brooklyn Bridge, 205
Brothers Grimm, 232
Brownies, 157
Browning pistol, 178
Brunei, 141
buddhas, 244
Buddha statue, 193
Buddhism, 162
Buddhist festivals, 168
Buddhist temples, 200
Bugatti Royale, 212
Bugs Bunny, 270
buildings and structure, 199–207
building styles, 198–99
bullet trains, 215
Bunyan, Paul, 170
burgers, 98
Burj, Dubai, 202–3
Burkina Faso, 132
burning at the stake, 184
Burton, Richard, 153
Burundi, 134
buses, 213
Bush, George, 67
Bussell, Darcey, 261
butterfly (swimming stroke), 295
Byzantine architecture, 198

C

cables, 88
Cabot, John, 153
Cairo, Egypt, 38
calendar, 16–18
Californium, 78
calorie counts, 96
Cambodia, 141
Cameroon, 132
Canadian, 214
Canadian law, 182
cancer (crab), 172
Canis Major, 21
Canis Major Dwarf galaxy, 21
canoeing, 294
Canterbury Tales, 228
cantilever bridges, 204
Cape Verde, 130
Capello, Fabio, 289
Capricorn (goat), 172
carbon dioxide pollution, 71
car ferries, 210
Caribbean Sea, 44
Carolingian architecture, 198
Carroll, Lewis, 232–33
Carter, Howard, 193
Casals, Pablo, 154
Casper the Ghost, 270
Caspian Sea, 41
catacombs of Alexandria, 207
catamarans, 210
cathedrals, 162
celebrities, 154
cellos, 252
cell phones, 89
cell phone throwing, 281
Celsius, 84, 85
cement manufacturing, 71
centaurs, 170
centisecond, 15
Central African Republic, 133
Central America, 120–23
Ceres, 161
cesspits, 189
chain gang, 184
Chairman Mao, 151
chamber pots, 189
champagne bottles, 99
champion divers, 55
Channel crossing, 217
channel tunnel, 207
chapels, 162
Chappe, Claude, 226
Charles, Jacques, 217
Chaucer, Geoffrey, 228
checks, 193
Chichén Itzá, 16, 119, 207
Chief Crazy Horse, 245
children, 156
children's books, 232
Chile, 123
Chilvers, Peter, 81
China, 139
Chinese alphabets, 225
Chinese boarding school, 241
Chinese calendar, 17
Chinese empire, 106
Chinese folk religions, 162
Chinese gods, 160
Chinese language, 224
Christian festivals, 168
Christianity, 162, 166–67
Christianity timeline, 166
Christmas, 168
Christ the Redeemer, 207, 245
chronologies, 229
chronon, 15
Chrysler Building, 199
churches, 162, 200–201
Churchill, Winston, 97
Cinderella, 232
cinema, 264–65
circus history, 256
Cirque du Soleil, 256
Citizen Kane, 268
city populations, 118
clarinets, 252
Classen, Cindy, 299
classical music, 252–53
Cliff Palace (Mesa Verde), Colorado, 119
climate, 42–43
Clinton
Bill, 67
Hilary, 144–5
cloud layers, 44
clovers, 172
CN Tower, 202
coal, 194, 195
coastlines, 41
coat of arms, 149
Cochran, Jacqueline, 152
Codex Hammer, 228
Codex Leicester, 228
Cody, Samuel F., 216
Coelacanth, 68
Coffeyville, Kansas, 45
cog railway, 214
coins, 192
collecting, 246–47
collectors, 246
Colombia, 123
colonialism, 102
Colosseum, 207

Colossus of Rhodes, 206
Colt, Samuel, 80
Colt revolver, 80
Columbia, 29
Columbus, Christopher, 150, 153
columns, 201
combined gun and plow, 178
Comet Hale-Bopp, 25
comic books, 236
comic books and films, 267
comics, 236
comic strips, 236
Commonwealth Bay, Antarctica, 44
communication, 226–27
Comoros, 141
computers, 86–87
  data, 86
  games, 191
  games and films, 266
  speak, 86
  timeline, 86
Concorde, 216
conflict and crime, **179–85**
conga, 258
conspiracy theories, 175
constellations, 21
container ships, 210
continents, 37
convents, 162
conversions, 84
Cook, James, 153
Cook, Thomas, 220
Coral Sea, 181
cosmic calendar, 12
Côte d'Ivoire, 132
countries' pets, 66–67
countries' populations, 117
country development, 117
court of appeals, 182
court terminology, 183
cousins, 148
cowboy inventions, 80
credit cards, 193
Crick, Francis, 151
crime, 179–85
  and punishment lasts, 306
Croatia, 128
crocodiles, 62
crop circles, 175
Cruise, Tom, 272, 273
cruise ships, 210
crustacean sizes, 57
Crux Australis, 21
Cuba, 100, 101, 110, 121
cubism, 242
Cub Scouts, 157
Cukor, George, 155
Curtiss, Glenn, 216
Cutty Sark, 211
cymbals, 253
Cyprus, 129
Cyrillic alphabets, 224
Czech Republic, 127

D

da Gama, Vasco, 153
dagoba, 162
dance, 258–59
dance films, 258
dance marathons, 259
dangerous plants, 51
Dartmoor, 185
Darfur, 176–7
Darwin, Charles, 150
da Vinci, Leonardo, 80, 228
Davis, Shani, 299
days, 14
Daytona, 276–7, 297
deadly snakes, 62
Dead Sea, 37
death cap, 51
death penalty, 183
deaths, 304
decathlon, 284
deep sea divers, 57
deep-sea trenches, 41
de la Hoya, Oscar, 292
Deltawerken flood barrier, 207
Demeter, 161
Democratic Republic of Congo, 133
Denmark, 124
density, 76
Depp, Johnny, 272
desert climate, 43
deserts, 36
Desert Shield/Storm/Sabre/Kuwait, 180
detective stories, 229
diamonds, 192
Diana, 161
diaries, 230
Dickens, Charles, 67, 188
dictionaries, 229
Dietrich, Marlene, 272
digestive system, 92
digital watches, 13
Dingley Hall, 190
dinosaurs, 68, 99
directories, 229
Disney, Walt, 270
Disneyland, 220
district courts, 182
Diva festival, 169
divorces, 148
Djibouti, 131
DNA testing, 185
documentary films, 266
dodo bird, 69
Dolin, Anton, 261
domes, 201
Dominica, 122
Dominican Republic, 121
Donald Duck, 270
Dona Paz, 218
double bass, 250, 252
Dowell, Anthony, 261
Dr. Seuss, 233
dragons, 171
drums, 250, 253
ducking stool, 184
dumper trucks, 213
Dunbar armored robbery, 184
Duncan, Lee, 67
Duomo Cathedral, 201
DVD, 274

E

Earhart, Amelia, 152, 216
Earth, 22, 34–47
  elements, 79
  layers, 34
  observation satellites, 29
earthquakes, 47
  detectors, 46
Easter Island, 174
Easter Sunday, 168
East Timor, 141
eating insects, 61
eBooks, 229
Ecuador, 123
Eden Project, 207
Edison, Thomas, 251
education, 240–41
education and the arts, 240–47
Egypt, 130
Eiffel, Gustave, 202
Eiffel Tower, 202, 220
Einstein, Albert, 150
El Alamein, 180
El Cid, 170
electric cars, 213
electric chair, 183
electronic books, 229
elements, 78–79
El Salvador, 120
Emmy Awards (Oscars), 155
emperor penguins, 59
Empire State Building, 203
Empress of Ireland, 218
Encke, Johann, 25
encyclopedias, 229
endangered and extinct, 68–69
endangered animals, 69
Endeavor, 211
energy, 194–95
English language, 224
entertainment lasts, 306
environment, 70–71
environmental art, 242
epic poems, 234
Epiphany (Twelfth Night), 168
epoch, 15
Epsom Derby, 301
Equatorial Guinea, 133
Eritrea, 130
Estonia, 126
Ethiopia, 130
Etruscan architecture, 198
euphonium, 252
euro coins, 192
Europe, 124–29
  colonialism, 103
Eurostar, 215
Everglades, 221
execution, 183
exhibitions, 220
ex-planet, 23
Explorer of the Seas, 211
explorers, 153
Expo 2005, 244
Exposition Internationale des Arts Décoratifs et Industriels, 244
Exposition Universelle, 244
expressionism, 242
extinct, 68–69
Exxon Valdez, 71

F

face transplants, 97
Fahrenheit, 85
fairies, 170
fairy tale authors, 232
families and relationships, 148
famous cars, 212–13
famous cat lovers, 67
famous dog lovers, 67
famous last words, 304
famous people, 150–51
Fantasy Entertainment Complex, 201
farm animals, 65
fastest dogs, 66
Federal Bureau of Investigation (FBI), 185
federal court, 182
femtosecond, 15
femur, 93
ferries, 210
Festival of Britain, 244
festivals, 168, 220
Fiji, 143
film, 264–71
  budgets, 265
  songs, 269
  stars, 272–73
  winners, 268–69
fingerprinting, 185
Finland, 124
fire engines, 213
First Impressionist Exhibition, 244
fish sizes, 57
flamenco dancing, 259
flightless birds, 59
Flintstones, 270
flogging, 184
fluegelhorn, 252
flutes, 252
flying animals, 58–59
flying frogs, 28
flying mammals, 59
follicle mites, 64
Fonteyn, Margot, 261
food and drink, 98–99
football, 289
Ford, Henry, 212
forest destruction, 70
Formula One World Championship, 297
Fossett, Steve, 153, 217
fossil fuel burning, 71
Four Freedoms, 111
Fox, Terry, 155
Foyt, A.J., 297
France, 125
Frank, Anne, 230
Franklin, Benjamin, 155, 188
Freedom of the Seas, 211
freestyle (swimming), 295
French horn, 252
French Open, 291
French Revolution, 104
freshwater lakes, 39
friary, 162
Friday the 13th, 173
frogs, 63
frog sizes, 63
front crawl, 295
funiculars, 214
fussy sleepers, 188

G

Gabon, 133
Galapagos Islands, 221
galleons, 210
galleys, 210
Gallipoli, 180
Gambia, 131
Gandhi, Mahatma, 150
garbage and recycling, 72–73
gas burning, 71
Gates, Bill, 151, 228
Gateshead Millennium Bridge, 204
Gatling gun, 178
gazetteers, 229
Gemini (twins), 172
geological timeline, 34–35
Georgia, 128
Georgian architecture, 198
Georgia Superdome, 201
Germany, 124
Gettysburg, 180
geysers, 37
Ghan, 214, 215
Ghana, 132
giants, 95, 170
giant statues, 245
GI Joe, 190
Girl Guides, 157
Girl Scouts, 157
glaciers, 39
Gladstone, William, 155
glass slippers, 232
global warming, 70
glossary, 229
GM Terex, 213
goddesses, 160–61
gods, 160–61
Gods of the Vedas, 163
go-fast boats, 210
gold, 78
  refinery, 78
  salt shaker, 193
  stores, 193
Golden Arrow, 214
Golden Gate Bridge, 205
Golden Globe Awards, 155
Golden Raspberry Awards, 155
golden treasures, 193
golf, 286
Good Friday, 168
Google, 87
Goscinny, René, 232
Gothic architecture, 198
government types, 110
Grammy Awards, 155
Grand Coulee Dam, 195
Grand National steeplechase, 280, 301
Grand Prix, 297
Gray, John, 67
Great Barrier Reef, 221
Great Bed of Ware, 188
Great Britain, 211
great buildings, 200–201
Great Eastern, 211
Great Exhibition, 220, 244
Great Lakes, 38
Great Pyramid of Giza, 206, 207
great robberies, 184
Great Wall of China, 207
Great Western, 211
Greek alphabets, 224
Greek architecture, 198
Greek gods, 161
Greek Parthenon, 198
Greenwich Prime Meridian, 13
Gregorian calendar, 16
Grenada, 122
Grey, Beryl, 261
greyhounds, 66
  racing, 300
Griffith-Joyner, Florence, 285
Grimm, Jacob, 232
Grimm, Wilhelm, 232
Guadalcanal, 181
Guantanamo Bay, 185
guard dogs, 65
Guatemala, 120
Guggenheim Museum, 207
Guillem, Sylvie, 261
Guinea, 131
Guinea-Bissau, 132
guitars, 250
Gulf War, 180
Guru Granth Sahib, 164
Gutenberg Bible, 228
Guyana, 123

H

Hagia Sophia, 207
haiku, 235
Haiti, 121
Hale, George, 26
Halley, Edmond, 26
Halley's comet, 24–25
Hamilton, Lewis, 297
Hanging Gardens of Babylon, 206
Hanning, John, 153
Happy Birthday to You, 251
hard cheese, 178
harness racing, 300
harps, 252
Harry Potter, 156, 230
Hartland Bridge, 204
Hartono, Rudy, 290
Harvard University Library, 228, 240
Hastings, 180
Hathor, 160
Hawking, Stephen, 154
head line, 173
health and medicine, 96–97
heart line, 173
Hebrew alphabets, 224
Hebrew calendar, 17
Helium, 79
helper dogs, 65
Hemingway, Ernest, 67
Hendrix, Jimi, 255
Henie, Sonja, 299
Henry VII, 109
Hephaistos, 161
heptathlon, 284
Hera, 161

Heracles, 171
Hercules, 171
Herschel, William, 26
Hestia, 161
Heye, George Gustav, 246
Heyerdahl, Thor, 211
hieroglyphics, 226
higher education students, 240–41
high-tech architecture, 199
Hillary, Edmund, 153
Hindenburg disaster, 219
Hindu gods and goddesses, 163
Hinduism, 162
Hindustani language, 224
Hindu temples, 200
historical periods, 102
history timeline, 12–13, 104–5
Hitler, Adolph, 151, 154, 230
Hobby-Eberly telescope, 27
Hogan, Hulk, 293
holy places, 162
home, 189–95
Homer, 234
Honduras, 120
Hoover Dam, 207
horse races, 301
horseshoes, 172
Horus, 160
hot-air balloon flights, 217
household waste, 72
Houston Astrodome, 201
hovercraft, 210
Hubble, Edwin, 26
Hubble space telescope (HST), 27, 29
Hudson, Henry, 153
hula, 258
human body, 92–95
human organs, 92
human skeleton, 93
humerus, 93
Hungary, 128
Hussein, Saddam, 105,137, 184
hydroelectricity, 194, 195
hydrofoils, 210
hydrogen, 79, 92
  balloon flights, 217
hydroplanes, 210

I

iPhone, 89
iPod, 251, 254
iceberg density, 76
icebergs, 41
ice hockey, 299
Iceland, 125
ice skating, 299
identikit, 185
Iliad, 234
illustrators, 233
imaginary lands, 231
Inca empire, 107
incineration, 73
India, 138
Indianapolis 500, 297
Indian calendar, 17
Indian Ocean, 47
Indian schoolchildren, 156
Indiana Jones, 262–3
Indonesia, 141
Industrial Revolution, 103
Inglis, Mark, 155
in-laws, 148
insects, 60–61
  life expectancy, 60
intelligent dogs, 67
international caps, 288
International Date Line, 13
International Monetary Fund, 111
international organizations, 111
International Space Station, 13, 220
International System of Units (SI), 82
international youth organizations, 157
Internet, 86–87
inventions, 80–81
Iran, 137
Iraq, 137
Iraq Central Bank, 184
Ireland, 124
Isis, 160
Islam, 162
Islamic calendar, 17
Islamic festivals, 169
Israel, 136
Italy, 126
Iyar, 169

J

Jacobean architecture, 198
jail sentences, 185
Jamaica, 121
James the Great, 165
James the Less, 165
Japan, 140
  alphabet, 225
  architecture, 199
  language, 224
Jesus Christ, 167
Jewish festivals, 169
Joan of Arc, 184
jockeys, 301
John (disciple), 165
Johnson, Amy, 216
Jolie, Angelina, 156
Jordan, 137
Jordan, Michael, 279
joule, 84
Judaism, 162
Judas Iscariot, 165
Jude, 165
junks, 210
Juno, 161
Jupiter, 22, 161
Jutland, 181
juvenile courts, 182

K

Kain, Karen, 261
Kalashnikov, 178
Kangchenjunga, 36
Kansai International Airport, 207
Katsura Palace, 199
Kazakhstan, 136
Keller, Helen, 155
Kentucky Derby, 301
Kenya, 135
Khan, Jahangir, 291
Khayyám, Omar, 234
King, Martin Luther, 151
King Arthur, 170
King Herod, 100
King Kong, 273
Kintai-Kyo Bridge, 204
Kiribati, 142
Kislev, 169
kitchen, 189
Knights of the Round Table, 166
Kon-Tiki, 211
Koran, 164
Kosovo, 112–3, 129
Kursk, 218
Kuwait, 137
Kyrgyzstan, 138

L

Labors of Hercules, 170
ladders, 172
Lake District, 221
lakes, 38–39
Laki, Iceland, 46
land, 36–37
  battles, 180
  pollution, 70
landfills, 73
landlocked countries, 116
language, 224–25
  dictionaries, 229
  and literature, 224–37
Laos, 140
Large Binocular Telescope, 27
last lists, 304–7
Last Supper, 165
latitude, 13
Latvia, 127
law, 182–83
law courts, 182
lawn tennis, 290, 291
leaders, 108–9
Leaning Tower of Pisa, 207
leap seconds, 14
Lebanon, 137
Ledger, Heath, 302–3
legal language, 182
legendary heroes, 170–71
LeMay, Harold, 246
Lent, 168
Leo (lion), 172
Leonard, Sugar Ray, 292
Lepanto, 181
leprechauns, 170
Leshan Giant Buddha, 245
Les Misérables, 257
Lesotho, 134
Levi's jeans, 80
Leyte Gulf, 181
Liberia, 132
Liberty of the Seas, 211
Libra (scales), 172
libraries, 228–29
Library of Congress, 228
Libya, 130

Liechtenstein, 127
life expectancy records, 95
life line, 173
life sciences, 50–73
lighthouses, 200
light speed, 20
limbo, 258
limousines, 213
Lindbergh, Charles, 216
Lindy Hop, 258
line dancing, 258
liners, 210
Liston, Sonny, 292
literature, **224–37**
Lithium, 79
Lithuania, 127
Livingstone, David, 153
Loch Ness Monster, 175
London Bridge, 205
longest bridges, 204
longitude, 13
Losar, 168
lost cities, 119
Louisiana Superdome, 201
Louis XIV, 246
Lovell, James, 154
Lowell, Percival, 26
Lüger, 178
lunar cycle, 17
Lusitania, 211, 218
Luxembourg, 124

M

Macedonia, 129
Machu Picchu, Peru, 119
Madagascar, 135
Madame Butterfly, 253
Magellan, Ferdinand, 153
Maglev train, 214
magpies, 172
Mahabharata, 234
major wars, 180
Malawi, 134
Malaysia, 140
Maldives, 141
Mali, 131
Malta, 126
mammals, 54–55
man and beast, 64–65
Mandela, Nelson, 151
man eaters, 65
mannerism, 242
Manville, Tommy, 148
Mao Tse-tung, 151
Mao Zedong, 151
marathon, 180, 284–85
Marie Celeste, 211
marine mammals, 56
marine mammal sizes, 56
Markova, Alicia, 261
marriages, 148–49
Mars, 22, 161
Marshall Islands, 143
Mary Rose, 218
Massier, Charles, 26
Masters, 286
mathematical symbols, 82
mathematics, 82–83
Matthew, 165
Maundy (Holy) Thursday, 168
Mauretania, 211
Mauritania, 131
Mauritius, 135
Mauser, 178
Mausoleum at Halicarnassus, 206
Maxim gun, 178
Mayan calendar, 16
Mayan empire, 107
Mayan gods, 161
Mayan months, 16
Mayflower, 211
McKay, Heather, 291
McNamara, Frank X., 193
measures, 84–85
medal winners, 181
medical milestones, 96–97
medicine, 96–97
Medieval Ages, 102
Medieval art styles, 242
meeting houses, 162
mega multiples, 82
Melba, Nellie, 253
Melbourne Cup, 301
melting points, 78
Mercalli scale, 84
Mercedes, 212
Mercury, 22
mermaids, 171
meteorite craters, 34
meter, 85
metric measurements, 99
Mexico, 120
Michelangelo, 154
Mickey Mouse, 190, 270
Micronesia, 142
microsecond, 15
microwave ovens, 189
Middle Ages, 102
mile running, 284
military animals, 65
military satellites, 29
Milky Way, 21
Millennium Dome, 201
millisecond, 15
minerals, 34–35
Minerva, 161
MINI, 213
Minnie Mouse, 190
mirrors, 172
Mitchell, Helen, 253
Model T Ford, 212
modern living, 103
Mogul empire, 107
Mohs scale, 34
Mohs' scale, 84
Moldova, 128
Molotov cocktail, 178
Monaco, 125
Mona Lisa, 184
monarchs, 109
monastery, 162
Monet, Claude, 154
money, 192
Mongolia, 138
monkeys, 55
monographs, 229
Monopoly, 191
monorail, 214
Montgolfier, Etienne, 217
Montgolfier, Joseph, 217
Montgomery, Lucy Maud, 232
Month, 160
months, 14
Mont Pelée, Martinique, 46
Moon, 24
Moorish/Islamic architecture, 198
Morse, Samuel, 226
Morse code, 88, 226
Morse keys, 227
Moscow, 180
Moses, 165
mosque, 162
mosques, 200
most wanted, 185
motor cycle racing, 297
Motown, 248–9
mountain biking, 296
mountain climate, 42
mountains, 36
Mount Everest, 153
Mount Rushmore, 245
movie monsters, 272–73
movie screens, 265
movie stars, 272
Mozambique, 135
Mozart, Wolfgang Amadeus, 156
Mt. Rainier, Washington, 45
MTV Video Music Awards, 155
Muhammad Ali, 292
Multi-Purpose Arena, 201
Munch, Edvard, 242
museums and monuments, 244–45
musical instrument records, 250
musical terms, 251
music and performance 261, 250–61
Muslims, 162, 169
Myanmar, 140, 158–9
mysterious monsters, 175
mysterious places, 174
mythical creatures, 170

N

nails, 93
names, 146–47
Namibia, 134
nanosecond, 15
Naseby, 180
national parks, 221
natural disasters, 46–47
natural gas, 194
Nauru, 143
Navigator of the Seas, 211
Nazca Lines, 174
Nefertum, 160
Nelson, Horatio, 154, 201
neoclassical/Federalist architecture, 198
neoclassicism, 242
Nepal, 139
nephews, 148
Neptune, 23, 161
Netherlands, 125
Newbery Medal, 232
Newgate, 185
newspapers and magazines, 236–37
Newton, Isaac, 26
New Zealand, 142

Nicaragua, 120
nicotine, 51
nieces, 148
Niger, 131
Nigeria, 132
Nijinsky, Vaslav, 261
Nile River, 38
Nina, 211
Nisan, 169
Nobel Prize, 155
Nobel Prize for literature, 231
Norman architecture, 198
Normandie, 211
North America, **120–21**
North Atlantic Treaty Organization, 111
North Korea, 139
North Pole, 152
novellas, 229
novels, 229
nuclear power, 194, 195
nuclear weapons, 178
nucleus, 78
number 13, 173
nunneries, 162
Nureyev, Rudolf, 261
nursery rhyme book, 232

O

Obama, Barack, 144–5
obelisks, 201
Oberammergau, 257
oboes, 252
observatories, 26
Oceanic, 211
ocean liners, 210
oceans, 40–41
Odyssey, 234
ohm, 84
oil, 194, 195
oil tankers, 210
oil tanker spills, 71
oldest animal, 53
oldest people, 94
Olympic cycling, 296
Olympic Games, 220, 278, 282–85
Olympic rowing, 294
Olympic swimming, 294
Olympic water sports, 294
Oman, 137
operas, 253
opera terms, 252
opium, 51
Orbiting Frog Otolith satellite (OFO-A), 28
orchestras, 250, 252
Organization for Economic Cooperation and Development, 111
organs, 250
Orient Express, 214
Orion, 21
Oscars, 155, **268–69**
Osiris, 160
Osmium, 78
Ottoman empire, 107
Owen, Richard, 99
oxygen, 92

P

package tours, 220
Paedocypris progenetica, 57
pagoda, 162
paintings, 243
Pakistan, 138
Palau, 142
Pali Canon, 164
palmistry, 173
Palm Sunday, 168
Panama, 120
Panama Canal, 207
Pankhurst, Emmeline, 150
Papua New Guinea, 142
parachute fire escape, 80
Paraguay, 123
Paris Exhibition, 220
particle detector, 74–75
patron saints, 167
Pavlova, Anna, 261
peacock feathers, 58
pelota, 290
Penny Black stamp, 227
Pentecost, 168
people, 147–57
Pepys, Samuel, 230
percussion instruments, 253
Perrault, Charles, 232
Peru, 123
Peruvian Andes mountains, 38
Peter (disciple), 165
pets, 66–67
Pharos of Alexandria, 207
Philadelphia Centennial Exposition, 244
Philip (disciple), 165
Philippines, 140
Phillips, Thomas, 246
phobias, 96
phonetic alphabets, 225
photographs, 243
phrasebooks, 229
pianos, 250
piccolo, 252
picosecond, 15
Pincay, Laffit, 301
Pinta, 211
Pisces (fishes), 172
plague carriers, 64
planet Earth, 34–47
plants, 50–51
Platinum, 78
plays, 256
playwrights, 256
Pluto, 23, 26, 27, 28
Plutonium, 78
poets and poetry, 234–35
poets laureate, 235
Poland, 127
polar exploration, 105, 152
Polar Express, 271
polka, 258
pollution, 70–71
Polo, Marco, 153
polygons, 83
Pompeii, Italy, 119
Pont d'Avignon, 204
Pont Neuf, 204
pool, 293
pop and rock, 254–55
pop art, 242
popes, 166
Popeye, 270
popular first names, 146
population density, 117
popup books, 229
pop-up toasters, 189
Porcelain Pagoda of Nanking, 207
Porlock, Alice, 154
Porsche, Ferdinand, 212
portable radio, 275
Portugal, 126
Poseidon, 161
postal firsts, 227
postimpressionism, 242
Potassium, 79
potatoes, 51
Potter, Beatrix, 232
Potter, Harry, 202–3
Po Valley, 180
Powell, Asafa, 15
pre-Columbian architecture, 198
predictions and prophecies, 172–73
prehistoric ages, 102
prehistoric architecture, 198
President, 211
presidents, 108
Presley, Elvis, 175, 254
Prime numbers, 83
Princess Alice, 218
Principe, 133
printed books, 229
priory, 162
prisons, 185
Prix de L'Arc de Triomphe, 301
psychological profiling, 185
Ptah, 160
Pulitzer, Joseph, 155
Pulitzer Prize, 155
punishments, 184
Putin, Vladimir, 154
pyramids, 20

Q

Qatar, 137
quasars, 20
Queen Elizabeth, 211
Queen Mary, 211
Quimby, Harriet, 152, 216
quotations, 229

R

Ra, 160
racket sports, 290–91
Radcliffe, Daniel Jacob, 156
radio, 274–75
rail disasters, 218
rail networks, 215
rain gauges, 45
Rambert, Marie, 261
Ratatouille, 271
realism/naturalism, 242
record-breaking plants, 51
recreation injuries, 189
recycling, 72–73
Reeve, Christopher, 155
Reformation, 102
refrigerators, 189
refugee camp, 156
regular solids, 83

religious buildings, 162
Renaissance, 102
Renaissance architecture, 198
Renaissance art styles, 242
reptiles, 62–63
Republic of Congo, 132
Reshef, 160
Rezazadeh, Hossein, 293
Richter scale, 47, 84
ricin, 51
rivers, 38–39
road and rail tunnels, 205
road disasters, 218
road kill recipes, 98
Robin Hood
Robinson, Sugar Ray, 292
rocks, 34–35
Rococo, 242
  architecture, 198
rodeo, 300
Rodriguez, Alex, 286
Rolls-Royce, 212
Roman architecture, 198
Roman baths, 220
Roman empire, 106
Romanesque architecture, 198
Roman gods, 161
Romania, 129
Roman numerals, 82
romanticism, 242
roofs, 201
Roosevelt, Theodore, 64
Rosh Hashana, 169
rowing, 294
Rowling, J.K., 230, 232
royal lasts, 306
Rubáiyat, 234
rubber-tired metro, 214
rugby, 287
rulers, 108–9
Runyan, Maria, 155
Russia, 137
Russian language, 224
Russian Revolution, 105
Russian State Library, 228
Rwanda, 134

S

sacred texts, 164–65
Sagan, Carl, 12
Sagittarius (archer), 172
Sagrada Familia Cathedral, 200
sailing, 294
  vessels, 210
salamander, 63
Salamis, 181
Salchow, Ulrich, 299
Samoa, 143
San Marino, 126
Santa Maria, 211
Sao Tome, 133
satellites, 88
Saturday Night Fever, 258
Saturn, 23
Saudi Arabia, 137
Scarlatti, Domenico, 67
Schlumpf, Fritz, 246
Schlumpf, Hans, 246
schools, 241
Schulz, Charles, 67
Schumacher, Michael, 297
science
  and crime detection, 185
  and technology, 76–89
Scorpio (scorpion), 172
scouts, 157
scrabble, 191
screen legends, 272
sea, 56–57
  battles, 181
  creatures, 57
  density, 76
  elements, 79
Seaborg, Glen Theodore, 78
second, 15
Securitas depot robbery, 184
Sekhmet, 160
semaphore, 226
Senegal, 131
September 11, 2001, 219
sequels, 229
Serengeti National Park, 221
Seth, 160
seven wonders
  medieval world, 207
  modern, 207
Seychelles, 141
Shakespeare, William, 150, 228
sharks, 56, 57
sheep, 64
Shemini Atzeret, 169
ships, 210–11
shipwrecks, 218
shrapnel, 178
Shrek, 271
shrines, 163
Shuttleworth, Mark, 220
Sidis, William James, 156
Sierra Leone, 132
sign language, 227
signs of the zodiac, 172
Sikkhism, 162
Simpsons, 270
Singapore, 140
singing parts, 252
Sing Sing, 185
Sir Gawain and the Green Knight, 234
Sivan, 169
ski jumping, 299
skin, 93
Sky Dome, 201
skyscrapers, 202–3, 210
sleep facts, 97
Sleeping Beauty's Castle, 220
Slovakia, 128
Slovenia, 129
snake facts, 63
snooker, 293
snowboarding, 298
soap operas, 275
soccer, 281, 288
Sodium, 79
solar day, 15
solar energy, 195
solar power, 74
solar system, 22
solar system 1, 22–23
solar system 2, 24–25
solar year, 15
Solomon Islands, 142
Somalia, 131
Somme, 180
songs, 251
Sony Reader, 229
Sotomayor, Javier, 284
sound barrier, 217
sound levels, 77
South Africa, 135
South America, **122–23**
South Korea, 139
South Pole, 152
space, 20–31
  dogs, 28
  exploration, 28–29
  junk, 29
  rockets, 29
  tourism, 31, 220
Spain, 126
Spangler, James Murray, 188
Spanish Armada, 181, 218
Spanish language, 224
spectrum colors, 77
speeds, 279
Sphinx, 207, 245
spider ladder, 80
spiders, 60–61
spilling salt, 172
Spitz, Mark, 294
sports, 278–301
  crowds, 281
  events, 280–81
  injuries, 189
  teams, 278
  tourism, 220
squash, 291
Sri Lanka, 138
St. George, 171
St. Lucia, 122
stage names, 273
Stalingrad, 180
stamp collections, 247
stamps, 227
Stanley, Henry Morton, 153
Stanley Cup, 299
stars, 20–21
Star Wars, 266
statue of justice, 182
Statue of Liberty, 245
statues, 245
Steiff teddy bear, 190
Stetson hat, 80
Stine, R.L., 232
stocks and pillory, 184
Stonehenge, 174, 207
stoning, 184
strange laws, 183
strings, 252
Strite, Charles, 189
submarines, 210
subway disasters, 218
subways, 215
Sudan, 131, **176–7**
Sukkoth (Feast of the Tabernacles), 169
Sultana, 218
Summer Olympics, 282
Sun, 20
Sundance Awards, 155
Superior Dome, 201
Superman actors, 272
supernovae, 20
Supersaurus, 68
Supreme Court, 182

Suriname, 122
surnames, 146
surrealism, 242
surveillance, 185
suspension bridges, 204
Swaziland, 134
Sweden, 124
Swedish Treskilling Yellow stamp, 227
swimming strokes, 295
swing bridges, 204
Swiss Re Building, 199
Switzerland, 127
Sydney Harbour Bridge, 205
symbolism, 242
synagogues, 163, 200
Syria, 136

T

tabernacles, 163
table tennis, 290
Tacoma Dome, 201
Taglioni, Maria, 261
Taiwan, 139
Taj Mahal, 207
Tajikistan, 138
taking the waters, 220
tallest buildings, 202
Tambora, Indonesia, 46
Tammuz, 169
Tanzania, 134
Tarzan, 295
Tasman, Abel, 153
Taurus (bull), 172
Teatro Olimpico, 256
techno toy, **186–87**
teddy bear, 190
Teddy Girl, 190
Tek Sing, 218
telecommunications, 88–89
telecom timeline, 88
telegraph messages, 88
telephone bell, 89
telescopes, 26
television, 274–75
temperature conversions, 84
Temple of Artemis, 206
temples, 163
ten commandments165, 165
tennis scoring, 291
Teotihuacán, 174
Tereshkova, Valentina, 152
Terracotta Army, 238–39
test cricket, 287
Thailand, 140
theater, 256–57
theater disasters, 256
The Charleston, 258
thermometer, 45
thesaurus, 229
Thomas, 165
Thoth, 160
threatened animals, 69
ThrustSSC, 213
Thursday, 14
tibia, 93
tidal energy, 195
tigers, 69
time, 12–13
  periods, 14–15
  pyramid, 16
  words, 15
  zones, 13
timpani/kettledrums, 253
Tin Lizzie, 212
tires, 213
Titan, 25
Titania's Palace, 190
Titanic, 211, 218, 307
titanium, 76
Tito, Denis, 220
toads, 63
Togo, 133
toilet paper, 188
toilets, 189
tolls, 171
Tom and Jerry, 270
Tommy gun, 178
Tonga, 143
Tony Awards, 155
top food fish, 56
top food plants, 50
Torah, 164
tornados, 45
tortoises, 63
Tour de France, 296
tourism, 220–21
tourist countries, 221
Toutatis, 24
Tower Bridge, 205
toys and games, 190–91
Toy Story, 271
track and field records, 285
Trafalgar, 181
Train à Grande Vitesse (TGV), 215
trains, 214–15
translations, 230
transportation
  disasters, 218–19
  lasts, 307
  and travel, 210–21
transport beasts, 65
Trans-Siberian Express, 214
travel, 210–21
  guides, 229
travelers, 153
travelers' checks, 193
Travolta, John, 258
Treasures of Tutankhamun, 244
trees, 50–51
triangles, 253
Trinidad, 122
trombones, 252
tropical climate, 43
trumpets, 252
tsunami, 40
tubas, 250, 252
Tunisia, 130
Turkey, 136
Turkmenistan, 138
Turner Prize, 155
turtles, 63
Tutankhamun's mask, 193
tutu, 261
Tuvalu, 143
TV, 274–75
Twain, Mark, 67, 233
twelve disciples, 165

U

Uganda, 134
Ukraine, 128
Ultrasaurus, 68
Uluru, 35
UN Convention on the Rights of the Child, 157
unexplained, 174–75
unicorns, 170
United Arab Emirates, 136
United Kingdom, 125
United Nations, 111
United Nations Children's Fund, 111
United Nations Educational, Scientific, and Cultural Organization, 111
United States, 120
universe, 12, 20–21
Unsen, Japan, 46
Uranus, 23
urine, 92
Uruguay, 123
Ushiku Daibutsu, 245
US independence, 104
US Open, 291
US presidents, 108
Uzbekistan, 139

V

vacuum cleaner, 188
vampires, 171
van Beethoven, Ludwig, 154
Vanuatu, 143
Vatican City State, 126
Vedas, 164
Venezuela, 122
Venus, 22, 161
Verne, Jules, 152
Vespucci, Amerigo, 37
Vesta, 161
Vesuvius, Italy, 46
Victor, 211
Vietnam, 140
violas, 252
violins, 252
Virgo (virgin), 172
volcanic eruptions, 46
Volkswagen Beetle, 212–13
volt, 84
volume conversions, 84
Voyager of the Seas, 211
Vulcan, 161
vulnerable animals, 69

W

wars, 180
washing machines, 189
Washington Monument, 201
waste reduction, 73
water dangers, 56–57
waterfalls, 38
Waterloo, 180
Watson, James, 151
Watson, Thomas, 86
watt, 84
wave height scale, 40
wealth, 192–93

weapons, 178
weather, 44–45
weddings, 148
Wegman, William, 67
weightlifting, 293
weights, 84–85
weird weapons, 178
Weissmuller, Johnny, 295
Welles, Orson, 268
Wellington Monument, 201
Wembley Stadium, 201
werewolves, 171
Western architecture, 198
western art styles, 242
whales, 56
wheel sports, 296–97
White, E.B., 233
White Lightning Electric Streamliner, 213
Whitsunday, 168
Wilhelm Gustloff, 218
Williams, Serena, 291
Williams, Venus, 291
Williamson, Corliss, 287
Wimbledon, 291
wind energy, 195
wind farm, 195
windmills, 195
wine bottles, 99
Winehouse, Amy, 155
Winter Olympics, 298–99
wireless communications, 88
witches, 184
Witherspoon, Reese, 269
women voters, 110
wonders of the Ancient World, 206–7
Woods, Tiger, 286
Woodstock Festival, 255
work and home, 189–95
world
  cities, 118–19
  civilizations, 106–7
  countries, 116–17
  empires, 106–7
  fairs, 244
  forests, 50
  oldest people, 94
  politics, 110–11
  religions, 162–63
World Bank, 111
World Cup, 281, 288
World Health Organization, 111
World's Columbian Exposition, 244
World Series, 286
World Trade Center, 219
World Trade Organization, 111
World War II, 41
worldwide death causes, 96
World Wildlife Fund, 111
worst battles, 180
Wrangell-St. Elias, 221
wrestling, 293
Wright, Orville, 216
Wright, Wilbur, 216

X

Xingu, 221

Y

yachts, 210
Yager, Carol, 94
Yankee Doodle, 251
Yeager, Charles, 217
yearbooks, 229
Yellowstone, 221
Yemen, 136
Yeti, 175
YMCA, 157
Yom Kippur (Day of Atonement), 169
Yoon-mi, Kim, 299
Yorktown, 180
YWCA, 157

Z

Zambia, 134
Zeus, 161
Zeus statue, 206
Zimbabwe, 135
zoetrope, 270
zoo shopping list, 52

Author's acknowledgments

The author would like to thank the following people, organizations and publications for kindly supplying information for this book.

Academy of Motion Picture Arts and Sciences (AMPAS)*
American Film Institute
American Forests
Amnesty International
Association of Leading Visitor Attractions
Alexander Ash
Caroline Ash
Nicholas Ash
Box Office Mojo
BP Statistical Review of World Energy 2006
Richard Braddish
Thomas Brinkhoff
British Broadcasting Corporation (BBC)
The British Council
British Film Institute
British Library
British Museum
British Phonographic Industry (BPI)
Central Intelligence Agency (CIA)
Richard Chapman
Christian Research
Christie's
Computer Industry Almanac
Department for Environment, Food and Rural Affairs (DEFRA)
Earth Impact Database
The Economist
Emporis
Energy Information Administration
Ethnologue
Euromonitor
Food and Agriculture Organization of the United Nations (FAO)
Global Education Digest (UNESCO)
Global Forest Resources Assessment (FAO)
Gold Fields Mineral Services
Nathalie Golden
Russell E. Gough
Monica Grady
Robert Grant
Greyhound Racing Association of America
Home Accident Surveillance System (HASS)
Home Office
Human Development Report (United Nations)
Imperial War Museum
International Centre for Prison Studies
International Federation of Audit Bureaux of Circulations
The International Institute for Strategic Studies, *The Military Balance 2006–2007*
International Olympic Committee (IOC)
International Telecommunication Union (ITU)
International Union for the Conservation of Nature (IUCN)
Internet Movie Database (IMDb)
Internet World Stats
London Zoo
Dr. Benjamin Lucas
Mattel, Inc.
Chris Mead
Mike Melvill
National Aeronautics and Space Administration (NASA)
National Basketball Association (NBA)
National Football League (NFL)
National Statistics
Natural History Museum
AC Nielsen
The Nobel Foundation
Organisation for Economic Co-operation and Development (OECD)
Organisation Internationale des Constructeurs d'Automobiles (OICA)
Felicity Page
Parker Brothers
Patent Office
Periodical Publishers Association
Tony Pattison
Population Reference Bureau
Recording Industry Association of America (RIAA)
Dafydd Rees
Louise Reip
Royal Astronomical Society
Royal Observatory, Greenwich
Screen Digest
Screen International
Robert Senior
Sotheby's
Time magazine
Tree Register of the British Isles
United Nations (UN)
United Nations Children's Fund (UNICEF)
United Nations Educational, Scientific and Cultural Organization (UNESCO)
United Nations Environment Programme
United Nations Population Division (UNPD)
U.S. Census Bureau International Data Base
U.S. Geological Survey
U.S. Patent Office
Variety
Lucy T. Verma
Ward's Motor Vehicle Facts & Figures 2006
WebElements
Whitaker's Almanack 2007
World Association of Girl Guides and Girl Scouts
World Association of Newspapers
World Bank
World Christian Database
World Gazetteer
World Health Organization (WHO)
World of Learning
World Organization of the Scout Movement
World Tourism Organization (WTO)

population data
© by Stefan Helders
www.world-gazetteer.com

Country names
The following abbreviations are used for country names on page 285
BUL: Bulgaria
CHN: China
CUB: Cuba
CZE: Czech Republic
DEN: Denmark
ETH: Ethiopia
FRA: France
GBR: Great Britain
GDR: German Democratic Republic (1955–90)
MAR: Morocco (Maroc)
QAT: Qatar
ROM: Romania
RUS: Russian Federation
UKR: Ukraine
U.S.: United States of America
USSR: Union of Soviet Socialist Republics (1922–91)

Picture acknowledgments

L = left, R = right, C = center, T = top, B = bottom

Page **2** Flirt Collection/Photolibrary; **4** Robert Harding Travel/Photolibrary; **8** Robert Harding Travel/Photolibrary; **10** Roberto Schmidt/AFP/Getty Images; **11T** Jeremy Swinborne/iStockphoto; **12C** Jeremy Horner/Corbis; **14TL** Eileen Tweedy/The Art Archive; **15B** David Taylor/Getty Images; **16C** Charles & Josette Lenars/Corbis; **17TR** REGIS MADEC/Thaiworldview.com; **18** NASA/EPA/Corbis; **19B** NASA; **19TC** NASA; **20TR** NASA; **20BR** NASA; **20C** NASA; **20CR** NASA; **22BL** NASA; **22CL** NASA; **22CR** NASA; **22C** NASA; **22TR** NASA; **23BL** NASA; **23BC** NASA; **23BR** NASA; **23TL** NASA; **24CL** Gianni Dagli Orti/Corbis; **24C** NASA; **24TR** NASA; **24TC** NASA; **25CL** NASA; **25C** NASA; **26CL** Roger Ressmeyer/Corbis; **26TR** Bettmann/Corbis; **27C** NASA; **28R** NASA; **29TL** NASA; **30CL** NASA; **30C** NASA; **31TR** NASA; **32** Mark Webster/Oxford Scientific/Photolibrary; **34C** Charles & Josette Lenars/Corbis; **35T** Timothy Ball/iStockphoto; **36BL** Theo Allofs/ZEFA/Corbis; **36TL** iStockphoto; **37CL** Robyn Glover/iStockphoto; **38B** Andre Klaassen/iStockphoto; **38T** Frank Leung/iStockphoto; **40T** Daniel Leclair/Reuters/Corbis; **41C** Stewart Westmorland/Corbis; **41BL** John Pitcher/iStockphoto; **44TR** Shaun Lowe/iStockphoto; **44TC** Clint Spencer/iStockphoto; **46B** Gary Braasch/Corbis; **47T** Koch Valerie/iStockphoto; **48** Marian Bacon/Animals Animals/Photolibrary; **50TR** Peter Fuchs/iStockphoto; **51BL** Frans Lanting/Corbis; **51C** Jon Rasmussen/iStockphoto; **52CR** Richard Nowitz/Corbis; **53TR** Brad Thompson/iStockphoto; **54TL** Jim Jurica/iStockphoto; **55R** iStockphoto; **55BL** iStockphoto; **56CL** Amos Nachoum/Corbis; **57TR** Will Burgees/Reuters/Corbis; **57CL** Don Bayley/iStockphoto; **58TR** Tim Davis/Corbis; **58BL** Anastasiya Maksymenko/iStockphoto; **59B** Tim Davis/Corbis; **60TL** Thomas Bedenk/iStockphoto; **61CL** Dan Guravich/Corbis; **61TR** Will Schmitz/iStockphoto; **62B** Jeremy Edwards/iStockphoto; **63TR** Steve Geer/iStockphoto; **64CR** Jose Carlos Pires Pereira/iStockphoto; **65TR** Wolfgang Kaehler/Corbis; **66B** Nico Smit/iStockphoto; **66TR** iStockphoto; **68T** Christoph Ermel/iStockphoto; **69BR** Jameson Weaton/iStockphoto; **70TR** Wayne Lawler/ Ecoscene/Corbis; **70B** Loic Bernard/iStockphoto; **72B** Roger Milley/iStockphoto; **73BC** Marcelo Wain/iStockphoto; **73CR** Nathan Watkins/iStockphoto; **74** Maximilien Brice/CERN/ Science Photo Library; **75TR** Les Cunliffe/iStockphoto; **76TR** Liz Van Steenburgh/iStockphoto; **76CR** Liz Van Steenburgh/iStockphoto; **78CR** Bettmann/Corbis; **78CL** Donall O Cleirigh/iStockphoto; **80L** Strauss/Curtis/Corbis; **81T** Alexander Kolomietz/iStockphoto; **84TL** Hulton-Deutch Collection/Corbis; **84R** Carole Gomez/iStockphoto; **85TR** Nogues Alain/Corbis/Sygma; **86L** iStockphoto; **87TL** Bettmann/Corbis; **87C** Courtesy of Apple; **89TL** Bettmann/Corbis; **89TR** Courtesy of Apple; **90** Jens Neith/ZEFA/Corbis; Carol Munoz/iStockphoto; **92TR** Stephen Sweet/iStockphoto; **93C** Maria Boytunoa/iStockphoto; **94C** Bettmann/Corbis; **95R** Bettmann/Corbis; **95BL** Corbis; **96TL** Maria Bibikova/iStockphoto; **97TR** David Pollack/Corbis; **97L** Roberta Casaliggi/iStockphoto; **98TL** SwimInk2/LCC/Corbis; **98CR** Kelly Cline/iStockphoto; **99TR** Mary Evans Picture Library; **100** Claudia Daut/Reuters/Corbis; **102CR** iStockphoto; **102TR** Jose Marafona/iStockphoto; **103R** David Lewis/iStockphoto; **104CL** Falk Kienas/iStockphoto; **104C** Eliza Snow/iStockphoto; **105T** Bettmann/Corbis; **106B** Karim Hesham/iStockphoto; **107TR** Jivko Kazakov/iStockphoto; **107TL** Francisco Orellana/iStockphoto; **108TR** Jack Tzekov/iStockphoto; **108CL** John Woodworth/iStockphoto; **109L** Palazzo Baberini. Rome/Dagli Orti/The Art Archive; **109C** John Steele/iStockphoto; **110TL** Corbis; **110CB** Wally McNamee/Corbis; **111TR** Natalia Bratslavsky/iStockphoto; **112** Dimitar Dilkoff/AFP/Getty Images; **116BR** Bob Krist/Corbis; **116T** Arne Thaysen/iStockphoto; **117BR** Ivan Mateev/iStockphoto; **118B** James Rabinowitz/Corbis; **119T** Yann Arthus-Bertrand/Corbis; **120TL** Randy Mayes/iStockphoto; **121B** Steven Miric/iStockphoto; **122BL** Fabian Guignard/iStockphoto; **122BL** Dennis Sabo/iStockphoto; **124TC** Mike Morley/iStockphoto; **124BR** Emilia Kun/iStockphoto; **125TC** Rob Broek/iStockphoto; **126TL** iStockphoto; **126B** Stephen Hoerold/iStockphoto; **127TR** Ekatrina Fribus/iStockphoto; **128TL** Klemen Demsar/iStockphoto; **128BR** Marisa Allegra/iStockphoto; **129TR** Mark Weiss/iStockphoto; **130T** John Woodworth/iStockphoto; **131BR** Alan Toby/iStockphoto; **132BL** Paul Almasy/Corbis; **132TL** Andrew Cribb/iStockphoto; **133BL** Steven Tilson/iStockphoto; **134BR** Torleif Svensson/Corbis; **134TR** iStockphoto; **135TR** Michel de Nijs/iStockphoto; **136TL** iStockphoto; **136CR** John Sigler/iStockphoto; **137TR** iStockphoto; **138B** iStockphoto; **139TR** iStockphoto; **140TL** Stefan Tordenmalm/iStockphoto; **140B** Ondrej Cech/iStockphoto; **141C** Andy Green-AGMIT/iStockphoto; **142B** Lisa Kyle Young/iStockphoto; **142TR** Felix Mockel/iStockphoto; **143C** Matthew Scholey/iStockphoto; **144** Brian Snyder/Reuters/Corbis; **145TR** Sandra O'Claire/iStockphoto; **146TL** Frank May/DPA/Corbis; **147CR** Bettmann/Corbis; **148TR** Gianni Dagli Orti/Corbis; **148BL** Nik Wheeler/Corbis; **149LC** Dave Wirtzfeld/iStockphoto; **149LC** Dave Wirtzfeld/iStockphoto; **149LC** Dave Wirtzfeld/iStockphoto; **150TL** Historical Picture Archive/Corbis; **150CR** Bettmann/Corbis; **150CL** Peter Spiro/iStockphoto; **151B** iStockphoto; **152TL** Bettmann/Corbis; **153C** Jim Sugar/Corbis; **154TL** NASA; **155C** Shannon Stapleton/Corbis; **155BL** The Scotsman/Corbis/Sygma; **156T** Alison Wright/Corbis; **156BL** Nancy Kaszerman/Zuma/Corbis; **157B** Edward Parsons/UN/EPA/Corbis; **158** AFP/Getty Images; **160B** Sandro Vannini/Corbis; **161C** Richard A. Cooke/Corbis; **162C** Bennett Dean/Eye Ubiquitous/Corbis; **163R** Ashwin Kharidehal Abhirama/iStockphoto; **164TR** Corbis; **164L** Nancy Louie/iStockphoto; **165C** Elio Clol/Corbis; **166C** Fred de Noyelle/Godong/Corbis; **167TR** Robert Young/iStockphoto; **168BL** Earl & Nazima Kowall/Corbis; **169TR** Reuters/Corbis; **169C** Nikhil Gangavane/iStockphoto; **170L** iStockphoto; **170TR** Pam Wardlaw/iStockphoto; **170C** Geoffrey Hammond/iStockphoto; **172C** Christine Balderas/iStockphoto; **172L** iStockphoto; **173B** Sharon Dominick/iStockphoto; **174B** Jiri Vatka/iStockphoto; **175L** Joza Pojbic/iStockphoto; **176** Stuart Price/AFP/Getty Images; **177TR** Lise Gagne/iStockphoto; **178C** Owen Franklen/Corbis; **178T** Vladimir Melnik/iStockphoto; **180C** The Dmitri Baltermants Collection/Corbis; **181T** Fine Art Photography Library/Corbis; **182R** Jeff Gynane/iStockphoto; **183L** Tim Wright/Corbis;

183T Dan Mason/iStockphoto; **184T** Gerald French/Corbis; **184C** Dusty Cline/iStockphoto; **185B** Reuters/Corbis; **185T** Achim Prill/iStockphoto; **186** Jonathan Hordle/Rex Features; **187T** Joel Blitt/iStockphoto; **188CL** Sandro Vannini/Corbis; **188R** Bettmann/Corbis; **190BL** Christie's Images/Corbis; **190LR** Neema Frederic/Corbis Sygma; **192R** Tim Graham/Corbis; **192CB** Sascha Burkard/iStockphoto; **192L** iStockphoto; **193R** Archivo Iconografico, SA/Corbis; **194B** Eliza Snow/iStockphoto; **195CR** Eric Foltz/iStockphoto; **196** OMA/EPA/Corbis; **198L** Asier Villafranca Valasco/iStockphoto; **198B** Jim Jurica/iStockphoto; **199TC** Andrea Jemolo/Corbis; **199TR** Paul Hardy/Corbis; **200B** Roger Antrobus/Corbis; **201T** Pawel Libea/Corbis; **203T** Paul Cheyne/iStockphoto; **204T** iStockphoto; **205C** Donall O'Cleirigh/iStockphoto; **206B** Liu Liqun/Corbis; **208** Car Culture/Corbis; **210B** Tony Arruza/Corbis; **212C** Aston Martin; **213T** Bill Nation/Corbis Sygma; **214C** Tim Wimborne/Reuters/Corbis; **215TL** Thomas Hottner/iStockphoto; **215CR** Robert Churchill/iStockphoto; **216B** Underwood & Underwood/Corbis; **216T** Bettmann/Corbis; **217CR** Bettmann/Corbis; **218TL** Eileen Tweedy/Magdalene College, Cambridge/The Art Archive; **219BR** Hulton Deutsch Collection/Corbis; **219R** Reuters/Corbis; **220B** Jaques Langevin/Corbis; **220CL** Allison Marles/iStockphoto; **221T** Duncan Gilbert/iStockphoto; **222** MGM/Album/AKG-Images; **223T** Catherine dée Auvil/ iStockphoto; **224BL** Alison Wright/Corbis; **224T** Andres Balcazar/iStockphoto; **226C** Ian Poole/iStockphoto; **226TL** Robert Dawson/ iStockphoto; **228CR** Seth Joel/Corbis; **228T** iStockphoto; **229B** Amazon.com; **231TR** The Estate of C.S. Lewis, 1950; **232C** Blue Lantern Studio/Corbis; **234T** Blue Lantern Studio/Corbis; **235CL** Marisa Allegra Williams/ iStockphoto; **235BR** Rey Rojo/iStockphoto; **236R** Marvel Characters Inc./Corbis; **238** Danny Lehman/Corbis; **239TR** iStockphoto; **240C** Joseph Sohm; ChromoSohm Inc./Corbis; **241T** Michael S Yamashita/Corbis; **242CR** Gillet Luc/iStockphoto; **242TL** Adrian Beesley/ iStockphoto; **243TR** Archivo Iconografico, SA/Corbis; **244C** Laryn Bakker/iStockphoto; **244BR** Matej Michelizza/iStockphoto; **247TL** Gabe Palmer/Corbis; **247CR** iStockphoto; **247BR** Olga Shelego/iStockphoto; **248** Michael Ochs Archives/Getty Images; **250TR** Dave Bartruff/Corbis; **251C** Bettmann/Corbis; **253TR** David Lees/ Corbis; **253C** Corbis; **254CR** Bettmann/Corbis; **254CL** Courtesy of Apple; **255C** Bettmann/Corbis; **255TR** Henry Dilz/Corbis; **256B** Jonathan Drake/Reuters/Corbis; **256BR** Luke Daniek/iStockphoto; **258TL** Sunset Boulevard/Corbis; **258C** Josef Philipp/iStockphoto; **259R** Fernando Mañoso/EFE/Corbis; **260B** Robbie Jack/Corbis; **261TL** Robbie Jack/Corbis; **261R** Diane Diederich; **262** Paramount/Everett/Rex Features; **264TL** Swim Ink 2/LLC/Corbis; **265CR** Yann Arthus-Bertrand/Corbis; **266TR** Trapper Frank/Corbis Sygma; **267TR** MGM/United Artists/Sony/The Kobal Collection; **267BL** Warner Bros/The Kobal Collection; **268CR** RKO/The Kobal Collection; **269CR** Michael Goulding/Orange County Register/Corbis; **270CR** Disney/The Kobal Collection; **271T** Album/AKG-Images; **272C** Michael Caronna/ Reuters/Corbis; **272TL** Bettmann/Corbis; **273TR** RKO/The Kobal Collection; **274TL** iStockphoto; **275C** Dan Herrick/iStockphoto; **276** George Tiedemann/GT Images/Corbis; **277TR** Tracy Hebden/iStockphoto; **278B** Duomo/Corbis; **279TR** Bettmann/Corbis; **280BR** Historical Picture Archive/Corbis; **280CL** Historical Picture Archive/Corbis; **281T** iStockphoto; **282BR** Karl Weatherly/Corbis; **282C** Karl Mathis/EPA/Corbis; **284TL** Tim de Waele/Isosport/Corbis; **284C** Jorge Delgado/iStockphoto; **285R** Duomo/Corbis; **286TL** Tomasso DeRosa/Corbis; **286BR** Simon Bruty/SI/Newsport/Corbis; **287TR** Jeff Lewis/Icon SMI/Corbis; **288TR** AFP/Getty Images; **289CR** Matt A. Brown/Newsport/Corbis; **290T** Susan Mullane/Newsport/Corbis; **290CR** Jim Sugar/Corbis; **290CL** Jolande Gerritsen/iStockphoto; **291C** Jolande Gerritsen/iStockphoto; **292TR** Bettmann/Corbis; **292BL** Duomo/Corbis; **294BL** Andy Clark/Reuters/Corbis; **294TR** David Gray/Reuters/Corbis; **295BR** Maggie Hallahan/Corbis; **296BL** Pichon P/Corbis/Sygma; **296TC** Eric Gaillard/Reuters/Corbis; **297T** Bryn Lennon/Getty Images; **298TR** Olivier Marie/EPA/Corbis; **300BL** Kevin R Morris/Corbis; **300TR** Kelly-Mooney Photography/Corbis; **301CR** Steve Boyle/Newsport/Corbis; **302** Universal Studios/Kime French/AKG-Images; **304CR** Gianni Dagli Orti/Corbis; **305TR** Corbis; **306CR** Archivo Iconografico, SA/Corbis; **306BC** Ralph White/Corbis; **307TL** Bettmann/Corbis